THE
OBJECTIVIST
NEWSLETTER

THE OBJECTIVIST NEWSLETTER

Volumes 1–4
1962–1965

The Objectivist® is a registered trademark of Leonard Peikoff.
© Copyright 1962, 1963, 1964, 1965 by Ayn Rand
© Copyright 1990 renewed by the Estate of Ayn Rand

All rights reserved.
This book or any part thereof may not be reproduced in any form without the written permission of the Estate of Ayn Rand.
Send requests and inquiries to the publisher.

Published by the Ayn Rand Institute
6 Hutton Centre Drive, Suite 600, Santa Ana, CA 92707

ISBN 978-0-9960101-9-1
Library of Congress Catalog Card Number: 90-61904

TABLE OF CONTENTS

VOLUME 1 — JANUARY TO DECEMBER, 1962

January

Choose Your Issues—by Ayn Rand.
Books: PLANNED CHAOS by Ludwig von Mises, reviewed by Barbara Branden.
Intellectual Ammunition Department: Reason and Emotion — by Nathaniel Branden.
The Crisis Over Berlin—by Alan Greenspan.

February

Antitrust: The Rule of Unreason—by Ayn Rand.
Books: ECONOMICS IN ONE LESSON by Henry Hazlitt, reviewed by Robert Hessen.
I.A.D. Ethical hedonism—by Leonard Peikoff.
I.A.D. Individual rights versus society—by Nathaniel Branden.
I.A.D. Property rights—by Nathaniel Branden.

March

"Have Gun, Will Nudge"—by Ayn Rand.
Books: PROSPERITY THROUGH FREEDOM by Lawrence Fertig, reviewed by Edith Efron.
I.A.D. Capitalism and religion—by Barbara Branden.
I.A.D. The psychological meaning of man's "need" of approval—by Nathaniel Branden.

April

Counterfeit Individualism—by Nathaniel Branden.
Books: TEN THOUSAND COMMANDMENTS by Harold Fleming, reviewed by Ayn Rand.
Child Labor and the Industrial Revolution—by Robert Hessen.
I.A.D. Leading a rational life in an irrational society—by Ayn Rand.

May

Who Will Protect Us from Our Protectors?—by Ayn Rand.
Books: THE ANTI-CAPITALISTIC MENTALITY by Ludwig von Mises, reviewed by Edith Efron.
I.A.D. The "first cause" argument—by Nathaniel Branden.

June

"The National Interest, c'est moi"—by Ayn Rand.
I.A.D. Monopolies and laissez-faire capitalism—by Nathaniel Branden.
Doctors and the Police State—by Leonard Peikoff (Special Supplement).

July

Benevolence versus Altruism—by Nathaniel Branden.
Books: THE DECLINE OF AMERICAN LIBERALISM by Arthur A. Ekirch, Jr., reviewed by Robert Hessen.
I.A.D. Doesn't life require compromise?—by Nathaniel Branden.
"Account Overdrawn"—by Ayn Rand.

August

The "Conflicts" of Men's Interests—by Ayn Rand.
I.A.D. Depressions and laissez-faire capitalism—by Nathaniel Branden.
Introducing Objectivism—by Ayn Rand.
The New Enemies of "The Untouchables"—by Ayn Rand.

September

The Pull Peddlers—by Ayn Rand.
Books: PLANNING FOR FREEDOM by Ludwig von Mises, reviewed by Nathaniel Branden.
I.A.D. Isn't everyone selfish?—by Nathaniel Branden.

October

"To Young Scientists"—by Ayn Rand.
Books: NINETY-THREE by Victor Hugo, reviewed by Ayn Rand.
THE GIRL HUNTERS by Mickey Spillane, reviewed by Ayn Rand.
I.A.D. Does man possess instincts?—by Nathaniel Branden.
War and Peace—by Ayn Rand.
"Through Your Most Grievous Fault"—by Ayn Rand.

November

Social Metaphysics—by Nathaniel Branden.
Books: EAST MINUS WEST = ZERO by Werner Keller, reviewed by Edith Efron.
The Esthetic Vacuum of Our Age—by Ayn Rand.
Women and the Industrial Revolution—by Robert Hessen.

December

The Monument Builders—by Ayn Rand.
Books: THE ROOSEVELT MYTH by John T. Flynn, reviewed by Barbara Branden.
I.A.D. The obligations of parents and children—by Nathaniel Branden.

VOLUME 2 — JANUARY TO DECEMBER, 1963

January

Collectivized Ethics—by Ayn Rand.
"The Stolen Concept"—by Nathaniel Branden.
I.A.D. Capital punishment—by Nathaniel Branden.
I.A.D. Are certain things unknowable?—by Nathaniel Branden.

February

The Ethics of Emergencies—by Ayn Rand.
Books: REASON AND ANALYSIS by Brand Blanshard, reviewed by Nathaniel Branden.

March

Mental Health versus Mysticism and Self-Sacrifice—by Nathaniel Branden.
"How *not* to fight against Socialized Medicine"—by Ayn Rand.

April

Man's Rights—by Ayn Rand.
I.A.D. Agnosticism—by Nathaniel Branden.

May

The Contradiction of Determinism—by Nathaniel Branden.
Books: ARISTOTLE by John Herman Randall, Jr., reviewed by Ayn Rand.

June

Collectivized "Rights"—by Ayn Rand.
I.A.D. Public education—by Nathaniel Branden.
I.A.D. Inherited wealth—by Nathaniel Branden.
I.A.D. "Right-to-work" laws—by Barbara Branden.

July

Vast Quicksands—by Ayn Rand.
Books: THE FEMININE MYSTIQUE by Betty Friedan, reviewed by Edith Efron.
I.A.D. Demonstration and irrationality—by Nathaniel Branden.

August

"The Divine Right of Stagnation"—by Nathaniel Branden.
Books: THE LANGUAGE OF DISSENT by Lowell B. Mason, reviewed by Ayn Rand.
The Assault on Integrity—by Alan Greenspan.

September

Racism—by Ayn Rand.
Books: HUMAN ACTION by Ludwig von Mises, reviewed by Nathaniel Branden.

October

The Goal of My Writing—by Ayn Rand.
I.A.D. The psychological appeal of altruism—by Nathaniel Branden.

November

The Goal of My Writing (Part II)—by Ayn Rand.
Books: TA TA, TAN TAN by Valentin Chu, reviewed by Robert Hessen.
I.A.D. Labor unions and the standard of living—by Nathaniel Branden.
I.A.D. Capitalism's practicality—by Nathaniel Branden.

December

The Nature of Government—by Ayn Rand.
A Report to Our Readers—by Nathaniel Branden.

VOLUME 3—JANUARY TO DECEMBER, 1964

January

The Anatomy of Compromise—by Ayn Rand.
Books: ROOSEVELT'S ROAD TO RUSSIA by George N. Crocker, reviewed by Beatrice Hessen.
I.A.D. The Objectivist concept of free will versus the traditional concepts—by Nathaniel Branden.

February

The Psychology of Pleasure—by Nathaniel Branden.
I.A.D. Government financing in a free society—by Ayn Rand.

March

How to Judge a Political Candidate—by Ayn Rand.
Books: THE TYRANNY OF TESTING by Banesh Hoffman, reviewed by Joan Blumenthal.

April

The Property Status of Airwaves—by Ayn Rand.
I.A.D. The psychological primacy of the choice to think — by Nathaniel Branden.
I.A.D. The moral meaning of risking one's life — by Nathaniel Branden.

May

Pseudo-Self-Esteem—by Nathaniel Branden.
Books: THE GREATEST PLOT IN HISTORY by Ralph de Toledano, reviewed by Edith Efron.
I.A.D. Patents and copyrights—by Ayn Rand.

June

The Cult of Moral Grayness—by Ayn Rand.
Pseudo-Self-Esteem (Part II)—by Nathaniel Branden.

July

The Argument from Intimidation—by Ayn Rand.
Social Metaphysical Fear—by Nathaniel Branden.

August

Is Atlas Shrugging?—by Ayn Rand.

September

"Extremism" or The Art of Smearing—by Ayn Rand.
Books: A HISTORY OF WESTERN PHILOSOPHY by W. T. Jones, PHILOSOPHIC CLASSICS ed. Walter Kaufmann, A HISTORY OF PHILOSOPHY by Wilhelm Windelband; reviewed by Leonard Peikoff.

October

Psycho-Epistemology—by Nathaniel Branden.
Books: THE GOD OF THE MACHINE by Isabel Paterson, reviewed by Ayn Rand.
Book Report: DAY OF THE GUNS by Mickey Spillane, a commentary by Ayn Rand.

November

Introduction to THE VIRTUE OF SELFISHNESS—by Ayn Rand.
Psycho-Epistemology (Part II)—by Nathaniel Branden.

December

"It Is Earlier Than You Think"—by Ayn Rand.
A Report to our Readers—1964—by Nathaniel Branden.

VOLUME 4—JANUARY TO DECEMBER, 1965

January

Bootleg Romanticism—by Ayn Rand.

February

Rogues' Gallery—by Nathaniel Branden.
I.A.D. Who is the final authority in ethics?—by Ayn Rand.

March

Art and Moral Treason—by Ayn Rand.
Rogues' Gallery (Part II)—by Nathaniel Branden.

April

The Psycho-Epistemology of Art—by Ayn Rand.
A Message to our Readers—by Nathaniel Branden.

May

The New Fascism: Rule by Consensus—by Ayn Rand.
Books: ECONOMICS AND THE PUBLIC WELFARE by Benjamin M. Anderson, reviewed by Martin Anderson.

June

The New Fascism: Rule by Consensus (Part II)—by Ayn Rand.
From the "Horror File."

July

The Cashing-In: The Student "Rebellion"—by Ayn Rand.
Alienation—by Nathaniel Branden.

August

The Cashing-In: The Student "Rebellion" (Part II)—by Ayn Rand.
Alienation (Part II)—by Nathaniel Branden.

September

The Cashing-In: The Student "Rebellion" (Part III)—by Ayn Rand.
Alienation (Part III)—by Nathaniel Branden.

October

The Obliteration of Capitalism—by Ayn Rand.
Books: THE DEMOCRAT'S DILEMMA by Philip M. Crane, reviewed by Joan Meltzer.

November

What Is Capitalism?—by Ayn Rand.
I.A.D. What is psychological maturity?—by Nathaniel Branden.

December

What is Capitalism? (Part II)—by Ayn Rand.
A Report to our Readers—1965—by Nathaniel Branden.

THE OBJECTIVIST NEWSLETTER

Edited and Published by AYN RAND and NATHANIEL BRANDEN

VOL. 1 NO. 1   JANUARY, 1962

CHECK YOUR PREMISES
By AYN RAND

Choose Your Issues

Objectivism is a philosophical movement; since politics is a branch of philosophy, Objectivism advocates certain political principles—specifically, those of laissez-faire capitalism—as the consequence and the ultimate practical application of its fundamental philosophical principles. It does not regard politics as a separate or primary goal, that is: as a goal that can be achieved without a wider ideological context.

Politics is based on three other philosophical disciplines: metaphysics, epistemology and ethics—on a theory of man's nature and of man's relationship to existence. It is only on such a base that one can formulate a consistent political theory and achieve it in practice. When, however, men attempt to rush into politics without such a base, the result is that embarrassing conglomeration of impotence, futility, inconsistency and superficiality which is loosely designated today as "conservatism." Objectivists are *not* "conservatives." We are *radicals for capitalism;* we are fighting for that philosophical base which capitalism did not have and without which it was doomed to perish.

A change in a country's political ideas has to be preceded by a change in its cultural trends; a *cultural* movement is the necessary precondition of a *political* movement. Today's culture is dominated by the philosophy of mysticism (irrationalism)—altruism—collectivism, the base from which only *statism* can be derived; the statists (of any brand: communist, fascist or welfare) are merely cashing in on it—while the "conservatives" are scurrying to ride on the enemy's premises and, somehow, to achieve political freedom by stealth. It can't be done.

Neither a man nor a nation can have a practical policy without any basic principles to integrate it, to set its goals and guide its course. Just as the United States, having abandoned its own principles, is floundering aimlessly in international affairs, is unable to act and is merely *reacting* to the issues chosen and raised by Soviet Russia—so, in domestic affairs, the "conservatives" are unable to act and are merely *reacting* to the issues chosen and raised by the statists, thus accepting and helping to propagate the statists' premises.

When the statists proclaim that their slave-system will achieve material prosperity, the "conservatives" concede it and rush to urge people to sacrifice their "materialistic" concerns in order to preserve freedom—thus helping the statists (and their own audiences) to evade the fact that only freedom makes it possible for men to achieve material prosperity. When the statists announce that our first duty is to support the entire population of the globe—the "conservatives" rush into debates on whether Asia, Africa or South America should be the first recipient of our handouts. When the statists set up a "Peace Corps" to send young Americans into unpaid (though tax-supported) servitude to foreign nations—"conservative" youth rush to propose an *"effective* Peace Corps." When certain statist groups, counting, apparently, on a total collapse of American self-esteem, dare go so far as to urge America's surrender into slavery without a fight, under the slogan *"Better Red Than Dead"*—the "conservatives" rush to proclaim that they prefer to be dead, thus helping to spread the idea that our only alternative is communism or destruction, forgetting that the only proper answer to an ultimatum of that kind is: *"Better See The Reds Dead."*

While public attention is distracted by headlines about the latest whim of Khrushchev or of some other tribal chief, while the "conservatives" gallop obediently down any sidetrack set up by their enemies, two enormously dangerous issues are sneaking up on us, undiscussed, unopposed and unfought. They seem to be a double move planned by the statists, one to destroy intellectual freedom, the other to destroy economic freedom. The chief means to the first is the Federal Communications Commission, to the second—the Anti-Trust laws.

When a government official—Mr. Newton N. Minow, Chairman of the F.C.C.—cynically threatens "those few of you who really believe that the public interest is merely what interests the public," the principle (and precedent) he seeks to establish is clear: that the public is not the judge of its own interest, but *he* is; that the people's vote of approval, freely and *individually* cast in the form of preference for certain television programs, is to be superseded by *his* edict; that television stations are not to be guided by their viewers' wishes (he calls them "the nation's whims") nor by their own wishes, but by *his*—under penalty of having their licenses revoked for unspecified and unspecifiable offenses (which action, somehow, is *not* to be regarded as a whim).

One can easily see what would happen to our entire communications industry (including the press) if such a precedent were accepted in one of its branches—and one would expect the intellectuals of a free country to raise their voices in such a protest that it would sweep Mr. Minow out of Washington. Instead, most of the press congratulated him on his "courage"—the courage of an armed bureaucrat who threatens the livelihood, property and professions of legally disarmed victims.

The Anti-Trust laws—an unenforceable, uncompliable, unjudicable mess of contradictions—have for decades kept American businessmen under a silent, growing reign of terror. Yet these laws were created and, to this day, are upheld by the "conservatives," as a grim monument to their lack of political philosophy, of economic knowledge and of any concern with principles. Under the Anti-Trust laws, a man becomes a criminal from the moment he goes into business, no matter what he does. For instance, if he charges prices which some bureaucrats judge as too high, he can be prosecuted for monopoly or for a successful "intent to monopolize"; if he charges prices lower than those of his competitors, he can be prosecuted for "unfair competition" or "restraint of trade"; and if he charges the same prices as his competitors, he can be prosecuted for "collusion" or "conspiracy." There is only one difference in the legal treatment accorded to a criminal or to a businessman: the criminal's rights are protected much more securely and objectively than the businessman's.

The full, brutal injustice of that legislation has now come into the open: seven distinguished businessmen (in the so-called "Electrical Conspiracy" case) were sentenced to jail for breaking a law which they could not avoid breaking without breaking a number of other laws. To my knowledge, no public voices were raised to defend them. Instead, the headlines screamed abuse at helpless, legally throttled, martyred victims who were deprived even of the opportunity of self-defense (by the threat of treble damages).

In subsequent columns, I shall discuss these two issues at greater length. For the present, I will merely point out that in the F.C.C. and in the Anti-Trust Division the government possesses the legal weapons it needs to transform this country into a totalitarian state—and if the "conservatives" do not

(continued on page 4)

Copyright © 1961 by The Objectivist Newsletter, Inc.

BOOKS

Planned Chaos* by Ludwig von Mises

Reviewed by **BARBARA BRANDEN**

Ludwig von Mises, the most distinguished economist of our age, is an intransigent advocate of freedom and capitalism. With brilliant lucidity and ruthless logic, *Planned Chaos* discusses the major collectivist ideologies of the twentieth century, as they have been put into practice in various countries: interventionism (the so-called "mixed economy"), fascism, nazism, socialism, communism. Originally written as an epilogue to *Socialism* (an encyclopedic and devastating analysis of the fallacies of collectivist economic doctrines), *Planned Chaos* is now available as a separate book.

A central point of *Planned Chaos* is Professor Mises' eloquent refutation of one of the most disastrous myths of the twentieth century: the belief that capitalism and socialism are *not* the only alternative economic systems, that there is a "third way." This alleged "third way" is interventionism, the *hampered* market economy, in which the state "seeks to influence the market by the intervention of its coercive power, but it does not want to eliminate the market altogether."

Professor Mises demonstrates that interventionism, politically and economically, is unstable, impractical and futile. Unless it is abandoned and the free market restored, it leads necessarily to full socialism. As one illustration, he cites the futility of government enforced minimum wage rates: if minimum rates are fixed at the market level, they are useless; if they are raised above the level the free market would have determined, the result is permanent unemployment of a great part of the potential labor force, which cannot be absorbed into the market at economically unjustified wages. In the latter case, the government then has no choice but to add new regulations in the hope of making its initial regulation work. Since any interference with the free market produces harmful economic consequences, a government which will not abandon interventionist policies faces the constant necessity of taking further measures in the attempt to eliminate the consequences of past measures—until all economic freedom has been legislated out of existence and socialism has replaced capitalism.

Socialism, in this century, has taken two different forms. "The one pattern—we may call it the Marxian or Russian pattern—is purely bureaucratic. All economic enterprises are departments of the government just as the administration of the army and the navy or the postal system. . . . The second pattern—we may call it the German or *Zwangswirtschaft* system—differs from the first one in that it, seemingly and nominally, maintains private ownership of the means of production, entrepreneurship, and market exchange. . . . But the government tells these seeming entrepreneurs what and how to produce, at what prices and from whom to buy, at what prices and to whom to sell. The government decrees at what wages laborers should work and to whom and under what terms the capitalists should entrust their funds. Market exchange is but a sham." Thus socialism, nazism and fascism are equally "leftist"; they differ, not in basic principle or goal, but only in techniques of implementation.

The American New Deal and the Fair Deal (and, one may add, the New Frontier) have followed the pattern of the nazi or fascist variety of socialism. Many New Dealers consciously and admittedly adopted Mussolini's corporate state as their model. Today, the state is not moving in the direction of making all economic enterprises departments of the government, but in the direction of making private ownership *nominal*, of telling "seeming entrepreneurs what and how to produce, at what prices and from whom to buy, at what prices and to whom to sell." (Consider, for example, the government's farm policy, or President Kennedy's recent efforts to dictate steel prices.)

The nazi slogan: "The commonweal ranks above private profit," would be unreservedly endorsed by any socialist, and by any advocate of interventionism. This slogan implies, Mises states, "that profit-seeking business harms the vital interests of the immense majority and that it is the sacred duty of popular government to prevent the emergence of profits by public control of production and distribution." If the nazis, the socialists and the interventionists are agreed in their estimate of "profit-seeking business," it is not astonishing that they are agreed in their estimate of how the "menace" of profit seeking should be dealt with: the annihilation of the freedom that makes profit seeking possible—that is, the annihilation of freedom.

Those who advocate interventionism deceive themselves and/or seek to deceive others if they pretend that the end they will achieve is anything other than totalitarian statism. The interventionist aims at the substitution of governmental force for the choices of individuals dealing by voluntary agreement on the free market. As Professor Mises points out: "If a man were to say: 'I do not like the mayor elected by majority vote; therefore I ask the government to replace him by the man I prefer,' one would hardly call him a democrat. But if the same claims are raised with regard to the market, most people are too dull to discover the dictatorial aspirations involved."

For the reader who seeks to untangle the twisted pretensions of interventionism and to understand the fundamental political-economic alternative now confronting the world, *Planned Chaos* offers invaluable material. In an age when men are told that all extremes are evil, that one must neither demand complete freedom nor accept full slavery, but must endorse a "middle of the road," Mises demonstrates that nothing but one or the other extreme *is possible*. "The issue," he writes, "is always the same: the government *or* the market. There is no third solution." The choice is coercion—or voluntary trade; slavery—or freedom.

Excerpts from Ayn Rand's lecture, *America's Persecuted Minority: Big Business*

(see Objectivist Calendar, p. 4)

The smallest minority on earth is the individual. Those who deny individual rights, cannot claim to be defenders of minorities.

■ ■

Every ugly, brutal aspect of injustice toward racial or religious minorities is being practiced toward businessmen. For instance, consider the evil of judging people by a double-standard and of denying to some the rights granted to others. Today's "liberals" recognize the workers' (the majority's) right to their livelihood (their wages), but deny the businessmen's (the minority's) right to *their* livelihood (their profits). If workers struggle for higher wages, this is hailed as "social gains"; if businessmen struggle for higher profits, this is damned as "selfish greed." If the workers' standard of living is low, the "liberals" blame it on the businessmen; but if the businessmen attempt to improve their economic efficacy, to expand their markets and to enlarge the financial returns of their enterprises, thus making higher wages and lower prices possible, the same "liberals" denounce it as "commercialism." If a *non-commercial* foundation—that is: a group which did not have to *earn* its funds—sponsors a television show, advocating its particular views, the "liberals" hail it as "enlightenment," "education," "art" and "public service"; if a businessman sponsors a television show and wants it to reflect *his* views, the "liberals" scream, calling it "censorship," "pressure" and "dictatorial rule." When three locals of the International Brotherhood of Teamsters deprived New York City of its milk supply for fifteen days—no moral indignation or condemnation was heard from the "liberal" quarters; but just imagine what would happen if *businessmen* stopped that milk supply for one hour—and how swiftly they would be struck down by that legalized lynching or pogrom known as "trust-busting."

---

* Published by F.E.E., $2.00. Available from NBL BOOK SERVICE, INC., 165 East 35th St., New York 16, N.Y. (N.Y.C. residents add 3% sales tax; outside the U.S., add 15¢.)

INTELLECTUAL AMMUNITION DEPARTMENT

[*Subscribers are invited to send in the questions that they find themselves unable to answer in philosophical or political discussions. As many questions as space permits will be answered. No questions will be answered by mail.*]

■ **Objectivism advocates the moral principle that man should be guided exclusively by reason. But what about the emotional side of human nature?**

To answer this question, one must begin—as in all philosophical issues—by giving precise definitions to the concepts involved.

Reason is the faculty that perceives, identifies and integrates the evidence of reality provided by man's senses. Reason is man's tool of cognition, the faculty by means of which he acquires knowledge—the knowledge he needs in order to act and to deal with existence.

An *emotion* is the psychosomatic form in which man experiences his estimate of the relationship of things to himself. An emotion is a *value*-response. It is the automatic psychological result of a man's value-judgments.

Just as love is man's emotional response to that which he values—so fear is his response to that which threatens his values. Just as desire is the consequence of love: man's wish to achieve and possess that which he regards as his good—so hatred is the consequence of fear: his wish for the destruction of that which endangers his good. Just as happiness is the consequence of fulfilled desire, the emotion that results from the achievement of one's values—so suffering is the emotion that results from the frustration of one's desire or the destruction of one's values.

Man's value-judgments are not innate. Having no innate knowledge of what is true or false, man can have no innate knowledge of what is good or evil. His values, and his emotions, are the product of the conclusions he has drawn or accepted, that is: of his *basic premises*.

A man's basic premises and values may be rational (that is, consonant with the facts of reality) or irrational, contradictory and self-defeating; he may hold them consciously or subconsciously, explicitly or implicitly, he may have chosen them independently and by deliberation or absorbed them uncritically from the assertions of others, by a process of cultural osmosis. But whatever the case, it is a man's basic premises that determine what he will regard as good or evil, desirable or undesirable, *for* him or *against* him, conducive or inimical to his welfare. Thus a man's values—and his emotions—are the product of the thinking he has done or has failed to do.

Reason and emotion—thinking and feeling—are not two contradictory or mutually inimical faculties, but their functions are not interchangeable. *Emotions are not tools of cognition*. What one *feels* in regard to any fact or issue is irrelevant to the question of whether one's judgment of it is true or false, right or wrong. It is not by means of one's feelings that one perceives reality.

In the psychology of a rational man, the relationship of cognition and evaluation—of reason and emotion—is that of cause and effect. *Irrationality* consists of the attempt to reverse this relationship: to let one's emotions—one's *wishes* or *fears*—determine one's thinking, guide one's actions and serve as one's standard of judgment, which means: the attempt to judge what is true or false by the standard of what is "pleasant" or "unpleasant." Philosophically, this attempt is the cause of mysticism; psychologically, it is the cause of neurosis.

The man who asserts that reason and emotion are antagonists is merely confessing that *his* emotions are the product of values which he knows to be irrational and which he does not care to change. When, in response to the statement that men should be guided by reason, a man demands: "But what about the emotional side of human nature?"—the meaning of his demand is: "But what about my irrational wishes?" The man who knows that the values behind his emotions and desires are rational, does not find his reason clashing with his emotions and does not regard rationality as an "inhibiting restriction." *He* is the only man capable of experiencing profound, intense, undivided emotions—because there are no contradictions, no conflicts, among the values from which they come.

If, in any issue, you find that your emotions clash with your reason and you are tempted to reject reason—*identify what this means*. Reason is your faculty of perceiving reality; to act against reason is to act against reality. To attempt the irrational is to attempt to make the impossible succeed.

When you hear such bromides as: "The heart is superior to the mind"—"There is something higher than reason"—"Men cannot live by logic"—"Rational analysis kills"—remind yourself of what reason is, then translate these bromides into their actual meaning, as follows: "The heart is superior to reality"—"There is something higher than reality"—"Men cannot live in accordance with reality"—"Knowledge of reality kills." Then remember that the most consistent exponent of these beliefs is a schizophrenic.

Emotions do not have to be your enemies, your torturers and your destroyers—which is what they become when you follow them blindly. Emotions are the means of experiencing the enjoyment of life. But they offer that experience only to the man who does not substitute his emotions for his mind.

—NATHANIEL BRANDEN

An excerpt from Nathaniel Branden's forthcoming book, *Who is Ayn Rand?*
(see Objectivist Calendar, p. 4)

The Objectivist ethics is especially significant for the psychotherapist because it is the first *psychological* morality. It is the first morality to define the issue of good and evil in terms of the actions of one's consciousness—that is, in terms of the manner in which one *uses* one's consciousness. It ties virtue and vice to the action directly subject to man's volition: the choice to think or not to think. The evils that a man may commit existentially, in action, are made possible only by the primary evil committed inside his consciousness: evasion, the refusal to think, the rejection of reason—just as the good that a man may achieve is made possible by his choice to think, to identify, to integrate, to accept reason as an absolute.

The Objectivist morality does not require infallibility or omniscience of man: it merely requires that he choose to be conscious—that is, to perceive reality. The issue is a *moral* one, because man is a being who has to be conscious *by choice*.

This approach to morality is reflected in the Objectivist treatment of desires. Altruistic moralities tell man to sacrifice his desires. Hedonistic moralities tell man to indulge them. Other schools of morality tell man to seek a compromise, to mediate among his desires and the other claims upon him. But all of these schools share a fundamental premise, whether one consults Plato, Epicurus, Augustine, Calvin, Hobbes, Hume, Kant, Bentham, Nietzsche or Dewey: they all, implicitly or explicitly, regard desires and emotions as irreducible primaries, as the given—then proceed to tell man what attitude to take toward them. The Objectivist morality recognizes that man's desires and emotions proceed from and are caused by his premises, that his premises are the result of his thinking—and that the issue of morality is not to be fought over desires and emotions (which are only a consequence), but over the thinking a man has done or has failed to do. Objectivism teaches man that his mind and his emotions do not have to be antagonists, that his conscious convictions and his desires do not have to clash; it teaches man how they are to be *integrated*, how to bring them into non-contradictory harmony; it teaches man how *he* can determine the *content* of his desires and emotions. (It defines the principles involved; to develop their full implementation is the task of the science of psychology.)

The Crisis Over Berlin
By ALAN GREENSPAN

Over a piece of real estate scarcely a tenth the size of Rhode Island, the Russians have brought the world to the brink of war. One would reasonably conclude from the Soviets' unrelenting pressure on West Berlin that they fear the city is a threat which can overrun the whole communist empire. As absurd as it may sound, the Russians are right: West Berlin *is* a threat to the whole communist system. But the threat is not military; it is ideological. The city, with its broad boulevards, new buildings and prosperous industries, stands as a monument to freedom and free enterprise amid the drabness of East Germany. It is hardly imaginable that the communists can vaunt the wonders of their "workers' paradise" while the glitter of West Berlin makes a mockery of their pretensions. West Berlin must be destroyed, threaten the Soviets. The city must be reduced to the level of its surroundings. Its spirit must be broken. Communism cannot stand the comparison.

This is the cause of the Berlin crisis. The Russians will not, and cannot, let up until they have brought the city under communist rule. The Soviet allegation that West Berlin is a military threat because of the Western garrison stationed there is too absurd for rebuttal. The city is surrounded and militarily indefensible. The charge that West Berlin is a base for spies should be—but probably is not—true. The claim that West Berlin harbors hoodlums who kidnap East Berliners cannot really be taken seriously. The Russians will never acknowledge the real reason for their continual provocations and threats toward West Berlin. To acknowledge it would be to admit that communism is a failure in the area in which it vociferously avers superiority: the ability to achieve material prosperity.

History rarely offers so controlled an experiment in rival economic systems as has been seen in Berlin during the last decade. In the late 1940's, when the rest of Western Europe was sinking under a morass of socialistic experiments, West Germany, including West Berlin, turned instead to free enterprise (at least predominantly). The results were dramatic: from a country defeated and devastated by war, it arose to become spectacularly prosperous. Meanwhile, East Germany and East Berlin barely emerged from the rubble.

As the discrepancies in freedom and material well-being between the two halves of Germany grew, the exodus from the Eastern sector became a torrent. West Berlin was a showplace of free enterprise, and the exit to freedom. Finally, in desperation, the gauleiters of East Berlin cynically slammed shut the escape hatch and built a wall which turned the "workers' paradise" of East Germany into a huge concentration camp.

While the communists have been quick to grasp the ideological significance of Berlin, the "global strategists" of the West evidently cannot, or will not. The welfare statists both in this country and abroad, who are responsible for the formulation of Western foreign policy, have laboriously evaded coming to grips with the meaning and nature of the issue at stake. Their mental block is not difficult to understand: West Berlin is more than an affront to the communist world—it is a slap in the face to their own socialist programs at home. They are caught between their fear of a communist victory—and their terror of identifying that *capitalism* is the only alternative, and that *that* is the issue at stake in West Berlin. The contradiction they refuse to resolve or acknowledge has paralyzed them and made them blusteringly ineffectual against the Russians.

West Berliners, sensing compromise and abandonment in our overeagerness to confer with the Russians—and knowing whose are the lives we are willing to "negotiate"—are beginning to leave in droves. The flow of new capital investment in the city is slowly drying up. To make matters worse, the West German government is offering subsidies to keep people from leaving. The subsidies, contemptuously labeled "jitter bonuses" by the people, serve only to accelerate the exodus.

Mr. Greenspan is President of Townsend-Greenspan & Co., Inc., New York, economic consultants.

The story of West Berlin is at once a salute to the efficacy of a free economy and a tragic commentary on the destructiveness of compromise, of mixed premises and mixed purposes, of an ostensible fight for freedom by Western leaders who do not wish to know or have anyone else know what is being fought for. West Berlin is a symbol of crisis for *both* the East and the West.

Choose Your Issues *(from page 1)*

know it, the present administration seems to know it. The "trial balloons" are being sent up with growing frequency.

Any person who claims to be an advocate of freedom and who wonders what practical action he can take, should choose *these* two issues as his first concern: they involve the fundamental principles of our culture. He should study these issues, watch their developments and make himself heard in public, on any scale open to him, great or modest, from private discussions to national forums. It is with these two issues that the "practical" fight for freedom should begin.

OBJECTIVIST CALENDAR

■ In June, 1962, Random House will publish *Who is Ayn Rand?* by Nathaniel Branden. This book discusses: the moral revolution of *Atlas Shrugged,* and the relevance of Ayn Rand's philosophy to the cultural and political crisis of our time; the application of Objectivism to basic problems of psychology; the esthetic principles underlying Ayn Rand's novels, and her concept of man's relationship to existence, which holds the key to her literary method. The title essay—contributed by Barbara Branden—is a biographical study, concerned primarily with Ayn Rand's intellectual and artistic development.

■ *Nathaniel Branden Lectures* has incorporated under the new name of NATHANIEL BRANDEN INSTITUTE. In addition to offering lecture courses, the Institute will publish papers and essays on the Objectivist philosophy and its application to the social sciences. The first of these, published in December, 1961, is "The Objectivist Ethics" by Ayn Rand, a paper originally given at the University of Wisconsin 1961 Symposium on "Ethics in Our Time." (This paper is now available from THE OBJECTIVIST NEWSLETTER, INC. Price $1. N.Y.C. residents add 3% sales tax.)

■ The next New York series of "Basic Principles of Objectivism" will be given at the Hotel Roosevelt, 45th St. & Madison Ave., at 7:30 P.M. on twenty consecutive Tuesday evenings, beginning February 13. Registration is now open.

■ Barbara Branden will speak on N.Y.C. radio station WBAI-FM (99.5 on the dial) on Friday, January 5, at 7 P.M. Her topic: "The Moral Antagonism of Capitalism and Socialism." This program will be rebroadcast on Saturday, January 6, at 9:15 A.M.

■ Ayn Rand gave a lecture at the Ford Hall Forum, Boston, on Sunday, December 17. Her topic: "America's Persecuted Minority: Big Business."

■ In mid-September, New American Library brought out *The Fountainhead* with a new jacket design; a second printing of this edition, in October, brought the total number of paperback copies in print to over 1,000,000. New American Library also published a paperback edition of *Anthem,* in September; the first printing was over 300,000 copies; six weeks later, a second printing was announced.

Published monthly at 165 East 35th Street, New York 16, N.Y. Subscription rate: in United States, its possessions, Canada and Mexico, $5 for one year; other countries, $6.

Ayn Rand and Nathaniel Branden, *Editors and Publishers*
Barbara Branden, *Managing Editor*
Elayne Kalberman, *Circulation Manager*
PRINTED BY CARNEGIE PRESS, INC., NEW YORK CITY

THE OBJECTIVIST NEWSLETTER

Edited and Published by AYN RAND and NATHANIEL BRANDEN

VOL. 1 NO. 2   FEBRUARY, 1962

CHECK YOUR PREMISES
By AYN RAND

Antitrust: the Rule of Unreason

It is a grave error to suppose that a dictatorship rules a nation by means of strict, rigid laws which are obeyed and enforced with rigorous, military precision. Such a rule would be evil, but almost bearable; men could endure the harshest edicts, provided these edicts were known, specific and stable; it is not the known that breaks men's spirits, but the unpredictable. A dictatorship has to be capricious; it has to rule by means of the unexpected, the incomprehensible, the wantonly irrational; it has to deal not in death, but in *sudden* death; a state of chronic uncertainty is what men are psychologically unable to bear.

The American businessmen have had to live in that state for seventy years. They were condemned to it by that judicial version of the doctrine of Original Sin which presumes men to be guilty with little or no chance to be proved innocent and which is known as the Antitrust laws.

No business-hating collectivist could have gotten away with creating so perfect an instrument for the destruction of capitalism and the delivery of businessmen into the total power of the government. It took the so-called "conservatives," the alleged defenders of capitalism, to create the Antitrust laws. And it takes the intellectual superficiality of today's "conservatives" to continue supporting these laws, in spite of their meaning, record and results.

The alleged purpose of the Antitrust laws was to protect competition; that purpose was based on the socialistic fallacy that a free, unregulated market will inevitably lead to the establishment of coercive monopolies. But, in fact, no coercive monopoly has ever been or ever can be established by means of free trade on a free market. Every coercive monopoly was created by government intervention into the economy: by special privileges, such as franchises or subsidies, which closed the entry of competitors into a given field, by legislative action. (For a full demonstration of this fact, I refer you to the works of the best economists.) The Antitrust laws were the classic example of a moral inversion prevalent in the history of capitalism: an example of the victims, the businessmen, taking the blame for the evils caused by the government, and the government using its own guilt as a justification for acquiring wider powers, on the pretext of "correcting" the evils.

Since *"free* competition *enforced* by law" is a grotesque contradiction in terms, Antitrust grew into a haphazard accumulation of non-objective laws, so vague, complex, contradictory and inconsistent that any business practice can now be construed as illegal, and by complying with one law a businessman opens himself to prosecution under several others. No two jurists can agree on the meaning and application of these laws. No one can give an exact definition of what constitutes "restraint of trade" or "intent to monopolize" or any of the other, similar "crimes." No one can tell what the law forbids or permits one to do. The interpretation is left entirely up to the courts. "The courts in the United States have been engaged ever since 1890 in deciding case by case exactly what the law proscribes. No broad definition can really unlock the meaning of the statute . . ." (A. D. Neale, *The Antitrust Laws of the U.S.A.*, Cambridge University Press, 1960, p. 13.)

Thus a businessman has no way of knowing in advance whether the action he takes is legal or illegal, whether he is guilty or innocent. Yet he has to act; he has to run his business.

Retroactive law—which means: a law that punishes a man for an action which was not legally defined as a crime at the time he committed it—is a form of persecution practiced only in dictatorships and forbidden by every civilized legal code. It is not supposed to exist in the United States and it is not applied to anyone—except to businessmen. A case in which a man cannot know until he is convicted whether the action he took in the past was legal or illegal, is certainly a case of retroactive law.

At first, Antitrust was merely a potential club, a "big stick" over businessmen's heads; but it soon became actual. From their hesitant, sluggish beginnings in a few vaguely semi-plausible cases, Antitrust prosecutions accelerated by a progression of logical steps to such judicial decisions as: that established businesses have to share with any newcomer the facilities it had taken them years to create, if the lack of such facilities imposes a real hardship on the would-be competitor (*Associated Press* case, 1945)—that business concerns have no right to pool their patents and that the penalty for such pools is either the compulsory licensing of their patents to any and all comers or the outright confiscation of the patents; and if a businessman, who is a member of such a pool, sues a competitor who has infringed his patent, the competitor not only wins the case, but collects treble damages from the man whose patent he had infringed (*Kobe v. Dempsey Pump Company*, 1952)—that if a would-be competitor's efficiency is so low that he is unable even to pay a royalty on the patents owned by stronger companies, he is entitled to such patents royalty-free (*General Electric* case, 1948)—that business concerns must, not merely make a gift of their patents to any rival, but must also *teach* him how to use these patents (*I.C.I. and duPont* case, 1952)—that a business concern must not anticipate increases in the demand for its product and must not be prepared to meet them by expanding its capacity "before others entered the field," because this might *discourage* newcomers (*ALCOA* case, 1945).

Is the basic line clear? Do you observe the nature of the principle that dictated the decisions in these cases?

A. D. Neale identifies it as follows: "There is an element of pure 'underdoggery' in the law; an element of throwing the weight of the enforcement authorities into the scale on the side of the weaker parties, which has *little to do with the economic control of monopoly."* (P. 461).

I identify it as: the penalizing of ability for being ability, the penalizing of success for being success, and the sacrifice of productive genius to the demands of envious mediocrity.

Who were the profiteers of Antitrust? Many businessmen supported it from the start: some innocently, some not. These last were the kind who seek to rise, not by free trade and productive ability, but by *political favor and pull,* which means: not by merit, but by *force.* They are the typical products of a "mixed economy" and their numbers multiply as the economy grows more "mixed."

The other group of profiteers was the bureaucrats and the statists. As the trend toward statism grew, the statists found an invaluable instrument for the persecution and the eventual enslavement of businessmen. Observe that the most outrageous Antitrust cases date from the 1940's. Power, in a statist sense, means *arbitrary* power. An *objective* law protects a country's freedom; only a *non-objective* law can give a statist the chance he seeks: a chance to impose *his* arbitrary will—*his* policies, *his* decisions, *his* interpretations, *his* enforcement, *his* punishment or favor—on disarmed, defenseless victims.

(continued on page 6)

Copyright © 1962 by The Objectivist Newsletter, Inc.

BOOKS

*Economics in One Lesson** by Henry Hazlitt

Reviewed by R. HESSEN

Economists, most notably Professor Ludwig von Mises, have repeatedly demonstrated that the only economic system consonant with a free and prosperous society is laissez-faire capitalism. But the influence of statist theorists and historians in the past few decades has resulted in the medley of errors, half-truths, misconceptions and misrepresentations which constitutes most laymen's "knowledge" of capitalism and its history.

It is the extraordinary merit of Henry Hazlitt to have detected the central fallacy involved in most of the popular errors and to have patiently presented and refuted scores of the standard arguments against free enterprise. In *Economics in One Lesson,* he has written the finest primer available for students of capitalism. Clear, vigorous, logical and thoroughly engrossing, the book has richly earned its status as a classic in the literature of freedom.

"The whole argument of this book," writes Hazlitt, "may be summed up in the statement that in studying the effects of any given economic proposal we must trace not merely the immediate results but the results in the long run, not merely the primary consequences but the secondary consequences, and not merely the effects on some special group, but the effects on everyone."

When people clamor for a protective tariff, an export subsidy, a minimum wage law, or a farm price-support law, what they *see* is only the immediate benefit to the businessmen or workers or farmers whom the new law is designed to aid. What they *fail to see* is that some taxpayer, consumer or property-owner must bear the cost and burden of the dole or restriction; that every dollar taken in taxes and spent by the government means there is one less dollar to be spent by the individual who earned it; that "temporary" subsidies to unprofitable farms or industries will either merely *delay* their collapse or lead to a *permanent* subsidization of inefficient production methods or of surplus goods.

The blindly irresponsible, range-of-the-moment nature of the statists' economic theories can best be illustrated by the following popular fallacies:

(a) The notion that a little inflation is necessary to stimulate economic growth. When warned that inflation (by eroding the purchasing power of money) has calamitous cumulative long-range effects on savings, prices and wages, the inflationists shrug it off with the Keynesians' insipid wisecrack: "In the long run we will all be dead." Hazlitt retorts: "Today is already the tomorrow which the bad economist yesterday urged us to ignore."

(b) The notion that machines are a threat to the livelihood of workers, and that the unions and the government should halt automation in the name of maintaining or achieving full employment. In answer, Hazlitt cites the fact that in England in 1760, 7900 people were engaged in the home production of cotton textiles. If the workers or a short-sighted government had been able to bar the introduction of Arkwright's cotton-spinning machinery, they would have barred the day, just 27 years later, when 320,000 persons were employed in the newly-mechanized industry, an increase of 4,400 per cent.

Hazlitt demonstrates that technological unemployment is a temporary phenomenon; that new machines create more jobs than they destroy; that a rising standard of living and an increase in the general economic welfare can be achieved, not by an increase in employment as such, but only by an increase in *production.* "It is . . . no trick," he writes, "to employ everybody, even (or especially) in the most primitive economy. Full employment—very full employment; long, weary, back-breaking employment—is characteristic of precisely the nations that are most retarded industrially."

These are a few random samples of Hazlitt's critical acuity. I suggest that before sending any economic queries to our Intellectual Ammunition Department, you read this book; it will give you most of the basic answers.

Antitrust: the Rule of Unreason (from page 5)

He does not have to exercise his power too frequently nor too openly; he merely has to have it and let his victims know that he has it; fear will do the rest.

In the light of this, consider the *new* phase of Antitrust enforcement. In February of 1961, in Philadelphia, seven businessmen, representing some of America's greatest industrial concerns, were sentenced to jail in the "Electrical Conspiracy" case. This case involved twenty-nine companies manufacturing electrical equipment. The charge against them was that they had made secret agreements to fix prices and rig bids. But without such agreements, the larger companies could have set their prices so low that the smaller ones would have been unable to match them and would have gone out of business, whereupon the larger companies would have faced prosecution, under these same Antitrust laws, for "intent to monopolize."

It is evil enough to impose ruinous fines under laws which the victims have no way to comply with, laws which everyone concedes to be non-objective, contradictory and undefinable. It is obscene, under such laws, to impose jail sentences on men of distinguished achievement, outstanding ability and unimpeachable moral character, who had spent their lives on so responsible a task as industrial production.

But *this,* perhaps, is the clue to the purpose of that disgraceful verdict. It created in the public's mind the impression that industrial production is some sort of sinister underworld activity and that businessmen, by their nature and profession, are to be treated as criminals.

Such was the obvious implication of the disgusting howling that went on in the press. The same humanitarians who rush to the defense of any homicidal dipsomaniac, did not hesitate to release all of their repressed hatred and malice on seven silent, defenseless men whose profession was *business.* That the leftist press would enjoy it, is understandable and, at least, consistent. But what is one to think of the alleged "conservative" press? Take a look at the February 17, 1961, issue of *Time* magazine; with its story about the verdict, *Time* published photographs of six of the victims—six faces with intelligence and determination as their common characteristic—and under them, the caption: "A drama that U.S. business will long remember to its shame."

The same humanitarians of the press who clamor that penitentiaries are a useless, vengeful form of cruelty to juvenile switch-blade killers questing for "kicks" and that these sensitive victims of society should be "given a chance" and should be sent to garden rest-homes for rehabilitation—these same humanitarians have remained silent while a bill is proposed in Congress to the effect that an executive convicted of an Antitrust violation may not, thereafter, be given employment by any business concern and is thus to be deprived of the right to earn a living.

No, all this is not the result of a communist conspiracy. It is the result of something much harder to fight: the result of a culture's cynical, goal-less disintegration, which can benefit no one but the communists and the random little power-lusters of the moment, who fish in muddy waters.

It is futile to wonder about the policies or the intentions of the present administration. Whether the whole administration or any one of its members is consciously dedicated to the destruction of American business, does not matter. What matters is that if any of them *are,* they have the machinery to accomplish it and no opposition: a culture without goals, values or political principles can offer no opposition to anything.

(continued on page 8)

---

* Published by Harper & Bros., $3.75. Available from NBL BOOK SERVICE, INC., 165 East 35th St., New York 16, N.Y., for $2.95 (N.Y.C. residents add 3% sales tax; outside the U.S., add 15¢).

Mr. Hessen received his M.A. in History from Harvard University, and is now on the staff of NATHANIEL BRANDEN INSTITUTE.

INTELLECTUAL AMMUNITION DEPARTMENT

[Subscribers are invited to send in the questions that they find themselves unable to answer in philosophical or political discussions. As many questions as space permits will be answered. No questions will be answered by mail.]

■ **Why does Objectivism reject ethical hedonism?**

Ethical hedonism is the doctrine that pleasure is the standard of moral value, the criterion to be used in determining good and evil, virtue and vice—that the right action in any situation is the action which produces the most pleasure (and/or the least pain).

Hedonists disagree about many questions, such as: Should one pursue short-range or long-range pleasure? Should one pursue one's own selfish pleasure (egoistic hedonism)—or "the greatest happiness of the greatest number" (the Utilitarianism of Bentham and Mill)? But the doctrine of pleasure as the ethical standard is the fundamental uniting them all.

The feeling of pleasure, however, like any emotional response, is not a psychological primary; it is a consequence, an *effect*, of one's previously formed value-judgments. To say, therefore, that men should determine their values by the standard of what gives them pleasure, is to say: Men should determine their values by the standard of whatever they already value. This means that hedonism is a circular and content-less morality which can define no values or virtues and has to count on whatever random values any man happens to have acquired.

In practice, men have no way of obeying the tenets of hedonism, except by taking *their already formed feelings*—their desires and aversions, their loves and fears—as *the given*, as irreducible primaries the satisfaction of which is the purpose of morality, regardless of whether the value-judgments that caused these feelings are rational or irrational, consistent or contradictory, consonant with reality or in flagrant defiance of it.

Objectivism holds that such a policy is suicidal; that if man is to survive, he needs the guidance of an *objective* and *rational* morality, a code of values based on and derived from man's nature as a specific type of living organism, and the nature of the universe in which he lives. Objectivism rejects any subjectivist ethics that begins, not with facts, but with: "I (we, they) *wish* . . ." Which means: it rejects hedonism of any variety. —LEONARD PEIKOFF

■ **What is the Objectivist answer to those who claim that the rights of the individual must be subordinated and sacrificed to the interests of society?**

There is no term that has been used more indiscriminately than the term "society," and with so total a lack of understanding of its meaning.

"Society" is an abstraction; in a political context, it denotes a group or number of individual men who live in the same geographical area and who deal with one another. Society is not a separate entity endowed with some sort of autonomous existence, apart from the individual men of whom it is composed. Society as such does not exist; only individual men exist.

What, therefore, does it mean to declare that man must live for society? It means that one individual must sacrifice himself to other individuals. What does it mean to declare that the rights of society supersede the rights of the individual? It means that some men's rights are to be sacrificed for the sake of other men. What does it mean to declare that public good comes above individual good? It means that some gang of men have a good lobby in Washington, have had themselves designated as "the public," and are now empowered to swing a club over the heads of other men who, for the time being, are *not* the public.

For precisely the same reasons that it is evil to sacrifice one individual to another individual, it is evil to sacrifice him to two individuals or two hundred or two billion. Numbers do not change the moral principle involved. If one man has no claim to the life of another, neither does a group of men have such a claim. As Kira, the heroine of *We The Living*, observes: "If you write a whole line of zeroes, it's still—nothing."

■ **Why do Objectivists maintain that without property rights, no other rights are possible?**

The right of property is the right of use and disposal. If one is not free to use that which one has produced, one does not possess the right of liberty. If one is not free to make the products of one's work serve one's chosen goals, one does not possess the right to the pursuit of happiness. And—since man is not a ghost who exists in some non-material manner—if one is not free to keep and to consume the products of one's work, one does not possess the right of life. In a society where men are not free privately to own the material means of production, their position is that of slaves whose lives are at the absolute mercy of their rulers. —NATHANIEL BRANDEN

An excerpt from Nathaniel Branden's forthcoming book, *Who is Ayn Rand?*

The principle of justice, which is central in the ethical philosophy of Ayn Rand, is the principle most conspicuously avoided in the ethics of altruism. The question of justice is one which the advocates of altruism clearly prefer not to hear raised. Their reticence is not difficult to understand, when one remembers what altruism advocates. Just as altruism teaches that wealth does not have to be earned, so it teaches that love does not have to be earned. . . .

One of the foremost contemporary spokesmen for this "non-commercial" view of human relationships is psychologist Erich Fromm who, with impressive consistency, is a socialist, a devotee of Zen Buddhism and an advocate of the theory that love should be liberated from such unspiritual concepts as the "deserved" and the "undeserved." "In essence, all human beings are identical," he declares in *The Art of Loving*. "We are all part of One; we are One. This being so, it should not make any difference whom we love." Fromm criticizes capitalism for what he (correctly) terms its *"fairness ethics."* It is capitalism, he holds, that makes the practice of love so difficult. He writes: "It may even be said that the development of fairness ethics is the particular ethical contribution of capitalist society. . . . In pre-capitalist societies, the exchange of goods was determined either by direct force, by tradition, or by personal bonds of love and friendship. In capitalism, the all-determining factor is the exchange on the market. . . . If our whole social and economic organization is based on each one seeking his own advantage, if it is governed by the principle of egotism tempered only by the ethical principle of fairness, how can one do business, how can one act within the framework of existing society and at the same time practice love? . . . The *principle* underlying capitalist society and the *principle* of love are incompatible." It is socialism, he argues, that will make love possible . . .

Here one may observe, in unusually explicit statement, the diametrical opposite of Ayn Rand's view of proper human relationships as expressed by the "trader principle." Ayn Rand does not believe that fairness (justice) "tempers" or "limits" self-interest, as Fromm evidently does; she regards fairness or justice as indispensable to, *and inseparable from*, self-interest. Nor does she think that, in regard to moral worth, "all human beings are identical." She draws moral distinctions between a hero and a scoundrel, or a murderer and his victim. Nor does she think that "it should not make any difference whom we love." In her ethics, it should and does make a difference.

To love, she states, is to *value*; love, properly, is the consequence and expression of admiration—"the emotional price paid by one man for the joy he receives from the virtues of another." Love is not alms, but a moral tribute.

(continued on page 8)

Mr. Peikoff is presently completing his doctoral dissertation in philosophy at New York University.

OBJECTIVIST CALENDAR

- Ayn Rand will give her lecture on "America's Persecuted Minority: Big Business" at Columbia University, Wollman Auditorium, Ferris Booth Hall, on Thursday, February 15, 8 P.M. The lecture is open to the public, admission free.

- On March 1, Ayn Rand will begin a twelve-week series of radio programs for the Columbia University station WKCR (590 kc AM, 89.9 mc FM). Under the general title of "Ayn Rand on Campus," these programs will be broadcast weekly, on Thursday, at 8:30 P.M. to 9:30 P.M. The format will be as follows: on six alternate weeks, Miss Rand will give one of the lectures she has delivered at various universities. On the other six programs, Professor John Hospers of the Philosophy Department of Brooklyn College will discuss Objectivism and the lecture of the preceding week, with Ayn Rand, Nathaniel Branden and Barbara Branden. Professor Hospers is the author of: *Meaning and Truth in the Arts—An Introduction to Philosophical Analysis—Human Conduct: an introduction to the problems of ethics.*

The schedule of the programs is as follows:

March 1—"America's Persecuted Minority: Big Business." (This program will be a recording of Ayn Rand's lecture at Columbia University on February 15.)

March 8 — Discussion of preceding lecture by Prof. Hospers, Ayn Rand and Nathaniel Branden.

March 15 — "The Objectivist Ethics."

March 22 — Discussion by Prof. Hospers, Ayn Rand and Nathaniel Branden.

March 29 — "The Intellectual Bankruptcy of Our Age."

April 5 — Discussion by Prof. Hospers, Ayn Rand and Nathaniel Branden.

April 12 — "Conservatism: an Obituary."

April 19 — Discussion by Prof. Hospers, Ayn Rand and Barbara Branden.

April 26 — "Our Esthetic Vacuum."

May 3 — Discussion by Prof. Hospers, Ayn Rand and Barbara Branden.

May 10 — "Faith and Force: the Destroyers of the Modern World."

May 17 — Concluding remarks by Prof. Hospers and Ayn Rand.

These programs will be available to Educational radio stations and University stations, for cost of tape and postage. If a station in your community is interested, its representative may write to: Bruce E. Goldman, President, WKCR, 208 Ferris Booth Hall, Columbia University, New York 27, N.Y.

- In addition to the forthcoming series given in New York by Nathaniel Branden Institute on "Basic Principles of Objectivism," which begins on February 13, the Institute began a new Tape Transcription series of the same course in Indianapolis on January 20 and in Boston on January 23. Tape series are also scheduled to begin in Los Angeles on February 9 and in Washington, D.C., on February 11. Mr. Branden will deliver the opening night's lecture of the Washington series in person.

- On January 2, Ayn Rand addressed Professor John Hospers' class in Ethics, at Brooklyn College; and on January 10, she addressed his graduate seminar. The subject of discussion on both occasions was the Objectivist ethics.

- In December, the Presidents' Professional Association, Inc. (affiliated with the American Management Association, Inc.) made a video-tape recording of a talk by Ayn Rand on "Capitalism *versus* Communism." This recording is to be used on closed-circuit television by the P.P.A.'s educational discussion-groups for presidents of industrial concerns.

- Random House has brought out the fifth printing of *Atlas Shrugged* in its hardcover edition; in paperback, New American Library has ordered its tenth printing (100,000 copies), to be brought out in February.

Antitrust: the Rule of Unreason (from page 6)

Intentionally or not, the purpose achieved by those jail sentences is: intimidation—or, more precisely: terrorization. The Antitrust laws give the government the power to prosecute and convict any business concern in the country any time it chooses. The threat of sudden destruction, of unpredictable retaliation for unnamed offenses, is a much more potent means of enslavement than explicit dictatorial laws. It demands more than mere obedience; it leaves men no policy save one: *to please* the authorities; to please—blindly, uncritically, without standards or principles; to please—in any issue, matter or circumstance, for fear of an unknowable, unprovable vengeance. Anyone possessing such a stranglehold on businessmen, possesses a stranglehold on the wealth and the material resources of the country, which means: a stranglehold on the country.

Businessmen are already helpless and almost silenced. It is only the intellectuals who still have a chance to be heard. That is why I suggest to you the following test: if you hear an alleged "conservative" who quibbles bravely over taxes, budgets or school-aid, but supports the Antitrust laws—you may be sure that he is futile as a fighter for capitalism. To combat petty larceny as a crucial danger, at a time when murder is being committed, is to sanction the murder.

What should we do? We should demand a re-examination and revision of the entire issue of Antitrust. We should challenge its philosophical, political, economic and *moral* base. We should have a Civil Liberties Union—for businessmen. The repeal of the Antitrust laws should be our ultimate goal; it will require a long intellectual and political struggle; but, in the meantime and as a first step, we should urge that the jail-penalty provisions of these laws be abolished.

Businessmen are the one group that distinguishes capitalism and the American way of life from the totalitarian statism that is swallowing the rest of the world. All the other social groups—workers, professional men, scientists, soldiers—exist under dictatorships, even though they exist in chains, in terror, in misery and in progressive self-destruction. *But there is no such group as businessmen under a dictatorship.* Their place is taken by armed thugs: by bureaucrats and commissars. So if you want to fight for freedom, you must begin by fighting for its unrewarded, unrecognized, unacknowledged, yet best representatives—the American businessmen.

Excerpt from: *Who is Ayn Rand?* (from page 7)

If love did *not* imply admiration, if it did not imply an acknowledgment of moral qualities that the recipient of love possessed—what meaning or significance would love have, and why would Fromm or anyone consider it desirable? Only one answer is possible, and it is not an attractive one: when love is divorced from values, then "love" becomes, not a tribute, but a moral blank check: a promise that one will be forgiven anything, that one will not be abandoned, that one will be taken care of.

Published monthly at 165 East 35th Street, New York 16, N.Y.

Subscription rate: In United States, its possessions, Canada and Mexico, $5 for one year; other countries, $6. Trial subscriptions: 4 months $2. 6 months $3.

Additional copies of this Newsletter: single copy 50¢ (coins, not stamps); 10—99 copies, 25¢ each plus postage (for first-class delivery add 1¢ per copy, for third-class delivery add ½¢ per copy); 100 or more copies, 15¢ each plus postage (same as above).

For change of address send old address and new address with zone number if any. Allow us two weeks to process new subscriptions and change of address.

Ayn Rand and Nathaniel Branden, Editors and Publishers
Barbara Branden, Managing Editor
Elayne Kalberman, Circulation Manager

PRINTED BY CARNEGIE PRESS, INC., NEW YORK CITY

THE OBJECTIVIST NEWSLETTER

Edited and Published by AYN RAND and NATHANIEL BRANDEN

VOL. 1 NO. 3   MARCH, 1962

CHECK YOUR PREMISES
By AYN RAND
"Have Gun, Will Nudge"

Mr. Newton N. Minow, Chairman of the F.C.C., is performing a great, educational public service—though not in the way he intends. He is giving the public an invaluable object lesson on the nature and results of a "mixed economy."

The basic evil in any theory of a "mixed economy"—an economy of freedom mixed with controls—is the evasion of the fact that a government holds a legal monopoly on the use of physical force and that political power is the power of coercion. While a dictatorship rests on a blunt acknowledgment of this fact, on the motto that "might is right"—a "mixed economy" rests on pretending that no such distinction exists, that might and right can be safely scrambled together if we all agree never to raise this issue.

The current policy of the F.C.C. has provided a spectacle of not raising that issue, on a grand scale.

First, Mr. Minow announces that any television or radio station which does not satisfy his unstated criterion of an unspecified public service, will lose its license, that is: will be silenced forever. Then, while the victims mumble feeble protests, vaguely referring to *censorship,* Mr. Minow assumes an air of injured innocence and asserts that his sole intention is "to nudge, to exhort, to urge those who decide what goes on the air to appeal to our higher as well as our lower tastes." And President Kennedy declares: "Mr. Minow has attempted not to use *force,* but to use *encouragement* in persuading the networks to put on better children's programs, more public service programs."

No one has stepped forward to ask Mr. Kennedy whether his word usage is correct; and, if it is, whether we should claim that a holdup man who points a gun, is not attempting to use force, but to use encouragement in persuading a citizen to hand over his wallet.

No one has challenged Mr. Minow's description of censorship: "I dislike censorship as much as anyone else. Yet today we have censorship in a very real sense . . . There is censorship by ratings, by advertisers, by networks, by affiliates which reject programming offered to their area. I want to free expression rather than stifle it. All sections of the community should be served rather than have them cut out by censorship which decrees they cannot see or hear something." (*Show Business Illustrated,* September 19, 1961.)

Let's see whether we can adopt Mr. Minow's concept of censorship: it would mean that the failure of a bad play is "censorship by the box office"—that the frustration of a lady who, weighing three hundred pounds, does not get a chance to model filmy negligees, is "censorship by advertisers"—that the plight of an inventor who finds no backers for his perpetual motion machine, is "censorship by bankers"—that the bankruptcy of a manufacturer who offers us gadgets which we don't buy, is "censorship by consumers"—and that free expression is stifled, whenever a manuscript molders in its author's trunk, cut out by "the censorship of publishers" who decree that we cannot read or hear something. What, then, is non-censorship? Mr. Minow's edicts.

So long as people evade the difference between economic power and political power, between a private choice and a government order, between intellectual persuasion and physical force—Mr. Minow has reason to assume that he can safely stretch their evasions all the way to the ultimate inversion: to the claim that a *private* action is coercion, but a *government* action is freedom.

It is true, as Mr. Minow assures us, that he does not propose to establish censorship; what he proposes is much worse. Censorship, in its old-fashioned meaning, is a government edict that forbids the discussion of some specific subjects or ideas—such, for instance, as sex, religion or criticism of government officials—an edict enforced by the government's scrutiny of all forms of communication prior to their public release. But for stifling the freedom of men's minds the modern method is much more potent; it rests on the power of non-objective law; it neither forbids nor permits anything; it never defines or specifies; it merely delivers men's lives, fortunes, careers, ambitions into the arbitrary power of a bureaucrat who can reward or punish at whim. It spares the bureaucrat the troublesome necessity of committing himself to rigid rules—and it places upon the victims the burden of discovering how to please him, with a fluid unknowable as their only guide.

No, a federal commissioner may never utter a single word for or against any program. But what do you suppose will happen if and when, with or without his knowledge, a third-assistant or a second cousin or just a nameless friend from Washington whispers to a television executive that the commissioner does not like producer X or does not approve of writer Y or takes a great interest in the career of starlet Z, or is anxious to advance the cause of the United Nations?

What makes it possible to bring a free country down to such a level? If you doubt the connection between altruism and statism, I suggest that you count how many times—in the current articles, speeches, debates and hearings—there appeared the magic formula which makes all such outrages possible: *"The Public Interest."*

What is the public interest? No specific definition has ever been or ever can be given by anyone. Since the concept is not used in its literal meaning, to designate the personal

(continued on page 10)

BOOKS

Prosperity Through Freedom*
by Lawrence Fertig

Reviewed by EDITH EFRON

For fourteen years, Lawrence Fertig has been combating collectivism in America by popularizing the basic principles of free enterprise in his column for the Scripps-Howard newspapers. His latest book, *Prosperity Through Freedom,* applies these principles to a wide range of current events, and offers a highly readable survey of the economics behind the headlines.

The most interesting aspect of the book is journalistic rather than theoretical. Filled with statistics, quotations from liberal and libertarian theorists, and information gathered from an impressive number of American and foreign sources, this book provides an arsenal of factual ammunition for advocates of free enterprise.

In a section which examines the myth of Soviet superiority, Mr. Fertig reports in some detail on an important, but little known, study of Russian industry published by Professor G. Warren Nutter under the auspices of the National Bureau of Economic Research, in 1957. Accepting Soviet figures at their face value, Professor Nutter shows that in such basic industries as electric power, natural gas, steel ingots, cement, freight cars, and others, the Soviet time-lag behind the United States was greater in 1955 than it was in 1913. In certain instances, the rate of deterioration is startling. In 1913, the Russian time-lag behind the U.S. in the production of crude petroleum was only 14 years; by 1937, the lag had widened to 26 years; and by 1955, the lag was up to 34 years. Again in 1913, the Russian lag in the production of freight cars was only 33 years; by 1937, the lag had increased to 57 years; and by 1955, the Russians were behind by 69 years. The Nutter study concludes that, according to their own "public relations" statistics, the Russians are about 35 years behind us in quantity of goods produced and about 55 years behind us in production per capita — and the lags have generally been increasing. Professor Nutter's wry concluding comment is worth quoting: "It hardly seems likely that Soviet authorities have practiced the art of understatement in heralding their achievements."

In another fascinating section of Mr. Fertig's book, called "How Our Experts Almost Ruined Germany," he reveals the details of the fiscal advice given to the West German government in 1948 by a commission of American economists. The commissioners' report was declassified only in April, 1961, and one can understand the State Department's reluctance to make its contents known. The report recommended deficit spending and a cheap money policy. It advocated inflationary measures and criticized Germany's "excessive concern for price stability." It objected to granting industry high depreciation allowances, on the grounds that "it was an expenditure of tax funds which would otherwise have been collected by the government." And it concluded that "the nostalgic hopes . . . looking toward a revival of the nineteenth century role of a capital market are doomed to disappointment."

The report landed in a German wastebasket. The West German government did precisely the opposite; in the words of Economics Minister Erhard, it "re-introduced the old rules of a free economy, the rules of *laissez-faire*." The result was "the miracle of German recovery." And what happened to the spurned American commissioners? They went home, reports Mr. Fertig, to continue advocating the same destructive policies for America. One of these commissioners, Professor Walter W. Heller, is now head of President Kennedy's Council of Economic Advisers.

Regrettably, Mr. Fertig is not entirely consistent as a theorist. His advocacy of capitalism is diluted by an occasional concession to economic interventionism. For instance, he challenges particular policies of the Federal Reserve System or the specific administration of the Antitrust laws, but he does not challenge the basic principle or the validity of such institutions. It is also regrettable that he did not present his research in a more scholarly form; more detailed references would have been desirable.

For readers who are swamped by statist-slanted news stories, however, *Prosperity Through Freedom* will be a welcome corrective, a lead to a better understanding of current events, and an eminently valuable book.

"Have Gun, Will Nudge" (from page 9)

interest of every citizen of a country, but is used to imply and establish a *conflict,* the opposition of *private* interests to *public* interest—its use can convey only one meaning: the right of some men (those who, by some undefined criterion, are *the public*) to sacrifice the interests of other men (of those who, for unspecified reasons, are *not* the public). Once that collectivist formula becomes the moral standard of a society, the rest is only a matter of time.

Mr. Paul Rand Dixon, F.T.C. Chairman, has announced: "Private rights are important but the public interest is a greater right."

An article entitled "His Master's Voice?" by Shirley Scheibla in *Barron's* magazine for January 1, 1962, offers the following warning: "The [Communications] Act gives the [Federal Communications] Commission a broad grant of authority to regulate broadcasting 'in the public interest.' Since neither Congress nor the courts ever have been able to agree on a working definition of what constitutes the 'public interest,' the commissioners need only decide that it is served by the way they happen to vote."

That such is the ultimate goal of our present trend, is indicated in Mr. Minow's "vast wasteland" speech of May 9, 1961. While all the concrete-bound, range-of-the-moment modern mentalities have been clamoring over the issue of Westerns *versus* spelling-bees, the ominous key-sentence of that speech has been passed by in comparative silence: the threat to "those few of you who really believe that the public interest is merely what interests the public."

Here is an open declaration that the public is not competent to judge its own interest. Who, then, is? Who will be its guardian and determine its interest, which supersedes any individual rights? Mr. Newton N. Minow.

(continued on page 12)

---

* Published by Henry Regnery Co., $3.95. Available from NBL BOOK SERVICE, INC., 165 East 35th St., New York 16, N.Y., for $3.25 (N.Y.C. residents add 3% sales tax; outside the U.S., add 15¢).

Edith Efron is a journalist whose articles have appeared in such publications as Life, Look, and The New York Times Magazine.

INTELLECTUAL AMMUNITION DEPARTMENT

[*Subscribers are invited to send in the questions that they find themselves unable to answer in philosophical or political discussions. As many questions as space permits will be answered. No questions will be answered by mail.*]

■ **Should a rational advocate of capitalism co-operate with those "conservatives" who base their advocacy of capitalism on religious faith?**

Reason is the faculty that perceives, identifies and integrates the evidence of reality provided by man's senses. To base one's convictions on reason, is to base them on the facts of reality. *Faith* is the acceptance of an idea without evidence or proof, or in spite of evidence to the contrary.

To rest one's advocacy of capitalism on faith, is to concede that *reason* is on the side of one's enemies. Such a position implies that a free society cannot be rationally justified—that there are no *rational* arguments why men should not murder and enslave one another—that logic is on the side of dictatorships, firing squads and concentration camps, but men should renounce logic in favor of such "irrationalities" as freedom, justice, individual rights, achievement, prosperity and progress.

The implications of tying capitalism to faith have come nakedly into the open in the explicit irrationalism of many "conservative" groups. Intending to bring the mystical concept of Original Sin into political theory, they declare that man is depraved by nature, that reason is impotent, that man should not attempt to create a perfect political system or to establish a rational society on earth—but should settle for capitalism, instead.

The communists allege that *their* political philosophy is rational and has been scientifically proved. The mystical "conservatives" concede it and retreat into the world of the supernatural, surrendering *this* world to communism—a victory that the communists' irrational ideology could never win on its own merits.

Collectivism gained its intellectual influence and appeal by promising a *scientific* approach to social problems—a promise which it could not and did not keep. Today, disillusioned by the horrors which collectivism has achieved in practice, people, particularly young people, are seeking a rational alternative—which, in fact, only capitalism can provide. But instead of proof, logic or science, today's mystical "conservatives" have nothing better to offer than appeals to faith, revelation and the supernatural. In our age, in the presence of the triumphs of science, no thinking man will listen to the voices from the Dark Ages speaking of Original Sin and the futility of human endeavor; no thinking man will reject reason and the achievements of man's mind. If the "conservatives" succeeded in convincing him that he must accept capitalism on faith or not at all, he would, properly, answer: Not at all.

To claim that capitalism rests on religious faith is to contradict the fundamental principles of the United States; in America, religion is a private matter which must not be brought into political issues.

One need not be an atheist in order to fight for capitalism—provided one keeps the two issues separate. A rational advocate of capitalism *can* co-operate with religious people who share his political principles, but only in a strictly secular movement, that is: only in a movement that does not claim religion as the base and justification of its political principles.

The greatest single threat to capitalism today is the attempt to put capitalism, mysticism and Original Sin over on the public as one "package deal." No attacks by collectivists could do more to discredit capitalism than is done by this kind of attempt. Its result can be only to consign capitalism to the "lunatic fringe" of political thought and to remove it from the realm of serious, civilized discussion.

A rational advocate of capitalism should repudiate any individual or group that links capitalism to the supernatural. He commits treason to his own cause if and when he co-operates with the mystical "conservatives," if and when he sanctions them as creditable spokesmen for the cause of freedom.   —BARBARA BRANDEN

■ **What is the Objectivist view of the claim, made by many social theorists today, that man's primary psychological need is to receive the approval and esteem of other men?**

Before one can make any statement concerning man's fundamental needs, it is necessary to define precisely the meaning of "need" in this context. A living organism's *needs* are those things which the organism requires, by its nature, for its survival and well-being. Thus we can observe that man needs food, water, air, etc. Such needs are *objectively demonstrable,* and the standard by which one judges them to be needs is clear-cut and unequivocal: that which man's survival *in fact* requires.

The same principle applies to man's psychological needs. It can be shown that man has a need of self-esteem—a need to be confident of his judgment and his capacity to deal with reality. Man's mind is his basic means of survival. The absence of confidence in one's own mind results in a state of neurosis characterized by varying degrees of anxiety, ineffectuality, helplessness—that is, of incompetence to deal with existence. Again, the standard establishing this need is the requirements of man's survival.

A *desire* or a *wish* is not equivalent to a *need;* the fact that a great many men may desire a thing, does not prove that it represents a need inherent in human nature.

No advocate of the theory that man's primary psychological need is to receive the approval of other men, has offered any *proof* of such a claim; it is generally offered as an assertion which, presumably, one is to accept as self-evident.

Now consider the exact implications of this theory; taken literally, it means: (a) that man's survival, well-being and mental health require that no other consideration, such as, for instance, truth, facts, reason or reality, ever be permitted to take precedence over social approval —and that in the event of any clash, it is truth, facts, reason and reality that are to be sacrificed; (b) that if a man sees his fellow men pursuing a course of self-destruction, he should join them — in the interests of his survival — rather than risk their opprobrium; (c) that if a man remains loyal to his own rational judgment, in defiance of the opposition of others, he jeopardizes his psychological

(continued on page 12)

OBJECTIVIST CALENDAR

- On March 1, Ayn Rand will appear on the CBS-TV network program "The Great Challenge: America's Continuing Revolution." 10 to 11 P.M., EST. (See your local listings.)
- Ayn Rand will speak at the Massachusetts Institute of Technology, Cambridge, Mass., on March 14; and at Brown University, Providence, Rhode Island, on March 15.
- Nathaniel Branden will give public readings of three plays by Ayn Rand. April 2: *The Night of January 16th* (original version). April 9: *Ideal*. April 16: *Think Twice*. Those who live in the Greater New York area will shortly receive an announcement giving them full details.
- Correction: Ayn Rand's series of radio programs for the Columbia University station WKCR will be broadcast only on FM (89.9 on your dial).

"Have Gun, Will Nudge" (from page 10)

Consider the implications. If the public is not competent to judge television programs and its own entertainment—how can it be competent to judge political issues? Or economic problems? Or nuclear policies? Or international affairs? And since—on the above premise—the answer is that it can't, shouldn't its guardians protect it from those books and newspapers which, in the guardians' judgment, are not consonant with the public interest and would only confuse the poor incompetent that's unable to judge?

Today—when rule by precedent has all but replaced rule by law, and nothing protects us from enslavement but the fragile barrier of custom—consider the consequences of a precedent such as Mr. Minow is seeking to establish.

Bear in mind what I said about the issue of Antitrust last month, when you evaluate the significance of the following: the article "His Master's Voice?" mentions that General Electric and Westinghouse have both applied for renewal of their broadcasting licenses, and: "Although FCC officials are unable to explain how they would improve program quality by forcing these two companies out of the field, the Commission currently is pondering whether the applications should be turned down on the ground that both firms have been convicted of antitrust violations."

Do you observe the nature of the pincer-movement or the squeeze-play—and the nature of the possibilities inherent in non-objective law?

For the special consideration of all those who are engaged in any branch of the communications industry, I submit the following: In January, 1961, in a case involving censorship of motion pictures (Times Film Corp *v.* City of Chicago), the Supreme Court ruled in favor of the censor, by a majority of one (in a five to four decision). The dissenting opinion, written by Chief Justice Warren, stated: "The decision presents a real danger of eventual censorship for every form of communication, be it newspapers, journals, books, magazines, television, radio or public speeches.... I am aware of no constitutional principle which permits us to hold that the communication of ideas through one medium may be censored while other media are immune.... It is not permissible, as I read the Constitution, for government to release one movie and refuse to release another because of an official's concept of the prevailing need or the public good."

That is the reason why one should fight against the terrorization and enslavement of television. *That* is the issue at stake in the F.C.C. hearings—not the issue of whether today's television programs are good or bad (most of them are atrocious, particularly in the public affairs department)—not the issue of whether some cowboys, gangsters and private-eyes should be sacrificed in favor of more newsreels, slanted documentaries and panel discussions of political topics, with big close-ups of selfless public servants from Washington.

Intellectual Ammunition (from page 11)

well-being, but if he surrenders his judgment in obedience to widely-held beliefs which he knows to be false, he secures his psychological well-being; (d) that an abject second-hander, such as Peter Keating, is the epitome of mental health, whereas a man of independence and integrity, such as Howard Roark, is neurotically self-destructive because he always asks "What *is* true?" and not "What do others *believe* is true?"

To hold the approval of others as one's primary motive and goal, is to be a selfless, mindless, blind parasite incapable of thought and unfit for survival. That a great many men, who dread the responsibility of independent judgment, have chosen this state, is undeniable. But the inescapable result of this state is anxiety, insecurity, the sense of inner emptiness—neurotic symptoms that testify to the incompatibility of such dependence with mental health. The normalcy or healthiness of a psychological condition is not established by its statistical prevalence, but by its appropriateness to the requirements of man's survival. At one time, bubonic plague was dismayingly widespread, but this did not lead physicians to regard it as man's normal or healthy condition. If a person declares that gaining the approval of others is the dominating concern of his life, it is the responsibility of psychologists to recognize his state as a *disease,* and to discover and correct the underlying premises that *cause* his fear of independence—rather than to announce that this fear is an intrinsic attribute of human nature.

Man's survival and his mental health demand that he place *nothing* above his own rational judgment. It was not the parasitical practitioners of "togetherness" who brought mankind out of the cave. And it is not men of intransigent rationality and sovereign intellect who collapse in anxiety and neurosis, crying that they have no sense of personal identity.

How would Objectivism answer the person who claims that man's deepest psychological need is to receive the approval and esteem of others? This Objectivist would tell him: "Speak for yourself, brother." —NATHANIEL BRANDEN

Published monthly at 165 East 35th Street, New York 16, N.Y.
Subscription rate: In United States, its possessions, Canada and Mexico, $5 for one year; other countries, $6. Trial subscriptions: 4 months $2. 6 months $3.
Additional copies of this Newsletter: single copy 50¢ (coins, not stamps); 10 — 99 copies, 25¢ each plus postage (for first-class delivery add 1¢ per copy, for third-class delivery add ½¢ per copy); 100 or more copies, 15¢ each plus postage (same as above).
For change of address send old address and new address with zone number if any. Allow us two weeks to process new subscriptions and change of address.

Ayn Rand and Nathaniel Branden, Editors and Publishers
Barbara Branden, Managing Editor
Elayne Kalberman, Circulation Manager
PRINTED BY CARNEGIE PRESS, INC., NEW YORK CITY

THE OBJECTIVIST NEWSLETTER

Edited and Published by AYN RAND and NATHANIEL BRANDEN

VOL. 1 NO. 4   APRIL, 1962

Counterfeit Individualism
By NATHANIEL BRANDEN

The theory of individualism is a central component of the Objectivist philosophy. Individualism is at once an ethical-political concept and an ethical-psychological one. As an ethical-political concept, individualism upholds the supremacy of individual rights, the principle that man is an end in himself, not a means to the ends of others. As an ethical-psychological concept, individualism holds that man should think and judge independently, valuing nothing higher than the sovereignty of his intellect.

The philosophical base and validation of individualism, as Ayn Rand has shown in *Atlas Shrugged*, is the fact that individualism, ethically, politically and psychologically, is an objective requirement of man's proper survival, of man's survival *qua* man, *qua* rational being. It is implicit in, and necessitated by, a code of ethics that holds *man's life* as its standard of value.

The advocacy of individualism as such is not new; what is new is the Objectivist validation of the theory of individualism and the definition of a consistent way to practice it.

Too often, the ethical-political meaning of individualism is held to be: doing whatever one wishes, regardless of the rights of others. Writers such as Nietzsche and Max Stirner are sometimes quoted in support of this interpretation. Altruists and collectivists have an obvious vested interest in persuading men that such is the meaning of individualism, that the man who refuses to be sacrificed intends to sacrifice others.

The contradiction in, and refutation of, such an interpretation of individualism is this: since the only rational base of individualism as an ethical principle is the requirements of man's survival *qua* man, one man cannot claim the moral right to violate the rights of another. If he denies inviolate rights to other men, he cannot claim such rights for himself; he has rejected the base of rights. No one can claim the moral right to a contradiction.

Individualism does not consist merely of rejecting the belief that man should live for the collective. A man who seeks escape from the responsibility of supporting his life by his own thought and effort, and wishes to survive by conquering, ruling and exploiting others, is not an individualist. An individualist is a man who lives for his own sake *and by his own mind*; he neither sacrifices himself to others nor sacrifices others to himself; he deals with men as a trader—not as a looter; as a Producer—not as an Attila.

It is the recognition of this distinction that altruists and collectivists wish men to lose: the distinction between a trader and a looter, between a Producer and an Attila.

If the meaning of individualism, in its ethical-political context, has been perverted and debased predominantly by its avowed antagonists, the meaning of individualism, in its ethical-psychological context, has been perverted and debased by its professed *supporters*: by those who wish to dissolve the distinction between an independent *judgment* and a subjective *whim*. These are the alleged "individualists" who equate individualism, not with independent *thought*, but with "independent *feelings*." There are no such things as "independent *feelings*." There is only an independent mind.

An individualist is, first and foremost, a *man of reason*. It is upon the ability to think, upon his rational faculty, that man's life depends; rationality is the precondition of independence and self-reliance. An "individualist" who is neither independent nor self-reliant, is a contradiction in terms; individualism and independence are logically inseparable. The basic independence of the individualist consists of his loyalty to his own *mind*: it is his perception of *the facts of reality*, his *understanding*, his *judgment*, that he refuses to sacrifice to the unproved assertions of others. *That* is the meaning of intellectual independence—and that is the essence of an individualist. He is dispassionately and intransigently *fact*-centered.

Man needs knowledge in order to survive, and only reason can achieve it; men who reject the responsibility of thought and reason, can exist only as parasites on the thinking of others. And a parasite is not an individualist. The irrationalist, the whim-worshipper who regards knowledge and objectivity as "restrictions" on his freedom, the range-of-the-moment hedonist who acts on his private feelings, is not an individualist. The "independence" that an irrationalist seeks is *independence from reality*—like Dostoevsky's *Underground* man who cries: "What do I care for the laws of nature and arithmetic, when, for some reason, I dislike those laws and the fact that twice two makes four?"

To the irrationalist, existence is merely a clash between *his* whims and the whims of *others;* the concept of an *objective* reality has no reality to him.

Rebelliousness or unconventionality as such do not constitute proof of individualism. Just as individualism does not consist merely of rejecting collectivism, so it does not consist merely of the absence of conformity. A conformist is a man who declares, "It's true because *others* believe it"—but an individualist is *not* a man who declares, "It's true because *I* believe it." An individualist declares, "I believe it because I see in reason that it's true."

There is an incident in *The Fountainhead* that is worth recalling in this connection. In the chapter on the life and career of collectivist Ellsworth Toohey, Ayn Rand describes the various groups of writers and artists that Toohey organized: there was ". . . a woman who never used capitals in her books, and a man who never used commas . . . and another who wrote poems that neither rhymed nor scanned . . . There was a boy who used no canvas, but did something with bird cages and metronomes . . . A few friends pointed out to Ellsworth Toohey that he seemed guilty of inconsistency; he was so deeply opposed to individualism, they said, and here were all these writers and artists of his, and every one of them was a rabid individualist. 'Do you really think so?' said Toohey, smiling blandly."

What Toohey knew—and what students of Objectivism would do well to understand—is that such subjectivists, in their rebellion against "the tyranny of reality," are less independent and more abjectly parasitical than the most commonplace Babbitt whom they profess to despise. They originate or create nothing; they are profoundly *selfless*—and they struggle to fill the void of the egos they do not possess, by means of the only form of "self-assertiveness" they recognize: defiance for the sake of defiance, irrationality for the sake of irrationality, destruction for the sake of destruction, whims for the sake of whims.

A psychotic is scarcely likely to be accused of conformity; but neither a psychotic nor a subjectivist is an exponent of individualism.

Observe the common denominator in the attempts to corrupt the meaning of individualism as an ethical-political concept and as an ethical-psychological concept: the attempt to divorce individualism from *reason*. But it is only in the context of reason and man's needs as a rational being that the principle

(continued on page 16)

BOOKS

*Ten Thousand Commandments**
by Harold Fleming

Reviewed by AYN RAND

Antitrust is a peculiar underground in American life: it is a secret torture chamber where executions take place in open, public sight, yet remain unseen, rendered invisible by such a screen of unintelligible legal complexities that few laymen can hope to see through it. Harold Fleming has split that screen—by means of a brilliantly incisive common sense—and has presented a coherent view of the chaos beneath. His book is a primer for laymen, condensed with unusual skill, simplicity and accuracy. If you want to grasp the essentials of Antitrust—its issues, methods and meaning—I suggest that you begin by reading *Ten Thousand Commandments*. No abstract estimates, such as "injustice," "persecution," "terrorization," can convey the nature of what is going on, without the shocking facts. These facts have to be read to be believed.

"The trouble," writes Mr. Fleming, "isn't simply that almost every businessman in the United States could now, by the new rules, be haled into court by government officials and be fined, branded a criminal . . . and subjected to treble damage suits by competitors and customers. It is that the policies and practices by which American business has grown so phenomenally productive have one and all in recent years been damned, discouraged, and suppressed."

Mr. Fleming shows how the alleged crime of "injury to *competition*" was switched into "injury to *competitors*"—by a succession of court decisions reinterpreting non-objective, undefinable statutes—and injury to *actual* competitors was switched into injury to *potential* competitors. The alleged crime of abusing an undefined "monopoly power" (the abuse consisting of "excluding" competitors) was switched into the crime of *"intent"* to abuse it, and then into the crime of possessing *"an opportunity for abuse,"* regardless of whether a business concern ever took that opportunity or not. "Thus it seems that a company may now find itself violating the Sherman Act even though (1) it 'excludes' competitors only by keeping ahead of them (Alcoa case); (2) it doesn't even keep ahead of them (Tobacco case); and (3) it doesn't try to (Griffith case)."

The alleged crime of "conspiracy" was switched from an actual secret agreement into a presumed "meeting of the minds"—then into "consciously parallel action" of independent companies—and then: "In the Schine case the high Court said, 'The concerted action of the parent company, its subsidiaries, and the named officers and directors in that endeavor was a conspiracy which was not immunized by reason of the fact that the members were closely affiliated rather than independent.' That would seem to mean that it is illegal for the officers of different departments of an integrated company to cooperate."

What is the net result of this nightmare? "Since the essential purpose of all the variegated attacks has been to hamper the more successful business for the benefit of the less successful business, the result has been not to clarify the law, but to dissolve it. . . . What is left is merely a rule that the bigger companies are almost invariably wrong on some count or other and the little companies almost invariably right."

It would be hard to find a clearer indication of the fact that the morality of altruism—the sacrifice of success to failure, of ability to need—is the basic cause and motive power of Antitrust. It is unfortunate that Mr. Fleming does not seem to grasp the full meaning of his own statement. In the last two chapters of his book, attempting to explain and evaluate the monstrous facts he has presented, he resorts to some vague, superficial generalities, such as the suggestion that some sort of "Freudian" fear is the motive for the persecution of businessmen.

But he is too good a reporter to let his theory interfere with the facts he is presenting. And his book is so good that the inadequacy of his explanation can be safely overlooked. The facts speak for themselves.

Child Labor and the Industrial Revolution
By R. HESSEN

The least understood and most widely misrepresented aspect of the history of capitalism is child labor.

One cannot evaluate the phenomenon of child labor in England during the Industrial Revolution of the late eighteenth and early nineteenth century, unless one realizes that the introduction of the factory system offered a livelihood, a means of survival, to tens of thousands of children who would not have lived to be youths in the pre-capitalistic eras.

The factory system led to a rise in the general standard of living, to rapidly falling urban death rates and decreasing infant mortality—and produced an unprecedented population explosion.

In 1750, England's population was 6 million; it was 9 million in 1800 and 12 million in 1820, a rate of increase without precedent in any era. The age distribution of the population shifted enormously; the proportion of children and youths increased sharply. "The proportion of those born in London dying before five years of age" fell from 74.5% in 1730-49 to 31.8% in 1810-29. (Mabel C. Buer, *Health, Welfare and Population in the Early Days of the Industrial Revolution*, p. 30.) Children who hitherto would have died in infancy now had a chance for survival.

Both the rising population and the rising life expectancy give the lie to the claims of socialist and fascist critics of capitalism that the conditions of the laboring classes were progressively deteriorating during the Industrial Revolution.

One is both morally unjust and ignorant of history if one blames capitalism for the condition of children during the Industrial Revolution, since, in fact, capitalism brought an enormous improvement over their condition in the preceding age. The source of that injustice was ill-informed, emotional novelists and poets, like Dickens and Mrs. Browning; fanciful medievalists, like Southey; political tract writers posturing as economic historians, like Engels and Marx. All of them painted a vague, rosy picture of a lost "golden age" of the working classes, which, allegedly, was destroyed by the Industrial Revolution. Historians have not supported their assertions. Investigation and common sense have deglamorized the pre-factory system of domestic industry. In that system, the worker made a costly initial investment, or paid heavy rentals, for a loom or frame, and bore most of the speculative risks involved. His diet was drab and meager, and even subsistence often depended on whether work could be found for his wife and children. There was nothing romantic or enviable about a family living and working together in a badly lighted, improperly ventilated, and poorly constructed cottage.

How did children thrive before the Industrial Revolution? In 1697, John Locke wrote a report for the Board of Trade on the problem of poverty and poor-relief. Locke estimated that a laboring man and his wife in good health could support no more than two children, and he recommended that *all children over three years of age* (!) should be taught to earn their living at working schools for spinning and knitting, where they would be given food. "What they can have at home, from their parents," wrote Locke, "is seldom more than bread and water, and that very scantily too."

Professor Ludwig von Mises reminds us: "The factory owners did not have the power to compel anybody to take a factory job. They could only hire people who were ready to work for the wages offered to them. Low as these wage rates were, they were nonetheless much more than these paupers could earn in any other field open to them. It is a distortion of facts to say that the factories carried off the housewives from the nurseries and the kitchen and the children from their

(continued on page 16)

---

* Published by F.E.E. Available for $1.50 plus 15¢ postage from NBL BOOK SERVICE, INC., 165 East 35th St., New York 16, N.Y. (N.Y.C. residents add 5¢ sales tax).

INTELLECTUAL AMMUNITION DEPARTMENT

[Subscribers are invited to send in the questions that they find themselves unable to answer in philosophical or political discussions. As many questions as space permits will be answered. No questions will be answered by mail.]

■ **How does one lead a rational life in an irrational society, such as we have today?**

I will confine my answer to a single, fundamental aspect of this question. I will name only one principle, the opposite of the idea which is so prevalent today and which is responsible for the spread of evil in the world. That principle is: *Never fail to pronounce moral judgment.*

Nothing can corrupt and disintegrate a culture or a man's character as thoroughly as does the precept of *moral agnosticism*, the idea that one must never pass moral judgment on others, that one must be morally tolerant of anything, that the good consists of never distinguishing good from evil.

It is obvious who profits and who loses by such a precept. It is not justice or equal treatment that you grant to men when you abstain equally from praising men's virtues and from condemning men's vices. When your impartial attitude declares, in effect, that neither the good nor the evil may expect anything from you—whom do you betray and whom do you encourage?

But to pronounce moral judgment is an enormous responsibility. To be a judge, one must possess an unimpeachable character; one need not be omniscient or infallible, and it is not an issue of errors of knowledge; one needs an unbreached integrity, that is: the absence of any indulgence in conscious, willful evil. Just as a judge in a court of law may err, when the evidence is inconclusive, but may not evade the evidence available, nor accept bribes, nor allow any personal feeling, emotion, desire or fear to obstruct his mind's judgment of the facts of reality—so every rational person must maintain an equally strict and solemn integrity in the courtroom within his own mind, where the responsibility is more awesome than in a public tribunal, because *he*, the judge, is the only one to know when he has been impeached.

There is, however, a court of appeal from one's judgments: objective reality. A judge puts himself on trial every time he pronounces a verdict. It is only in today's reign of amoral cynicism, subjectivism and hooliganism that men may imagine themselves free to utter any sort of irrational judgment and to suffer no consequences. But, in fact, a man is to be judged by the judgments he pronounces. The things which he condemns or extols exist in objective reality and are open to the independent appraisal of others. It is his own moral character and standards that he reveals, whenever he blames or praises. If he condemns America and extols Soviet Russia—or if he attacks businessmen and defends juvenile delinquents—or if he denounces a great work of art and praises trash—it is the nature of his own soul that he confesses.

It is their fear of *this* responsibility that prompts most people to adopt an attitude of indiscriminate moral neutrality. It is the fear best expressed in the precept: "Judge not, that ye be not judged." But that precept, in fact, is an abdication of moral responsibility: it is a moral blank check one gives to others in exchange for a moral blank check one expects for oneself.

There is no escape from the fact that men have to make choices; so long as men have to make choices, there is no escape from moral values; so long as moral values are at stake, no moral neutrality is possible. To abstain from condemning a torturer, is to become an accessory to the torture and murder of his victims.

The moral principle to adopt in this issue, is: *"Judge, and be prepared to be judged."*

The opposite of moral neutrality is not a blind, arbitrary, self-righteous condemnation of any idea, action or person that does not fit one's mood, one's memorized slogans or one's snap-judgment of the moment. Indiscriminate tolerance and indiscriminate condemnation are not two opposites: they are two variants of the same evasion. To declare that "everybody is white" or "everybody is black" or "everybody is neither white nor black, but gray," is not a moral judgment, but an escape from the responsibility of moral judgment.

To judge means: to evaluate a given concrete by reference to an abstract principle or standard. It is not an easy task; it is not a task that can be performed automatically by one's feelings, "instincts" or hunches. It is a task that requires the most precise, the most exacting, the most ruthlessly objective and *rational* process of thought. It is fairly easy to grasp abstract moral principles; it can be very difficult to apply them to a given situation, particularly when it involves the moral character of another person. When one pronounces moral judgment, whether in praise or in blame, one must be prepared to answer "Why?" and to prove one's case—to oneself and to any rational inquirer.

The policy of always pronouncing moral judgment does not mean that one must regard oneself as a missionary charged with the responsibility of "saving everyone's soul"—nor that one must give unsolicited moral appraisals to all those one meets. It means: (a) that one must know clearly, in full, verbally identified form, one's own moral evaluation of every person, issue and event with which one deals, and act accordingly; (b) that one must make one's moral evaluation known to others, when it is rationally appropriate to do so.

This last means that one need not launch into unprovoked moral denunciations or debates, but that one *must* speak up in situations where silence can objectively be taken to mean agreement with or sanction of evil. When one deals with irrational persons, where argument is futile, a mere "I don't agree with you" is sufficient to negate any implication of moral sanction. When one deals with better people, a full statement of one's views may be morally required. But in no case and in no situation may one permit one's own values to be attacked or denounced, and keep silent.

Moral values are the motive power of a man's actions. By pronouncing moral judgment, one protects the clarity of one's own perception and the rationality of the course one chooses to pursue. It makes a difference whether one thinks that one is dealing with human errors of knowledge or with human evil.

Observe how many people evade, rationalize and drive their minds into a state of blind stupor, in dread of discovering that those they deal with—their "loved ones" or friends or business associates or political rulers—are not merely mistaken, but *evil*. Observe that this dread leads them to sanction, to help and to spread the very evil whose existence they fear to acknowledge.

If people did not indulge in such abject evasions as the claim that some contemptible liar "means well"—that a mooching bum "can't help it"—that a juvenile delinquent "needs love"—that a criminal "doesn't know any better"—that a power-seeking politician is moved by patriotic concern for "the public good"—that communists are merely "agrarian reformers"—the history of the past few decades, or centuries, would have been different.

Ask yourself why totalitarian dictatorships find it necessary to pour money and effort into propaganda for their own helpless, chained, gagged slaves, who have no means of protest or defense. The answer is that even the humblest peasant or the lowest savage would rise in blind rebellion, were he to realize that he is being immolated, not to some incomprehensible "noble purpose," but to plain, naked human evil.

Observe also that moral neutrality necessitates a progressive sympathy for vice and a progressive antagonism to virtue. A man who struggles not to acknowledge that evil is evil, finds it increasingly dangerous to acknowledge that the good is the good. To him, a person of virtue is a threat that can topple all of his evasions—particularly when an issue of justice is involved, which demands that he take sides. It is then that such formulas as "Nobody is ever fully right or fully wrong" and "Who am I to judge?" take their lethal effect. The man who begins by saying: "There is some good in the worst of

(continued on page 16)

OBJECTIVIST CALENDAR

- Nathaniel Branden will address the Psychology Club at Brooklyn College on April 9, 12:30 P.M., in Room 3127, Ingersoll Hall. His subject is "Self-Esteem and Social Approval." Open to the public; admission free.

- Nathaniel Branden will offer a seven lecture course on contemporary psychological theories, at NATHANIEL BRANDEN INSTITUTE, beginning April 23. He will present the essentials of his own theory of neurosis in the concluding two lectures. Those who live in the Greater New York area will receive an announcement giving them full details. Later this year, the course will be made available via tape recordings to NBI groups across the country.

- Paintings by Frank O'Connor and Joan Blumenthal will be on exhibit in the Robert Brackman Student Show at the Art Students League, 215 West 57th St., New York City, April 23 through April 28. Weekdays: 9 A.M. to 10 P.M.; Saturdays: 9 A.M. to 4 P.M.

- Ayn Rand will speak at Boston University on April 25. Her subject is "The Esthetic Vacuum of Our Age."

- Ayn Rand's lecture on "America's Persecuted Minority: Big Business" has been published by NATHANIEL BRANDEN INSTITUTE and is available from THE OBJECTIVIST NEWSLETTER. Price: 50¢ (N.Y.C. residents add 2¢ sales tax).

Counterfeit Individualism (from page 13)

of individualism can be justified. Torn out of this context, any advocacy of "individualism" becomes as arbitrary and irrational as the advocacy of collectivism.

This is the basis of Objectivism's total opposition to any alleged "individualists" who attempt to equate individualism with subjectivism.

And this is the basis of Objectivism's total repudiation of any self-styled "Objectivists" who permit themselves to believe that any compromise, meeting ground or rapprochement is possible between Objectivism and that counterfeit individualism which consists of declaring: "It's right because *I* feel it" or "It's good because *I* want it" or "It's true because *I* believe it."

Child Labor (from page 14)

play. These women had nothing to cook with and to feed their children. These children were destitute and starving. Their only refuge was the factory. It saved them, in the strict sense of the term, from death by starvation." (*Human Action*, p. 615.)

Factory children went to work at the insistence of their parents. The children's hours of labor were very long, but the work was often quite easy—usually just attending a spinning or weaving machine and retying threads when they broke. It was not on behalf of such children that the agitation for factory legislation began. The first child labor law in England (1788) regulated the hours and conditions of labor of the miserable children who worked as chimney sweeps—a dirty, dangerous job which long antedated the Industrial Revolution, and which was not connected with factories. The first Act which applied to factory children was passed to protect those who had been sent into virtual slavery by the parish authorities, *a government body*: they were deserted or orphaned pauper children who were legally under the custody of the poor-law officials in the parish, and who were bound by these officials into long terms of unpaid apprenticeship in return for a bare subsistence.

Conditions of employment and sanitation are acknowledged to have been best in the larger and newer factories. As successive Factory Acts, between 1819 and 1846, placed greater and greater restrictions on the employment of children and adolescents, the owners of the larger factories, which were more easily and frequently subject to visitation and scrutiny by the Factory Inspectors, increasingly chose to dismiss children from employment rather than be subjected to elaborate, arbitrary and ever-changing regulations on how they might run a factory which employed children. The terrible result of this bureaucratic meddling was that these dismissed children, who needed to work in order to survive, were forced to seek jobs in smaller, older and more out-of-the-way factories, where the conditions of employment, sanitation and safety were markedly inferior. Those who could not find new jobs were reduced to the status of their counterparts a hundred years before, that is, to irregular agricultural labor, or worse—in the words of Professor von Mises, to "infest the country as vagabonds, beggars, tramps, robbers and prostitutes."

Child labor was not ended by legislative fiat; child labor ended when it became economically unnecessary for children to earn wages in order to survive—when the income of their parents became sufficient to support them. The emancipators and benefactors of those children were not bureaucrats, but manufacturers and financiers. Their efforts and investments in machinery led to a rise in real wages, to a growing abundance of goods at lower prices and to an incomparable improvement in the general standard of living.

The proper answer to the critics of the Industrial Revolution is given by Professor T. S. Ashton: "There are today on the plains of India and China men and women, plague-ridden and hungry, living lives little better, to outward appearance, than those of the cattle that toil with them by day and share their places of sleep by night. Such Asiatic standards, and such unmechanized horrors, are the lot of those who increase their numbers without passing through an industrial revolution." (*The Industrial Revolution*, p. 161.)

Let me add that the Industrial Revolution and its consequent prosperity, were the achievement of capitalism and cannot be achieved under any other politico-economic system. As proof, I offer you the current spectacle of Soviet Russia which combines industrialization—and famine.

Intellectual Ammunition (from page 15)

us," goes on to say: "There is some bad in the best of us"—then: "There's *got to* be some bad in the best of us"—and then: "It's the best of us who make life difficult—why don't they keep silent?—who are *they* to judge?"

And then, on some gray, middle-aged morning, such a man realizes suddenly that he has betrayed all the values he had loved in his distant spring, and wonders how it happened, and slams his mind shut to the answer, by telling himself hastily that the fear he had felt in his worst, most shameful moments was right and that values have no chance in this world.

An irrational society is a society of moral cowards—of men paralyzed by the loss of moral standards, principles and goals. But since men have to act, so long as they live, such a society is ready to be taken over by anyone willing to set its direction. The initiative can come from only two types of men: either from the man who is willing to assume the responsibility of asserting rational values—or from the thug who is not troubled by questions of responsibility.

No matter how hard the struggle, there is only one choice that a rational man can make in the face of such an alternative.

—AYN RAND

Published monthly at 165 East 35th Street, New York 16, N.Y.
Subscription rate: in United States, its possessions, Canada and Mexico, $5 for one year; other countries, $6. Trial subscriptions: 4 months $2. 6 months $3.
Additional copies of this Newsletter: single copy 50¢ (coins, not stamps); 10 — 99 copies, 25¢ each plus postage (for first-class delivery add 1¢ per copy, for third-class delivery add ½¢ per copy); 100 or more copies, 15¢ each plus postage (same as above).
For change of address send old address and new address with zone number if any. Allow us two weeks to process new subscriptions and change of address.

Ayn Rand and Nathaniel Branden, Editors and Publishers
Barbara Branden, Managing Editor
Elayne Kalberman, Circulation Manager
PRINTED BY CARNEGIE PRESS, INC., NEW YORK CITY

THE OBJECTIVIST NEWSLETTER

Edited and Published by AYN RAND and NATHANIEL BRANDEN

VOL. 1 NO. 5   MAY, 1962

CHECK YOUR PREMISES
By AYN RAND

Who Will Protect Us from Our Protectors?

Objectivists hold that the political philosophy of collectivism is based on a view of man as a congenital incompetent, a helpless, mindless creature who must be fooled and ruled by a special elite with some unspecified claim to superior wisdom and a lust for power.

Those who are inclined to doubt it, would do well to study President Kennedy's message to Congress of March 15, 1962, on the subject of "Protection for Consumers." It is an extraordinarily revealing and enlightening document.

"The Federal Government [is] by nature the highest spokesman for all the people," said President Kennedy. Leaving aside, for the moment, the highly ambiguous implications of such a sweeping statement, let us take him at his word—and see where it will lead us.

The first moral obligation of any spokesman, high or low, is to practice what he preaches. Let us attempt, therefore, to apply the ethical principles enunciated in Mr. Kennedy's message, to the policies of the Federal Government and of our political leaders.

Mr. Kennedy starts by promulgating a queer concept: *"the rights of the consumers."* These rights, apparently, are something other than the rights possessed by *all* men, and belong only to consumers, or: to men in their capacity as consumers. Since the only other human capacity relevant in this context is that of *producers*, it appears that consumers possess these rights, but producers do not. What are these rights? Mr. Kennedy lists them as follows: (1) *The right to safety*—(2) *The right to be informed*—(3) *The right to choose*—(4) *The right to be heard.* Apparently, the producers have no right to safety, no right to be informed, no right to choose, no right to be heard. Let us accept even that for a moment—for a very brief moment—and let us consider only these consumers' "rights," as Mr. Kennedy defines them.

(1) *"The right to safety—to be protected against the marketing of goods which are hazardous to health or life."*

It is true that such marketing is immoral. It is also true that our *safety* is critically imperiled today — but ptomaine poisoning is not the worst danger threatening us. So, by the same principle, shouldn't the government be prevented from selling us the kind of policies which are *hazardous* to health, wealth, liberty or life?

(2) *"The right to be informed—to be protected against fraudulent, deceitful or grossly misleading information, advertising, labelling, or other practices, and to be given the facts he needs to make an informed choice."*

Quite true. But the most critical choice we have to make today—a choice whose consequences are much more crucial than those of buying the wrong kind of laundry detergent—a choice in which our future, our freedom, our work, our property and our lives are at stake—is the choice of a candidate and a political program at election time. So shouldn't our political leaders refrain from *fraudulent, deceitful or grossly misleading* promises, slogans, generalities, evasions, equivocations, or other practices—and shouldn't they *give us the facts we need to make an informed choice?* Is there any other field today as swamped with confusion and misinformation as the field of politics—yet is there any other field in which the need for an informed choice is so enormously urgent?

(3) *"The right to choose—to be assured, wherever possible, access to a variety of products and services at competitive prices . . ."*

This is a highly dubious formulation—since nobody can claim a *"right"* to the products and services of others. But let us assume that Mr. Kennedy merely meant that *variety* is desirable. If so, shouldn't we have access to a variety of political ideas and viewpoints? Shouldn't we be offered some choice other than the stale, gray statism of two indistinguishable political parties?

(4) *"The right to be heard—to be assured that consumer interests will receive full and sympathetic consideration in the formulation of Government policy . . ."*

This applies to any opponent of businessmen. But when, in the last few decades, has any opponent of statism been *heard* in Washington? When has he received *full and sympathetic consideration* from the government or from those privileged pressure groups and cliques which are fostered, aided and abetted by the government? When has he received anything but smears, threats, defamations, denunciations, license-revoking or Antitrust suits?

To "protect" these "consumers' rights," Mr. Kennedy asked for more power and more money: for "new legislative authority" and "increased appropriations," to create new and/or enlarged government agencies with new and/or wider powers.

A double standard of ethics—a demand that some men practice what others do not have to practice—is morally indefensible. Yet that double standard underlies Mr. Kennedy's entire message, which seems to be addressed to the psychology of those concrete-bound people who cannot see past the range of the moment or connect one specific issue to another or look for fundamental moral principles.

"The march of technology—" said Mr. Kennedy, "affecting for example, the foods we eat, the medicines we take, and the many appliances we use in our homes—has increased the difficulties of the consumer along with his opportunities . . . Many of the new products used every day in the home are highly complex. The housewife is called upon to be an amateur electrician, mechanic, chemist, toxicologist, dietician and mathematician—but she is rarely furnished the information she needs to perform these tasks proficiently."

Well, the march of collectivism and statism—affecting every aspect of our lives, surrendering an ever-growing degree of arbitrary power to the government—has increased the difficulties of the voter (though not his opportunities). When the government was restricted to its proper function—that of policeman and umpire—an honestly applied common sense was sufficient for a voter to make an intelligent choice. But when the government controls every aspect of a complex industrial civilization, and the voter is asked to choose the men who will determine the fate of industry, science, art and every other human activity—what knowledge will be sufficient to make *that* choice? Today, the voter—that same housewife, for instance—is called upon to be an amateur philosopher, psychologist, sociologist, economist, industrial expert, nuclear physicist, TV program director, urban planner, jungle missionary, to name only a few—but she is rarely furnished the information she needs to perform these tasks proficiently.

"Important steps are being taken," said Mr. Kennedy, "to help assure more adequate protection for the savings that prudent consumers lay aside . . ."

(continued on page 18)

BOOKS

*The Anti-Capitalistic Mentality**
by Ludwig von Mises

Reviewed by **EDITH EFRON**

At a time when "conservative" and "liberal" thought alike manifests a violent opposition to *laissez-faire* capitalism, it is important to understand not only the overt "intellectual" hostility that capitalism provokes, but also the covert psychological motivation that underlies this hostility. In a book entitled *The Anti-Capitalistic Mentality*, Professor Ludwig von Mises discusses some crucial aspects of this motivation.

In any statist or religious-caste society, where men are not equal before the law, says Professor von Mises, an individual's wealth or poverty, fame or ignominy, may be attributable to "the system," and do not necessarily reflect his intelligence, productiveness or competence. But in a *laissez-faire* capitalist society, where men are equal before the law, where they earn their wealth and distinction by trading their skills and achievements in a free market, a man's long-range failure, like his long-range success, *is* an objective reflection of his ability. It is precisely this inexorable rule of capitalism—"to each according to his ability"—that wounds the self-esteem of the "frustrated mediocrity," and engenders the widespread hatred for the *laissez-faire* system.

Ironically, Mises points out, the most passionately voiced charge against capitalism claims that it is an "unjust" system. The man who hates and fears *laissez faire* does not confess that what he resents is precisely the implacable justice of this system. He prefers to evade the fact that reason and effort are the cause of both an individual's and a nation's wealth; and he projects, instead, a wishful fantasy as an alternative theory.

Industrial production and wealth, asserts the anti-capitalist, are not to be attributed to any individual's creative thought or action, but are a "free gift of nature." Such "gifts" as refrigerators, automobiles, lifesaving drugs and cyclotrons multiply automatically across the centuries through the intervention of impersonal agencies called "Science," "Technology" and "Progress," and each man is morally entitled to his "fair share" of these "gifts."

"The doctrines of Marx received approval," writes Mises, "simply because they adopted this popular interpretation of events and clothed it with a pseudophilosophical veil. . . . In the scheme of Marx, the 'material productive forces' are a superhuman entity independent of the will and actions of men." Only the State, according to this "gift of nature" theory of wealth, can achieve "social justice" by wresting the "gifts" from the hands of the evil, greedy rich, who have appropriated more than their "fair share," and by redistributing them "fairly" among the virtuous, non-greedy poor.

Such is the rationale of the Welfare State, which gives the apathetic bum his "fair share" of the wages of the hard-working laborer, and gives the incompetent businessman his "fair share" of a great corporation's patents. Such, too, is the rationale of our foreign aid program which is righteously determined to give the "backward nations" their "fair share" of America's productivity—a notion that makes sense, Mises observes, only if one assumes that "the Lord presented mankind with a definite quantity of machines and expected that these contrivances would be distributed equally among the various nations." The driving motive of these irrational policies, Mises states bluntly, is the desire to destroy the hated system which rewards men according to their abilities, and to substitute one which will "give to the frustrated mediocrity 'according to his needs.'"

---

* Published by D. Van Nostrand Co., $3.75. Available from NBL BOOK SERVICE, INC., 165 East 35th St., New York 16, N.Y., for $2.95 (N.Y.C. residents add 3% sales tax; outside the U.S., add 15¢).

Edith Efron is a journalist whose articles have appeared in such publications as Life, Look, *and* The New York Times Magazine.

The "gift of nature" theory of wealth may be temporarily soothing to precarious egos, but it is not a safe guide to action in practical reality. Industrial wealth does not, in fact, fall like perpetual manna from the Marxian skies. Indeed, it is blatantly absent in the socialist nations which are officially committed to that theory. In this country, Mises demonstrates, the continued pursuit of a subverted "justice" which penalizes the productive for the sake of the non-productive, must destroy our industrial wealth as it destroys the free market and free political institutions, which are its preconditions. The choice before us, he concludes, is: the adoption of *laissez-faire* capitalism or an inevitable collapse into dictatorship and barbarism.

This challenging and informative book contains an excellent analysis of the operation of a free-market economy, as well as a provocative discussion of the impact of the anti-capitalistic mentality on America's cultural and intellectual life. There are occasional points in the book to which one must take exception: for instance, one must dispute the author's psychological theory which attributes creativeness to a primary human desire to escape discomfort; one must also question his apparent (and puzzling) regard for such mystical philosophers as Croce, Bergson and Whitehead. But these are minor flaws in a book that provides a cogent and illuminating analysis of the most dangerous trend in our society.

Who Will Protect Us from Our Protectors?
(from page 17)

Protection—from whom? The only real threat to people's savings, which shrinks them and can wipe them out, is *inflation*. Inflation is not caused by the actions of private citizens, but *by the government:* by an artificial expansion of the money supply required to support deficit spending. No private embezzlers or bank robbers in history have ever plundered people's savings on a scale comparable to the plunder perpetrated by the fiscal policies of statist governments. Should this knowledge have been withheld from us?

"Excessive and untimely use of credit," said Mr. Kennedy, "arising out of ignorance of its true cost is harmful both to the stability of the economy and to the welfare of the public. Legislation should therefore be enacted requiring lenders and vendors to disclose to borrowers in advance the actual amounts and rates which they will be paying for credit."

Nobody forces a man to borrow money and nobody hides from him the cost of such credit, though it may be difficult to compute; a borrower who is neither lazy nor irresponsible can compute it. But which one of us can compute *his* share of the cost of the government's "excessive and untimely use of credit"? Which one of us can compute what he pays to the government in hidden taxes with every purchase he makes? And if any of the proposals in Mr. Kennedy's message become laws, shouldn't they carry a provision requiring the government to disclose what part of a product's price represents the cost of the additional bureaus and bureaucrats assigned to "protect" us?

Mr. Kennedy gave special emphasis to the issue labeled "Truth in Packaging." The consumers, he said, "have the right to know what is in the package they buy . . . a right to expect that packages will carry reliable and readily usable information about their contents."

Doesn't this principle apply to the kind of political packages or package-deals that are put over on us daily? Don't we have a right to expect *reliable and readily usable information* about the content of the packages labeled "New Deal," "Fair Deal," "New Frontier"?

The consumer may not realize, said Mr. Kennedy, that "changes in the customary size or shape of the package" may deceive him. If the new size or shape of a carton contains half-an-ounce less breakfast cereal than did the old one, what damage does the consumer suffer, compared to the disasters that result from changes in the customary meaning of political terms, concepts and principles? And if the consumer does not know "whether the 'large economy size' is really a bargain," has he any way of knowing whether a gigantic Welfare State economy is a bargain? *(continued on page 19)*

INTELLECTUAL AMMUNITION DEPARTMENT

[*Subscribers are invited to send in the questions that they find themselves unable to answer in philosophical or political discussions. As many questions as space permits will be answered. No questions will be answered by mail.*]

■ **Since everything in the universe requires a cause, must not the universe itself have a cause, which is God?**

There are two basic fallacies in this argument. The first is the assumption that, if the universe required a causal explanation, the positing of a "God" would provide it. To posit God as the creator of the universe is only to push the problem back one step farther: Who then created God? Was there a still earlier God who created the God in question? We are thus led to an infinite regress—the very dilemma that the positing of a "God" was intended to solve. But if it is argued that no one created God, that God does not require a cause, that God has existed eternally—then on what grounds is it denied that the universe has existed eternally?

It is true that there cannot be an infinite series of antecedent causes. But recognition of this fact should lead one to reappraise the validity of the initial question, *not* to attempt to answer it by stepping outside the universe into some gratuitously invented supernatural dimension.

This leads to the second and more fundamental fallacy in this argument: the assumption that the universe as a whole *requires* a causal explanation. It does not. The universe is the total of that which exists. Within the universe, the emergence of new entities can be explained in terms of the actions of entities that already exist: the cause of a tree is the seed of the parent tree; the cause of a machine is the purposeful reshaping of matter by men. All actions presuppose the existence of entities—and all emergences of new entities presuppose the existence of entities that caused their emergence. All causality presupposes the existence of *something that acts as a cause*. To demand a cause for all of existence is to demand a contradiction: if the cause exists, it is part of existence; if it does *not* exist, it cannot be a cause. *Nothing* cannot be the cause of *something*. *Nothing* does not exist. Causality presupposes existence, existence does not presuppose causality: there can be no cause "outside" of existence or "anterior" to it. The *forms* of existence may change and evolve, but the *fact* of existence is the irreducible primary at the base of all causal chains. Existence—not "God"—is the First Cause.

Just as the concept of causality applies to events and entities within the universe, but not to the universe as a whole—so the concept of time applies to events and entities within the universe, but not to the universe as a whole. The universe did not "begin"—it did not, at some point in time, "spring into being." Time is a measurement of motion. Motion presupposes entities that move. If nothing existed, there could be no time. Time is "in" the universe; the universe is not "in" time.

The man who asks: "Where did existence come from?" or: "What caused it?"—is the man who has never grasped that *existence exists*. This is the mentality of a savage or a mystic who regards existence as some sort of incomprehensible *miracle*—and seeks to "explain" it by reference to *non-existence*.

Existence is all that exists, the non-existent does not exist; there is nothing for existence to have come out of—and *nothing* means *nothing*. If you are tempted to ask: "What's outside the universe?"—recognize that you are asking: "What's outside of existence?" and that the idea of "something outside of existence" is a contradiction in terms; *nothing* is outside of existence, and "nothing" is not just another kind of "something"—it is *nothing*. Existence exists; you cannot go outside it, you cannot get under it, on top of it or behind it. Existence exists—and *only* existence exists: *there is nowhere else to go.*

—**NATHANIEL BRANDEN**

Who Will Protect Us from Our Protectors?

(from page 18)

Speaking of the labeling of drugs, Mr. Kennedy said that the consumers "should be able to identify the drug by a simple, common name in order to avoid confusion . . ."

The simple, common name for all the political theories and measures advanced in Washington in the past decades is: *socialism*. And if no political mislabeling was involved, how are we to explain the fact that Norman Thomas and the Socialist party never won a popular vote of significant size, yet all the planks of their early platforms have now been enacted into law by two political parties which did not attach that label to the package they were selling?

Perhaps the most ominously dangerous issue in Mr. Kennedy's message is the unstressed, unobtrusive package-deal which equates *harmful* drugs with *ineffectual* drugs—and proposes to place both under the control of bureaucrats who would have the power to bar from the market any drug they chose to designate as "ineffectual." Mr. Kennedy did not specify who would be entrusted with such totalitarian authority over so complex, so crucial, so controversial an activity as medical research. He referred to that proposed ruler or group of rulers only as "an impartial scientific source."

It is not necessary to comment on the fate of any great scientific innovator delivered into the power of his professional colleagues. One example is sufficient: if Mr. Kennedy's proposal had been put into effect in the nineteenth century, the world would never have heard of Pasteur, who was violently opposed by the best "scientific sources," by virtually the entire medical profession of his time.

No first-rate man or first-rate mind will devote his life to the excruciating task of pursuing new knowledge (or to any task), if the value and future of his work are to be determined by the arbitrary judgment of any one man or group, whose verdict is final and backed by the power of a gun. Such would be the end of medical research in the United States. And such is the reward, proposed by our President, for those independent scientists and drug manufacturers whose great, lifesaving achievements he cited in the same message.

There are two unstated premises on which the message is built, the "undisclosed" ingredients within the package we are expected to absorb: (1) the axiom that private citizens are, by nature, either helpless fools or ruthless scoundrels, but *government officials can do no wrong*; (2) businessmen, by nature, are the people's enemy. The second premise is necessary to make people accept the first.

The first premise makes a moral double standard possible: it divides men into two different species, the rulers and the subjects, each living by a different moral code. It is the basic social premise of statism, best expressed in the concept of "The Divine Right of Kings."

But in order to justify it, the statists have to rouse people to an hysterical fear of some malevolent enemy who threatens them with constant, unpredictable dangers. In my lecture on *America's Persecuted Minority: Big Business*, I said: "Every dictatorship or potential dictatorship needs some minority group as a scapegoat which it can blame for the nation's troubles and use as a justification of its own demands for dictatorial powers. In Soviet Russia, the scapegoat was the bourgeoisie; in Nazi Germany, it was the Jewish people; in America, it is the businessmen." I submit Mr. Kennedy's message in evidence.

Dishonest or unprincipled individuals exist in every group or profession, and they exist among businessmen as well as among bureaucrats. But Mr. Kennedy charges *all* businessmen with collective guilt for individual crimes, and absolves *all* bureaucrats. If he decries the crooked businessmen who attempt to defraud the public, what about corrupt government officials? Consider the number of known cases of bribery, pull-peddling, favor-dispensing, five-percenting, deep-freezes, vicuña coats, etc. Consider the notorious cases of bribery of government inspectors, such as building inspectors, for in-

(continued on page 20)

Who Will Protect Us from Our Protectors?

(from page 19)

stance. Then project the possibilities inherent in placing more industries under the control of government inspectors endowed with wider, more autocratic powers—and ask yourself whom or what this would "protect."

The truth of the matter is that there is no such thing as "consumers' rights," just as there can be no "rights" belonging to some special group or race and to no others. There are only *the rights of man*—rights possessed by every individual man and by *all* men as individuals. The right to be protected from physical injury or fraud belongs to *all* men, not merely to "consumers," and does not require any special protection other than that provided by *the criminal law*.

Observe that all the alleged threats to our "safety," listed in Mr. Kennedy's message, are not political or economic matters, but matters that belong to the jurisdiction of the criminal code. If a businessman—or any other citizen—willfully and knowingly cheats or injures others ("consumers" or otherwise), it is a matter to be *proved* and punished in a criminal court. But the precedent which Mr. Kennedy is here attempting to establish is the legal hallmark of a dictatorship: *preventive law*—the concept that a man is guilty until he is proved innocent by the permissive rubber stamp of a commissar or a Gauleiter.

What protects us from any private citizen who may choose to turn criminal and injure or defraud us? *That*, precisely, is the proper duty of a government. But if the government assumes a totalitarian power and its officials are not subject to any law, then *who will protect us from our protectors?* What will be our recourse against the dishonesty, vindictiveness, cupidity or stupidity of a bureaucrat?

If matters such as *science* are to be placed into the unanswerable power of a single bureau, what will guarantee the superior wisdom, justice and integrity of the bureaucrats? Why, the vote of the people, a statist would answer—of the people who choose the ruler who then appoints the bureaucrats—of the same people whom Mr. Kennedy does not consider competent to choose electric toasters, credit contracts, face lotions, laxative tablets or canned vegetables.

Available at Your Bookstore in Mid-May

Who is Ayn Rand?

by Nathaniel Branden

Content:

¶ The moral revolution of ATLAS SHRUGGED, and the relevance of Ayn Rand's philosophy to the cultural and political crisis of our time.

¶ The application of Objectivism to basic problems of psychology.

¶ The esthetic principles underlying Ayn Rand's novels, and her concept of man's relationship to existence, which holds the key to her literary method.

¶ The title essay—contributed by Barbara Branden—is a biographical study, concerned primarily with Ayn Rand's intellectual and artistic development.

Random House $3.95

OBJECTIVIST CALENDAR

■ Nathaniel Branden will address the Young Republican Club at C.C.N.Y. on May 3, 12:15 P.M., in Room 106, Wagner Hall, 133rd St. & St. Nicholas Terrace. His subject is "The Ethical Philosophy of *Atlas Shrugged*." Open to the public; admission free.

■ Ayn Rand will participate in the Public Affairs Forum of Sarah Lawrence College on May 7. The subject of the Forum is "Which Way America?" Admission is restricted to Sarah Lawrence students.

■ Nathaniel Branden will deliver his address on "The Ethical Philosophy of *Atlas Shrugged*" to the Philosophy Club of the University of Delaware, on May 9, 8 P.M. Open to the public; admission free.

■ Ayn Rand will deliver a lecture on capitalism to the Economics Club of Hunter College at the Uptown (Bronx) Campus, on May 16, 12:15 P.M. Admission is restricted to Hunter College students.

■ NATHANIEL BRANDEN INSTITUTE will offer a 10 lecture course on the "History of Ancient Philosophy," to be given by Leonard Peikoff, starting May 24. Tracing the philosophic ideas and movements from ancient Greece to the Renaissance, Mr. Peikoff's course is the first of a three-part series on the history of Western philosophy; his courses on "Modern Philosophy" and "Contemporary Philosophy" will be offered at a later date. Full details concerning the present course will be sent shortly to residents in the Greater New York area and in Philadelphia.

■ Ayn Rand addressed the New Enterprise Club of the Harvard University Graduate School of Business Administration, on April 25, on the subject of capitalism.

■ NATHANIEL BRANDEN INSTITUTE will offer a new 20 lecture course to be given by Mr. Branden this fall. Entitled "Basic Principles of Objectivist Psychology," the course will present the first detailed, systematic exposition of Mr. Branden's psychological theories.

■ Ayn Rand's lecture on "The Intellectual Bankruptcy of Our Age" has been published by NATHANIEL BRANDEN INSTITUTE and is available from THE OBJECTIVIST NEWSLETTER. Price: 50¢ (N.Y.C. residents add 2¢ sales tax).

Other activities: Phillip J. Smith, a student of NATHANIEL BRANDEN INSTITUTE, informs us that the *Phillip J. Smith Acting Studio* will offer a production of Noel Coward's *Hay Fever*. Several N.B.I. students will be in the cast. Time: May 11 and 12, 8:30 P.M. Place: Goddard-Riverside Center, 100 West 77th St. (Junior High School 44). Admission: $1.25.

"The Objectivist Ethics" by Ayn Rand

The first non-fiction presentation of the fundamentals of the Objectivist moral philosophy. Originally delivered by Ayn Rand at a symposium on Ethics at the University of Wisconsin. Published by NATHANIEL BRANDEN INSTITUTE. Available from THE OBJECTIVIST NEWSLETTER. Price $1. (N.Y.C. residents add 3¢ sales tax.)

Published monthly at 165 East 35th Street, New York 16, N.Y.
Subscription rate: In United States, its possessions, Canada and Mexico, $5 for one year; other countries, $6. Trial subscriptions: 4 months $2. 6 months $3.
Additional copies of this Newsletter: single copy 50¢ (coins, not stamps); 10 — 99 copies, 25¢ each plus postage (for first-class delivery add 1¢ per copy, for third-class delivery add ½¢ per copy); 100 or more copies, 15¢ each plus postage (same as above).
For change of address send old address and new address with zone number if any. Allow us two weeks to process new subscriptions and change of address.

Ayn Rand and Nathaniel Branden, Editors and Publishers
Barbara Branden, Managing Editor
Elayne Kalberman, Circulation Manager
PRINTED BY CARNEGIE PRESS, INC., NEW YORK CITY

THE OBJECTIVIST NEWSLETTER

Edited and Published by AYN RAND and NATHANIEL BRANDEN

VOL. 1 NO. 6   JUNE, 1962

CHECK YOUR PREMISES
By AYN RAND

"The National Interest, *c'est moi*"

"He was looking at them with the anger of a man declaring that the country's troubles were a personal affront to him. So many men seeking favors had been afraid of him that he now acted as if his anger were a solution to everything, as if his anger were omnipotent, as if all he had to do was to get angry."

Any resemblance of this passage from *Atlas Shrugged*, published in 1957, to any political leader of today is purely coincidental — since it is blind chance that determines what particular individual rises to power in a society that abandons principles. But the philosophical, political and psychological principles behind that passage are *not* coincidental; principles, like laws of nature, continue to operate, whether men choose to recognize them or not—and those of you who have seen President Kennedy on television on April 11, have seen a concrete illustration, as eloquent as and much cruder than a work of fiction could offer you.

The President of the United States was denouncing the steel industry, with the trembling intensity and rage of a spoiled, petulant child stamping its foot at a universe that had disobeyed its whims. The same man who had repeatedly declared, in a manner of gravely courteous tolerance, that he would always be willing to negotiate with Khrushchev or any other foreign aggressor on any continent, was pouring violent abuse upon a group of American citizens. But since these citizens were *businessmen*, he felt, apparently, that it was safe to attack them. Who hasn't?

The temper tantrums of any one man do not necessarily indict a culture; but what *does* indict it is the fact that most of the press accepted the meaning of that tantrum on *his* terms. "The ruler is *angry!*" was the leitmotif of the press comments, which proceeded to speculate on what Mr. Kennedy's displeasure might do to the steel industry and to all business, as if such concepts as "rights" or "law" had never existed, as if we were a country where the emotional moods of the ruler are of paramount public significance, where his frown or smile determines one's fate. "The Kennedys do not like to lose," wrote the liberal James Reston in *The New York Times*. "They do not like to be crossed." Change the name to read: "The Bourbons do not like to lose," and ask yourself whether the spirit of that comment would be appropriate to the reign of Louis XV (or to the reign of the Hitlers or the Khrushchevs who "do not like to lose or to be crossed," either).

What has brought a free country to this state?

There were two key statements made by the two antagonists in the steel crisis, which contain the essence of the whole issue and the clue to its cause.

On April 11, in his televised news conference, President Kennedy declared that "price and wage decisions in this country . . . are and ought to be freely and privately made," then added: "But *the American people have a right to expect, in return for that freedom,* a higher sense of business responsibility for the welfare of their country . . ." (Italics mine.)

On April 12, in *his* televised news conference, Mr. Roger M. Blough, board chairman of United States Steel, was asked by a reporter whether the increase in steel prices "was designed to check expanded government influence in collective bargaining," and answered: *"I know nothing about politics."*

Though Mr. Blough's statement did provoke some comments, Mr. Kennedy's did not. It was neither noticed nor discussed nor protested. Yet that abstract statement is more disastrously important than inflation, foreign competition or any other concrete problem of the immediate moment by means of which men blind themselves to their future. I call it, therefore, to the attention of those who still understand the power of ideas and the importance of principles.

"The American people have a right to expect, *in return for that freedom* . . ." Here is an explicit declaration by the President of the United States that *freedom* is not an inalienable right of the individual, but a conditional favor or privilege granted to him by society (by "the people" or the collective) —a privilege which he has to purchase by performing some sort of duty *in return*. Should he fail in that duty, "the people" have *the right* to abrogate his freedom and return him to his natural condition of slavery. Rights, by this concept, are the property of the collective, not of the individual; the individual's life, liberty and effort belong to "the people" who have "the right" to dispose of him and to dictate the terms of his existence in any way they please. *This* is the basic principle of collectivism and statism. A statement of that nature could not have been mere rhetorical carelessness on the part of Mr. Kennedy who prides himself on his knowledge of history.

Where were the "conservatives" on April 11, when Mr. Kennedy slapped the Declaration of Independence in its philosophical face? Where were those alleged defenders of the American way of life who claim "tradition," if nothing better, as their chief loyalty? Where were the Republicans? According to the press reports, they were "not available for comment." After all, what's freedom, rights, or the American way of life, when compared to the embarrassment of having to defend the selfish *profits* of *big business*?

It is in the midst of such an intellectual atmosphere that the representative of the undefended victims—who, for one half hour, on April 12, had the chance to achieve a major cultural turning point and, by asserting his "selfish" rights in defiance of overbearing statism, to help save the rights of all of us — found nothing better to say than: *"I know nothing about politics."*

In this day and age —when political issues are a matter of life or death, when the humblest longshoreman or sharecropper has no moral right to evade the responsibility of political judgment—the head of one of America's largest industrial companies declared that politics does not concern him.

If Mr. Blough saw no threat to free enterprise in Mr. Kennedy's policies, how can he expect his workers or the man in the street to see it? If he did not choose to uphold *his* property rights, how can he expect struggling young people to uphold theirs? If he did not care to fight for capitalism, whom does he expect to fight for it?

Those two television news conferences presented, in condensed form, the whole tragic history of the destruction of capitalism and its causes: while the representative of statism, the politician, was asserting his principles with arrogant self-righteousness—the representative of capitalism, the industrialist, was evading the existence of principles, abstractions, moral values, philosophy, and was attempting to fight in terms of a single, concrete, "practical" issue, thus sanctioning and supporting the philosophical premises of his adversary.

If you wish to know the futility of fighting without a philosophical base, and the impotence of the businessmen's "con-

(continued on page 22)

"The National Interest, c'est moi" *(from page 21)*

servative" intellectual advisers—the steel crisis has given you a dramatic demonstration.

And if you are still inclined to doubt that capitalism is being destroyed by the altruist morality, observe that there was no way to fight Mr. Kennedy's policy without challenging its root, that undefined, undefinable, collectivist formula which strikes its victims like the knife of a sacrificial ritual: *"The National Interest."*

If you thought that that formula was to be invoked only against "selfish businessmen," you have now heard it invoked against labor unions as well.

On February 23, during the steel industry's contract negotiations, Secretary of Labor Arthur J. Goldberg announced, as a "definitive" statement of the Kennedy Administration's philosophy, that the government henceforth would "define and assert the national interest" in regard to collective bargaining. Declaring that labor-management relations should no longer be resolved "on the old testing ground of clash of selfish interest," he made it explicitly clear that from now on *three clashing interests* would be involved: the selfish interest of management, the selfish interest of labor and the (unselfish?) interest of "the nation," as represented by the government.

It is significant that labor leaders were the first to protest against this doctrine in no uncertain terms. The majority of labor leaders have always been much more acute philosophically, much more sensitive to the long-range implications of political principles than the leaders of industry. Labor leaders objected to Mr. Goldberg's manifesto promptly and forcefully. Said George Meany, president of the A.F.L.-C.I.O.: "When he says the role of the government is to assert the national interest, he is infringing on the rights of free people and free society, and I don't agree with him whatsoever."

By contrast, observe the statements of industrial leaders, which came a day later. The men who voiced the best objections to Mr. Goldberg's doctrine asked not to be identified by name. "From a broad philosophical standpoint," said one of them, "most businessmen feel that in a competitive system you serve the national interest in pursuing your private interest." This, of course, is the proper answer and touches on the core of the whole issue. But the man who said it had to remain anonymous. On the other hand, observe that those "middle-of-the-road" industrialists who *agreed* with Mr. Goldberg and supported his doctrine, did not hesitate to air their views openly, under their own names. Observe also that one of them was Joseph L. Block, chairman of Inland Steel.

But the truly disgraceful touch was provided by the statement of the National Association of Manufacturers, the alleged spokesman for industry. After a few cautious generalities, objecting to Mr. Goldberg, that statement declared: "The real remedy is to subject labor organizations to legal restrictions on the attainment and use of monopoly power."

At a time when the government is openly assuming a totalitarian-statist role, the spokesman for its chained victims is asking that the government be granted wider powers! Unable or unwilling to liberate the enslaved, their spokesman proposes, as a "remedy," to spread enslavement to the rest of society and thus silence the only powerful economic group which is still free to speak and to assert its rights.

Voluntary slavery is precisely the goal of Mr. Kennedy's policy and the means by which he intends to rule. Observe the hypocritical euphemism of such a phrase as the government's intention *"to define and assert the national interest."* Anybody can "define and assert" anything he pleases—so this is obviously not what the phrase is intended to mean. It means—and is so intended to be understood—that "the national interest" is whatever the government chooses to say it is and that any assertion of the government's wishes is a command, whether the law has given the government the power to issue such a command or not. It means that the government possesses enough undefined, arbitrary powers, granted to it by undefined, non-objective laws, to crack down on any dissenter and punish any disobedience in any manner it pleases. It means that law has become superfluous and that *fear* has taken its place.

What Mr. Kennedy was projecting in his televised tantrum was the spiteful anger of a man who had believed himself safe in feeling that "the national interest, *c'est moi.*"

In the February issue of this newsletter, I wrote: "The Antitrust laws give the government the power to prosecute and convict any business concern in the country any time it chooses. The threat of sudden destruction, of unpredictable retaliation for unnamed offenses, is a much more potent means of enslavement than explicit dictatorial laws. It demands more than mere obedience; it leaves men no policy save one: *to please* the authorities; to please—blindly, uncritically, without standards or principles; to please—in any issue, matter or circumstance, for fear of an unknowable, unprovable vengeance."

You have now seen this in practice — in a cruder, more cynically obvious practice than I would have ventured to predict. Mr. Kennedy was threatening the steel companies with retaliation by means of: Antitrust prosecutions, grand jury investigation, Senate and House Committees investigations, Department of Justice investigation, Federal Trade Commission investigation, the "reconsidering" of tax legislation favorable to industry, etc., etc.—including, for full scare effect, the melodramatic touch of F.B.I. agents awakening newspaper reporters in the middle of the night to question them about the public statement of one of the steel industrialists. No, Mr. Kennedy was not afraid of creating in the public mind the connotations of a totalitarian state: he was *seeking* to create them.

So long as a government holds discretionary powers to dispense punishments or favors, who will ever be able to prove or to know what goes on behind the scenes of any clash between government and private citizens? On April 14, the day after the steel industry's surrender, *The New York Times* reported that the President and his advisers had been privately "bringing every form of *persuasion* to bear on the industry, trying to hold back the companies that had not yet raised prices and *induce* the others to roll back the price increase." (Italics mine.) *Time* magazine of April 20 wrote as follows: "Every New Frontiersman who had a friend, old college mate or former colleague in the steel industry was summoned to join in an all-out campaign to persuade the holdouts to keep on holding out. 'Everyone in the Administration who knew anyone called him,' said a White House aide." Who can tell what deals were made, what favors were granted, whose fate was determined, whose interests were sacrificed to whom—in those private conversations and by such methods?

Is *this* a government of laws and not of men?

No, Congress never passed any law giving Mr. Kennedy the power to dictate prices and wages. But it passed many non-objective laws which gave him the power to make legality obsolete. The German Reichstag voted itself out of existence. Our Congress seems to have achieved the same end piecemeal, gradually and cumulatively.

It is obvious that the goal of the Kennedy Administration is to achieve a statist dictatorship without ever calling it by that name, without any official declaration or identification, counting on demagogic slogans to extort people's subservience, with a minimum show of force and a maximum illusion of "voluntary" obedience. And the future of this country now depends on whether enough people will realize the grotesquely evil contradiction in the concept of "voluntary action at the point of a governmental gun."

"It's extremely important," said Dr. Ferris in *Atlas Shrugged*, "to get those patents turned over to us *voluntarily*. Even if we had a law permitting outright nationalization, it would be much better to get them as a gift. We want to leave to people the illusion that they're still preserving their private property rights. And most of them will play along. They'll sign the Gift Certificates. Just raise a lot of noise about its being a patriotic duty and that anyone who refuses is a prince of greed, and they'll sign."

As a novelist, I had always regarded myself as belonging to the literary school of Romanticism. I did not know that the Kennedy Administration would transform my work into that of a rank Naturalist.

INTELLECTUAL AMMUNITION DEPARTMENT

[Subscribers are invited to send in the questions that they find themselves unable to answer in philosophical or political discussions. As many questions as space permits will be answered. No questions will be answered by mail.]

■ **In a society of laissez-faire capitalism, what would prevent the formation of powerful monopolies able to gain control over the entire economy?**

One of the worst fallacies in the field of economics—propagated by Karl Marx and accepted by almost everyone today, including many businessmen—is that the development of monopolies is an inescapable and intrinsic result of the operation of a free, unregulated economy. In fact, the exact opposite is true. It is a free market that makes monopolies impossible.

It is imperative that one be clear and specific in one's understanding of the meaning of "monopoly." When people speak, in an economic or political context, of the dangers and evils of monopoly, what they mean is a *coercive* monopoly—that is: exclusive control of a given field of production which is closed to and exempt from competition, so that those controlling the field are able to set arbitrary production policies and charge arbitrary prices, independent of the market, immune from the law of supply and demand. Such a monopoly, it is important to note, entails more than the *absence* of competition; it entails the *impossibility* of competition. That is a coercive monopoly's characteristic attribute—and is essential to any condemnation of such a monopoly.

In the whole history of capitalism, no one has been able to establish a coercive monopoly by means of competition on a free market. There is only one way to forbid entry into a given field of production: by *law*. Every single coercive monopoly that exists or ever has existed—in the United States, in Europe or anywhere else in the world—*was created and made possible only by an act of government*: by special franchises, licenses, subsidies, by *legislative* actions which granted special privileges (*not* obtainable on a free market) to a man or a group of men, and forbade all others to enter that particular field.

A coercive monopoly is not the result of *laissez faire*; it can result only from the *abrogation* of *laissez faire* and from the introduction of the *opposite* principle—the principle of *statism*.

In this country, a utility company is a coercive monopoly: the government grants it a franchise for an exclusive territory, and no one else is allowed to engage in that service in that territory; a would-be competitor, attempting to sell electric power, would be stopped by law. A telephone company is a coercive monopoly. As recently as World War II, the government ordered the two then existing telegraph companies, Western Union and Postal Telegraph, to merge into one monopoly.

One of the best illustrations of the fact that a coercive monopoly requires the abrogation of the principle of *laissez faire* is given by Ayn Rand in her "Notes on the History of American Free Enterprise." She writes:

"The Central Pacific—which was built by the 'Big Four' of California, on federal subsidies—was the railroad which was guilty of all the evils popularly held against railroads. For almost thirty years, the Central Pacific controlled California, held a monopoly and permitted no competitor to enter the state. It charged disastrous rates, changed them every year, and took the entire profit of any California farmer or shipper, who had no other railroad to turn to. How was this made possible? It was done through the power of the California legislature. The Big Four controlled the legislature and held the state closed to competitors by legal restrictions—such as, for instance, a legislative act which gave the Big Four exclusive control of the entire coast line of California and forbade any other railroad to enter any port. During these thirty years, many attempts were made by private interests to start competing railroads in California and break the monopoly of the Central Pacific. These attempts were defeated—not by methods of free trade and free competition, but by *legislative action*.

"This thirty-year monopoly of the Big Four and the practices in which they engaged are always quoted as an example of the evils of big business and Free Enterprise. Yet the Big Four were not free enterprisers; they were not businessmen who had achieved power by means of unregulated trade. They were typical representatives of what is now called 'a mixed economy.' They achieved power by legislative interference into business; none of their abuses would have been possible in a free, unregulated economy."

In the comparatively free days of American capitalism, in the late-nineteenth-early-twentieth century, there were many attempts to "corner the market" on various commodities (such as cotton and wheat, to mention two famous examples)—then close the field to competition and gather huge profits by selling at exorbitant prices. All such attempts failed. The men who tried it were compelled to give up—or go bankrupt. They were defeated, not by legislative action—but by the action of the free market.

The question is often asked: What if a large, rich company kept buying out its smaller competitors or kept forcing them out of business by means of undercutting prices and selling at a loss—would it not be able to gain control of a given field and then start charging high prices and be free to stagnate with no fear of competition? The answer is: No, it would not be able to do it. If a company assumed heavy losses in order to drive out competitors, then began to charge high prices to regain what it had lost, this would serve as an incentive for new competitors to enter the field and take advantage of the high profitability, without any losses to recoup. The new competitors would force prices down to the market level. The large company would have either to abandon its attempt to establish monopoly prices—or else go bankrupt fighting off the competitors that its own policies would attract.

It is a matter of historical fact that no "price war" has ever succeeded in establishing a monopoly or in maintaining prices *above* the market level, outside the law of supply and demand. ("Price wars" *have*, however, acted as spurs to the economic efficiency of competing companies—and have thereby resulted in enormous benefits to the public, in terms of better products at lower prices.)

What is frequently forgotten by people, in considering an issue of this kind, is the crucial role of the capital market in a free economy. As Alan Greenspan observes in his article "Bad History" (*Barron's*, February 5, 1962): "If entry [into a given field of production] is not impeded by Government regulations, franchises or subsidies, the ultimate regulator of competition in a free economy is the capital market. So long as capital is free to flow, it will tend to seek those areas of maximum rate of return." Investors are constantly seeking the most profitable uses of their capital. If, therefore, some field of production is seen to be highly profitable (particularly when the profitability is due to high prices rather than to low costs), businessmen and investors necessarily will be attracted to that field; and, as the supply of the product in question is increased relative to the demand for it, prices fall accordingly. "The capital market," writes Mr. Greenspan, "acts as a regulator of prices, not necessarily of profits. It leaves any individual producer free to earn as much as he can by lowering his costs and by increasing his efficiency relative to others. Thus it constitutes the mechanism which generates greater incentives to increased productivity, thereby leading to a rising standard of living."

The free market does not permit inefficiency or stagnation—with economic impunity—in any field of production. Consider, for instance, a well-known incident in the history of the American automobile industry. There was a period when Henry Ford's Model-T held an enormous part of the automobile market. But when Ford's company attempted to stagnate and to resist stylistic changes—"You can have any color of the Model-T you want, so long as it's black"—General Motors, with its more attractively styled Chevrolet, cut into a major segment of Ford's market. And the Ford Company was com-

(continued on page 24)

Intellectual Ammunition (from page 23)

pelled to change its policies in order to compete. One will find examples of this principle in the history of virtually every industry.

Now if one considers the only kind of monopoly that *can* exist under capitalism, a *non*-coercive monopoly, one will perceive that its prices and production policies are not independent of the wider market in which it operates, but are fully bound by the law of supply and demand; that there is no particular reason for or value in retaining the designation of "monopoly" when one uses it in a non-coercive sense; and that there are no rational grounds on which to condemn such "monopolies."

For instance, if a small town has only one drug store, which is barely able to survive, the owner might be described as enjoying a "monopoly"—except that no one would think of using the term in this context. There is no economic need or market for a second drug store, there is not enough trade to support it. But if that town grew, its one drug store would have no way, no power, to prevent other drug stores from being opened.

It is often thought that the field of mining is particularly vulnerable to the establishment of monopolies, since the materials extracted from the earth exist in limited quantity and since, it is believed, some firm might gain control of all the sources of some raw material. Well, observe that International Nickel of Canada produces more than two-thirds of the world's nickel—yet it does *not* charge monopoly prices. It prices its product *as though* it had a great many competitors —and the truth is that it *does* have a great many competitors. Nickel (in the form of alloy and stainless steels) is competing with aluminum and a variety of other materials. The seldom recognized principle involved is this: no single product, commodity or material is or can be indispensable to an economy *regardless of price*. A commodity can be only *relatively* preferable to other commodities. For example, when the price of bituminous coal rose (which was due to John L. Lewis' forcing an economically unjustified wage raise), this was instrumental in bringing about a large-scale conversion to the use of oil and gas in many industries. The free market is its own protector.

Now if a company were able to gain and hold a non-coercive monopoly, if it were able to win all the customers in a given field, not by special government-granted privileges, but by sheer productive efficiency—by its ability to keep its costs low and/or to offer a better product than any competitor could—there would be no grounds on which to condemn such a monopoly. On the contrary, the company that achieved it would deserve the highest praise and esteem.

The history of the Aluminum Company of America prior to World War II is a case in point. Seeking constantly to expand its market, Alcoa kept its prices as low as possible; this policy required enormous productive efficiency and cost-cutting. Alcoa was the only producer of primary aluminum and, as such, was a monopoly; but it was not a coercive monopoly; nothing prevented other companies from attempting to compete with it, except the fact that they could not match its productive efficiency. The pricing policies of Alcoa were entirely subject to the law of supply and demand: aluminum had to compete with steel, with copper, with cement, and with many other construction materials; and had Alcoa attempted to raise its prices—this would have served as an engraved invitation to competitors to enter Alcoa's own field.

No one can morally claim the *right* to compete in a given field, if he cannot match the productive efficiency of those with whom he hopes to compete. There is no reason why people should buy inferior products at higher prices in order to maintain less efficient companies in business. Under capitalism, any man or company that can surpass competitors, is free to do so. It is in this manner that the free market rewards ability and works for the benefit of everyone— except those who seek the undeserved.

A bromide commonly cited in this connection by opponents of capitalism is that of the old corner grocer who is thrown out of business by the big chain store. What is the clear implication of their protest? It is that the people who live in the neighborhood of the old grocer have to continue buying from him, even though a chain store could give them better service at lower prices and thereby let them save money. Thus both the owners of the chain store and the people in the neighborhood are to be penalized—in order to protect the stagnation of the old grocer. *By what right?* If that grocer is unable to compete with the chain store, then, properly, he has no choice but to move elsewhere or go into another line of business or seek employment from the chain store. Capitalism, by its nature, entails a constant process of motion, of growth, of progress; no one has a *vested right* to a position, if others can do better than he can.

When people denounce the free market as "cruel," the fact they are decrying is that the market is ruled by a single moral principle: *justice*. And *that* is the root of their hatred for capitalism.

There is only one kind of monopoly that men may rightfully condemn—the only kind for which the designation of "monopoly" is economically significant: a *coercive* monopoly. (Observe that in the *non*-coercive meaning of the term, *every* man may be described as a "monopolist"—since he is the exclusive owner of his own effort and product. But it is not *this* that is denounced as evil—except by socialists.)

In the issue of monopolies, as in so many other issues, capitalism is commonly blamed for the evils perpetrated by its destroyers: it is not free trade on a free market that creates coercive monopolies, but government legislation, government action, government controls. If men are concerned about the evils of monopolies, let them identify the actual villain in the picture and the actual cause of the evils: government intervention into the economy. Let them recognize that there is only one way to destroy monopolies: by the separation of State and Economics—that is, by instituting the principle that the government may not abridge the freedom of production and trade.

—NATHANIEL BRANDEN

OBJECTIVIST CALENDAR

■ On June 19, Professor John Hospers of the Philosophy Department of Brooklyn College will deliver a special guest lecture in NATHANIEL BRANDEN INSTITUTE'S spring series on "Basic Principles of Objectivism." Professor Hospers is the author of: *Meaning and Truth in the Arts—An Introduction to Philosophical Analysis—Human Conduct: an introduction to the problems of ethics*. The subject of his lecture at the Institute is: Objectivism and its relation to other contemporary ethical systems. Place: Hotel Roosevelt, 45th St. and Madison Ave., New York City. Time: 7:30 P.M. Admission: $3.50. (This is lecture #19 in the present series.)

■ In February of this year, New American Library issued the tenth printing of *Atlas Shrugged*—100,000 copies. In April, an *eleventh* printing was issued—95,000 copies.

■ On May 11, Ayn Rand conducted a seminar on capitalism for the Management Course, Postgraduate Unit, of the American Management Association.

Published monthly at 165 East 35th Street, New York 16, N.Y.
Subscription rate: In United States, its possessions, Canada and Mexico, $5 for one year; other countries, $6. Trial subscriptions: 4 months $2. 6 months $3.
Additional copies of this Newsletter: single copy 50¢ (coins, not stamps); 10 — 99 copies, 25¢ each plus postage (for first-class delivery add 1¢ per copy, for third-class delivery add ½¢ per copy); 100 or more copies, 15¢ each plus postage (same as above).
For change of address send old address and new address with zone number if any. Allow us two weeks to process new subscriptions and change of address.

Ayn Rand and Nathaniel Branden, Editors and Publishers
Barbara Branden, Managing Editor
Elayne Kalberman, Circulation Manager
PRINTED BY CARNEGIE PRESS, INC., NEW YORK CITY

SPECIAL SUPPLEMENT

THE OBJECTIVIST NEWSLETTER

Edited and Published by AYN RAND and NATHANIEL BRANDEN

VOL. 1 NO. 6 SPECIAL SUPPLEMENT JUNE, 1962

Doctors and the Police State

By LEONARD PEIKOFF

Having eroded the value of everyone's savings through decades of inflationary deficit spending, the statists have now decided to pose as champions of their own victims—specifically, of those over 65 years of age. The Kennedy Administration's King-Anderson bill proposes to finance hospital and nursing home care for the aged out of the tax money collected through the Federal Social Security system.

Nobody bothers much any more to deny that this is only a first step. There is no principle by which the State can claim to be responsible for the hospital expenses of the aged, but not for their doctors' bills—or for the costs of those under 65 with chronic diseases—or for the psychiatric expenses of those in mental institutions—or for the dental expenses of the unemployed—or, ultimately, for *everyone's* medical expenses. The leaders of the Canadian province of Saskatchewan name their purposes more openly: Premier Woodrow S. Lloyd has announced that, as of July 1 of this year, full-scale socialized medicine will be instituted throughout the province.

The statists in both countries seek to counter the protests of the medical profession by claiming that government-financed medicine is compatible with perfect freedom for the doctors. Said Secretary Ribicoff: "It should be absolutely no concern to a physician where a patient gets the money . . ."

The truth is, that it is a matter of life and death concern. He who pays the money for a service is *morally obligated* to see that he receives full value in return; he *must* set the terms, conditions and standards governing his expenditures. If he does not, he is an irresponsible wastrel. If it is the government that does the paying, then the government has to decide who is qualified to receive its money—how much a particular service is worth—under what conditions that service is necessary and under what conditions it is merely a squandering of State funds—whether a controversial new surgical technique, or a controversial drug, or a controversial method of psychotherapy, is a failure which should not be supported or a success which deserves the taxpayers' money.

In a free society, a man cannot force his terms on others; those who dissent are free to deal elsewhere. A patient who disapproves of a doctor's methods of treatment can seek out another doctor; a doctor who considers a patient's demands irrational is not compelled to give in to them. And, in the long run, it is the best and ablest doctors—those who achieve the cures and demonstrate their value—that rise to the top and set the example for the rest of the profession.

But when the government sets the terms, they are enforced by the police power of the State. The standards of the government become the laws of the country, and no others are *legally* permitted. Should any doctor object to the decrees of the officials who staff the State Health Board—should he attempt to act on his own best judgment and make an unauthorized use of the drugs, the hospital beds, the operating rooms being paid for by the State—he becomes thereby a criminal, and he is legally subject to retribution: to loss of license, or fine, or jail-sentence. There is no one to whom he can turn: the government is his sole employer. He either submits—or he leaves medicine—or he escapes from the country.

The proposal to pay medical expenses with State funds has only one meaning: it is a proposal to enslave the doctors.

That there may be medical men on the State Health Board changes nothing. There are, undoubtedly, journalists in the bureau which controls the press in Soviet Russia; this does not make the editors of *Pravda* free men.

By what moral principle are the doctors to be deprived of their right to practice their profession as free men? By the principle of *altruism*: the principle that man is a sacrificial animal, that the only justification of his existence is the service he renders to others, and that any consideration or concern for the men who *provide* the services is irrelevant. "This is too important a matter," declared Premier Lloyd in explanation of his refusal to drop his plan, "to leave the decision to a relatively small group who have power because they have special skills." Thus, the men with invaluable skills are to have no say in the matter; they are to have no say *because* they are men with invaluable skills.

The doctors in both countries have been enormously generous; in protesting the enslavement of medicine, they have made it abundantly clear, in repeated statements, that they will continue *voluntarily* to treat the needy without charge in the future as they have in the past. The altruist-statists, however, are still not satisfied. They oppose the "means test." States Premier Lloyd: "Doctors have a fine tradition of providing services without charge to those who are unable to pay but many people feel uncomfortable in asking for and obtaining something for which they cannot pay." How will government medicine solve this problem? Since the State does all the paying, anyone who is upset at being a charity case does not have to think about or even to assert his need; he has only to pretend that the benefits are his by right, and evade the whole question of where the money is coming from. It is not the *needy* who are the objects of such solicitous concern in the present campaign; it is the *dishonest* needy. The man who demands something for nothing and, when he gets it, considers it an affront to have to say thank-you, is a parasite. It is in the name of the sensibilities of parasites that the doctors are to be enslaved.

When altruism reaches so corrupt a stage, its full meaning comes out into the open. The emphasis changes from love to obedience, from handouts to handcuffs, from the Welfare State to the Police State.

It is happening now in the United States. Some two hundred New Jersey doctors, led by Dr. J. Bruce Henriksen, signed a petition of protest against the King-Anderson bill. They declared that they would continue voluntarily to treat the indigent aged without charge, but that they would refuse to treat anyone whose medical care was financed under the government's plan. The meaning of their action was clear-cut; it cannot be evaded and it had nothing to do with the needy. It was the action free men have always taken to protest an advancing dictatorship: the statement that they will not sanction, help, or participate in the growth of slavery.

What was the response they received? "Greedy private doctors," charged Zalmen J. Lichtenstein, executive director of the Golden Ring Council of Senior Citizens. "A breach of ethics as bad as anything else I could imagine," declared New Jersey Governor Hughes. "A vicious scheme," cried Vincent J. Murphy, president of the New Jersey A.F.L.-C.I.O. "A disgrace to the country," announced Secretary Goldberg to a convention in Atlantic City.

"The attitude of these doctors in opposition to a basic national need is shocking," said Secretary Ribicoff. "In trying to blackmail the Congress and the American people by refusing to treat older people, they are violating the Hippocratic oath . . ." The relevant portion of this oath reads: "That

I will lead my life and practice my art in uprightness and honor." In Secretary Ribicoff's view, it is *blackmail* for a man to ask anything in exchange for his services, even if all he asks is that he be left free to provide them voluntarily. It is a betrayal of uprightness for a man to refuse to sanction conditions which he considers evil. It is a betrayal of honor for a man to fight for his professional integrity, for his right to use his own mind, make his own decisions, and act on his own independent judgment. Who, then, is the man of uprightness and honor? The man who abdicates his intellectual responsibility. What is the proof of his love for mankind? His willingness to submit unconditionally to the demands of the State.

Harry S. Truman summarized the humanitarian viewpoint in its most eloquent form. Asked what he thought of the doctors' revolt, he replied: "I think they ought to be hit over the head with a club."

The club was not long in coming. On May 7, the New Jersey State Assembly voted overwhelmingly in favor of a resolution condemning the protesting doctors. On the same day, six New Jersey Democrats, led by Assemblyman John J. Kijewski, introduced in the Assembly a bill to make the doctors' protest *illegal;* the penalties it proposed for any doctor who refuses services to anyone "solely because of the prospective or intended method for payment of such services" include: loss of license, up to $100 fine, and/or *ninety days in jail.* Alfred E. Clark, reporting the proposed bill in the May 6 issue of *The New York Times,* commented: "Governor Hughes' statement left no doubt that the measure would have his backing."

Socialized medicine is a controversial, political issue. The controversy is over philosophical questions: over the right code of morality, the proper functions of government, the relation of the individual to society. The disagreement between the two sides is a matter of opposing *ideas*. The Kijewski bill proposed to make it a *matter of law* that no doctor is entitled to a viewpoint on this question if his ideas do not agree with those of the President. It proposed to define a new crime in the United States and to threaten a man with jail for committing it: *the crime of upholding political opinions opposed to those of the officials of the State.*

The bill was intended to come to a vote about a week after its introduction in the Legislature. For that week, it was an open question whether or not the New Jersey jail cells were soon to start admitting political prisoners. The doctors saw what was coming and named the issue. Dr. Ralph M. L. Buchanan, president of the New Jersey Medical Society, declared: "This bill violates and outrages the Constitution of the United States and imperils the basic rights of every citizen." Dr. Henriksen was even more succinct: "The fact that this bill was even thought of shows that we are nearer the police state than we thought."

At the end of that week, the news was released: at the request of the Governor, the bill had been withdrawn from the Assembly. Someone had discovered that they couldn't get away with it yet. It was a reprieve for the country—but only that. A decade ago, they would not have dared to contemplate such legislation. A decade from now—unless the trend is reversed—they will be able to pass it.

America has always been the haven which men throughout the world have sought in their flight from tyrannies at home. When socialized medicine swept through Britain and continental Europe, doctors moved here by the thousands in order to escape. Fifteen hundred doctors have come here from Cuba alone since Castro took over. The pattern is now repeating itself in Saskatchewan. The province's nine hundred doctors have informed the Premier and the public that they will not practice their profession under the socialist plan. Dr. J. C. Houston spoke for them all when he said about that plan: "It raises the vital question: 'Is the state created to serve the individual or is the individual created to serve the state?' If the latter viewpoint is accepted then professional freedom and indeed all freedom is destroyed. The light grows dim."

Mr. Peikoff is an Associate Lecturer of NATHANIEL BRANDEN INSTITUTE; *he has taught philosophy at Hunter College, Long Island University, and New York University; he is presently completing his doctoral dissertation in philosophy at New York University.*

Throughout the province, in medical clinics and doctors' offices, cardboard signs have been appearing with the following message: "Unless agreement is reached between the present government and the medical profession, this office will close as of July 1." Winnipeg *Free Press* columnist Pat O'Dwyer reports on the doctors' intentions: "They will leave the province, especially the ablest young specialists, and those doctors who came here from the British Isles to get away from state medicine." What is their destination? Many of them are heading for the United States. This country, they think, is safe and free. If America collapses into slavery, there will be no haven to seek anywhere any longer.

What will happen to the caliber of medical practice in this country, if the socialists take over? Consider the reports coming out of England, Holland, Hungary, and all the rest of the countries which have embraced socialized or semi-socialized medicine. The degrees and details vary; the essence of the pattern remains the same: First, the government announces free medical care for everyone—then there is a sudden, insatiable, endless stampede, as malingerers, neurotics and the authentically sick all clamor, in one howling mass, for medical attention—then the doctors, crushed by impossible overloads, abandon, in despair, the attempt to treat each patient's problem thoroughly and conscientiously; increasingly, doctors turn into traffic directors, routing people out of their offices in three to five minute appointments per patient, making instantaneous diagnoses, dispensing routine prescriptions, and then calling for the next man; meanwhile the bureaucrats, dismayed by the endless flow of money pouring into the bottomless pit of patients, begin to clamp down more and more severely—the doctors who use expensive new techniques, or exceed their quota of drugs, are fined for wasting the "people's resources"—the restrictions and the forms in triplicate multiply—the doctors become part-time clerks—the bureaucrats and their friends multiply—the doctors begin to check a patient's political contacts before they prescribe—and, in the end, the patients who have no contacts but really need medical attention start running to non-socialized countries, if they can find any.

There is no conflict between the interests of patients and the interests of doctors. The enslavement of the medical profession does not benefit the patients; it merely deprives them of doctors: the most dedicated, able and independent quit the profession or never enter it. The words of Dr. Hendricks, a surgeon in *Atlas Shrugged* who has gone on strike against socialized medicine, are singularly appropriate here:

"That a man who's willing to work under compulsion is too dangerous a brute to entrust with a job in the stockyards—never occurred to those who proposed to help the sick by making life impossible for the healthy. I have often wondered at the smugness with which people assert their right to enslave me, to control my work, to force my will, to violate my conscience, to stifle my mind—yet what is it that they expect to depend on, when they lie on an operating table under my hands? . . . Let them discover the kind of doctors that their system will now produce. Let them discover, in their operating rooms and hospital wards, that it is not safe to place their lives in the hands of a man whose life they have throttled. It is not safe, if he is the sort of man who resents it—and still less safe, if he is the sort who doesn't."

It is not an easy task to convert a free country into a totalitarian dictatorship; those who attempt it know that they must move gradually, by a series of precedent-setting steps. The Kennedy Administration has been urging a national campaign of letters to newspapers and petitions to Congress in support of their medical plans. The American Medical Association has asked for a similar campaign in defense of the doctors. For anyone who sees the nature of the issue, the side to choose is clear—and the need for action, imperative. No one who values his life—or his freedom—should remain silent.

Published monthly at 165 East 35th Street, New York 16, N.Y.
Subscription rate: in/United States, its possessions, Canada and Mexico, $5 for one year; other countries, $6. Trial subscriptions: 4 months $2. 6 months $3.
Additional copies of this supplement: single copy 25¢ (coins, not stamps); 10-99 copies, 15¢ each plus postage (for first-class delivery add 1¢ per copy, for third-class delivery add ½¢ per copy); 100-999 copies, 10¢ each plus postage (same as above); 1000 or more copies, 7¢ each plus postage (same as above).

THE OBJECTIVIST NEWSLETTER

Edited and Published by AYN RAND and NATHANIEL BRANDEN

VOL. 1 NO. 7   JULY, 1962

Benevolence versus Altruism

By NATHANIEL BRANDEN

A disastrous confusion in the minds of most people concerning the nature of altruism is the belief that altruism represents or derives from the principle of benevolence, good will and kindness toward others. Advocates of altruism take great pains to encourage this belief—to establish a "package-deal," as it were—so as to conceal from their victims the actual meaning of the altruist morality.

Such a view of altruism is worse than mistaken: like the perversion entailed in the technique of the "Big Lie," it represents the exact *opposite* of the truth; altruism and benevolence are not merely different, they are *mutually inimical and contradictory*.

The literal philosophical meaning of altruism is: *placing others above self*. As an ethical principle, altruism holds that man must make the welfare of others his primary concern and must place their interests above his own; it holds that man has no right to exist for his own sake, that service to others is the moral justification of his existence, that self-sacrifice is his foremost duty and highest virtue.

The essence of altruism is the concept of *self-sacrifice*. It is the *self* that altruism regards as evil: *selflessness* is its moral ideal. Thus, it is an *anti-self* ethics—and this means: anti-man, anti-personal happiness, anti-individual rights.

A morality that tells man that he is to regard himself as a sacrificial animal, is *not* an expression of benevolence or good will.

By the nature of the altruist ethics, it can engender only fear and hostility among men: it forces men to accept the role of victim or executioner, as objects of sacrifice or profiteers on human sacrifices—and leaves men no standard of justice, no way to know what they can demand and what they must surrender, what is theirs by right, what is theirs by favor, what is theirs by someone's sacrifice—thereby casting men into an *amoral* jungle. Contrary to the pretensions of altruism's advocates, it is human brotherhood and good will among men that altruism makes *impossible*.

Benevolence, good will and respect for the rights of others proceed from an *opposite* code of morality: from the principle that man the individual is not an object of sacrifice but an entity of *supreme value;* that each man exists for his own sake and is not a means to the ends of others; that *no one has the right to sacrifice anyone*.

Men of self-esteem, uncorrupted by the altruist morality, are the only men who can and do value human life—because they value their own life, because they are secure in the knowledge of their right to it, and because, to them, *"human being"* is a designation of honor. It is one's view of *oneself* that determines one's view of man and of human stature. The respect and good will that men of self-esteem feel toward other human beings is profoundly egoistic; they feel, in effect: "Other men are of value because they are of the same species as myself." In revering living entities, they are revering their *own* life. This is the psychological base of any emotion of sympathy and any feeling of "species solidarity."

But this causal relation cannot be reversed: a man must *first* value himself; only then can he value others. If a man does not value himself, *nothing* can have value for him.

When the advocates of a morality of rational self-interest express opposition to the creed of self-sacrifice, altruists commonly reply with some such evasion as: "You mean that if you found an abandoned baby in the street, you wouldn't do anything to help?"—or: "If you saw a man run over by a car, you wouldn't call a doctor?" The evasion consists of equating any help to others with altruism—and any *motive* for helping others with the motive demanded by altruism.

If, in an issue where no self-sacrifice is involved, a rational man helps a fellow human being in an emergency, and does so, not as a moral obligation, but out of good will and regard for the value of a human life—it is worse than absurd to equate his action with the policy of a man who accepts the tenet that to serve others is the purpose of his existence, that he has no right to live on any other terms, that anyone's suffering, need or helplessness has first claim on him. The motives of the two men are opposite: whereas the rational man's policy toward help to others rests on the value of an individual life, the other man's policy rests on the premise that an individual life *has no value*, that it is an object of sacrifice. Altruism does not declare: Help others when no self-sacrifice is entailed—or: Help those in whom you see positive value. Altruism declares: Help others, *any* others, because such is your only moral function—otherwise, you are *nothing*—and do not presume to pass judgment on the worthiness of those who demand your help—*theirs* is the *right*, yours is the *duty*. But if the altruists' view of man is correct, if the individual is a *zero*—then why should anyone be concerned with helping him? It is only the rational man's view of the individual's value that can provide an incentive or reason to help anyone—but *his* view is incompatible with the creed of self-sacrifice.

If helping that baby or accident victim actually required self-sacrifice—that is, the sacrifice of some higher value of one's own (for example, if one's own child immediately and desperately needed one's attention)—then, no, one should not do it. But normally, when no such sacrifice is involved, one *would* render help, not as an altruistic duty, but out of loyalty to the value of living entities and to the human potential that the baby or the accident victim represents. One would properly refuse help only if one knew some major evil about the person in trouble: if, for example, one saw a Hitler or a Khrushchev drowning, one would be *immoral* if one jumped into the water to save him; if the motive that would prompt one to save a person from drowning is concern for the value of human life, one does not save a mass-murderer.

Altruists cannot claim that they *do* value an individual life, offering as evidence their concern for those who are in need. If concern for human life were their actual motive, they would not be so contemptuously indifferent to—nor so eagerly willing to sacrifice—those who are *able* to live. They would not advocate the enslavement of the healthy for the benefit of the diseased. *Life* is an attribute of individual organisms; no one who values human life would preach that man has no right to exist for his own sake.

It is worth stressing that the entire issue of helping others is a *marginal* one; it is only the ethics of altruism that has made it a crucial question; it is not the central focus of a *rational* code of morality nor the source of a man's virtue nor the justification of anyone's existence. Man does not live for the purpose of combating disaster.

More grotesque than the altruists' claim to be spokesmen for benevolence and good will among men, is their declaration that altruism is the base of *love*, that love is selfless, that the essence of love is self-sacrifice. Love is one of the most profound forms of *self-assertion*: to love, is to value—one falls

(continued on page 28)

Copyright © 1962 by The Objectivist Newsletter, Inc.

BOOKS

The Decline of American Liberalism

by Arthur A. Ekirch, Jr.

Reviewed by **R. HESSEN**

How is it possible that one hundred and fifty years ago liberalism meant the advocacy of freedom and economic *laissez faire* and that today it means the creed of totalitarian statism? Many people are aware of this total reversal, but few, especially today's liberals, know, or care to know, how or why it came about.

In an engrossing book, distinguished for its scholarship, Professor Ekirch provides the evidence for understanding and explaining how two mutually antagonistic creeds share the name of liberalism and how one led to the other.

The Decline of American Liberalism surveys the rise and demise of liberal ideology and institutions in America. It charts the transition from the nineteenth-century liberalism of limited government, states' rights, strict interpretation of the Constitution, and economic *laissez faire*—the ideology of Jefferson and John Randolph—to the twentieth-century liberalism of omnipotent government, the usurpation and/or destruction of states' and individual rights, the unchecked rise of the Executive branch to discretionary power, the abdication of Congress to the status of a rubber stamp and the self-appointment of the Supreme Court as a lawmaking body—the legacy of Hamilton, Marshall, Lincoln, Theodore Roosevelt, Wilson and Franklin D. Roosevelt.

How was the shift from liberty to tyranny made possible? The definition of liberalism by Professor Ekirch provides a major clue to the answer. "Perhaps it is best therefore if we think of liberalism, not as a well-defined political or economic system, but as a collection of ideas or principles which go to make up an attitude or 'habit of mind.'"

It was the vagueness, gaps, contradictions and errors in its "collection of ideas" which proved the undoing of nineteenth-century liberalism. Although Professor Ekirch seems to share some of those errors, being a liberal himself, the facts he presents tell an eloquent story. Nineteenth-century liberal ideologists cherished the hope of the *"automatic* perfection" of mankind; they saw man as a creature "determined by environment" and they expected man to reach perfection by perfecting the environment through social reform. Again, men like Jefferson and Randolph mistakenly thought that freedom and culture required individual economic self-sufficiency and an agrarian society; they argued against extension of the powers of the federal government, *primarily* in order to prevent the use of its powers to create an industrial society. Thus the best of the classical liberals failed to appreciate capitalism and to conceive the possibility of industrialism spreading without government favors and handouts.

Ekirch shows that the death of nineteenth-century liberalism was keynoted by the Civil War. Before the war, only Southerners blatantly defended totalitarianism—Henry Hughes, a sociologist, conceived of "perfection in terms of an authoritarian, socialist order." Now, Northern liberals acquiesced in Lincoln's abrogations of individual rights, because they saw ideological advantages to be derived from the war. During this period, one detects the birth of the distinguishing attribute of the *modern* liberal: the willingness (and sometimes eagerness) to condone or advocate the initiation of physical force to achieve his ideals. "Emerson, like Whitman, nevertheless hoped and believed that the conflict would free the nation from an excessive reliance on a crude materialism and infuse it with a new ethical and idealistic purpose"—a sentiment to be echoed by Wilson's ideologue, Herbert Croly, to justify World War I: "The American nation needs the tonic of a serious moral adventure."

Ekirch brilliantly portrays a crucial moment in liberalism's decline when he exposes the Populists and Theodore Roosevelt's Progressives as usurpers of the liberal mantle. He demonstrates that ". . . the progressives were essentially nationalists, moving to a state socialism along European lines and owing relatively little to the American tradition of liberal individualism." Yet they were the bridge to the domestic and foreign policies of Wilson—for the liberals willingly accepted the Progressives as ideological pacemakers. This led, in domestic policy, to ". . . the paradox that much of the regulatory legislation, which was passed with the idea of restoring free competition, had precisely the opposite effect. In other words, government legislation was the greatest single factor in the decline of the very liberal economy that it sought to preserve and protect." And in foreign policy, it led to Wilson using deceit to drag an unwilling nation into war.

In recommending this book, one must register dissent from some of Professor Ekirch's interpretations. He conceives of government as an instrument of positive good—not simply as a policeman, but as a source of public welfare. At times, he seems to ascribe America's economic progress to government intervention in the economy. Finally, he fails to distinguish between economic power and political power, between wealth *earned* and wealth *acquired* through political favors such as exclusive franchises, subsidies and tariffs. He "package-deals" the two types; he quotes a nineteenth-century solution offered by E. L. Godkin, but fails fully to appreciate its truth or relevance. "Godkin asserted that the answer to bribery and corruption was to end the power of members of Congress to bestow great privileges upon private individuals and business corporations. . . . 'It [the government] cannot touch them without breeding corruption.'"

Such flaws as one may find in this book are largely confined to the interpretation of economic history, but Professor Ekirch is primarily an historian of ideas—and it is in this realm that his book has great merit. Those who want evidence of the cause and effect relationship between ideas and institutions, will find *The Decline of American Liberalism* extremely valuable, as will all those who are alarmed by the erosion of individual rights and economic freedom. Today's headlines provide a grim epilogue and confirmation: liberalism is in its last stages of decline; America is galloping toward a fascist dictatorship, with a liberal, Kennedy, as jockey. This book will show you what kind of ideas brought us here—and give you a clue to the ideas needed to change our course.

Benevolence versus Altruism (from page 27)

in love with the person who embodies and reflects one's own deepest values. Love is the *opposite* of selflessness.

As proof, ask yourself what your reaction would be if the man or woman you loved were to tell you: "Don't imagine that I want to marry you out of any selfish expectation of pleasure. Don't imagine that I see anything to admire in you, or that I find your company interesting, or that I enjoy our relationship in any manner whatever. In fact, I find you boring and thoroughly unappealing. But I wouldn't be so *selfish* as to seek anything personally valuable from our marriage. Don't imagine that your thoughts or feelings are of any *actual* interest to me, or that I do any of the things I do for you because I *care* about your happiness—don't think there's anything in it for *me* whether you're happy or not. I'm not an egoist, after all. I'm marrying you out of pity, out of charity, as a *duty*, because I know that you *need* me. I'm marrying you out of compassion for your flaws, not admiration for your virtues—I'm doing it as an act of *self-sacrifice.*"

No? You wouldn't feel romantically inspired? So much for the theory that love is selfless.

Altruism is the antithesis of love, just as it is the antithesis of *any* positive value in human relationships.

The choice is not: selfishness or good will among men. The choice is: altruism or good will, benevolence, kindness, love and human brotherhood.

---

* Published by Longmans, Green & Co., $7.50. Available from NBL BOOK SERVICE, INC., 165 East 35th St., New York 16, N.Y., for $5.95 (N.Y.C. residents add 3% sales tax; outside the U.S., add 15¢).

Mr. Hessen received his M.A. in History from Harvard University, and is now on the staff of NATHANIEL BRANDEN INSTITUTE.

INTELLECTUAL AMMUNITION DEPARTMENT

[Subscribers are invited to send in the questions that they find themselves unable to answer in philosophical or political discussions. As many questions as space permits will be answered. No questions will be answered by mail.]

■ **Doesn't life require compromise?**

A compromise is an adjustment of conflicting claims by mutual concessions. This means that both parties to a compromise have some valid claim and some value to offer each other. And *this* means that both parties agree upon some fundamental principle which serves as a base for their deal.

It is only in regard to concretes or particulars, implementing a mutually accepted basic principle, that one may compromise. For instance, one may bargain with a buyer over the price one wants to receive for one's product, and agree on a sum somewhere between one's demand and his offer. The mutually accepted basic principle, in such case, is the principle of trade, namely: that the buyer must pay the seller for his product. But if one wanted to be paid and the alleged buyer wanted to obtain one's product for nothing, no compromise, agreement or discussion would be possible, only the total surrender of one or the other.

There can be no compromise between a property owner and a burglar; offering the burglar a single teaspoon of one's silverware would not be a compromise, but a total surrender—the recognition of his *right* to one's property. What value or concession did the burglar offer in return? And once the principle of unilateral concessions is accepted as the base of a relationship by both parties, it is only a matter of time before the burglar would seize the rest. As an example of this process, observe the present foreign policy of the United States.

There can be no compromise between freedom and government controls; to accept "just a few controls" is to surrender the principle of inalienable individual rights and to substitute for it the principle of the government's unlimited, arbitrary power, thus delivering oneself into gradual enslavement. As an example of this process, observe the present domestic policy of the United States.

There can be no compromise on basic principles or on fundamental issues. What would you regard as a "compromise" between life and death? Or between truth and falsehood? Or between reason and irrationality?

Today, however, when people speak of "compromise," what they mean is not a legitimate mutual concession or a trade, but precisely the betrayal of one's principles—the unilateral surrender to any groundless, irrational claim. The root of that doctrine is *ethical subjectivism*, which holds that a *desire* or a *whim* is an irreducible moral primary, that every man is entitled to any desire he might feel like asserting, that all desires have equal moral validity, and that the only way men can get along together is by giving in to anything and "compromising" with anyone. It is not hard to see who would profit and who would lose by such a doctrine.

The immorality of this doctrine—and the reason why the term "compromise" implies, in today's general usage, an act of moral treason—lies in the fact that it requires men to accept ethical subjectivism as the basic principle superseding all principles in human relationships and to sacrifice anything as a concession to one another's whims.

The question "Doesn't life require compromise?" is usually asked by those who fail to differentiate between a basic principle and some concrete, specific wish. Accepting a lesser job than one had wanted is *not* a "compromise." Taking orders from one's employer on how to do the work for which one is hired, is *not* a "compromise." Living within one's income, is *not* a "compromise." Failing to have a cake after one has eaten it, is *not* a "compromise."

Integrity does not consist of loyalty to one's subjective whims, but of loyalty to rational principles. A "compromise" (in the unprincipled sense of that word) is not a breach of one's comfort, but a breach of one's convictions. A "compromise" does not consist of doing something one dislikes, but of doing something one knows to be evil. Accompanying one's husband or wife to a concert, when one does not care for music, is *not* a "compromise"; surrendering to his or her irrational demands for social conformity, for pretended religious observance or for generosity toward boorish in-laws, *is*. Working for an employer who does not share one's ideas, is *not* a "compromise"; pretending to share his ideas, *is*. Accepting a publisher's suggestions to make changes in one's manuscript, when one sees the rational validity of his suggestions, is *not* a "compromise"; making such changes in order to please him or to please "the public," against one's own judgment and standards, *is*.

The excuse, given in all such cases, is that the "compromise" is only temporary and that one will reclaim one's integrity at some indeterminate future date. But one cannot correct a husband's or wife's irrationality by giving in to it and encouraging it to grow. One cannot achieve the victory of one's ideas by helping to propagate their opposite. One cannot offer a literary masterpiece, "when one has become rich and famous," to a following one has acquired by writing trash. If one found it difficult to maintain one's loyalty to one's own convictions at the start, a succession of betrayals—which helped to augment the power of the evil one lacked the courage to fight—will not make it easier at a later date, but will make it virtually impossible.

There can be no compromise on moral principles. "In any compromise between food and poison, it is only death that can win. In any compromise between good and evil, it is only evil that can profit." *(Atlas Shrugged)* The next time you are tempted to ask: "Doesn't life require compromise?" translate that question into its actual meaning: "Doesn't life require the surrender of that which is true and good to that which is false and evil?" The answer is that *that* precisely is what life forbids—if one wishes to achieve anything but a stretch of tortured years spent in progressive self-destruction.

—AYN RAND

"Account Overdrawn"
By AYN RAND

The entire policy of the Kennedy Administration—with its opening of "New Frontiers" to the realm of the unearned, its handouts, its frantic search for new recipients who demand handouts, its ticker-tape parades for foreign recipients who nationalize the property of American businessmen—rests on a single hope: the *"economic growth"* of the United States.

You have heard that concept invoked by the Administration as a magic formula or a mystic prayer in every plan, project, budget or demand for power to spend wealth which is not yet in existence, but which is to be provided by our "economic growth." It is time to ask yourself concretely and specifically: just what *is* "economic growth?"

Economic growth is the rise of an economy's productivity. What causes that rise? "The most important factor," wrote *Time* (April 27, 1962), "is new machinery and equipment. Other factors enter in, including higher levels of education and skill among workers, more efficient means of transportation and communication, research that pays off in new products or new techniques."

What is the common denominator of all the items on this interesting list, presented by a magazine that could hardly be called a staunch advocate of capitalism? *Human ability*. The intelligence, the efficiency, the skill, the knowledge, the creative inventiveness of the men who take part in a country's economy. Who channels that ability into "new machinery and equipment, new products or new techniques?" *The businessmen*.

It is on the productive ability of the American businessmen —on the hope that that ability will continue to function—that the whole grandiose edifice of Mr. Kennedy's plans is built.

(continued on page 30)

"Account Overdrawn" (from page 29)

How does Mr. Kennedy treat these providers and benefactors who are indispensable to him according to his own reiterated pronouncements? "My father always told me," said Mr. Kennedy, "that all businessmen were sons-of-bitches, but I never believed it till now!"

On May 28, a great many people apparently came to believe it, too, and, giving up the aspiration to achieve the status of sons-of-bitches, decided to sell their shares of America's doghouses.

"Why, Mr. Kennedy," said the falling stock market, paraphrasing Francisco d'Anconia, "what's the matter? Why do you seem to be upset? Profits are the root of all evil—so I just got tired of being evil."

Most of the commentators, in the press and in Washington, professed to be puzzled by the stock market drop. "There was no economic reason for it," they cried. "Our economy is sound!" While some government officials were beginning to express doubt, others went on declaring that "economic growth" is just around the corner.

In style, content and implication, one of the most curious comments was made by James Reston (*The New York Times*, June 3, 1962). In a gentle, swimmy mixture of pleas and threats, he wrote the following: "At least a moratorium on ugly charges of bad faith is indicated. . . . The psychological slump at the moment, therefore, is probably more important than the stock market slump—in fact, it is probably responsible for the stock market slump. . . . If you go on telling the Yankees they are a lousy ball team you can soon land them in the second division, and if you go on insisting that Kennedy is anti-business the darned thing could easily happen, to the detriment of everybody."

Believe it or not, it is the businessmen who are guilty, as usual; they are guilty of making "ugly charges of bad faith" against Mr. Kennedy, who is innocent of such tactics ("Kennedy is not anti-business now, but he is Irish," Mr. Reston explains.) The rest may be taken to mean, interchangeably, either: (a) that businessmen must not let their "psychological slump" affect Mr. Kennedy who'll crack down on them if they don't cheer up—or (b) that Mr. Kennedy is suffering from a "psychological slump" and needs sympathy, reassurance and encouragement from businessmen.

Well, let us take a look at some of the "darned things" which *did* happen—and then ask ourselves whose psychological endurance had borne too much for too long.

In February, 1962, the F.C.C. hearings featured Mr. Newton N. Minow's demand for dictatorial power over the radio and television industry, while he charged businessmen (industry executives and sponsors alike) with bad taste, incompetence, commercialism, greed for profits, and policies contrary to "the public interest."

In March, proposing "protection for consumers," Mr. Kennedy demanded the power to control the food and drug industries, declaring to the nation that businessmen, in their pursuit of profit, are not to be trusted to give people an honest measure of untainted food or an effective, lifesaving drug.

In April, Mr. Kennedy exploded against the steel industry, denouncing the "steel executives whose pursuit of private power and profit exceeds their sense of public responsibility . . . ," damning them for disobeying the wishes he had no right to assert, and declaring, in effect, that the urgent needs of business (such as maintenance, modernization, fighting foreign competition, etc.) are to be left at the mercy of the government's whim in some indeterminate future—that prices are to conform, not to the demands of the market, but to the demands of *his* policies—that profits are the first item to be sacrificed to the "national interest"—and that the antitrust boys would work-over any dissenter.

How long did Mr. Kennedy expect to be able to damn profits and to demand sacrifices, before people would take him at his word? Well, they did: they sacrificed their hope of profits—in the stock market.

There was a grim justice in the stock market's fall. It was the only form in which people could still express a protest, consciously or subconsciously, against the persecution and destruction of American business. And no amount of evasion on the part of the New Frontiersmen can hide the fact that the steel crisis *was* the immediate cause of that fall; logically and chronologically, the evidence was too dramatic to misinterpret. If, in the face of political outrages, you had wondered: "How can the American people stand for it?"—you have now seen a preview of the manner in which people declare that they can't.

On May 28, 1962, the United States economy suffered a heart attack. As of this writing, the attack was not fatal and the patient seemed to rally. But, as with all heart attacks, there is now no way to know whether the next one will strike in an hour, a day or a year. Only one thing is certain: it was a warning, not to be ignored. The catastrophe which the advocates of capitalism had been predicting theoretically for the past decades is now discernible in practical, factual reality.

There are two roads ahead of us, with no "middle."

When the blow strikes, the statists will declare that free enterprise—the enterprise of chained, hampered, paralyzed, terrorized, antitrust-gagged men—has had its chance and has failed, and that they, the statists, in selfless service to the "public interest," must impose on us an emergency system of totalitarian controls.

Or: when the blow strikes, all those who value America, freedom, civilization, individual rights and their own lives, will unite on a single political program—placing the blame where it belongs—a program which will declare that statist controls have had their chance and have failed, and that there is only one way to save a collapsing economy: *to start decontrolling*.

OBJECTIVIST CALENDAR

■ A weekly column by Ayn Rand now appears each Sunday in the *Los Angeles Times*. The column began on June 17.

■ NATHANIEL BRANDEN INSTITUTE's fall course of lectures on "Basic Principles of Objectivism" is scheduled to begin in New York City on Tuesday, October 9, and in Philadelphia on Monday, October 15.

At present, the Tape Transcription Course on "Basic Principles of Objectivism" is scheduled for fourteen cities this fall: Boston; Washington; Indianapolis; Miami; Chicago; St. Louis; Kansas City, Kansas; Lincoln, Nebraska; Houston; Dallas; Los Angeles; San Diego; Toronto; Winnipeg.

The INSTITUTE invites requests for interviews from individuals who are potentially interested in handling this course, as business representatives, in other cities in the United States and Canada. Write for information to: NATHANIEL BRANDEN INSTITUTE, Tape Transcription Division, 165 East 35th St., New York 16, N.Y.

■ Ayn Rand's lecture on "Conservatism: An Obituary" has been published by NATHANIEL BRANDEN INSTITUTE and is available from THE OBJECTIVIST NEWSLETTER. Price: 50¢ (N.Y.C. residents add 2¢ sales tax).

Published monthly at 165 East 35th Street, New York 16, N.Y.
Subscription rate: In United States, its possessions, Canada and Mexico, $5 for one year; other countries, $6. Trial subscriptions: 4 months $2. 6 months $3.
Additional copies of this Newsletter: single copy 50¢ (coins, not stamps); 10 — 99 copies, 25¢ each plus postage (for first-class delivery add 1¢ per copy, for third-class delivery add ½¢ per copy); 100 or more copies, 15¢ each plus postage (same as above).
For change of address send old address and new address with zone number if any. Allow us two weeks to process new subscriptions and change of address.

Ayn Rand and Nathaniel Branden, Editors and Publishers
Barbara Branden, Managing Editor
Elayne Kalberman, Circulation Manager
PRINTED BY CARNEGIE PRESS, INC., NEW YORK CITY

THE OBJECTIVIST NEWSLETTER

Edited and Published by AYN RAND and NATHANIEL BRANDEN

VOL. 1 NO. 8   AUGUST, 1962

CHECK YOUR PREMISES
By AYN RAND

The "Conflicts" of Men's Interests

Some students of Objectivism find it difficult to grasp the Objectivist principle that "there are no conflicts of interests among rational men."

A typical question runs as follows: "Suppose two men apply for the same job. Only one of them can be hired. Isn't this an instance of a conflict of interests, and isn't the benefit of one man achieved at the price of the sacrifice of the other?"

There are four interrelated considerations which are involved in a rational man's view of his interests, but which are ignored or evaded in the above question and in all similar approaches to the issue. I shall designate these four as: (a) "Reality," (b) "Context," (c) "Responsibility," (d) "Effort."

(a) *"Reality."* The term "interests" is a wide abstraction that covers the entire field of ethics. It includes the issues of: man's values, his desires, his goals and their actual achievement in reality. A man's "interests" depend on the kind of goals he chooses to pursue, his choice of goals depends on his desires, his desires depend on his values—and, for a rational man, his values depend on the judgment of his mind.

Desires (or feelings or emotions or wishes or whims) are not tools of cognition; they are not a valid standard of value, nor a valid criterion of man's interests. The mere fact that a man desires something does not constitute a proof that the object of his desire is *good*, nor that its achievement is actually to his interest.

To claim that a man's interests are sacrificed whenever a desire of his is frustrated—is to hold a subjectivist view of man's values and interests. Which means: to believe that it is proper, moral and possible for man to achieve his goals, regardless of whether they contradict the facts of reality or not. Which means: to hold an irrational or mystical view of existence. Which means: to deserve no further consideration.

In choosing his goals (the specific values he seeks to gain and/or keep), a rational man is guided by his thinking (by a process of reason)—not by his feelings or desires. He does not regard desires as irreducible primaries, as the given, which he is destined irresistibly to pursue. He does not regard "because I *want* it" or "because I *feel* like it" as a sufficient cause and validation of his actions. He chooses and/or identifies his desires by a process of reason, and he does not act to achieve a desire until and unless he is able rationally to validate it *in the full context of his knowledge* and of his other values and goals. He does not act until he is able to say: "I want it because it is *right*."

The Law of Identity (A is A) is a rational man's paramount consideration in the process of determining his interests. He knows that the contradictory is the impossible, that a contradiction cannot be achieved in reality and that the attempt to achieve it can lead only to disaster and destruction. Therefore, he does not permit himself to hold contradictory values, to pursue contradictory desires and goals, or to imagine that the pursuit of a contradiction can ever be to his interest.

Only an irrationalist (or mystic or subjectivist—in which category I place all those who regard faith, feelings or desires as man's standard of value) exists in a perpetual conflict of "interests." Nothing but conflicts of interests is possible to him. Not only do his alleged interests clash with those of other men, but they clash also with one another.

No one finds it difficult to dismiss from philosophical consideration the problem of a man who wails that life entraps him in an irreconcilable conflict because he cannot eat his cake and have it, too. That problem does not acquire intellectual validity by being expanded to involve more than cake—whether one expands it to the whole universe, as in the doctrines of Existentialism, or only to a few random whims and sundry evasions, as in most people's views of their own interests.

When a person reaches the stage of claiming that *man's interests conflict with reality*, the concept "interests" ceases to be meaningful—and his problem ceases to be philosophical and becomes psychological.

(b) *"Context."* Just as a rational man does not hold any conviction out of context—that is: without relating it to the rest of his knowledge and resolving any possible contradictions—so he does not hold or pursue any desire out of context. And he does not judge what is or is not to his interest out of context, on the range of any given moment.

Context-dropping is one of the chief psychological tools of evasion. In regard to one's desires, there are two major ways of context-dropping: the issue of *range* and the issue of *means*.

A rational man sees his interests in terms of a lifetime and selects his goals accordingly. This does not mean that he has to be omniscient, infallible or clairvoyant. It means that he does not live his life short-range and does not drift like a bum pushed by the spur of the moment. It means that he does not regard any moment as cut off from the context of the rest of his life, and that he allows no conflicts or contradictions between his short-range and long-range interests. He never loses sight of the fact that his life has to be an integrated whole—and he does not become his own destroyer by pursuing a desire today which wipes out all his values tomorrow.

A rational man does not indulge in wistful longings for ends divorced from means. He does not hold a desire without knowing (or learning) and considering the means by which it is to be achieved. Since he knows that nature does not provide man with the automatic satisfaction of his desires, that a man's goals or values have to be achieved by his own effort, that the lives and efforts of other men are not his property and are not there to serve his wishes—a rational man never holds a desire or pursues a goal, which cannot be achieved directly or *indirectly* by his own effort.

It is with a proper understanding of this *"indirectly"* that the crucial social issue begins.

Living in a society, instead of on a desert island, does not relieve a man of the responsibility of supporting his own life. The only difference is that he supports his life by *trading* his products or services for the products or services of others. And, in this process of trade, a rational man does not seek or desire any more or any less than his own effort can earn. What determines his earnings? The free market, that is: the voluntary choice and judgment of the men who are willing to trade him their effort in return.

When a man trades with others, he is counting—explicitly or implicitly—on their rationality, that is: on their ability to recognize the objective value of his work. (A trade based on any other premise is a con game or a fraud.) Thus, when a rational man pursues a goal in a free society, he does not place himself at the mercy of the whims, the favors or the prejudices of others; he depends on nothing but his own

(continued on page 32)

The "Conflicts" of Men's Interests (from page 31)

effort: *directly*, by doing objectively valuable work—*indirectly*, through the objective evaluation of his work by others.

It is in this sense that a rational man never holds a desire or pursues a goal which cannot be achieved by his own effort. He trades value for value. He never seeks or desires the *unearned*. If he undertakes to achieve a goal that requires the cooperation of many people, he never counts on anything but his own ability to persuade them and their voluntary agreement.

Needless to say, a rational man never distorts or corrupts his own standards and judgment in order to appeal to the irrationality, stupidity or dishonesty of others. He knows that such a course is suicidal. He knows that one's only practical chance to achieve any degree of success or anything humanly desirable lies in dealing with those who are rational, whether there are many of them or few. If, in any given set of circumstances, any victory is possible at all, it is only reason that can win it. And, in a free society, no matter how hard the struggle might be, it is reason that ultimately wins.

Since he never drops the context of the issues he deals with, a rational man accepts that struggle as *to his interest*—because he knows that freedom is to his interest. He knows that the struggle to achieve his values includes the possibility of defeat. He knows also that there is no alternative and no automatic guarantee of success for man's effort, neither in dealing with nature nor with other men. So he does not judge his interests by any particular defeat nor by the range of any particular moment. He lives and judges long-range. And he assumes the full responsibility of knowing what conditions are *necessary* for the achievement of his goals.

(c) *"Responsibility."* This last is the particular form of intellectual responsibility that most people evade. That evasion is the major cause of their frustrations and defeats.

Most people hold their desires without any context whatever, as ends hanging in a foggy vacuum, the fog hiding any concept of means. They rouse themselves mentally only long enough to utter an *"I wish,"* and stop there, and wait, as if the rest were up to some unknown power.

What they evade is *the responsibility of judging the social world*. They take the world as the given. "A world I never made" is the deepest essence of their attitude—and they seek only to adjust themselves uncritically to the incomprehensible requirements of those unknowable others who did make the world, whoever those might be.

But humility and presumptuousness are two sides of the same psychological medal. In the willingness to throw oneself blindly on the mercy of others there is the implicit privilege of making blind demands on one's masters.

There are countless ways in which this sort of "metaphysical humility" reveals itself. For instance, there is the man who wishes to be rich, but never thinks of discovering what means, actions and conditions are required to achieve wealth. Who is he to judge? He never made the world—and "nobody gave him a break."

There is the girl who wishes to be loved, but never thinks of discovering what love is, what values it requires, and whether she possesses any virtues to be loved for. Who is she to judge? Love, she feels, is an inexplicable favor—so she merely longs for it, feeling that somebody has deprived her of her share in the distribution of favors.

There are the parents who suffer deeply and genuinely, because their son (or daughter) does not love them, and who, simultaneously, ignore, oppose or attempt to destroy everything they know of their son's convictions, values and goals, never thinking of the connection between these two facts, never making an attempt to understand their son. The world they never made and dare not challenge, has told them that children love parents automatically.

There is the man who wants a job, but never thinks of discovering what qualifications the job requires or what constitutes doing one's work well. Who is he to judge? He never made the world. Somebody owes him a living. How? *Somehow*.

A European architect of my acquaintance was talking, one day, of his trip to Puerto Rico. He described—with great indignation at the universe at large—the squalor of the Puerto Ricans' living conditions. Then he described what wonders modern housing could do for them, which he had daydreamed in detail, including electric refrigerators and tiled bathrooms. I asked: "Who would pay for it?" He answered, in a faintly offended, almost huffy tone of voice: "Oh, that's not for me to worry about! An architect's task is only to project what *should* be done. Let somebody else think about the money."

That is the psychology from which all "social reforms" or "welfare states" or "noble experiments" or the destruction of the world have come.

In dropping the responsibility for one's own interests and life, one drops the responsibility of ever having to consider the interests and lives of others—of those others who are, somehow, to provide the satisfaction of one's desires.

Whoever allows a "somehow" into his view of the means by which his desires are to be achieved, is guilty of that "metaphysical humility" which, psychologically, is the premise of a parasite. As Nathaniel Branden pointed out in a lecture, *"somehow"* always means *"somebody."*

(d) *"Effort."* Since a rational man knows that man must achieve his goals by his own effort, he knows that neither wealth nor jobs nor any human values exist in a given, limited, static quantity, waiting to be divided. He knows that all benefits have to be produced, that the gain of one man does not represent the loss of another, that a man's achievement is not earned at the expense of those who have not achieved it.

Therefore, he never imagines that he has any sort of unearned, unilateral claim on any human being—and he never leaves his interests at the mercy of any one person or single, specific concrete. He may need clients, but not any one particular client—he may need customers, but not any one particular customer—he may need a job, but not any one particular job.

If he encounters competition, he either meets it or chooses another line of work. There is no job so low that a better, more skillful performance of it would pass unnoticed and unappreciated; not in a *free* society. Ask any office manager.

It is only the passive, parasitical representatives of the "humility metaphysics" school who regard any competitor as a threat, because the thought of earning one's position by personal merit is not part of their view of life. They regard themselves as interchangeable mediocrities who have nothing to offer and who fight, in a "static" universe, for someone's causeless favor.

A rational man knows that one does not live by means of "luck," "breaks" or favors, that there is no such thing as an "only chance" or a single opportunity, and that this is guaranteed precisely by the existence of competition. He does not regard any concrete, specific goal or value as irreplaceable. He knows that only persons are irreplaceable—only those one loves.

He knows also that there are no conflicts of interests among rational men even in the issue of love. Like any other value, love is not a static quantity to be divided, but an unlimited response to be earned. The love for one friend is not a threat to the love for another, and neither is the love for the various members of one's family, assuming they have earned it. The most exclusive form—romantic love—is not an issue of competition. If two men are in love with the same woman, what she feels for either of them is not determined by what she feels for the other and is not taken away from him. If she chooses one of them, the "loser" could not have had what the "winner" has earned.

It is only among the irrational, emotion-motivated persons, whose love is divorced from any standards of value, that chance rivalries, accidental conflicts and blind choices prevail. But then, whoever wins, does not win much. Among the emotion-driven, neither love nor any other emotion has any meaning.

Such, in brief essence, are the four major considerations involved in a rational man's view of his interests.

(continued on page 35)

INTELLECTUAL AMMUNITION DEPARTMENT

[*Subscribers are invited to send in the questions that they find themselves unable to answer in philosophical or political discussions. As many questions as space permits will be answered. No questions will be answered by mail.*]

- **Are periodic depressions inevitable in a system of laissez-faire capitalism?**

It is characteristic of the enemies of capitalism that they denounce it for evils that are, in fact, the result not of capitalism but of statism: evils that result from and are made possible only by government intervention in the economy.

In the June issue of THE OBJECTIVIST NEWSLETTER, I discussed a flagrant example of this policy: the charge that capitalism leads to the establishment of coercive monopolies. The most notorious instance of this policy is the claim that capitalism, by its nature, inevitably leads to periodic depressions.

Statists repeatedly assert that depressions (the phenomenon of the so-called business cycle, of "boom and bust") are inherent in *laissez faire,* and that the great crash of 1929 was the final proof of the failure of an unregulated, free-market economy. What is the truth of the matter?

A depression is a large-scale decline in production and trade; it is characterized by a sharp drop in productive output, in investment, in employment and in the value of capital assets (plants, machinery, etc.). Normal business fluctuations, or a temporary decline in the rate of industrial expansion, do not constitute a depression; a depression is a nation-wide contraction of business activity—and a general decline in the value of capital assets—of major proportions.

There is nothing in the nature of a free-market economy to cause such an event. The popular explanations of depression as caused by "over-production," "under-consumption," monopolies, labor-saving devices, maldistribution, excessive accumulations of wealth, etc., have been exploded as fallacies many times. (See, in this connection, Carl Snyder, *Capitalism the Creator,* Macmillan, 1940.)

Readjustments of economic activity, shifts of capital and labor from one industry to another, due to changing conditions, occur constantly under capitalism. This is entailed in the process of motion, growth and progress that characterizes capitalism. But there always exists the possibility of profitable endeavor in one field or another, there is always the need and demand for goods, and all that can change is what kind of goods it becomes most profitable to produce.

In any one industry, it is possible for supply to exceed demand, in the context of all the other existing demands. In such a case, there is a drop in prices, in profitableness, in investment and in employment in that particular industry; capital and labor tend to flow elsewhere, seeking more rewarding uses. Such an industry undergoes a period of stagnation, as a result of unjustified, that is, uneconomic, unprofitable, unproductive investment.

In a free economy that functions on a gold standard, such unproductive investment is severely limited; unjustified speculation does not rise, unchecked, until it engulfs an entire nation. In a free economy, the supply of money and credit needed to finance business ventures is determined by *objective* economic factors. It is the banking system that is the guardian of economic stability. The principles governing money supply operate to forbid large-scale unjustified investment.

Most businesses finance at least part of their undertakings by means of bank loans. Banks function as an investment clearing house, investing the savings of their customers in those enterprises which promise to be most successful. Banks do not have unlimited funds to loan; they are limited in the credit they can extend by the amount of their gold reserves. In order for banks to remain successful, to make profits and thus attract the savings of investors, they must make their loans judiciously: they must seek out those ventures which they judge to be most sound and potentially profitable. If banks fail in their judgment too consistently, their loans are not repaid and they go bankrupt.

If, in a period of increasing speculation, banks are confronted with an inordinate number of requests for loans, then, in response to the shrinking availability of money, they (a) raise their interest rates and (b) scrutinize more severely the ventures for which loans are requested, setting more exacting standards of what constitutes a justifiable investment. As a consequence, funds are more difficult to obtain, and there is a temporary curtailment and contraction of business investment. Businessmen are often unable to borrow the funds they desire and have to reduce plans for expansion. The purchase of common stocks, which reflects investors' estimates of the future earnings of companies, is similarly curtailed; overvalued stocks fall in price. Businesses engaged in uneconomic ventures, now unable to obtain additional credit, go bankrupt; a further waste of productive factors is stopped and economic errors are liquidated.

At worst, the economy may experience a mild recession, that is, a general slight decline in investment and production. In an unregulated economy, readjustments occur quite swiftly, and then production and investment again begin to climb. The temporary recession is not harmful but beneficial; it is the state of an economic system in the process of curtailing disease and returning to health.

The impact of such a recession may be significantly felt in a few industries, but it does not wreck an entire economy. A nation-wide depression, such as occurred in the United States in the thirties, would not have been possible in a fully free society. It was made possible only by government intervention in the economy—more specifically, by government manipulation of the money supply.

The government's policy consisted, in essence, of anesthetizing the regulators, inherent in a free banking system, that prevent runaway speculation and consequent economic collapse.

All government intervention in the economy is based on the belief that economic laws need not operate, that principles of cause and effect can be suspended, that everything in existence is "flexible" and "malleable," except a bureaucrat's whim, which is omnipotent. Reality, logic and economics must not be allowed to get in the way.

This was the implicit premise that led to the establishment, in 1913, of the Federal Reserve System—a government bank with control (through complex and often indirect means) over the individual banks throughout the country. The Federal Reserve undertook to free individual banks from the "limitations" imposed on them by the amount of their own individual reserves, to free them from the laws of the market—and to arrogate to government officials the right to decide how much credit they wished to make available at what times.

A "cheap money" policy was the guiding idea and goal of these officials. Banks were no longer to be limited in making loans by the amount of their gold reserves. Interest rates were no longer to rise in response to increasing speculation and increasing demands for funds. Credit was to remain readily available—until and unless the Federal Reserve decided otherwise. (For a discussion of the means by which the Federal Reserve controls credit availability, see Snyder; see also Benjamin M. Anderson, *Economics and the Public Welfare,* Van Nostrand, 1949—the best financial and economic history of the United States from 1914 through 1946.)

The government argued that by taking control of money and credit out of the hands of private bankers, and by contracting or expanding credit at will, guided by considerations other than those influencing the "selfish" bankers, it could—in conjunction with other interventionist policies—so control investment as to guarantee a state of virtually constant prosperity. Many bureaucrats believed that the government could keep the economy in a state of unending boom.

To borrow an invaluable metaphor from Alan Greenspan:

(continued on page 34)

Intellectual Ammunition Department *(from page 33)*

if, under *laissez faire*, the banking system and the principles controlling the availability of funds act as a fuse that prevents a blowout in the economy—then the government, through the Federal Reserve System, *put a penny in the fuse-box*. The result was the explosion known as the Crash of 1929.

Throughout most of the 1920's, the government compelled banks to keep interest rates artificially and uneconomically low. As a consequence, money was poured into every sort of speculative venture. By 1928, the warning signals of danger were clearly apparent: unjustified investment was rampant and stocks were increasingly over-valued. The government chose to ignore these danger signals. A free banking system would have been compelled, by economic necessity, to put the brakes on this process of runaway speculation; credit and investment, in such a case, would be drastically curtailed; the banks which made unprofitable investments, the enterprises which proved unproductive, and those who dealt with them, would suffer—but that would be all; the country as a whole would not be dragged down. However, the "anarchy" of a free banking system had been abandoned—in favor of "enlightened" government planning.

The boom and the wild speculation—which had preceded every major depression—were allowed to rise unchecked, involving, in a widening network of malinvestments and miscalculations, the entire economic structure of the nation. People were investing in virtually everything and making fortunes overnight—*on paper*. Profits were calculated on hysterically exaggerated appraisals of the future earnings of companies. Credit was extended with promiscuous abandon, on the premise that somehow the goods would be there to back it up—it was like the policy of a man who passes out rubber checks, counting on the hope that he will somehow find a way to obtain the necessary money and to deposit it in the bank before anyone presents his checks for collection.

But A is A—and reality is not infinitely elastic. In 1929, the country's economic and financial structure had become impossibly precarious. By the time the government finally and frantically raised the interest rates, it was too late. It is doubtful whether anyone can state with certainty what events first set off the panic—and it does not matter: the crash had become inevitable; any number of events could have pulled the trigger. But when the news of the first bank and commercial failures began to spread, uncertainty swept across the country in widening waves of terror. People began to sell their stocks, hoping to get out of the market with their gains, or to obtain the money they suddenly needed to pay bank loans that were being called in—and other people, seeing this, apprehensively began to sell *their* stocks—and, virtually overnight, an avalanche hurled the stock market downward, prices collapsed, securities became worthless, loans were called in, many of which could not be paid, the value of capital assets plummeted sickeningly, fortunes were wiped out, and, by 1932, business activity had come almost to a halt. The law of causality had avenged itself.

Such, in essence, was the nature and cause of the 1929 depression.

It provides one of the most eloquent illustrations of the disastrous consequences of a "planned" economy. In a free economy, when an individual businessman makes an error of economic judgment, *he* (and perhaps those who immediately deal with him) suffers the consequences; in a controlled economy, when a central planner makes an error of economic judgment, the whole country suffers the consequences.

It was not the Federal Reserve, it was not government intervention that took the blame for the 1929 depression—it was capitalism. Freedom—cried statists of every breed and sect—had had its chance and had failed. The voices of the few thinkers who pointed to the real cause of the evil were drowned out in the denunciations of businessmen, of the profit motive, of capitalism.

Had men chosen to understand the cause of the crash, the country would have been spared much of the agony that followed. The depression was prolonged for tragically unnecessary years by the same evil that had caused it: government controls and regulations.

Contrary to popular misconception, controls and regulations began long before the New Deal; in the 1920's, the "mixed economy" was already an established fact of American life. But the trend toward statism began to move faster under the Hoover Administration—and, with the advent of Roosevelt's New Deal, it accelerated at an unprecedented rate. The economic adjustments needed to bring the depression to an end were prevented from taking place—by the imposition of strangling controls, increased taxes and labor legislation. This last had the effect of forcing wage rates to unjustifiably high levels, thus raising the businessman's costs at precisely the time when costs needed to be lowered, if investment and production were to revive.

The National Industrial Recovery Act, the Wagner Act, and the abandonment of the gold standard (with the government's subsequent plunge into inflation and an orgy of deficit spending) were only three of the many disastrous measures enacted by the New Deal for the avowed purpose of pulling the country out of the depression; all had the opposite effect. (For a study of the many regulations and policies which prevented business recovery, see Snyder; Anderson; and Hans F. Sennholz, *How Can Europe Survive?*, Van Nostrand, 1955.)

As Alan Greenspan points out in "Stock Prices and Capital Evaluation,"* the obstacle to business recovery did not consist exclusively of the specific New Deal legislation passed; more harmful still was the general atmosphere of *uncertainty* engendered by the Administration. One had no way to know what law or regulation would descend on one's head at any moment, one had no way to know what sudden shifts of direction government policy might take, one had no way to plan long-range.

To act and produce, businessmen require *knowledge*, the possibility of rational calculation, not "faith" and "hope"—above all, not "faith" and "hope" concerning the unpredictable twistings within a bureaucrat's head.

Such advances as business was able to achieve under the New Deal collapsed in 1937—as a result of an intensification of uncertainty regarding what the government might choose to do next. Unemployment rose to more than ten million and business activity fell almost to the low point of 1932, the worst year of the depression.

It is part of the official New Deal mythology that Roosevelt "got us out of the depression." How was the problem of the depression finally "solved"? By the favorite expedient of all statists in times of emergency: a war.

The depression precipitated by the stock market crash of 1929 was not the first in American history—though it was incomparably more severe than any that had preceded it. If one studies the earlier depressions, the same basic cause and common denominator will be found: in one form or another, by one means or another, government manipulation of the money supply. It is typical of the manner in which interventionism grows that the Federal Reserve System was instituted as a proposed antidote against those earlier depressions—which were themselves products of monetary manipulation by the government.

The financial mechanism of an economy is the sensitive center, the living heart, of business activity. In no other area can government intervention produce quite such disastrous consequences. (For a general discussion of the business cycle and its relation to government manipulation of the money supply, see Ludwig von Mises, *Human Action*, Yale University Press, 1949.)

One of the most striking facts of history is men's failure to learn from it. For further details, see the policies of the present Administration. —**NATHANIEL BRANDEN**

---

*A paper delivered before a joint session of the American Statistical Association and the American Finance Association in 1959.

The "Conflicts" of Men's Interests *(from page 32)*

Now let us return to the question originally asked—about the two men applying for the same job—and observe in what manner it ignores or opposes these four considerations.

(a) *"Reality."* The mere fact that two men desire the same job does not constitute proof that either of them is entitled to it or deserves it, and that his interests are damaged if he does not obtain it.

(b) *"Context."* Both men should know that if they desire a job, their goal is made possible only by the existence of a business concern able to provide employment—that that business concern requires the availability of more than one applicant for any job—that if only one applicant existed, he would not obtain the job, because the business concern would have to close its doors—and that their competition for the job *is* to their interest, even though one of them will lose in that particular encounter.

(c) *"Responsibility."* Neither man has the moral right to declare that he doesn't want to consider all those things, he just wants a job. He is not entitled to any desire or to any "interest" without knowledge of what is required to make its fulfillment possible.

(d) *"Effort."* Whoever gets the job, has earned it (assuming that the employer's choice is rational). This benefit is due to his own merit—not to the "sacrifice" of the other man who never had any vested right to that job. The failure to give to a man what had never belonged to him can hardly be described as "sacrificing his interests."

All of the above discussion applies only to the relationships among rational men and only to a free society. In a free society, one does not have to deal with those who are irrational. One is free to avoid them.

In a non-free society, no pursuit of any interests is possible to anyone; nothing is possible but gradual and general destruction.

Introducing Objectivism*
By AYN RAND

[*This is the first column by Ayn Rand, which appeared in the* Los Angeles Times, *on June 17, 1962.*]

At a sales conference at Random House, preceding the publication of *Atlas Shrugged*, one of the book salesmen asked me whether I could present the essence of my philosophy while standing on one foot. I did, as follows:

1. *Metaphysics:* Objective Reality
2. *Epistemology:* Reason
3. *Ethics:* Self-interest
4. *Politics:* Capitalism

If you want this translated into simple language, it would read: 1. "Nature, to be commanded, must be obeyed" or "Wishing won't make it so." 2. "You can't eat your cake and have it, too." 3. "Man is an end in himself." 4. "Give me liberty or give me death."

If you held these concepts with total consistency, as the base of your convictions, you would have a full philosophical system to guide the course of your life. But to hold them with total consistency—to understand, to define, to prove and to apply them—requires volumes of thought. Which is why philosophy cannot be discussed while standing on one foot—nor while standing on two feet on both sides of every fence. This last is the predominant philosophical position today, particularly in the field of politics.

In the space of a column, I can give only the briefest summary of my position, as a frame-of-reference for all my future columns. My philosophy, Objectivism, holds that:

1. Reality exists as an objective absolute—facts are facts, independent of man's feelings, wishes, hopes or fears.
2. Reason (the faculty which identifies and integrates the material provided by man's senses) is man's only means of

* Copyright 1962 by Times-Mirror Co., Los Angeles.

perceiving reality, his only source of knowledge, his only guide to action, and his basic means of survival.

3. Man—every man— is an end in himself, not the means to the ends of others. He must exist for his own sake, neither sacrificing himself to others nor sacrificing others to himself. The pursuit of his own *rational* self-interest and of his own happiness is the highest moral purpose of his life.

4. The ideal political-economic system is *laissez-faire* capitalism. It is a system where men deal with one another, not as victims and executioners, nor as masters and slaves, but as *traders,* by free, voluntary exchange to mutual benefit. It is a system where no man may obtain any values from others by resorting to physical force, and *no man may initiate the use of physical force against others.* The government acts only as a policeman that protects man's rights; it uses physical force *only* in retaliation and *only* against those who initiate its use, such as criminals or foreign invaders. In a system of full capitalism, there should be (but, historically, has not yet been) a complete separation of state and economics, in the same way and for the same reasons as the separation of state and church.

Capitalism was the system originated in the United States. Its success, its progress, its achievements are unprecedented in human history. America's political philosophy was based on man's right to his own life, to his own liberty, to the pursuit of his own happiness, which means: on man's right to exist for his own sake. That was America's *implicit* moral code, but it had not been formulated explicitly. This was the flaw in her intellectual armor, which is now destroying her. America and capitalism are perishing for lack of a moral base.

The destroyer is the morality of altruism.

Altruism holds that man has no right to exist for his own sake, that service to others is the only moral justification of his existence, and that self-sacrifice is his highest moral duty. The political expression of altruism is collectivism or *statism,* which holds that man's life and work belong to the state— to society, to the group, the gang, the race, the nation—and that the state may dispose of him in any way it pleases for the sake of whatever it deems to be its own tribal, collective good.

"From her start, America was torn by the clash of her political system with the altruist morality. Capitalism and altruism are incompatible; they cannot co-exist in the same man or in the same society. Today, the conflict has reached its ultimate climax; the choice is clear-cut: either a new morality of rational self-interest, with its consequences of freedom, justice, progress and man's happiness on earth—or the primordial morality of altruism, with its consequences of slavery, brute force, stagnant terror and sacrificial furnaces." *(For the New Intellectual)*

You may observe the practical results of altruism and statism all around us in today's world—such as the slave-labor camps of Soviet Russia, where twenty-one million political prisoners work on the construction of government projects and die of *planned* malnutrition, human life being cheaper than food—or the gas chambers and mass slaughter of Nazi Germany—or the terror and starvation of Red China—or the hysteria of Cuba where the government offers men for sale —or the wall of East Berlin where human beings leap from roofs or crawl through sewers in order to escape, while guards shoot at fleeing *children*.

Observe these atrocities, then ask yourself whether any of it would be possible if men had not accepted the idea that man is a sacrificial animal to be immolated for the sake of the "public good." Read the speeches of those countries' political leaders and ask yourself what arguments would be left to them if the word "sacrifice" were regarded not as a moral ideal, but as the anti-human evil which it is.

And *then*, listen to the speeches of our present Administration—and ask yourself the same question.

[*If you would like the Ayn Rand column to appear in your city, write the editors of your local newspapers.*]

The New Enemies of "The Untouchables"*

By AYN RAND

[*This is the fourth column, which appeared in the* Los Angeles Times, *on July 8, 1962.*]

When a culture is dominated by an irrational philosophy, a major symptom of its decadence is the inversion of all values. This can always be seen clearly in the field of art, the best barometer of a culture. In today's flood of criticism and abuse, unleashed against the television industry, it is the best program that has been singled out for the most persistent denunciations. That program is "The Untouchables."

The moral meaning and psychological motives of those denunciations are of much deeper significance than the superficiality of the attackers might indicate.

The attacks are spearheaded by the statists inside and outside the F.C.C., who propose to place television and radio under total government control, to establish censorship-by-license-revoking, and to dictate the content of programs by bureaucratic edict, which means: by force. Simultaneously and as a justification for it, they clamor that the television industry is corrupting the public taste by presenting too many shows that feature force and violence.

Crime stories and Westerns are the main target of the statists' attack, in alliance with sundry busybodies of all political denominations, who are always to be found in any pro-censorship movement of the left or the right.

The truth of the matter is the exact opposite of their allegations: the appeal of crime stories and Westerns does not lie in the element of violence, but in the element of moral conflict and moral purpose.

Crime stories and Westerns are the last remnant of romanticism on our airwaves. No matter how primitive their terms, they deal with the most realistic issue of man's life: the battle of good and evil. They present man as a purposeful being who is able to choose his goals, to fight for his values, to resist disaster, to struggle and to win. The best of such stories offer the invaluable elements of a purposeful plot structure, of ingenuity and suspense, of the daring, the unusual, the exciting.

Compare this with what passes for serious drama on today's television screens: slack-faced, loose-lipped characters with unseeing eyes and unfocused minds, who utter self-consciously ungrammatical lines and jerk hysterically through a sprawling mess of pointless happenings, purporting to show man's helplessness or loneliness or essential depravity—all of it adding up to a scream of "I couldn't help it!"—or to a maudlin, mawkish whine of sympathy for some subhuman object who doesn't know why he murders people, he just does—with, occasionally, some stale corn to the effect that life is a rat race.

There are "sophisticated" crime stories, produced by the same modern mentality, which present both the criminals and the detectives as cynical, larcenous, indistinguishable barroom buddies, with brutal fist fights as a substitute for plot—and there are those queer mongrels: the "psychological" Westerns that present a hostility-sublimating sheriff and a cattle rustler with an Oedipus complex. These may indeed appeal to the lowest element of the public's taste. But they come up and perish, unnoticed, every season. It is not by means of fist fights, chases or gun duels that the successful, popular shows hold audiences glued to TV sets year after year.

"The Untouchables" is one of the most successful programs and fully deserves its success. It is a profoundly moral show. In writing, acting and direction, it is a masterpiece of stylized characterization. It captures the essence of the gangster psychology: the irrationality, the hysteria, the chronic terror, the panic. These gangsters are neither glamorized strongmen nor innocent "victims of society"; they are scared rats. They are presented as loathsome, but not frightening, because not powerful; they are presented as contemptible. No child or adult could ever feel inspired to emulate a Frank Nitti.

* Copyright 1962 by Times-Mirror Co., Los Angeles.

But Robert Stack's superlative portrayal of Eliot Ness is the most inspiring image on today's screen, the only image of a real hero.

By the austere, unsmiling grimness of his manner, the total self-confidence even in moments of temporary defeat, so total that it can afford to be unstressed, the controlled intensity, the quietly absolute dedication to the moral justice of his task, Stack conveys the integrity of a truly untouchable man—a man whom evil cannot tempt, because it has nothing to offer him. By the faint, occasional hints of a bitterly patient weariness, he projects that fighting evil is not a lark or a glamorous adventure, but a grim job and a deadly battle. And the constantly intense perceptiveness of his attitude—the attitude of a man fully in control and a mind fully in focus—projects the nature of that battle: man's intellect versus brute force.

Compare "The Untouchables" to the militant mindlessness of today's "serious" dramas and ask yourself which is more likely to give men hope, courage and an hour's refueling for the battle against the sordid ugliness of today's headlines. And, if moral influence on children is your concern, ask yourself which will help to shape a child's moral character: the conviction that justice, values, struggles and victories are possible, and that there are heroes he can live up to—or the conviction that nothing is possible and anything is permissible, that the good he desperately longs for is an illusion, but the evil that tempts him will bring him loving sympathy, that nobody can help what he does and there is no way out of the incomprehensible terror with which life seems to confront him. Which will shape his soul? Which made you, perhaps, renounce yours?

In view of the virtues of "The Untouchables," what is it that the "touchables" resent and denounce? Precisely its virtues. Not its criminals, but the triumph over criminals. Not the violence, but the moral absolutism.

It is part of today's profound revolt against man, against the intellect, against human efficacy and, above all, against moral values.

OBJECTIVIST CALENDAR

- Due to the unprecedented volume of orders for reprints of the June Special Supplement: *Doctors and the Police State,* by Leonard Peikoff, we are able to offer a special reprint rate: single copy, 25¢; 10-99 copies, 15¢ each plus postage (for first-class delivery add 1¢ per copy, for third-class delivery add ½¢ per copy); 100-999 copies, 10¢ each plus postage; 1,000 or more, 7¢ each plus postage; 10,000 and over, 4¢ each plus postage.
- This summer, NATHANIEL BRANDEN INSTITUTE offers a ten lecture course on "Principles of Efficient Thinking," given by Barbara Branden in Philadelphia (began July 2) and New York City (began July 10).
- On August 25, the Bobbs-Merrill Co. will publish a new soft-cover, quality edition of *The Fountainhead,* priced at $2.95, as part of their new line of Charter Books. This will make *The Fountainhead* available simultaneously in hardcover, quality paperback and regular paperback editions.

Other activities: In response to *The Executive's Coloring Book* and *The JFK Coloring Book,* two students of NATHANIEL BRANDEN INSTITUTE, Francesca Knight and Lois Roberts, have prepared *The Bureaucrat's Coloring Book.* Published by Athene Press, it is available from The Bookmailer, 232 East 35th St., New York 16, N. Y. Price: $2.00.

Published monthly at 165 East 35th Street, New York 16, N. Y.
Subscription rate: in United States, its possessions, Canada and Mexico, $5 for one year; other countries, $6. Trial subscriptions: 4 months $2. 6 months $3.
Additional copies of this Newsletter: single copy 50¢ (coins, not stamps); 10 — 99 copies, 25¢ each plus postage (for first-class delivery add 1¢ per copy, for third-class delivery add ½¢ per copy); 100 or more copies, 15¢ each plus postage (same as above).
For change of address send old address and new address with zone number if any. Allow us two weeks to process new subscriptions and change of address.

Ayn Rand and Nathaniel Branden, Editors and Publishers
Barbara Branden, Managing Editor
Elayne Kalberman, Circulation Manager

PRINTED BY STANDARD GRAPHICS, NEW YORK CITY

THE OBJECTIVIST NEWSLETTER

Edited and Published by AYN RAND and NATHANIEL BRANDEN

VOL. 1 NO. 9   SEPTEMBER, 1962

CHECK YOUR PREMISES
By AYN RAND
The Pull Peddlers

America's foreign policy is so grotesquely irrational that most people believe there must be some sensible purpose behind it. The extent of the irrationality acts as its own protection: like the technique of the "Big Lie," it makes people assume that so blatant an evil could not possibly be as evil as it appears to them and, therefore, that *somebody* must understand its meaning, even though they themselves do not.

The sickening generalities and contradictions cited in justification of the foreign aid program fall roughly into two categories which are offered to us simultaneously: the "idealistic" and the "practical," or mush and fear.

The "idealistic" arguments consist of appeals to altruism and swim out of focus in a fog of floating abstractions about our duty to support the "underdeveloped" nations of the entire globe, who are starving and will perish without our selfless help.

The "practical" arguments consist of appeals to fear and emit a different sort of fog, to the effect that our own selfish interest requires that we go bankrupt buying the favor of the "underdeveloped" nations, who, otherwise, will become a dangerous threat to us.

It is useless to point out to the advocates of our foreign policy that it's either-or: either the "underdeveloped" nations are so weak that they are doomed without our help, in which case they cannot become a threat to us—or they are so strong that with some other assistance they can develop to the point of endangering us, in which case we should not drain our economic power to help the growth of potential enemies who are that powerful.

It is useless to discuss the contradiction between these two assertions, because neither of them is true. Their proponents are impervious to facts, to logic and to the mounting evidence that after two decades of global altruism, our foreign policy is achieving the exact opposite of its alleged goals: it is wrecking our economy—it is reducing us internationally to the position of an impotent failure who has nothing but a series of compromises, retreats, defeats and betrayals on his record—and, instead of bringing progress to the world, it is bringing the bloody chaos of tribal warfare and delivering one helpless nation after another into the power of communism.

When a society insists on pursuing a suicidal course, one may be sure that the alleged reasons and proclaimed slogans are mere rationalizations. The question is only: what is it that these rationalizations are hiding?

Observe that there is no consistent pattern in the erratic chaos of our foreign aid. And although in the long run it leads to the benefit of Soviet Russia, Russia is not its direct, immediate beneficiary. There is no consistent winner, only a consistent loser: the United States.

In the face of such a spectacle, some people give up the attempt to understand; others imagine that some omnipotent conspiracy is destroying America, that the rationalizations are hiding some malevolent, fantastically powerful giant.

The truth is worse than that: the truth is that the rationalizations are hiding nothing—that there is nothing at the bottom of the fog but a nest of scurrying cockroaches.

I submit in evidence an article in the editorial section of *The New York Times*, of July 15, 1962, entitled: "Role of Foreign Lobbies."

"A 'non-diplomatic corps' of foreign agents," states the article, "has bloomed in recent years [in Washington] . . .

"Lobbying in Congress to obtain—or prevent—the passage of legislation of interest to their foreign clients, seeking to pressure the Administration into adopting certain political or economic policies, or attempting to mold public opinion through a myriad of methods and techniques, this legion of special agents has become an elusive shadow for operating in Washington and the width and the length of the land."

"Lobbying" is the activity of attempting to influence legislation by privately influencing the legislators. It is the result and creation of a "mixed economy"—of government by pressure groups. Its methods range from mere social courtesies and cocktail-party or luncheon "friendships" to favors, threats, bribes, blackmail.

All lobbyists, whether serving foreign or domestic interests, are required—by laws passed in the last three decades—to register with the government. The registrations have been growing at such a rate—with the foreign lobbyists outnumbering the domestic ones—that legislators are beginning to be alarmed. The Senate Foreign Relations Committee has announced that it is preparing an investigation of these foreign agents' activities.

The *N. Y. Times* article describes foreign lobbying as follows: "The theory behind this whole enterprise is that for a fee or a retainer and often for hundreds of thousands of dollars in advertising, publicity and expense money, a foreign Government or a foreign economic or political interest *can purchase a favorable legislation in the United States Congress, a friendly policy of the Administration* or a positive image in the eyes of the American public opinion, leading in turn to *profitable political or economic advantage.*" (Italics mine.)

Who are these lobbyists? Men with political pull—with "access" to influential Washington figures—American men hired by foreign interests. The article mentions that most of these men are "Washington lawyers" or "New York public relations firms."

Russia is one of these foreign interests and is served by registered lobbyists in Washington; but she is merely cashing in on the situation, like the others. The success of her conspiracy in this country is the result, not the cause, of our self-destruction; she is winning by default. The cause is much deeper than that.

The issue of lobbies has attracted attention recently through the struggle of foreign lobbyists to obtain sugar quotas from the American government. "Their efforts," states the article, "were centered on Representative Harold D. Cooley, Democrat of North Carolina, chairman of the House Committee on Agriculture, who at least until this year held almost the complete power in the distribution of quotas. It has never been too clear what criteria Mr. Cooley used in allocating these quotas, and, by the same token, it is impossible to determine what was the actual effect of the lobbyists' entreaties on him.

"But in offering their services to foreign governments or sugar growers' associations, these representatives were, in effect, offering for sale their real or alleged friendship with Mr. Cooley."

This is the core and essence of the issue of lobbying—and of our foreign aid—and of a "mixed economy."

(continued on page 38)

Copyright © 1962 by The Objectivist Newsletter, Inc.

BOOKS

Planning for Freedom* by Ludwig von Mises
Reviewed by NATHANIEL BRANDEN

The economic essays of Ludwig von Mises are always a pleasure to read. They combine elegant simplicity with patient and devastating logical rigor. A collection of his essays and addresses, in a new, enlarged edition, has recently been published by the Libertarian Press. It is entitled *Planning for Freedom*. We recommend it enthusiastically to our readers.

The essays cover a wide range of subjects: Nazism or fascism as a variety of socialism; minimum wage rates as a cause of mass unemployment; Keynesianism as a resurrection of the theories of nineteenth-century "money cranks"; the fallacy of the belief that labor unions can raise the general standard of living; the nature of profit and loss; the dominance of collectivist teachings in our universities—to mention only a few.

In one of the most interesting essays of the book, "Profit and Loss," Mises writes:

"It is not the capital employed that creates profits and losses. Capital does not 'beget profit' as Marx thought. The capital goods as such are dead things that in themselves do not accomplish anything. If they are utilized according to a good idea, profit results. If they are utilized according to a mistaken idea, no profit, or losses, result. It is the entrepreneurial decision that creates either profit or loss. It is mental acts, the mind of the entrepreneur, from which profits ultimately originate. Profit is a product of the mind, of success in anticipating the future state of the market. It is a spiritual and intellectual phenomenon."

Elsewhere in the same essay, Mises writes:

"The average wage earner thinks that nothing else is needed to keep the social apparatus of production running and to improve and to increase output than the comparatively simple routine work assigned to him. He does not realize that the mere toil and trouble of the routinist is not sufficient. Sedulousness and skill are spent in vain if they are not directed . . . by the entrepreneur's foresight and are not aided by the capital accumulated by capitalists. The American worker is badly mistaken when he believes that his high standard of living is due to his own excellence. He is neither more industrious nor more skillful than the workers of Western Europe. He owes his superior income to the fact that his country clung to 'rugged individualism' much longer than Europe. It was his luck that the United States turned to an anti-capitalistic policy as much as forty or fifty years later than Germany. His wages are higher than those of the workers of the rest of the world because the capital equipment per head of the employee is highest in America and because the American entrepreneur was not so much restricted by crippling regimentation as his colleagues in other areas. The comparatively greater prosperity of the United States is an outcome of the fact that the New Deal did not come in 1900 or 1910, but only in 1933."

Advocates of government intervention in the economy take great pains to evade acknowledging the dictatorial nature of their proposals. But Mises never permits this issue to be forgotten. In an essay entitled "Laissez Faire or Dictatorship," he writes:

"Professor Harold Laski, the former chairman of the British Labor Party, determined the objective of planned direction of investment as 'the use of the investor's savings will be in housing rather than in cinemas.' It does not matter whether or not one agrees with the professor's personal view that better houses are more important than moving pictures. The fact is that consumers, by spending part of their money for admission to the movies, have made another choice. If the masses of Great Britain, the same people whose votes swept the Labor Party into power, were to stop patronizing the moving pictures and to spend more for comfortable homes and apartments, profit-seeking business would be forced to invest more in building homes and apartment houses, and less in the production of swanky pictures. What Professor Laski aimed at is to defy the wishes of the consumers and to substitute his own will for theirs. He wanted to do away with the democracy of the market and to establish the absolute rule of a production czar. He might pretend that he is right from a 'higher' point of view, and that as a superman he is called upon to impose his own set of values on the masses of inferior men. But then he should have been frank enough to say so plainly."

In "Economic Teaching at the Universities," originally published in 1952, Mises recounts an incident that is strikingly timely today:

"A few years ago a House of Representatives Subcommittee on Publicity and Propaganda in the Executive Departments, under the chairmanship of Representative Forest A. Harness, investigated Federal propaganda operations. On one occasion the Committee had as a witness a government-employed doctor. When asked if his public speeches throughout the country presented both sides of the discussion touching compulsory national health insurance, this witness answered: 'I don't know what you mean by both sides.'"

Planning for Freedom is chiefly concerned with exposing the disastrous effects of government intervention in economics. As an introduction to the issues involved in capitalism versus the "mixed economy," it is an ideal companion piece to Mises' *Planned Chaos* and Henry Hazlitt's *Economics in One Lesson*.

The Pull Peddlers (from page 37)

The trouble is not that "it has never been too clear what criteria Mr. Cooley used in allocating these quotas"—but that it has never been and never can be too clear what criteria he was expected to use by the legislation that granted him these powers. No criteria can ever be defined in this context; such is the nature of non-objective law and of all economic legislation.

So long as a concept such as "the public interest" (or the "social" or "national" or "international" interest) is regarded as a valid principle to guide legislation—lobbies and pressure groups will necessarily continue to exist. Since there is no such entity as *"the public,"* since the public is merely a number of individuals, the idea that "the public interest" supersedes private interests and rights, can have but one meaning: that the interests and rights of some individuals take precedence over the interests and rights of others.

If so, then all men and all private groups have to fight to the death for the privilege of being regarded as "the public." The government's policy has to swing like an erratic pendulum from group to group, hitting some and favoring others, at the whim of any given moment—and so grotesque a profession as lobbying (selling "influence") becomes a full-time job. If parasitism, favoritism, corruption and greed for the unearned did not exist, a "mixed economy" would bring them into existence.

Since there is no rational justification for the sacrifice of some men to others, there is no objective criterion by which such a sacrifice can be guided in practice. All "public interest" legislation (and any distribution of money taken by force from some men for the unearned benefit of others) comes down ultimately to the grant of an undefined, undefinable, non-objective, arbitrary power to some government officials.

The worst aspect of it is not that such a power can be used dishonestly, but that *it cannot be used honestly*. The wisest man in the world, with the purest integrity, cannot find a criterion for the just, equitable, rational application of an unjust, inequitable, irrational principle. The best that an honest official can do is to accept no material bribe for his arbitrary decision; but this does not make his decision and its consequences more just or less calamitous.

A man of clear-cut convictions is impervious to anyone's influence. But when clear-cut convictions are impossible, per-

(continued on page 40)

---

* Published by Libertarian Press, $2.00. Available from NBL BOOK SERVICE, INC., 165 East 35th St., New York 16, N.Y. (N.Y.C. residents add 3% sales tax; outside the U.S., add 15¢.)

INTELLECTUAL AMMUNITION DEPARTMENT

[*Subscribers are invited to send in the questions that they find themselves unable to answer in philosophical or political discussions. As many questions as space permits will be answered. No questions will be answered by mail.*]

- **Isn't everyone selfish?**

Some variety of this question is often raised as an objection to those who advocate an ethics of rational self-interest. For example, it is sometimes claimed: "Everyone does what he really *wants* to do—otherwise, he wouldn't do it." Or: "No one ever *really* sacrifices himself. Since every purposeful action is motivated by some value or goal that the actor desires, one always acts *selfishly*, whether one knows it or not."

To untangle the intellectual confusion involved in this viewpoint, let us consider what facts of reality *give rise* to such an issue as selfishness versus self-sacrifice, or egoism versus altruism, and what the concept of "selfishness" means and entails.

The issue of selfishness versus self-sacrifice arises in an *ethical* context. Ethics is a code of values to guide man's choices and actions—the choices and actions that determine the purpose and course of his life. In choosing his actions and goals, man faces constant alternatives. In order to choose, he requires a standard of value—a purpose which his actions are to serve or at which they are to aim. " 'Value' presupposes an answer to the question: of value to whom and for what?" What is to be the goal or purpose of a man's actions? Who is to be the intended *beneficiary* of his actions? Is he to hold, as his primary moral purpose, the achievement of *his own* life and happiness—or should his primary moral purpose be to serve the wishes and needs of *others*?

The clash between egoism and altruism lies in their conflicting answers to these questions. Egoism holds that man is an end in himself; altruism holds that man is a means to the ends of others. Egoism holds that, morally, the beneficiary of an action should be the person who acts; altruism holds that, morally, the beneficiary of an action should be someone *other* than the person who acts.

To be selfish is to be motivated by concern for one's self-interest. This requires that one consider what constitutes one's self-interest and how to achieve it—what values and goals to pursue, what principles and policies to adopt. If a man were not concerned with this question, he could not be said objectively to be concerned with or to desire his self-interest; one cannot be concerned with or desire that of which one has no knowledge.

Selfishness entails: (a) a hierarchy of values set by the standard of one's self-interest, and (b) the refusal to sacrifice a higher value to a lower one or to a non-value.

A genuinely selfish man knows that only reason can determine what is, in fact, to his self-interest, that to pursue contradictions or attempt to act in defiance of the facts of reality is self-destructive—and self-destruction is not to his self-interest. "To think, is to man's self-interest; to suspend his consciousness, is not. To choose his goals in the full context of his knowledge, his values and his life, is to man's self-interest; to act on the impulse of the moment, without regard for his long-range context, is not. To exist as a productive being, is to man's self-interest; to attempt to exist as a parasite, is not. To seek the life proper to his nature, is to man's self-interest; to seek to live as an animal, is not." (*Who is Ayn Rand?*)

Because a genuinely selfish man chooses his goals by the guidance of reason—and because the interests of rational men do not clash—other men may often benefit from his actions. But the benefit of other men is not his primary purpose or goal; his *own* benefit is his primary purpose and the conscious goal directing his actions.

To make this principle fully clear, let us consider an extreme example of an action which, in fact, is selfish, but which conventionally might be called self-sacrificial: a man's willingness to die to save the life of the woman he loves. In what way would such a man be the beneficiary of his action?

The answer is given in *Atlas Shrugged*—in the scene when Galt, knowing he is about to be arrested, tells Dagny: "If they get the slightest suspicion of what we are to each other, they will have you on a torture rack—I mean, physical torture—before my eyes, in less than a week. I am not going to wait for that. At the first mention of a threat to you, I will kill myself and stop them right there. . . . I don't have to tell you that if I do it, it won't be an act of self-sacrifice. I do not care to live on their terms, I do not care to obey them and I do not care to see you enduring a drawn-out murder. There will be no values for me to seek after that—and I do not care to exist without values." If a man loves a woman so much that he does not wish to survive her death, if life can have nothing more to offer him at that price, then his dying to save her is not a sacrifice.

The same principle applies to a man, caught in a dictatorship, who willingly risks death to achieve freedom. To call his act a "self-sacrifice," one would have to assume that he *preferred* to live as a slave. The selfishness of a man who is willing to die, if necessary, fighting for his freedom, lies in the fact that he is unwilling to go on living in a world where he is no longer able to act on his own judgment—that is, a world where *human* conditions of existence are no longer possible to him.

The selfishness or unselfishness of an action is to be determined objectively: it is not determined by the *feelings* of the person who acts. Just as feelings are not a tool of cognition, *so they are not a criterion in ethics*.

Obviously, in order to act, one has to be moved by *some* personal motive; one has to "want," in *some* sense, to perform the action. The issue of an action's selfishness or unselfishness depends, not on whether or not one wants to perform it, but on *why* one wants to perform it. By what standard was the action chosen? To achieve what goal?

If a man proclaimed that he *felt* he would best benefit others by robbing and murdering them, men would not be willing to grant that his actions were altruistic. By the same logic and for the same reasons, if a man pursues a course of blind self-destruction, his *feeling* that he has something to gain by it does not establish his actions as selfish.

If, motivated solely by a sense of charity, compassion, duty or altruism, a person renounces a value, desire or goal in favor of the pleasure, wishes or needs of another person whom he values less than the thing he renounced—*that* is an act of self-sacrifice. The fact that a person may feel that he "wants" to do it, does not make his action selfish or establish objectively that he is its beneficiary.

Suppose, for example, that a son chooses the career he wants by rational standards, but then renounces it in order to please his mother who prefers that he pursue a different career, one that will have more prestige in the eyes of the neighbors. The boy accedes to his mother's wish because he has accepted that such is his moral duty: he believes that his duty as a son consists of placing his mother's happiness above his own, even if he knows that his mother's demand is irrational and even if he knows that he is sentencing himself to a life of misery and frustration. It is absurd for the advocates of the "everyone is selfish" doctrine to assert that since the boy is motivated by the desire to be "virtuous" or to avoid guilt, no self-sacrifice is involved and his action is really selfish. What is evaded is the question of *why* the boy feels and desires as he does. Emotions and desires are not causeless, irreducible primaries: they are the product of the premises one has accepted. The boy "wants" to renounce his career only because he has accepted the ethics of altruism; he believes that it is immoral to act for his self-interest. *That* is the principle directing his actions.

Advocates of the "everyone is selfish" doctrine do not deny that, under the pressure of the altruist ethics, men can knowingly act against their own long-range happiness. They merely assert that in some higher, undefinable sense such men are

(continued on page 40)

The Pull Peddlers (from page 38)

sonal influences take over. When a man's mind is trapped in the foggy labyrinth of the non-objective, that has no exits and no solutions, he will welcome any quasi-persuasive, semi-plausible argument. Lacking certainty, he will follow anyone's facsimile thereof. He is the natural prey of social "manipulators," of propaganda-salesmen, of lobbyists.

When any argument is as inconclusive as any other, the subjective, emotional or "human" element becomes decisive. A harried legislator may conclude, consciously or subconsciously, that the friendly man who smiled at him at the cocktail party last week was a good person who would not deceive him and whose opinion can be trusted safely. It is by considerations such as these that officials may dispose of your money, your effort and your future.

Although cases of actual corruption do undoubtedly exist among legislators and government officials, they are not a major motivating factor in today's situation. It is significant that in such cases as have been publicly exposed, the bribes were almost pathetically small. Men who held the power to dispose of millions of dollars, sold their favors for a thousand-dollar rug or a fur coat or a refrigerator.

The truth, most likely, is that they did not regard it as bribery or as a betrayal of their public trust; they did not think that their particular decision could matter one way or another, in the kind of causeless choices they had to make, in the absence of any criteria, in the midst of the general orgy of tossing away an apparently ownerless wealth. Men who would not sell out their country for a million dollars, are selling it out for somebody's smile and a vacation trip to Florida. "It is of such pennies and smiles that the destruction of your country is made."

The general public is helplessly bewildered. The "intellectuals" do not care to look at our foreign policy too closely. They feel guilt; they sense that their own worn-out ideologies, which they dare not challenge, are the cause of the consequences which they dare not face. The more they evade, the greater their eagerness to grasp at any fashionable straw or rationalization and to uphold it with glassy-eyed aggressiveness. The threadbare cloak of altruism serves to cover it up and to sanction the evasions by a fading aura of moral righteousness. The exhausted cynicism of a bankrupt culture, of a society without values, principles, convictions or intellectual standards, does the rest: it leaves a vacuum, for anyone to take over and use.

The motive power behind the suicidal bleeding of the greatest country in the world is not an altruistic fervor or a collectivist crusade any longer, but the manipulations of little lawyers and public relations men pulling the mental strings of lifeless automatons.

These—the lobbyists in the pay of foreign interests, the men who could not hope to get, in any other circumstances, the money they are getting now—are the real and only profiteers on the global sacrifice, as their ilk has always been at the close of every altruistic movement in history. It is not the "underdeveloped" nations nor the "underprivileged" masses nor the starving children of jungle villages who benefit from America's self-immolation—it is only the men who are too small to start such movements and small enough to cash in at the end.

It is not any "lofty ideal" that the altruism-collectivism doctrine accomplishes or can ever accomplish. Its end-of-trail is as follows: "A local railroad had gone bankrupt in North Dakota, abandoning the region to the fate of a blighted area, the local banker had committed suicide, first killing his wife and children—a freight train had been taken off the schedule in Tennessee, leaving a local factory without transportation at a day's notice, the factory owner's son had quit college and was now in jail, awaiting execution for a murder committed with a gang of raiders—a way station had been closed in Kansas, and the station agent, who had wanted to be a scientist, had given up his studies and become a dishwasher—that he, James Taggart, might sit in a private barroom and pay for the alcohol pouring down Orren Boyle's throat, for the waiter who sponged Boyle's garments when he spilled his drink over his chest, for the carpet burned by the cigarettes of an ex-pimp from Chile who did not want to take the trouble of reaching for an ashtray across a distance of three feet." (*Atlas Shrugged*)

Intellectual Ammunition Department (from page 39)

still acting "selfishly." A definition of "selfishness" that includes or permits the possibility of knowingly acting against one's long-range happiness, is a contradiction in terms.

It is only the legacy of mysticism that permits men to imagine that they are still speaking meaningfully when they declare that one can seek one's happiness in the renunciation of one's happiness.

The basic fallacy in the "everyone is selfish" argument consists of an extraordinarily crude equivocation. It is a psychological truism—a tautology—that all purposeful behavior is motivated. But to equate *"motivated* behavior" with *"selfish* behavior" is to blank out the distinction between an elementary fact of human psychology and the phenomenon of *ethical choice*. It is to evade the central *problem* of ethics, namely: by *what* is man to be motivated?

A genuine selfishness—that is: a genuine concern with discovering what is to one's self-interest, an acceptance of the responsibility of achieving it, a refusal ever to betray it by acting on the blind whim, mood, impulse or feeling of the moment, an uncompromising loyalty to one's judgment, convictions and values—represents a profound moral achievement. Those who assert that "everyone is selfish" commonly intend their statement as an expression of cynicism and contempt. But the truth is that their statement pays mankind a compliment it does not deserve.

(The doctrine that man is selfish by nature is called "psychological egoism." For an interesting critique of this doctrine, treating aspects somewhat different from those discussed above, see John Hospers, *Human Conduct: an Introduction to the Problems of Ethics*, Harcourt, Brace & World, New York, 1961, pp. 141-155.)
—**NATHANIEL BRANDEN**

OBJECTIVIST CALENDAR

- Early in September, Bantam Books will publish, in paperback, a new translation of Victor Hugo's great novel *Ninety-Three*, with an introduction by Ayn Rand. The introduction deals with the issue of Romanticism in literature, and offers a philosophical evaluation of Hugo's novels.
- NATHANIEL BRANDEN INSTITUTE's fall course of lectures on "Basic Principles of Objectivism" is scheduled to begin in New York City on Tuesday, October 9, and in Philadelphia on Monday, October 15.

NBI's Tape Transcription Division has now scheduled the following starting dates for "Basic Principles of Objectivism" in other cities: Kansas City, Kansas, October 2; San Francisco, October 2; San Diego, October 4; Los Angeles, October 5; Boston, October 15; Chicago, November 2; Toronto, November 5; Washington, November 18. Mr. Branden will deliver the opening night's lecture in person in San Francisco, San Diego, Los Angeles, Chicago, Toronto and Washington. Additional starting dates will be listed here next month.

Published monthly at 165 East 35th Street, New York 16, N. Y.
Subscription rate: in United States, its possessions, Canada and Mexico, $5 for one year; other countries, $6. Trial subscriptions: 4 months $2. 6 months $3.
Additional copies of this Newsletter: single copy 50¢ (coins, not stamps); 10 — 99 copies, 25¢ each plus postage (for first-class delivery add 1¢ per copy, for third-class delivery add 1/2¢ per copy); 100 or more copies, 15¢ each plus postage (same as above).
For change of address send old address and new address with zone number if any. Allow us two weeks to process new subscriptions and change of address.

Ayn Rand and Nathaniel Branden, Editors and Publishers
Barbara Branden, Managing Editor
Elayne Kalberman, Circulation Manager
PRINTED BY STANDARD GRAPHICS, NEW YORK CITY

THE OBJECTIVIST NEWSLETTER

Edited and Published by AYN RAND and NATHANIEL BRANDEN

VOL. 1 NO. 10   OCTOBER, 1962

CHECK YOUR PREMISES
By AYN RAND

"To Young Scientists"

In March of this year, I gave a lecture on "The Objectivist Ethics" at the Massachusetts Institute of Technology, with a special introduction which I wrote for the students who are to be America's future scientists. Now, at the beginning of a new school year, I want to repeat that message, addressing it to all those who are starting out on their careers in science.

We are living in an age when every social group is struggling frantically to destroy itself—and doing it faster than any of its rivals or enemies could hope for—when every man is his own most dangerous enemy, and the whole of mankind is rolling, at supersonic speed, back to the Dark Ages, with a nuclear bomb in one hand and a rabbit's foot in the other.

The most terrible paradox of our age is the fact that the destruction of man's mind, of reason, of logic, of knowledge, of civilization, is being accomplished in the name and with the sanction of *science*.

It took centuries and volumes of writing to bring our culture to its present state of bankruptcy—and volumes would have to be written to expose, counteract and avert the disaster of a total intellectual collapse. But of all the deadly theories by means of which you are now being destroyed, I would like to warn you about one of the deadliest and most crucial: the alleged dichotomy of science and ethics.

You have heard that theory so often and from so many authorities that most of you now take it for granted, as an axiom, as the one absolute taught to you by those who proclaim that there are no absolutes. It is the doctrine that man's science and ethics—or his knowledge and values, or his body and soul—are two separate, antagonistic aspects of his existence, and that man is caught between them, as a precarious, permanent traitor to their conflicting demands.

Science, they tell you, is the province of reason—but ethics, they say, is the province of a higher power, which man's impotent, fallible intellect must not be so presumptuous as to challenge. What power? Why, *feelings*.

Before you accept that doctrine, identify concretely and specifically what it means. (Remember that ethics is a code of values to guide man's choices and actions, the choices and actions that determine the purpose and course of his life.) It means that *you*, as scientists, are competent to discover new knowledge—but not competent to judge for what purpose that knowledge is to be used. *Your* judgment is to be disqualified, if, when and *because* it is rational—while human purposes are to be determined by the representatives of non-reason. *You* are to create the means—but *they* are to choose the ends. *You* are to work and think and strain all the power, energy and ingenuity of your mind to its utmost logical best, and produce great achievements—but those "superior" others will dispose of your achievements, by the grace and guidance of their *feelings*. Your *mind* is to be the tool and servant of their *whims*. You are to create the H-bomb—but a blustering Russian anthropoid will decide when he *feels* like dropping it and on whom. Yours is not to reason why—yours is just to do and provide the ammunition for others to die.

From Plato's *Republic* onward, all statist-collectivists have looked longingly up at an ant hill as at a social ideal to be reached. An ant hill is a society of interdependent insects, where each particular kind or class is physiologically able to perform only one specific function: some are milch cows, some are toilers, a few are rulers. Collectivist planners have dreamed for a long time of creating an ideal society by means of eugenics—by breeding men into various castes physiologically able to perform only one specific function. *Your* place, in such a society, would be that of toiling milch-brains, of human computers who would produce anything on demand and would be biologically incapable of questioning the orders of the anthropoid who'd throw them their food rations.

Does your self-esteem accept such a prospect?

No, I am not saying that that dream will ever be achieved physiologically. But I am saying that it has already been achieved politically and intellectually: politically, among your so-called colleagues in Soviet Russia—intellectually, in the mind of any man who accepts the science-ethics dichotomy.

I believe that many of you were attracted to the field of science precisely by reason of that dichotomy: in order to escape from the hysterical mystic-subjectivist-emotionalist shambles to which philosophers have reduced the field of ethics—and in order to find a clean, intelligible, rational, *objective* realm of activity.

You have not found it—not because it doesn't exist, but because it cannot be found without the help of a clean, intelligible, rational, *objective* philosophy, part of which is ethics. It cannot be found until you realize that man cannot exist as half-scientist, half-brute—that *all* the aspects of his existence are, can be and *should* be subject to the study and the judgment of his intellect—and that of all human disciplines, it is *ethics*, the discipline which sets his goals, that should be elevated into a science.

No man and no class of men can live without a code of ethics. But if there are degrees of urgency, I would say that it is *you*, the scientists, who need it most urgently. The nature of your power and of your *responsibility* is too obvious to need restatement. You can read it in every newspaper headline. It is obvious why you should know—before you start out—to what purpose and service you choose to devote the power of your mind.

If you do not care to know—well, I would like to say that there is a character in *Atlas Shrugged* who was dedicated to *you* as a warning, with the sincere hope that it would not be necessary. His name is Dr. Robert Stadler.

Many things have happened since March of this year to demonstrate the ultimate consequences of the science-ethics dichotomy.

If a professional soldier were to accept a job with Murder, Inc. and claim that he is merely practicing his trade, that it is not his responsibility to know who is using his services or for what purpose—he would be greeted by a storm of indignation and regarded as a moral psychopath. Yet at his bloodiest worst, he could not perpetrate a fraction of the horrors achieved by any haughty ascetic of science who merely places a slip of paper with some mathematical computations into the hands of Khrushchev or Mao Tse-tung or any of their imitators in America, and, having read no newspapers since 1914, declares himself to be "above the battle."

It is thus that the world reached the nightmare spectacle which surpasses any horror story of science fiction: two Soviet capsules circling in "outer space," as the alleged triumph of an advanced science—while here on earth, a young boy lies bleeding to death and screaming for help, at the foot of the wall in East Berlin, shot for attempting to escape and left there by the prehistorical monsters from 20-thousand centuries deep: the Soviet rulers.

(continued on page 46)

BOOKS

*Ninety-Three** by Victor Hugo

Reviewed by **AYN RAND**

[*Reprinted from the* Los Angeles Times *of September 16.*]

"Then, without haste, slowly, proudly, he stepped over the window sill, and, not turning, standing straight, his back against the rungs of the ladder, with the flames behind him and the abyss ahead, he began to descend the ladder in silence with the majesty of a phantom. . . . With each step he made toward the men whose eyes, aghast, stared at him through the darkness, he seemed to grow taller. . . .

"When he came down, when he had reached the last rung of the ladder and placed his foot on the ground, a hand fell on his shoulder. He turned.

"'I arrest you,' said—

"'You are right.' . . ."

I heard this scene when I was seven years old, lying awake in the darkness, listening intently to a voice reading aloud behind the closed door of the nursery. It was my mother reading a French novel to my grandmother in the living room, and all I could hear was a few snatches. But they gave me the sense of some tremendous drama resolving events of unimaginable importance.

When people look back at their childhood or youth, their wistfulness comes from the memory, not of what their lives had been in those years, but of what life had then promised to be. The expectation of some undefinable splendor, of the unusual, the exciting, the great, is an attribute of youth—and the process of aging is the process of that expectation's gradual extinction.

One does not have to let it happen. But that fire dies for lack of fuel, under the gray weight of disappointments, when one discovers that the adults do not know what they are doing, nor care—that a person one respected is an abject coward—that a public figure one admired is a posturing mediocrity—that a literary classic one had looked forward to reading is a minute analysis of people one would not want to look at twice, like a study in depth of a mud puddle.

But there are exceptions.

I did not ask what book that scene came from, since I was not supposed to be listening. It remained in my mind as a brilliant flash; I did not expect to find it again nor to learn the mystery of such questions as who was arrested and why.

I was thirteen when I found it, with a sudden shock of recognition, in the closing chapters of a magnificent novel. It was *Ninety-Three* by Victor Hugo.

That scene was not as good as I had thought—it was better. It was incomparably better than anything I could have imagined. It was the climax of so enormous a drama, the resolution of such profound moral conflicts, that it left one stunned by the experience of what great literature is really like; after which, one does not settle for any lesser values, neither in books nor in life.

Now, some forty years later, I was asked to write an introduction for a new translation of *Ninety-Three*. It has just been published, in paperback, by Bantam Books. I almost envy the readers who can discover Hugo for the first time.

I quote from my introduction: "The distance between his world and ours is astonishingly short—he died in 1885—but the distance between his universe and ours has to be measured in esthetic light-years. . . . He is as invisible to the neo-barbarians of our age as the art of Rome was to their spiritual ancestors, and for the same reasons. Yet Victor Hugo is the greatest novelist in world literature."

The background of *Ninety-Three* is the French Revolution. The title refers to 1793, the year of the terror. The theme is that which is most signally lacking in today's culture: man's loyalty to values.

Three figures dominate the violence of a ruthless civil war: an intransigent aristocrat, who leads a royalist rebellion against the revolution—his nephew and heir, a young revolutionary who commands the republican army sent to crush the rebellion—an ex-priest, now a dedicated leader of the revolution, who is sent to watch the political loyalty of the young commander, his former pupil, the only man he ever loved.

Their story is told, not by the sloppy stream of an unfocused consciousness, but by the purposeful drive of a focused mind, which means: by the mounting suspense of a brilliantly integrated plot-structure.

You may read any number of more "realistic" accounts of the French Revolution, but Hugo's is the one you will remember. He is not a reporter of the momentary, but an artist who projects the essential and fundamental. He is not a statistician of gutter trivia, but a Romanticist who presents life "as it might be and ought to be." He is the worshiper and the superlative portrayer of man's greatness.

If you are struggling to hold your vision of man above the gray ashes of our century, Hugo is the fuel you need.

One cannot preserve that vision or achieve it without some knowledge of what is greatness and some image to concretize it. Every morning, when you read today's headlines, you shrink a little in human stature and hope. Then, if you turn to modern literature for a nobler view of man, you are confronted by those cases of arrested development—the juvenile delinquents aged 30 to 60—who still think that depravity is daring or shocking, and whose writing belongs, not on paper, but on fences.

If you feel, as I do, that there's nothing as boring as depravity, if you seek a glimpse of human grandeur—turn to a novel by Victor Hugo.

*The Girl Hunters** by Mickey Spillane

Reviewed by **AYN RAND**

[*Reprinted from the* Los Angeles Times *of September 2.*]

Mickey Spillane is one of the best writers of our time. He has won an enormous popular following—but no acknowledgment. He stands as a measure of the gulf between the public and its alleged intellectual leaders.

Being the most popular, he has suffered the most vicious injustice on the part of the "intellectuals"—which is a clue to their psychology and to the state of our culture. Like "The Untouchables," like any outstanding exponent of the Romantic school of art, he has been subjected to a sustained campaign of smears, attacks and denunciations—not for errors, but for achievements, not for flaws, but for his artistic virtues.

Most of today's "intellectuals"—the statist-collectivists, the worshipers of "the masses," the servants of "the people"—are savagely antagonistic to the people's standards and to every authentic, popular value in art.

They feel hatred for any projection of man as a clean, self-confident, efficacious being. They extol depravity; they relish the sight of man spitting in his own face. The object of their deepest hatred (and fear) is moral values. Their view of life is best symbolized by a middle-aged professor who seduces a twelve-year old girl—and whose story is treated humorously.

It is absurd that the same aesthetes, who acclaim the above obscenity as "adult" and "artistic," should voice concern over the "immoral" influence of Mickey Spillane.

They allege that "sex and violence" are the cause of his popular appeal. What they hate him for is the fact that Mickey Spillane is an intransigent moral crusader.

Detective fiction presents, in simple, primitive essentials, the conflict of good and evil; that is the root of its appeal. Mickey Spillane is a moral absolutist. His characterizations are excellent and drawn in black-and-whites; there are no slippery half-tones, no cowardly evasions, no cynicism—and no forgiveness; there are no doubts about the evil of evil.

Spillane's view of life has a strong element of tragic bitterness: he projects the belief that evil is powerful (a view with which I do not agree), but that man has the capacity to fight

(continued on page 46)

---

* Published by Bantam Books, 75¢.

* Published by E. P. Dutton & Co., $3.50.

Both books are available from NBL BOOK SERVICE, INC., 165 East 35th St., New York 16, N. Y., for a combined discount price of $3.75. Separately, *The Girl Hunters* is $3.15. *Ninety-Three* is $1.00 (includes postage and handling). N. Y. C. residents add 3% sales tax.

INTELLECTUAL AMMUNITION DEPARTMENT

[*Subscribers are invited to send in the questions that they find themselves unable to answer in philosophical or political discussions. As many questions as space permits will be answered. No questions will be answered by mail.*]

■ **Does man possess instincts?**

The function which the concept of "demon" served for the primitive savage and the concept of "God" serves for the theologian, is served for many psychologists by the concept of "instinct"—a term denoting nothing scientifically intelligible, while creating the illusion of causal understanding. What a savage could not comprehend, he "explained" by postulating a demon; what a theologian cannot comprehend, he "explains" by postulating a God; what many psychologists cannot comprehend, they "explain" by postulating an instinct.

Instinct theory enjoyed an enormous vogue in the eighteenth and nineteenth centuries and in the early years of the twentieth. Although its influence has been declining for the past several decades, it is still a major pillar of the Freudian school of psychoanalysis.

Observing certain types of behavior which they believed to be characteristic of the human species, instinct theorists decided that the cause of such behavior is innate, unchosen and unlearned tendencies which drive man to act as he does. Thus, they spoke of a survival instinct, a parental instinct, an acquisitive instinct, a pugnacity instinct, and so forth. They seldom attempted to define precisely what they understood an instinct to be; still less did they trouble to explain how it functioned; predominantly, they vied with one another in compiling lists of the instincts their particular theory presumed man to possess, promising to account thereby for the ultimate sources of all human action.

That mysterious force, "instinct," is not a thought or an action or an emotion or a need. The attempt, on the part of some theorists, to identify an instinct as a "compound reflex" has been recognized as unsupportable and has collapsed. A reflex is a specific, definable neuro-physiological phenomenon, the existence of which is empirically demonstrable; it is not a dumping-ground for un-understood behavior. Today, the concept of "instinct" remains as obscure as when it was first introduced into psychology.

To account for man's actions in terms of undefinable "instincts" is to contribute nothing to human knowledge: it is only to confess that one does not know why man acts as he does. To observe that men engage in sexual activities and to conclude that man has a "sex instinct"—to observe that men pursue food when they are hungry and to conclude that man has a "hunger instinct"—to observe that some men act destructively and to conclude that man has a "destructive instinct"—to observe that men usually seek out one another's company and to conclude that man has a "gregarious instinct" —is to *explain* nothing. It is merely to place oneself in the same psycho-epistemological category as the physician in the anecdote who "explains" to a distraught mother that the reason why her child will not drink milk is that "the child is just not a milk-drinker."

The history of instinct theory, in the past fifty years, is the history of intense efforts, on the part of its supporters, to twist the meaning of their formulations, of language and of the facts of reality, in order to protect their doctrines from science's growing recognition that traits and activities alleged to be "instinctive" are either: (a) not universal to the species, but are the product of particular men's acquired attitudes or beliefs, as in the case of pugnacity; or (b) the product of simple reflexes, such as a baby's sucking reflex; and/or (c) the product of learning, such as sexual behavior. (The sexual *need*, of course, is innate; but a need is not an "instinct.")

The concept of "instinct" was first used to account for complex patterns of animal behavior, such as migratory, mating and maternal behavior, that appeared inexplicable. But the concept is no less misleading when applied to animals. "Instincts" *explain* nothing. An excellent example of the type of analysis, in this sphere, that is replacing "explanation via instincts" may be found in Morgan and Stellar's *Physiological Psychology* (McGraw-Hill, 1950, pp. 402-417). Discussing the migratory behavior of salmon, the authors write:

"Their place of birth and early growth is far up in the headwaters of streams. In their second year they migrate downstream to the ocean and there spend two or three years. After that they reenter the river, usually the one from which they came, and proceed up the river and its tributaries to its headwaters. There they spawn and die. . . . The question is how they do it.

"The first phase of migration is controlled by light. The salmon has some photosensitive receptors deep in its skin. . . . In the young salmon these receptors are first covered by a layer of pigment, but gradually the pigment is lost. Then, of course, the photosensitive receptors are stimulated and the fish reacts negatively, *i.e.*, avoids light. Since the upper streams are shallow, this light-avoidance reaction eventually takes the salmon downstream to the deep ocean, where it gets away from a lot of light. Because the waters of the river emptying into the ocean are somewhat colder, contain somewhat more oxygen, and are less salty, the salmon tends to stay in the general region of the ocean into which the river runs.

"Eventually the salmon matures sexually and its gonads put out more sex hormones. These raise its activity and probably its general metabolism, which in turn leads it to choose the colder and more oxygenated water at the mouth of the river. Once the salmon gets back into the river it has a strong tendency to swim against the current, a reaction known as a *rheotropism*. As the fish swims upstream and comes to each branch of the river, it chooses the one that is colder. . . . The salmon arrives eventually at one of the headwaters of the stream, usually the one that is coldest. There it lays its eggs and dies, thus closing one cycle and beginning another. Because of the factor of temperature in the route of migration upstream, it turns out that salmon tend to return to the same places in which they were born. Thus what may seem to be a mysterious instinct or a phenomenal memory for their places of birth is really a matter of reaction to particular stimuli in their environment."

Now consider the nature of *human* behavior.

Man is born with *needs*, but he is not born with a knowledge of those needs or a knowledge of how to satisfy them. The needs of man as an organism are those things required by his nature for his survival and well-being. Man is born with a need for food, shelter and clothing, for instance—but until his mind has recognized these needs, until it has chosen food, shelter and clothing as values and learned how they can be obtained, his body will not proceed to obtain them. His body does not act "by instinct." It does not have the power to pursue goals of its own volition, independent of man's consciousness, knowledge and values.

All purposeful action aims at the achievement of a value. If a man performs the action of plowing a field, it is because he considers the plowed field a value; if he conducts a scientific experiment, it is because he considers the experiment a value; if he purchases an automobile, it is because he considers the automobile a value; if he takes a walk for the sheer pleasure of bodily motion, it is because he considers the pleasure of bodily motion a value; if he writes a treatise, it is because he has a value to gain: the objectification of his ideas and their communication to other minds. *Value* and *action* imply and necessitate each other; it is in the nature of a value that action is required to achieve and/or maintain it; it is in the nature of a consciously initiated action that its motive and purpose is the achievement and/or maintenance of a value.

But values are not innate. Man does not possess them at birth. At birth, man's mind is *tabula rasa*. Having no innate knowledge of what is true or false, man can have no innate knowledge of what is good for him or evil. Just as his knowledge must be acquired, so his values must be chosen.

(continued on page 44)

Intellectual Ammunition Department (from page 43)

If such a thing as an "instinct" could exist, it could be only some sort of innate, automatic knowledge, some sort of "frozen intelligence" inscribed in the nervous system at birth. Instinct theory thus amounts to a resurrection of the doctrine of innate ideas, which has been thoroughly discredited by both philosophy and biology, as a legacy of mysticism.

Unsatisfied, unfilled needs can set up a state of tension or disquietude or pain in man, thus prompting him to seek biologically appropriate activity, such as protecting himself against the elements. But the necessity of learning what *is* the appropriate activity cannot be by-passed.

Man must *discover* that the pain in his stomach is his body's reaction to lack of nourishment, he must discover that food will provide that nourishment, he must discover that food may be obtained by hunting or planting seed; he possesses no "hunger instinct" to provide him with this knowledge automatically and to send him in pursuit of that which he does not yet know he needs.

His body provides him only with signals of pain or pleasure; but it does not tell him their causes, it does not tell him how to alleviate one or achieve the other. *That* must be learned by his mind.

Man must *discover* the actions his life requires; he has no "instinct of self-preservation." It was not an "instinct" that taught man to make fire, to build bridges, to perform surgery, to design a telescope: it was his capacity to think. And if a man chooses *not* to think—if he chooses to risk his life in senseless dangers, to close his eyes rather than open his mind at the sight of any problem, to seek escape from consciousness in alcohol or drugs, to act in willfully stubborn defiance of his own objective self-interest—he has no "instinct" that will force his mind to function, no "instinct" that will compel him to value his life sufficiently to perform the one act that can protect and maintain it: the act of reasoning.

Man possesses a nature: as a living organism of a specific kind, he has specific needs and capacities. But how well his needs will be satisfied and to what extent his capacities will be used in the service of his life, depends, not on his "instincts," but on his knowledge, his premises and his rationality.

As members of the same species, confronted with the same reality, men perform many actions that appear to be virtually universal. But the universality of an action is not proof that it represents an unlearned, unchosen "innate tendency"— whatever this might mean.

The concept of "instinct" is disastrous to scientific theory, because—by offering a *pseudo*-explanation—it halts further inquiry and thus stands as an obstacle to a genuine understanding of the causes of human behavior.

But its practical consequences for psychology—particularly in the field of psychotherapy—are still more tragic.

Orthodox psychoanalysis, the chief stronghold of instinct theory today, has—in its interpretation of neurosis via "instincts and their vicissitudes"—virtually resurrected the doctrine of Original Sin. Psychoanalysis teaches that the source of man's suffering lies, not in Adam, but in one's "instincts" —that one is born with a racially-inherited sewer of irrational impulses and immoral drives, that mental illness is the result of one's inability to escape (through successful repression and sublimation) one's innate desires for murder, rape and incest, and that mental health begins with the admission that such desires are inherent in one's nature as man.

Persons suffering from a neurosis—from anxiety, compulsions, masochism, homosexuality—commonly experience the desperately hopeless sense that their problems are insolvable, that their neurosis is an intrinsic part of them, that there is no escape from it. The theory of an "id," or any equivalent view of human motivation in terms of inherited "instincts," is scarcely calculated to discourage such a feeling. Yet to combat that feeling is the first task of successful psychotherapy.

Patients caught in the bewildering and frightening grip of emotions and desires whose cause they cannot understand, need to learn that the cause lies in their conscious or subconscious *premises;* that those premises were *acquired,* not innate; and that irrational or mistaken premises can be corrected and changed.

Instinct theory is incompatible with a scientific system of psychology. A scientific psychology must discard it as the last, dying convulsion of medieval demonology.

—NATHANIEL BRANDEN

War and Peace
By AYN RAND

[*Reprinted from the* Los Angeles Times *of June 24.*]

One of the ugliest characteristics of today's world is the mixture of frantic war preparations with hysterical peace propaganda, and the fact that *both come from the same source* —from the same political philosophy. If mankind is ever to achieve peace, the first step will be made when people realize that today's peace movements are *not* advocates of peace.

Professing love and concern for the survival of mankind, these movements keep screaming that nuclear weapons have made war too horrible to contemplate, that armed force and violence should be abolished as a means of settling disputes among nations, and that war should be outlawed in the name of humanity. Yet these same peace movements do not oppose dictatorships; the political views of their members range through all shades of the statist spectrum, from "welfare statism" to socialism to communism. This means that these movements are opposed to the use of coercion by one nation against another, but not by the government of a nation against its own citizens; it means that they are opposed to the use of force and violence against *armed* adversaries, but not against the *disarmed.*

Under any political system, in any organized society, the government holds a legal monopoly on the use of physical force. *That* is the crucial difference between a government and any private organization. Private individuals or groups deal with one another peacefully, by means of trade, persuasion, discussion and voluntary agreements; they cannot resort to force; those who do, are criminals—and it is the proper duty of the government to restrain them.

In a free, civilized society, the use of physical force is outlawed by the recognition of men's inalienable, individual rights. The power of the government is limited by law to the role of a policeman that protects men's rights and uses force only against those who initiate its use. *This* is the basic political principle of the only social system that banishes force from human relationships: *laissez-faire* capitalism.

But a statist system—whether of a communist, fascist, Nazi, socialist or "welfare" type—is based on the opposite principle: on the government's unlimited power, which means: on the rule of brute force. The differences among statist systems are only a matter of time and degree; the principle is the same. Under statism, the government is not a policeman, but a legalized criminal that holds the power to use physical force in any manner and for any purpose it pleases against legally disarmed, defenseless victims.

Nothing can ever justify so monstrously evil a theory. Nothing can justify the horror, the brutality, the plunder, the destruction, the starvation, the slave-labor camps, the torture chambers, the wholesale slaughter of statist dictatorships. Yet *this* is what today's alleged peace-lovers are willing to advocate or tolerate—in the name of love for humanity.

Statism is a system of institutionalized violence and perpetual civil war, that leaves men no choice but to fight to seize power over one another. In a full dictatorship, that civil war takes the form of bloody purges, as in Nazi Germany and Soviet Russia. In a "mixed economy," it takes the form of "pressure group" warfare, each group fighting for legislation to extort its own advantages by *force* from all other groups.

Statism is nothing more than gang rule. A statist dictatorship is a gang devoted to looting the effort of the productive citizens of its own country. When statist rulers exhaust their own country's economy and run out of loot, they attack their neighbors. All the major wars of history were started by the more controlled economies of the time against the freer ones. For instance, World War I was started by monarchist Germany and Czarist Russia, which were "mixed economies" of a predominantly statist kind. World War II was started by the alliance of Nazi Germany with Soviet Russia and their joint attack on Poland.

Observe that in World War II, Germany and Russia dismantled entire factories in conquered countries, to ship them home—while the freest one of the "mixed economies," the semi-capitalistic United States, sent billions worth of lend-lease equipment, including entire factories, to its allies. Germany and Russia needed war; the United States did not and gained nothing. Yet it is capitalism that today's peace-lovers oppose and statism that they advocate—in the name of peace.

There is no moral justification for the vicious doctrine that some men have the right to rule others by force. But so long as men continue to believe that some sort of alleged "noble purpose" can justify it—violence, bloodshed and wars will continue.

It is true that nuclear weapons have made wars too horrible to contemplate. But it makes no difference to a man whether he is killed by a nuclear bomb or is led to a Nazi gas chamber or a Soviet firing squad, with no voices raised to defend him. Will such a man feel any love or concern for the survival of mankind? Or will he be more justified in feeling that a cannibalistic mankind, which tolerates dictatorships, does not deserve to survive?

Let those who are seriously concerned with peace, those who do love *man* and do care about his survival, realize that war cannot be outlawed by lawless statist thugs and that it is not war but *force* that has to be outlawed.

"Through Your Most Grievous Fault"
By AYN RAND

[*Reprinted from the* Los Angeles Times *of August 19.*]

The death of Marilyn Monroe shocked people, with an impact different from their reaction to the death of any other movie star or public figure. All over the world, people felt a peculiar sense of personal involvement and of protest, like a universal cry of "Oh, no!"

They felt that her death had some special significance, almost like a warning which they could not decipher—and they felt a nameless apprehension, the sense that something terribly wrong was involved.

They were right to feel it.

Marilyn Monroe, on the screen, was an image of pure, innocent, childlike joy in living. She projected the sense of a person born and reared in some radiant Utopia, untouched by suffering, unable to conceive of ugliness or evil, facing life with the confidence, the benevolence and the joyous self-flaunting of a child or a kitten who is happy to display its own attractiveness as the best gift it can offer the world, and who expects to be admired for it, not hurt.

In real life, Marilyn Monroe's probable suicide—or worse: a death that might have been an accident, suggesting that, to her, the difference did not matter—was a declaration that we live in a world which made it impossible for her kind of spirit, and for the things she represented, to survive.

If there ever was a victim of society, Marilyn Monroe was that victim—of a society that professes dedication to the relief of the suffering, but kills the joyous.

None of the objects of the humanitarians' tender solicitude, the juvenile delinquents, could have had so sordid and horrifying a childhood as did Marilyn Monroe.

To survive it and to preserve the kind of spirit she projected on the screen—the radiantly benevolent sense of life, which cannot be faked—was an almost inconceivable psychological achievement that required a heroism of the highest order. Whatever scars her past had left were insignificant by comparison.

She preserved her vision of life through a nightmare struggle, fighting her way to the top. What broke her was the discovery, at the top, of as sordid an evil as the one she had left behind—worse, perhaps, because incomprehensible. She had expected to reach the sunlight; she found, instead, a limitless swamp of malice.

It was a malice of a very special kind. If you want to see her groping struggle to understand it, read the magnificent article in a recent issue of *Life* magazine. It is not actually an article, it is a verbatim transcript of her own words—and the most tragically revealing document published in many years. It is a cry for help, which came too late to be answered.

"When you're famous, you kind of run into human nature in a raw kind of way," she said. "It stirs up envy, fame does. People you run into feel that, well, who is she—who does she think she is, Marilyn Monroe? They feel fame gives them some kind of privilege to walk up to you and say anything to you, you know, of any kind of nature—and it won't hurt your feelings—like it's happening to your clothing. . . . I don't understand why people aren't a little more generous with each other. I don't like to say this, but I'm afraid there is a lot of envy in this business."

"Envy" is the only name she could find for the monstrous thing she faced, but it was much worse than envy: it was the profound hatred of life, of success and of all human values, felt by a certain kind of mediocrity—the kind who feels pleasure on hearing about a stranger's misfortune. It was hatred of the good for being the good—hatred of ability, of beauty, of honesty, of earnestness, of achievement and, above all, of human joy.

Read the *Life* article to see how it worked and what it did to her:

An eager child, who was rebuked for her eagerness—"Sometimes the [foster] families used to worry because I used to laugh so loud and so gay; I guess they felt it was hysterical."

A spectacularly successful star, whose employers kept repeating: "Remember you're not a star," in a determined effort, apparently, not to let her discover her own importance.

A brilliantly talented actress, who was told by the alleged authorities, by Hollywood, by the press, that she could not act.

An actress, dedicated to her art with passionate earnestness —"When I was 5—I think that's when I started wanting to be an actress—I loved to play. I didn't like the world around me because it was kind of grim—but I loved to play house and it was like you could make your own boundaries"—who went through hell to make her own boundaries, to offer people the sunlit universe of her own vision—"It's almost having certain kinds of secrets for yourself that you'll let the whole world in on only for a moment, when you're acting"—but who was ridiculed for her desire to play serious parts.

A woman, the only one, who was able to project the glowingly innocent sexuality of a being from some planet uncorrupted by guilt—who found herself regarded and ballyhooed as a vulgar symbol of obscenity—and who still had the courage to declare: "We are all born sexual creatures, thank God, but it's a pity so many people despise and crush this natural gift."

A happy child who was offering her achievement to the world, with the pride of an authentic greatness and of a kitten depositing a hunting trophy at your feet—who found herself answered by concerted efforts to negate, to degrade, to ridicule, to insult, to destroy her achievement—who was unable to conceive that it was her best she was punished for, not her worst —who could only sense, in helpless terror, that she was facing some unspeakable kind of evil.

How long do you think a human being could stand it?

That hatred of values has always existed in some people, in any age or culture. But a hundred years ago, they would have been expected to hide it. Today, it is all around us; it is the style and fashion of our century.

Where would a sinking spirit find relief from it?

The evil of a cultural atmosphere is made by all those who share it. Anyone who has ever felt resentment against the good for being the good and has given voice to it, is the murderer of Marilyn Monroe.

"To Young Scientists" *(from page 41)*

No, this is not the worst evil on today's earth; there is one still worse: the conscience of those Western scientists who are still willing to associate on civilized terms with those colleagues of theirs who champion unilateral disarmament.

If you are now starting on a career in science, you do not have to share the guilt of those men, but you do have to reclaim the field and the honor of science.

There is only one way to do it: by accepting the moral principle that one does not surrender one's mind into blind servitude to thugs, and one does not accept the job of munitions-maker for Attila's conquest of the world; not for any Attila, actual or potential, foreign or domestic.

There is only one way to implement that principle. Throughout history, with only a few exceptions, governments have claimed the "right" to rule men by means of physical force, that is: by terror and destruction. When the potential of terror and destruction reaches today's scale, it should convince every *human* being that if mankind is to survive, Attila's concept of government must be discarded, along with the alleged "right" of any men to impose their ideas or wishes on others by *initiating* the use of physical force. This means that men must establish a free, noncoercive society, where the government is only a policeman protecting *individual* rights, where force is used only in retaliation and self-defense, where no gang can seize the legalized power to unleash a reign of terror. Such a society does not have to be invented: it had existed, though not fully. Its name is capitalism.

Needless to say, capitalism does not force individuals or nations into the collectivist slave pen of a world government. The so-called One World is merely "one neck ready for one leash." Capitalism leaves men free for self-defense, but gives no one the political means to initiate force or war.

This—not physical, but *political* disarmament, the renunciation of legalized brute force as a way of life—is the only means of saving the world from nuclear destruction.

The Girl Hunters *(from page 42)*

it and that no allowances, concessions or compromises are morally conceivable or possible (with which I do agree). His hero, Mike Hammer, is a moral avenger, passionately dedicated to justice, to the defense of the wronged and to the destruction of evil.

That bitter, but intensely moralistic view of life is the key to the secret of Mickey Spillane's unparalleled popularity throughout the world. He is the true voice of the people, in the twentieth century. Men everywhere feel trapped by the spread of an uncontested, incomprehensible evil. They have borne so much injustice, seen so many cynically indifferent faces and stored so much frustrated indignation, that the image of Mike Hammer becomes their embodied dream, like an answer to the cry for help they are too inarticulate to utter.

As a writer, Mickey Spillane has a brilliant literary talent. Few modern writers can approach his originality, his imagination, his sense of drama, the ingenuity of his plot-structures. His style is uneven, not yet fully disciplined; but his best passages are literarily superior to the work of most of today's so-called "serious" writers.

All these values can be enjoyed again in *The Girl Hunters*—a new novel by Mickey Spillane, which brings Mike Hammer back after an absence of ten years. It will be published on September 27.

One expects the unexpected from Mickey Spillane—and one gets it. The story opens with Mike Hammer as a drunken bum who has gone to pieces under the pressure of self-reproach for a tragic disaster. What caused it and what brings him back, you will have to find out for yourself.

Though beautifully written and extremely dramatic, Mike Hammer as a bum is somewhat out of character—(and here is one admirer of Mike's who objects to it)—but, fortunately, his recovery is fairly speedy. It is also somewhat out of character for Mickey Spillane to keep reminding Mike that he's not what he used to be—because he is. Both of them are. The old vitality, the energy, the pace, the excitement come breaking through, almost in spite of the author's intention.

I almost wish Mike would tell Mickey that it would take a much worse man than he, Mickey, is, to keep Mike Hammer down.

The Girl Hunters is not fully up to the standard of Spillane's best novels, *The Long Wait* and *One Lonely Night*. It is marred by an oddly inconclusive ending, after a brilliantly sustained suspense. The mystery is solved, but the story is not fully consummated dramatically; it seems to demand a sequel—and if this was the author's intention, then he fully succeeded in arousing the readers' interest.

There is a certain air of maturity about this novel, which is both a virtue and a flaw. It is a virtue in respect to Spillane's style, which has become more polished and more controlled. It is a flaw in respect to a certain stress of bitterness: a faint overconcern with the psychology of hatred, a faint dimming of adventurous enjoyment.

"Maturity" is a slightly disturbing concept when applied to Spillane. Maturity of technique is always a value. But maturity of spirit can have many meanings, some of them undesirable. And in spirit—in the sense of life they have created, in their exuberant energy, in the spontaneous enthusiasm they project and evoke—both Mike Hammer and Mickey Spillane should remain timelessly young.

OBJECTIVIST CALENDAR

■ Ayn Rand's column for the *Los Angeles Times* will be syndicated nationally by the Times-Mirror Co. The general release date will be announced shortly. If you would like the column to appear in your city, write the editors of your local newspapers.

■ On October 2, Ayn Rand will begin a new weekly half-hour radio program for the Columbia University station WKCR (89.9 on your FM dial). Entitled "Ayn Rand on Campus," the program will be heard every Tuesday, at 8:30 P.M. It will present talks by Miss Rand and discussions with guest speakers. The program will be syndicated and will be available to radio stations at a nominal charge. If you would like to hear it in your city, ask your local stations to contact WKCR, Columbia University, New York 27, N. Y.

■ In addition to the cities listed here last month, NBI's Tape Transcription Division has scheduled the following cities and starting dates for "Basic Principles of Objectivism": Winnipeg, October 4; St. Louis, October 7; Newark, Delaware, October 16; Buffalo, November 13.

■ On October 11, Nathaniel Branden will address the Ayn Rand Literary Club of New York University. His lecture will be based on several of his articles which have appeared in THE OBJECTIVIST NEWSLETTER. Time: 3 P.M. Place: Washington Square Room, Loeb Student Center, New York University at Washington Square. Public invited, admission free.

■ A reminder to New York students of NBI: "Basic Principles of Objectivism" begins October 9, 7:30 P.M., at the Hotel Roosevelt; "Basic Principles of Objectivist Psychology" begins October 18, 7:30 P.M., at the Biltmore Hotel.

■ On October 26, Ayn Rand will address the annual meeting of The American Society for Aesthetics. The three-day meeting will be held in Boston and Cambridge, Thursday, October 25 through Saturday, October 27. Miss Rand will speak on Friday, 8 P.M., in the Fogg Museum Auditorium of Harvard University. Her topic: "Art as Sense of Life." Prof. John Hospers will comment on her paper. Public invited, admission free.

Published monthly at 165 East 35th Street, New York 16, N. Y.
Subscription rate: in United States, its possessions, Canada and Mexico, $5 for one year; other countries, $6. Trial subscriptions: 4 months $2. 6 months $3.
Additional copies of this Newsletter: single copy 50¢ (coins, not stamps); 10 — 99 copies, 25¢ each plus postage (for first-class delivery add 1¢ per copy, for third-class delivery add ½¢ per copy); 100 or more copies, 15¢ each plus postage (same as above).
For change of address send old address and new address with zone number if any. Allow us two weeks to process new subscriptions and change of address.

Ayn Rand and **Nathaniel Branden**, Editors and Publishers
Barbara Branden, Managing Editor
Elayne Kalberman, Circulation Manager

PRINTED BY STANDARD GRAPHICS, NEW YORK CITY

Reprinted articles: Copyright 1962 by Times-Mirror Co., Los Angeles

THE OBJECTIVIST NEWSLETTER

Edited and Published by AYN RAND and NATHANIEL BRANDEN

VOL. 1 NO. 11   NOVEMBER, 1962

Social Metaphysics
By NATHANIEL BRANDEN

There is an invisible killer loose in the world. It has claimed more victims than any other disease in history. Yet most of its symptoms are commonly regarded as normal. That is the secret of its deadliness.

These symptoms may be observed all around one: in the lives of all those who are dominated by an obsessive concern with gaining the approval and avoiding the disapproval of their fellow men; who lack a self-generated sense of personal identity and who feel themselves to be metaphysical outcasts, cut off from reality; whose first impulse, when confronted with an issue or called upon to pass a judgment, is to ask not "What is true?" but "What do others say is true?"; who have no firm, unyielding concept of existence, reality, facts, *as apart from* the judgments, beliefs, opinions, feelings of others.

When one understands the nature and causes of this phenomenon, one will understand why, for instance, the typical fate of an innovator is to be attacked, opposed and denounced by the society of his time; or why men are willing to follow blindly teachings and precepts that lead them to destruction; or why the line of poetry that best captures the inner sense of life of most men is "a stranger and afraid in a world I never made."

To understand this phenomenon, one must begin by considering three basic facts about human nature:

(1) *Man is a rational being.* Man's defining characteristic, which distinguishes him from all other living species, is his ability to *think*—to extend the range of his awareness beyond the perceptual concretes immediately confronting him—to rise to the *conceptual* level of consciousness—to abstract, to integrate, to grasp principles—to plan and act long-range.

(2) *Reason is man's basic means of survival.* At birth, man's mind is *tabula rasa*. Man has no innate knowledge of what is true or false, good or evil, conducive or inimical to his welfare, no innate knowledge of what values to select and what goals to pursue. He needs such knowledge in order to deal with reality successfully, in order to live—and only *reason* can provide it.

(3) *Man is a being of volitional consciousness.* Man's sensory-perceptual mechanism functions automatically; his conceptual faculty does not. Man must *initiate, sustain* and *direct* the process of reasoning—by volitional, self-generated effort.

These facts impose a solemn responsibility on man. Since his rational faculty does not function automatically, man must *choose* to initiate a reasoning process, he must *choose* to check and test his conclusions by constant observation and by a rigorous process of logic, and he must *choose* to be guided by his rational judgment. Since his consciousness is not infallible, he can make an error at any step of the way; if he leaves the error uncorrected and acts on it, he will be acting against reality—and suffering and self-destruction will be the result.

There are two ways, in essence, that a man can respond to these facts and to the responsibility they entail: he can accept and welcome them—or he can resent and dread them. The first response can lead to the achievement of self-esteem; the second—to neurosis.

Self-esteem is confidence in one's ability to deal with reality. If a man takes pleasure in the act of thinking, of developing the efficacy of his consciousness, of expanding the range of his knowledge, of choosing rational values and working for their achievement—that is: if he lives and acts as his nature requires—self-esteem will be the psychological result.

If a man seeks escape from this responsibility, if he evades the effort of thought, prefers a state of mental fog and drifts at the mercy of his blind feelings, he defaults on the process of proper human growth, sabotages his intellectual development and the efficacy of his consciousness—and sentences himself to the mounting terror of feeling that he is inadequate to and unfit for existence.

This state is not reached in a day, a week or a month; it is the cumulative result of a long succession of defaults, evasions and irrationalities—a long succession of failures to use one's mind properly.

Confronted with the choice to initiate the mental effort needed to pursue knowledge, to focus his mind, to think—or not to bother—the irrationalist characteristically chooses not to bother, *particularly if crucial issues are at stake.*

Confronted with the choice to stand by the judgment of his mind or to act on a wish he knows to be irrational, he characteristically sticks by his wish and defies his mind, invalidating its judgment.

Confronted with the choice between his own understanding and the assertions of others, he characteristically abandons his own understanding, finding it "safer" to pass the responsibility of judgment to others.

In all such cases, the basic choice involved is the same: to think or not to think.

There is no escape from the facts of reality, no escape from man's nature or the manner of survival his nature requires. Every living species that possesses awareness can survive only by the guidance of its consciousness; *that* is the role and function of consciousness in a living organism: to gain the knowledge needed to live. If a man rejects his distinctive form of consciousness, if he decides that thinking is too much effort, that choosing the values needed to guide his actions is too frightening a responsibility—then, if he wants to survive, he can do so only by means of the consciousness of others: by means of *their* perceptions, *their* judgments, *their* values.

He knows that he does not know what to do and that knowledge is required to make decisions in the face of the countless alternatives that confront him every day of his life. But *others* seem to know how to live, others have survived and are surviving around him, so the only way to survive, he feels, is to follow their lead and live by their knowledge; *they* know—they will spare him the risk and the effort; *they* know—somehow, they possess control of that mysterious unknowable: reality. He does not have to perceive the world as it is, and assume the responsibility of judgment; instead, he can look at people, watch what they do, guess what they see, get attuned to their manner of thinking and develop a skill for a special sight: *the world as perceived by others.*

Thus he is led to shape his soul in the image of a parasite inconceivable in other living species: not a parasite of body, but of *consciousness.*

What he seeks is not material support—some men of this type are financial moochers, but they are comparatively a minority, and the state of being a material parasite is only the consequence of a deeper, mental cause. He seeks a consciousness other than his own to replace the mind he has chosen to discard, he is begging humanity at large to take care of him on a level deeper than financial: to tell him how to live. This means: to set his goals, to choose his values, to prescribe his actions—never to leave him alone, at the mercy of his own unreliable mind. He may be willing to work, to obey and even to think (within a limited square), if others will assume responsibility for his ultimate direction.

A man of self-esteem and sovereign consciousness deals with reality, with nature, with an objective universe of facts; he holds his mind as his tool of survival and develops his

(continued on page 50)

Copyright © 1962 by The Objectivist Newsletter, Inc.

BOOKS

*East Minus West = Zero** by Werner Keller
Reviewed by EDITH EFRON

In 1920, after three years of Bolshevik rule, Russia was in chaos and the enslaved population was starving. Facing the economic havoc wrought by his government, Lenin declared: "Our program was right in theory, but impracticable."

In 1962, after 45 years of Bolshevik rule, Russia is widely believed to be a scientific and industrial rival of the United States and a military threat to the free world. Bolshevik theory, it is alleged, has somehow been made "practicable."

How?

In *East Minus West = Zero*, German historian Werner Keller gives the answer: by communist parasitism on the very capitalist system declared to be its mortal enemy, a parasitism which was—and still is—aided and abetted by the capitalists themselves.

The first architects of communist economic development, as this richly documented industrial-scientific history of Russia reveals, were businessmen. In 1921, Lenin launched a "New Economic Policy" and offered Westerners generous "concessions" in exchange for the rapid industrialization of Russia. English, German, Italian, Swedish, Danish and American firms "took the bait," as Mr. Keller puts it, and rushed to provide the new communist nation with airfields and railroads, with gold, copper and iron-mining installations, with ship, textile and aircraft factories, with oil refineries.

The most ambitious contributions to the "noble experiment" came from America. Replicas of complex American production centers were assembled, shipped and installed, like gigantic do-it-yourself-kits, in the heart of the primitive Russian wasteland. The Cleveland firm of Arthur G. Mackee provided the equipment for huge steel plants at Magnitogorsk; John K. Calder of Detroit equipped and installed the material for tractor plants at Chelyabinsk; Henry Ford and the Austin Company provided all the elements for a major automobile works at Gorki; Col. Hugh Cooper, creator of the Muscle Shoals dam, planned and built the giant hydroelectric installation of Dnieprostroi. The grandiose "Bolshevik achievements" of the 1930's—which glorified communism throughout the world—were all achievements of American capitalism.

Despite this artificial force-feeding, Russia remained industrially impotent, its peasant populace unable to understand, maintain or operate the complex transplants of capitalism. "We smashed a great deal of machinery," a grinning Khrushchev was to tell the world many years later.

Before the decade was up, the "Bolshevik colossus" was twice invaded by Finland, and, by 1941, Russia was desperately begging the West for aid against Hitler's armies. Again, capitalists rushed to save the collapsing communist dictatorship.

Under Lend-Lease, writes Mr. Keller, "the immense industrial potential of the United States was put freely at the disposal of the Soviet Union." Between 1941 and 1945, a vast flood of goods was flown and shipped to Russia: raw materials, machinery, tools, complete industrial plants, spare parts, textiles, clothing, tinned meat, sugar, flour and fats, as well as purely military supplies such as arms, trucks, tanks, aircraft and gasoline.

Lend-Lease was granted in the form of an interest-free loan, but not one cent has ever been repaid. It turned out to be an involuntary "gift" from capitalism to communism—a "gift" estimated at the incredible sum of $10,800,000,000.

While the communists were buying the fruits of capitalism, and begging them, they were also stealing them. Mr. Keller provides an extensive review of Russia's record during the 1920's and 30's: expropriation of foreign companies, ruthless breaking of contracts, stealing of patents, industrial espionage.

---

* Published by G. P. Putnam's Sons, $6.95. Available from NBL BOOK SERVICE, INC., 165 East 35th St., New York 16, N. Y., for $5.75 (N.Y.C. residents add 3% sales tax; outside the U. S., add 15¢).

Edith Efron is a journalist whose articles have appeared in such publications as Life, Look, *and* The New York Times Magazine.

But the most important sections of this book are those that provide documentation on the policy of world-wide stealing and looting which has been carried out systematically by the Russian government since the 1940's.

Throughout the war, writes Mr. Keller, America was "a veritable Eldorado for spies." Under the complaisant eye of the Roosevelt Administration, Russian Lend-Lease agents stole materials in astronomical quantities: classified documents, technical blueprints, military inventions, machinery and materials such as uranium and heavy water. They packed them into mammoth crates marked "diplomatic mail" and flew them to Russia by airlift.

"Nothing was done to stop the spies," writes Mr. Keller. "The government watched the activities of the Soviet agents with incredible tolerance. . . . The Americans themselves provided the transportation in which the Russians carried away the fruits of the most spectacular campaign of robbery ever undertaken."

The most calamitous theft of the period was Russia's rifling of the secrets of the atom bomb and the hydrogen bomb from American and British laboratories, with the aid of such spies as Fuchs, May, the Rosenbergs and Greenglass.

After the war, the communist dictatorship, protected by private agreements between Roosevelt and Stalin, plundered the bodies of the conquered nations with the rapacity of Attila. Russia collected "loot, loot on an unprecedented scale, loot from Europe and from the Far East"; from Manchuria: almost all the Japanese heavy industry, valued at $858,000,000; from the satellite states: minerals, machinery, petroleum and foodstuffs "in such quantities as to bring them to the verge of bankruptcy"; from Germany: iron and steel works, chemical works, shipyards, motor car factories, electric power stations, railway networks, armaments factories and the huge, underground V-2 works. Forty-one percent of Germany's industrial equipment was dismantled, packed and transported to Russia. Officially, Russia was awarded war damages totaling $10,000,000,000, which Germany paid. The property stolen in addition, says Mr. Keller, was worth four times that amount.

And the worst was yet to come. To exploit this fantastic accumulation of stolen equipment and scientific knowledge, labor was needed—and human beings, too, were looted. One million Poles, 380,000 Germans, and hundreds of thousands of Eastern Europeans (about 15 percent of the population of the Baltic States) were seized, like physical objects, and sent to Russian slave labor camps to work for "Bolshevik development." And—perhaps the most grotesque crime of all—on Tuesday, October 22, 1946, the Red Army moved to trap its ultimate prey: *human minds*. Six thousand German scientists were netted in a gigantic raid and were forcibly deported to Russia to work in the looted German aircraft and rocketry factories.

A few years later, the country which could not boast of one seminal thinker in the field of physics—*and which had officially rejected Einstein's theory of relativity because it clashed with Marxist ideology*—was producing atomic bombs, hydrogen bombs, intercontinental rockets, Sputniks, Luniks and manned satellites.

Thus was Bolshevik theory made "practicable."

The efficacy of the communist state is touted, today, by those who are eager to believe that a modern industrial system can be created by theft and maintained by force. Mr. Keller's book—particularly his analysis of the state of science, technology and industry under the communist dictatorship—demolishes this belief.

Scientific traditions existed in Czarist Russia, Mr. Keller points out in the introductory historical section of his book, but they were Western imports, artificial grafts on a primitive culture. Since the communist revolution of 1917, the alien legacy of free scientific inquiry has been under relentless attack. He describes the "human degradation and intellectual tyranny in the treatment of [Russia's] scientists" and the catastrophic effects of this tyranny on their work and on the material life of the nation. Official Lysenkoism has destroyed biology, genetics and agronomy; official Pavlovianism has retarded the theory and practice of medicine; biochemistry,

(continued on page 52)

The Esthetic Vacuum of Our Age
By AYN RAND

(Excerpts from a lecture delivered at the Creative Arts Festival of the University of Michigan.)

Prior to the nineteenth century, literature presented man as a helpless being whose life and actions were determined by forces beyond his control: either by fate and the gods, as in the Greek tragedies, or by an innate weakness, "a tragic flaw," as in the plays of Shakespeare. Writers regarded man as metaphysically impotent, incapable of achieving his goals or of directing the course of his life; their basic premise was *determinism*. On that premise, one could not project what might happen to men; one could only record what *did* happen —and chronicles were the appropriate literary form of such recording.

Man as a being of free will did not appear in literature until the nineteenth century. The *novel* was his proper literary form—and Romanticism was the great new movement in art. Romanticism saw man as a being able to choose his values, to achieve his goals, to control his own existence. The Romantic writers did not regard man as a plaything of unknowable forces; they regarded him as a product of his own value-choices. They did not record the events that *had* happened, but projected the events that *should* happen; they did not record the choices men *had* made, but projected the choices men *ought to make*.

The Romantic novel was the product of two factors, of *reason* and of *capitalism*: of the Aristotelian influence which, in the nineteenth century, gave man the confident power to choose his own goals—and of the politico-economic system that left him free to achieve them. With the resurgence of mysticism and collectivism, in the later part of the nineteenth century, the Romantic novel and the Romantic movement vanished gradually from the cultural scene.

Man's new enemy, in art, was Naturalism. Naturalism rejected the concept of free will and went back to a view of man as a helpless creature determined by forces beyond his control; only now the new ruler of man's destiny was held to be *society*. The Naturalists proclaimed that values have no power and no place, neither in human life nor in literature, that writers must present men "as they are," which meant: must record whatever they happen to see around them—that they must not pronounce value-judgments nor project abstractions, but must content themselves with a faithful transcription, a carbon copy, of any existing concretes.

This was a return to the literary principle of the chronicle— but since a novel was to be an *invented* chronicle, the novelist was faced with the problem of what to use as his standard of selection. When values are declared to be impossible, how is one to know what to record, what to regard as important or significant? Naturalism solved the problem by substituting *statistics* for a standard of value. That which could be claimed to be typical of a large number of men, in any given geographical area or period of time, was regarded as metaphysically significant and worthy of being recorded. That which was rare, unusual, exceptional, was regarded as unimportant and *unreal*.

Just as the new schools of philosophy became progressively dedicated to the negation of philosophy, so Naturalism was dedicated to the negation of art. Instead of presenting a *metaphysical* view of man and of existence, the Naturalists presented a *journalistic* view. In answer to the question: "What is man?"—they said: "This is what the village grocers are, in the south of France, in the year 1887," or: "This is what the inhabitants of the slums are, in New York, in 1921," or: "These are the folks next door."

Art—the integrator of metaphysics, the concretizer of man's widest abstractions—was shrinking to the level of a plodding, concrete-bound dolt who has never looked past the block he lives on or beyond the range of the moment.

It did not take long for the philosophical roots of Naturalism to come out into the open. At first, by the standard that substituted the *collective* for the *objective*, the Naturalists consigned the exceptional man to unreality and presented only the men who could be taken as typical of some group or another, high or low. Then, since they saw more misery than prosperity on earth, they began to regard prosperity as unreal and to present only misery, poverty, the slums, the lower classes. Then, since they saw more mediocrity than greatness around them, they began to regard greatness as unreal, and to present only the mediocre, the average, the common, the undistinguished. Since they saw more failure than success, they took success to be unreal and presented only human failure, frustration, defeat. Since they saw more suffering than happiness, they took happiness to be unreal and presented only suffering. Since they saw more ugliness than beauty, they took beauty to be unreal and presented only ugliness. Since they saw more vice than virtue, they took virtue to be unreal and presented only vice, crime, corruption, perversion, depravity.

Now, take a look at modern literature.

Man—the nature of man, the metaphysically significant, important, essential about man—is now represented by dipsomaniacs, drug addicts, sexual perverts, homicidal maniacs and psychotics. The subjects of modern literature are such themes as: the hopeless love of a bearded lady for a mongoloid pin-head in a circus side show—or: the problem of a married couple whose child was born with six fingers on her left hand—or: the tragedy of a gentle young man who just can't help murdering strangers in the park, for kicks.

All this is still presented to us under the Naturalistic heading of "a slice of life" or *"real* life"—but the old slogans have worn thin. The obvious question, to which the heirs of statistical Naturalism have no answer, is: if heroes and geniuses are not to be regarded as representative of mankind, by reason of their numerical rarity, why are freaks and monsters to be regarded as representative? Why are the problems of a bearded lady of greater universal significance than the problems of a genius? Why is the soul of a murderer worth studying, but not the soul of a hero?

The answer, of course, lies in the basic metaphysical premise of Naturalism, whether its practitioners ever chose it consciously or not: as an outgrowth of modern philosophy, that basic premise is anti-man, anti-mind, anti-life; and, as an outgrowth of the altruist morality, Naturalism is a frantic escape from moral judgment—a long, wailing plea for pity, for tolerance, for the forgiveness of anything.

The literary cycle has swung all the way around. What you read today is not Naturalism any longer: it is Symbolism; it is the presentation of a *metaphysical* view of man, as opposed to a journalistic or statistical view. But it is the Symbolism of the jungle. According to this modern view, *depravity* represents man's real, essential, metaphysical nature, while virtue does not; virtue is only an accident, an exception or an illusion; therefore, a *monster* is a consistent projection of man's essence, but a *hero* is not.

The Romanticists did not present a hero as a statistical average, but as an abstraction of man's best and highest potentiality, applicable to and achievable by all men, in various degrees, according to their individual choices. For the same reasons, in the same manner, but on an opposite metaphysical premise, today's writers do not present a monster as a statistical average, but as an abstraction of man's worst and lowest potentiality, which they regard as applicable to and essential in all men—not, however, as a potentiality, but as a hidden actuality. The Romanticists presented heroes as *"larger than life"*; now, monsters are presented as "larger than life" —or, rather, *man* is presented as *"smaller* than life."

If men hold a rational philosophy, including the conviction that they possess free will, the image of a hero guides and inspires them. If men hold an irrational philosophy, including the conviction that they are helpless automatons, the image of a monster serves to reassure them; they feel, in effect: "I am not *that* bad."

The philosophical meaning or the vested interest of presenting man as a loathsome monstrosity is the hope and the demand for a moral blank check.

Now consider a curious paradox: the same estheticians and intellectuals who advocate collectivism, with the subordination of all values and of everyone's life to the rule of "the masses," with art as the voice of "the people"—these same men are resentfully antagonistic toward all popular values in art. They

(continued on page 50)

The Esthetic Vacuum of Our Age *(from page 49)*

engage in virulent denunciations of the mass media, of the so-called "commercial" producers or publishers who happen to attract large audiences and to please the public. They demand government subsidies for the artistic ventures which "the people" do not enjoy and do not choose to support voluntarily. They feel that any financially successful, that is, *popular,* work of art is automatically worthless, while any unpopular failure is automatically great—provided it is unintelligible. Anything that can be understood, they feel, is vulgar and primitive; only inarticulate language, smears of paint and the noise of radio static are civilized, sophisticated and profound.

The popularity or unpopularity, the box-office success or failure, of a work of art is not, of course, a criterion of esthetic merit. No value—esthetic, philosophical or moral—can be established by counting noses; fifty million Frenchmen can be as wrong as one. But while a crude "philistine," who takes financial *success* as proof of artistic merit, can be regarded merely as a mindless parasite on art—what is one to think of the standards, motives and intentions of those who take financial *failure* as the proof of artistic merit? If the snobbery of mere financial success is reprehensible, what is the meaning of a snobbery of failure? Draw your own conclusions.

If you wonder what is the ultimate destination toward which modern philosophy and modern art are leading you, you may observe its advance symptoms all around us. Observe that literature is returning to the art form of the pre-industrial ages, to the *chronicle*—that fictionalized biographies of "real" people, of politicians, baseball-players or Chicago gangsters, are given preference over works of imaginative fiction, in the theater, in the movies, in television—and that a favored literary form is *the documentary*. Observe that in painting, sculpture and music the current vogue, fashion and inspirational model is the primitive art of the jungle.

If you rebel against reason, if you succumb to the old bromides of the Witch Doctors, such as: "Reason is the enemy of the artist" or "The cold hand of reason dissects and destroys the joyous spontaneity of man's soul, his creative imagination, his *élan vital*"—I suggest that you take note of the following fact: by rejecting reason and surrendering to the unhampered sway of their unleashed emotions (and whims), the apostles of irrationality, the Existentialists, the Zen Buddhists, the non-objective artists, have not achieved a free, joyous, triumphant sense of life, but a sense of doom, nausea and screaming, cosmic terror. Then read the stories of O. Henry or listen to the music of Viennese operettas and remember that these were the products of the spirit of the nineteenth century—a century ruled by the cold, dissecting hand of reason. And then ask yourself: which psycho-epistemology is appropriate to man, which is consonant with the facts of reality and with man's nature?

Just as a man's esthetic preferences are the sum of his metaphysical values and the barometer of his soul, so art is the sum and the barometer of a culture. Modern art is the most eloquent demonstration of the cultural bankruptcy of our age.

Social Metaphysics *(from page 47)*

ability to think. But the man who has abandoned his mind lives, not in a universe of facts, but in a *universe of people;* people, not facts, are *his* reality; people, not reason, are *his* tool of survival. It is with *them* that he has to deal, it is on *them* that his consciousness must focus, it is they whom he must understand or please or placate or deceive or maneuver or manipulate or obey.

It is his success at this task that becomes his gauge of his fitness to exist—of his competence to live.

Having alienated himself from objective reality, he has no other standard of truth, rightness or personal worth. To grasp and successfully to satisfy the expectations, conditions, demands, terms, *values* of others, is experienced by him as his deepest, most urgent need. The *approval* of others is his only form of assurance that he is right, that he is doing well. The temporary diminution of his anxiety that their approval offers him, is his substitute for self-esteem.

This form of neurosis can exist in men in various degrees of intensity and destructiveness. It exists in the majority of people. The name I have given it is: *Social Metaphysics*.

This designation is literal. "Metaphysics" is one's view of the nature of reality. To the man I am describing, reality is *people:* in his mind, in his thinking, in the automatic connections of his consciousness, *people* occupy the place which, in the mind of a rational man, is occupied by *reality*.

Just as a rational man bases his self-esteem on his ability to deal with objective reality—so this man bases his self-value on his ability to deal with people.

"Social Metaphysics," then, may be defined and summarized as follows: *the psychological syndrome that characterizes an individual who holds the consciousnesses of other men, not objective reality, as his ultimate psycho-epistemological frame-of-reference*.

Not every social metaphysician begins by resenting the effort and responsibility of thought. Many begin by enjoying the process of thought, but too frequently blank out their minds in order to indulge some irrational wish or irrational fear—and soon they find that the areas of reality about which it is "safe" to think are progressively shrinking, and they proceed to evade more and more, reserving their thinking for matters that have little or no connection to their behavior and life. But however it was arrived at, what all social metaphysicians have in common is a fundamental breach between their consciousness and reality. This breach is what leads to social metaphysics, and is worsened by it, thus setting up a pattern of reciprocal reinforcement.

The popular image of a conventional "conformist" is merely the crudest and most obvious type of social metaphysician. There are many others.

There is the man who seeks power—who hates people for his own fear of them, and, despairing of ever winning a conventional social-metaphysical form of success within the "system," knows no other concept of "security" save that of being able to *force* the consciousnesses he dreads, to *compel* obedience, approval, "love."

There is the "rebellious" social metaphysician who proudly, scornfully and loudly denounces and rejects the traditional value-system of his Babbitt background—and runs in abject surrender to the unshaven value-system of Greenwich Village (or its equivalent), instead.

There is the "independent" social metaphysician, the "counterfeit individualist" who is opposed to *all* values, whose only notion of self-expression is his *whims*—who, having no concept of objective reality, sees existence as a clash between *his* whims and the whims of *others*—and who is so terrified at the prospect of being disliked that he feels obliged to insult people in advance.

Then, at the other end of the social metaphysical continuum, there is the man who uses his own judgment and holds independent, rational convictions in many isolated aspects of his life, particularly in his professional work—but who is aware of an obsessive fear of others, particularly in the area of fundamental value-judgments, without ever understanding the cause of his fear—who fights and resists it by repression or will power, at the cost of enormous emotional suffering, never identifying the nature of the treason that has put him in bondage, and thus never breaking through to freedom and full sovereignty.

Perhaps the worst form of self-degradation and the worst punishment that all social metaphysicians endure, is their contempt for their own judgment. A man of sovereign consciousness places nothing higher than reality, and no judgment of reality higher than his own; he does not accept an idea as true or valid unless he recognizes it to be so by his own rational understanding. If a social metaphysician judges an idea to be true, the fact that he used his own judgment tends to *invalidate* the idea. Any conviction he forms, lacks conviction for him *because* it is his own. Any idea advanced by others, tends to be extra-convincing because it is *not* his. He feels that others have a wisdom superior to his own, granted to them by the fact that they are *"non-himself."* He may not always give in to them, but his emotions will always pull him secretly to acknowledge their superiority. His own mind, to him, is not

(continued on page 52)

Women and the Industrial Revolution
By R. HESSEN

To condemn capitalism one must first misrepresent its history. The notion that industrial capitalism led to nothing but misery and degradation for women is an article of faith among critics of capitalism. It is as prevalent as the view that children were victimized and exploited by the Industrial Revolution—and it is as false.*

Let us examine the source of this view. To appreciate the benefits that capitalism brought to women, one must compare their status under capitalism with their condition in the preceding centuries. But the nineteenth-century critics of capitalism did not do this; instead, they distorted and falsified history, glamorizing the past and disparaging everything modern by contrast.

For instance, Richard Oastler, the most fanatical nineteenth-century enemy of capitalism, claimed that everyone was better off spiritually and materially in the Middle Ages than in the early nineteenth century. Describing medieval England, Oastler rhapsodized about the lost golden age: "Oh, what a beautiful ship was England once! She was well built, well manned, well provisioned, well rigged! All were then merry, cheerful and happy on board."

This was said of centuries in which "the bulk of the population were peasants in a servile condition, bound by status, not free to change their mode of life or to move from their birthplace" (M. C. Buer)—when people had only the promise of happiness in the life beyond the grave to succor them against decimating plagues, recurring famines and at best half-filled stomachs—when people lived in homes so infested with dirt and vermin that one historian's verdict about these cottages is: "From a health point of view the only thing to be said in their favor was that they burnt down very easily!" (Mabel C. Buer, *Health, Wealth and Population in the Early Days of the Industrial Revolution, 1760-1815;* London, 1926, pp. 250, 88.)

Oastler represented the viewpoint of the medievalists. The socialists, who agreed with them, were equally inaccurate historians.

For example, describing the conditions of the masses in the pre-industrial seventeenth and early eighteenth centuries, Friedrich Engels alleged: "The workers vegetated throughout a passably comfortable existence, leading a righteous and peaceful life in all piety and probity; and their material position was far better off than their successors."

This was written of an age characterized by staggeringly high mortality rates, especially among children—crowded towns and villages untouched by sanitation—infamously high gin consumption. The working class diet consisted mainly of oatmeal, milk, cheese and beer; while bread, potatoes, coffee, tea, sugar and meat were still expensive luxuries. Bathing was infrequent and laundering a rarity because soap was so costly, and clothing—which had to last a decade or generation—would not last if washed too often.

The most rapid change wrought by the Industrial Revolution was the shifting of textile production out of the home and into the factory. Under the previous system, called "domestic industry," the spinning and weaving was done in the worker's own home with the aid of his wife and children. When technological advances caused the shifting of textile production into factories, this led, says one critic of capitalism, "to the breakup of the home as a social unit." (Wanda Neff, *Victorian Working Women;* N. Y., 1920, p. 51.)

Mrs. Neff writes approvingly that "under the system of domestic industry the parents and the children had worked together, the father the autocratic head, pocketing the family earnings and directing their expenditure." Her tone turns to condemnation when she recounts: "But under the factory system the members of the family all had their own earnings, they worked in separate departments of the mill, coming home only for food and sleep. The home was little but a shelter."

The factories were held responsible for every social problem of that age, including promiscuity, infidelity and prostitution. Implicit in the condemnation of women working in the factories was the notion that a woman's place is in the home and that her only proper role is to keep house for her husband and to rear his children. The factories were blamed simultaneously for removing girls from the watchful restraints of their parents and for encouraging early marriages; and later for fostering maternal negligence and incompetent housekeeping, as well as for encouraging lack of female subordination and the desire for luxuries.

It is a damning indictment of the pre-factory system to consider what kind of "luxuries" the Industrial Revolution brought within reach of the working class budget. Women sought luxuries like shoes instead of clogs, hats instead of shawls, "delicacies" (like coffee, tea and sugar) instead of "plain food."

Critics denounced the increasing habit of wearing ready-made clothes, and they viewed the replacement of wools and linens by inexpensive cottons as a sign of growing poverty. Women were condemned for not making by hand that which they could buy more cheaply, thanks to the revolution in textile production. Dresses no longer had to last a decade—women no longer had to wear coarse petticoats until they disintegrated from dirt and age; cheap cotton dresses and undergarments were a revolution in personal hygiene.

The two most prevalent nineteenth-century explanations of why women worked in the factories were: (a) that their "husbands preferred to remain home idle, supported by their wives" and (b) that the factory system "displaced adult men and imposed on women 'the duty and burden of supporting their husbands and families.'" These charges are examined in *Victorian Wives and Mothers,* (London, 1957) a monumental study by Dr. Margaret Hewitt of the University of Exeter. Her conclusion is: "Neither of these assumptions proves to have any statistical foundation whatsoever." (p. 190)

In fact, women worked in the factories for far more conventional reasons; Dr. Hewitt enumerates them: many women worked because "their husbands' wages were insufficient to keep the home going"; others were widowed or deserted; others were barren, or had grown-up children; some had husbands who were unemployed, or employed in seasonal jobs; and a few chose to work in order to earn money for extra comforts in the home, although their husbands' wages were sufficient to cover necessities. (pp. 192, 194)

What the factory system offered these women was—*not* misery and degradation—but a means of survival, of economic independence, of rising above the barest subsistence. Harsh as nineteenth-century factory conditions were, compared to twentieth-century conditions, women increasingly preferred work in the factories to any other alternatives open to them, such as domestic service, or back-breaking work in agricultural gangs, or working as haulers and pullers in the mines; moreover, if a woman could support herself, she was not driven into early marriage.

Even Professor Trevelyan, who persistently disparaged the factories and extolled "the good old days," admitted: "... the women who went to work in the factories though they lost some of the best things in life [Trevelyan does not explain what he means], gained independence.... The money they earned was their own. The factory hand acquired an economic position personal to herself, which in the course of time other women came to envy."

And Trevelyan concluded: "The working class home often became more comfortable, quiet and sanitary by ceasing to be a miniature factory." (G. M. Trevelyan, *English Social History;* London, 1942, p. 487.)

Critics of the factory system still try to argue that the domestic spinners or weavers could have a creator's pride in their work, which they lost by becoming mere cogs in a huge industrial complex. Dr. Dorothy George easily demolishes this thesis: "It seems unlikely that the average weaver, toiling hour after hour throwing the shuttle backwards and forwards

(continued on page 52)

---

* See my article, "Child Labor and the Industrial Revolution" in THE OBJECTIVIST NEWSLETTER, April, 1962.

Mr. Hessen received his M.A. in History from Harvard University, and is now on the staff of NATHANIEL BRANDEN INSTITUTE.

Social Metaphysics *(from page 50)*

an instrument of certainty, but of self-doubt and mistrust. He feels: "Who am I to know?"—"Who am I to judge?"—"How can I tell?" His attitude amounts to: "How can I live my life by the guidance of nothing but so precarious, so puny, so feeble, so uncertain, so unreliable a thing as *my mind?*"

If one discusses the importance of reason with a social metaphysician, he frequently will ask: *"Whose* reason?"—and will proceed to complain that experts disagree in every field, so how can one tell what *is* reasonable? It will never occur to a man of sovereign consciousness to ask such a question as "Whose reason?"—and it never occurs to a social metaphysician that the answer is "One's own."

It is not difficult to understand the appeal that certain currently prevalent ideas have for the social metaphysician.

If he hears a contemporary school of philosophy declare that certainty is impossible to man—his emotions leap to agree; his chronic inner state, he learns, is not a sign of neurosis but of superior intellectual sophistication.

If he hears another contemporary school declare that the purpose of philosophy is to study and analyze, not the facts of reality, but other philosophers' *statements* about reality—he feels himself to be in familiar psychological territory; he understands the point of view.

If he hears a psychologist declare that "love is the only sane and satisfactory answer to the problem of human existence"—if he hears an advocate of altruism declare that men must seek self-esteem through their relationships with others—if he hears an advocate of collectivism declare that everyone should be guaranteed "minimum sustenance," that one's survival should not have to depend on one's own effort—he can truthfully answer that that is just what, with all his heart, he has always believed.

At the root of all the twists, complexities, evasions and neurotic devices of social metaphysics, is the desire to escape from the responsibility of a *volitional* consciousness and an *objective* reality—the desire to escape from reason and man's nature. And in the world of today, many dominant cultural voices will encourage the social metaphysician in his quest.

But it is a quest that cannot succeed. No escape is possible. And the social metaphysician knows it. He knows it, not as firm, conceptualized knowledge, but as an emotion of terror. The terror is his form of awareness that, when he rejects the task of becoming man, nothing else is left to him but the agonizing stillness of non-identity. He knows it, whether he has failed to gain anyone's approval or has succeeded in gaining immense popularity. The social metaphysician at the bottom envies the social metaphysician at the top—because he cannot hear the latter's silent screams for help. But the social metaphysician at the top, *he* hears them.

East Minus West = Zero *(from page 48)*

biophysics and pharmacology are stumbling far behind the level reached by these sciences in the free nations.

The Russians, states Mr. Keller, are competent, today, in physics and chemistry, but not as creative thinkers—"their best work is second-hand." Their technology, too, is "second-hand"; communist inventions are almost invariably blatant copies of Western inventions, with patent rights ignored.

As for Russia's alleged rate of economic growth, Mr. Keller makes it abundantly clear that even with the stolen intelligence, labor and machinery of three continents at its disposal, the Soviet economy is developing at a throttled pace; its growth rate, by generous estimate, is only half that of the United States.

Russia is, in fact, an insanely crippled economy; Mr. Keller calls it "a deformed cretin." Thanks to captive foreign scientists, Russia has produced Sputniks; thanks to her own, she cannot produce bread.

"Bolshevik-planned industry feeds on the industrial freedom of the rest of the world," declares Mr. Keller at the close of this remarkable book. "It would long ago have died a natural death, had it not been for the repeated injections of fresh life-blood which are still being pumped into it."

For 45 years, the U.S.S.R. has been pirating the *effects* of capitalist productiveness while systematically destroying the *cause* of this productiveness: man's free mind. But men cannot work under compulsion: the chained mind is neither inventive nor productive. Were the communist dictatorship to be deprived, today, of all capitalist supports, it would collapse once again under the weight of its own lethal contradiction.

For those Americans who are intent on fighting the suicidal idea that a dictatorship is more efficacious than a free economy—that Statism is "practicable"—Mr. Keller's book provides potent political ammunition. Clearly written, militantly factual, it is one of the most important documents on Russia to be published in our generation. It cannot be too strongly recommended.

Women and the Industrial Revolution *(from page 51)*

on work which was monotonous and exhausting, had the reactions which would satisfy a modern enthusiast for peasant arts." *(England in Transition;* London, 1947, p. 139.)

Finally, it was charged that factory work made women too concerned with material comforts at the expense of spiritual considerations.

The misery in which women lived before capitalism, might have made them cherish the New Testament injunction: "Love not the world, nor the things that are in the world." But the productive splendor of capitalism vanquished that view. Today, the foremost champions of that viewpoint are Professor Galbraith and the austerity-preachers behind the Iron Curtain.

OBJECTIVIST CALENDAR

■ Alan Greenspan's article, "Antitrust," a revised and expanded version of a paper delivered at the Antitrust Seminar of the National Association of Business Economists at Cleveland, Ohio, on September 25, 1961, has been published by NATHANIEL BRANDEN INSTITUTE and is available from THE OBJECTIVIST NEWSLETTER. Price: 50¢ (N.Y.C. residents add 2¢ sales tax).

■ Secretary-General Horace Turner of the International College of Surgeons ordered, on behalf of the I.C.S., 2700 reprints of Leonard Peikoff's "Doctors and the Police State," for distribution at the 13th Biennial International and 27th Annual North American Federation Conference of the I.C.S., held at the Waldorf-Astoria Hotel, Sept. 9-13, 1962. To date, over forty thousand reprints of this article have been purchased by medical associations and individual physicians.

■ Readers have inquired as to when *For the New Intellectual* will be available in paperback. New American Library informs us that the book will not be published in paperback until late 1963. Random House is now issuing a fifth printing of the hardcover edition.

Other activities: Daryn Kent, an NBI student, will play the title role in an off-Broadway production of *Medea* (a new version of the Jason-Medea myth), November 25 through December 1 at Caffe Cino, 31 Cornelia Street, New York, N. Y. Performances begin at 9 P.M. and 11 P.M.; on November 30 and December 1, an additional performance begins at 1 A.M.

Published monthly at 165 East 35th Street, New York 16, N. Y.
Subscription rate: in United States, its possessions, Canada and Mexico, $5 for one year; other countries, $6. Trial subscriptions: 4 months $2. 6 months $3.
Additional copies of this Newsletter: single copy 50¢ (coins, not stamps); 10 — 99 copies, 25¢ each plus postage (for first-class delivery add 1¢ per copy, for third-class delivery add 1/2¢ per copy); 100 or more copies, 15¢ each plus postage (same as above).
For change of address send old address and new address with zone number if any. Allow us two weeks to process new subscriptions and change of address.

Ayn Rand and Nathaniel Branden, Editors and Publishers
Barbara Branden, Managing Editor
Elayne Kalberman, Circulation Manager
PRINTED BY STANDARD PRESS & GRAPHICS, INC., NEW YORK CITY

THE OBJECTIVIST NEWSLETTER

Edited and Published by AYN RAND and NATHANIEL BRANDEN

VOL. 1 NO. 12   DECEMBER, 1962

CHECK YOUR PREMISES
By AYN RAND

The Monument Builders

What had once been an alleged ideal is now a ragged skeleton rattling like a scarecrow in the wind over the whole world, but men lack the courage to glance up and to discover the grinning skull under the bloody rags. That skeleton is socialism.

Fifty years ago, there might have been some excuse (though not justification) for the widespread belief that socialism is a political theory motivated by benevolence and aimed at the achievement of men's well-being. Today, that belief can no longer be regarded as an innocent error. Socialism has been tried on every continent of the globe. In the light of its results, it is time to question the motives of socialism's advocates.

The essential characteristic of socialism is the denial of individual property rights; under socialism, the right to property (which is the right of use and disposal) is vested in "society as a whole," *i.e.*, in the collective, with production and distribution controlled by the state, *i.e.*, by the government.

Socialism may be established by force, as in the Union of Soviet Socialist Republics—or by vote, as in Nazi (National Socialist) Germany. The degree of socialization may be total, as in Russia—or partial, as in England. Theoretically, the differences are superficial; practically, they are only a matter of time. The basic principle, in all cases, is the same.

The alleged goals of socialism were: the abolition of poverty, the achievement of general prosperity, progress, peace and human brotherhood. The results have been a terrifying failure—terrifying, that is, if one's motive is men's welfare.

Instead of prosperity, socialism has brought economic paralysis and/or collapse to every country that tried it. The degree of socialization has been the degree of disaster. The consequences have varied accordingly.

England, once the freest and proudest nation of Europe, has been reduced to the status of a second-rate power and is perishing slowly from hemophilia, losing the best of her economic blood: the middle class and the professions. The able, competent, productive, independent men are leaving by the thousands, migrating to Canada or the United States, in search of freedom. They are escaping from the reign of mediocrity, from the mawkish poorhouse where, having sold their rights in exchange for free dentures, the inmates are now whining that they'd rather be Red than dead.

In more fully socialized countries, *famine* was the start, the insignia announcing socialist rule—as in Soviet Russia, as in Red China, as in Cuba. In those countries, socialism reduced the people to the unspeakable poverty of the pre-industrial ages, to literal starvation, and has kept them on a stagnant level of misery.

No, it is not "just temporary," as socialism's apologists have been saying—for half a century. After forty-five years of government planning, Russia is still unable to solve the problem of feeding her population.

As far as superior productivity and speed of economic progress are concerned, the question of any comparisons between capitalism and socialism has been answered once and for all—for any honest person—by the present difference between West and East Berlin.

Instead of peace, socialism has introduced a new kind of gruesome lunacy into international relations—the "cold war," which is a state of chronic war with undeclared periods of peace between wantonly sudden invasions—with Russia seizing one-third of the globe, with socialist tribes and nations at one another's throats, with socialist India invading Goa, and communist China invading socialist India.

An eloquent sign of the moral corruption of our age is the callous complacency with which most of the socialists and their sympathizers, the "liberals," regard the atrocities perpetrated in socialistic countries and accept rule by terror as a way of life—while posturing as advocates of "human brotherhood." In the 1930's, they did protest against the atrocities of Nazi Germany. But, apparently, it was not an issue of principle, but only the protest of a rival gang fighting for the same territory—because we do not hear their voices any longer.

In the name of "humanity," they condone and accept the following: the abolition of all freedom and all rights, the expropriation of all property, executions without trial, torture chambers, slave-labor camps, the mass slaughter of countless millions in Soviet Russia—and the bloody horror of East Berlin, including the bullet-riddled bodies of fleeing children.

When one observes the nightmare of the desperate efforts made by hundreds of thousands of people struggling to escape from the socialized countries of Europe, to escape over barbed-wire fences, under machine-gun fire—one can no longer believe that socialism, in any of its forms, is motivated by benevolence and by the desire to achieve men's welfare.

No man of authentic benevolence could evade or ignore so great a horror on so vast a scale.

Socialism is not a movement of the people. It is a movement of the intellectuals, originated, led and controlled by the intellectuals, carried by them out of their stuffy ivory towers into those bloody fields of practice where they unite with their allies and executors: the thugs.

What, then, is the motive of such intellectuals? Power-lust. Power-lust—as a manifestation of helplessness, of self-loathing and of the desire for the unearned.

The desire for the unearned has two aspects: the unearned in matter and the unearned in spirit. (By "spirit" I mean: man's consciousness.) These two aspects are necessarily interrelated, but a man's desire may be focused predominantly on one or the other. The desire for the unearned in spirit is the more destructive of the two and the more corrupt. It is a desire for *unearned greatness;* it is expressed (but not defined) by the foggy murk of the term "*prestige.*"

The seekers of unearned material benefits are merely financial parasites, moochers, looters or criminals, who are too limited in number and in mind to be a threat to civilization, until and unless they are released and legalized by the seekers of unearned greatness.

Unearned greatness is so unreal, so neurotic a concept that the wretch who seeks it cannot identify it even to himself: to identify it, is to make it impossible. He needs the irrational, undefinable slogans of altruism and collectivism to give a semi-plausible form to his nameless urge and anchor it to reality—to support his own self-deception more than to deceive his victims. "The public," "the public interest," "service to the public" are the means, the tools, the swinging pendulums of the power-luster's self-hypnosis.

Since there is no such entity as "the public," since the public is merely a number of individuals, any claimed or implied conflict of "the public interest" with private interests means that the interests of some men are to be sacrificed to the interests and wishes of others. Since the concept is so conveniently undefinable, its use rests only on any given gang's ability to proclaim that "The public, *c'est moi*"—and to maintain the claim at the point of a gun.

(continued on page 55)

BOOKS

The Roosevelt Myth by John T. Flynn
Reviewed by BARBARA BRANDEN

In the years of his power and the years since his death, eulogies of Franklin D. Roosevelt and his alleged achievements grew and spread, mushrooming into an elaborate mythology. It is particularly the young people, children of the New Deal—too young during the 1930's and early 40's to have a first-hand knowledge of political events—who have been deluged by the massive propaganda effort, via textbooks, articles, lectures and speeches, conducted by those who share Roosevelt's ideology.

In the wake of the 1929 depression, many of the country's intellectual leaders were declaring that free enterprise had failed, that government must now take a more active part in directing the economic activities of the nation—that Americans must be given a new deal. Interventionist practices—the introduction of government controls into the economy—had been brought into American politics long before, and had been increasing since the turn of the century. But Roosevelt's administration was the first deliberately to embrace Interventionism as a ruling philosophy of government and as a consistent policy; *this* was the "New Deal" which Americans were given.

Who were the creators of this policy, and what motivated them? What was its effect on the American form of government and economic system? What legacy has it left to our day? Was it a *New* Deal—or something very old, with a long and bloody history in Europe?

In his carefully documented, comprehensive account of the New Deal years, John T. Flynn provides the answers to such questions, by providing the facts which the mythology of Roosevelt and his times was intended to conceal.

The New Deal—states the myth—saved a desperate country from total economic collapse, and pulled it out of the worst depression in history. What are the facts?

When Roosevelt was inaugurated in 1932, there were over eleven million persons unemployed, over sixteen million on relief, and a government debt of sixteen billion dollars. Roosevelt was elected on a platform which promised to end the deficits, curtail spending, abolish useless bureaus, assure a sound currency and reduce taxes.

In the first one hundred days of his administration, he produced a deficit larger than Hoover had produced in two years, and created a burgeoning network of new bureaus, boards, administrations, commissions and agencies. One of these agencies, dedicated to "fighting" the depression, was the Agricultural Adjustment Administration, headed by Henry Wallace. The AAA paid men $700,000,000 within two years to burn oats, kill millions of hogs and cut corn production—while the Department of Agriculture issued a bulletin "telling the nation that the great problem of our time was *our failure to produce enough food to provide the people with a mere subsistence diet*"—and while we imported oats, lard and corn from abroad.

By 1939, Roosevelt had spent more than seventeen billion dollars of borrowed public funds, he had gone off the gold standard, taxes had more than doubled—and there were over eleven million persons unemployed, over nineteen million on relief. The revival of business investment, essential to economic recovery, was nowhere in sight.

At a time when his carefully manufactured "public image" was that of a near-omniscient national savior, Roosevelt complained—after his cabinet informed him of the administration's failure to cope with the depression—"I am sick and tired of being told by Henry (Morgenthau) and everybody else what's the matter with the country while nobody suggests what I should do."

The New Deal—states the myth—was spearheaded and run by an intellectual, humanitarian elite, eminently competent to direct the course of the nation. With systematic detail,

---
* Published by The Devin-Adair Co., $4.50. Available from NBL BOOK SERVICE, INC., 165 East 35th St., New York 16, N.Y., for $3.90 (N.Y.C. residents add 3% sales tax; outside the U.S., add 15¢).

Flynn describes the hectic, carnival atmosphere that characterized the activities of this "elite":

—Roosevelt deciding that the price of gold should be raised to twenty-one cents, because twenty-one, being three times seven, is a "lucky number"—

—Harry Hopkins informing the President that the Civil Works Administration had "got four million at work but for God's sake don't ask me what they are doing"—

—Eleanor Roosevelt "gushing over the air for toilet preparations, mattresses and other products," for which gushing she received from $1,000 to $4,000 an appearance, and basking in the attentions of the young leaders of Communist front organizations, while entertaining them on the White House lawn—

—Henry Wallace, in search of his soul, sampling mystic cult after mystic cult, practicing vegetarianism and boomerang throwing, while directing the activities of the Department of Agriculture—

—Roosevelt admitting to Frances Perkins, his Secretary of Labor, that he knew nothing of economics and had never read a book on the subject—

—the Office of War Information dropping over North Africa such items as cakes of soap, coloring books, and pin buttons with a picture of Roosevelt colored to look like an Arab, in order to "sell" America to the North Africans—

—Leon Henderson, head of the Office of Price Administration, reporting that his work "was fun all the time even when I was mad."

"It was fun," comments Flynn, "pushing 130 million people around."

The New Deal—states the myth—secured our democratic system and restored its waning vitality. What are the facts?

Immediately upon his inauguration, Roosevelt reversed a central principle of his campaign: his pledge to resist the trend toward a powerful centralized government. The tentacles of government began to encircle business in a manner unprecedented in America.

Prominent New Dealers were extolling the fascist system of Mussolini. Roosevelt emulated that system through such means as the establishment of the National Recovery Administration. The NRA undertook to organize each industry into a trade association which would regulate production, prices, distribution, etc., under the supervision of the government.

Together, Flynn points out, the NRA and the AAA constituted "a plan to take the whole industrial and agricultural life of the country under the wing of government, organize it into vast farm and industrial cartels, as they were called in Germany, corporatives as they were called in Italy, and operate business and farms under plans made and carried out under the supervision of the government."

The New Deal tentacles began encircling Congress. Roosevelt removed from Congress, and placed in the hands of the Executive, a significant part of the former's constitutional prerogative of law-making. The countless bureaus created by Roosevelt's demand were soon vested with virtual law-making powers; there were so many of them, their duties so complex and varied, that it was impossible for Congress to police them all; gradually, directives and regulations began to issue forth from them "so that they actually became legislative and appropriating instrumentalities of a large area of government."

A further step toward concentrating power in the hands of the Executive was the policy of "blank-check legislation." Congress put billions of dollars into the President's hands, to be spent as and when he chose. "The great purse—which is the greatest of all the weapons in the hands of a free parliament to oppose the extravagance of a headstrong executive—had been handed over to him."

Some of Roosevelt's power grabs—such as his plan to pack the Supreme Court with dedicated New Dealers—were blocked by Congress. Some of them—such as the NRA—were ultimately declared unconstitutional. But the basic tenet of the New Deal, the underlying philosophy of *statism*, was unchallenged. The "New" Deal had brought to America that "modern" resurrection of medievalism and mercantilism which was practiced by such distinguished "liberals" as Bismarck, Hitler and Mussolini.

(continued on page 56)

INTELLECTUAL AMMUNITION DEPARTMENT

[*Subscribers are invited to send in the questions that they find themselves unable to answer in philosophical or political discussions. As many questions as space permits will be answered. No questions will be answered by mail.*]

■ **What are the respective obligations of parents to children, and children to parents?**

The key to understanding the nature of parental obligation lies in the moral principle that human beings must assume responsibility for the consequences of their actions.

A child is the responsibility of his parents, because (a) they brought him into existence, and (b) a child, by nature, cannot survive independently. (The fact that the parents might not have *desired* the child, in a given case, is irrelevant in this context; he is nevertheless the consequence of their chosen actions—a consequence that, as a possibility, was foreseeable.)

The essence of parental responsibility is: to equip the child for independent survival as an adult. This means, to provide for the child's physical and mental development and wellbeing: to feed, clothe and protect him; to raise him in a stable, intelligible, rational home environment, to equip him intellectually, training him to live as a rational being; to educate him to earn his livelihood (teaching him to hunt, for instance, in a primitive society; sending him to college, perhaps, in an advanced civilization).

When the child reaches the age of legal maturity and/or when he has been educated for a career, parental obligation ends. Thereafter, parents may still want to help their child, but he is no longer their responsibility.

A reasonable expectation that they will be able to afford the basic minimum necessary for food, clothing, shelter and education, should be the prerequisite of rational parents' decision to have children. However, parents are not morally at fault if, due to the father's illness or some other unforeseeable economic disaster, they are unable to provide for their child as they had expected to; in such a case, they are obliged simply to do the best they can.

If parents forgo other purchases in order to provide for their child's necessities, their action is *not* a sacrifice, and they have no moral right to regard it as such. One of the cruelest injustices that parents can perpetrate is to reproach a child for being a financial burden or for requiring time and attention, as if the child's legitimate needs were an imposition on them—to complain to the child of the "sacrifices" made for his sake, as if he were to feel apologetic or guilty—to state or imply that the child's mere existence is an unfair strain, as if the child had any choice in the matter.

Above the level of necessities, it is the standard of living of the parents that properly determines the standard of living of the child, appropriately scaled to his age and level of development. It is the responsibility of the child, as he grows older, to understand (if and when it is the case) that much of what he receives, above the ordinary, is an expression of his parents' benevolence and affection—and should be acknowledged as such in the form of reciprocated consideration and good will. If his parents are genuinely devoted to him, if they treat him justly and do their conscientious best to guide him, the appropriate response on the child's part is appreciation, affection, respect.

It is the child's further responsibility, as he grows older, to understand that his parents, too, have rights; that he may not make unlimited demands on them, as if their sole purpose were to live for and serve him; that he may not expect them to relinquish every other interest and value in order to work at satisfying any wish he may chance to conceive.

In accepting the basic necessities of food, clothing, etc., from his parents, the child does not incur an obligation to repay that support at some future date. The support is his by right. If, years later, when he is an adult, his parents encounter financial difficulty, it is not his *duty* to help them regardless of the cost to himself. There can be no *unchosen* obligations of this kind. If, however, they had treated him at all well and if he has maintained cordial relations with them, he properly would wish to help them to the extent that he reasonably and non-self-sacrificially can do so.

By virtue of their unique biological relationship, parents and child are normally predisposed to feel benevolence toward each other. Parents expect to feel love for their creation. A child wishes to feel love for his protectors. But this biological tie must never be "traded on"—that is, used as a moral blank check, as a substitute for personal value. Parents cannot demand love as a duty—"because we're your parents." A child cannot demand absolution of any irrationality—"because I'm your child." Emotions are not causeless. Love, respect, admiration have to be *earned*.

It is immensely valuable, from the point of view of the child's happiness and psychological development, that he find human beings whom he *can* love, respect and admire. One of the chief obligations of parents is to offer the child this opportunity. One of the chief obligations of the child— and of all human beings—is to recognize this opportunity if and when it exists.

—**NATHANIEL BRANDEN**

The Monument Builders (from page 53)

No such claim has ever been or can ever be maintained without the help of a gun—that is, without physical force. But, on the other hand, without that claim, gunmen would remain where they belong: in the underworld, and would not rise to the councils of state to rule the destinies of nations.

There are two ways of claiming that "The public, *c'est moi*": one is practiced by the crude material parasite who clamors for government handouts in the name of a "public" need and pockets what he has not earned; the other is practiced by his leader, the spiritual parasite, who derives his illusion of "greatness"—like a fence receiving stolen goods— from the power to dispose of that which he has not earned and from the mystic view of himself as the embodied voice of "the public."

Of the two, the material parasite is psychologically healthier and closer to reality: at least, he eats or wears his loot. But the only source of satisfaction open to the spiritual parasite, his only means to gain "prestige" (apart from giving orders and spreading terror), is the most wasteful, useless and meaningless activity of all: the building of public monuments.

Greatness is achieved by the productive effort of a man's mind in the pursuit of clearly defined, rational goals. But a delusion of grandeur can be served only by the switching, undefinable chimera of a public monument—which is presented as a munificent gift to the victims whose forced labor or extorted money had paid for it—which is dedicated to the service of all and none, owned by all and none, gaped at by all and enjoyed by none.

This is the ruler's only way to appease his obsession: "prestige." Prestige—in whose eyes? In anyone's. In the eyes of his tortured victims, of the beggars in the streets of his kingdom, of the bootlickers at his court, of the foreign tribes and their rulers beyond the borders. It is to impress all those eyes—the eyes of everyone and no one—that the blood of generations of subjects has been spilled and spent.

One may see, in certain Biblical movies, a graphic image of the meaning of public monument building: the building of the pyramids. Hordes of starved, ragged, emaciated men straining the last effort of their inadequate muscles at the inhuman task of pulling the ropes that drag large chunks of stone, straining like tortured beasts of burden under the whips of overseers, collapsing on the job and dying in the desert sands—that a dead Pharaoh might lie in an imposingly senseless structure and thus gain eternal "prestige" in the eyes of the unborn of future generations.

Temples and palaces are the only monuments left of mankind's early civilizations. They were created by the same means and at the same price—a price not justified by the fact that primitive peoples undoubtedly believed, while dying of starvation and exhaustion, that the "prestige" of their tribe, their rulers or their gods was of value to them somehow.

Rome fell, bankrupted by statist controls and taxation,

(continued on page 56)

The Monument Builders (from page 55)

while its emperors were building coliseums. Louis XIV of France taxed his people into a state of indigence, while he built the palace of Versailles, for his contemporary monarchs to envy and for modern tourists to visit. The marble-lined Moscow subway, built by the unpaid "volunteer" labor of Russian workers, including women, is a public monument, and so is the Czarist-like luxury of the champagne and caviar receptions at the Soviet embassies, which is needed—while the people stand in line for inadequate food rations—to "maintain the *prestige* of the Soviet Union."

The great distinction of the United States of America, up to the last few decades, was the modesty of its public monuments. Such monuments as did exist were genuine: they were not erected for "prestige," but were functional structures that had housed events of great historical importance. If you have seen the austere simplicity of Independence Hall, you have seen the difference between authentic grandeur and the pyramids of "public-spirited" prestige-seekers.

In America, human effort and material resources were not expropriated for public monuments and public projects, but were spent on the progress of the private, personal, individual well-being of individual citizens. America's greatness lies in the fact that her actual monuments *are not public*.

The skyline of New York is a monument of a splendor that no pyramids or palaces will ever equal or approach. But America's skyscrapers were not built by public funds nor for a public purpose: they were built by the energy, initiative and wealth of private individuals for personal profit. And, instead of impoverishing the people, these skyscrapers, as they rose higher and higher, kept raising the people's standard of living—including the inhabitants of the slums, who lead a life of luxury compared to the life of an ancient Egyptian slave or of a modern Soviet Socialist worker.

Such is the difference—both in theory and practice—between capitalism and socialism.

It is impossible to compute the human suffering, degradation, deprivation and horror that went to pay for a single, much-touted skyscraper of Moscow, or for the Soviet factories or mines or dams, or for any part of their loot-and-blood-supported "industrialization." What we do know, however, is that forty-five years is a long time: it is the span of two generations; we do know that, in the name of a promised abundance, two generations of human beings have lived and died in subhuman poverty; and we do know that today's advocates of socialism are not deterred by a fact of this kind.

Whatever motive they might assert, *benevolence* is one they have long since lost the right to claim.

The ideology of socialization (in a neo-fascist form) is now floating, by default, through the vacuum of our intellectual and cultural atmosphere. Observe how often we are asked for undefined "sacrifices" to unspecified purposes. Observe how often the present administration is invoking "the public interest." Observe what prominence the issue of international *"prestige"* has suddenly acquired and what grotesquely suicidal policies are justified by references to matters of "prestige." Observe that during the recent Cuban crisis—when the factual issue concerned nuclear missiles and nuclear war—our diplomats and commentators found it proper seriously to weigh such things as the "prestige," the personal feelings and the "face-saving" of the sundry socialist rulers involved.

There is no difference between the principles, policies and practical results of socialism—and those of any historical or prehistorical tyranny. Socialism is merely democratic absolute monarchy—that is, a system of absolutism without a fixed head, open to seizure of power by all comers, by any ruthless climber, opportunist, adventurer, demagogue or thug.

When you consider socialism, do not fool yourself about its nature. Remember that there is no such dichotomy as "human rights" versus "property rights." No human rights can exist without property rights. Since material goods are produced by the mind and effort of individual men, and are needed to sustain their lives, if the producer does not own the result of his effort, he does not own his life. To deny property rights means to turn men into property owned by the state. Whoever claims the "right" to "redistribute" the wealth produced by others is claiming the "right" to treat human beings as chattel.

When you consider the global devastation perpetrated by socialism, the sea of blood and the millions of victims, remember that they were sacrificed, not for "the good of mankind" nor for any "noble ideal," but for the festering vanity of some scared brute or some pretentious mediocrity who craved a mantle of unearned "greatness"—and that the monument to socialism is a pyramid of public factories, public theaters and public parks, erected on a foundation of human corpses, with the figure of the ruler posturing on top, beating his chest and screaming his plea for "prestige" to the starless void above him.

The Roosevelt Myth (from page 54)

Roosevelt followed their inspiration not only in his domestic policies, but also in his foreign policy: by resorting to war in order to "solve" his internal problems. He had found a solution to the depression in the spending of vast sums for National Defense.

"I say to you fathers and mothers and I will say it again and again and again. Your boys will not be sent into foreign wars." This was Roosevelt's promise to the American people in 1940. In 1941, states Flynn, he "exposed our fleet and our soldiers in Hawaii and the Philippine Islands to an attack which he knowingly invited."

It was Roosevelt—states the myth—who led us through a great war for democracy and freedom, and who saved the civilization of Europe.

Eleven billion dollars of American taxpayers' money was given to Russia during the war, in the form of Lend-Lease—dollars whose consequences, I might add, we can now see ninety miles from our shores. In secret agreements between Roosevelt and Stalin, sixteen European and Asiatic countries and over 725 million people were surrendered to Russian tyranny.

In his own economic convictions, John T. Flynn is not an advocate of *laissez-faire* capitalism; although he does not indicate his views clearly, he seems to sanction some form of mixed economy. But his ruthlessly factual presentation of the events of the New Deal period, and of the long-and-short-range consequences of its policies, make his book absorbing and eminently valuable.

When one is reading *The Roosevelt Myth*, one is heartened by a single thought: that by some near-miracle, America survived the New Deal. But then, when one reads today's newspapers and considers the present political scene, one realizes that that is the question still to be decided.

OBJECTIVIST CALENDAR

■ On December 16, Ayn Rand will give a talk at the Ford Hall Forum in Boston. Her subject: "The Fascist New Frontier." Time: 8 P.M. Place: Jordan Hall, 30 Gainsboro St. Open to the public.

■ Nathaniel Branden will address the Young Republican Club at C.C.N.Y. on December 20, 12:15 P.M., in Room 106, Wagner Hall, 133rd St. & St. Nicholas Terrace, New York City. His subject, "Collectivist Myths about Capitalism," is based on several of his articles in THE OBJECTIVIST NEWSLETTER. Open to the public.

Published monthly at 165 East 35th Street, New York 16, N. Y.
Subscription rate: in United States, its possessions, Canada and Mexico, $5 for one year; other countries, $6. Trial subscriptions: 4 months $2. 6 months $3.
Additional copies of this Newsletter: single copy 50¢ (coins, not stamps); 10 — 99 copies, 25¢ each plus postage (for first-class delivery add 1¢ per copy, for third-class delivery add ½¢ per copy); 100 or more copies, 15¢ each plus postage (same as above).
For change of address send old address and new address with zone number if any. Allow us two weeks to process new subscriptions and change of address.

Ayn Rand and Nathaniel Branden, Editors and Publishers
Barbara Branden, Managing Editor
Elayne Kalberman, Circulation Manager

PRINTED BY STANDARD PRESS & GRAPHICS, INC., NEW YORK CITY

THE OBJECTIVIST NEWSLETTER

Edited and Published by AYN RAND and NATHANIEL BRANDEN

VOL. 2 NO. 1   JANUARY, 1963

CHECK YOUR PREMISES
By AYN RAND
Collectivized Ethics

Certain questions, which one frequently hears, are not philosophical queries, but psychological confessions. This is particularly true in the field of ethics. It is especially in discussions of ethics that one must check one's premises (or remember them), and more: one must learn to check the premises of one's adversaries.

For instance, Objectivists will often hear a question such as: "What will be done about the poor or the handicapped in a free society?"

The altruist-collectivist premise, implicit in that question, is that men are "their brothers' keepers" and that the misfortune of some is a mortgage on others. The questioner is ignoring or evading the basic premises of Objectivist ethics and is attempting to switch the discussion onto his own collectivist base. Observe that he does not ask: *"Should* anything be done?" but: *"What* will be done?"—as if the collectivist premise had been tacitly accepted and all that remains is a discussion of the means to implement it.

Once, when Barbara Branden was asked by a student: "What will happen to the poor in an Objectivist society?"—she answered: "If *you* want to help them, you will not be stopped."

This is the essence of the whole issue and a perfect example of how one refuses to accept an adversary's premises as the basis of discussion.

Only individual men have the right to decide when or whether they wish to help others; society—as an organized political system—has no rights in the matter at all.

On the question of when and under what conditions it is morally proper for an individual to help others, I refer you to Galt's speech in *Atlas Shrugged*. What concerns us here is the collectivist premise of regarding this issue as political, as the problem or duty of "society as a whole."

Since nature does not guarantee automatic security, success and survival to any human being, it is only the dictatorial presumptuousness and the moral cannibalism of the altruist-collectivist code that permits a man to suppose (or idly to daydream) that *he* can somehow guarantee such security to some men at the expense of others.

If a man speculates on what "society" should do for the poor, he accepts thereby the collectivist premise that men's lives belong to society and that *he,* as a member of society, has the right to dispose of them, to set their goals or to plan the "distribution" of their efforts.

This is the psychological confession implied in such questions and in many issues of the same kind.

At best, it reveals a man's psycho-epistemological chaos; it reveals a fallacy which may be termed "the fallacy of the frozen abstraction" and which consists of substituting some one particular concrete for the wider abstract class to which it belongs—in this case, substituting a specific ethics (altruism) for the wider abstraction of "ethics." Thus, a man may reject the theory of altruism and assert that he has accepted a rational code—but, failing to integrate his ideas, he continues unthinkingly to approach ethical questions in terms established by altruism.

More often, however, that psychological confession reveals a deeper evil: it reveals the enormity of the extent to which altruism erodes men's capacity to grasp the concept of *rights* or the value of an individual life; it reveals a mind from which the reality of a human being has been wiped out.

Humility and presumptuousness are always two sides of the same premise, and always share the task of filling the space vacated by self-esteem in a collectivized mentality. The man who is willing to serve as the means to the ends of others, will necessarily regard others as the means to *his* ends. The more neurotic he is or the more conscientious in the practice of altruism (and these two aspects of his psychology will act reciprocally to reinforce each other), the more he will tend to devise schemes "for the good of mankind" or of "society" or of "the public" or of "future generations"—or of anything except actual human beings.

Hence the appalling recklessness with which men propose, discuss and accept "humanitarian" projects which are to be imposed by political means, that is, *by force,* on an unlimited number of human beings. If, according to collectivist caricatures, the greedy rich indulged in profligate material luxury, on the premise of "price no object"—then the social progress brought by today's collectivized mentalities consists of indulging in altruistic political planning, on the premise of "human lives no object."

The hallmark of such mentalities is the advocacy of some grand scale *public* goal, without regard to context, costs or means. *Out of context,* such a goal can usually be shown to be desirable; it has to be public, because the *costs* are not to be earned, but to be expropriated; and a dense patch of venomous fog has to shroud the issue of *means*—because the means are to be *human lives.*

"Medicare" is an example of such a project. "Isn't it desirable that the aged should have medical care in times of illness?" its advocates clamor. Considered out of context, the answer would be: yes, it is desirable. Who would have a reason to say no? And it is at this point that the mental processes of a collectivized brain are cut off; the rest is fog. Only the *desire* remains in his sight—it's the good, isn't it?—it's not for myself, it's for others, it's for the public, for a helpless, ailing public . . . The fog hides such facts as the enslavement and, therefore, the destruction of medical science, the regimentation and disintegration of all medical practice, and the sacrifice of the professional integrity, the freedom, the careers, the ambitions, the achievements, the happiness, the *lives* of the very men who are to provide that "desirable" goal—the doctors.

After centuries of civilization, most men—with the exception of criminals—have learned that the above mental attitude is neither practical nor moral in their private lives and may not be applied to the achievement of their private goals. There would be no controversy about the moral character of some young hoodlum who declared: "Isn't it desirable to have a yacht, to live in a penthouse and to drink champagne?"—and stubbornly refused to consider the fact that he had robbed a bank and killed two guards to achieve that "desirable" goal.

There is no moral difference between these two examples; the number of beneficiaries does not change the nature of the action, it merely increases the number of victims. In fact, the private hoodlum has a slight edge of moral superiority: he has no power to devastate an entire nation and *his* victims are not legally *disarmed.*

It is men's views of their public or *political* existence that the collectivized ethics of altruism has protected from the march of civilization and has preserved as a reservoir, a wildlife sanctuary, ruled by the mores of prehistorical savagery. If men have grasped some faint glimmer of respect for individual rights in their private dealings with one another, that

(continued on page 3)

Copyright © 1962 by The Objectivist Newsletter, Inc.

"The Stolen Concept"

By NATHANIEL BRANDEN

The distinguishing characteristic of twentieth-century philosophy is a resurgence of irrationalism—a revolt against reason.

Students in colleges today are assailed with pronouncements to the effect that factual certainty is impossible, that the contents of man's mind need bear no necessary relationship to the facts of reality, that the concept of "facts of reality" is an old-fashioned superstition, that reality is "mere appearance," that man can *know* nothing. It is with such intellectual equipment that their teachers arm them to deal with the problems of life.

In the prevalence of these claims, primordial mysticism is winning its ultimate triumph and (for the moment) is enjoying the last laugh—because men are now taught to accept, as the voice of *science,* the conclusion that man's reason is impotent to know the "real" world, and that the world knowable to reason is not "real."

In this article, I shall confine myself to the analysis of a single principle—a single fallacy—which is rampant in the writings of the neo-mystics and without which their doctrines could not be propagated.

We call it "the fallacy of the stolen concept."

To understand this fallacy, consider an example of it in the realm of politics: Proudhon's famous declaration that "All property is theft."

"Theft" is a concept that logically and genetically depends on the antecedent concept of "rightfully owned property"— and refers to the act of taking that property without the owner's consent. If no property is rightfully owned, that is, if nothing *is* property, there can be no such concept as "theft." Thus, the statement "All property is theft" has an internal contradiction: to use the concept "theft" while denying the validity of the concept "property," is to use "theft" as a concept to which one has no logical right—that is, as a *stolen concept.*

All of man's knowledge and all his concepts have a hierarchical structure. The foundation or ultimate base of this structure is man's sensory perceptions; these are the starting-point of his thinking. From these, man forms his first concepts and (ostensive) definitions—then goes on building the edifice of his knowledge by identifying and integrating new concepts on a wider and wider scale. It is a process of building one identification upon another—of deriving wider abstractions from previously known abstractions, or of breaking down wider abstractions into narrower classifications. Man's concepts are derived from and depend on earlier, more basic concepts which serve as their genetic roots. For example, the concept "parent" is presupposed by the concept "orphan"; if one had not grasped the former, one could not arrive at the latter, nor could the latter be meaningful.

The hierarchical nature of man's knowledge implies an important principle that must guide man's reasoning: When one uses concepts, one must recognize their genetic roots, one must recognize that which they logically depend on and presuppose.

Failure to observe this principle—as in "All property is theft"—constitutes the fallacy of the stolen concept.

Now let us examine a few of the more prevalent anti-reason tenets and observe how they rest on this fallacy.

Consider the laws of logic. In the Aristotelian school of thought, these laws are recognized as being abstract formulations of self-evident truths, truths implicit in man's first perceptions of reality, implicit in the very concept of existence, of being *qua* being; these laws acknowledge the fact that to be, is to be *something,* that a thing is itself. Among many contemporary philosophers, it is fashionable to contest this view—and to assert that the axioms of logic are "arbitrary" or "hypothetical."

To declare that the axioms of logic are "arbitrary" is to ignore the context which gives rise to such a concept as the "arbitrary." An arbitrary idea is one accepted by chance, caprice or whim; it stands in contradistinction to an idea accepted for logical reasons, *from which it is intended to be distinguished.* The existence of such a concept as an "arbitrary" idea is made *possible* only by the existence of logically necessary ideas; the former is not a primary; it is genetically dependent on the latter. To maintain that *logic* is "arbitrary" is to divest the concept "arbitrary" of meaning.

To declare that the axioms of logic are "hypothetical" (or merely "probable") is to be guilty of the same contradiction. The concept of the "hypothetical" (or the "probable") is not a primary; it acquires meaning only in contradistinction to the known, the certain, the logically established. Only when one knows something which is certain, can one arrive at the idea of that which is not; and only logic can separate the latter from the former.

"An axiom is a statement that identifies the base of knowledge and of any further statement pertaining to that knowledge, a statement necessarily contained in all others, whether any particular speaker chooses to identify it or not. An axiom is a proposition that defeats its opponents by the fact that they have to accept it and use it in the process of any attempt to deny it. Let the caveman who does not choose to accept the axiom of identity, try to present his theory without using the concept of identity or any concept derived from it . . ." (*Atlas Shrugged*)

When neo-mystics challenge the concept of "entity" and announce that, "naive" reason notwithstanding, all that exists is change and motion—("There is no *logical* impossibility in walking occurring as an isolated phenomenon, not forming part of any such series as we call a 'person,' " writes Bertrand Russell)—they are sweeping aside the fact that only the existence of entities makes the concepts "change" and "motion" *possible;* that "change" and "motion" presuppose *entities* which change and move; and that the man who proposes to dispense with the concept of "entity" loses his logical right to the concepts of "change" and "motion": having dropped their genetic root, he no longer has any way to make them meaningful and intelligible.

When neo-mystics assert that man perceives, not objective reality, but only an illusion or mere appearance—they evade the question of how one acquires such a concept as "illusion" or "appearance" without the existence of that which is *not* an illusion or mere appearance. If there were no *objective perceptions of reality,* from which "illusions" and "appearances" are intended to be distinguished, the latter concepts would be unintelligible.

When neo-mystics declare that man can never know the facts of reality, they are declaring that man is not *conscious.* If man cannot know the facts of reality, he cannot know *anything*—because there is nothing else to know. If he cannot perceive existence, he cannot perceive *anything*—because there is nothing else to perceive. To know nothing and to perceive nothing is to be *unconscious.* But to arrive—by a complex chain of "reasoning" and a long string of such concepts as "knowledge," "perceive," "evidence," "infer," "proof"—at the conclusion that one is not *conscious,* is scarcely epistemologically admissible.

"'We know that we know nothing,' they chatter, blanking out the fact that they are claiming knowledge—'There are no absolutes,' they chatter, blanking out the fact that they are uttering an absolute—'You cannot *prove* that you exist or that you're conscious,' they chatter, blanking out the fact that *proof* presupposes existence, consciousness and a complex chain of knowledge: the existence of something to know, of a consciousness able to know it, and of a knowledge that has learned to distinguish between such concepts as the proved and the unproved." (*Atlas Shrugged*)

Existence exists (that which is, is) and consciousness is conscious (man is able to perceive reality)—these are axioms at the base of all of man's knowledge and concepts. When neo-mystics contest or deny them, *all* of the concepts they use thereafter are stolen. They are entitled only to such concepts as they can derive from *non*-existence by means of *un*consciousness.

It is rational to ask: "*How* does man achieve knowledge?" It is not rational to ask: "*Can* man achieve knowledge?"— because the ability to ask the question presupposes a knowledge of man and of the nature of knowledge. It is rational to ask: "*What* exists?" It is not rational to ask: "Does *anything*

(continued on page 4)

INTELLECTUAL AMMUNITION DEPARTMENT

[*Subscribers are invited to send in the questions that they find themselves unable to answer in philosophical or political discussions. As many questions as space permits will be answered. No questions will be answered by mail.*]

■ **What is the Objectivist stand on capital punishment?**

In considering this issue, two separate aspects must be distinguished: the *moral* and the *legal*.

The moral question is: Does the man who commits willful murder, in the absence of any extenuating circumstances, *deserve* to have his own life forfeited? Here, the answer is unequivocally: *Yes*. Such a man deserves to die—not as "social revenge" or as an "example" to future potential murderers—but as the logical and just consequence of his own act: as an expression of the moral principle that no man may violate the rights of another with impunity, that no man may take the life of another and still retain the right to his own, that no man may profit from an evil of this kind or escape the consequences of having committed it.

However, the *legal question*: Should a legal system employ capital punishment?—is of a different order. There are grounds for debate—though *not* out of sympathy or pity for murderers.

If it were possible to be fully and irrevocably certain, beyond any possibility of error, that a man were guilty, then capital punishment for murder would be appropriate and just. But men are not infallible; juries make mistakes; *that* is the problem. There have been instances recorded where all the available evidence pointed overwhelmingly to a man's guilt, and the man was convicted, and then subsequently discovered to be innocent. It is the possibility of executing an *innocent* man that raises doubts about the legal advisability of capital punishment. It is preferable to sentence ten murderers to life imprisonment, rather than sentence one innocent man to death. If a man is unjustly imprisoned and subsequently proven to be innocent, some form of restitution is still possible; none is possible if he is dead.

The problem involved is that of establishing criteria of proof so rationally stringent as to forbid the possibility of convicting an innocent man.

It should be noted that the legal question of capital punishment is outside the sphere of philosophy proper; it is to be resolved by a special, separate discipline: the philosophy of law.

■ **Is there any validity to the claim that certain things are unknowable?**

The concept of the "unknowable" does not mean: that which is unknown at present. It means: that which, by its nature, *cannot* be known. To claim that a thing is unknowable entails a logical contradiction.

To claim that a thing is unknowable, one must first know that it exists—but then one already has knowledge of it, to that extent. Further, to pronounce a thing unknowable, one would have to know enough about it to justify one's pronouncement—but then the pronouncement and the justification would be in contradiction. If one makes such a pronouncement, or *any* pronouncement, *without* knowledge to justify it, then this is plain irrationalism.

The assertion that a thing is unknowable carries the necessary epistemological implication that the speaker is omniscient—that he has total knowledge of everything in the universe and, from his unique vantage point, is able to proclaim that certain things are inherently beyond the reach of man's knowledge and understanding.

The idea of the "unknowable" is indefensible—and its spokesmen can have no other purpose than to permit themselves flights into mysticism: to permit themselves beliefs for which they have no justification.

■ **What is the purpose of a definition?**

A definition, in identifying the specific meaning of a concept, isolates the facts of reality to which the concept refers and of which the concept is a mental integration.

Thus, the purpose of defining one's terms is to afford oneself the inestimable benefit of knowing what one is talking about.

—NATHANIEL BRANDEN

Collectivized Ethics (from page 1)

glimmer vanishes when they turn to public issues—and what leaps into the political arena is a caveman who can't conceive of any reason why the tribe may not bash in the skull of any individual if it so desires.

The distinguishing characteristic of such tribal mentality is: the axiomatic, the almost "instinctive" view of human life as the fodder, fuel or means for any public project.

The examples of such projects are innumerable: "Isn't it desirable to clean up the slums?" (dropping the context of what happens to those in the next income bracket)—"Isn't it desirable to have beautiful, planned cities, all of one harmonious style?" (dropping the context of *whose* choice of style is to be forced on the home-builders)—"Isn't it desirable to have an educated public?" (dropping the context of *who* will do the educating, *what* will be taught, and *what* will happen to dissenters)—"Isn't it desirable to liberate the artists, the writers, the composers from the burden of financial problems and leave them free to create?" (dropping the context of such questions as: *which* artists, writers and composers?—chosen by whom? —at whose expense?—at the expense of the artists, writers and composers who have no political pull and whose miserably precarious incomes will be taxed to "liberate" that privileged elite?)—"Isn't *science* desirable? Isn't it desirable for man to conquer space?"

And here we come to the essence of the unreality—the savage, blind, ghastly, bloody unreality—that motivates a collectivized soul.

The unanswered and unanswerable question in all of their "desirable" goals is: *To whom?* Desires and goals presuppose *beneficiaries*. Is science desirable? *To whom?* Not to the Soviet serfs who die of epidemics, filth, starvation, terror and firing squads—while some bright young men wave to them from space capsules circling over their human pigsties. And not to the American father who died of heart failure brought on by overwork, struggling to send his son through college—or to the boy who could not afford college—or to the couple killed in an automobile wreck, because they could not afford a new car—or to the mother who lost her child because she could not afford to send him to the best hospital—not to any of those people whose taxes pay for the support of our subsidized science and *public* research projects.

Science is a value only because it expands, enriches and protects man's life. It is not a value outside that context. Nothing is a value outside that context. And "man's life" means the single, specific, irreplaceable lives of individual men.

The discovery of new knowledge is a value to men only when and if they are free to use and enjoy the benefits of the previously known. New discoveries are a *potential* value to all men, but *not* at the price of sacrificing all of their *actual* values. A "progress" extended into infinity, which brings no benefit to anyone, is a monstrous absurdity. And so is the "conquest of space" by some men, when and if it is accomplished by expropriating the labor of other men who are left without means to acquire a pair of shoes.

Progress can come only out of men's surplus, that is: from the work of those men whose ability produces more than their personal consumption requires, those who are intellectually and financially able to venture out in pursuit of the new. Capitalism is the only system where such men are free to function and where progress is accompanied, not by forced privations, but by a constant rise in the general level of prosperity, of consumption and of enjoyment of life.

It is only to the frozen unreality inside a collectivized brain that human lives are interchangeable—and only such a brain can contemplate as "moral" or "desirable" the sacrifice of generations of living men for the alleged benefits which *public* science or *public* industry or *public* concerts will bring to the unborn.

(continued on page 4)

Collectivized Ethics *(from page 3)*

Soviet Russia is the clearest, but not the only, illustration of the achievements of collectivized mentalities. Two generations of Russians have lived, toiled and died in misery, waiting for the abundance promised by their rulers, who pleaded for patience and commanded austerity, while building public "industrialization" and killing public hope in five-year installments. At first, the people starved while waiting for electric generators and tractors; they are still starving, while waiting for atomic energy and interplanetary travel.

That waiting has no end—the unborn profiteers of that wholesale sacrificial slaughter will never be born—the sacrificial animals will merely breed new hordes of sacrificial animals—as the history of all tyrannies has demonstrated—while the unfocused eyes of a collectivized brain will stare on, undeterred, and speak of his vision of service to mankind, mixing interchangeably the corpses of the present with the ghosts of the future, but seeing no *men*.

Such is the status of reality in the soul of any Milquetoast who looks with envy at the achievements of industrialists and dreams of what beautiful public parks *he* could create if only everyone's lives, efforts and resources were turned over to *him*.

All public projects are mausoleums, not always in shape, but always in cost.

The next time you encounter one of those "public-spirited" dreamers who tells you rancorously that "some very desirable goals cannot be achieved without *everybody's* participation," tell him that if he cannot obtain everybody's *voluntary* participation, his goals had jolly well better remain unachieved—and that men's lives are not his to dispose of.

And, if you wish, give him the following example of the ideals he advocates. It is medically possible to take the corneas of a man's eyes immediately after his death and transplant them to the eyes of a living man who is blind, thus restoring his sight (in certain types of blindness). Now, according to collectivized ethics, this poses a social problem. Should we wait until a man's death to cut out his eyes, when other men need them? Should we regard everybody's eyes as public property and devise a fair method of distribution? Would you advocate cutting out a living man's eye and giving it to a blind man, so as to "equalize" them? No? Then don't struggle any further with questions about "public projects" in a free society. You know the answer. The principle is the same.

The Stolen Concept *(from page 2)*

exist?"—because the first thing one would have to evade is the existence of the question and of a being who is there to ask it. It is rational to ask: "*How* do the senses enable man to perceive reality?" It is not rational to ask: "*Do* the senses enable man to perceive reality?"—because if they do not, by what means did the speaker acquire his knowledge of the senses, of perception, of man and of reality?

One of the most grotesque instances of the stolen concept fallacy may be observed in the prevalent claim—made by neomystics and old-fashioned mystics alike—that the acceptance of reason rests ultimately on "an act of faith."

Reason is the faculty that identifies and integrates the material provided by the senses. Faith is the acceptance of ideas or allegations without sensory evidence or rational demonstration. "Faith in reason" is a contradiction in terms. "Faith" is a concept that possesses meaning only *in contradistinction* to reason. The concept of "faith" cannot *antecede* reason, it cannot provide the grounds for the acceptance of reason—it is the revolt *against* reason.

One will search in vain for a single instance of an attack on reason, on the senses, on the ontological status of the laws of logic, on the cognitive efficacy of man's mind, that does not rest on the fallacy of the stolen concept.

The fallacy consists of *the act of using a concept while ignoring, contradicting or denying the validity of the concepts on which it logically and genetically depends.*

This fallacy must be recognized and repudiated by all thinkers, if truth and reality are their goal.

In the absence of such recognition, the gates are left open to the most lethal form of mysticism—the mysticism that postures as "science."

Who are the neo-mystics' victims?

Any college student who enrolls in philosophy courses, eagerly seeking a rational, comprehensive view of man and existence—and who is led to surrender the conviction that his mind can have any efficacy whatever; or who, at best, gives up philosophy in disgust and contempt, concludes that it is a con game for pretentious intellectual role-players, and thus accepts the tragically mistaken belief that philosophy is of no practical importance to man's life on earth.

OBJECTIVIST CALENDAR

■ Nathaniel Branden will address the Kappa Nu Kappa Fraternity Forum at Wesleyan University (Middletown, Connecticut) on Sunday, January 6, 1963, 3 P.M. His subject: "Reason and Individualism in the Philosophy of Ayn Rand." Open to the public.

■ Nathaniel Branden will speak on the same subject to the Philosophy Club of Hollins College (Hollins, Virginia) on Friday, January 11, 8:15 P.M. Open to the public.

■ Ayn Rand will address the Ayn Rand Literary Society of New York University on Tuesday, February 12, 3 P.M. Her topic: "America's Persecuted Minority: Big Business." Place: Loeb Student Center, Washington Square, New York City. Open to the public.

■ Ayn Rand will deliver lecture #17, "The Esthetics of Literature," in the NATHANIEL BRANDEN INSTITUTE course on "Basic Principles of Objectivism." She will give the lecture in Philadelphia on Monday, February 18, 7:30 P.M., at the Drake Hotel, 1512 Spruce St.; and in New York City on Tuesday, February 19, 7:30 P.M., at the Hotel Roosevelt, 45th St. & Madison Ave. Visitors' admission: $3.50. This is a new lecture, and henceforth will be given regularly by Miss Rand.

■ NBI's Tape Transcription Division is now offering courses in sixteen cities in the United States and Canada.

In addition to those previously announced, Tape Transcription courses on "Basic Principles of Objectivism" began in Miami on December 7; in Clear, Alaska, on December 13; and in Tucson on December 10.

The Tape Transcription Division is currently making arrangements to offer courses in the following additional cities: Milwaukee; Denver; Amarillo; Atlanta; Valparaiso, Indiana. When starting dates are determined, they will be announced here.

■ The next New York course on "Basic Principles of Objectivism" will be given at the Hotel Roosevelt, at 7:30 P.M. on twenty consecutive Mondays, beginning February 11. Registration is now open.

■ In response to requests, a limited quantity of back issues of THE OBJECTIVIST NEWSLETTER has been reprinted, and is now available to subscribers. The cost of a single issue is 50¢. For quantity rates and postage costs, see the box at the bottom of this page.

Published monthly at 165 East 35th Street, New York 16, N. Y.
Subscription rate: in United States, its possessions, Canada and Mexico, $5 for one year; other countries, $6. Trial subscriptions: 4 months $2. 6 months $3.
Additional copies of this Newsletter: single copy 50¢ (coins, not stamps); 10 — 99 copies, 25¢ each plus postage (for first-class delivery add 1¢ per copy, for third-class delivery add ½¢ per copy); 100 or more copies, 15¢ each plus postage (same as above).
For change of address send old address and new address with zone number if any. Allow us three weeks to process new subscriptions and change of address.

Ayn Rand and Nathaniel Branden, Editors and Publishers
Barbara Branden, Managing Editor
Elayne Kalberman, Circulation Manager

PRINTED BY STANDARD PRESS & GRAPHICS, INC., NEW YORK CITY

THE OBJECTIVIST NEWSLETTER

Edited and Published by AYN RAND and NATHANIEL BRANDEN

VOL. 2 NO. 2   FEBRUARY, 1963

CHECK YOUR PREMISES
By AYN RAND

The Ethics of Emergencies

The psychological results of altruism may be observed in the fact that a great many people approach the subject of ethics by asking such questions as: "Should one risk one's life to help a man who is: a) drowning, b) trapped in a fire, c) stepping in front of a speeding truck, d) hanging by his fingernails over an abyss?"

Consider the implications of that approach. If a man accepts the ethics of altruism, he suffers the following consequences (in proportion to the degree of his acceptance):

1. Lack of self-esteem—since his first concern in the realm of values is not how to live his life, but how to sacrifice it.

2. Lack of respect for others—since he regards mankind as a herd of doomed beggars crying for someone's help.

3. A nightmare view of existence—since he believes that men are trapped in a "malevolent universe" where disasters are the constant and primary concern of their lives.

4. And, in fact, a lethargic indifference to ethics, a hopelessly cynical amorality—since his questions involve situations which he is not likely ever to encounter, which bear no relation to the actual problems of his own life and thus leave him to live without any moral principles whatever.

By elevating the issue of helping others into the central and primary issue of ethics, altruism has destroyed the concept of any authentic benevolence or good will among men. It has indoctrinated men with the idea that to value another human being is an act of selflessness, thus implying that a man can have no personal interest in others—that *to value* another means *to sacrifice* oneself—that any love, respect or admiration a man may feel for others is not and cannot be a source of his own enjoyment, but is a threat to his existence, a sacrificial blank check signed over to his loved ones.

The men who accept that dichotomy but choose its other side, the ultimate products of altruism's dehumanizing influence, are those psychopaths who do not challenge altruism's basic premise, but proclaim their rebellion against self-sacrifice by announcing that they are totally indifferent to anything living and would not lift a finger to help a man or a dog left mangled by a hit-and-run driver (who is usually one of their own kind).

Most men do not accept or practice either side of altruism's viciously false dichotomy, but its result is a total intellectual chaos on the issue of proper human relationships and on such questions as the nature, purpose or extent of the help one may give to others. Today, a great many well-meaning, reasonable men do not know how to identify or conceptualize the moral principles that motivate their love, affection or good will, and can find no guidance in the field of ethics, which is dominated by the stale platitudes of altruism.

On the question of why man is not a sacrificial animal and why help to others is not his moral duty, I refer you to *Atlas Shrugged*. This present discussion is concerned with the principles by which one identifies and evaluates the instances involving a man's *non-sacrificial* help to others.

"Sacrifice" is the surrender of a greater value for the sake of a lesser one or of a non-value. Thus, altruism gauges a man's virtue by the degree to which he surrenders, renounces or betrays his values (since help to a stranger or an enemy is regarded as more virtuous, less "selfish," than help to those one loves). The rational principle of conduct is the exact opposite: always act in accordance with the hierarchy of your values, and never sacrifice a greater value to a lesser one.

This applies to all choices, including one's actions toward other men. It requires that one possess a defined hierarchy of *rational* values (values chosen and validated by a rational standard). Without such a hierarchy, neither rational conduct nor considered value-judgments nor moral choices are possible.

Love and friendship are profoundly personal, selfish values: love is an expression and assertion of self-esteem, a response to one's own values in the person of another. One gains a profoundly personal, selfish joy from the mere existence of the person one loves. It is one's own personal, selfish happiness that one seeks, earns and derives from love.

A "selfless," "disinterested" love is a contradiction in terms: it means that one is indifferent to that which one values.

Concern for the welfare of those one loves is a rational part of one's selfish interests. If a man who is passionately in love with his wife spends a fortune to cure her of a dangerous illness, it would be absurd to claim that he does it as a "sacrifice" for *her* sake, not his own, and that it makes no difference to *him*, personally and selfishly, whether she lives or dies.

Any action that a man undertakes for the benefit of those he loves is *not a sacrifice* if, in the hierarchy of his values, in the total context of the choices open to him, it achieves that which is of greatest *personal* (and rational) importance to *him*. In the above example, his wife's survival is of greater value to the husband than anything else that his money could buy, it is of greatest importance to his own happiness and, therefore, his action is *not* a sacrifice.

But suppose he let her die in order to spend his money on saving the lives of ten other women, none of whom meant anything to him—as the ethics of altruism would require. *That* would be a sacrifice. Here the difference between Objectivism and altruism can be seen most clearly: if sacrifice is the moral principle of action, then that husband *should* sacrifice his wife for the sake of ten other women. What distinguishes the wife from the ten others? Nothing but her value to the husband who has to make the choice—nothing but the fact that *his* happiness requires her survival.

The Objectivist ethics would tell him: your highest moral purpose is the achievement of your own happiness, your money is yours, use it to save your wife, *that* is your moral right and your rational, moral choice.

Consider the soul of the altruistic moralist who would be prepared to tell that husband the opposite. (And then ask yourself whether altruism is motivated by benevolence.)

The proper method of judging when or whether one should help another person is by reference to one's own rational self-interest and one's own hierarchy of values: the time, money or effort one gives or the risk one takes should be proportionate to the value of the person in relation to one's own happiness.

To illustrate this on the altruists' favorite example: the issue of saving a drowning person. If the person to be saved is a stranger, it is morally proper to save him only when the danger to one's own life is minimal; when the danger is great, it would be immoral to attempt it: only a lack of self-esteem could permit one to value one's life no higher than that of any random stranger. (And, conversely, if one is drowning, one cannot expect a stranger to risk his life for one's sake, remembering that one's life cannot be as valuable to him as his own.)

If the person to be saved is not a stranger, then the risk one should be willing to take is greater in proportion to the greatness of that person's value to oneself. If it is the man or woman one loves, then one can be willing to give one's own life to save him or her—for the selfish reason that life without the loved person could be unbearable.

Conversely, if a man is able to swim and to save his drowning wife, but becomes panicky, gives in to an unjustified, irrational fear and lets her drown, then spends his life in loneliness and misery—one would not call him "selfish"; one would condemn him morally for his treason to himself and to his own values, that is: his failure to fight for the preservation of a value crucial to his own happiness. Remember that values are that which one acts to gain and/or keep, and that one's own happiness has to be achieved by one's own effort. Since one's own happiness is the moral purpose of one's life, the man who fails to achieve it because of his own default, because of his failure to fight for it, is morally guilty.

The virtue involved in helping those one loves is not "selflessness" or "sacrifice," but *integrity*. Integrity is loyalty to one's convictions and values; it is the policy of acting in accordance with one's values, of expressing, upholding and translating them into practical reality. If a man professes to love a woman, yet his actions are indifferent, inimical or damaging to her, it is his lack of integrity that makes him immoral.

The same principle applies to relationships among friends. If one's friend is in trouble, one should act to help him by whatever non-sacrificial means are appropriate. For instance, if one's friend is starving, it is not a sacrifice, but an act of integrity to give him money for food rather than buy some insignificant gadget for oneself, because his welfare is important in the scale of one's personal values. If the gadget means more than the friend's suffering, one had no business pretending to be his friend.

The practical implementation of friendship, affection and love consists of incorporating the welfare (the *rational* welfare) of the person involved into one's own hierarchy of values, then acting accordingly.

But this is a reward which men have to earn by means of their virtues and which one cannot grant to mere acquaintances or strangers.

What, then, should one properly grant to strangers? The generalized respect and good will which one should grant to a human being in the name of the potential value he represents—until and unless he forfeits it.

A rational man does not forget that *life* is the source of all values and, as such, a common bond among living beings (as against inanimate matter), that other men are potentially able to achieve the same virtues as his own and thus be of enormous value to him. This does not mean that he regards human lives as interchangeable with his own. He recognizes the fact that his own life is the *source*, not only of all his values, but of *his capacity to value*. Therefore, the value he grants to others is only a consequence, an extension, a secondary projection of the primary value which is himself.

"The respect and good will that men of self-esteem feel toward other human beings is profoundly egoistic; they feel, in effect: 'Other men are of value because they are of the same species as myself.' In revering living entities, they are revering their *own* life. This is the psychological base of any emotion of sympathy and any feeling of 'species solidarity.'" ("Benevolence versus Altruism" by Nathaniel Branden, THE OBJECTIVIST NEWSLETTER, July, 1962.)

Since men are born *tabula rasa*, both cognitively and morally, a rational man regards strangers as innocent until proved guilty, and grants them that initial good will in the name of their human potential. After that, he judges them according to the moral character they have actualized. If he finds them guilty of major evils, his good will is replaced by contempt and moral condemnation. (If one values human life, one cannot value its destroyers.) If he finds them to be virtuous, he grants them personal, individual value and appreciation, in proportion to their virtues.

It is on the ground of that generalized good will and respect for the value of human life that one helps strangers in an emergency—*and only in an emergency*.

It is important to differentiate between the rules of conduct in an emergency situation and the rules of conduct in the normal conditions of human existence. This does not mean a double standard of morality: the standard and the basic principles remain the same, but their application to either case requires precise definitions.

An emergency is an unchosen, unexpected event, limited in time, that creates conditions under which human survival is impossible—such as a flood, an earthquake, a fire, a shipwreck. In an emergency situation, men's primary goal is to combat the disaster, escape the danger and restore normal conditions (to reach dry land, to put out the fire, etc.).

By "normal" conditions I mean *metaphysically* normal, normal in the nature of things, and appropriate to human existence. Men can live on land, but not in water or in a raging fire. Since men are not omnipotent, it is metaphysically possible for unforeseeable disasters to strike them, in which case their only task is to return to those conditions under which their lives can continue. By its nature, an emergency situation is temporary; if it were to last, men would perish.

It is only in emergency situations that one should volunteer to help strangers, if it is in one's power. For instance, a man who values human life and is caught in a shipwreck, should help to save his fellow passengers (though not at the expense of his own life). But this does not mean that after they all reach shore, he should devote his efforts to saving his fellow passengers from poverty, ignorance, neurosis or whatever other troubles they might have. Nor does it mean that he should spend his life sailing the seven seas in search of shipwreck victims to save.

Or to take an example that can occur in everyday life: suppose one hears that the man next door is ill and penniless. Illness and poverty are not metaphysical emergencies, they are part of the normal risks of existence; but since the man is temporarily helpless, one may bring him food and medicine, *if* one can afford it (as an act of good will, not of duty) or one may raise a fund among the neighbors to help him out. But this does not mean that one must support him from then on, nor that one must spend one's life looking for starving men to help.

In the normal conditions of existence, man has to choose his goals, project them in time, pursue them and achieve them by his own effort. He cannot do it if his goals are at the mercy of and must be sacrificed to any misfortune happening to others. He cannot live his life by the guidance of rules applicable only to conditions under which human survival is impossible.

The principle that one should help men in an emergency cannot be extended to regard all human suffering as an emergency and to turn the misfortune of some into a first mortgage on the lives of others.

Poverty, ignorance, illness and other problems of that kind are not metaphysical emergencies. By the *metaphysical* nature of man and of existence, man has to maintain his life by his own effort; the values he needs—such as wealth or knowledge—are not given to him automatically, as a gift of nature, but have to be discovered and achieved by his own thinking and work. One's sole obligation toward others, in this respect, is to maintain a social system that leaves men free to achieve, to gain and to keep their values.

Every code of ethics is based on and derived from a metaphysics, that is: from a theory about the fundamental nature of the universe in which man lives and acts. The altruist ethics is based on a "malevolent universe" metaphysics, on the theory that man, by his very nature, is helpless and doomed—that success, happiness, achievement are impossible to him—that emergencies, disasters, catastrophes are the norm of his life and that his primary goal is to combat them.

As the simplest empirical refutation of that metaphysics—as evidence of the fact that the material universe is not inimical to man and that catastrophes are the exception, not the rule of his existence—observe the fortunes made by insurance companies.

Observe also that the advocates of altruism are unable to base their ethics on any facts of men's normal existence and that they always offer "lifeboat" situations as examples from which to derive the rules of moral conduct. ("What should you do if you and another man are in a lifeboat that can carry only one?" etc.)

(continued on page 8)

BOOKS

*Reason and Analysis** by Brand Blanshard
Reviewed by NATHANIEL BRANDEN

"Both reason as a source of knowledge and rationality as a practical ideal are today under attack. Indeed there has been no period in the past two thousand years when they have undergone a bombardment so varied, so competent, so massive and sustained as in the last half-century."

This statement is made by Brand Blanshard in the opening pages of *Reason and Analysis*. There is only one word in the statement that I would challenge: the word "competent." And I offer, in support of my disagreement, Professor Blanshard's own brilliant critique: when one has finished reading his analysis of the irrationalist movement in contemporary philosophy, "competent" is a word that scarcely seems applicable to those whose doctrines he so lucidly and devastatingly exposes.

His critique is directed specifically at "logical positivism and the linguistic philosophies that have succeeded it." (For a critical analysis of pragmatist epistemology, see his *The Nature of Thought*, Vol. 1, Macmillan, 1939.) He traces the development of positivism and linguistic analysis from their roots in Hume, sets forth their main contentions, and then proceeds to subject their arguments and conclusions to a scrutiny that is dispassionate, courteous, meticulous—and deadly.

As he observes, "the task of the expositor is a baffling one. He has no sooner, with some effort, mastered a particular position and matured his estimate of it than he is told that this position was abandoned some years or some weeks ago, and that he is therefore flogging dead horses." The movement "has been kaleidoscopic in the quickness of its changes, which have followed each other at such a pace that the writing and printing of books could not keep up with it and it has had to register its changes in a bewildering profusion of notes and articles."

These difficulties notwithstanding, one of the most impressive features of *Reason and Analysis* is the clarity of its exposition; Professor Blanshard exhibits a remarkable ability to impart intelligibility to positions not conspicuous for that attribute.

His historical account is superb. He discusses: the early positivism of Mach, with Mach's assertion that all scientific laws must merely describe relationships among our percepts, with the implicit dismissal of conceptual explanation as mythology or "metaphysics"—the conventionalism of Poincaré, with its announcement that the laws and definitions of mathematics say nothing about the real world, but merely express "conventions" adopted on the grounds of "convenience" —Russell's *Principia Mathematica* and the theory of logical atomism, with the banishment of *necessity* from logic and the assertion that no fact of reality necessarily entails any other—the verifiability theory of meaning of the Vienna Circle, which seeks to divorce "meaning" from consciousness or concepts, and which has, at various stages, dismissed as "meaningless" statements about the self, the minds of other men, the past, the future, electrons, moral values, and the nature of reality—the declaration of the logical positivists that no proposition known to be necessarily true refers to the facts of reality and no proposition that refers to the facts of reality can be known with certainty to be true—the linguistic analysis of Wittgenstein, with its pronouncement that the task of philosophy is not to solve philosophical problems, but to "*dis*solve" them, by "teasing out" the confusions in philosophers' use of language. And thus Professor Blanshard traces the main steps of modern philosophy's descent into a nightmare blend of neo-mysticism and unutterable triviality.

One of the most interesting chapters in his book is devoted to the verifiability theory of meaning. This is the much-touted doctrine that promised to bring an unprecedented precision and clarity to philosophical discourse. Unfortunately, the theory itself—as Professor Blanshard shows—is a masterpiece of unclarity and ambiguity. Cast in its most general form, it asserts that the meaning of any factual statement is the observations that would verify it. But what exactly does this mean? That, as it turns out, is the problem. There is not one "verifiability theory of meaning," but many—as attempt after attempt has been made, and reformulation after reformulation has been offered, in the vain effort to endow the theory with consistency, intelligibility, applicability, value or meaning. Professor Blanshard leads the reader through the main stages of these attempts, quietly dissecting and unmasking version after version, with the patience of a saint and the skill of a surgeon.

In *For the New Intellectual*, Ayn Rand observes that the dominant trend of modern philosophy has been a concerted attack on man's *conceptual* faculty. While Professor Blanshard does not draw this conclusion explicitly, his analysis provides ample evidence in support of Miss Rand's statement. From his presentation, one can see in what manner the central thrust of the verifiability doctrine, in all its stages, is in the direction of by-passing the conceptual form of cognition and reducing man's consciousness to the animal level of sensory perception.

One of the clearest instances of the subjectivism of positivist epistemology is its assertion that the laws of logic and mathematics are merely "conventions"—arbitrary rules of discourse, of the use of terms—that indicate nothing about the facts of reality. "The principles of logic and mathematics," A. J. Ayer informs us, "are true universally simply because we never allow them to be anything else." (I cannot refrain from observing that if a man were to make such a statement using the first person *singular* pronoun, his problem would surely be regarded as psychiatric; it is curious to note what men permit themselves when hiding behind the *plural* pronoun.)

Professor Blanshard analyzes the conventionalist or linguistic theory of logic and mathematics in exhaustive detail, exposing the almost endless series of contradictions which it engenders.

"To deny the law [of contradiction] means to say that it is false *rather than* true, that its being false excludes its being true. But this is the very thing that is supposedly denied. One cannot deny the law of contradiction without presupposing its validity in the act of denying it."

"We accept the law and must accept it, because 'nature has said it.' If we hold that a thing cannot at once have a property and not have it, it is because we *see* that it cannot. The law of contradiction is at once the statement of a logical requirement and the statement of an ontological truth."

In reversing the actual order of things, and declaring that our view of reality reflects our use of language, rather than vice versa, the positivists, Professor Blanshard observes, "are telling us in effect that the only reason why the Rocky Mountains do not appear in the Great Lakes is that the map forbids them to."

One of the dominant themes in twentieth-century philosophy is a profound hostility to metaphysics, to any comprehensive view of reality or any inquiry concerning the nature of things. Philosophers are conducting an impassioned crusade for myopia as the highest intellectual virtue—for the progressive shrinking of man's vision and the progressive divorcement of thought from reality. This trend has reached its apogee in that curious movement known as linguistic analysis.

The animus toward any sort of general principles extends to the linguistic analysts' view of their own activity. Nothing is more futile than the attempt to extract from a linguistic analyst an intelligble statement of what linguistic analysis *is*. To quote Professor Blanshard: The attempt to define this movement "is complicated . . . by the notorious reluctance of these philosophers to talk about what they are doing in general terms; if they are asked what philosophy means for them, they are apt to say, 'it is the sort of thing I am doing now,' and return to their work."

It is safe to say, however, that one of the chief contentions

---

* Published by Open Court Pub. Co., $8.00. Available from NBL BOOK SERVICE, INC., 165 East 35th St., New York 16, N. Y., for $6.25 (N.Y.C. residents add 3% sales tax; outside the U.S., add 15¢).

(continued on page 8)

The Ethics of Emergencies (from page 6)

The fact is that men do not live in lifeboats—and that a lifeboat is not the place on which to base one's metaphysics.

The moral purpose of a man's life is the achievement of his own happiness. This does not mean that he is indifferent to all men, that human life is of no value to him and that he has no reason to help others in an emergency. But it *does* mean that he does not subordinate his life to the welfare of others, that he does not sacrifice himself to their needs, that the relief of their suffering is not his primary concern, that any help he gives is an *exception*, not a rule, an act of generosity, not of moral duty, that it is *marginal* and *incidental*—as disasters are marginal and incidental in the course of human existence—and that *values*, not disasters, are the goal, the first concern and the motive power of his life.

Reason and Analysis (from page 7)

of the linguistic school is that earlier philosophers had misconceived the task of philosophy: they had falsely imagined that their task was to discover basic truths about existence, about man and the universe, about how man should conduct his life. The *actual* mission of philosophy, linguistic analysts tell us, is to explicate the usage of *words*, to identify the sort of "work" words do in "ordinary language," and, by analyzing deviations from this usage, to cure those "mental cramps" which the uninitiated think of as philosophical problems. The concept of philosophical problems as "mental cramps" is Wittgenstein's; what he proposes to offer, in place of philosophical answers, is *linguistic therapy*.

(In reading the various doctrines and versions of linguistic analysis, one is irresistibly reminded of a statement made by Hugh Akston in *Atlas Shrugged*: "People would not employ a plumber who'd attempt to prove his professional excellence by asserting that there's no such thing as plumbing—but, apparently, the same standards of caution are not considered necessary in regard to philosophy.")

Professor Blanshard writes: "The discussion of words in philosophy is prefatory and preparatory only. How expressions are used is not a philosophical problem. How they ought to be used *is* a philosophical problem, but not primarily one about words at all, but about the character and relations of the objects talked about."

In bringing to light the underlying irrationalism of the analytic movement, Professor Blanshard may be said to have administered some admirable philosophical "therapy" of his own, but not of the linguistic variety; his treatment is an unqualified success: the patient died—but philosophy survived.

It is necessary to mention that many of Professor Blanshard's own philosophical premises are deeply at variance with those of Objectivism. He is a representative of the Absolute Idealist school of thought, and there is much in his book with which an Objectivist cannot agree: for instance, his views concerning the nature of universals and the relation of thought to reality.

One may take issue with many of Professor Blanshard's own philosophical views, however, and still appreciate the enormous value of his book. No honest man can read it through to the end and retain any serious regard for the philosophical schools at which his critique is directed. Since these schools are currently dominant, it is scarcely to be expected that the book will receive the justice it deserves from the philosophical profession. The real beneficiaries of the book, and its most significant readers, will be the younger generation, the college students who are to be the writers, the teachers, the intellectuals of tomorrow. Struggling in the dense jungle of today's epistemological nihilism, they will find in *Reason and Analysis* a powerful weapon to help them cut their way through to a clearer view of the proper nature of philosophy.

OBJECTIVIST CALENDAR

■ On Monday, January 28, Ayn Rand will speak on "The Fascist New Frontier" over an educational radio network. Time: 7 P.M. to 8 P.M. The talk will be broadcast by the following FM radio-stations: WGBH in Boston; WHYY in Philadelphia; WAMU in Washington, D. C.; WFCR in Amherst, Mass.; WAMC in Albany, N. Y. In New York City, the talk will be broadcast on February 7, 2:30 P.M. on WRVR. In other cities, consult your local radio stations.

■ On February 6, Ayn Rand will address a meeting of the Ocean County Medical Society, Ocean County, N. J. Not open to the public.

■ On Monday, February 11, Nathaniel Branden will deliver the opening lecture of the course on "Basic Principles of Objectivism." Single admission: $3.50; High School and College Students: $2.75. Time: 7:30 P.M. Place: Hotel Roosevelt, 45th St. & Madison Ave., New York City.

Mr. Branden is introducing a considerable amount of new material into this twenty-lecture course; several lectures have been almost entirely re-written. A revised schedule of the lecture topics will be available at the February 11 lecture.

■ Dr. Allan Blumenthal, a psychiatrist in private practice in New York City, has joined the staff of NATHANIEL BRANDEN INSTITUTE as an associate lecturer. He will deliver lecture #16, "The Psychology of Sex," in the "Basic Principles of Objectivism" course in Philadelphia on Monday, February 11, 7:30 P.M., at the Drake Hotel, 1512 Spruce St. Visitors' admission: $3.50.

Nathaniel Branden and Dr. Blumenthal are currently preparing a new course of lectures that will deal with the application of the principles of Objectivist psychology to the nature and treatment of neurosis.

■ On Wednesday, February 13, Nathaniel Branden will address The Ayn Rand Club of Brooklyn College. His subject: "Reason and Self-Interest in the Objectivist Ethics." Time: 12:15 P.M. Place: 4200 Boylan Hall, Brooklyn College. Open to the public.

■ On Monday, February 18, Robert A. Hessen, a member of the staff of NBI and a contributor to this Newsletter, will address The Capitalist Club of Brooklyn College. His subject: "Collectivist Myths about the Industrial Revolution." Time: 12 noon. Place: 3146 Boylan Hall, Brooklyn College. Open to the public.

■ On Tuesday, February 26, Nathaniel Branden will address the Eleutherian Society at the University of Pennsylvania in Philadelphia. His subject: "Reason and Self-Interest in the Objectivist Ethics." Time: 7:30 P.M. Place: Benjamin Franklin Room, Houston Hall, University of Pennsylvania.

■ On Wednesday, February 27, Ayn Rand will address the Ayn Rand Club of Brooklyn College. Her subject: "The Fascist New Frontier." Time: 12 noon. Place: Whitman Auditorium, Brooklyn College. Open to the public.

■ Nathaniel Branden will deliver a new lecture (#19) in his current course on "Basic Principles of Objectivism." The lecture is entitled "The Neurosis of the Intellectual"; it will replace the previously scheduled "Objectivism and the History of Western Philosophy." Mr. Branden will give the lecture in Philadelphia on Monday, March 4, 7:30 P.M., at the Drake Hotel; and in New York City on Tuesday, March 5, 7:30 P.M., at the Hotel Roosevelt. Visitors' admission: $3.50.

A Reminder:

On Tuesday, February 12, 3 P.M., Ayn Rand will address the Ayn Rand Literary Society of New York University.

Ayn Rand will deliver lecture #17, "The Esthetics of Literature," in the current NBI courses: in Philadelphia on February 18, in New York City on February 19.

Published monthly at 165 East 35th Street, New York 16, N. Y.
Subscription rate: in United States, its possessions, Canada and Mexico, $5 for one year; other countries, $6.
Additional copies of this Newsletter: single copy 50¢ (coins, not stamps); 10 — 99 copies, 25¢ each plus postage (for first-class delivery add 1¢ per copy, for third-class delivery add ½¢ per copy); 100 or more copies, 15¢ each plus postage (same as above).
For change of address send old address and new address with zone number if any. Allow us three weeks to process new subscriptions and change of address.

Ayn Rand and Nathaniel Branden, Editors and Publishers
Barbara Branden, Managing Editor
Elayne Kalberman, Circulation Manager
PRINTED BY STANDARD PRESS & GRAPHICS, INC., NEW YORK CITY

THE OBJECTIVIST NEWSLETTER

Edited and Published by AYN RAND and NATHANIEL BRANDEN

VOL. 2 NO. 3   MARCH, 1963

Mental Health versus Mysticism and Self-Sacrifice

By NATHANIEL BRANDEN

The standard of mental health—of biologically appropriate mental functioning—is the same as that of physical health: man's survival and well-being. A mind is healthy to the extent that its method of functioning is such as to provide man with the control over reality that the support and furtherance of his life require.

The hallmark of this control is self-esteem. Self-esteem is the consequence, expression and reward of a mind fully committed to reason. Reason, the faculty that identifies and integrates the material provided by the senses, is man's basic tool of survival. Commitment to reason is commitment to the maintenance of a full intellectual focus, to the constant expansion of one's understanding and knowledge, to the principle that one's actions must be consistent with one's convictions, that one must never attempt to fake reality or place any consideration above reality, that one must never permit oneself contradictions—that one must never attempt to subvert or sabotage the proper function of consciousness.

The proper function of consciousness is: perception, cognition, and the control of action.

An unobstructed consciousness, an integrated consciousness, a thinking consciousness, is a *healthy* consciousness. A blocked consciousness, an evading consciousness, a consciousness torn by conflict and divided against itself, a consciousness disintegrated by fear or immobilized by depression, a consciousness dissociated from reality, is an *unhealthy* consciousness.

In order to deal with reality successfully—to pursue and achieve the values which his life requires—man needs self-esteem: he needs to be confident of his efficacy and worth.

Anxiety and guilt, the antipodes of self-esteem and the insignia of mental illness, are the disintegrators of thought, the distorters of values and the paralyzers of action.

When a man of self-esteem chooses his values and sets his goals, when he projects the long-range purposes that will unify and guide his actions—it is like a bridge thrown to the future, across which his life will pass, a bridge supported by the conviction that his mind is competent to think, to judge, to value, and that *he* is worthy of enjoying values.

This sense of control over reality is not the result of special skills, ability or knowledge. It is not dependent on *particular* successes or failures. It reflects one's *fundamental* relationship to reality, one's conviction of *fundamental* efficacy and worthiness. It reflects the certainty that, in essence and in principle, one is *right* for reality. Self-esteem is a *metaphysical* estimate.

It is this psychological state that traditional morality makes impossible, to the extent that a man accepts it.

Neither mysticism nor the creed of self-sacrifice is compatible with mental health or self-esteem. These doctrines are destructive existentially *and psychologically*.

(1) The maintenance of his life and the achievement of self-esteem require of man the fullest exercise of his reason—but morality, men are taught, rests on and requires *faith*.

Faith is the commitment of one's consciousness to beliefs for which one has no sensory evidence or rational proof.

When a man rejects reason as his standard of judgment, only one alternative standard remains to him: his feelings. A mystic is a man who treats his feelings as tools of cognition. Faith is the equation of *feeling* with *knowledge*.

To practice the "virtue" of faith, one must be willing to suspend one's sight and one's judgment; one must be willing to live with the unintelligible, with that which cannot be conceptualized or integrated into the rest of one's knowledge, and to induce a trance-like illusion of understanding. One must be willing to repress one's critical faculty and hold it as one's guilt; one must be willing to drown any questions that rise in protest—to strangle any thrust of reason convulsively seeking to assert its proper function as the protector of one's life and cognitive integrity.

Remember that all of man's knowledge and all his concepts have a hierarchical structure. The foundation and starting-point of man's thinking are his sensory perceptions; on this base, man forms his first concepts, then goes on building the edifice of his knowledge by identifying and integrating new concepts on a wider and wider scale. If man's thinking is to be valid, this process must be guided by *logic*, "the art of non-contradictory identification"—and any new concept man forms must be integrated without contradiction into the hierarchical structure of his knowledge. *To introduce into one's consciousness any idea that cannot be so integrated, an idea not derived from reality, not validated by a process of reason, not subject to rational examination or judgment—and worse: an idea that clashes with the rest of one's concepts and understanding of reality—is to sabotage the integrative function of consciousness, to undercut the rest of one's convictions and kill one's capacity to be certain of anything.* This is the meaning of John Galt's statement in *Atlas Shrugged* that "the alleged short-cut to knowledge, which is faith, is only a short-circuit destroying the mind."

There is no greater self-delusion than to imagine that one can render unto reason that which is reason's and unto faith that which is faith's. Faith cannot be circumscribed or delimited; to surrender one's consciousness by an inch, is to surrender one's consciousness in total. Either reason is an absolute to a mind or it is not—and if it is not, there is no place to draw the line, no principle by which to draw it, no barrier faith cannot cross, no part of one's life faith cannot invade: one remains rational until and unless one's *feelings* decree otherwise.

Faith is a malignancy that no system can tolerate with impunity; and the man who succumbs to it, will call on it in precisely those issues where he needs his reason most. When one turns from reason to faith, when one rejects the absolutism of reality, one undercuts the absolutism of one's consciousness—and one's mind becomes an organ one cannot trust any longer. It becomes what the mystics claim it to be: a tool of distortion.

(2) Man's need of self-esteem entails the need for a sense of control over reality—but no control is possible in a universe which, by one's own concession, contains the supernatural, the miraculous and the causeless, a universe in which one is at the mercy of ghosts and demons, in which one must deal, not with the *unknown*, but with the *unknowable;* no control is possible if man proposes, but a ghost disposes; no control is possible if the universe is a haunted house.

(3) His life and self-esteem require that the object and concern of man's consciousness be reality and this earth—but morality, men are taught, consists of scorning this earth and the world available to sensory perception, and of contemplating, instead, a "different" and "higher" reality, a realm inaccessible to reason and incommunicable in language, but attainable by revelation, by special dialectical processes, by that superior state of intellectual lucidity known to Zen-Buddhists as "No-Mind," or by death.

There is only one reality—the reality knowable to reason. And if man does not choose to perceive it, there is nothing

Copyright © 1963 by The Objectivist Newsletter, Inc.

else for him to perceive; if it is not of this world that he is conscious, then he is not conscious at all.

The sole result of the mystic projection of "another" reality, is that it incapacitates man psychologically for this one. It was not by contemplating the transcendental, the ineffable, the undefinable—it was not by contemplating the non-existent—that man lifted himself from the cave and transformed the material world to make a human existence possible on earth.

If it is a virtue to renounce one's mind, but a sin to use it; if it is a virtue to approximate the mental state of a schizophrenic, but a sin to be in intellectual focus; if it is a virtue to denounce this earth, but a sin to make it livable; if it is a virtue to mortify the flesh, but a sin to work and act; if it is a virtue to despise life, but a sin to sustain and enjoy it—then no self-esteem or control or efficacy are possible to man, *nothing* is possible to him but the guilt and terror of a wretch caught in a nightmare universe, a universe created by some metaphysical sadist who has cast man into a maze where the door marked "virtue" leads to self-destruction and the door marked "efficacy" leads to self-damnation.

(4) His life and self-esteem require that man take pride in his power to think, pride in his power to live—but morality, men are taught, holds pride, and specifically intellectual pride, as the gravest of sins. Virtue begins, men are taught, with humility: with the recognition of the helplessness, the smallness, the impotence of one's mind.

Is man omniscient?—demand the mystics. Is he infallible? Then how dare he challenge the word of God, or of God's representatives, and set himself up as the judge of—anything?

Intellectual pride is not—as the mystics preposterously imply it to be—a pretense at omniscience or infallibility. On the contrary, precisely because man must *struggle* for knowledge, precisely because the pursuit of knowledge requires an *effort,* the men who assume this responsibility properly feel pride.

Sometimes, colloquially, pride is taken to mean a pretense at accomplishments one has not in fact achieved. But the braggart, the boaster, the man who affects virtues he does not possess, is not proud; he has merely chosen the most humiliating way to reveal his humility.

Pride is one's response to one's power to achieve values, the pleasure one takes in one's own efficacy. And it is this that mystics hold as evil.

But if doubt, not confidence, is man's proper moral state; if self-distrust, not self-reliance, is the proof of his virtue; if fear, not self-esteem, is the mark of perfection; if guilt, not pride, is his goal—then mental illness is a moral ideal, the neurotics and psychotics are the highest exponents of morality, and the thinkers, the achievers, are the sinners, those who are too corrupt and too arrogant to seek virtue and psychological well-being through the belief that they are unfit to exist.

Humility is, of necessity, the basic virtue of a mystical morality: it is the only virtue possible to men who have renounced the mind.

Pride has to be earned; it is the reward of effort and achievement; but to gain the virtue of humility, one has only to abstain from thinking—nothing else is demanded—and one will feel humble quickly enough.

(5) His life and self-esteem require of man loyalty to his values, loyalty to his mind and its judgments, loyalty to his life—but the essence of morality, men are taught, consists of self-sacrifice: the sacrifice of one's mind to some higher authority, and the sacrifice of one's values to whomever may claim to require it.

It is not necessary, in this context, to analyze the almost countless evils entailed by the precept of self-sacrifice. Its irrationality and destructiveness have been thoroughly exposed in *Atlas Shrugged*. But there are two aspects of the issue that are especially pertinent to the subject of mental health.

The first is the fact that *self*-sacrifice means—and can only mean—*mind*-sacrifice.

A sacrifice, it is necessary to remember, means the surrender of a higher value in favor of a lower value or of a non-value. If one gives up that which one does not value in order to obtain that which one does value—or if one gives up a lesser value in order to obtain a greater one—this is not a sacrifice, but a *gain*.

Remember further that all of a man's values exist in a hierarchy; he values some things more than others; and, to the extent that he is rational, the hierarchical order of his values is rational: that is, he values things in proportion to their importance in serving his life and well-being. That which is inimical to his life and well-being, that which is inimical to his nature and needs as a living being, he *dis*-values.

Conversely, one of the characteristics of mental illness is a distorted value-structure; the neurotic does not value things according to their objective merit, in relation to his nature and needs; he frequently values the very things that will lead him to self-destruction. Judged by *objective* standards, he is engaged in a chronic process of self-sacrifice.

But if sacrifice is a virtue, it is not the neurotic but the rational man who must be "cured." He must learn to do violence to his own rational judgment—to reverse the order of his value-hierarchy—to surrender that which his mind has chosen as the good—to turn against and invalidate his own consciousness.

Do mystics declare that all they demand of man is that he sacrifice his *happiness*? To sacrifice one's happiness is to sacrifice one's desires; to sacrifice one's desires is to sacrifice one's values; to sacrifice one's values is to sacrifice one's judgment; to sacrifice one's judgment is to sacrifice one's mind—and it is nothing less than this that the creed of self-sacrifice aims at and demands.

The root of selfishness is man's right—and need—to act on his own judgment. If his judgment is to be an object of sacrifice—what sort of efficacy, control, freedom from conflict, or serenity of spirit will be possible to man?

The second aspect that is pertinent here, involves not only the creed of self-sacrifice but *all* the foregoing tenets of traditional morality.

An irrational morality, a morality set in opposition to man's nature, to the facts of reality and to the requirements of man's survival, necessarily forces men to accept the belief that there is an inevitable clash between the moral and the practical—that they must choose either to be virtuous or to be happy, to be idealistic or to be successful, but that they cannot be both. This view establishes a disastrous conflict on the deepest level of man's being, a lethal dichotomy that tears man apart: it forces him to choose between making himself *able* to live and making himself *worthy* of living. Yet self-esteem and mental health require that he achieve *both*.

If man holds life on earth as the good, if he judges his values by the standard of that which is proper to the existence of a rational being, then there is no clash between the requirements of survival and of morality—no clash between making himself able to live and making himself worthy of living; he achieves the second by achieving the first. But there *is* a clash, if man holds the renunciation of this earth as the good, the renunciation of life, of mind, of happiness, of self. Under an anti-life morality, man makes himself worthy of living to the extent that he makes himself unable to live—and to the extent that he makes himself able to live, he makes himself unworthy of living.

The answer given by many defenders of traditional morality is: "Oh, but people don't have to go to extremes!"—meaning: "We don't expect people to be *fully* moral. We expect them to smuggle *some* self-interest into their lives. We recognize that people have to live, after all."

The defense, then, of this code of morality is that few people will be suicidal enough to attempt to practice it consistently. *Hypocrisy* is to be man's protector against his professed moral convictions. What does *that* do to his self-esteem?

And what of the victims who are insufficiently hypocritical?

What of the child who withdraws in terror into an autistic universe because he cannot cope with the ravings of parents who tell him that he is guilty by nature, that his body is evil, that thinking is sinful, that question-asking is blasphemous, that doubting is depravity, and that he must obey the orders of a supernatural ghost because, if he doesn't, he will burn forever in hell?

Or the daughter who collapses in guilt over the sin of not wanting to devote her life to caring for the ailing father who has given her cause to feel only hatred?

Or the adolescent who flees into homosexuality because he has been taught that sex is evil and that women are to be worshipped, but not desired?

Or the businessman who suffers an anxiety attack because, after years of being urged to be thrifty and industrious, he has finally committed the sin of succeeding, and is now told that it shall be easier for a camel to pass through the eye of a needle than for a rich man to enter the kingdom of heaven?

Or the neurotic who, in hopeless despair, gives up the attempt to solve his problems because he has always heard it preached that this earth is a realm of misery, futility and doom, where no happiness or fulfillment is possible to man?

If the advocates of these doctrines bear a grave moral responsibility, there is a group who, perhaps, bears a graver responsibility still: the psychologists and psychiatrists who see the human wreckage of these doctrines, but who remain silent and do not protest—who declare that philosophical and moral issues do not concern them, that science cannot pronounce value-judgments—who shrug off their professional obligations with the assertion that a *rational* code of morality is impossible, and, by their silence, lend their sanction to spiritual murder.

"How **not** to fight against Socialized Medicine"

By AYN RAND

(This is a condensed version of a talk given by Miss Rand on February 6 at a meeting of the Ocean County Medical Society, Ocean County, N. J. The membership of that society includes Dr. J. Bruce Henriksen and his associates who, in May, 1962, signed his resolution declaring that they refused to participate in the care of patients under the provisions of the King-Anderson bill or similar legislation.)

I am happy to have this opportunity to express my admiration for Dr. Henriksen and the group of doctors who signed his resolution.

Dr. Henriksen and his group took a heroic stand. The storm of vicious denunciations unleashed against them at the time, showed that they had delivered a dangerous blow to the welfare-statists. More than any other single factor, it was Dr. Henriksen's group that demonstrated to the public the real nature of the issue, prevented the passage of the King-Anderson bill and saved this country from socialized medicine —so far.

Their action was an eloquent example of the fact that only a strong, uncompromising stand—a stand of *moral* self-confidence, on clear-cut, consistent principles—can win.

But there are grave danger signs that the medical profession as a whole—like every other group today—will ignore that example and pursue the usual modern policy of caution and compromise. Such a policy is worse than futile: it assists and promotes the victory of one's own enemies. The battle is not over. The King-Anderson bill will be brought up again, and if the doctors are defeated, they will be defeated by their own hand, or rather: by their own mind.

I want, therefore, to make certain suggestions to the medical profession—on the subject of how *not* to fight against socialized medicine.

The majority of people in this country—and in the world —do not want to adopt socialism; yet it is growing. It is growing because its victims concede its basic moral premises. Without challenging these premises, one cannot win.

The strategy of the Kennedy administration, and of all welfare-statists, consists of attempts to make people accept certain intellectual "package-deals," without letting them identify and differentiate the various elements—and equivocations—involved. The deadliest of such "package-deals" is the attempt to make people accept the collectivist-altruist principle of self-immolation under the guise of mere kindness, generosity or charity. It is done by hammering into people's minds the idea that *need* supersedes all rights—that the need of some men is a first mortgage on the lives of others— and that everything should be sacrificed to the undefined, undefinable grab bag known as *"the public interest."*

Doctors have no chance to win if they concede that idea and help their enemies to propagate it.

Yet the ideological policy of most spokesmen for the medical profession—such as the A.M.A.—is as permeated by the collectivist-altruist spirit as the pronouncements of the welfare-statists. The doctors' spokesmen declare, in net effect, that selfless service to their patients is the doctors' only goal, that concern for the needy is their only motive, and that "the public interest" is the only justification of their battle.

The sole difference is this: the voices of the welfare-statists are brazenly, self-righteously overbearing—while the voices of the doctors' spokesmen are guiltily, evasively apologetic.

Whom can one expect the people to believe and to follow?

People can always sense guilt, insincerity, hypocrisy. The lack of a morally righteous tone, the absence of moral certainty, have a disastrous effect on an audience—an effect which is not improved by the triviality of the arguments over political minutiae. And the terrible thing is that the doctors' spokesmen give an impression of guilty evasiveness while *the right is on their side*. They do it by being afraid to assert their rights.

They are afraid of it because they do not believe that they possess any rights—because they have conceded the enemy's premises—because they have no moral base, no intellectual guide lines, no ideology, no defense.

Consider, for instance, the outcome of the Canadian doctors' struggle in Saskatchewan. The doctors had gone on strike against the full-scale socialized medicine instituted by the provincial government. They won the battle—and lost the war; in exchange for a few superficial concessions, they surrendered the principle for which they had been fighting: to permit no socialized medicine in the Western hemisphere.

They surrendered, even though the overwhelming sympathy and support of the Canadian people were on their side (except for *the intellectuals* and the labor unions). They were defeated, not by the power of the socialists, but by the gaping holes in their own ideological armor.

They had been fighting, properly, in the name of individual rights, against the enslavement of medicine by totalitarian-statist controls. Then, under the pressure of the usual intellectual lynching, under the hysterical, collectivist charges of "anti-social selfishness and greed," they made a shocking change in their stand. Declaring, in effect, that their rebellion was not directed against socialized medicine as such, but against the high-handed, arbitrary manner in which the government had put it over, their spokesmen began to argue that the government plan did not represent "the will of the people." The ideological kiss of death was a statement by Dr. Dalgleish, the strikers' leader, who declared that if a *plebiscite* were taken and the people voted for it, the doctors would accept socialized medicine.

Could they deserve to win, after that? They could not and did not.

Consider the full meaning of Dr. Dalgleish's statement. It meant the total repudiation of individual rights and the acceptance of unlimited majority rule, of the collectivist doctrine that the people's vote may dispose of an individual in any way it pleases. Instead of a battle for the integrity of a doctor's professional judgment and practice, it became a battle over *who* should violate his integrity. Instead of a battle against the enslavement of medicine, it became a battle over *who* should enslave it. Instead of a battle for freedom, it became a battle over a choice of masters. Instead of a moral crusade, it became a petty quarrel over political technicalities.

This led to the ludicrous spectacle of the alleged individualists arguing for democratic mob-rule, and the socialists righteously upholding the parliamentary form of government.

Those who doubt the power of ideas, should note the fact that the doctors' surrender took place five days after Dr. Dalgleish's statement.

The text of the agreement reached between the doctors and the government, contained the following horrifying sentence: "The doctors fear that if the government becomes their only source of income they are in danger of becoming servants of the state and not *servants of their patients.*" (Italics mine.)

A more abject statement of self-abnegation could not be hoped for or extorted by the most extreme collectivist.

No self-respecting labor union would declare that its members are *"servants"* of their employers. It took so-called "conservatives" to declare that professional men—and of so responsible, so demanding, so unusually skilled a profession as medicine—are the "servants" of their patients or of anyone who pays them.

The concept of "service" has been turned into a collectivist "package-deal" by means of a crude equivocation and a cruder evasion. In the language of economics, the word "service" means *work* offered for trade on a free market, to be paid for by those who choose to buy it. In a free society, men deal with one another by voluntary, uncoerced exchange, by mutual consent to mutual profit, each man pursuing his own rational self-interest, none sacrificing himself or others; and all values—whether goods or services—are *traded*, not given away.

This is the opposite of what the word "service" means in the language of altruist ethics: to an altruist, "service" means unrewarded, self-sacrificial, unilateral *giving*, while receiving nothing in return. It is this sort of selfless "service" to "society" that collectivists demand of all men.

One of the grotesque phenomena of the twentieth century is the fact that the "package-deal" of "service" is most vociferously propagated by the "conservatives." Intellectually bankrupt, possessing no political philosophy, no direction, no goal, but clinging desperately to the ethics of altruism, such "conservatives" rest their case on a cheap equivocation: they proclaim that "service" to others (to one's customers or clients or patients or "consumers" in general) is the motive power and the moral justification of a free society—and evade the question of whether such "services" are or are not to be paid for.

But if "service" to the "consumers" is our primary goal, why should these masters pay us or grant us any rights? Why shouldn't they dictate the terms and conditions of our work?

If socialized medicine comes to the United States, it is such "conservatives" that the doctors would have to thank for it, as well as their own spokesmen who recklessly play with an intellectual poison of that kind.

Doctors are *not* the servants of their patients. No free man is a "servant" of those he deals with. Doctors are *traders*, like everyone else in a free society—and they should bear that title proudly, considering the crucial importance of the services they offer.

The pursuit of his own productive career is—and, morally, should be—the primary goal of a doctor's work, as it is the primary goal of any self-respecting, productive man. But there is no clash of interests among rational men in a free society, and there is no clash of interests between doctors and patients. In pursuing his own career, a doctor does have to do his best for the welfare of his patients. This relationship, however, cannot be reversed: one cannot sacrifice the doctor's interests, desires and freedom to whatever the patients (or their politicians) might deem to be their own "welfare."

Many doctors know this, but are afraid to assert their rights, because they dare not challenge the morality of altruism, neither in the public's mind nor in their own. Others are collectivists at heart, who believe that socialized medicine is morally right and who feel guilty while opposing it. Still others are so cynically embittered that they believe that the whole country consists of fools or parasites eager to get something for nothing—that morality and justice are futile—that ideas are impotent—that the cause of freedom is doomed—and that the doctors' only chance lies in borrowing the enemy's arguments and gaining a brief span of borrowed time.

This last is usually regarded as the "practical" attitude for "conservatives."

But nobody is as naive as a cynic, and nothing is as impractical as the attempt to win by conceding the enemy's premises. How many defeats and disasters will collectivism's victims have to witness before they become convinced of it?

In any issue, it is the most consistent of the adversaries who wins. One cannot win on the enemy's premises, because *he* is then the more consistent, and all of one's efforts serve only to propagate *his* principles.

Most people in this country are not moochers who seek the unearned, not even today. But if all their intellectual leaders *and the doctors themselves* tell them that doctors are only their "selfless servants," they will feel justified in expecting and demanding unearned services.

When a politician tells them that they are entitled to the unearned, they are wise enough to suspect his motives; but when the proposed victim, the doctor, says it too, they feel that socialization is safe.

If you are afraid of people's irrationality, you will not protect yourself by assuring them that their irrational notions are right.

The advocates of "Medicare" admit that their purpose is not help to the needy, the sick or the aged. Their purpose is to spare people "the embarrassment" of a means test—that is, to establish the principle and precedent that some people are entitled to the unrewarded services of others, not as charity, but as a *right*.

Can you placate, conciliate, temporize or compromise with a principle of that kind?

As doctors, what would you say if someone told you that you must not try to *cure* a deadly disease—you must give it *some* chance—you must reach a "compromise" with cancer or with coronary thrombosis or with leprosy? You would answer that it is a battle of life or death. The same is true of your political battle.

Would you follow the advice of someone who told you that you must fight tuberculosis by confining the treatment to its symptoms—that you must treat the cough, the high temperature, the loss of weight—but must refuse to consider or to touch its cause, the germs in the patient's lungs, in order not to antagonize the germs?

Do not adopt such a course in politics. The principle—and the consequences—are the same. It *is* a battle of life or death.

OBJECTIVIST CALENDAR

■ On Wednesday, March 6, Nathaniel Branden will address the Student Union of Cornell University. His subject: "Reason and Individualism in the Philosophy of Ayn Rand." Time: 8 P.M. Open to the public. Admission free. For further information, contact Mr. Michael Wachter, Willard Straight Hall, Program Dept., Cornell University, Ithaca, N. Y.

■ On Monday, March 11, Alan Greenspan will address the Society of Capitalists of Brooklyn College. His subject: "Anti-Antitrust." Time: 12:15 P.M. Place: 3146 Boylan Hall, Brooklyn College. Open to the public. Admission free.

■ On Wednesday, March 20, Nathaniel Branden will address the Ayn Rand Club of Brooklyn College. His subject: "The Literary Method of Ayn Rand." Time: 12 noon. Place: 4200 Boylan Hall, Brooklyn College. Open to the public. Admission free.

George Reisman's article, "The Revolt Against Affluence: Galbraith's Neo-Feudalism," which was originally published in *Human Events*, has been reprinted in pamphlet form by NATHANIEL BRANDEN INSTITUTE and is available from THE OBJECTIVIST NEWSLETTER. Price: 50¢ (N.Y.C. residents add 2¢ sales tax).

Other activities: On March 30, Deborah Odzer, an NBI student, will give a solo dance concert. Time: 8:30 P.M. Place: Judson Hall, 165 West 57th St., New York City. Admission: $2.50.

Published monthly at 165 East 35th Street, New York 16, N. Y.
Subscription rate: in United States, its possessions, Canada and Mexico, $5 for one year; other countries, $6.
Additional copies of this Newsletter: single copy 50¢ (coins, not stamps); 10 — 99 copies, 25¢ each plus postage (for first-class delivery add 1¢ per copy, for third-class delivery add ½¢ per copy); 100 or more copies, 15¢ each plus postage (same as above).
For change of address send old address and new address with zone number if any. Allow us three weeks to process new subscriptions and change of address.

Ayn Rand and Nathaniel Branden, Editors and Publishers
Barbara Branden, Managing Editor
Elayne Kalberman, Circulation Manager
PRINTED BY STANDARD PRESS & GRAPHICS, INC., NEW YORK CITY

THE OBJECTIVIST NEWSLETTER

Edited and Published by AYN RAND and NATHANIEL BRANDEN

VOL. 2 NO. 4   APRIL, 1963

CHECK YOUR PREMISES
By AYN RAND

Man's Rights

If one wishes to advocate a free society—that is, capitalism—one must realize that its indispensable foundation is the principle of individual rights. If one wishes to uphold individual rights, one must realize that capitalism is the only system that can uphold and protect them. And if one wishes to gauge the relationship of freedom to the goals of today's intellectuals, one may gauge it by the fact that the concept of individual rights is evaded, distorted, perverted and seldom discussed, most conspicuously seldom by the so-called "conservatives."

"Rights" are a moral concept—the concept that provides a logical transition from the principles guiding an individual's actions to the principles guiding his relationship with others—the concept that preserves and protects individual morality in a social context—the link between the moral code of a man and the legal code of a society, between ethics and politics. *Individual rights are the means of subordinating society to moral law.*

Every political system is based on some code of ethics. The dominant ethics of mankind's history were variants of the altruist-collectivist doctrine which subordinated the individual to some higher authority, either mystical or social. Consequently, most political systems were variants of the same statist tyranny, differing only in degree, not in basic principle, limited only by the accidents of tradition, of chaos, of bloody strife and periodic collapse. Under all such systems, morality was a code applicable to the individual, but not to society. Society was placed *outside* the moral law, as its embodiment or source or exclusive interpreter—and the inculcation of self-sacrificial devotion to social duty was regarded as the main purpose of ethics in man's earthly existence.

Since there is no such entity as "society," since society is only a number of individual men, this meant, in practice, that the rulers of society were exempt from moral law; subject only to traditional rituals, they held total power and exacted blind obedience—on the implicit principle of: "The good is that which is good for society (or for the tribe, the race, the nation), and the ruler's edicts are its voice on earth."

This was true under all statist systems and under all variants of the altruist-collectivist ethics, mystical or social. "The Divine Right of Kings" summarizes the political theory of the first—"*Vox populi, vox dei*" of the second. As witness: the theocracy of Egypt, with the Pharaoh as an embodied god—the unlimited majority-rule or *democracy* of Athens—the welfare-state run by the Emperors of Rome—the Inquisition of the late Middle Ages—the absolute monarchy of France—the welfare-state of Bismarck's Prussia—the gas-chambers of Nazi Germany—the slaughterhouse of the Soviet Union.

All these political systems were expressions of the altruist-collectivist ethics—and their common characteristic is the fact that society stood above the moral law, as an omnipotent, sovereign whim-worshiper. Thus, politically, all these systems were variants of an *amoral* society.

The most profoundly revolutionary achievement of the United States of America was *the subordination of society to moral law*.

The principle of man's individual rights represented the extension of morality into the social system—as a limitation on the power of the state, as man's protection against the brute force of the collective, as the subordination of *might* to *right*. The United States was the first *moral* society in history.

All previous systems had regarded man as a sacrificial means to the ends of others, and society as an end in itself. The United States regarded man as an end in himself, and society as a means to the peaceful, orderly, *voluntary* co-existence of individuals. All previous systems had held that man's life belongs to society, that society can dispose of him in any way it pleases, and that any freedom he enjoys is his only by favor, by the *permission* of society, which may be revoked at any time. The United States held that man's life is his by *right* (which means: by moral principle and by his nature), that a right is the property of an individual, that society as such has no rights, and that the only moral purpose of a government is the protection of individual rights.

A "right" is a moral principle defining and sanctioning a man's freedom of action in a social context. There is only *one* fundamental right (all the others are its consequences or corollaries): a man's right to his own life. Life is a process of self-sustaining and self-generated action; the right to life means the right to engage in self-sustaining and self-generated action—which means: the freedom to take all the actions required by the nature of a rational being for the support, the furtherance, the fulfillment and the enjoyment of his own life. (Such is the meaning of the right to life, liberty and the pursuit of happiness.)

The concept of a "right" pertains only to action—specifically, to freedom of action. It means freedom from physical compulsion, coercion or interference by other men.

Thus, for every individual, a right is the moral sanction of a *positive*—of his freedom to act on his own judgment, for his own goals, by his own *voluntary, uncoerced* choice. As to his neighbors, his rights impose no obligations on them except of a *negative* kind: to abstain from violating his rights.

The right to life is the source of all rights—and the right to property is their only implementation. Without property rights, no other rights are possible. Since man has to sustain his life by his own effort, the man who has no right to the product of his effort has no means to sustain his life. The man who produces while others dispose of his product, is a slave.

Bear in mind that the right to property is a right to action, like all the others: it is not the right *to an object*, but to the action and the consequences of producing or earning that object. It is not a guarantee that a man *will* earn any property, but only a guarantee that he will own it if he earns it. It is the right to gain, to keep, to use and to dispose of material values.

The concept of individual rights is so new in human history that most men have not grasped it fully to this day. In accordance with the two theories of ethics, the mystical or the social, some men assert that rights are a gift of God—others, that rights are a gift of society. But, in fact, the source of rights is man's nature.

The Declaration of Independence stated that men "are endowed by their Creator with certain inalienable rights." Whether one believes that man is the product of a Creator or of nature, the issue of man's origin does not alter the fact that he is an entity of a specific kind—a rational being—that he cannot function successfully under coercion, and that rights are a necessary condition of his particular mode of survival.

"The source of man's rights is not divine law or congressional law, but the law of identity. A is A—and Man is Man. *Rights* are conditions of existence required by man's nature for his proper survival. If man is to live on earth, it is *right* for him to use his mind, it is *right* to act on his own free judgment, it is *right* to work for his values and to keep the product of his work. If life on earth is his purpose, he has a *right* to live as a rational being: nature forbids him the irrational." *(Atlas Shrugged)*

To violate man's rights means to compel him to act against his own judgment, or to expropriate his values. Basically, there is only one way to do it: by the use of physical force. There are two potential violators of man's rights: the criminals and the government. The great achievement of the United States was to draw a distinction between these two—by forbidding to the second the legalized version of the activities of the first.

The Declaration of Independence laid down the principle that "to secure these rights, governments are instituted among men." This provided the only valid justification of a government and defined its only proper purpose: to protect man's rights by protecting him from physical violence.

Thus the government's function was changed from the role of ruler to the role of servant. The government was set to protect man from criminals—and the Constitution was written to protect man from the government. The Bill of Rights was not directed against private citizens, but against the government—as an explicit declaration that individual rights supersede any public or social power.

The result was the pattern of a civilized society which—for the brief span of some hundred and fifty years—America came close to achieving. A civilized society is one in which physical force is banned from human relationships—in which the government, acting as a policeman, may use force *only* in retaliation and *only* against those who initiate its use.

This was the essential meaning and intent of America's political philosophy, implicit in the principle of individual rights. But it was not formulated explicitly, nor fully accepted nor consistently practiced.

America's inner contradiction was the altruist-collectivist ethics. Altruism is incompatible with freedom, with capitalism and with individual rights. One cannot combine the pursuit of happiness with the moral status of a sacrificial animal.

It was the concept of individual rights that had given birth to a free society. It was with the destruction of individual rights that the destruction of freedom had to begin.

A collectivist tyranny dare not enslave a country by an outright confiscation of its values, material or moral. It has to be done by a process of internal corruption. Just as in the material realm the plundering of a country's wealth is accomplished by inflating the currency—so today one may witness the process of inflation being applied to the realm of rights. The process entails such a growth of newly-promulgated "rights" that people do not notice the fact that the meaning of the concept is being reversed. Just as bad money drives out good money, so these "printing-press rights" negate authentic rights.

Consider the curious fact that never has there been such a proliferation, all over the world, of two contradictory phenomena: of alleged new "rights" and of slave-labor camps.

The "gimmick" was the switch of the concept of rights from the political to the economic realm.

The Democratic Party platform of 1960 summarizes the switch boldly and explicitly. It declares that a Democratic Administration "will reaffirm the economic bill of rights which Franklin Roosevelt wrote into our national conscience sixteen years ago."

Bear clearly in mind the meaning of the concept of *"rights"* when you read the list which that platform offers:

"1. The right to a useful and remunerative job in the industries or shops or farms or mines of the nation.

"2. The right to earn enough to provide adequate food and clothing and recreation.

"3. The right of every farmer to raise and sell his products at a return which will give him and his family a decent living.

"4. The right of every businessman, large and small, to trade in an atmosphere of freedom from unfair competition and domination by monopolies at home and abroad.

"5. The right of every family to a decent home.

"6. The right to adequate medical care and the opportunity to achieve and enjoy good health.

"7. The right to adequate protection from the economic fears of old age, sickness, accidents and unemployment.

"8. The right to a good education."

A single question added to each of the above eight clauses would make the issue clear: *At whose expense?*

Jobs, food, clothing, recreation (!), homes, medical care, education, etc., do not grow in nature. These are man-made values—goods and services produced by men. *Who* is to provide them?

If some men are entitled *by right* to the products of the work of others, it means that those others are deprived of rights and condemned to slave-labor.

Any alleged "right" of one man, which necessitates the violation of the rights of another, is not and cannot be a right.

No man can have a right to impose an unchosen obligation, an unrewarded duty or an involuntary servitude on another man. There can be no such thing as *"the right to enslave."*

A right does not include the material implementation of that right by other men; it includes only the freedom to earn that implementation by one's own effort.

Observe, in this context, the intellectual precision of the Founding Fathers: they spoke of the right to *the pursuit* of happiness—*not* of the right to happiness. It means that a man has the right to take the actions he deems necessary to achieve his happiness; it does *not* mean that others must make him happy.

The right to life means that a man has the right to support his life by his own work (on any economic level, as high as his ability will carry him); it does *not* mean that others must provide him with food, clothing and shelter.

The right to property means that a man has the right to take the economic actions necessary to earn property, to use it and to dispose of it; it does *not* mean that others must provide him with property.

The right of free speech means that a man has the right to express his ideas without danger of suppression, interference or punitive action by the government. It does *not* mean that others must provide him with a lecture hall, a radio station or a printing press through which to express his ideas.

Any undertaking that involves more than one man, requires the *voluntary* consent of every participant. Every one of them has the *right* to make his own decision, but none has the right to force his decision on the others.

There is no such thing as "a right to a job"—there is only the right of free trade, that is: a man's right to take a job if another man chooses to hire him. There is no "right to a home," only the right of free trade: the right to build a home or to buy it. There are no "rights to a 'fair' wage or a 'fair' price" if no one chooses to pay it, to hire a man or to buy his product. There are no "rights of consumers" to milk, shoes, movies or champagne if no producers choose to manufacture such items (there is only the right to manufacture them oneself). There are no "rights" of special groups, there are no "rights of farmers, of workers, of businessmen, of employees, of employers, of the old, of the young, of the unborn." There are only *the Rights of Man*—rights possessed by every individual man and by *all* men as individuals.

Property rights and the right of free trade are man's only "economic rights" (they are, in fact, *political* rights)—and there can be no such thing as "an *economic* bill of rights." But observe that the advocates of the latter have all but destroyed the former.

Remember that rights are moral principles which define and protect a man's freedom of action, but impose no obligations on other men. Private citizens are not a threat to one another's rights or freedom. A private citizen who resorts to physical force and violates the rights of others is a criminal—and men have legal protection against him.

Criminals are a small minority in any age or country. And the harm they have done to mankind is infinitesimal when compared to the horrors—the bloodshed, the wars, the persecutions, the confiscations, the famines, the enslavements, the wholesale destructions—perpetrated by mankind's governments. A government is the most dangerous threat to man's rights: it holds a legal monopoly on the use of physical force against legally disarmed victims. When unlimited and unrestricted by individual rights, a government is men's deadliest enemy. It is not as protection against *private* actions, but against governmental actions that the Bill of Rights was written.

(Continued on page 16)

INTELLECTUAL AMMUNITION DEPARTMENT

[*Subscribers are invited to send in the questions that they find themselves unable to answer in philosophical or political discussions. As many questions as space permits will be answered. No questions will be answered by mail.*]

■ **What is the Objectivist view of agnosticism?**

Of any position one might take concerning the question of the existence of God, agnosticism is, epistemologically, the least tenable.

Agnosticism is the refusal to commit oneself one way or the other concerning the existence of God.

In judging this policy, it is necessary to remember that no theist has ever been able to adduce evidence in support of his belief in God; that all of the theist's alleged proofs, such as the "argument from a first cause," the "argument from design," "the ontological argument," etc., have been refuted by philosophers many times; that no theist has ever succeeded even in providing an intelligible and non-contradictory definition of what he *means* by "God"; and that one can believe in God only as an act of faith.

Faith is the acceptance of ideas without sensory evidence or rational proof.

A man of reason does not accept ideas on faith. He knows that all of one's conclusions must be based on and derived from the facts of reality. He is, therefore, an atheist.

His position is this: "I accept or consider only that for which there is rational evidence. If a theist wishes to assert the existence of God, the burden of proof is on him. But I do not regard his *feeling* that God exists as relevant or admissible to a rational discussion."

The position of the theist and the atheist, then, is unequivocal and clear-cut: the theist, in the absence of rational grounds for believing in God, believes in God *on faith;* the atheist, in the absence of rational grounds for believing in God, does *not* believe in God. In logic these two positions exhaust the possibilities. Agnosticism is not a *third* position, it is the *evasion* of a position.

To understand the nature—and motive—of this evasion, consider the argument that the agnostic offers in self-justification. He states, in effect: "Granted that the existence of God cannot be proved—neither can it be *dis*proved. One cannot prove that God does *not* exist. All we can say is that we do not know whether or not God exists; and perhaps we can never know. Atheism is as much an act of faith as theism."

An agnostic does not distinguish between—but treats as equally valid—an atheist's demand for *reasons* and a theist's assertion of his *feelings*.

An atheist's refusal to believe that for which no evidence exists, is classified by the agnostic as an "act of faith."

What the agnostic demands of the atheist is proof of a negative—proof of the non-existence of God. *But it is impossible to prove a negative and irrational to demand it.*

"Proving a negative" means: proving the non-existence of that for which *no evidence of any kind exists.*

Proof, logic, reason, thinking, knowledge pertain to and deal only with that which exists. They cannot be applied to that which does *not* exist. Nothing can be relevant or applicable to the non-existent. The non-existent is *nothing.*

A *positive* statement, based on facts that have been erroneously interpreted, can be refuted—by means of exposing the errors in the interpretation of the facts. Such refutation is the *disproving* of a *positive*, not the proving of a negative.

As an example of the irrationality of the demand for proof of a negative, project the following situation.

Suppose that you attend a gathering with a friend. At this gathering, a stranger suddenly confronts you and charges you with having committed a murder. You indignantly deny it—but the stranger insistently repeats his charge.

"What murder?" you demand. Your accuser does not answer. "Who was killed?" you demand. Your accuser does not answer. "Why do you suspect me?" you demand.

Your accuser smiles slyly and answers, "I believe **that you** have committed a murder. Can you prove that you didn't?"

You turn away—and see that the friend with whom you came is looking at you tensely. You cry to him, *"You* don't believe I'm a murderer, do you?"

Your friend answers nervously, "No, of course I don't. I mean . . . he hasn't given any *evidence* that you're a murderer, he's just asserted it. . . . But . . . on the other hand . . . you haven't proved you're *not* a murderer, have you? I guess I'd have to say I don't know whether you're a murderer or not."

Thereafter, your friend is very fair and conscientious; he makes it clear to everyone that he does not believe that you *are* a murderer; he is, he explains, an agnostic in the matter.

If you were the victim of such a nightmare, you would feel that some monstrous injustice—specifically, an epistemological injustice—had been perpetrated against you. And you would be right.

That is the evil of uttering an arbitrary claim and offering, as its sole defense, the challenge: "Prove that it *isn't* so!"

In the pursuit of knowledge, there is no place for *whims*. Every claim, statement or proposition has to be based on the facts of reality; nothing may be claimed causelessly, groundlessly, *arbitrarily.*

Even a hypothesis has to have some factual basis, some factual evidence indicating that it might be true. A hypothesis based on nothing but a blind guess is not admissible into rational consideration. Reason deals only with that which exists; any hypothesis or supposition that some hitherto unknown fact may exist, has to be based on the evidence of facts *known* to exist.

Rational demonstration, an appeal to facts, is necessary to support even the claim that a thing is *possible*. It is a breach of logic to assert that that which has not been proven to be impossible is, therefore, possible. An absence does not constitute proof of anything. Nothing can be derived from nothing.

The theist believes in the existence of God—without reason; the agnostic believes in the possibility of God's existence—without reason.

But the theist who openly bases his belief on faith is closer to reality in one respect: he does not pretend to be rational.

The motive of the agnostic is not difficult to discern; it consists of the following premise: "If anyone asserts anything, regardless of whether or not he offers reasons, who am I to judge the truth or falsehood of his claim? Particularly if it is a claim voiced by a great many people. Why do I have to take a stand? I'll only antagonize them. Better to play it safe and commit myself to nothing." (For an analysis of this psychology, I refer the reader to my article on "Social Metaphysics" in the November 1962 issue of THE OBJECTIVIST NEWSLETTER.)

The agnostic grants respectful consideration to the assertion of God's existence, not because he has any rational grounds for doing so, but because millions of men profess theism—and he dreads to assume the responsibility of judging them as *entirely* wrong.

When a person makes an assertion for which no rational grounds are given, his statement is —*epistemologically*—without cognitive content. *It is as though nothing had been said.* This is equally true if the assertion is made by two billion people.

— NATHANIEL BRANDEN

NEWSLETTER ARTICLE REPRINTS

Two articles by Nathaniel Branden, "Does Man Possess Instincts?" and "Social Metaphysics: The Psychology of Dependence," (originally published in this NEWSLETTER), have been reprinted in pamphlet form by NBI and are available from this NEWSLETTER. Price: 25¢ each. (N.Y.C. residents add 1¢ sales tax.)

Man's Rights (*from page 14*)

Now observe the process by which that protection is being destroyed.

The process consists of ascribing to private citizens the specific violations constitutionally forbidden to the government (which private citizens have no power to commit) and thus freeing the government from all restrictions. The switch is becoming progressively more obvious in the field of free speech. For years, the collectivists have been propagating the notion that a private individual's refusal to finance an opponent is a violation of the opponent's right of free speech and an act of "censorship."

It is "censorship," they claim, if a newspaper refuses to employ or publish writers whose ideas are diametrically opposed to its policy.

It is "censorship," they claim, if businessmen refuse to advertise in a magazine that denounces, insults and smears them.

It is "censorship," they claim, if a TV sponsor objects to some outrage perpetrated on a program he is financing—such as the incident of Alger Hiss being invited to denounce former Vice-President Nixon.

And then there is Newton N. Minow who declares: "There is censorship by ratings, by advertisers, by networks, by affiliates which reject programming offered to their areas." It is the same Mr. Minow who threatens to revoke the license of any station that does not comply with his views on programming—and who claims that *that* is not censorship.

Consider the implications of such a trend.

"Censorship" is a term pertaining only to governmental action. No private action is censorship. No private individual or agency can silence a man or suppress a publication; only the government can do so. The freedom of speech of private individuals includes the right not to agree, not to listen and not to finance one's own antagonists.

But according to such doctrines as the "economic bill of rights," an individual has no right to dispose of his own material means by the guidance of his own convictions—and must hand over his money indiscriminately to any speakers or propagandists, who have a "right" to his property.

This means that the ability to provide the material tools for the expression of ideas deprives a man of the right to hold any ideas. It means that a publisher has to publish books he considers worthless, false or evil—that a TV sponsor has to finance commentators who choose to affront his convictions—that the owner of a newspaper must turn his editorial pages over to any young hooligan who clamors for the enslavement of the press. It means that one group of men acquires the "right" to unlimited license—while another group is reduced to helpless irresponsibility.

But since it is obviously impossible to provide every claimant with a job, a microphone or a newspaper-column, *who* will determine the "distribution" of "economic rights" and select the recipients, when the owners' right to choose has been abolished? Well, Mr. Minow has indicated *that* quite clearly.

And if you make the mistake of thinking that this applies only to big property owners, you had better realize that the theory of "economic rights" includes the "right" of every would-be playwright, every beatnik poet, every noise-composer and every non-objective artist (who have political pull) to the financial support you did not give them when you did not attend their shows. What else is the meaning of the project to spend your tax-money on subsidized art?

And while people are clamoring about "economic rights," the concept of political rights is vanishing. It is forgotten that the right of free speech means the freedom to advocate one's views and to bear the possible consequences, including disagreement with others, opposition, unpopularity and lack of support. The political function of "the right of free speech" is to protect dissenters and unpopular minorities from forcible suppression—*not* to guarantee them the support, advantages and rewards of a popularity they have not gained.

The Bill of Rights reads: "Congress shall make no law . . . abridging the freedom of speech, or of the press. . ." It does not demand that private citizens provide a microphone for the man who advocates their destruction, or a passkey for the burglar who seeks to rob them, or a knife for the murderer who wants to cut their throats.

Such is the state of one of today's most crucial issues: *political* rights versus "*economic* rights." It's either-or. One destroys the other. But there are, in fact, no "economic rights," no "collective rights," no "public-interest rights." The term "individual rights" is a redundancy: there is no other kind of rights and no one else to possess them.

Those who advocate *laissez-faire* capitalism are the only advocates of man's rights.

OBJECTIVIST CALENDAR

■ An article by Ayn Rand, "The Money-Making Personality," appears in the April issue of *Cosmopolitan*.

■ As part of a New American Library series, "The Writer Speaks," Ayn Rand has recorded a half hour radio broadcast entitled "Literature and Philosophy." Future schedulings include: Baltimore, March 31, 7:30 P.M., WBAI(FM); Providence, March 31, 5:20 P.M., WHIM; Seattle, March 31, 8:00 P.M., KING(AM); New York, April 1, 11:00 A.M. and 11:00 P.M., WNYC; Seattle, April 3, 10:00 P.M., KING(FM); Terre Haute, April 21, 7:30 P.M., WTHI(FM); Philadelphia, April 28, 6:30 P.M., WCAU. Additional schedulings will be announced in future issues of the NEWSLETTER.

This program has, to date, been broadcast in the following cities: Albuquerque, Detroit, Poughkeepsie, Denver, Atlanta, Lafayette, Washington, D. C., Chicago. (We regret that we did not receive this information in time to list it in earlier CALENDARS.)

■ Beginning Tuesday, April 16, NBI will offer a ten lecture course on "The Esthetics of the Visual Arts," to be given by Mary Ann Rukavina. This course is open to students who have taken "Basic Principles of Objectivism"; to others, by special arrangement only.

■ NBI's Tape Transcription Division has scheduled the following starting dates for Barbara Branden's course, "Principles of Efficient Thinking": San Francisco, March 19; San Diego, March 21; Toronto, April 8; Chicago, April 17; Washington, D. C., April 28.

Mr. Branden's course, "Basic Principles of Objectivist Psychology," began in Philadelphia on March 5 and in Los Angeles on March 6.

■ On Wednesday, April 24, Mary Ann Rukavina will address the Society of Capitalists at Brooklyn College. Her subject: "A Critical Evaluation of Modern Art." Time: 12 noon. Place: 3146 Boylan Hall, Brooklyn College. Open to the public; admission free.

■ On Wednesday, April 24, Nathaniel Branden will address the Ayn Rand Philosophical Society of the Drexel Institute of Technology. His subject: "The Psychology of Dependence." Time: 8:00 P.M. Place: the Grand Hall of the Drexel Activity Center, 32nd St. & Chestnut, Philadelphia. Open to the public; admission free.

■ On Wednesday, May 1, Nathaniel Branden will address the Ayn Rand Special Projects Group at Brooklyn College. His subject: "Mental Health versus Mysticism and Self-Sacrifice." Time: 12 noon. Place: 4200 Boylan Hall, Brooklyn College. Open to the public; admission free.

■ On Tuesday, March 26, Nathaniel Branden addressed the Edgemont High School's Fourth Annual Senior Forum, in Pawling, New York. His subject: "The Objectivist Ethics."

■ NBI is planning a Ball to be held in June, for students and their guests, celebrating the INSTITUTE's fifth anniversary. All present and former students will receive more information shortly.

Published monthly at 165 East 35th Street, New York 16, N. Y.
Subscription rate: in United States, its possessions, Canada and Mexico, $5 for one year; other countries, $6.
Additional copies of this Newsletter: single copy 50¢ (coins, not stamps); 10 — 99 copies, 25¢ each plus postage (for first-class delivery add 1¢ per copy, for third-class delivery add ½¢ per copy); 100 or more copies, 15¢ each plus postage (same as above).
For change of address send old address and new address with zone number if any. Allow us three weeks to process new subscriptions and change of address.

Ayn Rand and Nathaniel Branden, Editors and Publishers
Barbara Branden, Managing Editor
Elayne Kalberman, Circulation Manager

PRINTED BY STANDARD PRESS & GRAPHICS, INC., NEW YORK CITY

THE OBJECTIVIST NEWSLETTER

Edited and Published by AYN RAND and NATHANIEL BRANDEN

VOL. 2 NO. 5   MAY, 1963

The Contradiction of Determinism

By NATHANIEL BRANDEN

One of the most important and fundamental elements in the Objectivist philosophy is the concept of man as a being of volitional consciousness.

In briefest essence, that concept may be summarized as follows:

Reason is the faculty on which man's life depends—but it is a faculty whose exercise is not automatic. The mere fact of being confronted with physical objects will not force man to abstract and identify their common properties, to integrate his abstractions into still wider abstractions, to apply his knowledge to each new particular he encounters. The stimulation of a sensory receptor may be sufficient to produce a sensation—but it is not sufficient to produce a syllogism. *Thinking* is an activity that must be initiated, sustained and directed by man's volitional, self-generated effort.

To quote from *Atlas Shrugged*: "Reason does not work automatically; thinking is not a mechanical process; the connections of logic are not made by instinct. The function of your stomach, lungs or heart is automatic; the function of your mind is not. In any hour and issue of your life, you are free to think or to evade that effort. But you are not free to escape from your nature, from the fact that *reason* is your means of survival—so that for you, who are a human being, the question 'to be or not to be' is the question 'to think or not to think.'"

Such is man's basic freedom of choice. This choice—given the context of his knowledge and of the existential possibilities confronting him—controls all of man's other choices, and directs the course of his actions.

This view of man's nature stands in sharp opposition to the view that dominates our culture in general and the social sciences in particular: the doctrine of psychological determinism.

Psychological determinism denies the existence of any element of freedom or volition in man's consciousness. It holds that every action, desire and thought of man is determined by forces beyond his control. It holds that, in relation to his actions, decisions, values and conclusions, man is ultimately and essentially *passive;* that man is merely a *reactor* to internal and external pressures; that those pressures determine the course of man's actions and the content of his convictions, just as physical forces determine the course of every particle of dust in the universe. It holds that, in any given situation or moment, only one "choice" is psychologically possible to man, the inevitable result of all the antecedent determining forces impinging on him, just as only one action is possible to the speck of dust; that man has no *actual* power of choice, no *actual* freedom or self-responsibility. Man, according to this view, has no more actual volition than a stone: he is merely confronted with more complex alternatives and is manipulated by more complex forces.

One of the foremost spokesmen for determinism, Sigmund Freud, writes in *The Ego and the Id:* "What we call our ego is essentially passive . . . We are 'lived' by unknown and uncontrollable forces."

The issue of free will versus determinism is the most crucial question in any study of the nature of man. Before one can draw any further conclusions about the activities or state proper to him, it is necessary to know: Does man possess free will, that is, volitional control over the function of his consciousness and therefore control over his actions—or is man an automaton, a complex robot operated by forces over which he has no control, a robot whose every action and reaction is determined by what reality or experience or environment or inanimate matter or an inherited Id or other people happen to have imprinted on him, a robot who, at any given moment, is pushed by whatever sum such influences may have added up to, and is powerless to resist them?

Above all, this question has to be answered before one ventures into any of the "normative" sciences, that is, sciences that prescribe or recommend certain courses of action for men, sciences such as ethics, education, political philosophy, law.

If man has freedom of choice, one can advise him which actions to take and which to avoid; one can teach him to distinguish between rational pursuits and irrational ones, between good and evil; one can hold him responsible for his actions, one can praise him or blame him accordingly, one can reward him for virtues or punish him for crimes.

But if man has no freedom of choice, no power of control over his actions, then ethics and law are the first two sciences that have to be abandoned: it would be senseless to expect man to observe any moral code, if he has no power to choose his actions; it would be senseless to admire or condemn any human action, be it an act of heroism or of knavery, if the actors could not help it in either case; it would be sheer brutality to punish any criminal, if he could not have acted differently, if the most cold-bloodedly premeditated murder were, in fact, an act of involuntary manslaughter determined by a complex mechanism of fate.

A different system of education results from the conviction that one is teaching and dealing with *minds*—or that one is doing the work of an animal trainer. A different political system results from the conviction that man is a rational being—or an emotion-dominated brute who is unfit to direct his own life, and can be manipulated and "conditioned" to accept and function under any conditions of existence his rulers decree.

In this article, I shall not attempt to offer either a full presentation of the Objectivist theory of volition or an exhaustive refutation of determinism; the latter theory is vulnerable to attack on more counts than can be covered in the space of a brief article. I shall confine myself to the analysis of a central and insuperable contradiction in the determinist position—an *epistemological* contradiction—a contradiction implicit in any variety of determinism, whether the alleged determining forces be physical, psychological, environmental or divine.

The determinist concept of mind maintains that whether a man thinks or not, whether he takes cognizance of the facts of reality or not, whether he holds facts above his feelings or his feelings above facts—all are determined by forces outside his control; in any given moment or situation, his method of mental functioning is the inevitable product of an endless chain of antecedent factors; *he* has no choice in the matter.

That which a man does, declare the advocates of determinism, he *had* to do—that which he believes, he *had* to believe—if he focuses his mind, he *had* to—if he evades the effort of focusing, he *had* to—if he is guided solely by reason, he *had* to be—if he is ruled instead by feeling or whim, he *had* to be—*he couldn't help it*.

But if this were true, no *knowledge* would be possible to man. No theory could claim greater plausibility than any other—including the theory of psychological determinism.

Man is neither omniscient nor infallible. This means: (a) that he must work to *achieve* his knowledge, and (b) that the mere presence of an idea inside his mind, does not prove that the idea is true; many ideas may enter a man's mind which are false. But if man believes what he *has* to believe, if he is not free to test his beliefs against reality and to validate or reject them—*if the actions and content of his mind are determined by factors that may or may not have anything to*

(continued on page 19)

BOOKS

*Aristotle** by John Herman Randall, Jr.

Reviewed by AYN RAND

If there is a philosophical Atlas who carries the whole of Western civilization on his shoulders, it is Aristotle. He has been opposed, misinterpreted, misrepresented, and—like an axiom—used by his enemies in the very act of denying him. Whatever intellectual progress men have achieved rests on his achievements.

Aristotle may be regarded as the cultural barometer of Western history. Whenever his influence dominated the scene, it paved the way for one of history's brilliant eras; whenever it fell, so did mankind. The Aristotelian revival of the thirteenth century brought men to the Renaissance. The intellectual counter-revolution turned them back toward the cave of his antipode: Plato.

There is only one fundamental issue in philosophy: the cognitive efficacy of man's mind. The conflict of Aristotle versus Plato is the conflict of reason versus mysticism. It was Plato who formulated most of philosophy's basic questions—and doubts. It was Aristotle who laid the foundation for most of the answers. Thereafter, the record of their duel is the record of man's long struggle to deny and surrender or to uphold and assert the validity of his particular mode of consciousness.

Today, philosophy has sunk below the level of Aristotle versus Plato, down to the primitive gropings of Parmenides versus Heraclitus, whose disciples were unable to reconcile the concept of intellectual certainty with the phenomenon of change: the Eleatics, who claimed that change is illogical; that in any clash between mind and reality, reality is dispensable and, therefore, change is an illusion—versus the Heraclitean Sophists, who claimed that mind is dispensable, that knowledge is an illusion and nothing exists but change. Or: consciousness without existence versus existence without consciousness. Or: blind dogmatism versus cynical subjectivism. Or: Rationalism versus Empiricism.

Aristotle was the first man who integrated the facts of identity and change, thus solving that ancient dichotomy. Or rather, he laid the foundation and indicated the method by which a full solution could be reached. In order to resurrect that dichotomy thereafter, it was necessary to ignore and evade his works. Ever since the Renaissance, the dichotomy kept being resurrected, in one form or another, always aimed at one crucial target: the concept of *identity*—always leading to some alleged demonstration of the deceptiveness, the limitations, the ultimate impotence of reason.

It took several centuries of misrepresenting Aristotle to turn him into a strawman, to declare the strawman invalidated and to release such a torrent of irrationality that it is now sweeping philosophy away and carrying us back past the pre-Socratics, past Western civilization, into the prehistorical swamps of the Orient, via Existentialism and Zen Buddhism.

Today, Aristotle is the forgotten man of philosophy. Slick young men go about droning the wearisome sophistries of the fifth century B.C., to the effect that man can know nothing, while unshaven young men go about chanting that they *do* know by means of their whole body from the neck down.

It is in this context that one must evaluate the significance of an unusual book appearing on such a scene—*Aristotle* by John Herman Randall, Jr.

Let me hasten to state that the above remarks are mine, not Professor Randall's. He does not condemn modern philosophy as it deserves—he seems to share some of its errors. But the theme of his book is the crucial relevance and importance of Aristotle to the philosophical problems of our age. And his book is an attempt to bring Aristotle's theories back into the light of day—of *our* day—from under the shambles of misrepresentation by medieval mystics and by modern Platonists.

―――――――

*Published by Columbia University Press. Available in hard or soft cover from NBL BOOK SERVICE, 165 East 35th St., New York 16, N. Y. Hardcover: $4.10 (publisher's price: $5.00). Softcover: $1.60 plus 15¢ postage. (N.Y.C. residents add 3% sales tax; outside the U.S., add 15¢.)

"Indeed," he writes, "[Aristotle's] may well be the most passionate mind in history: it shines through every page, almost every line. His crabbed documents exhibit, not 'cold thought,' but the passionate search for passionless truth. For him, there is no 'mean,' no moderation, in intellectual excellence. The 'theoretical life' is not for him the life of quiet 'contemplation,' serene and unemotional, but the life of *nous*, of *theoria*, of intelligence, burning, immoderate, without bounds or limits."

Indicating that the early scientists had discarded Aristotle in rebellion against his religious interpreters, Professor Randall points out that their scientific achievements had, in fact, an unacknowledged Aristotelian base and were carrying out the implications of Aristotle's theories.

Blaming the epistemological chaos of modern science on the influence of Newton's mechanistic philosophy of nature, he writes: "It is fascinating to speculate how, had it been possible in the seventeenth century to reconstruct rather than abandon Aristotle, we might have been saved several centuries of gross confusion and error. . . . Where we are often still groping, Aristotle is frequently clear, suggestive, and fruitful. This holds true of many of his analyses: his doctrine of natural teleology; his view of natural necessity as not simple and mechanical but hypothetical; his conception of the infinite as potential, not actual; his notion of a finite universe; his doctrine of natural place; his conception of time as not absolute, but rather a dimension, a system of measurement; his conception that place is a coordinate system, and hence relative. On countless problems, from the standpoint of our present theory, Aristotle was right, where the nineteenth-century Newtonian physicists were wrong."

Objecting to "the structureless world of Hume in which 'anything may be followed by anything,'" Professor Randall writes: "To such a view, which he found maintained by the Megarians, Aristotle answers, No! Every process involves the operation of determinate powers. There is nothing that can become anything else whatsoever. A thing can become only what it has the specific power to become, only what it already *is*, in a sense, potentially. And a thing can be understood only as that kind of thing that has that kind of a specific power; while the process can be understood only as the operation, the actualization, the functioning of the powers of its subject or bearer."

To read a concise, lucid presentation of Aristotle's system, written by a distinguished modern philosopher—written in terms of basic principles and broad fundamentals, as against the senseless "teasing" of trivia by today's alleged thinkers—is so rare a value that it is sufficient to establish the importance of Professor Randall's book, in spite of its flaws.

Its flaws, unfortunately, are numerous. Professor Randall describes his book as "a philosopher's delineation of Aristotle." Since there are many contradictory elements and many obscure passages in Aristotle's own works (including, in some cases, the question of their authenticity), it is a philosopher's privilege (within demonstrable limits) to decide which strands of a badly torn fabric he chooses to present as significantly "Aristotelian." But nothing—particularly not Aristotle—is infinite and indeterminate. And while Professor Randall tries to separate his presentation from his interpretation, he does not always succeed. Some of his interpretations are questionable; some are stretched beyond the limit of the permissible.

For instance, he describes Aristotle's approach to knowledge as follows: "Knowing is for him an obvious fact. . . . The real question, as he sees it, is, 'In what kind of a world is knowing possible?' What does the fact of knowing imply about our world?" *This* is a form of "the prior certainty of consciousness"—the notion that one can first possess knowledge and then proceed to discover what that knowledge is of, thus making the world a derivative of consciousness—a Cartesian approach which would have been inconceivable to Aristotle and which Professor Randall himself is combating throughout his book.

Most of the book's flaws come from the same root: from Professor Randall's inability or unwillingness to break with modern premises, methods and terminology. The perceptiveness he brings to his consideration of Aristotle's ideas, seems to vanish whenever he attempts to equate Aristotle with modern trends. To claim, as he does, that: "In modern terms,

Aristotle can be viewed as a behaviorist, an operationalist, and a contextualist" (and, later, as a "functionalist" and a "relativist"), is either inexcusable or so loosely generalized as to rob those terms of any meaning.

Granted that those terms have no specific definitions and are used, like most of today's philosophical language, in the manner of "mobiles" which *connote*, rather than denote—even so, their accepted "connotations" are so anti-Aristotelian that one is forced, at times, to wonder whether Professor Randall is trying to put something over on the moderns or on Aristotle. There are passages in the book to support either hypothesis.

On the one hand, Professor Randall writes: "That we can know things as they are, that such knowledge is possible, is the fact that Aristotle is trying to explain, and not, like Kant and his followers, trying to deny and explain away." And: "Indeed, any construing of the fact of 'knowledge,' whether Kantian, Hegelian, Deweyan, Positivistic, or any other, seems to be consistent and fruitful, and to avoid the impasses of barren self-contradiction, and insoluble and meaningless problems, only when it proceeds from the Aristotelian approach, and pushes Aristotle's own analyses further . . . only, that is, in the measure that it is conducted upon an Aristotelian basis." (Though one wonders what exactly would be left of Kant, Hegel, Dewey or the Positivists, if they were stripped of their non-Aristotelian elements.)

On the other hand, Professor Randall seems to turn Aristotle into some foggy combination of a linguistic analyst and a Heraclitean, as if language and reality could be understood as two separate, unconnected dimensions—in such passages as: "When [Aristotle] goes on to examine what is involved in 'being' anything . . . he is led to formulate two sets of distinctions: the one set appropriate to understanding any 'thing' or *ousia* as a subject of discourse, the other set appropriate to understanding any 'thing' or *ousia* as the outcome of a process, as the operation or functioning of powers, and ultimately as sheer functioning, activity."

It is true that Aristotle holds the answer to Professor Randall's "structuralism-functionalism" dichotomy and that his answer is vitally important today. But his answer eliminates that dichotomy altogether—and one cannot solve it by classifying him as a "functionalist" who believed that things are "sheer process."

The best parts of Professor Randall's book are Chapters VIII, IX and XI, particularly this last. In discussing the importance of Aristotle's biological theory and "the biological motivation of Aristotle's thought," he brings out an aspect of Aristotle which has been featured too seldom in recent discussions and which is much more profound than the question of Aristotle's "functionalism": the central place given to living entities, to the phenomenon of *life*, in Aristotle's philosophy.

For Aristotle, *life* is not an inexplicable, supernatural mystery, but a fact of nature. And consciousness is a natural attribute of certain living entities, their natural power, their specific mode of action—*not* an unaccountable element in a mechanistic universe, to be explained away somehow in terms of inanimate matter, nor a mystic miracle incompatible with physical reality, to be attributed to some occult source in another dimension. For Aristotle, "living" and "knowing" are facts of reality; man's mind is neither unnatural nor supernatural, but *natural*—and *this* is the root of Aristotle's greatness, of the immeasurable distance that separates him from other thinkers.

Life—and its highest form, man's life—is the central fact in Aristotle's view of reality. The best way to describe it is to say that Aristotle's philosophy is *"biocentric."*

This is the source of Aristotle's intense concern with the study of living entities, the source of the enormously "pro-life" attitude that dominates his thinking. In some oddly undefined manner, Professor Randall seems to share it. This, in spite of all his contradictions, seems to be his real bond with Aristotle.

"Life is the end of living bodies," writes Professor Randall, "since they exist for the sake of living." And: "No kind of thing, no species is subordinated to the purposes and interests of any other kind. In biological theory, the end served by the structure of any specific kind of living thing is the good—ultimately, the 'survival'—of that kind of thing." And, discussing the ends and conclusions of natural processes: "Only in human life are these ends and conclusions consciously intended, only in men are purposes found. For Aristotle, even God has no purpose, only man!"

The blackest patch in this often illuminating book is Chapter XII, which deals with ethics and politics. Its contradictions are apparent even without reference to Aristotle's text. It is astonishing to read the assertion that: "Aristotle's ethics and politics are actually his supreme achievement." They are not, even in their original form—let alone in Professor Randall's version which transforms them into the ethics of pragmatism.

It is shocking to read the assertion that Aristotle is an advocate of the "welfare state." Whatever flaws there are in Aristotle's political theory—and there are many—he does not deserve that kind of indignity.

Professor Randall, who stresses that knowledge must rest on empirical evidence, should take cognizance of the empirical fact that throughout history the influence of Aristotle's philosophy (particularly of his epistemology) has led in the direction of individual freedom, of man's liberation from the power of the state—that Aristotle (via John Locke) was the philosophical father of the Constitution of the United States and thus of *capitalism*—that it is Plato and Hegel, not Aristotle, who have been the philosophical ancestors of all totalitarian and welfare states, whether Bismarck's, Lenin's or Hitler's.

An "Aristotelian statist" is a contradiction in terms—and this, perhaps, is a clue to the conflict that mars the value of Professor Randall's book.

But, if read critically, this book is of great value in the study of Aristotle's philosophy. It is a concise and comprehensive presentation which many people need and look for, but cannot find today. It is of particular value to college students: by providing a frame-of-reference, a clear summary of the whole, it will help them to grasp the meaning of the issues through the fog of the fragmentary, unintelligible manner in which most courses on Aristotle are taught today.

Above all, this book is important culturally, as a step in the right direction, as a recognition of the fact that the great physician needed by our dying science of philosophy is Aristotle—that if we are to emerge from the intellectual shambles of the present, we can do it only by means of an *Aristotelian* approach.

"Clearly," writes Professor Randall, "Aristotle did not say everything; though without what he first said, all words would be meaningless, and when it is forgotten they usually are."

The Contradiction of Determinism *(from page 17)*

do with reason, logic and reality—then he can never know if his conclusions are true or false.

Knowledge is the correct identification of the facts of reality; and in order for man to know that the contents of his mind *do* constitute knowledge, in order for him to know that he has identified the facts of reality correctly, he requires a means of testing his conclusions. The means is the process of *reasoning*—of testing his conclusions against reality and checking for contradictions. It is thus that he validates his conclusions. But this validation is possible only if his *capacity* to judge is free—that is, non-conditional (given a normal brain state). If his capacity to judge is *not* free, there is no way for a man to discriminate between his beliefs and those of a raving lunatic.

But then how did the advocates of determinism acquire *their* knowledge? What is its validation? Determinists are conspicuously silent on this point.

If the advocates of determinism insist that their choice to think and their acceptance of reason is *conditional*, dependent on factors outside their control—which means: that they are *not* free to test their beliefs against the facts of reality—then they cannot claim to *know* that their theory is true; they can only report that they feel helpless to believe otherwise. Nor can they claim that their theory is highly probable; they can only acknowledge the inner compulsion that forbids them to doubt that it is highly probable.

Some advocates of determinism, evidently sensing this epistemological dilemma, have sought to escape it by asserting that, although they are determined to believe what they believe, the factor determining them is *logic*. But by what means do they know this? Their beliefs are no more subject to their control than a lunatic's. They and the lunatic are equally the pawn of deterministic forces. Both are incapable of judging their judgments.

(continued on page 20)

The Contradiction of Determinism (from page 19)

One of the defining characteristics of psychosis is *loss* of volitional control over rational judgment—but, according to determinism, that is man's normal, metaphysical state. There *is* no escape from determinism's epistemological dilemma.

A mind that is not free to test and validate its conclusions—a mind whose judgment is not free—can have no way to tell the logical from the illogical, *no way to ascertain that which compels and motivates it,* no right to claim knowledge of any kind; such a mind is disqualified for such appraisals by its very nature. The very *concept* of logic is possible only to a volitional consciousness; an automatic consciousness could have no need of it and could not conceive of it.

The concepts of logic, thought and knowledge are not applicable to machines. A machine does not reason; it performs the actions its builder sets it to perform, and those actions alone. If it is set to register that two plus two equal four, it does so; if it is set to register that two plus two equal five, it does so; it has no power to correct the orders and information given it. If "self-correctors" are built into it, it performs the prescribed acts of "self-correction," and no others; if the "self-correctors" are set incorrectly, it cannot correct itself; it cannot make any independent, self-generated contribution to its own performance. If man, who is not "set" invariably to be right, were merely a super-complex machine, engineered by his heredity and operated by his environment, pushed, pulled, shaped and molded by his genes, his toilet training, his parental upbringing and his cultural history, then no premise reached by him could claim objectivity or truth—including the premise that man is a machine.

If, as a staunch determinist such as Baron Holbach states in his *System of Nature,* man's "ideas come to him involuntarily"—if man is "wise or foolish, reasonable or irrational, without his will being for anything in these various states"—then by what right does he or any other determinist claim his "involuntary" ideas as *knowledge?* A determinist can only announce: "Destiny forces me to believe" etc. He cannot claim to *know* anything.

Those who expound determinism must either assert that they arrived at their theory by mystical revelation, and thus exclude themselves from the realm of reason—or they must assert that *they* are an exception to the theory they propound, and thus exclude their theory from the realm of truth.

That knowledge is possible to man, cannot be contested without self-contradiction. It is a truth that must be accepted even in the act of seeking to dispute it. Any theory that necessitates the conclusion that man can know nothing, is self-invalidating and self-refuting by that very fact. Yet such is the conclusion to which the theory of determinism inescapably leads. Thus, a rationally espoused determinism is a contradiction in terms.

In appraising any theory of the nature of man's mind and its operations, it is necessary to consider this: since the theory is itself a product of man's mind, its claim to truth must be compatible with its own existence and content. Otherwise, the theory is contradictory and nonsensical (Russell's theory of types notwithstanding). For example, if a man were to declare, as an alleged fact of reality: "Man is incapable of knowing any facts"—the logical absurdity of his statement would be obvious. The epistemological contradiction of determinism is—in a subtler and more complex way—of the identical order.

Determinism is a theory whose claim to truth is incompatible with its own content. It exhibits what may be termed *the fallacy of self-exclusion.*

A number of thinkers, attacking the theory of classical associationism, pointed out that the associationist theory of mind does not allow the possibility of ever establishing associationism as true; that the theory does not allow the possibility of *any* knowledge. But associationism is merely one version of psychological determinism. What has not been recognized is that the same objection applies to—and invalidates—*any* version of determinism.

It does not matter whether man's mind is alleged to be passively under the sway of the "laws of association"—or of conditioned reflexes—or of environmental pressures—or of Original Sin. *Any* theory of mind that denies man's volitional control over his faculty of judgment, collapses under the weight of the same inescapable and insuperable contradiction.

Only because man *is* a being of volitional consciousness—only because he *is* free to initiate and sustain a reasoning process, is knowledge—in contradistinction to irresistible, unchosen beliefs—possible to him.

The advocates of psychological determinism have repeatedly insisted that science demands the acceptance of their doctrine. The exact opposite is true. The doctrine of psychological determinism would make not only the normative sciences but *all* science impossible.

OBJECTIVIST CALENDAR

■ On Sunday, May 19, at 2 P.M., Ayn Rand's lecture on "The Fascist New Frontier" will be broadcast over radio station WNIB/FM (97.1) in Chicago.

This lecture, originally given at the Ford Hall Forum in Boston, has been published by NBI and is available from THE OBJECTIVIST NEWSLETTER. Price: 50¢. (N.Y.C. residents add 2¢ sales tax.)

■ On Monday, June 3, Ayn Rand will deliver lecture #17 in the current NBI course on "Basic Principles of Objectivism." The title of her lecture: "The Esthetics of Literature." Time: 7:30 P.M. Place: Hotel Roosevelt, 45th St. & Madison Ave., New York City. Visitor's admission: $3.50.

■ Beginning Thursday, June 6, NBI will offer, in New York City, a ten lecture course on "Principles of Efficient Thinking," to be given by Barbara Branden. This course is open to students who have taken "Basic Principles of Objectivism"; to others, by special arrangement only.

■ At present, the Tape Transcription Division of NBI offers courses on Objectivism in the following cities: Atlanta; Boston; Buffalo; Chicago; Clear, Alaska; Indianapolis; Kansas City, Kansas; Los Angeles; Miami; Newark, Delaware; Philadelphia; St. Louis; San Diego; San Francisco; Toronto; Tucson; Valparaiso; Washington, D.C.; Winnipeg. NBI invites requests for interviews (in New York City) from individuals who are potentially interested in handling courses, as business representatives, in other cities in the United States and Canada. Write for information to: NATHANIEL BRANDEN INSTITUTE, Tape Transcription Division, 165 East 35th St., New York 16, N. Y.

■ In February of this year, New American Library issued the 14th printing of *The Fountainhead*—100,000 copies.

■ Readers have asked when *Who is Ayn Rand?* will be available in paperback. The book will not be published in a paperback edition for at least a year, and perhaps longer.

■ Ayn Rand's weekly column in the *Los Angeles Times* was discontinued by mutual consent on December 23, 1962. Miss Rand was unable to continue her column due to the pressure of other commitments.

A Reminder:

On October 2, 1962, Ayn Rand began a weekly half-hour radio program for the Columbia University station WKCR/FM (89.9). Entitled: "The Ayn Rand Program," it is heard in New York every Tuesday, at 8:30 P.M. It presents talks by Miss Rand and discussions with guest speakers. The program is now being broadcast in a number of cities and is available to other radio stations at a nominal charge. If you would like to hear it in your city, ask your local stations to contact WKCR, Columbia University, New York 27, N. Y.

Published **monthly** at 165 East 35th Street, New York 16, N. Y.
Subscription rate: in United States, its possessions, Canada and Mexico, $5 for one year; other countries, $6.
Additional copies of this Newsletter: single copy 50¢ (coins, not stamps); 10 — 99 copies, 25¢ each plus postage (for first-class delivery add 1¢ per copy, for third-class delivery add ½¢ per copy); 100 or more copies, 15¢ each plus postage (same as above).
For change of address send old address and new address with zone number if any. Allow us three weeks to process new subscriptions and change of address.

Ayn Rand and Nathaniel Branden, Editors and Publishers
Barbara Branden, Managing Editor
Elayne Kalberman, Circulation Manager
PRINTED BY STANDARD PRESS & GRAPHICS, INC., NEW YORK CITY

THE OBJECTIVIST NEWSLETTER

Edited and Published by AYN RAND and NATHANIEL BRANDEN

VOL. 2 NO. 6   JUNE, 1963

CHECK YOUR PREMISES
By AYN RAND

Collectivized "Rights"

(*This article is a continuation of the discussion begun in my article "Man's Rights" in the April 1963 issue of this* NEWSLETTER.)

[In "Man's Rights," I covered the following points:

A "right" is a moral principle defining and sanctioning a man's freedom of action in a social context, *i.e.*, freedom from physical compulsion, coercion or interference by other men.

The source of rights is neither mystical nor social; rights, like morality, are derived from man's nature and are a necessity of a rational being's mode of survival.

A man's right to his own life is the base of all other rights.

A right does not include the material implementation of that right by other men; it includes only the freedom to earn that implementation by one's own effort.

Without property rights no other rights can be practiced.

The principle of rights is the means of subordinating society to moral law, as the individual's protection against the brute force of the collective.

The only proper purpose of a government is to protect individual rights, *i.e.*, to protect men from physical force.

The destruction of freedom requires the destruction of rights, and the statists are now striving to accomplish it by means of intellectual subversion, specifically: (a) by switching the concept of rights from the political to the economic realm (claiming the "right" of some men to be supported by the forced labor of others) and (b) by ascribing to private citizens the violations constitutionally forbidden to the government (such as the issue of "censorship"), thus freeing the government from any restrictions.]

Rights are a moral principle defining proper social relationships. Just as a man needs a moral code in order to survive (in order to act, to choose the right goals and to achieve them), so a society (a group of men) needs moral principles in order to organize a social system consonant with man's nature and with the requirements of his survival.

Just as a man *can* evade reality and act on the blind whim of any given moment, but can achieve nothing save progressive self-destruction—so a society *can* evade reality and establish a system ruled by the blind whims of its members or its leaders, by the majority gang of any given moment, by the current demagogue or by a permanent dictator. But such a society can achieve nothing save the rule of brute force and a state of progressive self-destruction.

What subjectivism is in the realm of ethics, collectivism is in the realm of politics. Just as the notion that "Anything I do is right because *I* chose to do it," is not a moral principle, but a negation of morality—so the notion that "Anything society does is right because *society* chose to do it," is not a moral principle, but a negation of moral principles and the banishment of morality from social issues.

When *"might"* is opposed to *"right,"* the concept of "might" can have only one meaning: the power of brute, physical force—which, in fact, is not a "power" but the most hopeless state of impotence; it is merely the "power" to destroy; it is the "power" of a stampede of animals running amuck.

Yet *that* is the goal of most of today's intellectuals. At the root of all their conceptual switches, there lies another, more fundamental one: the switch of the concept of rights from the individual to the collective—which means: the replacement of "The Rights of Man" by "The Rights of Mob."

Since only an individual man can possess rights, the expression "individual rights" is a redundancy (which one has to use for purposes of clarification in today's intellectual chaos). But the expression "collective rights" is a contradiction in terms.

Any group or "collective," large or small, is only a number of individuals. A group can have no rights other than the rights of its individual members. In a free society, the "rights" of any group are derived from the rights of its members through their voluntary, individual choice and *contractual* agreement, and are merely the application of these individual rights to a specific undertaking. Every legitimate group undertaking is based on the participants' right of free association and free trade. (By "legitimate," I mean: non-criminal and freely formed, that is, a group which no one was *forced* to join.)

For instance, the right of an industrial concern to engage in business is derived from the right of its owners to invest their money in a productive venture—from their right to hire employees—from the right of the employees to sell their services—from the right of all those involved to produce and to sell their products—from the right of the customers to buy (or not to buy) those products. Every link of this complex chain of contractual relationships rests on individual rights, individual choices, individual agreements. Every agreement is delimited, specified and subject to certain conditions, that is, dependent upon a mutual trade to mutual benefit.

This is true of all legitimate groups or associations in a free society: partnerships, business concerns, professional associations, labor unions (*voluntary* ones), political parties, etc. It applies also to all agency agreements: the right of one man to act for or represent another or others is derived from the rights of those he represents and is delegated to him by their voluntary choice, for a specific, delimited purpose—as in the case of a lawyer, a business representative, a labor union delegate, etc.

A group, as such, has no rights. A man can neither acquire new rights by joining a group nor lose the rights which he does possess. The principle of individual rights is the only moral base of all groups or associations.

Any group that does not recognize this principle is not an association, but a gang or a mob.

Any doctrine of group activities that does not recognize individual rights is a doctrine of mob rule or legalized lynching.

The notion of "collective rights" (the notion that rights belong to groups, not to individuals) means that "rights" belong to some men, but not to others—that some men have the "right" to dispose of others in any manner they please—and that the criterion of such privileged position consists of numerical superiority.

Nothing can ever justify or validate such a doctrine—and no one ever has. Like the altruist morality from which it is derived, this doctrine rests on mysticism: either on the old-fashioned mysticism of faith in supernatural edicts, like "The Divine Right of Kings"—or on the social mystique of modern collectivists who see society as a super-organism, as some supernatural entity apart from and superior to the sum of its individual members.

The amorality of that collectivist mystique is particularly obvious today in the issue of *national* rights.

A nation, like any other group, is only a number of individuals and can have no rights other than the rights of

(continued on page 23)

INTELLECTUAL AMMUNITION DEPARTMENT

[*Subscribers are invited to send in the questions that they find themselves unable to answer in philosophical or political discussions. As many questions as space permits will be answered. No questions will be answered by mail.*]

■ **Should education be compulsory and tax-supported, as it is today?**

The answer to this question becomes evident if one makes the question more concrete and specific, as follows: Should the government be permitted to remove children forcibly from their homes, with or without the parents' consent, and subject the children to educational training and procedures of which the parents may or may not approve? Should citizens have their wealth expropriated to support an educational system which they may or may not sanction, and to pay for the education of children who are not their own? To anyone who understands and is consistently committed to the principle of individual rights, the answer is clearly: *No*.

There are no moral grounds whatever for the claim that education is the prerogative of the State—or for the claim that it is proper to expropriate the wealth of some men for the unearned benefit of others.

The doctrine that education should be controlled by the State is consistent with the Nazi or Communist theory of government. It is not consistent with the American theory of government.

The totalitarian implications of State education (preposterously described as "free education") have in part been obscured by the fact that in America, unlike Nazi Germany or Soviet Russia, private schools are legally tolerated. Such schools, however, exist not by right but only by *permission*.

Further, the facts remain that: (a) most parents are effectively compelled to send their children to State schools, since they are taxed to support these schools and cannot afford to pay the additional fees required to send their children to private schools; (b) the *standards* of education, controlling *all* schools, are prescribed by the State; (c) the growing trend in American education is for the government to exert wider and wider control over every aspect of education. As an example of this last: when many parents, who objected to the pictographic method of teaching schoolchildren to read, undertook to teach their children at home by the phonetic method—a proposal was made *legally to forbid* parents to do so. What is the implication of this, if not that the child's mind belongs to the State?

When the State assumes *financial* control of education, it is logically appropriate that the State should progressively assume control of the *content* of education—since the State has the responsibility of judging whether or not its funds are being used "satisfactorily." But when a government enters the sphere of *ideas*, when it presumes to prescribe in issues concerning intellectual *content*, that is the death of a free society.

To quote Isabel Paterson in *The God of the Machine:*

"Educational texts are necessarily selective, in subject matter, language and point of view. Where teaching is conducted by private schools, there will be a considerable variation in different schools; the parents must judge what they want their children taught, by the curriculum offered. Then each must strive for objective truth . . . Nowhere will there be any inducement to teach the 'supremacy of the state' as a compulsory philosophy. But every politically controlled educational system will inculcate the doctrine of state supremacy sooner or later, whether as the divine right of kings, or the 'will of the people' in 'democracy.' Once that doctrine has been accepted, it becomes an almost superhuman task to break the stranglehold of the political power over the life of the citizen. It has had his body, property, and mind in its clutches from infancy."

The disgracefully low level of education in America today is the predictable result of a State-controlled school system. Schooling, to a marked extent, has become a status symbol and a ritual. More and more people are entering college—and fewer and fewer people are emerging properly educated. Our educational system is like a vast bureaucracy, a vast civil service, in which the trend is toward a policy of considering everything about a teacher's qualifications (such as the number of his publications) *except his teaching ability;* and of considering everything about a student's qualifications (such as his "social adaptability") *except his intellectual competence.*

The solution is to *bring the field of education into the market-place.*

There is an urgent *economic need* for education. When educational institutions have to compete with one another in the quality of the training they offer—when they have to compete for the value that will be attached to the diplomas they issue—educational standards will necessarily rise. When they have to compete for the services of the best teachers, the teachers who will attract the greatest number of students, then the calibre of teaching—and of teachers' wages—will necessarily rise. (Today, the most talented teachers often abandon their profession and enter private industry, where they know their efforts will be better rewarded.) When the economic principles that have resulted in the superlative efficiency of American industry are permitted to operate in the field of education, the result will be a revolution, in the direction of unprecedented educational development and growth.

Education should be liberated from the control or intervention of government, and turned over to *profit-making* private enterprise, not because education is unimportant, but because education is so *crucially important.*

What must be challenged is the prevalent belief that education is some sort of "natural right"—in effect, a free gift of nature. There *are* no such free gifts. But it is in the interests of Statism to foster this delusion—in order to throw a smokescreen over the issue of whose freedom must be sacrificed to pay for such "free gifts."

As a result of the fact that education has been tax-supported for such a long time, most people find it difficult to project an alternative. Yet there is nothing unique about education that distinguishes it from the many other human needs which are filled by private enterprise. If, for many years, the government had undertaken to provide all the citizens with shoes (on the grounds that shoes are an urgent necessity), and if someone were subsequently to propose that this field should be turned over to private enterprise, he would doubtless be told indignantly: "What! Do you want everyone except the rich to walk around barefoot?"

But the shoe industry is doing its job with immeasurably greater competence than public education is doing *its* job.

To quote Isabel Paterson once more: "The most vindictive resentment may be expected from the pedagogic profession for any suggestion that they should be dislodged from their dictatorial position; it will be expressed mainly in epithets, such as 'reactionary,' at the mildest. Nevertheless, the question to put to any teacher moved to such indignation, is: Do you think nobody would *willingly* entrust his children to you and pay you for teaching them? Why do you have to extort your fees and collect your pupils by compulsion?"

■ **Does inherited wealth give some individuals an unfair advantage in a competitive economy?**

In considering the issue of inherited wealth, one must begin by recognizing that the crucial right involved is not that of the heir but of the original *producer* of the wealth. The right of property is the right of use and disposal; just as the man who produces wealth has the right to use it and dispose of it in his lifetime, so he has the right to choose who shall be its recipient after his death. No one else is entitled to make that choice. It is irrelevant, therefore, in this context, to consider the worthiness or unworthiness of any particular heir; his is not the basic right at stake; when people denounce inherited wealth, it is the *right of the producer* that they in fact are attacking.

It has been argued that, since the heir did not work to produce the wealth, he has no inherent right to it; that is true: the heir's is a *derived* right; the only *primary* right is the producer's. But if the future heir has no moral claim to the wealth, except by the producer's choice, *neither has anyone else*—certainly not the government or "the public."

In a *free* economy, inherited wealth is not an impediment or a threat to those who do not possess it. Wealth, it is necessary to remember, is not a static, limited quantity that can only be divided or looted; wealth is produced; its potential quantity is virtually unlimited.

If an heir is worthy of his money, that is, if he uses it productively, he brings more wealth into existence, he raises the general standard of living—and, to that extent, he makes the road to the top easier for any talented newcomer. The greater the amount of wealth, of industrial development, in existence, the higher the economic rewards (in wages and profits) and *the wider the market for ability*—for new ideas, products and services.

The *less* the wealth in existence, the longer and harder the struggle for everyone. In the beginning years of an industrial economy, wages are low; there is little market yet for unusual ability. But with every succeeding generation, as capital accumulation increases, the economic demand for men of ability rises. The existing industrial establishments desperately need such men; they have no choice but to bid ever higher wages for such men's services—and thus *to train their own future competitors*—so that the time required for a talented newcomer to accumulate his own fortune and establish his own business grows continually shorter.

If the heir is not worthy of his money, the only person threatened by it is himself. A free, competitive economy is a constant process of improvement, innovation, progress; it does not tolerate stagnation. If an heir who lacks ability acquires a fortune and a great industrial establishment from his successful father, he will not be able to maintain it for long; he will not be equal to the competition. In a free economy, where bureaucrats and legislators would not have the power to sell or grant economic favors, all of the heir's money would not be able to buy him protection for his incompetence; he would have to be good at his work or lose his customers to companies run by men of superior ability. There is nothing as vulnerable as a large, mismanaged company that competes with small, efficient ones. (See, in this connection, my discussion of monopolies in the June, 1962 issue of this NEWSLETTER.)

The personal luxuries or drunken parties that the incompetent heir may enjoy on his father's money, are of no *economic* significance. In business, he would not be able to stand in the way of talented competitors or serve as an impediment to men of ability. He would find no automatic security anywhere.

At the turn of the century, there was a popular phrase that is very eloquent with regard to the foregoing: "From shirtsleeves to shirtsleeves in three generations." If a self-made man rose by ability and left his business to unworthy heirs, his grandson went back to the shirtsleeves of obscure employment. (He did *not* end up with the governorship of a state.)

It is a *"mixed" economy*—such as the semi-socialist or semi-fascist variety we have today—that protects the nonproductive rich by freezing a society on a given level of development, by freezing people into classes and castes and making it increasingly more difficult for men to rise or fall or move from one caste to another; so that whoever inherited a fortune before the freeze, can keep it with little fear of competition, like an heir in a feudal society.

It is significant how many heirs of great industrial fortunes, the second and third generation millionaires, are welfare statists, clamoring for more and more controls. The target and victims of these controls are the men of ability who, in a free economy, would displace these heirs; the men with whom the heirs would be unable to compete.

As Ludwig von Mises writes in *Human Action*:

"Today taxes often absorb the greater part of the newcomer's 'excessive' profits. He cannot accumulate capital; he cannot expand his own business; he will never become big business and a match for the vested interests. The old firms do not need to fear his competition; they are sheltered by the tax collector. They may with impunity indulge in routine . . . In this sense progressive taxation checks economic progress and makes for rigidity. . . .

"The interventionists complain that big business is getting rigid and bureaucratic and that it is no longer possible for competent newcomers to challenge the vested interests of the rich old families. However, as far as their complaints are justified, they complain about things which are merely the result of their own policies."

—NATHANIEL BRANDEN

■ **What is the Objectivist stand on "right-to-work" laws?**

As advocates of laissez-faire capitalism, Objectivists are opposed to any legislation that abridges the freedom of production and trade. We are, therefore, opposed to the "right-to-work" laws.

The "right-to-work" laws prohibit employers and unions from contractually agreeing to and stipulating a closed and/or union shop. As such, these laws clearly represent an infringement of the rights of the parties involved; these laws rest on the principle that the government has the right to prescribe the terms of contractual agreements—which is a *Statist* concept. In a free society, an employer who voluntarily negotiates with a voluntary union, may sign any agreement with the union that he wishes. Although it is doubtful whether a closed and/or union shop agreement would ever be economically wise, that choice is the employer's to make. No one's *rights* are infringed by such an agreement; a worker does not have a *"right"* to a job with a given employer; if he does not or cannot meet the employer's terms, he is free to seek employment elsewhere.

Many "conservatives" champion "right-to-work" laws on the ground that today unions are so powerful they can virtually compel an employer's agreement to a closed and/or union shop. It is true that unions have such power. But they acquired it only by virtue of legislation, which had the effect of forcing men into unions whether they wished to join or not and of forcing employers to deal with these unions. Unions did not and could not achieve, in a free society, the monopolistic, destructive power they possess in today's "mixed economy." The guilty party is not unionism as such, but government controls.

The solution lies, not in passing new laws, but in repealing the laws that caused the disaster in the first place.

The defenders of freedom do not serve their own cause by trying to fight their battle on the enemy's terms, that is, by deciding that the solution to the evil of government intervention in the economy is more government intervention.

—BARBARA BRANDEN

Collectivized "Rights"   (from page 21)

its individual citizens. A free nation—a nation that recognizes, respects and protects the individual rights of its citizens—has a right to its territorial integrity, its social system and its form of government. The government of such a nation is not the ruler, but the servant or *agent* of its citizens and has no rights other than the rights *delegated* to it by the citizens for a specific, delimited task (the task of protecting them from physical force, derived from their right of self-defense).

The citizens of a free nation may disagree about the specific legal procedures or *methods* of implementing their rights (which is a complex problem, the province of political science and of the philosophy of law), but they agree on the basic principle to be implemented: the principle of individual rights. When a country's Constitution places individual rights outside the reach of public authorities, the sphere of political power is severely delimited—and thus the citizens may, safely and properly, agree to abide by the decisions of a majority vote in this delimited sphere. The lives and property of minorities or dissenters are not at stake, are not subject to vote and are not endangered by any majority decision; no man or group holds a blank check on power over others.

Such a nation has a right to its sovereignty (derived from the rights of its citizens) and a right to demand that its sovereignty be respected by all other nations.

(continued on page 24)

Collectivized "Rights" *(from page 23)*

But this right cannot be claimed by dictatorships, by savage tribes or by any form of absolutist tyranny. A nation that violates the rights of its own citizens cannot claim any rights whatsoever. In the issue of rights, as in all moral issues, there can be no double standard. A nation ruled by brute physical force is not a nation, but a horde—whether it is led by Attila, Genghis Khan, Hitler, Khrushchev or Castro. What rights could Attila claim and on what grounds?

This applies to all forms of tribal savagery, ancient or modern, primitive or "industrialized." Neither geography nor race nor tradition nor previous state of development can confer on some human beings the "right" to violate the rights of others.

The right of "the self-determination of nations" applies only to free societies or to societies seeking to establish freedom; it does not apply to dictatorships. Just as an individual's right of free action does not include the "right" to commit crimes (that is, to violate the rights of others), so the right of a nation to determine its own form of government does not include the right to establish a slave-society (that is, to legalize the enslavement of some men by others). *There is no such thing as "the right to enslave."* A nation *can* do it, just as a man *can* become a criminal—but neither can do it *by right.*

It does not matter, in this context, whether a nation was enslaved by force, like Soviet Russia, or by vote, like Nazi Germany. Individual rights are not subject to a public vote; a majority has no right to vote away the rights of a minority; the political function of rights is precisely to protect minorities from oppression by majorities (and the smallest minority on earth is the individual). Whether a slave-society was conquered or *chose* to be enslaved, it can claim no national rights and no recognition of such "rights" by civilized countries— just as a mob of gangsters cannot demand a recognition of its "rights" and a legal equality with an industrial concern or a university, on the ground that the gangsters *chose* by unanimous vote to engage in that particular kind of group activity.

Dictatorship nations are outlaws. Any free nation had the *right* to invade Nazi Germany and, today, has the *right* to invade Soviet Russia, Cuba or any other slave-pen. Whether a free nation chooses to do so or not is a matter of its own self-interest, *not* of respect for the non-existent "rights" of gang-rulers. It is not a free nation's *duty* to liberate other nations at the price of self-sacrifice, but a free nation has the right to do it, when and if it so chooses.

This right, however, is conditional. Just as the suppression of crimes does not give a policeman the right to engage in criminal activities, so the invasion and destruction of a dictatorship does not give the invader the right to establish another variant of a slave-society in the conquered country. A slave-country has no *national* rights, but the *individual* rights of its citizens remain valid, even if unrecognized, and the conqueror has no right to violate them. Therefore, the invasion of an enslaved country is morally justified only when and if the conquerors establish a *free* social system, that is, a system based on the recognition of individual rights.

Since there is no fully free country today, since the so-called "Free World" consists of various "mixed economies," it might be asked whether every country on earth is morally open to invasion by every other. The answer is: No. There is a difference between a country that recognizes the principle of individual rights, but does not implement it fully in practice, and a country that denies and flouts it explicitly. All "mixed economies" are in a precarious state of transition which, ultimately, has to turn to freedom or collapse into dictatorship. There are four characteristics which brand a country unmistakably as a dictatorship: one-party rule— executions without trial or with a mock trial, for political offenses—the nationalization or expropriation of private property—and censorship. A country guilty of these outrages forfeits any moral prerogatives, any claim to national rights or sovereignty, and becomes an outlaw.

Observe, on this particular issue, the shameful end-of-trail and the intellectual disintegration of modern "liberals."

Internationalism had always been one of the "liberals'" basic tenets. They regarded nationalism as a major social evil, as a product of capitalism and as the cause of wars. They opposed any form of national self-interest; they refused to differentiate between rational patriotism and blind, racist chauvinism, denouncing both as "fascist." They advocated the dissolution of national boundaries and the merging of all nations into "One World." Next to property rights, "national rights" were the special target of their attacks.

Today, it is "national rights" that they invoke as their last, feeble, fading hold on some sort of moral justification for the results of their theories—for the brood of little statist dictatorships spreading, like a skin disease, over the surface of the globe, in the form of so-called "newly emerging nations," semi-socialist, semi-communist, semi-fascist, and wholly committed only to the use of brute force.

It is the "national right" of such countries to choose their own form of government (any form they please) that the "liberals" offer as a moral validation and ask us to respect. It is the "national right" of Cuba to *its* form of government, they claim, that we must not violate or interfere with. Having all but destroyed the legitimate national rights of free countries, it is for dictatorships that the "liberals" now claim the sanction of "national rights."

And worse: it is not mere nationalism that the "liberals" champion, but *racism*—primordial tribal racism.

Observe the double standard: while, in the civilized countries of the West, the "liberals" are still advocating internationalism and global self-sacrifice—the savage tribes of Asia and Africa are granted the sovereign "right" to slaughter one another in racial warfare. Mankind is reverting to a pre-industrial, pre-historical view of society: to racial collectivism.

Such is the logical result and climax of the "liberals'" moral collapse which began when, as a prelude to the collectivization of property, they accepted the collectivization of rights.

Their own confession of guilt lies in their terminology. Why do they use the word *"rights"* to denote the things they are advocating? Why don't they preach what they practice? Why don't they name it openly and attempt to justify it, if they can?

The answer is obvious.

OBJECTIVIST CALENDAR

■ On May 7, Nathaniel Branden addressed the student body of Green Mountain College, in Poultney, Vermont. His subject: "Reason and Individualism in the Philosophy of Ayn Rand."

■ On May 13, Ayn Rand addressed the annual meeting of The Medical Society of New Jersey, in Atlantic City. Her subject: "How *not* to fight against Socialized Medicine."

■ On June 6, in New York City, NBI begins a ten-lecture course, "Principles of Efficient Thinking," given by Barbara Branden. This course begins in Los Angeles, via tape transcription, on June 28.

■ Between June 29 and July 5, Nathaniel Branden will visit Pittsburgh, Columbus, Cincinnati, Cleveland and Detroit, for the purpose of interviewing prospective representatives for NBI's Tape Transcription Division; these representatives are to act as business managers for the lecture series given in their cities. Mr. Branden will be available for interviews as follows: Pittsburgh—June 29; Columbus—June 30 and July 1; Cincinnati—July 2; Cleveland—July 3 and 4; Detroit— July 5. Interested persons are invited to write to NATHANIEL BRANDEN INSTITUTE, 120 East 34th St., New York 16, N. Y., for further details and to arrange appointments.

Published monthly at 120 East 34th Street, New York 16, N. Y.
Subscription rate: in United States, its possessions, Canada and Mexico, $5 for one year; other countries, $6.
Additional copies of this Newsletter: single copy 50¢ (coins, not stamps); 10 — 99 copies, 25¢ each plus postage (for first-class delivery add 1¢ per copy, for third-class delivery add 1/2¢ per copy); 100 or more copies, 15¢ each plus postage (same as above).
For change of address send old address and new address with zone number if any. Allow us three weeks to process new subscriptions and change of address.

Ayn Rand and Nathaniel Branden, Editors and Publishers
Barbara Branden, Managing Editor
Elayne Kalberman, Circulation Manager
PRINTED BY STANDARD PRESS & GRAPHICS, INC., NEW YORK CITY

THE OBJECTIVIST NEWSLETTER

Edited and Published by AYN RAND and NATHANIEL BRANDEN

VOL. 2 NO. 7   JULY, 1963

CHECK YOUR PREMISES
By AYN RAND

Vast Quicksands

Objectivists have been maintaining that all the evils and abuses popularly ascribed to capitalism were caused, necessitated and made possible, not by the free market, but by government intervention into the economy. The alleged cure for such evils, administered by the advocates of a "mixed economy," consisted of blaming the businessmen for the sins of the bureaucrats and of granting wider powers to the bureaucrats—thus making the country swallow a full, "unmixed" glass of the poison which was destroying it.

Those who could not discern this process in history, can now see it taking place before their eyes.

On his last day in office, May 31, Newton N. Minow wrote a letter to President Kennedy, recommending that the F.C.C. be abolished and the entire broadcasting industry of the United States be placed in the power of a single Czar.

For about two years, Mr. Minow and his intellectual henchmen in the nation's press have been attacking and denouncing the television industry as a "vast wasteland" of dullness, conformity, stagnation and bad taste. Many of these accusations were true; with very rare exceptions, today's television is in a miserable state intellectually and esthetically. But what caused it and who is to blame? In a series of intellectual lynch-parties, known as public hearings, an assortment of "liberal" witnesses blamed the usual scapegoat: *businessmen*; specifically, network executives and sponsors.

The cynicism of that entire performance was best expressed by the fact that the majority of the press praised Mr. Minow's "courage"—the courage of a bureaucrat who was threatening to revoke the licenses of his victims while denouncing them for their timidity.

Although some voices did protest that Mr. Minow was "exceeding" his authority, no one challenged the nature of that authority: the fact that the F.C.C. holds an undefined power to enforce an undefinable criterion of broadcasting—*"the public interest."*

No one named the obvious fact that when men are caught in the trap of non-objective law, when their work, future and livelihood are at the mercy of a bureaucrat's whim, when they have no way of knowing what unknown "influence" will crack down on them for which unspecified offense, *fear* becomes their basic motive, if they remain in the industry at all—and compromise, conformity, staleness, dullness, the dismal grayness of the middle-of-the-road are all that can be expected of them. Independent thinking does not submit to bureaucratic edicts, originality does not follow "public policies," integrity does not petition for a license, heroism is not fostered by fear, creative genius is not summoned forth at the point of a gun.

Non-objective law is the most effective weapon of human enslavement: its victims become its enforcers and enslave themselves.

If you want to see a graphic picture of how it works in practice, read a brilliant article, "TV: the Timid Giant" by Edith Efron, in the May 18, 1963 issue of *TV Guide*. It is an objective, impersonal report—and it reveals a nightmare spectacle of terror, a terror accepted as "normal," the more terrible because part of it is terror of admitting that one is terrorized.

"They [TV newsmen] contend that there are 'taboos' in the coverage of national affairs. They insist that these taboos are 'tacit' and unstated—and that they are not being imposed explicitly by the networks but are imposed by many men on themselves, in cautious 'self-censorship.'"

And: "Some staff men blame the trouble on pressure groups. 'They're so organized,' says Chet Huntley, 'that they can create real havoc within a network. After some controversial stories, you've got six weeks of absolute agony ahead of you, with yelling and meetings and endless correspondence, and lawyers and suits, and shipping scripts back and forth to the F.C.C. It's real agony.'"

And: "Says a newscaster: 'The broadcasters are afraid because they're regulated. The F.C.C. can refuse to renew a station's license any time it pleases. People don't know what their Constitutional rights are.'"

And: "If one were to boil down all these different types of diagnoses of the TV industry's trouble into one phrase, it would be: *floating political anxiety*. It is an anxiety caused by a continuous awareness of *potential* political danger—a danger that might spring from any one of dozens of possible sources—a danger that might strike tomorrow, next week, next year, or never. It is so omnipresent an emotion that the men in TV have apparently grown used to it, and automatically act to inhibit direct coverage of national affairs."

The article quotes both "conservative" and "liberal" newsmen. Both feel desperately frustrated; both find the situation close to unbearable. But none has a solution to offer—and none challenges the root of the evil: government licensing.

Yet it is obvious that neither pressure groups nor "Big Business" nor "Big Labor" could terrorize and enslave the entire TV industry without the help of political power. In a free country, pressure groups would be merely private organizations with no power other than that of persuasion—and their influence would depend on the justice of their cause. No group of cranks or of hidden special interests could become a threat to the business community of the whole nation, to networks and sponsors alike. But in a "mixed economy," every pressure group—rational, irrational or criminal—is a potential threat to everyone; every pressure group is a political lobby that can influence legislation and the appointment of F.C.C. commissioners; for an industry that depends on government licensing, every pressure group holds, not merely the power to disagree, but the power to destroy.

It is in the face of this monstrous situation and in the name of "curing" television's troubles that Mr. Minow proposes greater government power over the television industry.

Such is the technique of all statists: first, you tie a man hand and foot; then, you complain that he is unwilling to move; then you put him into a strait jacket. (And then you declare that capitalism has failed.)

Mr. Minow proposes what his "conservative" opponents lack the courage to propose: that the F.C.C. be abolished. But where an advocate of freedom would demand that the F.C.C. be abolished, period—Mr. Minow demands that it be replaced by a *single administrator* and a court.

The N. Y. Times of June 5 quotes him as follows: "The multi-member agency has great difficulty resolving differences among the members in their approach to basic policies. The result is to not formulate the policy—and to postpone the policy decision to resolution on a case by case basis, which all too often means inconsistent decisions, with the public and the regulated industry not knowing the ground rules. More important, its consequence is that vital planning and policy measures are not undertaken."

Consider carefully the meaning of this statement. A clear, objective principle or basic policy can unite hundreds or millions of men—as the philosophy of freedom united this

(continued on page 28)

BOOKS

*The Feminine Mystique** by Betty Friedan

Reviewed by **EDITH EFRON**

—Woman is a sexual being whose sole purpose in life is to submit passively to male dominance, and to breed.

—The only work for which she is psychologically suited is the rearing of children, and household chores.

—Her sexual capacity is destroyed by the use of her intellect and by the pursuit of a productive career.

These, says author Betty Friedan, are the basic tenets of the "feminine mystique"—a Freudian revision of the Victorian view of woman's nature—which was introduced into the United States twenty years ago, and is now accepted as scientific truth by the vast majority of the American population.

Mrs. Friedan's book—one of the most illuminating psycho-social studies ever to be published about the United States—analyzes this Freudian "mystique," describes its rapid passage through our cultural institutions, reports on the severe psychological damage it has inflicted on millions of American women, and prescribes radical solutions for its victims.

Freud's view of woman, writes Mrs. Friedan, was both an outgrowth of the Victorian view and a rebellion against it. He shared the Victorian idea that women were inferior, childish beings, "less than human, unable to think like men, born merely to breed and serve men." He interpreted feminine intellectual strivings and ambition as psychological sickness—a camouflaged desire to possess male sexual organs, or "penis envy." In opposition to Victorian views, however, he recognized that women had sexual desires, and he viewed sexual satisfaction as a crucial psychological need. He accordingly declared that the precondition for feminine sexual fulfillment was woman's acceptance of her dependency on man, and her sublimation of "penis envy" through motherhood.

The image Freud created of woman was a new one in the history of human thought. The older, conventional view of woman, says Mrs. Friedan, "split woman in two": she was the "good, pure woman on a pedestal"—or she was the evil "whore with desires of the flesh." Freud created a different dichotomy: the "good" woman now had "feminine," healthy desires of the flesh—and the "evil" woman had "unfeminine," unhealthy desires for a career.

The new Freudian doctrine was seized upon with enthusiasm by American social "scientists," who incorporated it as literal truth into their works and recklessly transmitted it to the nation as the new enlightenment.

Mrs. Friedan reports in detail on the astonishing battery of Freudian works in psychology, sociology and anthropology which appeared in the 1940's to lay the groundwork for the "mystique." Here are a few samples of the new "science":

In 1944, psychoanalyst Helene Deutsch published *The Psychology of Woman*, which announced that an intellectual woman had a "masculinity complex" and that "normal" femininity was to be achieved only by the renunciation of "originality" and of active goals.

In 1946, sociologist Mirra Komarovsky published her *Functional Analysis of Sex Roles*, which warned of the "risk" inherent in "awakening interests and abilities which . . . run counter to the present definition of femininity," and recommended "generalized dependency" as the ideal state for a young girl.

And throughout the 1940's and 50's, anthropologist Margaret Mead, who defined feminine "creativity" in terms of "the passive receptivity of the uterus," published volume after volume glorifying female savages for whom reproduction was the highest achievement.

The "prime target" of this barrage of Freudian writings, writes Mrs. Friedan, was the educational system. The Freudians were militantly opposed to educating women in the same manner as men, and they accused the nation's educators of over-training women's minds, of "defeminizing American women, of dooming them to frustration . . . to life without orgasm." They rapidly induced guilt in the educators, most of whom joined the Freudian camp in the 40's, and accepted the new challenge of protecting American girls from the hazards of education.

The author presents massive and horrifying evidence of the rapid deterioration of higher education for women, as the "mystique" was accepted throughout the academic world. All over the land, she writes, "college presidents and professors became more concerned with their students' future capacity for sexual orgasm than with their future use of trained intelligence."

In many colleges, girls were taught by Freudian educators that thinking was alien to their nature, that "abstractions," "quantitative thinking" and "innovation" were "masculine"—and that women should concentrate on developing such "feminine" attributes as: "the sense of the immediate," "the intuitive," "the emotional."

Within one generation, the "feminine mystique" became a national "psychological religion." And millions of American women living by this "religion" became the passive sexual beings Freud had declared them to be.

Education, marriage and birthrate statistics tell the disastrous story:

—In 1929, the proportion of women among American college students was 47%, but by 1958, it had dropped to 35%. By the mid-50's, 60% of the girls enrolled in colleges were leaving school before graduation in order to marry. The United States may now be the only nation in the world where the proportion of women receiving a higher education has decreased in the last twenty years.

—By the end of the 50's, the average marriage-age of the American woman was 20, and it is dropping into the teens. It is now lower than that of any other country in the Western world, and closely approximates the marriage-age in the "underdeveloped" countries.

—The annual birthrate of the United States is now nearly 3 times that of the Western European nations; nearly double that of Japan; and is rapidly approaching that of Africa and India.

Betty Friedan, in 1963, is the first to reveal the massive psychological disaster caused by the "feminine mystique," and the section of her book which is devoted to this expose, is a horrifying social document.

All over the country, she reports, women are in torment, and cannot grasp the nature of their suffering. They have so profoundly accepted the "mystique" that they can hardly put their frustration into words.

When they try to express it, they say, "I feel incomplete . . ." "I feel as if I don't exist . . ." "I don't feel alive . . ." "I don't know who I am . . ." Many of them refer to this inner emptiness as "the problem." Mrs. Friedan calls it "the problem without a name."

In an attempt to relieve the dread grey anguish, they turn to the only guide they know, the "mystique" itself, and seek even more desperately for the "fulfillment" it promised. They engage in "insatiable sex-seeking," make excessive sexual demands on their husbands, conduct extra-marital affairs, collapse into hopeless promiscuity—and are terrified by their inability to experience sexual pleasure. They breed compulsively and keep house compulsively to prove their femininity.

When these defenses fail, they develop psychosomatic ailments: chronic fatigue, bleeding blisters, bleeding ulcers, ovarian breakdowns, heart attacks. They become alcoholics. They are immobilized by fear, and are unable to make the simplest decisions. They collapse into suicidal depressions and psychosis.

"You'd be surprised," one doctor told Mrs. Friedan, "at the number of these happy suburban wives who simply go berserk one night and go shrieking through the streets without any clothes on."

What is "the problem without a name" that is destroying the lives and sanity of American women? It is, says Mrs. Friedan, "that diffuse feeling of purposelessness, non-existence,

(continued on page 27)

---

* Published by W. W. Norton Co., $5.95. Available from NBI BOOK SERVICE, INC., 120 East 34th St., New York 16, N. Y., for $4.95 (N. Y. C. resident add 4% sales tax; outside the U. S. add 15¢).

Edith Efron is a journalist whose articles have appeared in such publications as Life, Look, *and* The New York Times Magazine.

INTELLECTUAL AMMUNITION DEPARTMENT

[Subscribers are invited to send in the questions that they find themselves unable to answer in philosophical or political discussions. As many questions as space permits will be answered. No questions will be answered by mail.]

■ **How does one persuade a person who refuses to accept reason or logical demonstration?**

It is always necessary to remember that man is a being of volitional consciousness and, therefore, that one cannot *compel* a man to think or to be rational. To think or not to think, is man's basic act of choice—and the only consciousness over which one has such control is one's own. In intellectual discussions—and in *any* dealings with other human beings—one's obligation is to present one's position clearly, to offer logical arguments and to know that, within the context, one's case is sufficiently comprehensive. That is the limit of one's power and, therefore, of one's responsibility.

There are two errors that people often make in discussions or disagreements. The first is to persist too long, ignoring unequivocal evidence that one's opponent has no intention of being bound by reason. The second is to give up too soon, to take lack of instant agreement as *prima facie* evidence that one's opponent is irrational, and to be insufficiently concerned with the clarity and objectivity of one's own presentation.

(1) When, in a discussion, a person announces that he is a mystic or that he holds his beliefs "on faith"—or when he answers an argument with some such statement as "That's only reason," or "That's only logic," or "But I don't *feel* it" —that is the time to end the discussion and refuse to continue. One should always take a mystic or irrationalist at his word and treat him accordingly (which is what he dreads most). One should not grant one's intellectual sanction by continuing to argue and thus imply that a compromise or rapproachment between reason and mysticism is possible. One's attitude should be: I have only one means of knowledge or communication, reason; and I do not recognize or accept any other intellectual currency.

What often makes this issue difficult in practice, of course, is the fact that few irrationalists are so obliging as to identify themselves as such. The majority go through the motions of being rational, faking (for others and often for themselves) an honest desire for understanding and communication. This places the burden on the shoulders of any rational, conscientious man who will not want to condemn his opponent unfairly and will prefer to give the benefit of every possible doubt, stretching his generosity and sense of justice to the limit.

Since the possible forms of evasion, subterfuge and willful irrationality are virtually unlimited, there is no way to formulate a general rule that will guide one infallibly in recognizing them. But some of the more obvious signs of intellectual dishonesty include: refusing to answer specific questions or arguments, persistently running off to irrelevancies at crucial points in the discussion; appeals to authority, such as "But *nobody* believes that," or "But *everybody* believes such and such"; impugning the motives or intelligence of the opponent. Whenever one encounters this kind of attitude, one may know that one is not dealing with a person whose primary concern is the truth or falsehood of ideas.

It is a mistake to assume that everyone, no matter how irrational, can be reached intellectually "if only one knew the right words." Everyone is *not* reachable—because not everyone *wants* to be reached. (The fact that a psychotherapist, *sometimes*, not always, can break through a neurotic's defenses and bring him to reason, is irrelevant here; even the most skilled psychotherapist cannot succeed, if his patient persistently refuses to think; and, in any event, one cannot regard life as a mental hospital and one cannot deal with people as if they were psychological invalids.)

(2) Just as it is an error to ignore the fact that intellectual dishonesty is possible, so it is no less an error to regard any disagreement, regardless of context or circumstances, as proof of one's opponent's dishonesty. It is necessary always to remember that man is neither omniscient nor infallible and that honest errors of knowledge are possible. (Avowed mysticism, I hasten to add, does not belong in the category of honest errors.)

In any disagreement, a conscientious person's first concern is: Have I presented my case clearly? Have I been objective? Have I given the *reasons* for my convictions? Have I fully answered my opponent's questions or objections?

Very often, the person who least understands his own case and cannot *prove* his ideas (even though they may be true), is the person who is quickest to condemn his opponent as irrational or stupid when they fail to agree. He converts his own inner uncertainty or anxiety into an accusation against the other person.

How long one will persist in seeking to resolve an intellectual disagreement with someone, depends, in part, on the importance one attaches to the person involved. One is not obliged to try to educate or persuade every person one meets.

If, however, one chooses to discuss ideas at all and to advocate a philosophy of reason, it would be a gross contradiction to tolerate, as a legitimate "difference of opinion," explicit irrationalism on the part of the other person—or to demand less of oneself than full objectivity and rational clarity.

—NATHANIEL BRANDEN

The Feminine Mystique (from page 26)

non-involvement with the world that can be called anomie, or lack of identity."

She writes: "It is my thesis that the core of the problem for women today is . . . a problem of identity—a stunting or evasion of growth that is perpetuated by the feminine mystique."

The "mystique," she says, permits adolescent girls to escape their "terror of freedom" and the necessity to "face the question of their own identity"—to determine who they are and what they will be. It permits them "to escape identity altogether in the name of sexual fulfillment." The price paid for this evasion is the failure to develop "the firm core of self or 'I' without which a human being is not truly alive."

Mrs. Friedan concludes that American women have been "dehumanized" by an irrational doctrine, and offers the victims of the "mystique" psychologically valid advice. Women, like men, she says, have a crucial psychological need for purposeful intellectual activity and for life-long productive goals—and only these will produce in them the "self," the self-esteem, the sense of efficacy and mastery, which they now lack.

She counsels all American housewives to choose a career— not a "job" or a "hobby," but a life-long profession. She recommends that women return to school immediately for the education they forfeited.

She makes an additional suggestion to which one must take exception. She advocates a "G.I. Bill of Rights" for women, which would finance the housewives' return to school, and would be paid for by taxation. She has clearly failed to grasp the moral implications of her proposal: it would financially penalize those women who have been loyal to their human status, for the sake of those who have betrayed it.

Mrs. Friedan may have made this proposal because she does not understand the Statist implications of the phenomenon she is combating. In an early chapter of her book, she equates the "feminine mystique" with *"Kinder, Kuche, Kirche,"* the slogan with which the Nazis reduced women to breeding animals; and she asks why the Nazi view of woman received such unanimous support from the "thinkers" of America—why it was so readily integrated into the modern American culture. It is an excellent question, but Mrs. Friedan ends her book without answering it. The answer is this: Doctrines which deny mind, independence and individuality are magnetically attractive to Statist "intellectuals" in all societies; the "feminine mystique" was totally harmonious with the anti-reason, anti-individualism of modern American liberals.

Apart from this regrettable failure to understand the political context of her subject, Mrs. Friedan has written a brilliant, informative and culturally explosive book.

The Feminine Mystique should be read by every woman— and by every man—in America.

Vast Quicksands *(from page 25)*

nation at its birth. What is one to think of a *basic* policy on which seven men cannot agree (the seven members of the F.C.C.)? Such a policy, by its nature, has to be so arbitrary, irrational, undefinable and non-objective that no argument, persuasion or agreement is possible—and the contest is not one of principle but of personal whim. If so, then by what conceivable moral standard should such a policy be imposed on an entire industry and on an entire nation?

That which cannot be formulated into an objective law, cannot be made the subject of legislation—not in a free country, not if we are to have "a government of laws and not of men." An undefinable law is not a law, but merely a license for some men to rule others.

All regulatory agencies have the same problem; all of them practice the same tyrannical injustices, inconsistencies and whims as the F.C.C.; all of them spread the same kind of destruction. The evil is inherent in government regulations, in any attempt to impose government controls on an economy: it cannot be done justly, the injustice is in the nature of the principle, no law can cover it, and the attempt can only destroy all semblance of civilized legality.

This is where an entire nation (and every honest man within it) has to check its premises: either we correct the evil at its root and move to abolish the arbitrary powers of regulatory agencies—or we surrender to the first (or second or tenth) Newton Minow who will demonstrate without difficulty that regulatory commissions, committees and conferences do not work, and that if we wish to retain government controls, we can do so only by granting total power to a single autocrat.

After two years of speech-making and of brandishing the words "public interest" as if they were a simple, self-evident absolute, clear to all but the most anti-social reactionaries, Mr. Minow now admits that even seven "public servants" can't agree on just what is "in the public interest," and, therefore, that the public cannot possibly know it or agree on it, and, therefore, that a single autocrat should have the power to determine it and ram it down the public's throat by legalized force.

These, of course, are not the words Mr. Minow uses; he merely says that the public does not know "the ground rules," which a single autocrat should prescribe. He demands this power in the name of his often stated belief that "the public owns the airways." A group of owners who have no say about the ground rules governing the use of their property is a queer concept under a free economy—but not under socialism. Such is the nature of any "public ownership."

"More important," says Mr. Minow, "is that *vital planning* and *policy measures* are not undertaken." *Whose* policy measures? Vital planning—of *what?* Of the use of this country's airways? Of everything that is to be said, presented or broadcast over our radio and television stations? No act of Congress has ever granted any such "planning" authority to any government agency—nor would it have the Constitutional right to grant it.

But Mr. Minow intends, apparently, to claim that he is merely upholding the American principle of a division of powers. He declares that the F.C.C. cannot properly perform the functions of judge, legislator and administrator, which it had been performing—and, therefore, he proposes that it surrender its judicial function to a court.

According to *The N. Y. Times*, Mr. Minow expressed concern over the plight of the applicants for a television or radio channel and explained that: "Over the years, the commission has laid down many 'criteria' for choosing one applicant over another. . . . These criteria were mutually inconsistent and were applied in such a way that no one knew what the commission wanted in a station owner. Instead of this system, Mr. Minow proposes a single administrator to lay down the criteria. Then the administrative court would apply them in a legal contest among the competitors."

Consider carefully what *this* means. That single administrator would be a *lawmaker*. His "criteria" would have the force of law for the broadcasting industry. A court does not have the power to change the law, only to enforce compliance with the law. That administrative court would have no function and no power other than to judge which applicant best suits the Czar's edicts.

"The administrator would have had to articulate effective, logical policies," said Mr. Minow ingenuously, "or the administrative court would be at a loss in deciding the comparative case. And the court would have long ago established a coherent line of comparative decisions, rather than an unpredictable, crazy-quilt pattern."

Is Mr. Minow that ignorant of the record and history of another regulatory agency—the F.T.C.—and of the court decisions in antitrust cases? Or does he believe that the public's mind is so disintegrated that nobody will think of looking at that glaring precedent?

Such is Mr. Minow's proposal. "White House aides are now considering his ideas," states *The N. Y. Times*.

It is possible that the same short-range mentalities, among the broadcasting industry's executives, who accepted and endorsed the creation of the F.C.C. in the first place, might now accept and endorse Mr. Minow's proposal. Such mentalities might think that it is easier to court one autocrat and they might be willing to compete for his favor, each assuring himself that the Czar is really a nice fellow who won't let him down. If there were a way to save this country's freedom without saving such men, one would gladly leave them to their fate: they deserve what they are getting.

But there is no such way. It is not the broadcasting licenses of a few appeasers and cowards that are here at stake, but our freedom of speech. It is not necessary to point out what the establishment of such a precedent in the field of broadcasting would do to all the other media of communication and how swiftly it would do it. I shall merely remind you of the words of Chief Justice Warren in a dissenting opinion in a case involving movie censorship (Times Film Corp. *v.* City of Chicago, 1961): "The decision presents a real danger of eventual censorship for every form of communication, be it newspapers, journals, books, magazines, television, radio or public speeches. . . . I am aware of no constitutional principle which permits us to hold that the communication of ideas through one medium may be censored while other media are immune."

Mr. Minow's proposal is more urgent and deadly an issue than any headlined in today's newspapers. It is not an issue of narrow, journalistic politics. It is an issue that should unite, into a *philosophical* opposition, whatever advocates of freedom are still left among us, the non-traditional "conservatives," the non-totalitarian "liberals"—and any man of self-esteem who will not accept the prospect of a Czar ruling the realm of ideas.

OBJECTIVIST CALENDAR

■ Beginning Monday, July 8, NBI will offer a ten lecture course on "The Esthetics of the Visual Arts," in Philadelphia, to be given by Mary Ann Rukavina.

■ NBI's Tape Transcription Division has scheduled "Basic Principles of Objectivist Psychology," a twenty lecture course by Nathaniel Branden, to begin in Washington, D. C. on Sunday, July 14.

■ On June 14, NBI held its Fifth Anniversary Ball, for students and their guests, at the Hotel Roosevelt in New York City. Students from as far away as Texas and California attended. Originally, NBI had planned to hold the next Ball in celebration of the Institute's 10th anniversary; but the response to the June 14th Ball was such that plans are now under way to make the affair annual.

Published monthly at 120 East 34th Street, New York 16, N. Y.
Subscription rate: in United States, its possessions, Canada and Mexico, $5 for one year; other countries, $6.
Additional copies of this Newsletter: single copy 50¢ (coins, not stamps); 10 — 99 copies, 25¢ each plus postage (for first-class delivery add 1¢ per copy, for third-class delivery add ½¢ per copy); 100 or more copies, 15¢ each plus postage (same as above).
For change of address send old address and new address with zone number if any. Allow us three weeks to process new subscriptions and change of address.

Ayn Rand and Nathaniel Branden, Editors and Publishers
Barbara Branden, Managing Editor
Elayne Kalberman, Circulation Manager
PRINTED BY STANDARD PRESS & GRAPHICS, INC., NEW YORK CITY

THE OBJECTIVIST NEWSLETTER

Edited and Published by AYN RAND and NATHANIEL BRANDEN

VOL. 2 NO. 8   AUGUST, 1963

"The Divine Right of Stagnation"

By NATHANIEL BRANDEN

For every living species, growth is a necessity of survival. Life is motion, a process of self-sustaining action that an organism must carry on in order to remain in existence. This principle is equally evident in the simple energy-conversions of a plant and in the long-range, complex activities of man. Biologically, inactivity is death.

The nature and range of possible motion and development varies from species to species. The range of a plant's action and development is far less than an animal's; an animal's is far less than man's. An animal's capacity for development ends at physical maturity and thereafter its growth consists of the action necessary to maintain itself at a fixed level; after reaching maturity, it does not, to any significant extent, continue to grow *in efficacy*—that is, it does not significantly increase its ability to cope with the environment. But man's capacity for development does *not* end at physical maturity; his capacity is virtually limitless. His power to reason is man's distinguishing characteristic, his mind is man's basic means of survival—and his ability to think, to learn, to discover new and better ways of dealing with reality, to expand the range of his efficacy, *to grow intellectually*, is an open door to a road that has no end.

Man survives, not by adjusting himself to his physical environment in the manner of an animal, but by transforming his environment through *productive work*. "If a drought strikes them, animals perish—man builds irrigation canals; if a flood strikes them, animals perish—man builds dams; if a carnivorous pack attacks them, animals perish—man writes the Constitution of the United States." (Ayn Rand, *For the New Intellectual*.)

If life is a process of self-sustaining action, then this is the distinctly *human* mode of action and survival: to think—to produce—to meet the challenges of existence by a never-ending effort and inventiveness.

When man discovered how to make fire to keep himself warm, his need of thought and effort was not ended; when he discovered how to fashion a bow and arrow, his need of thought and effort was not ended; when he discovered how to build a shelter out of stone, then out of brick, then out of glass and steel, his need of thought and effort was not ended; when he moved his life expectancy from nineteen to thirty to forty to sixty to seventy, his need of thought and effort was not ended; so long as he lives, *his need of thought and effort is never ended*.

Every achievement of man is a value in itself, but it is also a stepping-stone to greater achievements and values. Life is growth; not to move forward, is to fall backward; life remains life, only so long as it advances. Every step upward opens to man a wider range of action and achievement—and creates the *need* for that action and achievement. There is no final, permanent "plateau." The problem of survival is never "solved," once and for all, with no further thought or motion required. More precisely, the problem of survival *is* solved, by recognizing that survival demands constant growth and creativeness.

Constant growth is, further, a *psychological* need of man. It is a condition of his mental well-being. His mental well-being requires that he possess a firm sense of control over reality, of control over his existence—the conviction that he is *competent* to live. And this requires, not omniscience or omnipotence, but the knowledge that one's *methods* of dealing with reality—the *principles* by which one functions—are *right*. Passivity is incompatible with this state. Self-esteem is not a value that, once achieved, is maintained automatically thereafter; like every other human value, including life itself, it can be maintained only by action. Self-esteem, the basic conviction that one is competent to live, can be maintained only so long as one is engaged in a process of growth, only so long as one is committed to the task of increasing one's efficacy. In living entities, nature does not permit stillness: when one ceases to grow, one proceeds to disintegrate—in the mental realm no less than in the physical.

Observe, in this connection, the widespread phenomenon of men who are old by the time they are thirty. These are men who, having in effect concluded that they have "thought enough," drift on the diminishing momentum of their past effort—and wonder what happened to their fire and energy, and why they are dimly anxious, and why their existence seems so desolately impoverished, and why they feel themselves sinking into some nameless abyss—and never identify the fact that, in abandoning the will to think, one abandons the will to live.

Man's need to grow—and his need, therefore, of the social or existential conditions that make growth possible—are facts of crucial importance to be considered in judging or evaluating any politico-economic system. One should be concerned to ask: Is a given politico-economic system pro-life or anti-life, conducive or inimical to the requirements of man's survival?

The great merit of capitalism is its unique appropriateness to the requirements of human survival and to man's need to grow. Leaving men free to think, to act, to produce, to attempt the untried and the new, its principles operate in a way that rewards effort and achievement, and penalizes passivity.

This is one of the chief reasons for which it is denounced.

In *Who is Ayn Rand?*, discussing the 19th century attacks on capitalism, I wrote: "In the writings of both medievalists and socialists, one can observe the unmistakable longing for a society in which man's existence will be automatically guaranteed to him—that is, in which man will not have to bear responsibility for his own survival. Both camps project their ideal society as one characterized by that which they call 'harmony,' by freedom from rapid change or challenge or the exacting demands of competition; a society in which each must do his prescribed part to contribute to the well-being of the whole, but in which no one will face the necessity of making choices and decisions that will crucially affect his life and future; in which the question of what one has or has not earned, and does or does not deserve, will not come up; in which rewards will not be tied to achievement and in which someone's benevolence will guarantee that one need never bear the consequences of one's errors. The failure of capitalism to conform to what may be termed this *pastoral* view of existence, is essential to the medievalists' and socialists' indictment of a free society. It is not a Garden of Eden that capitalism offers men."

Among the arguments used by those who long for a "pastoral" existence, is a doctrine which, translated into explicit statement, consists of: *the divine right of stagnation.*

This doctrine is illustrated in the following incident. Once, on a plane trip, I became engaged in conversation with an executive of a labor union. He began to decry the "disaster" of automation, asserting that increasing thousands of workers would be permanently unemployed as a result of new machines and that "something ought to be done about it." I answered that this was a myth that had been exploded many times; that the introduction of new machines invariably resulted in *increasing* the demand for labor as well as in raising the general standard of living; that this was demonstrable the-

(continued on page 32)

Copyright © 1963 by The Objectivist Newsletter, Inc.

BOOKS

The Language of Dissent by Lowell B. Mason

Reviewed by **AYN RAND**

Lowell B. Mason is an unusual—or paradoxical—figure on today's political scene: a pro-free-enterprise bureaucrat. To be exact, he is a distinguished lawyer who, for eleven years, held the post of Commissioner in the stronghold of anti-trust enforcement: the Federal Trade Commission.

Appointed by President Truman in 1945, he attempted in good faith to hold the F.T.C. to its officially alleged purpose: that of regulating the economy "in the public interest." He believed that free enterprise is compatible with government controls. He attempted to apply a scrupulously strict legality to the operations of an administrative agency—which is a contradiction in terms. As a result, he became famous as a lone dissenter, a rebel fighting a losing battle.

Many of his dissents from the Commission's rulings were upheld by the Courts of Appeals or by the Supreme Court. Thus, he was instrumental in protecting the nation from some of the more outrageous rulings and in saving the business lives of countless victims. But he was unable to stop the trend toward statism in the court interpretations of the antitrust laws, which went on accelerating during the 1940's and 50's. (That trend was a *philosophical* matter, which could not be changed by narrowly political means.)

In *The Language of Dissent*, Mr. Mason presents the conclusions he has drawn from his first-hand experience, and the texts of his official dissents, which are here made available to the public for the first time. Those readers who, under the influence of modern epistemology, may be inclined to regard any criticism of antitrust by its opponents as not fully objective, may now hear it from the horse's mouth—with my apologies to Mr. Mason, who had been a very brave horse indeed in an all but hopeless race.

What Mr. Mason discovered about the workings of bureaucracy is a principle which he entitles "Mason's law" and explains as follows: "Parkinson's law states that bureaucracy will arrogate to itself all employees available under the budget allowance regardless of the limitations of the task. Mason's law holds that bureaucracy will arrogate to itself all power available under a statute in spite of the limitations against tyranny in the Constitution. This it will do, quietly and unobtrusively, through decisions at the lowest rung of the quasi-judicial ladder where the issue seldom meets the eye of the public."

Observing the bureaucrats' ruthlessness, he describes their psychology as follows: "The governing elite accumulate tyrannical power, not for themselves, but for the state. The prospect of personal advantage could never drive them to do the things they do for the state, for in their private lives they are the souls of altruism. Abnegation of their self-interest gives them an aura of sanctity, and at the same time makes them unsympathetic to an economic system based on personal profit, such as free enterprise."

Administrative agencies, Mr. Mason points out, are intent on establishing *precedents* which "short-cut the Bill of Rights." Most of the Constitutional guarantees protecting the individual, have been infringed, suspended, negated or eroded in regard to businessmen; today, these guarantees are respected only in regard to criminals. The criminals' rights have legal protection, the businessmen's rights have none.

On this point, Mr. Mason makes a profoundly important observation: whenever a country's criminal laws are more lenient than its civil laws, it means that the country is accepting the basic principle of statism and is moving toward a totalitarian state. (Such a trend means that crimes against individuals are regarded as negligible, while the collectivist concept of "Crimes against the State" becomes paramount and supersedes all rights.)

In Soviet Russia, he points out, criminals were treated "with tolerance and circumspection. On the other hand, those accused of violating the state's political and economic commands were sentenced to death or exiled to Siberia without any semblance of trial as we know the word here in America.

"In this country one sees a growing acceptance of this thesis that violations of the economic commands of the state are more dangerous to our material welfare than criminal offenses, and therefore can be punished without due process. An administrative officer in Ohio (not a judge, but a deputy fire marshal) sentenced a man to jail after holding a secret inquisitorial proceeding. The defendant was not even allowed to have his own counsel present. The Supreme Court upheld the sentence because the trial 'was not a criminal trial. . .' it was 'an administrative investigation of incidents damaging to the economy. . .' "

Through Mr. Mason's colorful comments and through the dry, meticulous precision of the legal language of his dissents, the book offers a well-documented nightmare—a panorama of antitrust cases. There are the cases of victims picked at random—businessmen prosecuted and convicted for offenses which continue to be practiced with impunity by their competitors—while the bureaucrats refuse to apply their edicts impartially to an entire field of business (the *Moog Industries* case—and others). "To be dangerous," writes Mr. Mason, "a wicked precedent must be susceptible of being used or not used at the whim of an institution. . . . Whim is the essence of tyranny, for this gives the power to arbitrarily apply or not apply authority for no assigned reasons." What lay behind the choice of individual victims—whether blind chance or a competitor's scheming or a bureaucrat's malice—we will never be able to know.

There is the case of a company which was prosecuted for a policy it had adopted *on the advice of the F.T.C.* three years earlier (the *Carpel Frosted Foods* case). There are numerous cases of businessmen convicted by *ex post facto* law, that is, convicted for actions which were not illegal at the time when they were committed (the *Standard Oil* case) —and cases of the F.T.C. *refusing* to interpret or clarify a non-objective law in advance, then prosecuting the businessmen for the wrong guess (the *Minneapolis-Honeywell Regulator Co.* case).

The essence and spirit of antitrust is best captured in a story which Mr. Mason tells on himself. "As an administrator of two antitrust laws diametrically opposed to each other, it was not difficult for me to accuse everybody at a trade convention with being some kind of a lawbreaker. Either they were all charging everyone the same price, a circumstance indicating a violation of the Sherman Act, or they were *not* charging everyone the same price, a circumstance indicating a violation of the Robinson-Patman Act.

"Most businessmen took that kind of jibing in good grace. But at one convention a man interrupted my speech to say the Commission had recently sued him for doing both. To which I replied, 'Then in that event, how can you win? We shall probably find you guilty of one or the other!'

"His retort, 'You damn fools found me guilty of both!' "

It is funny—but horrible, because it is true.

In summing up that gruesome panorama, Mr. Mason begs the reader, with desperate eloquence, to grasp the danger and to oppose the growth of bureaucratic power. The last, solemn sentence of his report is: "I invite the reader of this book to concern himself with tyranny."

I invite all those who *are* concerned with tyranny to read this book. It is an important historical document and it offers irrefutable information on the subject of antitrust, which is confronting us with growing frequency—and growing fogginess—in today's news, as the major threat to this country's freedom.

I must, however, *dissent* from Mr. Mason on one point: on his belief in a "mixed economy," in the compatibility of free enterprise with government regulations and of justice with administrative law. To borrow his own phrase: "I am against it"—and I submit the content of his book as one of the best refutations of that belief.

---

* List price $5.00. Available from NBI BOOK SERVICE, INC., 120 East 34th St., New York 16, N. Y., for $4.25 (N.Y.C. residents add 4% sales tax; outside the U. S. add 15¢).

The Assault on Integrity
By ALAN GREENSPAN

Protection of the consumer against "dishonest and unscrupulous business practices" has become a cardinal ingredient of welfare statism. Left to their own devices, it is alleged, businessmen would attempt to sell unsafe food and drugs, fraudulent securities and shoddy buildings. Thus, it is argued, the Pure Food and Drug Administration, the Securities and Exchange Commission and the numerous building regulatory agencies are indispensable if the consumer is to be protected from the "greed" of the businessman.

But it is precisely the "greed" of the businessman or, more appropriately, his profit-seeking, which is the unexcelled protector of the consumer.

What collectivists refuse to recognize is that it is in the self-interest of every businessman to have a reputation for honest dealings and a quality product. Since the market value of a going business is measured by its money-making potential, reputation or "good-will" is as much an asset as its physical plant and equipment. For many a drug company, the value of its reputation, as reflected in the saleability of its brand name, is often its major asset. The loss of reputation through the sale of a shoddy or dangerous product would sharply reduce the market value of the drug company, though its physical resources would remain intact. The market value of a brokerage firm is even more closely tied to its good-will assets. Securities worth hundreds of millions of dollars are traded every day over the telephone. The slightest doubt as to the trustworthiness of a broker's word or commitment would put him out of business overnight.

Reputation, in an unregulated economy, is thus a major competitive tool. Builders who have acquired a reputation for top quality construction take the market away from their less scrupulous or less conscientious competitors. The most reputable securities dealers get the bulk of the commission business. Drug manufacturers and food processors vie with one another to make their brand names synonymous with fine quality.

Physicians have to be just as scrupulous in judging the quality of the drugs they prescribe. They, too, are in business and compete for trustworthiness. Even the corner grocer is involved: he cannot afford to sell unhealthy foods if he wants to make money. In fact, in one way or another, every producer and distributor of goods or services is caught up in the competition for reputation.

It requires years of consistently excellent performance to acquire a reputation and to establish it as a financial asset. Thereafter, a still greater effort is required to maintain it: a company cannot afford to risk its years of investment by letting down its standards of quality for one moment or one inferior product; nor would it be tempted by any potential "quick killing." Newcomers entering the field cannot compete immediately with the established, reputable companies, and have to spend years working on a more modest scale in order to earn an equal reputation. Thus the incentive to scrupulous performance operates on all levels of a given field of production. It is a built-in safeguard of a free enterprise system and the only real protection of consumers against business dishonesty.

Government regulation is not an alternative means of protecting the consumer. It does not build quality into goods, nor accuracy into information. Its sole "contribution" is to substitute force and fear for incentive as the "protector" of the consumer. The euphemisms of government press releases to the contrary notwithstanding, the basis of regulation is armed force. At the bottom of the endless pile of paper work which characterizes all regulation lies a gun. What are the results?

To paraphrase Gresham's Law: bad "protection" drives out good. The attempt to protect the consumer by force undercuts the protection he gets from incentive. First, it undercuts the value of reputation by placing the reputable company on the same basis as the unknown, the newcomer or the fly-by-nighter. It declares, in effect, that all are equally suspect and that years of evidence to the contrary do not free a man from that suspicion. Second, it grants an automatic (though, in fact, unachievable) guarantee of safety to the products of any company that complies with its arbitrarily set minimum standards. The value of a reputation rested on the fact that it was necessary for the consumers to exercise judgment in the choice of the goods and services they purchased. The government's "guarantee" undermines this necessity; it declares to the consumers, in effect, that no choice or judgment is required—and that a company's record, its years of achievement, is irrelevant.

The minimum standards which are the basis of regulation gradually tend to become the maximums as well. If the building codes set minimum standards of construction, a builder does not get very much competitive advantage by exceeding those standards and, accordingly, he tends to meet only the minimums. If minimum specifications are set for vitamins, there is little profit in producing something of above average quality. Gradually, even the attempt to maintain minimum standards becomes impossible, since the draining of incentives to improve quality ultimately undermines even the minimums.

The guiding purpose of the government regulator is to prevent rather than to create something. He gets no credit if a new miraculous drug is discovered by drug company scientists; he does if he bans Thalidomide. Such emphasis on the negative sets the framework under which even the most conscientious regulators must operate. The result is a growing body of restrictive legislation on drug experimentation, testing and distribution. As in all research, it is impossible to add restrictions to the development of new drugs without simultaneously cutting off the secondary rewards of such research—the improvement of existing drugs. Quality improvement and innovation are inseparable.

Building codes are supposed to protect the public. But by being forced to adhere to standards of construction long after they have been surpassed by new technological discoveries, builders divert their efforts to maintaining the old rather than adopting new and safer techniques of construction.

Regulation—which is based on force and fear—undermines the moral base of business dealings. It becomes cheaper to bribe a building inspector than to meet his standards of construction. A fly-by-night securities operator can quickly meet all the SEC requirements, gain the inference of respectability and proceed to fleece the public. In an unregulated economy, the operator would have had to spend a number of years in reputable dealings before he could earn a position of trust sufficient to induce a number of investors to place funds with him.

Protection of the consumer by regulation is thus illusory. Rather than isolating the consumer from the dishonest businessman, it is gradually destroying the only reliable protection the consumer has: competition for reputation.

While the consumer is thus endangered, the major victim of "protective" regulation is the producer: the businessman. Regulation which acts to destroy the competition of businessmen for reputation undermines the market value of the good will which businessmen have built up over the years. It is an act of expropriation of wealth created by integrity. Since the value of a business—its wealth—rests on its ability to make money, the acts of a government seizing a company's plant or devaluing its reputation are in the same category: both are acts of expropriation.

Moreover, "protective" legislation falls in the category of preventive law. Businessmen are being subjected to governmental coercion *prior* to the commission of any crime. In a free economy, the government may step in only when a fraud has been perpetrated, or a demonstrable damage has been done to a consumer; in such cases the only protection required is that of criminal law.

Government regulations do not eliminate potentially dishonest individuals, but merely make their activities harder to detect or easier to hush up. Furthermore, the possibility of individual dishonesty applies to government employees fully as much as to any other group of men. There is nothing to guarantee the superior judgment, knowledge and integrity of an inspector or a bureaucrat—and the deadly consequences of entrusting him with arbitrary power are obvious.

(continued on page 32)

Mr. Greenspan is President of Townsend-Greenspan & Co., Inc., New York, economic consultants.

Divine Right of Stagnation (from page 29)

oretically and observable historically. I remarked that automation increased the demand for skilled labor relative to unskilled labor, and that doubtless many workers would need to learn new skills. "But," he asked indignantly, "what about the workers who don't *want* to learn new skills? Why should *they* have troubles?"

The ambition, the far-sightedness, the drive to do better and still better, the living energy of creative men are to be throttled and suppressed—for the sake of men who have "thought enough" and "learned enough" and do not wish to be concerned with the future nor with the bothersome question of what their jobs depend on.

Alone on a desert island, bearing sole responsibility for his own survival, no man could permit himself the delusion that tomorrow is not his concern, that he can safely rest on yesterday's knowledge and skills, and that nature owes him "security." It is only in society—where the burden of one man's default can be passed to the shoulders of a man who did *not* default—that such a delusion can be indulged in. (And it is *here* that the morality of altruism becomes indispensable, to provide a sanction for such parasitism.)

The claim that men doing the same type of job should all be paid the same wages, regardless of differences in their performance or output, thus penalizing the superior worker in favor of the inferior—*this* is the doctrine of the divine right of stagnation.

The claim that men should keep their jobs or be promoted on grounds, not of merit, but of seniority, so that the mediocrity who is "in" is favored above the talented newcomer, thus blocking the newcomer's future and that of his potential employer—*this* is the doctrine of the divine right of stagnation.

The claim that an employer should be compelled to deal with a specific union which has an arbitrary power to exclude applicants for membership, so that the chance to work at a certain craft is handed down from father to son and no newcomer can enter to threaten the established vested interests, thus blocking progress in the entire field, like the guild system of the Middle Ages—*this* is the doctrine of the divine right of stagnation.

The claim that men should be retained in jobs that have become unnecessary, doing work that is wasteful or superfluous, to spare them the difficulties of retraining for new jobs—thus contributing, as in the case of railroads, to the virtual destruction of an entire industry—*this* is the doctrine of the divine right of stagnation.

The denunciation of capitalism for such "iniquities" as allowing an old corner grocer to be driven out of business by a big chain store, the denunciation implying that the economic well-being and progress of the old grocer's customers and of the chain store owners should be throttled to protect the limitations of the old grocer's initiative or skill—*this* is the doctrine of the divine right of stagnation.

The court's decree, under the antitrust laws, that a successful business establishment does not have a right to its patents, but must give them, royalty-free, to a would-be competitor who cannot afford to pay for them (*General Electric* case, 1948)—*this* is the doctrine of the divine right of stagnation.

The court's edict convicting and blocking a business concern for the crime of far-sightedness, the crime of anticipating future demand and expanding plant capacity to meet it, and of thereby possibly "discouraging" future competitors (*ALCOA* case, 1945)—*this* is the legal penalizing of growth, *this* is the penalizing of ability for being ability—and *this* is the naked essence and goal of the doctrine of the divine right of stagnation.

Capitalism, by its nature, entails a constant process of motion, growth and progress. It creates the optimum social conditions for man to respond to the challenges of nature in such a way as best to further his life. It operates to the benefit of all those who choose to be active in the productive process, whatever their level of ability. But it is not geared to the demands of stagnation. *Neither is reality.*

When one considers the spectacular success, the unprecedented prosperity, that capitalism has achieved in practice (even with hampering controls)—and when one considers the dismal failure of every variety of collectivism—it should be clear that the enemies of capitalism are not motivated, at root, by economic considerations. They are motivated by *metaphysical* considerations—by a rebellion against the *human* mode of survival, a rebellion against the fact that *life is a process of self-sustaining and self-generated action*—and by the dream that, if only they can harness the men who do *not* resent the nature of life, they will make existence tolerable for those who *do* resent it.

The Assault on Integrity (from page 31)

The hallmark of collectivists is their deeprooted distrust of freedom and of the free market processes; but it is their advocacy of so-called "consumer protection" that exposes the nature of their basic premises with particular clarity. By preferring force and fear to incentive and reward as a means of human motivation, they confess their view of man as a mindless brute functioning on the range of the moment, whose actual self-interest lies in "flying-by-night" and making "quick kills." They confess their ignorance of the role of intelligence in the production process, of the wide intellectual context and long-range vision required to maintain a modern industry. They confess their inability to grasp the crucial importance of the moral values which are the motive power of capitalism. Capitalism is based on self-interest and self-esteem; it holds integrity and trustworthiness as cardinal virtues and makes them pay off in the market place, thus demanding that men survive by means of virtues, not of vices. It is this superlatively moral system that the welfare statists propose to improve upon by means of preventive law, snooping bureaucrats and the chronic goad of fear.

OBJECTIVIST CALENDAR

■ On Saturday, August 17, Nathaniel Branden will appear on the "At Random" show in Chicago. CBS-TV Channel 2, 12 Midnight.

■ On August 2, 16 and 30, in Chicago, Nathaniel Branden will give readings (via tape transcriptions) of three plays by Ayn Rand. Place: Hotel Knickerbocker, 163 East Walton, Chicago, Illinois. Time: 8 P.M. Admission: $2.00 per play, or $5.00 for the series.

■ On August 7, 14 and 21, these readings of plays by Ayn Rand will be given in Los Angeles. Place: Institute of Aeronautics and Astronautics, 7660 Beverly Blvd., Los Angeles. Time: 8 P.M.

■ Ayn Rand's lecture, "How *not* to fight against Socialized Medicine," which was published in the March, 1963 issue of this NEWSLETTER, has been reprinted separately and is available at a special reprint rate: single copy, 25¢; 10-99 copies, 15¢ each plus postage (for first-class delivery add 1¢ per copy; for third-class delivery add ½¢ per copy); 100-999 copies, 10¢ each plus postage; 1000 or more copies, 7¢ each plus postage.

Published monthly at 120 East 34th Street, New York 16, N. Y.
Subscription rate: in United States, its possessions, Canada and Mexico, $5 for one year; other countries, $6.
Additional copies of this Newsletter: single copy 50¢ (coins, not stamps); 10—99 copies, 25¢ each plus postage (for first-class delivery add 1¢ per copy, for third-class delivery add ½¢ per copy); 100 or more copies, 15¢ each plus postage (same as above).
For change of address send old address and new address with zone number if any. Allow us three weeks to process new subscriptions and change of address.

Ayn Rand and Nathaniel Branden, Editors and Publishers
Barbara Branden, Managing Editor
Elayne Kalberman, Circulation Manager
PRINTED BY STANDARD PRESS & GRAPHICS, INC., NEW YORK CITY

THE OBJECTIVIST NEWSLETTER

Edited and Published by AYN RAND and NATHANIEL BRANDEN

VOL. 2 NO. 9   SEPTEMBER, 1963

CHECK YOUR PREMISES
By AYN RAND

Racism

Racism is the lowest, most crudely primitive form of collectivism. It is the notion of ascribing moral, social or political significance to a man's genetic lineage — the notion that a man's intellectual and characterological traits are produced and transmitted by his internal body chemistry. Which means, in practice, that a man is to be judged, not by his own character and actions, but by the characters and actions of a collective of ancestors.

Racism claims that the content of a man's mind (not his cognitive apparatus, but its *content*) is inherited; that a man's convictions, values and character are determined before he is born, by physical factors beyond his control. This is the caveman's version of the doctrine of innate ideas — or of inherited knowledge — which has been thoroughly refuted by philosophy and science. Racism is a doctrine of, by and for brutes. It is a barnyard or stock-farm version of collectivism, appropriate to a mentality that differentiates between various breeds of animals, but not between animals and men.

Like every form of determinism, racism invalidates the specific attribute which distinguishes man from all other living species: his rational faculty. Racism negates two aspects of man's life: reason and choice, or mind and morality, replacing them with chemical predestination.

The respectable family that supports worthless relatives or covers up their crimes in order to "protect the family name" (as if the moral stature of one man could be damaged by the actions of another) — the bum who boasts that his great-grandfather was an empire-builder, or the small-town spinster who boasts that her maternal great-uncle was a state senator and her third-cousin gave a concert at Carnegie Hall (as if the achievements of one man could rub off on the mediocrity of another) — the parents who search geneological trees in order to evaluate their prospective sons-in-law — the celebrity who starts his autobiography with a detailed account of his family history — all these are samples of racism, the atavistic manifestations of a doctrine whose full expression is the tribal warfare of prehistorical savages, the wholesale slaughter of Nazi Germany, the atrocities of today's so-called "newly-emerging nations."

The theory that holds "good blood" or "bad blood" as a moral-intellectual criterion, can lead to nothing but torrents of blood in practice. Brute force is the only avenue of action open to men who regard themselves as mindless aggregates of chemicals.

Modern racists attempt to prove the superiority or inferiority of a given race by the historical achievements of some of its members. The frequent historical spectacle of a great innovator who, in his lifetime, is jeered, denounced, obstructed, persecuted by his countrymen, and then, a few years after his death, is enshrined in a national monument and hailed as a proof of the greatness of the German (or French or Italian or Cambodian) race — is as revolting a spectacle of collectivist expropriation, perpetrated by racists, as any expropriation of material wealth perpetrated by communists.

Just as there is no such thing as a collective or racial mind, so there is no such thing as a collective or racial achievement. There are only individual minds and individual achievements — and a *culture* is not the anonymous product of undifferentiated masses, but the sum of the intellectual achievements of individual men.

Even if it were proved — which it is not — that the incidence of men of potentially superior brain power is greater among the members of certain races than among the members of others, it would still tell us nothing about any given individual and it would be irrelevant to one's judgment of him. A genius is a genius, regardless of the number of morons who belong to the same race — and a moron is a moron, regardless of the number of geniuses who share his racial origin. It is hard to say which is the more outrageous injustice: the claim of Southern racists that a Negro genius should be treated as an inferior because his race has "produced" some brutes — or the claim of a German brute to the status of a superior because his race has "produced" Goethe, Schiller and Brahms.

These are not two different claims, of course, but two applications of the same basic premise. The question of whether one alleges the superiority or the inferiority of any given race is irrelevant; racism has only one psychological root: the racist's sense of his own inferiority.

Like every other form of collectivism, racism is a quest for the unearned. It is a quest for automatic knowledge — for an automatic evaluation of men's characters that bypasses the responsibility of exercising rational or moral judgment — and, above all, a quest for *an automatic self-esteem* (or pseudo-self-esteem).

To ascribe one's virtues to one's racial origin, is to confess that one has no knowledge of the process by which virtues are acquired and, most often, that one has failed to acquire them. The overwhelming majority of racists are men who have earned no sense of personal identity, who can claim no individual achievement or distinction, and who seek the illusion of a "tribal self-esteem" by alleging the inferiority of some other tribe. Observe the hysterical intensity of the Southern racists; observe also that racism is much more prevalent among the poor white trash than among their intellectual betters.

Historically, racism has always risen or fallen with the rise or fall of collectivism. Collectivism holds that the individual has no rights, that his life and work belong to the group (to "society," to the tribe, the state, the nation) and that the group may sacrifice him at its own whim to its own interests. The only way to implement a doctrine of that kind is by means of brute force — and *statism* has always been the political corollary of collectivism.

The absolute state is merely an institutionalized form of gang rule, regardless of which particular gang seizes power. And — since there is no rational justification for such rule, since none has ever been or can ever be offered—the mystique of racism is a crucial element in every variant of the absolute state. The relationship is reciprocal: statism rises out of prehistorical tribal warfare, out of the notion that the men of one tribe are the natural prey for the men of another — and establishes its own internal sub-categories of racism, a system of castes determined by a man's birth, such as inherited titles of nobility or inherited serfdom.

The racism of Nazi Germany — where men had to fill questionnaires about their ancestry for generations back, in order to prove their *"Aryan"* descent — has its counterpart in Soviet Russia, where men had to fill similar questionnaires to show that their ancestors had owned no property and thus to prove their *"proletarian"* descent. The Soviet ideology rests on the notion that men can be conditioned to communism *genetically* — that is, that a few generations conditioned by dictatorship will transmit communist ideology to their descendants, who will be communists *at birth*. The persecution

(continued on page 34)

BOOKS

*Human Action** by Ludwig von Mises

Reviewed by **NATHANIEL BRANDEN**

Through a long and distinguished career, Professor Ludwig von Mises has been a powerful advocate of laissez-faire capitalism. He has written many lucid and scholarly books dealing with the operation of a free market economy, and with the attacks levelled against it by supporters of collectivism. Among the most important of these books are: *The Theory of Money and Credit* (1912), a treatise on the nature, origin and functions of banking, credit and interest, and on the problems of inflation and deflation; *Socialism* (1922), a devastating refutation of every known version of socialist or collectivist economic theory; and *Omnipotent Government* (1944), an analysis of the historical and intellectual origins of the Nazi state, demonstrating the relationship between government regulation of the economy and aggressive nationalism.

In 1949, Professor Mises published *Human Action* — a definitive presentation of his economic theories. The book has had five printings, and recently has been re-issued in a new, revised edition. In scope and importance, it is clearly the climax of his previous works.

In *Human Action*, Professor Mises offers a systematic and comprehensive analysis of the nature of production and trade. He shows why a free economy is necessarily the most productive and efficient; why coercive interference with men's free choices in the market invariably leads to a lowering of the standard of living; why slavery is incompatible with an industrial civilization.

Among the many issues he discusses are: economic calculation in a market economy; the determinants of prices, wages and production policies; the gold standard; interest rates and credit expansion; the causes of depression; the impossibility of rational economic calculation in a socialist system (this demonstration is one of his most important achievements); the contradictions and destructiveness of interventionism; common misconceptions concerning the history and nature of capitalism; the economics of war; confiscatory taxation.

One of the great merits of the book is its encyclopedic character; it deals with virtually every major problem in economic theory. It contains many historical illustrations and references that provide further illumination — such as, for instance, a discussion of the "welfare state" policies of the disintegrating Roman Empire, and the manner in which these policies made the Empire vulnerable to the barbarian invaders (an analogy that is far from academic in our present political context).

Today, government officials and economists of the statist persuasion clearly believe that there are no economic laws, no immutable principles regarding production and trade — and that, given sufficient power, they may impose any regulations or controls they wish and still retain a high level of material prosperity. Thus, they believe that they can pass legislation which results in forcing wages above their market level, and yet escape the consequence of unemployment; they believe that they can dictate the pricing and production policies of industrialists, and yet suffer no consequent diminution of goods and services; they believe that they can indulge in unlimited deficit spending, and yet avoid inflation; they believe that they can manipulate the money supply, expanding credit at whim, and yet escape a depression; they believe that they can create an atmosphere of chronic uncertainty, and yet have men continue to invest and produce, happily and confidently. When their plans fail, when economic disaster occurs, they do not question their policies, they denounce the "selfish greed" of businessmen for thwarting the noble plans that would have worked if everyone had *wanted* them to work. It is the barbaric absurdity of these beliefs — the dream which sees economic laws as a myth and the social planner's whim as omnipotent — that Professor Mises brilliantly exposes. He delineates the principles that *necessarily* operate in an exchange economy, establishing the conditions on which successful material production *necessarily* depends. To put the matter another way: he brings the law of causality into the context of man's productive activity.

In justice to Professor Mises' position and our own, it must be mentioned that there are many sections of *Human Action* with which Objectivists cannot agree. These sections pertain, not to the sphere of economics as such, but to the philosophical framework in which his economic theories are presented. We must take the gravest exception, for example, to the general doctrine of praxeology; to the assertion that all value-judgments are outside the province of reason, that a scientific ethics is impossible; to the disavowal of the concept of inalienable rights; and to many of the psychological views expressed.

Notwithstanding these reservations, the book is of the first rank of importance, eminently deserving of careful study. It is a major economic classic. As a reference work, it belongs in the library of every advocate of capitalism.

Racism (from page 33)

of racial minorities in Soviet Russia, according to the racial descent and whim of any given commissar, is a matter of record; anti-semitism is particularly prevalent — only the official pogroms are now called "political purges."

There is only one antidote to racism: the philosophy of individualism and its politico-economic corollary, laissez-faire capitalism.

Individualism regards man — every man — as an independent, sovereign entity who possesses an inalienable right to his own life, a right derived from his nature as a rational being. Individualism holds that a civilized society, or any form of association, cooperation or peaceful co-existence among men, can be achieved only on the basis of the recognition of individual rights — and that a group, as such, has no rights other than the individual rights of its members. (See my articles "Man's Rights" and "Collectivized 'Rights' " in the April and June, 1963, issues of this NEWSLETTER.)

It is not a man's ancestors or relatives or genes or body chemistry that count in a free market, but only one human attribute: productive ability. It is by his own individual ability and ambition that capitalism judges a man and rewards him accordingly.

No political system can establish universal rationality by law (or by force). But capitalism is the only system that functions in a way which rewards rationality and penalizes all forms of irrationality, including racism.

A fully free, capitalist system has not yet existed anywhere. But what is enormously significant is the correlation of racism and political controls in the semi-free economies of the 19th century. Racial and/or religious persecutions of minorities stood in inverse ratio to the degree of a country's freedom. Racism was strongest in the more controlled economies, such as Russia and Germany — and weakest in England, the then freest country of Europe.

It is capitalism that gave mankind its first steps toward freedom and a rational way of life. It is capitalism that broke through national and racial barriers, by means of free trade. It is capitalism that abolished serfdom and slavery in all the civilized countries of the world. It is the capitalist North that destroyed the slavery of the agrarian-feudal South in the United States.

Such was the trend of mankind for the brief span of some hundred and fifty years. The spectacular results and achievements of that trend need no restatement here.

The rise of collectivism reversed that trend.

When men began to be indoctrinated once more with the notion that the individual possesses no rights, that supremacy, moral authority and unlimited power belong to the group, and

---

*List price $15.00. Available from NBI BOOK SERVICE, INC., 120 East 34th St., New York 16, N. Y., for $12.50 (N.Y.C. residents add 4% sales tax; outside the U.S. add 15¢).

that a man has no significance outside his group — the inevitable consequence was that men began to gravitate toward some group or another, in self-protection, in bewilderment and in subconscious terror. The simplest collective to join, the easiest one to identify — particularly for people of limited intelligence — the least demanding form of "belonging" and of "togetherness" is: *race*.

It is thus that the theoreticians of collectivism, the "humanitarian" advocates of a "benevolent" absolute state, have led to the rebirth and the new, virulent growth of racism in the 20th century.

In its great era of capitalism, the United States was the freest country on earth — and the best refutation of racist theories. Men of all races came here, some from obscure, culturally undistinguished countries, and accomplished feats of productive ability which would have remained stillborn in their control-ridden native lands. Men of racial groups that had been slaughtering one another for centuries, learned to live together in harmony and peaceful cooperation. America had been called "the melting pot," with good reason. But few people realized that America did not melt men into the gray conformity of a collective: she united them by means of protecting their right to individuality.

The major victims of such race prejudice as did exist in America were the Negroes. It was a problem originated and perpetuated by the non-capitalist South, though not confined to its boundaries. The persecution of Negroes in the South was and is truly disgraceful. But in the rest of the country, so long as men were free, even that problem was slowly giving way under the pressure of enlightenment and of the white men's own economic interests.

Today, that problem is growing worse — and so is every other form of racism. America has become race-conscious in a manner reminiscent of the worst days in the most backward countries of 19th century Europe. The cause is the same: the growth of collectivism and statism.

In spite of the clamor for racial equality, propagated by the "liberals" in the past few decades, the Census Bureau reported recently that "[the Negro's] economic status relative to whites has not improved for nearly 20 years." It had been improving in the freer years of our "mixed economy"; it deteriorated with the progressive enlargement of the "liberals'" Welfare State.

The growth of racism in a "mixed economy" keeps step with the growth of government controls. A "mixed economy" disintegrates a country into an institutionalized civil war of pressure groups, each fighting for legislative favors and special privileges at the expense of one another.

The existence of such pressure groups and of their political lobbies is openly and cynically acknowledged today. The pretense at any political philosophy, any principles, ideals or long-range goals is fast disappearing from our scene — and it is all but admitted that this country is now floating without direction, at the mercy of a blind, short-range power-game played by various statist gangs, each intent on getting hold of a legislative gun for any special advantage of the immediate moment.

In the absence of any coherent political philosophy, every economic group has been acting as its own destroyer, selling out its future for some momentary privilege. The policy of the businessmen has, for some time, been the most suicidal one in this respect. But it has been surpassed by the current policy of the Negro leaders.

So long as the Negro leaders were fighting against government-enforced discrimination — right, justice and morality were on their side. But that is not what they are fighting any longer. The confusions and contradictions surrounding the issue of racism have now reached an incredible climax.

It is time to clarify the principles involved.

The policy of the Southern states toward Negroes was and is a shameful contradiction of this country's basic principles. Racial discrimination, imposed and enforced by law, is so blatantly inexcusable an infringement of individual rights that the racist statutes of the South should have been declared unconstitutional long ago.

The Southern racists' claim of "states' rights" is a contradiction in terms: there can be no such thing as the "right" of some men to violate the rights of others. The constitutional concept of "states' rights" pertains to the division of power between local and national authorities, and serves to protect the states from the Federal government; it does not grant to a state government an unlimited, arbitrary power over its citizens or the privilege of abrogating the citizens' individual rights.

It is true that the Federal government has used the racial issue to enlarge its own power and to set a precedent of encroachment upon the legitimate rights of the states, in an unnecessary and unconstitutional manner. But this merely means that both governments are wrong; it does not excuse the policy of the Southern racists.

One of the worst contradictions, in this context, is the stand of many so-called "conservatives" (not confined exclusively to the South) who claim to be defenders of freedom, of capitalism, of property rights, of the Constitution, yet who advocate racism at the same time. They do not seem to possess enough concern with principles to realize that they are cutting the ground from under their own feet. Men who deny individual rights cannot claim, defend or uphold any rights whatsoever. It is such alleged champions of capitalism who are helping to discredit and destroy it.

The "liberals" are guilty of the same contradiction, but in a different form. They advocate the sacrifice of all individual rights to unlimited majority rule — yet posture as defenders of the rights of minorities. But the smallest minority on earth is the individual. Those who deny individual rights, cannot claim to be defenders of minorities.

This accumulation of contradictions, of short-sighted pragmatism, of cynical contempt for principles, of outrageous irrationality, has now reached its climax in the new demands of the Negro leaders.

Instead of fighting against racial discrimination, they are demanding that racial discrimination be legalized and enforced. Instead of fighting against racism, they are demanding the establishment of racial quotas. Instead of fighting for "color-blindness" in social and economic issues, they are proclaiming that "color-blindness" is evil and that "color" should be made a primary consideration. Instead of fighting for equal rights, they are demanding special race privileges.

They are demanding that racial quotas be established in regard to employment and that jobs be distributed on a racial basis, in proportion to the percentage of a given race among the local population. For instance, since Negroes constitute 25 per cent of the population of New York City, they demand 25 per cent of the jobs in a given establishment.

Racial quotas have been one of the worst evils of racist regimes. There were racial quotas in the universities of Czarist Russia, in the population of Russia's major cities, etc. One of the accusations against the racists in this country is that some schools practice a secret system of racial quotas. It was regarded as a victory for justice when employment questionnaires ceased to inquire about an applicant's race or religion.

Today, it is not an oppressor, but an oppressed minority group that is demanding the establishment of racial quotas. (!)

This particular demand was too much even for the "liberals." Many of them denounced it — properly — with shocked indignation.

Wrote *The N. Y. Times* (July 23, 1963): "The demonstrators are following a truly vicious principle in playing the 'numbers game.' A demand that 25 per cent (or any other percentage) of jobs be given to Negroes (or any other group) is wrong for one basic reason: it calls for a 'quota system,' which is in itself discriminatory.... This newspaper has long fought a religious quota in respect to judgeships; we equally oppose a racial quota in respect to jobs from the most elevated to the most menial."

As if the blatant racism of such a demand were not enough, some Negro leaders went still farther. Whitney M. Young Jr., executive director of the National Urban League, made the following statement (*N. Y. Times*, August 1):

"The white leadership must be honest enough to grant that throughout our history there has existed a special privileged class of citizens who received preferred treatment. That class
(continued on page 36)

Racism (from page 35)

was white. Now we're saying this: If two men, one Negro and one white, are equally qualified for a job, hire the Negro."

Consider the implications of that statement. It does not merely demand special privileges on racial grounds — it demands that white men be penalized *for the sins of their ancestors.* It demands that a white laborer be refused a job because his grandfather may have practiced racial discrimination. But perhaps his grandfather had *not* practiced it. Or perhaps his grandfather had not even lived in this country. Since these questions are not to be considered, it means that that white laborer is to be charged with *collective racial guilt,* the guilt consisting merely of the color of his skin.

But *that* is the principle of the worst Southern racist who charges all Negroes with collective racial guilt for any crime committed by an individual Negro, and who treats them all as inferiors on the ground that their ancestors were savages.

The only comment one can make about demands of that kind, is: "By what right?—By what code?—By what standard?"

That absurdly evil policy is destroying the moral base of the Negroes' fight. Their case rested on the principle of individual rights. If they demand the violation of the rights of others, they negate and forfeit their own. Then the same answer applies to them as to the Southern racists: there can be no such thing as the "right" of some men to violate the rights of others.

Yet the entire policy of the Negro leaders is now moving in that direction. For instance, the demand for racial quotas in schools, with the proposal that hundreds of children, white and Negro, be forced to attend school in distant neighborhoods — for the purpose of "racial balance." Again, this is pure racism. As opponents of this demand have pointed out, to assign children to certain schools by reason of their race, is equally evil whether one does it for purposes of segregation or integration. And the mere idea of using children as pawns in a political game should outrage all parents, of any race, creed or color.

The "civil rights" bill, now under consideration in Congress, is another example of a gross infringement of individual rights. It is proper to forbid all discrimination in government-owned facilities and establishments: the government has no right to discriminate against any citizens. And by the very same principle, the government has no right to discriminate *for* some citizens at the expense of others. It has no right to violate the right of private property by forbidding discrimination in privately owned establishments.

No man, neither Negro nor white, has any claim to the property of another man. A man's rights are not violated by a private individual's refusal to deal with him. Racism is an evil, irrational and morally contemptible doctrine — but doctrines cannot be forbidden or prescribed by law. Just as we have to protect a communist's freedom of speech, even though his doctrines are evil, so we have to protect a racist's right to the use and disposal of his own property. Private racism is not a legal, but a moral issue — and can be fought only by private means, such as economic boycott or social ostracism.

Needless to say, if that "civil rights" bill is passed, it will be the worst breach of property rights in the sorry record of American history in respect to that subject.

It is an ironic demonstration of the philosophical insanity and the consequently suicidal trend of our age, that the men who need the protection of individual rights most urgently — the Negroes — are now in the vanguard of the destruction of these rights.

A word of warning: do not become victims of the same racists by succumbing to racism; do not hold against all Negroes the disgraceful irrationality of some of their leaders. No group has any proper intellectual leadership today or any proper representation.

In conclusion, I shall quote from an astonishing editorial in *The N. Y. Times* of August 4 — astonishing because ideas of this nature are not typical of our age:

"But the question must be not whether a group recognizable in color, features or culture has its rights as a group. No, the question is whether any American individual, regardless of color, features or culture, is deprived of his rights as an American. If the individual has all the rights and privileges due him under the laws and the Constitution, we need not worry about groups and masses — those do not, in fact, exist, except as figures of speech."

OBJECTIVIST CALENDAR

■ On Saturday, September 28, Ayn Rand and Nathaniel Branden will appear on the Chicago television program, "Kup's Show" (ABC, Channel 7, 12 midnight-3:00 A.M.).

■ On Sunday, September 29, Ayn Rand will give a major public address at McCormick Place in Chicago. Her talk is entitled "America's Persecuted Minority: Big Business." (Those in the Chicago area desiring further information should write to: Mr. Edward L. Nash, Nash Productions, 55 E. Washington, Chicago 2, Illinois.)

■ On Wednesday, October 2, Ayn Rand will receive an honorary Doctor of Letters degree from Lewis and Clark College in Portland, Oregon. On October 1 and 2, the entire student body and faculty of the college will be engaged in a series of discussions of Miss Rand's books. Nathaniel Branden will participate in a discussion of *The Fountainhead* and *Atlas Shrugged.* On October 1, Miss Rand will deliver an introductory talk; on October 2, she will deliver a lecture entitled "Is Atlas Shrugging?" which will be open to the public. (Those in the Portland area desiring further information should write to: Office of the President, Lewis and Clark College, 0615 S.W. Palatine Hill Road, Portland 19, Oregon.)

■ On October 4, 8 and 9 respectively, NATHANIEL BRANDEN INSTITUTE will begin its fall series on "Basic Principles of Objectivism" in San Francisco, San Diego and Los Angeles. Mr. Branden will deliver the opening lecture in each city in person. Miss Rand will join Mr. Branden in extended question periods following each of these three lectures. The remainder of the course is given via tape transcription.

In addition, NBI's Tape Transcription Division has now scheduled the following starting dates for "Basic Principles of Objectivism" in the following cities: Lincoln (Nebraska), September 9; Cleveland, October 7; Dallas, October 7; Chicago, October 11; Milwaukee, October 13; Toronto, October 21; Philadelphia, October 24; Washington, D.C., October 27; Boston, November 1. Mr. Branden will deliver the opening night's lecture in person in Chicago, Milwaukee, Toronto, Philadelphia, Washington and Boston.

Starting dates in additional cities will be listed here as they are scheduled.

■ On Monday, October 14, the course on "Basic Principles of Objectivism" will begin in New York City. Place: Hotel Roosevelt. Time: 7:30 P.M. Miss Rand will participate in the question period which follows the lecture.

■ NBI is planning tape series in Portland, Oregon, in Seattle, Washington, and in neighboring towns around Los Angeles. Persons interested in acting as business managers for the lecture series given in these areas, are invited to write NBI's Tape Transcription Division, enclosing a detailed resume. Appointments for the purpose of interviewing prospective business managers will be arranged in Portland on September 30, October 1 and 2, and in Los Angeles on October 6, 7, 8 and 9.

—B. B.

Published monthly at 120 East 34th Street, New York 16, N.Y.
Subscription rate: in United States, its possessions, Canada and Mexico, $5 for one year; other countries, $6.
Additional copies of this Newsletter: single copy 50¢ (coins, not stamps); 10 — 99 copies, 25¢ each plus postage (for first-class delivery add 1¢ per copy, for third-class delivery add ½¢ per copy); 100 or more copies, 15¢ each plus postage (same as above).
For change of address send old address and new address with zone number if any. Allow us three weeks to process new subscriptions and change of address.

Ayn Rand and Nathaniel Branden, Editors and Publishers
Barbara Branden, Managing Editor
Elayne Kalberman, Circulation Manager
PRINTED BY STANDARD PRESS & GRAPHICS, INC., NEW YORK CITY

THE OBJECTIVIST NEWSLETTER

Edited and Published by AYN RAND and NATHANIEL BRANDEN

VOL. 2 NO. 10   OCTOBER, 1963

CHECK YOUR PREMISES
By AYN RAND
The Goal of My Writing

(*This is the first part of an address delivered at Lewis and Clark College, on October 1, 1963. The second part will appear in our next issue.*)

I have been asked to discuss the motive or purpose of my writing. It is a somewhat difficult assignment, because I know that it is a very complex subject — yet, to me, it feels like a simple, self-evident primary, obvious in every line I have ever written.

Knowing that the self-evident is usually the hardest to communicate, I shall begin by telling you an incident which may help to make it clearer.

Shortly after I met Nathaniel Branden, he and I had a telephone conversation about literature. He was then nineteen years old, and he told me that two novels had played an important role in his intellectual development: one was *The Fountainhead*, which he had read at the age of fourteen, the other was Romain Roland's *Jean Christophe*, which he had read at sixteen. In a very generalized way, these two novels may be said to deal with the same subject: the struggle of a creative genius against an inimical society. Mr. Branden said that both novels were of great value to him, that both had helped him to grasp and objectify certain issues — but that *The Fountainhead* had a deeper *personal* importance to him and he was struggling to identify all the reasons of the difference of his reaction.

I asked him: "Tell me, would you want to meet Jean Christophe in real life?"

He understood me at once. I heard a kind of small gasp of delighted astonishment over the telephone wire — and he answered: "No. No, not particularly. But I *would* want to meet Howard Roark."

This, I told him, was the primary meaning of literature to me — both in what I write and in what I like to read.

This is the motive and purpose of my writing: *the projection of an ideal man*. The portrayal of a moral ideal, as my ultimate literary goal, as an end in itself — to which any didactic, intellectual or philosophical values contained in a novel are only the means.

Let me stress this: my purpose is *not* the philosophical enlightenment of my readers, it is *not* the beneficial influence which my novels may have on people, it is *not* the fact that Howard Roark did help Mr. Branden's intellectual development. All these matters are important, but they are secondary considerations, they are merely consequences and effects, not first causes or prime movers — although a reader like Nathaniel Branden is as great a reward as a novelist could ever hope to find. My purpose, first cause and prime mover is the portrayal of Howard Roark (or John Galt or Hank Rearden or Francisco d'Anconia) *as an end in himself* — not as a means to any further end. Which, incidentally, is the greatest value I could ever offer a reader.

This is why I feel a very mixed emotion — part patience, part amusement and, at times, an empty kind of weariness — when I am asked whether I am primarily a novelist or a philosopher (as if these two were antonyms), whether my stories are propaganda vehicles for ideas, whether politics or the advocacy of capitalism is my chief purpose. All such questions are so enormously irrelevant, so far beside the point, so much *not* my way of coming at things.

My way is much simpler and, simultaneously, much more complex than that, speaking from two different aspects. The simple truth is that I approach literature as a child does: I write — and read — for the sake of the story. The complexity lies in the task of translating that attitude into adult terms.

The specific concretes, the *forms* of one's values, change with one's growth and development. The abstraction *"values"* does not. An adult's values involve the entire sphere of human activity, including philosophy — most particularly philosophy. But the basic principle — the function and meaning of values in man's life and in literature — remains the same.

My basic test for any story is: "Would I want to meet these characters and observe these events in real life? Is this story an experience worth living through for its own sake? Is the pleasure of contemplating these characters an end in itself?"

It's as simple as that. But that simplicity involves the total of man's existence.

It involves such questions as: What kind of men do I want to see in real life — and why? What kind of events, that is, human actions, do I want to see taking place — and why? What kind of experience do I want to live through, that is, what are my goals — and why?

It is obvious to what field of human knowledge all these questions belong: to the field of *ethics*. What is the good? What are the right actions for man to take? What are man's proper *values*?

Since my purpose is the presentation of an ideal man, I had to define and present the conditions which make him possible and which his existence requires. Since man's character is the product of his premises, I had to define and present the kind of premises and values that create the character of an ideal man and motivate his actions; which means that I had to define and present a rational code of ethics. Since man acts among and deals with other men, I had to present the kind of social system that makes it possible for ideal men to exist and to function — a free, productive, rational system, which demands and rewards the best in every man, and which is, obviously, laissez-faire capitalism.

But neither politics nor ethics nor philosophy are ends in themselves, neither in life nor in literature. Only Man is an end in himself.

It is not my purpose today to discuss the Objectivist theory of esthetics. But in order to indicate my frame-of-reference, let me give you the Objectivist definition of art — and of literature as one of its branches. Art is a selective re-creation of reality according to the artist's metaphysical values. By "metaphysical" values I mean those values which reflect an artist's fundamental view of the nature of man and the nature of reality, of the universe in which he lives and acts; or, to put it another way: an artist's fundamental view of man's relationship to existence.

For a brief presentation of my theory of art, I will refer you to the introduction I wrote for the new translation of Victor Hugo's novel *Ninety-Three*, published by Bantam Books. For a fuller presentation and validation of my theory, I will refer you to the lecture on *The Objectivist Esthetics* which I give at the Nathaniel Branden Institute.

For the purposes of today's discussion, I will ask you to bear in mind only two characteristics of art (and of literature), which almost all theories of esthetics recognize to be true: the fact that art is *selective* and the fact that an art work, as distinguished from a utilitarian object, serves no practical purpose other than that of *contemplation*.

I must mention, as an aside, that the Objectivist esthetics can demonstrate that such contemplation does have a purpose and does serve a need of man — only it is not a physical need of his existence, it is a profound need of his consciousness. But this is not the subject — though it is the deeper background — of today's discussion.

(continued on page 38)

Copyright © 1963 by The Objectivist Newsletter, Inc.

The Goal of My Writing *(from page 37)*

Now observe that the practitioners of the literary school diametrically opposed to mine—the school of Naturalism—claim that a writer must reproduce what they call "real life," allegedly "as it is," exercising no selectivity and no value-judgments. By "reproduce," they mean "photograph"; by "real life," they mean whatever given concretes they happen to observe; by "as it is," they mean "as it is lived by the people around them." But observe that these Naturalists — or the good writers among them — are extremely selective in regard to two attributes of literature: *style* and *characterization*. Without selectivity, it would be impossible to achieve any sort of characterization whatever, neither of an unusual man nor of an average one who is to be offered as statistically typical of a large segment of the population. Therefore, the Naturalists' opposition to selectivity applies to only one attribute of literature: the content or *subject*. It is in regard to his choice of subject that a novelist must exercise no choice, they claim.

Why?

The Naturalists have never given an answer to that question—not a rational, logical, non-contradictory answer. Why should a writer photograph his subjects indiscriminately and unselectively? Because they "really" happened? To record what really happened is the job of a reporter or of an historian, not of a novelist. To enlighten readers and educate them? That is the job of science, not of literature, of non-fiction writing, not of fiction. To improve men's lot by exposing their misery? But *that* is a value-judgment and a moral purpose and a didactic "message"—all of which are forbidden by the Naturalist doctrine. Besides, to improve anything one must know what constitutes an improvement — and to know that, one must know what is the good and how to achieve it — and to know that, one must have a whole system of value-judgments, a system of *ethics*, which is anathema to the Naturalists.

Thus, the Naturalists' position amounts to giving a novelist full esthetic freedom in regard to *means*, but not in regard to *ends*. He may exercise choice, creative imagination, value-judgments in regard to *how* he portrays things, but not in regard to *what* he portrays — in regard to style or characterization, but not in regard to *subject*. Man — the subject of literature — must not be viewed or portrayed selectively. Man must be accepted as the given, the unchangeable, the not-to-be-judged, the *status-quo*. But since we observe that men do change, that they differ from one another, that they pursue different values, who, then, is to determine the human *status-quo*? Naturalism's implicit answer is: everybody except the novelist.

The novelist — according to the Naturalist doctrine — must neither judge nor value. He is not a creator, but only a recording secretary whose master is the rest of mankind. Let others pronounce judgments, make decisions, select goals, fight over values and determine the course, the fate and the soul of man. The novelist is the only outcast and deserter of that battle. His is not to reason why — his is only to trot behind his master, notebook in hand, taking down whatever the master dictates, picking up such pearls or such swinishness as the master may choose to drop.

As far as I am concerned, I have too much self-esteem for a job of that kind.

I see the novelist as a combination of prospector and jeweler. The novelist must discover the potential, the gold mine, of man's soul, must extract the gold and then fashion as magnificent a crown as his ability and vision permit.

Just as men of ambition for material values do not rummage through city dumps, but venture out into lonely mountains in search of gold — so men of ambition for intellectual values do not sit in their backyards, but venture out in quest of the noblest, the purest, the costliest elements. I would not enjoy the spectacle of Benvenuto Cellini making mud-pies.

It is the selectivity in regard to subject — the most severely, rigorously, ruthlessly exercised selectivity — that I hold as the primary, the essential, the cardinal aspect of art. In literature, this means: *the story* — which means: the plot and the characters—which means: the kind of men and events that a writer chooses to portray.

The subject is not the only attribute of art, but it is the fundamental one, it is the end to which all the others are the means. In most esthetic theories, however, the end — the subject — is omitted from consideration, and only the means are regarded as esthetically relevant. Such theories set up a false dichotomy and claim that a slob portrayed by the technical means of a genius is preferable to a goddess portrayed by the technique of an amateur. I hold that *both* are esthetically offensive; but while the second is merely esthetic incompetence, the first is an esthetic crime.

There is no dichotomy, no necessary conflict between ends and means. The end does *not* justify the means — neither in ethics nor in esthetics. And neither do the means justify the end: there is no esthetic justification for the spectacle of Rembrandt's great artistic skill employed to portray a side of beef.

That particular painting may be taken as a symbol of everything I am opposed to in art and in literature. At the age of seven, I could not understand why anyone should wish to paint or to admire pictures of dead fish, garbage cans or fat peasant women with triple chins. Today, I understand the psychological causes of such esthetic phenomena — and the more I understand, the more I oppose them.

In art, and in literature, the end and the means, or the subject and the style, must be worthy of each other.

That which is not worth contemplating in life, is not worth re-creating in art.

Misery, disease, disaster, evil, all the negatives of human existence, are proper subjects of *study* in life, for the purpose of understanding and correcting them — but are not proper subjects of *contemplation* for contemplation's sake. In art, and in literature, these negatives are worth re-creating only in relation to some positive, as a foil, as a contrast, as a means of stressing the positive — but *not* as an end in themselves.

The "compassionate" studies of depravity — of dipsomaniacs, drug addicts, murderers, psychotics—which pass for literature today are the dead end and the tombstone of Naturalism. If their perpetrators still claim the justification that these things are "true" (most of them aren't)—the answer is that this sort of truth belongs in psychological case histories, not in literature. The picture of an infected ruptured appendix may be of great value in a medical textbook—but it does not belong in an art gallery. And an infected soul is a much more repulsive spectacle.

That one should wish to enjoy the contemplation of *values*, of the *good* — of man's greatness, intelligence, ability, virtue, heroism — is self-explanatory. It is the contemplation of the *evil* that requires explanation and justification; and the same goes for the contemplation of the mediocre, the undistinguished, the commonplace, the meaningless, the mindless.

At the age of seven, I refused to read the children's equivalent of Naturalistic literature — the stories about the children of the folks next door. They bored me to death. I was not interested in such people in real life; I saw no reason to find them interesting in fiction.

This is still my position today; the only difference is that today I know its full philosophical justification.

As far as literary schools are concerned, I would call myself a Romantic Realist.

Consider the significance of the fact that the Naturalists call Romantic art an "escape." Ask yourself what sort of metaphysics — what view of life — that designation confesses. An escape — from what? If the projection of value-goals — the projection of an improvement on the given, the known, the immediately available — is an "escape," then medicine is an "escape" from disease, agriculture is an "escape" from hunger, knowledge is an "escape" from ignorance, ambition is an "escape" from sloth, and life is an "escape" from death. If so, then a hardcore realist is a vermin-eaten brute who sits motionless in a mud puddle, contemplates a pigsty and whines that "such is life." If *that* is realism, then I am an escapist. So was Aristotle. So was Christopher Columbus.

There is a passage in *The Fountainhead* that deals with this issue: the passage in which Howard Roark explains to Steven Mallory why he chose him to do a statue for the Stoddard Temple. In writing that passage, I was consciously and deliberately stating the essential goal of my own work — as a kind of small, personal manifesto: "I think you're the best sculptor we've got. I think it, because your figures are not what men are, but what men could be — and should be. Because you've gone beyond the probable and made us see what is possible, but possible only through you. Because your fig-
(continued on page 39)

INTELLECTUAL AMMUNITION DEPARTMENT

[*Subscribers are invited to send in the questions that they find themselves unable to answer in philosophical or political discussions. As many questions as space permits will be answered. No questions will be answered by mail.*]

- **What is the psychological appeal of altruism for people who appear to be, not altruism's beneficiaries, but its victims?**

A morality which teaches man that he has no right to exist for his own sake but must sacrifice himself to others, has an obvious appeal for men who seek the unearned and wish to profit by someone else's sacrifice. We have thoroughly discussed the psychology of such men elsewhere, and it does not require elaboration here. Less obvious, however, is the psychology of men who do *not* appear to desire the unearned, but are willing to grant it to others, who may admit that the creed of altruism cannot be justified in reason, but who nonetheless are unwilling to repudiate a doctrine which demands that they regard themselves as objects of sacrifice.

The broadest explanation of this phenomenon is the fact that altruism is the only ethical code most men have ever known. They have no other concept of morality, and they lack the independence to challenge a doctrine which they have heard preached all their lives and which, in one form or another, has been dominant for centuries. They have always heard unselfishness equated with virtue, and selfishness made a synonym of evil. They find it unthinkable that so many men — so many authorities — could be wrong.

If and when they are compelled to realize that altruism is irrational, that it cannot be practiced consistently, that they must act against it some of the time in order to live — even then, the majority of men feel obliged to pay it lip-service as a noble ideal, and feel guilty over the failure to practice it more fully and to relinquish their desire for "selfish" happiness. They know, implicitly if not explicitly, that man needs *some* code of moral principles to guide his life; and if they reject the altruist morality, they face a prospect which fills them with dread: that of standing intellectually alone — of re-thinking the issue of morality from scratch — and of having to assume responsibility for *choosing* (instead of blindly and passively accepting) the values by which they are to live.

For a fuller discussion of this psychology, I refer the reader to my article on *Social Metaphysics* in the November 1962 issue of this NEWSLETTER.

In addition to the above, there is another, more specific reason why men are unwilling to break with the altruist morality. Altruism does not demand self-esteem of man; but an ethics of rational self-interest *does*.

An ethics of rational self-interest demands that man identify what *is* to his self-interest, that he choose meaningful, long-range goals, that he struggle to achieve his values, holding them above all lesser considerations, never surrendering them to the blind whim of the moment or to lethargy or to fear of the opposition of other men. Such an ethics tells man that he has the right to his own happiness — but it also tells him that his is the responsibility of *earning* that happiness.

If men lack the self-esteem and courage to assert their right to exist, altruism assures them that this is the virtue of selflessness. If they lack the independence, integrity and ambition to fight for their values, altruism assures them that this is the virtue of renunciation. If they dread the responsibility of relying on their own mind, and prefer to surrender it to the authority of others, altruism assures them that this is the virtue of faith.

It is illuminating, in this connection, to recall the scene, in *The Fountainhead*, of Peter Keating's last encounter with Catherine Halsey, the one girl whom he had loved, but had abandoned in order to enter a marriage that would grant him more prestige — the scene in which Keating finally perceives the abject selflessness of his entire life: "Katie, I wanted to marry you. It was the only thing I ever really wanted. And that's the sin that can't be forgiven — that I hadn't done what I wanted. . . . Katie, why do they always teach us that it's easy and evil to do what we want and that we need discipline to restrain ourselves? It's the hardest thing in the world — to do what we want. And it takes the greatest kind of courage. I mean, what we really want. As I wanted to marry you. Not as I want to sleep with some woman or get drunk or get my name in the papers. Those things — they're not even desires — they're things people do to escape from desires — because it's such a big responsibility, really to want something."

Altruism holds out to men the promise of that which is every neurotic's dream: *a way to by-pass the need of achieving self-esteem*. Altruism tells man that his moral worth is determined not by his intellectual integrity, nor by what he has achieved, nor by what he has made of himself — but only by what he has done for others. Altruism promises men that they can buy their way out of everything — irrationality, ineptitude, parasitism, dishonesty, self-contempt — if they will pay the price in service to others.

Thus, the natural prey of altruism is any man who suffers from a sense of guilt or inadequacy and who does not propose to deal with his problem rationally. It is irrelevant, in this context, whether the guilt is warranted or unwarranted, whether the man is productive or a parasite, whether he is admired by others or despised; what is relevant is that he suffers from a sense of unworthiness which he does not care to face. When altruism tells him that virtue consists of living for others, he is ready, sacrifice and check book in hand, grateful that he has been spared the necessity for thought, grateful that the solution is *so easy*.

If a man cheats in business, or is unfaithful to his wife, or betrays his standards in order to court popularity, or is arbitrary and vindictive in his dealings with subordinates — it is comforting to be told that altruism is the omnipotent moral purifier. Such a man's sacrifices may be genuinely painful to him — but less so than the effort of living as a rational being.

Consider the phenomenon of the hard-working, successful man who supports a dozen worthless relatives, whose wallet is always open to everyone, who is exploited and imposed on — yet who clings tenaciously to his burdens, is anxious and tensely resistant at the suggestion that he does not have to carry them, and resents any argument that altruism is not a moral ideal. To understand such a man, one must remember the following: the fact that a man is hard-working and productive, does not guarantee that he is without neurotic problems; he may feel guilty or anxious or lacking in self-esteem because of failures or irrationalities in other areas of his life; and this can lead him to a vested interest in altruism. Such a man is willing to give others a wealth *they* do not deserve — in order to receive from them a love or approval he feels *he* does not deserve. He is willing to give the *materially* unearned — in order to receive the *spiritually* unearned. This is why he does not want to be liberated from his exploiters; in their expressions of affection or admiration, in their eager forgiveness of his personal flaws, he hopes to find the self-esteem he does not possess.

Needless to say, neurotic devices do not work, and altruism does not in fact deliver anyone from guilt. It encourages men to evade their actual problems and keeps them in a state of chronic guilt over the sacrifices they have failed to make — and they go on blindly and vainly striving to appease a claimant that is a bottomless hole.

It is harder to achieve self-esteem than to practice self-sacrifice. But there is no substitute for self-esteem and no way to achieve it except by working to live up to one's highest potentiality as a rational, integrated, efficacious being. The secret appeal of altruism for many people is that it offers them the delusion that an alternative is possible.

— **NATHANIEL BRANDEN**

The Goal of My Writing (from page 38)

ures are more devoid of contempt for humanity than any work I've ever seen. Because you have a magnificent respect for the human being. Because your figures are the heroic in man."

Today, more than twenty years later, I would want to

(continued on page 40)

The Goal of My Writing (from page 39)

change — or, rather, to clarify — only two small points. First, the words "more devoid of contempt for humanity" are not too exact grammatically; what I wanted to convey was *"untouched"* by contempt for humanity, while the work of others was touched by it to some extent. Second, the words "possible only through you" should not be taken to mean that Mallory's figures were impossible metaphysically, in reality; I meant that they were possible only because *he* had shown the way to make them possible.

"Your figures are not what men are, but what men could be — and should be."

This line will make it clear whose great philosophical principle I had accepted and was following and had been groping for, long before I heard the name "Aristotle." It was Aristotle who said that fiction is of greater philosophical importance than history, because history represents things only as they are, while fiction represents them "as they *might be* and *ought to be*."

(To be continued in our next issue)

OBJECTIVIST CALENDAR

■ On October 4, 11 and 24, in Indianapolis, Nathaniel Branden will give readings (via tape transcriptions) of three plays by Ayn Rand. Place: Hotel Warren, 123 S. Illinois St. Time: 8:00 P.M. Admission: $2.00 per play or $5.00 for the series.

■ On October 10, in Clear, Alaska, NATHANIEL BRANDEN INSTITUTE's Tape Transcription Division will begin the twenty-lecture course on "Basic Principles of Objectivist Psychology."

■ In addition to the starting dates listed last month, NBI's Tape Transcription Division has scheduled the following starting dates for the course on "Basic Principles of Objectivism" in the following cities: Cincinnati, Oct. 14; St. Louis, Oct. 14; Valparaiso (Indiana), Oct. 15; Ithaca, Nov. 3. In Ithaca, Mr. Branden will give the opening night's lecture in person.

■ On October 23, in Valparaiso, NBI's Tape Transcription Division will begin Barbara Branden's course on "Principles of Efficient Thinking."

■ On October 22, "Basic Principles of Objectivist Psychology" will begin in New York City. Place: Hotel Roosevelt, 45th St. & Madison Avenue. Time: 7:30 P.M. Visitors' admission: $3.50.

■ Random House has recently issued the sixth printing of *Atlas Shrugged* in its hardcover edition.

Social Note:

Allan Gotthelf, on behalf of a group of NBI students, challenged Nathaniel Branden and a number of his associates to a game of baseball. For reasons not yet known, Mr. Branden accepted, and the game was held in Central Park on September 8. Mr. Gotthelf's and Mr. Branden's teams were respectively designated as "The Attilas" and "The Witch Doctors."

As the game progressed, players could be heard shouting: "Focus! Focus!" to members of their own team, and "You whim worshipers!" to members of the opposing team. There was little evidence, on the part of passers-by in the park, of any appreciation of the momentous issues at stake. Some onlookers appeared a bit puzzled by the fact that, whenever a player disagreed with the decision of the umpire, a public poll of everyone within the area was promptly taken in order to resolve the dispute.

The Attilas won by a score of 35 to 17. "This settles the issue of the superiority of brawn over brain, once and for all," a member of the Attilas was heard to remark. Mr. Branden was not available for comment. However, several Witch Doctors are protesting "unfair competition," inasmuch as a number of players on the Attila team are definitely known to have participated in this sport on previous occasions. Except for the fact that half of the NBI office staff is walking around on crutches, a good time was had by all.

— B. B.

A Suggestion

The contest between Senator Goldwater and Governor Rockefeller for the Presidential nomination of the Republican Party is becoming a very serious and important issue. Mr. Rockefeller has recently made a statement lumping all opponents of the welfare state with actual crackpots and smearing them as "the radical right lunatic fringe." Since we have only two major political parties, that statement — which he has failed to clarify or define — will disfranchise, if he is nominated, all those whose political convictions are to the right of his own, which includes all advocates of capitalism.

I say "disfranchise," because voters who take political philosophy seriously and hold reasoned convictions, cannot permit themselves to vote for a man who has, in effect, slapped their faces. Since the Democratic Party is fully committed to welfare statism, such voters will not be able to vote at all, not even in token of protest. (But it must be said that even the Democratic Party has not confronted them with an insult of that kind.)

Inasmuch as the majority of Republican voters are implicit (if confused) supporters of capitalism in various mixed degrees, Mr. Rockefeller's statement constitutes an attempt at an intellectual *coup d'etat*, which should be protested.

The most direct and effective form of protest is to vote for Senator Goldwater in the Republican Presidential primaries of 1964. The importance of such voting was demonstrated in the recent primaries, when Mr. Rockefeller's and Mayor Wagner's "prestige" was "saved" by 342 votes and 41 votes respectively, within their own parties.

Since only registered Republicans are entitled to vote in the Republican primaries, I suggest to all those who are interested in political action and specifically all those who advocate capitalism, that they should not fail to register in time.

If you are a registered voter, you must re-register if you have moved since the last election. If you are registered as an "Independent," but intend to vote for the Republican candidate, I suggest that you change your registration to "Republican." The last opportunity to do so, before the Presidential primaries, is *this* month; in New York, it is on October 10, 11 and 12, 1963.

A party registration does not commit you to vote for any of the party's candidates in the election. You are free to change your mind or to "cross party lines," according to your own judgment at the time.

In today's state of political confusion and contradictions, it is difficult to endorse any candidate with any degree of certainty. All one can say is that it appears, *at present*, that Senator Goldwater may become very much worth supporting, particularly in view of his recent stand on Cuba and the nuclear test treaty — and most particularly because he seems to be our last chance to preserve two-party government.

If, between now and nomination or election time, Senator Goldwater should change his stand, or adopt some major form of "me-too'ing" compromise, or tie his candidacy to some doctrine of a mystical nature — we will, of course, be free not to vote for him. At present, he is the best candidate in the field.

— **Ayn Rand**

Published **monthly** at 120 East 34th Street, New York 16, N. Y.
Subscription rate: in United States, its possessions, Canada and Mexico, $5 for one year; other countries, $6.
Additional copies of this Newsletter: single copy 50¢ (coins, not stamps); 10 — 99 copies, 25¢ each plus postage (for first-class delivery add 1¢ per copy, for third-class delivery add ½¢ per copy); 100 or more copies, 15¢ each plus postage (same as above).
For change of address send old address and new address with zone number if any. Allow us three weeks to process new subscriptions and change of address.

Ayn Rand and Nathaniel Branden, Editors and Publishers
Barbara Branden, Managing Editor
Elayne Kalberman, Circulation Manager
PRINTED BY STANDARD PRESS & GRAPHICS, INC., NEW YORK CITY

THE OBJECTIVIST NEWSLETTER

Edited and Published by AYN RAND and NATHANIEL BRANDEN

VOL. 2 NO. 11   NOVEMBER, 1963

CHECK YOUR PREMISES
By AYN RAND

The Goal of My Writing

(This is the second and final part of an address delivered at Lewis and Clark College, on October 1, 1963.)

Why must fiction represent things "as they might be and ought to be"?

My answer is in one statement of *Atlas Shrugged* — and in the implications of that statement: "As man is a being of self-made wealth, so he is a being of self-made soul."

Just as man's physical survival depends on his own effort, so does his psychological survival. Man faces two corollary, interdependent fields of action in which a constant exercise of choice and a constant creative process are demanded of him: the world around him and his own soul (by "soul," I mean his consciousness). Just as he has to produce the material values he needs to sustain his life, so he has to acquire the values of character that enable him to sustain it and that make his life worth living. He is born without the knowledge of either. He has to discover both — and translate them into reality — and survive by shaping the world and himself in the image of his values.

Growing from a common root, which is philosophy, man's knowledge branches out in two directions. One branch studies the physical world or the phenomena pertaining to man's physical existence; the other studies man or the phenomena pertaining to his consciousness. The first leads to abstract science, which leads to applied science or engineering, which leads to technology — to the actual production of material values. The second leads to art.

Art is the technology of the soul.

Art is the product of three philosophical disciplines: metaphysics, epistemology, ethics. Metaphysics and epistemology are the abstract base of ethics. Ethics is the applied science that defines a code of values to guide man's choices and actions — the choices and actions which determine the course of his life; ethics is the engineering that provides the principles and blue-prints. Art creates the final product. It builds the model.

Let me stress this analogy: art does not *teach* — it shows, it displays the full, concretized reality of the final goal. Teaching is the task of ethics. Teaching is not the purpose of an art work, any more than it is the purpose of an airplane. Just as one can learn a great deal from an airplane by studying it or taking it apart, so one can learn a great deal from an art work — about the nature of man, of his soul, of his existence. But these are merely fringe benefits. The primary purpose of an airplane is, not to *teach* man how to fly, but to give him the actual experience of flying. So is the primary purpose of an art work.

Although the representation of things "as they might be and ought to be" helps man to achieve those things in real life, this is only a secondary value. The *primary* value is that it gives him the experience of living in a world where things are *as they ought to be*. This experience is of crucial importance to him: it is his psychological life-line.

I quote from my lecture on *The Objectivist Esthetics*: "Since man's ambition is unlimited, since his pursuit and achievement of values is a life-long process — and the higher the values, the harder the struggle — man needs a moment, an hour or some period of time in which he can experience the sense of his completed task, the sense of living in a universe where his values have been successfully achieved. It is like a moment of rest, a moment to gain fuel to move farther. Art gives him that fuel." Art gives him the experience of seeing the full, immediate, concrete reality of his distant goals.

The importance of that experience is not in *what* he learns from it, but in *that* he experiences it. The fuel is not a theoretical principle, not a didactic "message," but the life-giving fact of experiencing a moment of *metaphysical* joy—a moment of love for existence.

A given individual may choose to move forward, to translate the meaning of that experience in the actual course of his own life; or he may fail to live up to it and spend the rest of his life betraying it. But whatever the case may be, the art work remains intact, an entity complete in itself, an achieved, realized, immovable fact of reality — like a beacon raised over the dark crossroads of the world, saying: *"This* is possible."

No matter what its consequences, that experience is not a way station one passes, but a stop, a value in itself. It is an experience about which one can say: "I am glad to have reached this in my life." There are not many experiences of that kind to be found in the modern world.

I have read a great many novels of which nothing remains in my mind but the dry rustle of scraps long since swept away. But the novels of Victor Hugo, and a very few others, were an unrepeatable experience to me, a beacon whose every brilliant spark is as alive as ever.

This aspect of art is difficult to communicate — it demands a great deal of the viewer or reader — but I believe that many of you will understand me introspectively.

There is a scene in *The Fountainhead* which is a direct expression of this issue. I was, in a sense, both characters in that scene, but it was written primarily from the aspect of myself as the consumer, rather than the producer, of art; it was based on my own desperate longing for the sight of human achievement. I regarded the emotional meaning of that scene as entirely personal, almost subjective — and I did not expect it to be shared by anyone. But that scene proved to be the one most widely understood and most frequently mentioned by the readers of *The Fountainhead*.

It is the opening scene of Part IV, between Howard Roark and the boy on the bicycle.

The boy thought that "man's work should be a higher step, an improvement on nature, not a degradation. He did not want to despise men; he wanted to love and admire them. But he dreaded the sight of the first house, poolroom and movie poster he would encounter on his way.... He had always wanted to write music, and he could give no other identity to the thing he sought.... Let me see that in one single act of man on earth. Let me see it made real. Let me see the answer to the promise of that music.... Don't work for my happiness, my brothers — show me yours — show me that it is possible — show me your achievement — and the knowledge will give me courage for mine."

This is the meaning of art in man's life.

It is from this perspective that I will now ask you to consider the meaning of Naturalism — the doctrine which proposes to confine men to the sight of slums, poolrooms, movie posters and on down, much farther down.

It is the Romantic or value-oriented vision of life that the Naturalists regard as "superficial"— and it is the vision which extends as far as the bottom of a garbage can that they regard as "profound."

It is rationality, purpose and values that they regard as naive — while sophistication, they claim, consists of discarding one's mind, rejecting goals, renouncing values, and writing four-letter words on fences and sidewalks.

Scaling a mountain, they claim, is easy — but rolling in the gutter is a noteworthy achievement.

(continued on page 42)

BOOKS

*Ta Ta, Tan Tan** by Valentin Chu

———————— Reviewed by **ROBERT A. HESSEN**

Science and logic are obsolete superstitions. Whims can supercede the laws of nature. Industrial production is a process which does not require intelligence or experience — only the will to succeed is necessary. Workmen can be starved, terrorized and systematically overworked without their efficiency or loyalty being affected.

These, explicitly, are the principles which guide the rulers of Communist China — yet she is regarded as the third greatest industrial and military power on earth. How can this be possible? Are freedom and rationality unnecessary for the development and growth of a complex industrial economy? Can dictators destroy the mind and still reap its product — material wealth? Judging from popular opinion about the strength of Red China, it would appear to be possible. In fact, however, it is not.

In his authoritative book, *Ta Ta, Tan Tan*, Valentin Chu, correspondent for *Time* magazine, demonstrates that Communist China's strength is illusory, that its policies have progressively weakened and crippled its economy, and thereby undercut the basis of any military threat to the West.

Mr. Chu demonstrates that the major evidence of China's progress is China's own propaganda releases — announcements of grandiose production goals, followed, a year later, by statistics which state that production has exceeded the goals. He shows that these statistics are frequently contradictory or meaningless, or, most often, deliberately falsified.

For instance, in 1958, 80 million people were ordered to produce steel in home-made backyard furnaces. "Believing that the mind could overcome matter and that science was 'useless superstition' in the face of mass fervor, Mao Tse-tung used the human-sea tactic to make up for the lack of technology and equipment." On paper, the results were all that Mao hoped for — impressive statistics that China had doubled its steel production in just one year. In reality, however, China's steel industry suffered a major setback — "steel" produced in the do-it-yourself furnaces turned out to be worthless, and tons of scarce raw materials had been wasted. In 1959, the government quietly admitted the fiasco and scrapped the project.

In 1958, another short-lived experiment was begun: the commune system, aimed at forcing the Chinese peasants into "self-supporting and self-contained agricultural-industrial-military units." Every vestige of freedom was deliberately destroyed. "There would be no more families. Husbands and wives would work, eat, and live separately with their own sexes in public dining halls and dormitories, and get a sex-break once a week in assigned rooms for an assigned length of time. The aged would live in 'Happy Homes.' Everyone would wake up, eat, go to the toilet, work, rest, exercise, drill, get indoctrinated, and go to sleep by the sound of a bugle, in military formation. In such a life no one would need to worry, for by the 'fifteen guarantees,' the state guaranteed to take a person from his mother's womb, raise, feed, clothe, indoctrinate, work him throughout his life, and when he dies, deep-bury him beneath the rice paddies so that his body chemicals would enrich the fatherland in a final gesture of loyalty."

Predictably, the results of Communist policies in agriculture have been disastrous. Today, China is experiencing the greatest famine in its history, which the Reds blame on natural calamities. Mr. Chu refutes their explanation: "It is not a momentary lack of food, but a pernicious exhaustion of the land and the people — the cumulative result of over a decade's abuse of nature and human nature."

In 1959, Party officials chose to evade the menace of locusts, which peasants had reported. Result: six million acres of crops were destroyed by locusts, at which point a sudden desperate drive to spray pesticides from airplanes was initiated—directed by frenzied and inexperienced bureaucrats. Result: 100,000 farm animals were killed.

———

*Published by W. W. Norton & Co., $4.95. Available from NBI BOOK SERVICE, INC., 120 East 34th St., New York 16, N.Y. for $4.25 (N.Y.C. residents add 4% sales tax; outside the U.S. add 15¢).

Believing that his whims could produce miracles, a Party functionary conscripted 6,000 people to construct a double-decker crop field, planting seeds in a layer of soil suspended on boards above the ground and using electric bulbs and fans to provide air and light for the soil beneath the boards. "Result: no harvest."

To forestall discontent, under-fed workers are told: "Under Party leadership, meals can be made without rice. There are difficulties but they can be overcome with sky-zooming zeal." In place of food, the populace is fed slogans — incessant exhortations to make still further sacrifices: "Two eat the rice of one; one does the work of two" or: "We must struggle amid hardship forever." Hardship is an understatement: since the Reds took over in 1949, 24 million people have been crippled and 73 million killed by overwork, accidents, exposure and disease. (These figures do not include an estimated 30 million who died in slave labor camps or in the recurrent waves of political executions.)

But eye-witness accounts by visitors to Communist China — the other major source of evidence of China's progress — do not mention slave labor camps, famine or industrial chaos. Like their counterparts who visited Nazi Germany and Soviet Russia in the 1930's, these visitors produce glowing reports of peace and prosperity. The Chinese Communists pay all their expenses, provide them with interpreter-guides, and then lead them on carefully planned tours of showcase areas: model farms and factories, or freshly painted towns from whose streets the hordes of beggars, prostitutes and rodents have been removed.

After three weeks of being wined and dined by top Communist officials, Field Marshal Montgomery concluded that food was not in short supply in Red China. A top U.N. expert on food and agricultural problems came to the same conclusion, based on food production statistics provided to him by the Reds — but soon after the publication of his book, in which he reported this conclusion, near-famine conditions forced the Communists to repudiate the statistics.

Ta Ta, Tan Tan (this title is the Communists' strategic slogan "Fight fight, talk talk") is an extremely valuable book. It brings China's history and prospects for the future into sharp focus. It is the product of years of research in Chinese and English language materials, and of personal interviews with hundreds of refugees from the Chinese mainland. Exceptionally well-written, lively and engrossing, *Ta Ta, Tan Tan* holds the reader fascinated by an account of events which sound like a macabre fantasy, but which are actually fact and history. It is a worthy companion to Werner Keller's study of Russia, *East Minus West Equals Zero* (reviewed in this NEWSLETTER, November, 1962).

It is regrettable that Mr. Chu occasionally permits himself to interject some irrelevant and dubious remarks, such as "Communism is idealism gone haywire" or the opinion that socialism will be temporarily necessary in China after the collapse of the Red regime, in order to restore the economy. Such remarks, however, do not detract from the massive and irrefutable evidence that in Red China the combination of socialism and mysticism has produced only death and destruction.

———

The Goal of My Writing (from page 41)

Those who seek the sight of beauty and greatness are motivated by *fear*, they claim — they who are the embodiments of chronic terror — while it takes courage to fish in cesspools.

Man's soul — they proclaim with self-righteous pride — is a sewer.

Well, they ought to know.

It is a significant commentary on the present state of our culture that I have become famous — and also have become the object of hatred, smears, denunciations — as virtually the only novelist who has declared that *her* soul is *not* a sewer, and neither are the souls of her characters, and neither is the soul of man.

The motive and purpose of my writing can best be summed up by saying that if a dedication page were to precede the total of my work, it would read: To the glory of Man.

And if anyone should ask me what it is that I have said to the glory of Man, I will answer only by paraphrasing Howard Roark. I will hold up a copy of *Atlas Shrugged* and say: "The explanation rests."

INTELLECTUAL AMMUNITION DEPARTMENT

[*Subscribers are invited to send in the questions that they find themselves unable to answer in philosophical or political discussions. As many questions as space permits will be answered. No questions will be answered by mail.*]

- **Do labor unions raise the general standard of living?**

One of the most widespread delusions of our age is the belief that the American worker owes his high standard of living to unions and to "humanitarian" labor legislation. This belief is contradicted by the most fundamental facts and principles of economics — facts and principles which are systematically evaded by labor leaders, legislators and intellectuals of the statist persuasion.

A country's standard of living, including the wages of its workers, depends on the productivity of labor; high productivity depends on machines, inventions and capital investment — which depend on the creative ingenuity of individual men — which requires, for its exercise, a politico-economic system that protects the individual's rights and freedom.

The productive value of physical labor as such is low. If the worker of today produces more than the worker of fifty years ago, it is not because the former exerts more physical effort; quite the contrary: the physical effort required of him is far less. The productive value of his effort has been multiplied many times by the tools and machines with which he works; they are crucial in determining the economic worth of his services. To illustrate this principle: consider what would be a man's economic reward, on a desert island, for pushing his finger the distance of half an inch; then consider the wages paid, for pushing a button, to an elevator operator in New York City. It is not muscles that make the difference.

As Ludwig von Mises observes: "American wages are higher than wages in other countries because the capital invested per head of the worker is greater and the plants are thereby in the position to use the most efficient tools and machines. What is called the American way of life is the result of the fact that the United States has put fewer obstacles in the way of saving and capital accumulation than other nations. The economic backwardness of such countries as India consists precisely in the fact that their policies hinder both the accumulation of capital and the investment of foreign capital. As the capital required is lacking, the Indian enterprises are prevented from employing sufficient quantities of modern equipment, are therefore producing much less per man hour and can only afford to pay wage rates which, compared with American wage rates, appear as shockingly low." (*Planning for Freedom*, 2nd ed., Libertarian Press, 1962, pp. 151-152.)

In a free market economy, employers must bid competitively for the services of workers, just as they must bid competitively for all the other factors of production. If an employer attempts to pay wages which are lower than his workers can obtain elsewhere, he will lose his workers and thus will be compelled to change his policy or go out of business; if, other things being equal, an employer pays wages which are above the market level, his higher costs will put him at a competitive disadvantage in the sale of his products, and again he will be compelled to change his policy or go out of business. Employers do not lower wages because they are cruel, nor raise wages because they are kind. Wages are not determined by the employer's *whim*. Wages are the prices paid for human labor and, like all other prices in a free economy, are determined by the law of supply and demand.

Since the start of the Industrial Revolution and capitalism, wage rates have risen steadily — as an inevitable economic consequence of rising capital accumulation, technological progress and industrial expansion. As capitalism created countless new markets, so it created an ever-widening market for labor: it multiplied the number and kinds of jobs available, increased the demand and competition for the worker's services, and thus drove wage rates upward.

It was the *economic self-interest* of employers that led them to raise wages and shorten working hours — not the pressure of labor unions. The eight hour day was established in most American industries long before unions acquired any significant size or economic power. At a time when his competitors were paying their workers between two and three dollars a day, Henry Ford offered five dollars a day, thereby attracting the most efficient labor force in the country, and thus raising his own production and profits. In the 1920's, when the labor movement in France and Germany was far more dominant than in the United States, the standard of living of the American worker was greatly superior. It was the consequence of economic *freedom*.

Needless to say, men have a right to organize into unions, provided they do so voluntarily, that is, provided no one is *forced* to join. Unions can have value as fraternal organizations, or as a means of keeping members informed of current market conditions, or as a means of bargaining more effectively with employers — particularly in small, isolated communities. It may happen that an individual employer is paying wages that, in the overall market context, are too low; in such a case, a strike, or the threat of a strike, can compel him to change his policy, since he will discover that he cannot obtain an adequate labor force at the wages he offers. However, the belief that unions can cause a *general* rise in the standard of living, is a myth.

Today, the labor market is no longer free. Unions enjoy a unique, near-monopolistic power over many aspects of the economy. This has been achieved through legislation which has forced men to join unions, whether they wished to or not, and forced employers to deal with these unions, whether they wished to or not. As a consequence, wage rates in many industries are no longer determined by a free market; unions have been able to force wages substantially above their normal market level. These are the "social gains" for which unions are usually given credit. In fact, however, the result of their policy has been (a) a curtailment of production, (b) widespread unemployment, and (c) the penalizing of workers in other industries, as well as the rest of the population.

(a) With the rise of wage rates to inordinately high levels, production costs are such that cut-backs in production are often necessary, new undertakings become too expensive, and growth is hindered. At the increased costs, marginal producers — those who have been barely able to compete in the market — find themselves unable to remain in business. The overall result: goods and services that would have been produced are not brought into existence.

(b) As a result of the high wage rates, employers can afford to hire fewer workers; as a result of curtailed production, employers need fewer workers. Thus, one group of workers obtains unjustifiably high wages at the expense of other workers who are unable to find jobs at all. This — in conjunction with minimum wage laws — is the cause of our widespread unemployment problem today. *Unemployment is the inevitable result of forcing wage rates above their free market level.* In a free economy, in which neither employers nor workers are subject to coercion, wage rates always tend toward the level at which all those who seek employment will be able to obtain it. In a frozen, controlled economy, this process is blocked. As a result of allegedly "pro-labor" legislation and of the monopolistic power that labor unions enjoy, unemployed workers are not free to compete in the labor market by offering their services for less than the prevailing wage rates; employers are not free to hire them. In the case of strikes, if unemployed workers attempted to obtain the jobs vacated by union strikers, by offering to work for a lower wage, they often would be subjected to threats and physical violence at the hands of union members. These facts are as notorious as they are evaded in most current discussions of the unemployment problem — particularly by government officials.

(c) When market conditions are such that producers whose labor costs have risen, cannot raise the prices of the goods they sell, a curtailment of production results, as indicated above; and the general population accordingly suffers a loss of potential goods and services. (The notion that producers can "absorb" such wage increases, by "taking them out of profits," without a detriment to future production, is worse than

(continued on page 44)

Intellectual Ammunition (from page 43)

economically naive; it is profits that make future production possible; the amount of profits that go, not into investment, but into the producer's personal consumption, is negligible in the overall economic context.) To the extent that market conditions *do* allow, producers whose labor costs have risen are obliged to raise the prices of their goods. Then, workers in other industries find that their living costs have gone up, that they must now pay higher prices for the goods they purchase. Then, they in turn demand a raise in *their* industries, which leads to new price rises, which leads to new wage increases, etc. (Union leaders typically express indignation whenever prices are raised; the only prices they consider it moral to raise are the prices paid for labor, that is, wages.) Non-unionized workers, and the rest of the population generally, face this same steady rise in their living costs; they are made to subsidize the unjustifiably high wages of union workers — and are the unacknowledged victims of the unions' "social gains." And one observes the spectacle of bricklayers receiving two or even three times the salary of office workers and professors.

It cannot be sufficiently emphasized that it is not unionism as such but government controls and regulations which make this state of affairs possible. In a free, unregulated economy, in a market from which coercion is barred, no economic group can acquire the power so to victimize the rest of the population. The solution does not lie in new legislation directed against unions, but in the repeal of the legislation that made the present evil possible.

See, in this connection, Barbara Branden's article condemning "right-to-work" laws, in the June 1963 issue of this NEWSLETTER.

The inability of unions to achieve real, widespread raises in wage rates — to raise the standard of living generally — is in part obscured by the phenomenon of inflation. As a consequence of the government's policy of deficit spending and credit expansion, the purchasing power of the monetary unit, the dollar, has diminished drastically across the years. *Nominal* wage rates have increased considerably more than *real* wage rates, that is, wages measured in terms of actual purchasing power.

What has further served to obscure this issue is the fact that real wage rates *have* risen considerably since the start of the century. In spite of destructive and increasing governmental restraints on the freedom of production and trade, major advances in science, technology and capital accumulation have been made and have raised the general standard of living. It should be added that these advances are less than would have occurred in a fully free economy and, as controls continue to tighten, such advances become slower and rarer — as witness current complaints about the rate of our "economic growth."

It is relevant to consider against what obstacles businessmen have had to fight and to go on producing — when one hears labor leaders proclaiming, in indignant tones, the workers' right to a "larger share" of the "national product." To paraphrase John Galt: A larger share — *provided by whom?* Blank out.

Economic progress, like every other form of progress, has only one ultimate source: man's *mind* — and can exist only to the extent that man is free to translate his thought into action.

Let anyone who believes that a high standard of living is the achievement of labor unions and government controls, ask himself the following question: If one had a "time machine" and transported the united labor chieftains of America, plus three million government bureaucrats, back to the tenth century — would *they* be able to provide the medieval serf with electric light, refrigerators, automobiles and television sets? When one grasps that they would *not*, one should identify who and what made these things possible.

(For excellent, more detailed discussions of these issues, see Ludwig von Mises, *Planning for Freedom*, especially the chapter entitled "Wages, Unemployment and Inflation"; and Henry Hazlitt, *Economics in One Lesson*, Harper, 1946, especially the chapters entitled "Minimum Wage Laws" and "Do Unions Really Raise Wages?")

Postscript: After completing the above, I noticed an article in *The New York Times* of September 8 that is too *apropos* to let pass without acknowledgment. The article, entitled "10 U.A.W. Leaders Find Unions are Losing Members' Loyalty," by Damon Stetson, reports that executives of the United Automobile Workers met to discuss the problem of workers' increasing lack of loyalty to union leadership and union solidarity. One U.A.W. official is quoted as declaring: "How can we get greater loyalty from the individual to the union? All the things we fought for, the corporation is now giving the workers. What we have to find are other things the workers want which the employer is not willing to give him, and we have to develop our program around these things as reasons for belonging to the union."

Is any comment necessary?

- **Is there any validity to the claim that laissez-faire capitalism becomes less practicable as society becomes more complex?**

This claim is the sort of collectivist bromide that "liberals" repeat ritualistically, without any attempt to prove or substantiate it. To examine it, is to perceive its absurdity.

The same condition of freedom that is necessary in order to *attain* a high level of industrial development — a high level of "complexity" — is necessary in order to *keep* it. To say that a society has become more complex, merely means that more men live in the same geographical area and deal with one another, that they engage in a greater volume of trading, and that they practice a greater number and diversity of productive activities. There is nothing in these facts which conceivably could justify the abandonment of economic freedom in favor of government "planning." On the contrary: the more "complex" an economy, the greater the number of choices and decisions that have to be made — and, therefore, the more blatantly impracticable it becomes for this process to be taken over by a central government authority. If there are degrees of irrationality, it would be more plausible to imagine that a primitive, pre-industrial economy could be managed, non-disastrously, by the state; but the notion of running a scientific, highly industrialized society with slave labor, is barbaric in the ignorance it reveals.

Observe that the same type of persons who espouse this doctrine, also declare that the under-developed nations of the world are not suited for economic freedom, that their primitive level of development makes socialism imperative. Thus, they simultaneously argue that a country should not be permitted freedom because it is too *un*developed economically — and that a country should not be permitted freedom because it is too *highly* developed economically.

Both positions are crude rationalizations on the part of statist mentalities who have never grasped what makes industrial civilization possible.
— NATHANIEL BRANDEN

OBJECTIVIST CALENDAR

- In addition to the starting dates listed last month, NATHANIEL BRANDEN INSTITUTE's Tape Transcription Division has scheduled the following starting dates in the following cities: Indianapolis, Nov. 8 — "Basic Principles of Objectivism"; Boston, Nov. 11 — "Principles of Efficient Thinking"; Toronto, Nov. 12 — "Basic Principles of Objectivist Psychology"; Los Angeles, Dec. 6 — "Basic Principles of Objectivist Psychology."

- This month, New American Library will issue a fourth printing of *Anthem* — 150,000 copies — bringing the total number of copies in print to over half a million.
— B.B.

Published monthly at 120 East 34th Street, New York 16, N. Y.
Subscription rate: in United States, its possessions, Canada and Mexico, $5 for one year; other countries, $6.
Additional copies of this Newsletter: single copy 50¢ (coins, not stamps); 10 – 99 copies, 25¢ each plus postage (for first-class delivery add 1¢ per copy, for third-class delivery add ½¢ per copy); 100 or more copies, 15¢ each plus postage (same as above).
For change of address send old address and new address with zone number if any. Allow us three weeks to process new subscriptions and change of address.

Ayn Rand and Nathaniel Branden, Editors and Publishers
Barbara Branden, Managing Editor
Elayne Kalberman, Circulation Manager
PRINTED BY STANDARD PRESS & GRAPHICS, INC., NEW YORK CITY

THE OBJECTIVIST NEWSLETTER

Edited and Published by AYN RAND and NATHANIEL BRANDEN

VOL. 2 NO. 12   DECEMBER, 1963

CHECK YOUR PREMISES
By AYN RAND

The Nature of Government

A government is an institution that holds the exclusive power to *enforce* certain rules of social conduct in a given geographical area.

Do men need such an institution — and why?

Since man's mind is his basic tool of survival, his means of gaining knowledge to guide his actions — the basic condition he requires is the freedom to think and to act according to his rational judgment. This does not mean that a man must live alone and that a desert island is the environment best suited to his needs. Men can derive enormous benefits from dealing with one another. A social environment is most conducive to their successful survival — *but only on certain conditions.*

"The two great values to be gained from social existence are: knowledge and trade. Man is the only species that can transmit and expand his store of knowledge from generation to generation; the knowledge potentially available to man is greater than any one man could begin to acquire in his own lifespan; every man gains an incalculable benefit from the knowledge discovered by others. The second great benefit is the division of labor: it enables a man to devote his effort to a particular field of work and to trade with others who specialize in other fields. This form of cooperation allows all men who take part in it to achieve a greater knowledge, skill and productive return on their effort than they could achieve if each had to produce everything he needs, on a desert island or on a self-sustaining farm.

"But these very benefits indicate, delimit and define what kind of men can be of value to one another and in what kind of society: only rational, productive, independent men in a rational, productive, free society." *(The Objectivist Ethics.)*

A society that robs an individual of the product of his effort, or enslaves him, or attempts to limit the freedom of his mind, or compels him to act against his own rational judgment — a society that sets up a conflict between its edicts and the requirements of man's nature — is not, strictly speaking, a society, but a mob held together by institutionalized gang-rule. Such a society destroys all the values of human co-existence, has no possible justification and represents, not a source of benefits, but the deadliest threat to man's survival. Life on a desert island is safer than and incomparably preferable to existence in Soviet Russia or Nazi Germany.

If men are to live together in a peaceful, productive, rational society and deal with one another to mutual benefit, they must accept the basic social principle without which no moral or civilized society is possible: the principle of individual rights. (See my articles on rights in the April and June issues of this NEWSLETTER.)

To recognize individual rights means to recognize and accept the conditions required by man's nature for his proper survival.

Man's rights can be violated only by the use of physical force. It is only by means of physical force that one man can deprive another of his life, or enslave him, or rob him, or prevent him from pursuing his own goals, or compel him to act against his own rational judgment.

The precondition of a civilized society is the barring of physical force from social relationships — thus establishing the principle that if men wish to deal with one another, they may do so only by means of *reason:* by discussion, persuasion and voluntary, uncoerced agreement.

The necessary consequence of man's right to life is his right to self-defense. In a civilized society, force may be used only in retaliation and only against those who initiate its use. All the reasons which make the initiation of physical force an evil, make the retaliatory use of physical force a moral imperative.

If some "pacifist" society renounced the retaliatory use of force, it would be left helplessly at the mercy of the first thug who decided to be immoral. Such a society would achieve the opposite of its intention: instead of abolishing evil, it would encourage and reward it.

If a society provided no organized protection against force, it would compel every citizen to go about armed, to turn his home into a fortress, to shoot any strangers approaching his door — or to join a protective gang of citizens who would fight other gangs, formed for the same purpose, and thus bring about the degeneration of that society into the chaos of gang-rule, *i.e.,* rule by brute force, into the perpetual tribal warfare of prehistorical savages.

The use of physical force — even its retaliatory use — cannot be left at the discretion of individual citizens. Peaceful co-existence is impossible if a man has to live under the constant threat of force to be unleashed against him by any of his neighbors at any moment. Whether his neighbors' intentions are good or bad, whether their judgment is rational or irrational, whether they are motivated by a sense of justice or by ignorance or by prejudice or by malice — the use of force against one man cannot be left to the arbitrary decision of another.

Visualize, for example, what would happen if a man missed his wallet, concluded that he had been robbed, broke into every house in the neighborhood to search it, and shot the first man who gave him a dirty look, taking the look to be a proof of guilt.

The retaliatory use of force requires *objective* rules of evidence to establish that a crime has been committed and to *prove* who committed it, as well as *objective* rules to define punishments and enforcement procedures. Men who attempt to prosecute crimes, without such rules, are a lynch mob. If a society left the retaliatory use of force in the hands of individual citizens, it would degenerate into mob rule, lynch law and an endless series of bloody private feuds or vendettas.

If physical force is to be barred from social relationships, men need an institution charged with the task of protecting their rights under an *objective* code of rules.

This is the task of a government — of a *proper* government — its basic task, its only moral justification and the reason why men do need a government.

A government is the means of placing the retaliatory use of physical force under objective control — i.e., under objectively defined laws.

The fundamental difference between private action and governmental action — a difference thoroughly ignored and evaded today — lies in the fact that a government holds a monopoly on the legal use of physical force. It has to hold such a monopoly, since it is the agent of restraining and combatting the use of force; and for that very same reason, its actions have to be rigidly defined, delimited and circumscribed; no touch of whim or caprice should be permitted in its performance; it should be an impersonal robot, with the law as its only motive power. If a society is to be free, its government has to be controlled.

Under a proper social system, a private individual is legally free to take any action he pleases (so long as he does not violate the rights of others), while a government official is bound by law in his every official act. A private individual may do anything except that which is legally *forbidden;* a government official may do nothing except that which is legally *permitted.*

This is the means of subordinating "might" to "right." This is the American concept of "a government of laws and not of men."

The nature of the laws proper to a free society and the source of its government's authority are both to be derived from the nature and purpose of a proper government. The basic principle of both is indicated in The Declaration of Independence: "to secure these [individual] rights, governments are instituted among men, deriving their just powers from the consent of the governed..."

Since the protection of individual rights is the only proper purpose of a government, it is the only proper subject of legislation: all laws must be based on individual rights and aimed at their protection. All laws must be *objective* (and objectively justifiable): men must know clearly, and in advance of taking an action, what the law forbids them to do (and why), what constitutes a crime and what penalty they will incur if they commit it.

The source of the government's authority is "the consent of the governed." This means that the government is not the *ruler,* but the servant or *agent* of the citizens; it means that the government as such has no rights except the rights *delegated* to it by the citizens for a specific purpose.

There is only one basic principle to which an individual must consent if he wishes to live in a free, civilized society: the principle of renouncing the use of physical force and delegating to the government his right of physical self-defense, for the purpose of an orderly, objective, legally-defined enforcement. Or, to put it another way, he must accept *the separation of force and whim* (any whim, including his own).

Now what happens in case of a disagreement between two men about an undertaking in which both are involved?

In a free society, men are not forced to deal with one another. They do so only by voluntary agreement and, when a time element is involved, by *contract.* If a contract is broken by the arbitrary decision of one man, it may cause a disastrous financial injury to the other — and the victim would have no recourse except to seize the offender's property as compensation. But here again, the use of force cannot be left to the decision of private individuals. And this leads to one of the most important and most complex functions of the government: to the function of an arbiter who settles disputes among men according to objective laws.

Criminals are a small minority in any semi-civilized society. But the protection and enforcement of contracts through courts of civil law is the most crucial need of a peaceful society; without such protection, no civilization could be developed or maintained.

Man cannot survive, as animals do, by acting on the range of the immediate moment. Man has to project his goals and achieve them across a span of time; he has to calculate his actions and plan his life long-range. The better a man's mind and the greater his knowledge, the longer the range of his planning. The higher or more complex a civilization, the longer the range of activity it requires — and, therefore, the longer the range of contractual agreements among men, and the more urgent their need of protection for the security of such agreements.

Even a primitive barter society could not function if a man agreed to trade a bushel of potatoes for a basket of eggs and, having received the eggs, refused to deliver the potatoes. Visualize what this sort of whim-directed action would mean in an industrial society where men deliver a billion-dollars-worth of goods on credit, or contract to build multi-million-dollar structures, or sign ninety-nine-year leases.

A unilateral breach of contract involves an indirect use of physical force: it consists, in essence, of one man receiving the material values, goods or services of another, then refusing to pay for them and thus keeping them by force (by mere physical possession), not by right — *i.e.,* keeping them without the consent of their owner. Fraud involves a similarly indirect use of force: it consists of obtaining material values without their owner's consent, under false pretenses or false promises. Extortion is another variant of an indirect use of force: it consists of obtaining material values, not in exchange for values, but by the threat of force, violence or injury.

Some of these actions are obviously criminal. Others, such as a unilateral breach of contract, may not be criminally motivated, but may be caused by irresponsibility and irrationality. Still others may be complex issues with some claim to justice on both sides. But whatever the case may be, all such issues have to be made subject to objectively defined laws and have to be resolved by an impartial arbiter, administering the laws, *i.e.,* by a judge (and a jury, when appropriate).

Observe the basic principle governing justice in all these cases: it is the principle that no man may obtain any values from others without the owners' consent — and, as a corollary, that a man's rights may not be left at the mercy of the unilateral decision, the arbitrary choice, the irrationality, *the whim* of another man.

Such, in essence, is the proper purpose of a government: to make social existence possible to men, by protecting the benefits and combatting the evils which men can cause to one another.

The proper functions of a government fall into three broad categories, all of them involving the issues of physical force and the protection of men's rights: *the police,* to protect men from criminals — *the armed services,* to protect

(continued on page 49)

A Report to Our Readers

By NATHANIEL BRANDEN

Since the publication of *Atlas Shrugged* and the establishment of NATHANIEL BRANDEN INSTITUTE, six years ago, I have received many inquiries concerning the spread of Objectivism and its impact on our culture.

These inquiries are somewhat difficult to answer — first, because six years is a very short time in the history of ideas; and second, because the manner in which new ideas penetrate a culture is so complex and indirect, with so many people and so many intermediate steps involved, that it is not easy to know what may be regarded as unequivocal signs of progress, particularly in the early stages.

There *are*, however, significant signs to be noted — signs which suggest, rather powerfully, that intense interest in the Objectivist philosophy is growing at a rapidly accelerating pace, that Objectivism has captured the mind and enthusiasm of the younger generation as no other contemporary intellectual trend has succeeded in doing.

Approximately 1,200,000 copies of *Atlas Shrugged* have been printed to date, in combined hard-cover and paper-back editions. No other book has challenged so many traditional beliefs in so many areas of human life — *Atlas Shrugged* has gone against almost every cultural trend of our time — and, six years after publication, it is steadily selling between 100,000 and 200,000 copies a year.

The sales of *The Fountainhead* — the book which twelve publishers had rejected as "too intellectual" and "non-commercial"— are now approaching 2,000,000 copies. Twenty years after publication, it is selling actively in a hard-cover edition, a deluxe paper-back edition and a popular-priced paper-back edition.

I cannot resist mentioning, parenthetically, that for many years Miss Rand was told by "conservative" acquaintances that in order to appeal to the public, one had to take a "moderate" position, that one dare not, for example, challenge the precepts of altruism or religion — this was said by the same "conservatives" who were wailing that no one really *cared* about capitalism, that young people in particular were indifferent and could not be reached.

When I established NBI, a few months after the publication of *Atlas Shrugged*, "Basic Principles of Objectivism" was given in a small hotel room to twenty-eight students. I could not have predicted, then, the rapid growth that was to follow. Perhaps the first indications appeared when, half way through that first course, several students asked me: "What other courses on Objectivism are you going to offer, when this one is finished?"

With a number of associates, who were to join NBI as lecturers, I began to plan for additional, more specialized courses in philosophy, psychology, economics and esthetics.

This year, throughout North America, approximately twenty-five hundred students will attend NBI courses. NBI's Tape Transcription Division is offering courses in more than thirty cities—from Los Angeles to Toronto to Clear, Alaska; and, within a few years, the figure promises to be close to a hundred.

The success of the Tape Division is one of the most eloquent indications of the intellectual impact of Objectivism, and of its students' level of motivation. In an age when educators commonly complain about the apathy of those they teach, one can conclude a great deal — philosophically and culturally — from the sight of one hundred people sitting around *a tape recorder*, listening to a lecture on epistemology or ethics or esthetics.

A growing stream of requests for its lecture courses is reaching NBI from Europe, Africa, Asia and Australia. Recently, an Indian psychologist came from India to the United States, on a fellowship to complete her studies at a university in Boston. Shortly after her arrival, as one of her first questions about America, she asked her hosts: "Can you tell me, please, how to contact the NATHANIEL BRANDEN INSTITUTE, so I can hear the lectures on Ayn Rand's philosophy?" She is now enrolled in the current Boston tape series.

Some time ago, I met the president of one of the largest lecture agencies in the country. He asked me a number of questions about NBI, about the courses we offered, the number of students, the fees. I mentioned that when I established NBI, there was no one from whom I could obtain professional advice — because the nature of the undertaking was virtually unprecedented. "I'll admit quite candidly," he told me, "that if you had come to me for advice then — I would have told you that what's happened is impossible. Lectures on *philosophy?*" He shook his head.

Last year, when I opened the lecture course in San Francisco for the first time, approximately one hundred people were in attendance. This year, Miss Rand was in San Francisco with me, and was to participate in the question period following the lecture. NBI engaged a lecture room to accommodate two hundred and fifty people. Five hundred people came. We managed, somehow, to seat four hundred (by means of a rather intense exercise in "togetherness"); we were compelled to turn the rest away. It was, as our San Francisco representative feverishly described it, "a horribly wonderful evening."

In Los Angeles—where the tape series had been given for several years—we were prepared. Again, Miss Rand was to join me in the question period. Our representative had engaged a lecture room that would hold six hundred people. Eleven hundred people came. We seated eight hundred. Then the rest were given the option of listening to the lecture in another room, via loudspeakers. Even though this would mean hearing the lecture while looking at a blank wall, almost all of them chose to remain. It was, for us, one of the most exciting and memorable occasions since the start of NBI.

A steadily increasing percentage of the people enrolled at NBI are college students. Many of them plan to enter the academic profession. They will be the teachers of tomorrow. A high percentage of NBI students are professional adults: lawyers, physicians, teachers, businessmen, writers, artists, engineers, psychologists, psychiatrists, research scientists. In many cases they are actively concerned with applying the ideas of Objectivism to their own fields.

When, last month, I went to Boston to deliver the opening lecture in the fall series, and I noted the professions of the students who were helping our representative to handle admissions, I felt a little like Dagny Taggart in Atlantis: the man and woman sitting at a table, processing visitors, were, respectively, a neurologist and an anesthesiologist; the man showing students to their seats was a bio-physicist; the NBI representative, handling new enrollments, was a researcher in bio-chemistry and genetics.

To a large extent, the response to Objectivism throughout the country has been underground. It has received little acknowledgment or commentary in the press. And such acknowledgment as it has received, with rare exceptions, has been in the context of smears, attacks and misrepresentations.

Writing in the leftist *New Leader* (September 26, 1960), one political antagonist warned his readers: "Objectivism, unlike most other past and present right-wing movements in this country, has more of an intellectual than an emotional appeal and is consequently attracting educated young people to its ranks." (This was one of the few factually accurate statements in his article.)

In another publication, of a similar political persuasion, *New University Thought* (Autumn, 1962), a teacher of English wrote — lengthily and with hysterical abusiveness — about the danger of Ayn Rand's influence on college students: ". . . for the past two or three semesters, no other author, not even the Luce-touted J. D. Salinger, has threatened to upset Miss Rand's commanding popularity. At first, I thought that perhaps my students' enthusiasm was hardly representative, but just recently I have had an opportunity to talk with several other college teachers, from various parts of the nation, and many of them informed me that they too have been troubled by Miss Rand's appeal.

"Some of the commentators on her ideas have tended to play down Miss Rand's apparent popularity, but I am not ready to do so, and I am genuinely disturbed by the similarity between my students' enthusiasm and the eagerness to talk about her books and her ideas which Gore Vidal noted when he was campaigning for Congress. She was 'the one writer' the voters he so futilely wooed were acquainted with and were eager to talk about; it is dismaying to contemplate the possibility that Ayn Rand is the single writer who engages the loyalties of the students I am perhaps ineffectually attempting to teach."

"All the students I talked with struck me as intelligent (three of them are in the honors program at my school), and most were quite able to verbalize the reasons of their admiration for Miss Rand."

Recently, when I spoke with a teacher of English at Yeshiva University, Professor Henry Grinberg, he reported the same trend. At the start of this semester, he gave his freshman English class the assignment of writing a paper on the book they had read during this past year which they had most enjoyed and which had most impressed or influenced them. "Twenty-five percent of my students," said Professor Grinberg, "wrote on one or another of Ayn Rand's novels." He did not say it with approval. He added: "When I was a young man, the students who experimented with new ideas were attracted, predominantly, to socialism and communism. But Ayn Rand seems to be capturing young people with *anti*-altruist ideas."

While Objectivism is attracting people of all ages and occupations, it is logical that its major following should be among the younger generation, and, most particularly, among college students. Of any group, this is the one most likely to be open to new ideas, most eager for a rational, intelligible view of life — and most dissatisfied with the intellectual and cultural *status quo*. This is the group that is least likely to have given up, in cynical resignation to the belief that no solutions are possible.

It is among this group that one can observe the signs of a growing disillusionment with and revolt against the prevailing dogmas of our age: irrationalism in philosophy, depravity-worship in art, and statism in politics. If the supporters of these dogmas, the intellectuals whose views are expressed by the bankruptcy of our present culture, are concerned about the younger generation's response to Objectivism — they have good grounds to be: they know what it signifies about the future.

A neutral commentator, John Chamberlain, reviewing *For the New Intellectual* in *The Wall Street Journal* (March 24, 1961), wrote: "Seated about in booths in college-town snack shops, the young Randites talk about their intellectual leader as their fathers and mothers a generation ago talked about Karl Marx, or John Maynard Keynes, or Thorstein Veblen." "Whether this [Objectivism] amounts to a rearguard action that is destined to universal defeat, or whether Ayn Rand possesses in her own intransigent head the philosophy of the future, will be hotly argued. Nevertheless, she has been gaining many followers among the young. And it is normally a matter of two decades before the young take over the seats of power in the name of what they have learned to believe 20 years ago."

The mail we receive at NBI and at this NEWSLETTER often provides an illuminating insight into the steps of Objectivism's motion through the country. "I heard some people arguing about *Atlas Shrugged* at a dinner party — the book sounded interesting — so I went out and bought it." "I first read *Atlas Shrugged* because people told me it was an evil book that no one should read." "After fighting with my professor for a month, I finally obtained permission to do my term paper [or thesis] on [some aspect of] Objectivism." "I first discovered the works of Ayn Rand when they were recommended in a course on psychology." "At the end of the first class, my professor of philosophy suddenly announced, without explanation or context, when no reference had been made to the subject, that if anyone turned in a paper on Objectivism, that student would automatically fail." "Can you recommend additional readings to supplement our discussion of Objectivism in an ethics seminar?" "My psychiatrist suggested that I read *Atlas Shrugged* as a helpful adjunct to psychotherapy." "I first heard about Ayn Rand when Galt's speech was quoted in a political science class."

Through these letters, I have learned of attempts to suppress discussion of Objectivism in classrooms — and also, of the increasing frequency with which Ayn Rand's works appear on lists of required or recommended readings. The attempts at suppression — no less than the recommended readings — are signs of Objectivism's growing impact.

At the start of the first lecture on "Basic Principles of Objectivism," I tell my favorite story concerning the spread of Objectivism. An acquaintance of mine, in Winnipeg, Canada, fell into a philosophical discussion with a young woman whom he met at a gathering. He did not refer to Ayn Rand and he did not mention Objectivism explicitly; but it was the ideas of Objectivism that he was in fact expounding. A week or so later, he happened to meet the young woman again, and she told him of the following incident. It seems that she was undergoing psychotherapy at the time, and — thinking about their conversation — she walked into her psychiatrist's office and said to him, without explanation: "Doctor, what do the words 'objective reality' mean to you?" Her psychiatrist answered: "They mean that you've been talking to someone who is an admirer of Ayn Rand."

Several years ago, a reporter from a magazine called me to ask about the Ayn Rand clubs that were springing up on campuses around the country. He assumed that it was I who was organizing them. Neither Miss Rand nor I had even known of their existence. Since that time, we have learned that many more such clubs have been formed and are being formed constantly. None have any connection with NBI; they are organized by college students acting independently, on their own initiative, for the purpose of discussing and studying Ayn Rand's philosophy.

While there is an increasing interest in Objectivism among members of the academic profession, it appears to be primarily the students who are bringing Objectivism into the universities. More than one professor has declared that he was obliged to read *Atlas Shrugged* because of the questions raised in his classes. For reasons that scarcely need elaboration here, these students' questions are often embarrassing to established academic doctrine and to supporters of the intellectual *status quo*. But the hostility that students sometimes encounter is, if anything, hastening rather than slowing the spread of Objectivism; these students recognize that anger, ridicule and evasion are *not* intellectual weapons.

Among the academic profession, there are distinguished exceptions. I had the pleasure, this past October, of witnessing an occasion where it was not the students who brought Objectivism to the college, but the college that brought Objectivism to the students. I accompanied Miss Rand to Lewis and Clark College in Portland, Oregon, where she had been invited to receive an honorary degree of Doctor of Humane Letters. During our two-day visit there, the entire college was involved in hearing lectures on and participating in discussions of Objectivism; in preparation for the occasion, the entire faculty and student body had read *Atlas Shrugged,* and many had read *The Fountainhead* as well. The man who originated the proposal to confer the degree on Miss Rand and who arranged the study program on Objectivism, was the president of Lewis and Clark College, Dr. John R. Howard. President Howard had read *Atlas Shrugged* some years earlier—and chose to express his estimate of it in action.

I asked President Howard how he first came to read *Atlas Shrugged*. He answered: "A few years ago, when I was president of a college in Illinois, there was a student with whom I was engaged in a rather protracted discussion, involving some disagreement between us. One day, the student walked into my office, put a book down on my desk, and said: 'President Howard, here is a book that you absolutely have to read.' The book was *Atlas Shrugged*."

This is the manner in which new ideas penetrate a culture—by each man acting to further his convictions, within the range possible to him, whether the range be wide or modest. That student took the action possible and appropriate to him; so did President Howard. Obviously, if President Howard were not the man of intellectual independence and integrity he is, the student's action would not have had the consequence it did. But, sooner or later, men of initiative and independence will find one another — and it is thus that cultural revolutions are made.

Such, then, are some of the signs of the spread of Objectivism during the past six years. I plan, at a future date, to write another such report, as more evidence accumulates — perhaps a year from now. I invite our readers to send me any information that may be relevant to such a report.

There is one final point I should like to mention here. It belongs in a "progress report" such as this.

NATHANIEL BRANDEN INSTITUTE and THE OBJECTIVIST NEWSLETTER are *profit-making* institutions, and have been so from the start of their existence. I am the sole owner of NBI; Miss Rand and I are co-owners of the NEWSLETTER. Neither organization has ever run at a deficit — nor received any sort of outside financial help. Both have been entirely self-supporting.

It is notorious that organizations and journals concerned with disseminating ideas — whether of the right or of the left, politically — are in chronic need of financial help. Such organizations are constantly sending out SOS's to their supporters and subscribers, pleading for money, wailing that without charitable contributions they cannot survive.

We are proud of the fact that we *can* — that there *is* an economic market for *our* ideas.

If this sounds like a boast, it is. We have earned it.

The Nature of Government (from page 46)

men from foreign invaders — *the law courts,* to settle disputes among men according to objective laws.

These three categories involve many corollary and derivative issues — and their implementation in practice, in the form of specific legislation, is enormously complex. It belongs to the field of a special science: the philosophy of law. Many errors and many disagreements are possible in the field of implementation, but what is essential here is the principle to be implemented: the principle that the purpose of law and of government is the protection of individual rights.

Today, this principle is forgotten, ignored and evaded. The result is the present state of the world, with mankind's retrogression to the lawlessness of absolutist tyranny, to the primitive savagery of rule by brute force.

In unthinking protest against this trend, some people are raising the question of whether government as such is evil by nature and whether anarchy is the ideal social system. Anarchy, as a political concept, is a naive floating abstraction: for all the reasons discussed above, a society without an organized government would be at the mercy of the first criminal who came along and who would precipitate it into the chaos of gang warfare. But the possibility of human immorality is not the only objection to anarchy: even a society whose every member were fully rational and faultlessly moral, could not function in a state of anarchy; it is the need of *objective* laws and of an arbiter for honest disagreements among men that necessitates the establishment of a government.

A recent variant of anarchistic theory, which is befuddling some of the younger advocates of freedom, is a weird absurdity called "competing governments." Accepting the basic premise of the modern statists — who see no difference between the functions of government and the functions of industry, between force and production, and who advocate government ownership of business — the proponents of "competing governments" take the other side of the same coin and declare that since competition is so beneficial to business, it should also be applied to government. Instead of a single, monopolistic government, they declare, there should be a number of different governments in the same geographical area, competing for the allegiance of individual citizens, with every citizen free to "shop" and to patronize whatever government he chooses.

Remember that forcible restraint of men is the only service a government has to offer. Ask yourself what a competition in forcible restraint would have to mean.

One cannot call this theory a contradiction in terms, since it is obviously devoid of any understanding of the terms "competition" and "government." Nor can one call it a floating abstraction, since it is devoid of any contact with or reference to reality and cannot be concretized at all, not even roughly or approximately. One illustration will be sufficient: suppose Mr. Smith, a customer of Government A, suspects that his next-door neighbor, Mr. Jones, a customer of Government B, has robbed him; a squad of Police A proceeds to Mr. Jones' house and is met at the door by a squad of Police B, who declare that they do not accept the validity of Mr. Smith's complaint and do not recognize the authority of Government A. What happens then? You take it from there.

The evolution of the concept of "government" has had a long, tortuous history. Some glimmer of the government's proper function seems to have existed in every organized society, manifesting itself in such phenomena as the recognition of some implicit (if often non-existent) difference between a government and a robber-gang — the aura of respect and of moral authority granted to the government as the guardian of "law and order"— the fact that even the most evil types of government found it necessary to maintain some semblance of order and some pretense at justice, if only by routine and tradition, and to claim some sort of moral justification for their power, of a mystical or social nature. Just as the absolute monarchs of France had to invoke "The Divine Right of Kings," so the modern dictators of Soviet Russia have to spend fortunes on propaganda to justify their rule in the eyes of their enslaved subjects.

In mankind's history, the understanding of the government's proper function is a very recent achievement: it is only two-hundred years old and it dates from the Founding Fathers of the American Revolution. Not only did they identify the nature and the needs of a free society, but they devised the means to translate it into practice. A free society — like any other human product — cannot be achieved by random means, by mere wishing or by the leaders' "good intentions." A complex legal system, based on *objectively* valid principles, is required to make a society free and *to keep it free* — a system that does not depend on the motives, the moral character or the intentions of any given official, a system that leaves no opportunity, no legal loop-hole for the development of tyranny.

The American system of checks and balances was just such an achievement. And although certain contradictions in the Constitution did leave a loop-hole for the growth of statism, the incomparable achievement was the concept of a constitution as a means of limiting and restricting the power of the government.

Today, when a concerted effort is made to obliterate this point, it cannot be repeated too often that the Constitution is a limitation on the government, not on private individuals — that it does not prescribe the conduct of private individuals, only the conduct of the government — that it is not a charter *for* government power, but a charter of the citizens' protection *against* the government.

Now consider the extent of the moral and political inversion in today's prevalent view of government. Instead of being a protector of man's rights, the government is becoming their most dangerous violator; instead of guarding freedom, the government is establishing slavery; instead of protecting men from the initiators of physical force, the government is initiating physical force and coercion in any manner and issue it pleases; instead of serving as the instrument of *objectivity* in human relationships, the government is creating a deadly, subterranean reign of uncertainty and fear, by means of non-objective laws whose interpretation is left to the arbitrary decisions of random bureaucrats; instead of protecting men from injury by whim, the government is arrogating to itself the power of unlimited whim — so that we are fast approaching the stage of the ultimate inversion: the stage where the government is *free* to do anything it pleases, while the citizens may act only by *permission;* which is the stage of the darkest periods of human history, the stage of rule by brute force.

It has often been remarked that in spite of its material progress, mankind has not achieved any comparable degree of moral progress. That remark is usually followed by some pessimistic conclusion about human nature. It is true that the moral state of mankind is disgracefully low. But if one considers the monstrous moral inversions of the governments (made possible by the altruist-collectivist morality) under which mankind has had to live through most of its history, one begins to wonder how men have managed to preserve even a semblance of civilization, and what indestructible vestige of self-esteem has kept them walking upright on two feet.

One also begins to see more clearly the nature of the political principles that have to be accepted and advocated, as part of the battle for man's intellectual Renaissance.

OBJECTIVIST CALENDAR

■ Beginning Thursday, December 5, NBI will offer a ten lecture course on "The Economics of a Free Society," to be given by Alan Greenspan. This course is open to students who have taken "Basic Principles of Objectivism"; to others, by special arrangement only.

■ NBI's Tape Transcription Division has scheduled starting dates for "Basic Principles of Objectivism" in the following cities: Pittsburgh, November 24; Denver, December 4; Urbana, Ill., December 16; Amarillo, January 14.

■ Ayn Rand's address, "The Goal of My Writing," published in two parts in this NEWSLETTER (October and November 1963), has been reprinted and is now available as a single pamphlet. Price: 50¢.

■ Two articles by Robert A. Hessen, "Child Labor and the Industrial Revolution" and "Women and the Industrial Revolution," published in this NEWSLETTER (April and November 1962), have been reprinted as a single pamphlet under the title "The Effects of the Industrial Revolution on Women and Children." A bibliography of suggested additional readings on the Industrial Revolution has been added to this reprint. Price: 25¢.

—B.B.

NOTE TO NEW SUBSCRIBERS

The regular length of THE OBJECTIVIST NEWSLETTER is four pages. This is a special issue.

Published monthly at 120 East 34th Street, New York 16, N. Y.
Subscription rate: in United States, its possessions, Canada and Mexico, $5 for one year; other countries, $6.
Additional copies of this Newsletter: single copy 50¢ (coins, not stamps); 10 — 99 copies, 25¢ each plus postage (for first-class delivery add 1¢ per copy, for third-class delivery add ½¢ per copy); 100 or more copies, 15¢ each plus postage (same as above).
For change of address send old address and new address with zone number if any. Allow us three weeks to process new subscriptions and change of address.

Ayn Rand and Nathaniel Branden, Editors and Publishers
Barbara Branden, Managing Editor
Elayne Kalberman, Circulation Manager

THE OBJECTIVIST NEWSLETTER

Edited and Published by AYN RAND and NATHANIEL BRANDEN

VOL. 3 NO. 1   JANUARY, 1964

CHECK YOUR PREMISES
By AYN RAND

The Anatomy of Compromise

A major symptom of a man's—or a culture's—intellectual and moral disintegration is the shrinking of vision and goals to the concrete-bound range of the immediate moment. This means: the progressive disappearance of abstractions from a man's mental processes or from a society's concerns. The manifestation of a disintegrating consciousness is the inability to think and act in terms of *principles*.

A principle is "a fundamental, primary or general truth, on which other truths depend." Thus a principle is an abstraction which subsumes a great number of concretes. It is only by means of principles that one can set one's long-range goals and evaluate the concrete alternatives of any given moment. It is only principles that enable a man to plan his future and to achieve it.

The present state of our culture may be gauged by the extent to which principles have vanished from public discussion, reducing our cultural atmosphere to the sordid, petty senselessness of a bickering family that haggles over trivial concretes, while betraying all its major values, selling out its future for some spurious advantage of the moment.

To make it more grotesque, that haggling is accompanied by an aura of hysterical self-righteousness, in the form of belligerent assertions that one must compromise with anybody on anything (except on the tenet that one must compromise)—and by panicky appeals to "practicality."

But there is nothing as impractical as a so-called "practical" man. His view of practicality can best be illustrated as follows: if you want to drive from New York to Los Angeles, it is "impractical" and "idealistic" to consult a map and to select the best way to get there; you will get there much faster if you just start out driving at random, turning (or cutting) any corner, taking any road in any direction, following nothing but the mood and the weather of the moment.

The fact is, of course, that by this method you will never get there at all. But while most people do recognize it in regard to the course of a journey, they are not so perceptive in regard to the course of their life and of their country.

There is only one science that could produce blindness on so large a scale, the science whose job it was to provide men with sight: philosophy. Since modern philosophy, in essence, is a concerted attack against the conceptual level of man's consciousness—a sustained attempt to invalidate reason, abstractions, generalizations and any integration of knowledge—men have been emerging from universities, for many decades past, with the helplessness of epistemological savages, with no inkling of the nature, function or practical application of principles. These men have been groping blindly for some direction through the bewildering mass of (to them) incomprehensible concretes in the daily life of a complex industrial civilization—groping, struggling, failing, giving up and perishing, unable to know in what manner they had acted as their own destroyers.

It is, therefore, important—for those who do not care to continue that suicidal process—to consider a few rules about the working of principles in practice and about the relationship of principles to goals.

The three rules listed below are by no means exhaustive; they are merely the first leads to the understanding of a vast subject.

1. In any *conflict* between two men (or two groups) who hold the *same* basic principles, it is the more consistent one who wins.

2. In any *collaboration* between two men (or two groups) who hold *different* basic principles, it is the more evil or irrational one who wins.

3. When opposite basic principles are clearly and openly defined, it works to the advantage of the rational side; when they are *not* clearly defined, but are hidden or evaded, it works to the advantage of the irrational side.

1. When two men (or groups) hold the same basic principles, yet oppose each other on a given issue, it means that at least one of them is inconsistent. Since basic principles determine the ultimate goal of any long-range process of action, the person who holds a clearer, more consistent view of the end to be achieved, will be more consistently right in his choice of means; and the contradictions of his opponent will work to his advantage, psychologically and existentially.

Psychologically, the inconsistent person will endorse and propagate the same ideas as his adversary, but in a weaker, diluted form—and thus will sanction, assist and hasten his adversary's victory, creating in the minds of their disputed following the impression of his adversary's greater honesty and courage, while discrediting himself by an aura of evasion and cowardice.

Existentially, every step or measure taken to achieve their common goal will necessitate further and more crucial steps or measures in the same direction (unless the goal is rejected and the basic principles reversed)—thus strengthening the leadership of the consistent person and reducing the inconsistent one to impotence.

The conflict will follow that course regardless of whether the basic principles shared by the two adversaries are right or wrong, good or bad, rational or irrational.

For instance, consider the conflict between the Republicans and the Democrats (and, within each party, the same conflict between the "conservatives" and the "liberals"). Since both parties hold altruism as their basic moral principle, both advocate a welfare state or mixed economy as their ultimate goal. Every government control imposed on the economy (regardless in whose favor) necessitates the imposition of further controls, to alleviate—momentarily—the disasters caused by the first control. Since the Democrats are more consistently committed to the growth of government power, the Republicans are reduced to helpless "me-too'ing," to inept plagiarism of any program initiated by the Democrats, and to the disgraceful confession implied in their claim that they seek to achieve "the same ends" as the Democrats, but by different means.

It is precisely those ends (altruism-collectivism-statism) that ought to be rejected. But if neither party chooses to do it, the logic of the events created by their common basic principles will keep dragging them both further and further to the left. If and when the "conservatives" are kicked out of the game altogether, the same conflict will continue between the "liberals" and the avowed socialists; when the socialists win, the conflict will continue between the socialists and the communists; when the communists win, the ultimate goal of altruism will be achieved: universal immolation.

(continued on page 4)

BOOKS

*Roosevelt's Road to Russia**

by George N. Crocker

Reviewed by **BEATRICE HESSEN**

Behind closed doors at Casablanca, Quebec, Cairo, Teheran and Yalta, Franklin D. Roosevelt made military and territorial concessions to the Soviet Union which led to the enslavement of almost half the world's population. Today, although the effects of those concessions are very much a reality, few people are aware of what actually happened at the war-time conferences. An important and courageous book, *Roosevelt's Road to Russia*, by George N. Crocker, exposes those events and the disastrous nature of Roosevelt's decisions.

"The story of World War II and its aftermath," Crocker points out, "is a drama of human will." It is widely believed that the exigencies of war alone shaped Roosevelt's decisions—that military considerations made him powerless to do other than he did. Crocker proves otherwise. From the evidence presented in his well-documented account, a portrait of Roosevelt emerges which reveals recklessness, irresponsibility, a gross indifference to the consequences of his actions, and, perhaps, a sneaking admiration for dictatorship.

At Teheran (1943), Stalin proposed a plan for the partition of Poland which would insure Soviet domination of the country. Roosevelt, motivated by insatiable political ambitions, had only one reservation: the 1944 Presidential election was approaching and seven million American Poles would protest. After he had explained this situation to Stalin, an agreement was reached: Roosevelt would go along with the partition of Poland, and it would be kept secret until after the election. ("I like this man," Roosevelt said of Stalin, "and I want to keep on good terms with him.") The result: eleven million Poles were sold out to the Soviet Union and millions more to a Polish communist regime. Safely in office for his fourth term, Roosevelt proudly revealed to Congress that the solution to the Polish problem was "agreed to by Russia, by Britain and *by me*."

Stalin knew that for communism to spread throughout Eastern Europe, it was crucial to keep American and British troops out of key areas on V-E Day. Roosevelt's attitude toward Stalin's demands is epitomized by his statement to Ambassador William C. Bullitt: "I have just a hunch that Stalin doesn't want anything but security for his country, and I think that if I give him everything I possibly can and ask nothing from him in return, noblesse oblige, he won't try to annex anything and will work for a world democracy and peace." Roosevelt played his "hunch." The result: American troops idly stood by, watching the spectacle of a Red Army "liberation" of Berlin and Prague, while the people of Czechoslovakia, Hungary, Rumania, Bulgaria and Yugoslavia saw that tryranny was not to end—only their masters would change.

Stalin maintained that the Baltic States, invaded and annexed in 1940 by the Soviet Union, should become permanent possessions of his country. Again, he met no opposition from Roosevelt, who agreed to sign away permanently the liberty of the people of Latvia, Lithuania and Estonia. In 1945, while millions were strangling within the Soviet orbit, Roosevelt said in a cable to Churchill: "I would minimize the general Soviet problem as much as possible because these problems, in one form or another, seem to arise every day and most of them straighten out." As Crocker observes: "It is possible that Roosevelt was so constituted psychologically that he could easily insulate his mind against jarring facts..."

At Yalta (February, 1945), Roosevelt was "cocksure, ill-prepared, and as at Teheran, with no strategy beyond his old obsession that the important thing was for Stalin to 'like' him..."

Before he left for Yalta, Roosevelt had been advised by his Pacific commanders that Japan was on the verge of collapse, and he knew that the success of the atomic bomb was a 99% certainty. Yet, he induced Stalin to enter the Pacific war by making an inexplicable and pathologically gratuitous offer of South Sakhalin, the Chinese ports of Dairen and Port Arthur, Outer Mongolia and the Kurile Islands in the Pacific, as well as vast quantities of military equipment. When Roosevelt returned from Yalta, he told Congress, with shameless duplicity, that: "This Conference concerned itself only with the European war and the political problems of Europe, and not with the Pacific war." Russia entered the war with Japan two days after the atomic bomb was dropped on Hiroshima—in time to plunder the industrial resources of Manchuria, to occupy North Korea, and to arm the Chinese communists with captured Japanese weapons. Today, Soviet submarine bases stretch across the Kurile Islands, cutting the route between Japan and Alaska.

At Cairo (1943), Chiang Kai-shek pleaded with Roosevelt for full-scale American support in order to withstand both the Japanese and the communist Chinese. But, as Crocker points out, "A strengthened Chinese Nationalist government would hardly fit in with Stalin's long-term plans for China." Roosevelt, therefore, forced Chiang Kai-shek to form a coalition with the communists, on the grounds that he did not consider Chiang's government "the modern democracy that ideally it should be." (Apparently, Roosevelt believed that empowering the communists would bring China closer to the democratic ideal.) Also, Roosevelt withheld much of the military support he had promised. These decisions plus his Asian concessions at Yalta strengthened the Chinese communists and led to the eventual enslavement of 600 million people.

Roosevelt's faith in Stalin was not diminished by the dictator's naked use of force, and Roosevelt did not shrink from emulating it. At Yalta, he promised Stalin that American troops in Europe would track down Russian nationals who had escaped during the war, and send them back to the Soviet Union. Two million Russians who had fled Soviet tyranny—who faced either execution or slave labor camps upon return—were herded into boxcars by American soldiers and sent back to Russia. *This was the Roosevelt who is remembered as a humanitarian, motivated by a love of liberty and justice.*

"This war," states Crocker, "was to end in perhaps the most terrifying peace in all history. The mass deportation of millions of innocent civilians, the partitions, the spoliation and plunder, and the destruction of moral and spiritual values were to be on an unprecedented scale."

In 1943, on a national radio broadcast, Roosevelt described Stalin—the known executioner of millions, the former ally of Nazi Germany—as a man "who combines a tremendous, relentless determination with a stalwart good humor. I believe he is truly representative of the heart and soul of Russia; and I believe that we are going to get along very well with him and the Russian people—very well indeed."

Today, we are told by the liberals that we can get along very well with the Russian people by emphasizing our similarities and evading our differences—by signing treaties and sending wheat, and by ignoring the bloody testimonies to Soviet tyranny around the world.

Crocker demonstrates that Roosevelt delivered half the world into slavery. Will some future historian recount that, a generation later, admirers of Roosevelt's policies delivered the other half to the same fate? This engrossing and powerful book should be read by everyone concerned about the destructive course of America's foreign policy.

―――――――

*Published by Henry Regnery Company. Available from NBI BOOK SERVICE, 120 East 34th St., New York 16, N. Y. Paperbound: $2.00 plus 15¢ postage. (N.Y.C. residents add 4% sales tax.)

―――――――

Beatrice Hessen received her M.A. in Literature from Columbia University, and is presently Manager of NBI BOOK SERVICE.

INTELLECTUAL AMMUNITION DEPARTMENT

[Subscribers are invited to send in the questions that they find themselves unable to answer in philosophical or political discussions. As many questions as space permits will be answered. No questions will be answered by mail.]

■ **What is the difference between the Objectivist concept of free will and the traditional concepts?**

I shall confine myself to answering this question literally—*i.e.*, to distinguishing the Objectivist *concept* of free will from traditional concepts; I shall not attempt to offer a full presentation and proof of the Objectivist theory.

"Free will"—in the widest sense of the term—is the doctrine which holds that man is capable of performing actions that are not determined by forces outside his control; that man has the power of making choices which are, causally, *primaries*—*i.e.*, not necessitated by antecedent factors. The nature of these choices, to what human faculty they pertain, how they operate and what are their limits—are issues on which various theories of free will differ. But what the principle of volition rejects is the doctrine that man's thoughts, desires, actions and character are ultimately imposed on him by physical, psychological, environmental or divine necessity. In its older form, this doctrine, which the concept of free will opposes, was called "fatalism." In its modern form, it is called "determinism."

Objectivism locates man's free will in a single action of his consciousness, in a single basic choice: to focus his mind or to suspend it; to think or not to think.

Man's sensory-perceptual mechanism functions automatically; no act of volition is required for man's brain to integrate sensations into perceptions. Man's freedom of choice pertains to the exercise of his *conceptual* faculty. It is the process of *abstract reasoning* that must be initiated, directed and sustained—volitionally.

Man is the most developed and complex of biological entities. All life entails and exhibits self-regulated action, but in man the principle of self-regulation reaches its highest expression: *man has the power to regulate the action of his own consciousness*. Man has the power to exercise his rational faculty—or to suspend it.

It is *this* choice that is a causal primary.

What a man thinks about, depends on his values, interests and context; it depends on antecedent causes; but whether or not, in a given situation, he chooses to think at all, is an issue of his free will. (The capacity to make this choice presupposes a normal brain state; a condition of disease can render *any* human faculty inoperative.)

This choice—given the context of a man's knowledge and of the existential possibilities confronting him—controls all of a man's other choices, and directs the course of his actions.

It is not thus that free will has been viewed by other theorists.

Historically, the most common view of free will locates man's freedom in his choice of *actions*. This is the view of Epicurus and of the modern Existentialists, for instance. According to this position, man is capable (at least, under certain circumstances) of choosing a particular course of action by direct free will; so that the choice, say, to go to the store for a loaf of bread or to join a political party, can be a causal primary, a "first cause" in consciousness.

The objections to this view are clearly overwhelming. When a man chooses to pursue a given course of action, the cause of his action is the mental operations that precede his choice; these mental operations express and are the result of his values, premises, knowledge and thinking—whether he is fully aware of it or not. Sometimes, through incompetence at introspection, a man is ignorant of the causes of his action; sometimes—when a man acts instantly and impulsively—the preceding mental operations are so rapid that he is unconscious of them. But the choice to perform an action is not and cannot be an irreducible, causal primary.

In the Objectivist theory of volition, a man is responsible for his actions, not because his actions are directly subject to his free will, but because they proceed from his values and premises, which in turn proceed from his thinking or non-thinking. His actions are free because they are under the control of a faculty that is free—*i.e.*, that functions volitionally.

Now consider the theory of free will advanced by Thomas Aquinas. Aquinas declares that the mind has an innate compulsion to think, to pursue truth and to desire that which reason clearly perceives to be right—that man has no choice in the matter—but that man is "*self*-determined," because the forces that compel him are *in*ternal rather than *ex*ternal.

Strictly speaking, this is not a theory of free will at all: the issue is not *which* forces compel man's choices, but *whether* man's choices are compelled. If the primary function of man's consciousness, the act of thinking, is not in man's control, then man is not a self-responsible being. It is true that *if* a man chooses to think and *if*, when he reaches a conclusion, he chooses to remain in focus and to hold nothing above the judgment of his mind—he will act in accordance with that judgment. But these precisely are the decisions that must be made volitionally: man's nature will not force them upon him.

Aquinas' theory has a second part, which consists of the claim that in the many practical instances where there is no conclusive evidence of what is right or wrong, or where, at any rate, a mind is ignorant of it, the "will" has the power to choose arbitrarily, to *desire* one thing rather than another, to generate such a desire by whim, motivated by nothing.

The attempt to ascribe free will to man's desires, is not defensible. A desire is a value-response, the automatic product of an estimate (conscious or subconscious)—and an estimate is the product of an individual's values and premises (conscious or subconscious), as the individual applies them to a given situation. (See my article on reason and emotion in the January 1962 issue of this NEWSLETTER.) Man is not free to create, destroy or change his desires and emotions by arbitrary whim, independent of his values and premises; he can alter his desires and emotions only by revising the thinking or non-thinking that produced his values and premises; *they* are the cause of his desires and emotions.

Another, very common view of free will sees man's freedom in the ability to choose among conflicting desires. This view regards desires as the given, as the inherent in man's nature—and locates man's volition in the freedom to act on one desire rather than another. But again, this is clearly untenable. Desires are not primaries; they proceed from a man's values and premises. Values and premises cannot be changed at will; they can be altered—but only by a new process of thought.

Such, then, is the distinctive nature of the Objectivist theory of free will: it locates man's volition, not in the sphere of action or desire, but in the sphere of cognition—in the choice to activate his mind or to suspend it.

For a discussion of why any attempt to deny that man possesses this freedom collapses under the weight of insuperable contradictions, I refer the reader to my article on determinism in the May 1963 issue of this NEWSLETTER.

—**NATHANIEL BRANDEN**

The Anatomy of Compromise (from page 1)

There is no way to stop or change that process except at the root: by a change of basic principles.

The evidence of that process is mounting in every country on earth. And, observing it, the unthinking begin to whisper about some mysterious occult power called a "historical necessity" which, in some unspecified way, by some unknowable means, has preordained mankind to collapse into the abyss of communism. But there are no fatalistic "historical necessities": the "mysterious" power moving the events of the world is the awesome power of men's principles—which is mysterious only to the "practical" modern savages who were taught to discard it as "impotent."

But—it might be argued—since the advocates of a mixed economy are also advocating freedom, at least in part, why does the irrational part of their mixture have to win? This leads us to the fact that—

2. In any collaboration between two men (or groups) who hold different basic principles, it is the more evil or irrational one who wins.

The rational (principle, premise, idea, policy or action) is that which is consonant with the facts of reality; the irrational is that which contradicts the facts and attempts to get away with it. A collaboration is a joint undertaking, a common course of action. The rational (the good) has nothing to gain from the irrational (the evil) except a share of its failures and crimes; the irrational has everything to gain from the rational: a share of its achievements and values. An industrialist does not need the help of a burglar in order to succeed; a burglar needs the industrialist's achievement in order to exist at all. What collaboration is possible between them and to what end?

If an individual holds mixed premises, his vices undercut, hamper, defeat and ultimately destroy his virtues. What is the moral status of an honest man who steals once in a while? In the same way, if a group of men pursues mixed goals, its bad principles drive out the good. What is the political status of a free country whose government violates the citizens' rights once in a while?

Consider the case of a business partnership: if one partner is honest and the other is a swindler, the latter contributes nothing to the success of the business; but the reputation of the former disarms the victims and provides the swindler with a wide-scale opportunity which he could not have obtained on his own.

Now consider the collaboration of the semi-free countries with the communist dictatorships, in the United Nations. To identify that institution is to damn it, so that any criticism is superfluous. It is an institution allegedly dedicated to peace, freedom and human rights, which includes Soviet Russia—the most brutal aggressor, the bloodiest dictatorship, the largest-scale mass-murderer and mass-enslaver in all history—among its charter members. Nothing can be added to that fact and nothing can mitigate it. It is so grotesquely evil an affront to reason, morality and civilization that no further discussion is necessary, except for a glance at the consequences.

Psychologically, the U.N. has contributed a great deal to the gray swamp of demoralization—of cynicism, bitterness, hopelessness, fear and nameless guilt—which is swallowing the Western world. But the communist world has gained a moral sanction, a stamp of civilized respectability from the Western world—it has gained the West's assistance in deceiving its victims—it has gained the status and prestige of an equal partner, thus establishing the notion that the difference between human rights and mass slaughter is merely a difference of political opinion.

The declared goal of the communist countries is the conquest of the world. What they stand to gain from a collaboration with the (relatively) free countries is the latter's material, financial, scientific and intellectual resources; the free countries have nothing to gain from the communist countries. Therefore, the only form of common policy or compromise possible between two such parties is the policy of property owners who make piecemeal concessions to an armed thug in exchange for his agreement not to rob them.

The U.N. has delivered a larger part of the globe's surface and population into the power of Soviet Russia than Russia could ever hope to conquer by armed force. The treatment accorded to Katanga versus the treatment accorded to Hungary, is a sufficient example of U.N. policies. An institution allegedly formed for the purpose of using the united might of the world to stop an aggressor, has become the means of using the united might of the world to force the surrender of one helpless country after another into the aggressor's power.

Who, but a concrete-bound epistemological savage, could have expected any other results from such an "experiment in collaboration"? What would you expect from a crime-fighting committee whose board of directors included the leading gangsters of the community?

Only a total evasion of basic principles could make this possible. And this illustrates the reason why—

3. When opposite basic principles are clearly and openly defined, it works to the advantage of the rational side; when they are *not* clearly defined, but are hidden or evaded, it works to the advantage of the irrational side.

In order to win, the rational side of any controversy requires that its goals be understood and has nothing to hide, since reality is its ally; the irrational side has to deceive, to confuse, to evade, to hide its goals. Fog, murk and blindness are not the tools of reason; they are the only tools of irrationality.

No thought, knowledge or consistency is required in order to destroy; unremitting thought, enormous knowledge and a ruthless consistency are required in order to achieve or create. Every error, evasion or contradiction helps the goal of destruction; only reason and logic can advance the goal of construction. The *negative* requires an absence (ignorance, impotence, irrationality); the *positive* requires a presence, an existent (knowledge, efficacy, thought).

The spread of evil is the symptom of a vacuum. Whenever evil wins, it is only by default: by the moral failure of those who evade the fact that there can be no compromise on basic principles.

"In any compromise between food and poison, it is only death that can win. In any compromise between good and evil, it is only evil that can profit." (*Atlas Shrugged*)

OBJECTIVIST CALENDAR

■ New American Library has published Ayn Rand's *For the New Intellectual* in a paperback edition. First printing: 200,000 copies.

■ Random House is issuing a third printing of *Who Is Ayn Rand?*

■ NBI's Tape Transcription Division has scheduled "Basic Principles of Objectivism" to begin in San Jose, California, on January 12.

■ Two articles, "Doctors and the Police State" by Leonard Peikoff, and "How *Not* to Fight Against Socialized Medicine" by Ayn Rand, published in this NEWSLETTER (June 1962 and March 1963), have been reprinted as a single pamphlet under the title "The Forgotten Man of Socialized Medicine: The Doctor." Price: 50¢. Special quantity rates to members of the medical profession.

—B.B.

Published monthly at 120 East 34th Street, New York 16, N. Y.
Subscription rate: in United States, its possessions, Canada and Mexico, $5 for one year; other countries, $6.
Additional copies of this Newsletter: single copy 50¢ (coins, not stamps); 10 – 99 copies, 25¢ each plus postage (for first-class delivery add 1¢ per copy, for third-class delivery add ½¢ per copy); 100 or more copies, 15¢ each plus postage (same as above).
For change of address send old address and new address with zone number if any. Allow us three weeks to process new subscriptions and change of address.

Ayn Rand and Nathaniel Branden, Editors and Publishers
Barbara Branden, Managing Editor
Elayne Kalberman, Circulation Manager

THE OBJECTIVIST NEWSLETTER

Edited and Published by AYN RAND and NATHANIEL BRANDEN

VOL. 3 NO. 2   FEBRUARY, 1964

The Psychology of Pleasure
By NATHANIEL BRANDEN

Pleasure, for man, is not a luxury, but a profound psychological need.

Pleasure (in the widest sense of the term) is a metaphysical concomitant of life, the reward and consequence of successful action—just as pain is the insignia of failure, destruction, death.

Through the state of enjoyment, man experiences the value of life, the sense that life is worth living, worth struggling to maintain. In order to live, man must act to achieve values. Pleasure or enjoyment is at once an emotional payment for successful action and an incentive to continue acting.

Further, because of the metaphysical meaning of pleasure to man, the state of enjoyment gives him a direct experience of his own efficacy, of his competence to deal with the facts of reality, to achieve his values, to live. Implicitly contained in the experience of pleasure is the feeling: "I am in control of my existence" — just as implicitly contained in the experience of pain is the feeling: "I am helpless." As pleasure emotionally entails a sense of efficacy, so pain emotionally entails a sense of impotence.

Thus, in letting man experience, in his own person, the sense that *life* is a value and that *he* is a value, pleasure serves as the emotional fuel of man's existence.

Just as the pleasure-pain mechanism of man's body works as a barometer of health or injury, so the pleasure-pain mechanism of his consciousness works on the same principle, acting as a barometer of what is for him or against him, what is beneficial to his life or inimical. But man is a being of volitional consciousness, he has no innate ideas, no automatic or infallible knowledge of what his survival depends on. He must choose the values that are to guide his actions and set his goals. His emotional mechanism will work according to the kind of values he chooses. It is his values that determine what a man feels to be for him or against him; it is his values that determine what a man seeks for pleasure.

If a man makes an error in his choice of values, his emotional mechanism will not correct him: it has no will of its own. If a man's values are such that he desires things which, in fact and in reality, lead to his destruction, his emotional mechanism will not save him, but will, instead, urge him on toward destruction: he will have set it in reverse, against himself and against the facts of reality, against his own life. Man's emotional mechanism is like an electronic computer: man has the power to program it, but no power to change its nature—so that if he sets the wrong programming, he will not be able to escape the fact that the most self-destructive desires will have, for him, the emotional intensity and urgency of life-saving actions. He has, of course, the power to change the programming—but only by changing his values.

A man's basic values reflect his conscious or subconscious view of himself and of existence. They are the expression of (a) the degree and nature of his self-esteem or lack of it, and (b) the extent to which he regards the universe as open to his understanding and action or closed—*i.e.*, the extent to which he holds a benevolent or malevolent view of existence. Thus, the things which a man seeks for pleasure or enjoyment are profoundly revealing psychologically; they are the index of his character and soul. (By "soul," I mean: a man's consciousness and his basic motivating values.)

There are, broadly, five (interconnected) areas that allow man to experience the enjoyment of life: productive work, human relationships, recreation, art, sex.

Productive work is the most fundamental of these: through his work man gains his basic sense of control over existence—his sense of efficacy—which is the necessary foundation of the ability to enjoy any other value. The man whose life lacks direction or purpose, the man who has no creative goal, necessarily feels helpless and out of control; the man who feels helpless and out of control, feels inadequate to and unfit for existence; and the man who feels unfit for existence is incapable of enjoying it.

One of the hallmarks of a man of self-esteem, who regards the universe as open to his effort, is the profound pleasure he experiences in the productive work of his mind; his enjoyment of life is fed by his unceasing concern to grow in knowledge and ability—to think, to achieve, to move forward, to meet new challenges and overcome them—to earn the pride of a constantly expanding efficacy.

A different kind of soul is revealed by the man who, predominantly, takes pleasure in working only at the routine and familiar, who is inclined to enjoy working in a semi-daze, who sees happiness in freedom from challenge or struggle or effort: the soul of a man profoundly deficient in self-esteem, to whom the universe appears as unknowable and vaguely threatening, the man whose central motivating impulse is a longing for safety, not the safety that is won by efficacy, but the safety of a world in which efficacy is not demanded.

Still a different kind of soul is revealed by the man who finds it inconceivable that work—*any* form of work—can be enjoyable, who regards the effort of earning a living as a necessary evil, who dreams only of the pleasures that begin when the work-day ends, the pleasure of drowning his brain in alcohol or television or billiards or women, *the pleasure of not being conscious*: the soul of a man with scarcely a shred of self-esteem, who never expected the universe to be comprehensible and takes his lethargic dread of it for granted, and whose only form of relief and only notion of enjoyment is the dim flicker of undemanding sensations.

Still another kind of soul is revealed by the man who takes pleasure, not in achievement, but in destruction, whose action is aimed, not at attaining efficacy, but at *ruling* those who have attained it: the soul of a man so abjectly lacking in self-value, and so overwhelmed by terror of existence, that his sole form of self-fulfillment is to unleash his resentment and hatred against those who do not share his state, those who are *able* to live—as if, by destroying the confident, the strong and the healthy, he could convert impotence into efficacy.

A rational, self-confident man is motivated by a love of values and by a desire to achieve them. A neurotic is motivated by fear and by a desire to escape it. This difference in motivation is reflected, not only in the things each type of man will seek for pleasure, but in the nature of the pleasure they will experience.

The emotional quality of the pleasure experienced by the four men described above, for instance, is not the same. The quality of any pleasure depends on the mental processes that give rise to and attend it, and on the nature of the values involved. The pleasure of using one's consciousness properly, and the "pleasure" of being unconscious, are not the same—just as the pleasure of achieving real values, of gaining an authentic sense of efficacy, and the "pleasure" of temporarily diminishing one's sense of fear and helplessness, are not the same. The man of self-esteem experiences the pure, unadulterated enjoyment of using his faculties properly and of achieving actual values in reality—a pleasure of which the other three men can have no inkling, just as he has no inkling of the dim, murky state which *they* call "pleasure."

This same principle applies to all forms of enjoyment. Thus, in the realm of human relationships, a different form of pleasure is experienced, a different sort of motivation is involved, and a different kind of character is revealed, by the man who seeks for enjoyment the company of human beings of intelligence, integrity and self-esteem, who share his exacting standards—and by the man who is able to enjoy himself only with human beings who have no standards whatever and with whom, therefore, he feels free to be himself—or by the man who finds pleasure only in the company of people he despises, to whom he can compare himself favorably—or by the man who finds pleasure only among people he can deceive and manipulate, from whom he derives the lowest neurotic substitute for a sense of genuine efficacy: a sense of power.

For the rational, psychologically healthy man, the desire for pleasure is the desire to celebrate his control over reality. For the neurotic, the desire for pleasure is the desire to escape from reality.

Now consider the sphere of recreation. For instance, a party. A rational man enjoys a party as an emotional reward for achievement, and he can enjoy it only if *in fact* it involves activities that are enjoyable, such as seeing people whom he likes, meeting new people whom he finds interesting, engaging in conversations in which something worth saying and hearing is being said and heard. But a neurotic can "enjoy" a party for reasons unrelated to the real activities taking place; he may hate or despise or fear all the people present, he may act like a noisy fool and feel secretly ashamed of it — but he will feel that he is enjoying it all, because people are emitting the vibrations of approval, or because it is a social distinction to have been invited to this party, or because *other* people appear to be gay, or because the party has spared him, for the length of an evening, the terror of being alone.

The "pleasure" of being drunk is obviously the pleasure of escaping from the responsibility of consciousness. And so are the kind of social gatherings, held for no other purpose than the expression of hysterical chaos, where the guests wander around in an alcoholic stupor, prattling noisily and senselessly, and enjoying the illusion of a universe where one is not burdened with purpose, logic, reality or awareness.

Observe, in this connection, the modern "beatniks"—for instance, their manner of dancing. What one sees is not smiles of authentic enjoyment, but the vacant, staring eyes, the jerky, disorganized movements of what looks like decentralized bodies, all working very hard—with a kind of flat-footed hysteria—at projecting an air of the purposeless, the senseless, the mindless. *This* is the "pleasure" of unconsciousness.

Or consider the *quieter* kind of "pleasures" that fill many peoples' lives: family picnics, ladies' tea-parties or "coffee-klatches," charity bazaars, vegetative kinds of vacation—all of them occasions of quiet boredom for all concerned, in which the *boredom* is the value. Boredom, to such people, means safety, the known, the usual, the routine—the absence of the new, the exciting, the unfamiliar, the *demanding*.

What is a *demanding* pleasure? A pleasure that demands the use of one's mind; not in the sense of problem-solving, but in the sense of exercising discrimination, judgment, awareness.

One of the cardinal pleasures of life is offered to man by works of art. Art, at its highest potential, as the projection of things "as they might be and ought to be," can provide man with an invaluable emotional fuel. But, again, the kind of art works one responds to, depends on one's deepest values and premises.

A man can seek the projection of the heroic, the intelligent, the efficacious, the dramatic, the purposeful, the stylized, the ingenious, the challenging; he can seek the pleasure of *admiration*, of looking up to great values. Or he can seek the satisfaction of contemplating gossip-column variants of the folks next door, with nothing demanded of him, neither in thought nor in value-standards; he can feel himself pleasantly warmed by projections of the known and familiar, seeking to feel a little less of "a stranger and afraid in a world [he] never made." Or his soul can vibrate affirmatively to projections of horror and human degradation, he can feel gratified by the thought that he's not as bad as the dope-addicted dwarf or the crippled lesbian he's reading about; he can relish an art which tells him that man is evil, that reality is unknowable, that existence is unendurable, that no one can help anything, that his secret terror is *normal*.

Art projects an implicit view of existence—and it is one's *own* view of existence that determines the art one will respond to. The soul of the man whose favorite play is *Cyrano de Bergerac* is radically different from the soul of the man whose favorite play is *Waiting for Godot*.

Of the various pleasures that man can offer himself, the greatest is *pride*—the pleasure he takes in his own achievements and in the creation of his own character. The pleasure he takes in the character and achievements of another human being is that of *admiration*. The highest expression of the most intense union of these two responses—pride and admiration—is romantic love. Its celebration is sex.

It is in this sphere above all—in a man's romantic-sexual responses—that his view of himself and of existence stands eloquently revealed. A man falls in love with and sexually desires the person who reflects his own deepest values.

There are two crucial respects in which a man's romantic-sexual responses are psychologically revealing: in his choice of partner—and in the *meaning*, to him, of the sexual act.

A man of self-esteem, a man in love with himself and with life, feels an intense need to find human beings he can admire —to find a spiritual equal whom he can love. The quality that will attract him most is self-esteem — self-esteem and an unclouded sense of the value of existence. To such a man, sex is an act of celebration, its meaning is a tribute to himself and to the woman he has chosen, the ultimate form of experiencing concretely and in his own person the value and joy of being alive.

The need for such an experience is inherent in man's nature. But if a man lacks the self-esteem to earn it, he attempts to *fake* it—and he chooses his partner (subconsciously) by the standard of her ability to help him fake it, to give him the illusion of a self-value he does not possess and of a happiness he does not feel.

Thus, if a man is attracted to a woman of intelligence, confidence and strength, if he is attracted to a heroine, he reveals one kind of soul; if, instead, he is attracted to an irresponsible, helpless scatterbrain, whose weakness enables him to feel masculine, he reveals another kind of soul; if he is attracted to a frightened slut, whose lack of judgment and standards allows him to feel free of reproach, he reveals another kind of soul.

The same principle, of course, applies to a woman's romantic-sexual choices.

The sexual act has a different meaning for the person whose desire is fed by pride and admiration, to whom the pleasurable self-experience it affords is an end in itself—and for the person who seeks in sex the proof of masculinity (or femininity), or the amelioration of despair, or a defense against anxiety, or an escape from boredom.

Paradoxically, it is the so-called pleasure-chasers—the men who seemingly live for nothing but the sensation of the moment, and are concerned only with having "a good time"—who are psychologically incapable of enjoying pleasure as an end in itself. The neurotic pleasure-chaser imagines that, by going through the motions of a celebration, he will be able to make himself feel that he has something to celebrate.

One of the hallmarks of the man who lacks self-esteem— and the real punishment for his moral and psychological default —is the fact that all his pleasures are pleasures of escape from the two pursuers whom he has betrayed and from whom there is no escape: reality and his own mind.

Since the function of pleasure is to afford man a sense of his own efficacy, the neurotic is caught in a deadly conflict: he is compelled, by his nature as man, to feel a desperate need for pleasure, as a confirmation and expression of his control over reality—but he can find pleasure only in an *escape* from reality. That is the reason why his pleasures do not work, why they bring him, not a sense of pride, fulfillment, inspiration, but a sense of guilt, frustration, hopelessness, shame. The effect of pleasure on a man of self-esteem is that of a reward and a confirmation. The effect of pleasure on a man who lacks self-esteem is that of a threat—the threat of anxiety, the shaking of the precarious foundation of his *pseudo*-self-value, the sharpening of the ever-present fear that the structure will collapse and he will find himself face to face with a stern, absolute, unknown and unforgiving reality.

One of the commonest complaints of patients who seek psychotherapy, is that nothing has the power to give them pleasure, that authentic enjoyment seems impossible to them. This is the inevitable dead end of the policy of pleasure-as-escape.

To preserve an unclouded capacity for the enjoyment of life, is an unusual moral and psychological achievement. Contrary to popular belief, it is the prerogative, not of mindlessness, but of an unremitting devotion to the act of perceiving reality, and of a scrupulous intellectual integrity. It is the reward of self-esteem.

INTELLECTUAL AMMUNITION DEPARTMENT

[*Subscribers are invited to send in the questions that they find themselves unable to answer in philosophical or political discussions. As many questions as space permits will be answered. No questions will be answered by mail.*]

■ **What would be the proper method of financing the government in a fully free society?**

This question is usually asked in connection with the Objectivist principle that the government of a free society may not initiate the use of physical force and may use force only in retaliation against those who initiate its use. Since the imposition of taxes does represent an initiation of force, how, it is asked, would the government of a free country raise the money needed to finance its proper services?

In a fully free society, taxation—or, to be exact, payment for governmental services—would be *voluntary*. Since the proper services of a government—the police, the armed forces, the law courts—are demonstrably needed by individual citizens and affect their interests directly, the citizens would (and should) be willing to pay for such services, as they pay for insurance.

The question of how to implement the principle of voluntary government financing—how to determine the best means of applying it in practice—is a very complex one and belongs to the field of the philosophy of law. The task of political philosophy is only to establish the nature of the principle and to demonstrate that it is practicable. The choice of a specific method of implementation is more than premature today — since the principle will be practicable only in a *fully* free society, a society whose government has been constitutionally reduced to its proper, basic functions. (For a discussion of these functions, see my article on "The Nature of Government" in the December 1963 issue of this NEWSLETTER.)

There are many possible methods of voluntary government financing. A government lottery, which has been used in some European countries, is one such method. There are others.

As an illustration (and *only* as an illustration), consider the following possibility. One of the most vitally needed services, which only a government can render, is the protection of contractual agreements among citizens. Suppose that the government were to protect—*i.e.*, to recognize as legally valid and enforceable—only those contracts which had been insured by the payment, to the government, of a premium in the amount of a legally fixed percentage of the sums involved in the contractual transaction. Such an insurance would not be compulsory; there would be no legal penalty imposed on those who did not choose to take it—they would be free to make verbal agreements or to sign uninsured contracts, if they so wished. The only consequence would be that such agreements or contracts would not be legally enforceable; if they were broken, the injured party would not be able to seek redress in a court of law.

All credit transactions are *contractual agreements*. A credit transaction is any exchange which involves a passage of time between the payment and the receipt of goods or services. This includes the vast majority of economic transactions in a complex industrial society. Only a very small part of the gigantic network of credit transactions ever ends up in court, but the entire network is made possible by the existence of the courts, and would collapse overnight without that protection. *This is a government service which people need, use, rely upon and should pay for*. Yet, today, this service is provided gratuitously and amounts, in effect, to a subsidy.

When one considers the magnitude of the wealth involved in credit transactions, one can see that the percentage required to pay for such governmental insurance would be infinitesimal —much smaller than that paid for other types of insurance— yet it would be sufficient to finance all the other functions of a proper government. (If necessary, that percentage could be legally increased in time of war; or other, but similar, methods of raising money could be established for *clearly defined* wartime needs.)

This particular "plan" is mentioned here only as an illustration of a possible method of approach to the problem— *not* as a definitive answer nor as a program to advocate at present. The legal and technical difficulties involved are enormous: they include such questions as the need of an ironclad constitutional provision to prevent the government from dictating the *content* of private contracts (an issue which exists today and needs much more objective definitions) — the need of objective standards (or safeguards) for establishing the amount of the premiums, which cannot be left to the arbitrary discretion of the government, etc.

Any program of voluntary government financing is the last, *not* the first, step on the road to a free society — the last, *not* the first, reform to advocate. It would work only when the basic principles and institutions of a free society have been established. It would not work today.

Men would pay voluntarily for insurance protecting their contracts. But they would not pay voluntarily for insurance against the danger of aggression by Cambodia. Nor would the plywood manufacturers of Wisconsin and their workers pay voluntarily for insurance to assist the development of the plywood industry of Japan which would put them out of business.

A program of voluntary government financing would be amply sufficient to pay for the legitimate functions of a proper government. It would not be sufficient to provide unearned support for the entire globe. But no type of taxation is sufficient for that — only the suicide of a great country might be and then only temporarily.

Just as the growth of controls, taxes and "government obligations" in this country was not accomplished overnight — so the process of liberation cannot be accomplished overnight. A process of liberation would be much more rapid than the process of enslavement had been, since the facts of reality would be its ally. But still, a gradual process is required — and any program of voluntary government financing has to be regarded as a goal for a distant future.

What the advocates of a fully free society have to know, at present, is only the principle by which that goal can be achieved.

The principle of voluntary government financing rests on the following premises: that the government is *not* the owner of the citizens' income and, therefore, cannot hold a blank check on that income — that the nature of the proper governmental services must be constitutionally defined and delimited, leaving the government no power to enlarge the scope of its services at its own arbitrary discretion. Consequently, the principle of voluntary government financing regards the government as the servant, not the ruler, of the citizens — as an *agent* who must be paid for his services, not as a benefactor whose services are gratuitous, who dispenses something for nothing.

This last, along with the notion of compulsory taxation, is a remnant of the time when the government was regarded as the omnipotent ruler of the citizens. An absolute monarch, who owned the work, income, property and lives of his subjects, had to be an unpaid "benefactor," protector and dispenser of favors. Such a monarch would have considered it demeaning to be paid for his services — just as the atavistic mentalities of his descendants-in-spirit (the remnants of Europe's ancient feudal aristocracy, and the modern welfare statists) still consider an earned, *commercial* income as demeaning and as morally inferior to an unearned one which is acquired by mooching or looting, by charitable donations or governmental force.

When a government, be it a monarch or a "democratic" parliament, is regarded as a provider of gratuitous services, it is only a question of time before it begins to enlarge its services and the sphere of the gratuitous (today, this process is called the growth of "the public sector of the economy") until it becomes, and has to become, the instrument of pressure-group warfare — of economic groups looting one another.

The premise to check (and to challenge) in this context is the primordial notion that any governmental services (even the legitimate ones) should be given to the citizens gratuitously. In order fully to translate into practice the American concept of the government as a *servant* of the citizens, one has to regard the government as a *paid servant*. Then, on that basis, one can proceed to devise the appropriate means of tying government revenues directly to the government services rendered.

It may be observed, in the example given above, that the cost of such voluntary government financing would be automatically proportionate to the scale of an individual's economic activity; those on the lowest economic levels (who seldom, if ever, engage in credit transactions) would be virtually exempt — though they would still enjoy the benefits of legal protection, such as that offered by the armed forces, by the police and by the courts dealing with criminal offenses. These benefits may be regarded as a bonus to the men of lesser economic ability, made possible by the men of greater economic ability — *without any sacrifice of the latter to the former.*

It is in their own interests that the men of greater ability have to pay for the maintenance of armed forces, for the protection of their country against invasion; their expenses are not increased by the fact that a marginal part of the population is unable to contribute to these costs. Economically, that marginal group is non-existent as far as the costs of war are concerned. The same is true of the costs of maintaining a police force: it is in their own interests that the abler men have to pay for the apprehension of criminals, regardless of whether the specific victim of a given crime is rich or poor.

It is important to note that this type of free protection for the non-contributors represents an *indirect benefit* and is merely a marginal consequence of the contributors' own interests and expenses. This type of bonus cannot be stretched to cover *direct* benefits, or to claim — as the welfare statists are claiming — that direct hand-outs to the non-producers are in the producers' own interests.

The difference, briefly, is as follows: if a railroad were running a train and allowed the poor to ride without payment in the seats left empty, it would not be the same thing (nor the same principle) as providing the poor with first-class carriages and special trains.

Any type of *non-sacrificial* assistance, of social bonus, gratuitous benefit or gift value possible among men, is possible only in a free society, and is proper so long as it is non-sacrificial. But, in a free society, under a system of voluntary government financing, there would be no legal loop-hole, no legal possibility, for any "redistribution of wealth" — for the unearned support of some men by the forced labor and extorted income of others — for the draining, exploitation and destruction of those who are able to pay the costs of maintaining a civilized society, in favor of those who are unable or unwilling to pay the cost of maintaining their own existence.

—AYN RAND

A "THANK YOU" NOTE

As an appropriate postscript to my article, "A Report to Our Readers," in the December 1963 issue of this NEWSLETTER, I want to report — and to acknowledge with sincere appreciation — that the mail response from our readers has been greater than to any other piece we have published. We have received many more letters than I am able to answer personally.

I want, therefore, to thank you in this form for the enthusiasm of your letters — and to say that I will write another report for our December 1964 issue. Any relevant information that you care to send me, will always be welcome.

—Nathaniel Branden

OBJECTIVIST CALENDAR

■ An interview with Ayn Rand will appear in the March issue of *Playboy*, which will be available on the newsstands in late February.

■ On Thursday evening, February 13, the course on "Basic Principles of Objectivism" will begin in New York City. Place: Hotel Roosevelt. Time: 7:30 P.M. Admission: $3.50; for college and high school students, $2.75. Ayn Rand will participate in the question period which follows the lecture.

■ NBI's Tape Transcription Division has scheduled the following starting dates: "Basic Principles of Objectivism" in Youngstown, February 7, in San Francisco, February 12, and in Seattle, February 14; "Basic Principles of Objectivist Psychology" in Lincoln, February 10, and in San Diego, March 11; "The Economics of a Free Society" in Boston, February 17, in San Francisco, March 6, and in Los Angeles, March 11; "A Critical Analysis of Modern Psychology" in Chicago, February 18.

■ In the past, those who wished to become business representatives for NBI's Tape Transcription Division, have been advised that they must be personally interviewed in New York. NBI has now made arrangements for such interviews to be conducted by our representatives in Los Angeles, Chicago and Toronto, as well as in New York. Interested persons should contact: Mr. Peter S. Crosby, 924½ Maltman Ave., Los Angeles 26, Calif.; Mr. Edward L. Nash, 33 East Cedar, Chicago 11, Illinois; or Mrs. H. E. Hirschfeld, 178 Old Yonge St., Willowdale, Ontario, Canada; or the NBI office in New York.

—B.B.

Published monthly at 120 East 34th Street, New York 16, N.Y.
Subscription rate: in United States, its possessions, Canada and Mexico, $5 for one year; other countries, $6.
Additional copies of this Newsletter: single copy 50¢ (coins, not stamps); 10 — 99 copies, 25¢ each plus postage (for first-class delivery add 1¢ per copy, for third-class delivery add ½¢ per copy); 100 or more copies, 15¢ each plus postage (same as above).
For change of address send old address and new address with zone number if any. Allow us three weeks to process new subscriptions and change of address.

Ayn Rand and Nathaniel Branden, Editors and Publishers
Barbara Branden, Managing Editor
Elayne Kalberman, Circulation Manager

THE OBJECTIVIST NEWSLETTER

Edited and Published by AYN RAND and NATHANIEL BRANDEN

VOL. 3 NO. 3   MARCH, 1964

CHECK YOUR PREMISES
By AYN RAND

How to Judge a Political Candidate

The political ignorance and intellectual disintegration of our age become appallingly evident in a major election year. They range from the lethargic passivity of those who ignore elections as of no consequence—to the frantic hysteria of those who believe that the life or death of a nation is determined on a single Tuesday in November.

In view of the general confusion on this subject, it is advisable to remind prospective voters of a few basic considerations, as guidelines in deciding what one can properly expect of a political candidate, particularly of a presidential candidate.

One cannot expect, nor is it necessary, to agree with a candidate's *total* philosophy—only with his *political* philosophy (and only in terms of essentials). It is not a Philosopher-King that we are electing, but an executive for a specific, delimited job. It is only *political* consistency that we can demand of him; if he advocates the right political principles for the wrong metaphysical reasons, the contradiction is *his* problem, not ours.

A contradiction of that kind will, of course, hamper the effectiveness of his campaign, weaken his arguments and dilute his appeal—as any contradictions undercut any man's efficacy. But we have to judge him as we judge any work, theory or product of mixed premises: by his dominant trend.

A vote for a candidate does not constitute an endorsement of his entire position, not even of his entire political position, only of his basic political principles. It is only in terms of principles that a candidate can offer us a program and indicate his future course—*not* in terms of floating abstractions, stale generalities and contradictory promises about a miscellaneous collection of concrete, out-of-context, range-of-the-moment issues. A candidate's view on whether the U.S. should or should not withdraw from the U.N. is *not* a principle; his view on whether a nation should or should not protect its sovereignty *is* a principle, which covers many issues besides the U.N.

Since it is only by means of principles that men can judge the alternatives confronting them and project their future, a political campaign conducted in terms of concretes means a candidate's demand for a blank check on power. A parliamentary form of government cannot function successfully nor for long in a society that loses or rejects its understanding of basic principles.

The nature and source of today's intellectual and political disintegration can best be illustrated by the following incident. A liberal journalist told me recently that his liberal friends regard him as a conservative because, in a few specific instances, he has opposed the growth of government power. "Do you mean," I asked him, "that the liberals admit that a pro-government-power stand is the *explicit* criterion of their political position?" "Oh, no," he answered, "they would never say that!

They merely support the extension of government power in one particular issue after another."

This is the method by which the world is being destroyed—the means by which men permit themselves to perpetrate atrocities without having to know what they are doing.

This is the psychology of men who scream, when a country collapses into dictatorship: "I'm not to blame! I merely wanted the government to control prices, wages, profits, industry, science, health, art, education, television and the press! I never advocated a dictatorship!"

This is the ultimate product of the philosophy of Pragmatism: the psycho-epistemological savage who believes that reality is indeterminate, that facts are fluid, that A will not be A so long as he refuses to identify it, that concretes will not add up to a sum if he rejects abstractions and principles.

Do you remember James Taggart? "This was the way he had lived all his life—keeping his eyes stubbornly, safely on the immediate pavement before him, craftily avoiding the sight of his road, of corners, of distances, of pinnacles. He had never intended going anywhere . . . he had never wanted his years to add up to any sum—what had summed them up?—why had he reached some unchosen destination where one could no longer stand still or retreat?" (*Atlas Shrugged*)

It is by such intellectuals and by their series of single, concrete, disintegrated steps that the United States is being pushed toward an unchosen destination: toward socialist-fascist statism.

The degree of evasion required to permit modern intellectuals not to see their ultimate goal—in the light of the historical evidence of the past fifty years—is almost inconceivable. It is Pragmatism that has made it semi-possible for them, by granting them permission to be *unprincipled on principle*.

I say "semi-possible," because two facts contradict the "sincerity" of their intellectual blank-out, indicating that they *do* know and *do* see in some horrid, subconscious, subverbal manner: (a) the hysterical intensity of their refusal to integrate their piecemeal goals, to identify their direction in *conceptual* terms, and the howling torrent of abuse which they unleash against anyone who does so; (b) the consistency of their unnamed, unadmitted policy: the fact that in any given issue, with exceedingly rare exceptions, they are on the side of greater government power.

Their "instincts" are right in one respect: the issue of freedom vs. statism—or individual rights vs. government controls, or capitalism vs. socialism—*is* the basic issue of political philosophy. It is *the* root, *the* start, *the* fundamental which is involved in every specific measure, by which all else is determined, by the side of which all other considerations are trivia.

It is the basic—and, today, the only—issue by which a candidate must be judged: freedom vs. statism.

If a candidate evades, equivocates and hides his stand under a junk-heap of random concretes, we must add up those concretes and judge him accordingly. If his stand is mixed, we must evaluate it by asking: Will he protect freedom or destroy the last of it? Will he accelerate, delay or stop the march toward statism?

By this standard, one can see why Barry Goldwater is the best candidate in the field today.

No, he is not an advocate of laissez-faire capitalism—this is one of the contradictions in his stand. Like all of today's political figures, he is the advocate of a mixed economy. But the difference between him and the others is this: they believe that some (undefined) element of freedom is compatible with government controls; he believes that some (undefined) government controls are compatible with freedom. Freedom is his *major* premise.

In his book, *The Conscience of a Conservative*, he wrote: "I have little interest in streamlining government or in making it more efficient, for I mean to reduce its size. I do not undertake to promote welfare, for I propose to extend freedom. My aim is not to pass laws, but to repeal them . . . And if I should later be attacked for neglecting my constituents' 'interests,' I shall reply that I was informed their main interest is liberty . . ."

In his address to the Economic Club of New York, on January 15, 1964, he said: "I would, also, seek to find for the federal government more of a role in removing restrictions than in imposing new ones — at every level of the economy... No matter the detail, I stand on the side of such principles. I stand on the side of individual responsibility and individual choice and creativity. I stand against the gray sameness of growing government, against the conformity of collectivism — no matter the excuses it uses."

This stand outweighs the lesser flaws of his campaign (and of his book). Some of his specific steps may be wrong; his direction is right.

In an age of moral collapse, like the present, men who seek power for power's sake rise to leadership everywhere on earth and destroy one country after another. Barry Goldwater is singularly devoid of power lust. Even his antagonists admit it with grudging respect. He is seeking, not to rule, but to liberate a country.

In a world ravaged by dictatorships, can we afford to pass up a candidate of that kind?

There are many smaller issues with which one has to disagree in Sen. Goldwater's domestic policy (most of them stemming from his mixed economy position), many regrettable contradictions which undercut the effectiveness of his case for free enterprise. But in his foreign policy he stands out as a giant against this country's disgraceful record of the past three decades.

That the United States of America should be brought down to a level where it is being insulted and defied by *Panama*, belongs in a nightmare version of a farce by Gilbert and Sullivan — and makes it unnecessary to debate the merits of our foreign policy or the competence of those bi-partisan statesmen whose efforts have led to this climax. When Barry Goldwater keeps stressing the theme of "national honor," it is the first and only sound of hope — the sound of a human step — in the truly unbelievable abyss of a great nation's gratuitous, suicidal self-abasement.

At a time when most of our political leaders keep apologizing for America's greatness to the bloodiest communist thugs from every rat hole of the globe, and keep draining her wealth to support her enemies — can we reject a candidate who, with profound pride, asserts America's self-interest and self-esteem?

Now consider Sen. Goldwater's chief competitor for the Republican presidential nomination.

The worst thing one can say about Gov. Rockefeller is that he seems to be "sincere." He has absorbed the liberals' pragmatic, concrete-bound mentality to such an extent that he does not even have the good grace to be evasive about it: he is aggressively self-righteous. His political position may be described as "the extreme, militant middle."

Consider the full meaning of the fact that he has repudiated the support of all those voters whose political convictions are to the right of his own — all opponents of the welfare state, all advocates of capitalism — lumping them together under the smear-label of "the radical right lunatic fringe." Consider the depth of moral, ideological and political ignorance implicit in that action.

A candidate does *not* have to agree with all those who vote for him — *they* have to agree with him (at least to a limited extent). It is his function to offer a program — *theirs* is only to accept or reject it at the polls. Under a two-party system, any candidate will necessarily have an enormously mixed following. To judge a candidate, not by his own views, but by the views of his followers — over whose irrationality, inconsistency, stupidity or dishonesty he has no control, whose contradictory demands he could not possibly reconcile — is worse than unjust: it is absurdly evil. It is a repudiation of the entire concept of national elections and parliamentary government.

A voter's choice does not commit him to a total agreement with a candidate — and certainly cannot commit a candidate to an agreement with every voter who supports him. Under a two-party system, a voter's choice is and has to be merely an approximation — a choice of the candidate whom he regards as closer to his own views; often, particularly in recent time, a voter chooses merely the lesser of two evils.

If a candidate disagrees with some group, he is free to say so. But to attack, to smear and to repudiate the support of any legitimate group means to disfranchise its members, since they have no other party to vote for and since they cannot, in honor, vote for a man who slaps their faces.

If a candidate were to be judged by and held responsible for the views of every voter who joined his side, no man of integrity would ever enter a political campaign: a man of integrity does not give to others a blank check on his own convictions or an ideological power-of-attorney. And more: on such a premise, no writer, speaker, teacher or philosopher, no man propagating ideas, could ever enter public life.

It is not astonishing that this premise is being spread by modern liberals. And it is not astonishing that liberal Republicans have fallen for it, among their many other acts of abject "me-too'ing."

Richard Nixon, who postures as a crusader against communism, repudiated the support of some "rightist" groups — whose worst sin allegedly was an over-zealous opposition to communism — during his California campaign of 1962, which he lost, as he deserved to, regardless of whether one approves or disapproves of those particular groups. Gov. Rockefeller did it wholesale.

This policy, strictly speaking, is not "me-too'ing," since the Democrats have not employed it against any potential followers of their own. It is worse than "me-too'ing": it is an attempt to be more liberal than the liberals or "more royalist than the king."

What, exactly, is the evil of the so-called "radical right?" As that sloppy term is used today, the "radical right" may be accused of including ignorant, small-town groups of fanatics. But political ignorance and fanaticism are hardly the monopoly of the "right." The worst element associated with some "rightists" is crackpot groups of racists. But the main, active body of racists in this country, who not merely preach, but practice and enforce race persecutions by political means, is in the South and belongs to the Democratic Party. We have not heard the Democratic leadership repudiate their votes. Why don't the liberal intellectuals, the mainstay of the Democratic Party, demand such a repudiation?

It is obvious that the smear campaign against the "radical right" is a booby-trap set by the liberals to disfranchise all antagonists of the welfare state and to destroy the Republican Party as a vehicle of political opposition.

Gov. Rockefeller's attack on the "radical right" was a smear because he failed to specify what he meant by that label or to define what political principles it subsumed.

In a TV interview, "Meet the Press," on September 15, 1963, Gov. Rockefeller kept stressing his concern with the Republican Party's need to clarify "basic principles" and "basic national purposes." When pressed to define what he meant by "the radical right," he answered: "Such positions as abandonment of the income tax.... Another one is rolling back the social progress of this nation, the social gains." And, after more prodding by questioners, he elaborated: "The best illustration was what happened at the Young Republican Convention in San Francisco a number of months ago, where a man was elected, a Young Republican was elected on a platform to abolish the income tax, to withdraw from the United Nations, I don't know whether he included impeachment of Earl Warren, but that is part of this whole concept, and the idea that General Eisenhower was a crypto-communist."

This, believe it or not, is what Gov. Rockefeller regards as *basic principles* (!).

"Concrete-bound" is too mild a term for an epistemological and ethical method of this kind.

About fifty per cent of the American people believe one or more of the above listed items. And *these* are the beliefs which

(continued on page 12)

BOOKS

*The Tyranny of Testing** by Banesh Hoffman

Reviewed by **JOAN BLUMENTHAL**

A young man planning a career in medicine applied for admission to the Bronx High School of Science, the finest scientific high school in the United States. He was given a routine multiple-choice entrance test — and was rejected. After spending a year at an inferior school, he reapplied, was admitted, and graduated in the top 10 percent of his class.

He next sought a New York State Regents Scholarship to finance his premedical studies. Again, he was given a multiple-choice test — and was rejected. Without the scholarship, he worked his way through premedical school, and graduated, winning his college's most coveted award.

He then applied for a New York State Regents Scholarship to finance his medical studies. He was given a multiple-choice test — and was rejected. On the basis of his scholastic achievements, however, he was admitted to an outstanding medical school.

This three-time loser in multiple-choice contests proved that he had the ability the qualifying tests repeatedly failed to uncover. He was fortunate enough to achieve his goal despite them. One can only speculate on the number of careers thwarted by tests which claim the power to predict a candidate's success or failure.

There are few Americans growing into adulthood today whose careers will not be subject to the dictates of the multiple-choice test. This type of test is used to assess the character, personality, aptitudes and knowledge of examinees ranging from kindergarten children to vice presidents of industry. At stake are student promotions, college admissions, scholarship awards, employment and professional advancement. The number of multiple-choice tests administered annually in the United States is not known. A *New York Times* estimate placed the figure for 1960 at almost 130 million. It is still growing.

In *The Tyranny of Testing*, Dr. Banesh Hoffman, physicist and professor of mathematics, denounces the wide-spread use of multiple-choice tests, on the grounds that they discriminate against the candidate of unusual intellectual ability.

The victim, says Dr. Hoffman, is the candidate who is "strong-minded, non-conformist, unusual, original or creative." Such a candidate is frustrated by the very nature of the tests: he is required to answer questions by choosing one of a number of given alternatives, and receives credit only if he selects the answer declared "correct" by the test-maker; he must choose among prefabricated formulations, none of which may be exact, and is given no opportunity to demonstrate the reasoning that lies behind his choices. The author observes: "The more profoundly gifted the candidate is, the more his resentment will rise against the mental strait jacket into which the testers would force his mind."

This intellectual victimization is made possible by the non-objectivity of these so-called "objective" examinations. Multiple-choice tests are called "objective" because the questions allegedly deal with factual material allowing of only one correct answer. In fact, as Dr. Hoffman demonstrates, multiple-choice tests "degenerate into subjective guessing games" in which the candidate — particularly the more discerning candidate — must try to read the mind of the test-maker and determine his intent.

---

*Published by Crowell-Collier Press, $3.95. Available from NBI BOOK SERVICE, 120 East 34th St., New York 16, N. Y. for $3.35. (N.Y.C. residents add 4% sales tax; outside the U.S. add 15¢).

Joan Blumenthal has done graduate work in art history at New York University. Her paintings have been exhibited in Los Angeles, Winnipeg, Toronto and New York.

The author cites this example:

Emperor is the name of
(A) a string quartet
(B) a piano concerto
(C) a violin sonata

The candidate with average musical knowledge quickly selects answer B, having in mind Beethoven's *Emperor Concerto*. But the candidate with greater musical knowledge knows that answer A is also correct: there is an *Emperor Quartet* by Haydn. The knowledgeable candidate is apparently faced with the choice between two correct answers; he is actually faced with the choice between two estimates of the test-maker: either the test-maker is ignorant or maliciously tricky.

This situation is by no means unique. So often is there no single, unequivocally correct choice, that teachers preparing students for these "multiple-guess" tests advise: "When in doubt, don't think — just pick."

In one of the most shocking sections of his book, Dr. Hoffman reports on the method by which these "objective" tests are "validated." This method is so absurd that it imposes a considerable strain on the mind attempting to grasp it. It is most simply described by means of a specific illustration: in screening applicants for medical school, for example, the testers will attempt to determine which candidates possess the qualities "necessary" for success in medicine. (The qualities considered "necessary" are based on psychologists' observations of successful doctors.) If successful doctors are said to possess quality X, the testers will prepare a multiple-choice question intended to reveal whether or not the candidate has this quality. The question, with alternative answers, is then pre-tested on successful doctors. If a majority of them select answer Y, then it becomes the "wanted" answer — the evidence of the possession of quality X. The question is "revalidated" over a period of years: as long as the majority of those who become successful doctors are those who predominantly selected answer Y when they were candidates for medical school, the question remains "valid" and answer Y remains the "wanted" answer.

Given such a "validation" procedure, there is nothing to prevent the "wanted" answer from being untrue. Using an extreme, but logically possible example, Dr. Hoffman illustrates this point: if "90 percent of the freshmen who earn high grades believe that Shakespeare wrote *Omlet* and not *King Lear*, then the 'best' answer will simply have to be *Omlet*, and that is that." And worse: when an exceptional student rejects the "wanted" answer in favor of one which is correct, but requires specialized knowledge, while 99.9 percent pick another answer, "statistics will damn him overwhelmingly."

The mental processes forced upon the candidate by this method of testing are perceptively described by Dr. Hoffman: the candidate must try to pick the answer "he believes most of the best candidates will pick, and mind you, he must pick not the answer he thinks they will honestly believe to be the best, but the answer he thinks they themselves will be guessing that the other best candidates will guess that they themselves will guess."

In this tortuous mental process Objectivists will recognize the psycho-epistemology of the accomplished social metaphysician.

In his article, "Social Metaphysics" (THE OBJECTIVIST NEWSLETTER, November, 1962), Mr. Branden defined this neurosis as "the psychological syndrome that characterizes an individual who holds the consciousnesses of other men, not objective reality, as his ultimate psycho-epistemological frame-of-reference." In rewarding the candidates who conform to the opinions of a certain majority, multiple-choice testers sanction

(continued on page 12)

How to Judge (from page 10)

Gov. Rockefeller considers "every bit as dangerous to American principles and American institutions as the radical left" (*i.e.*, as communism).

Another eloquent symptom of Mr. Rockefeller's mentality is his repeated insistence that the "radical right" is a small minority which deserves no consideration because it stands outside "the mainstream of American thought." A "mainstream of *thought*" is a crudely collectivistic concept, which can have only one meaning: the intellectual *status quo*. Mr. Rockefeller—who likes to assume the posture of an intellectual — does not seem to have grasped the fact that every innovator or non-conformist stands outside the intellectual *status quo* of any given moment.

It would be enlightening to observe the results, if young people who attend Rockefeller rallies were to begin asking that self-proclaimed champion of minority rights: "What about *intellectual* minorities, Mr. Rockefeller?"

There is one particular item of Barry Goldwater's position with which I explicitly and emphatically disagree: his appeal for "party unity," his insistence that Republicans must support *any* candidate nominated by the convention. It is impossible for any honest advocate of capitalism to vote for Gov. Rockefeller: he has read us out of the party and out of the nation. It is impossible to sanction him as a champion of individualism and free enterprise. It is precisely in the name of "party loyalty" that those who are Republicans must oppose him: his nomination would destroy the Republican Party's significance, its role as an *opposition party;* his election would deliver the country into the power of a single party with two indistinguishable branches.

There are many forms of protest open to us, if Gov. Rockefeller gets the Republican nomination: we can vote for a write-in candidate of our own choice — or vote a straight Republican ticket, leaving the presidential and vice-presidential spaces blank — or vote a mixed ticket — or vote for any Democrat who is not fully committed to statism — or not vote at all. But we cannot vote for the proposition that we, as advocates of capitalism, are lunatics — or for the candidate who so regards us.

Barry Goldwater is the first Republican candidate in over three decades who has not shown any inclination toward "me-too'ism." The difficulty of his campaign is that he has to educate his audiences, to teach them the meaning and nature of free enterprise, as he goes along. It is an almost unbearable double burden, an almost impossible task at which he is not too expert, particularly since he is not an advocate of full capitalism. He is a man of action, a first-rate political fighter, but not a theoretician or a teacher.

An election campaign is not the cause, but the effect and the product of a culture's intellectual trends. It is, perhaps, too early to fight for capitalism on the level of practical politics, in a culture devoid of any intellectual base for capitalism. The only element that Sen. Goldwater can count on is the subconscious basic premises (the "sense of life") of the American people, which are strongly individualist and anti-collectivist. But subconscious premises are precarious, unpredictable factors which, through ignorance, may seek expression in their own opposite. It is regrettable that his theoretical advisers are not up to his courageous attempt.

His battle can serve as an object lesson to those young people who declare, in effect, that "ideas and education are all very well, but we want *action*, political action." They can observe the problems of a political campaign without a firm ideological base. Sen Goldwater has undertaken a heroic task; they ought to help him. The best way to help is by fighting the smears and misrepresentations of his position — by acting as volunteer interpreters and clarifiers at any opportunity they can find, by filling in the theoretical information which his audiences need and lack.

Whether he wins or loses, it is not the last battle for capitalism, but the first — or, rather, the first, somewhat experimental, step in the direction of its return.

The Tyranny of Testing (from page 11)

those who substitute this aberration for the thinking process.

Although Dr. Hoffman calls multiple-choice tests "subjective," he does not explicitly indict them on philosophical grounds. Yet, it is the wide acceptance of philosophical subjectivism in our culture that makes such a phenomenon possible. When subjectivists reject reason and logic as the criteria of knowledge, they open the door to epistemological collectivism — the position that truth is determined by majority opinion.

The Tyranny of Testing is a remarkable study of the insidious operation of statistically-validated tests. In education, in business, in the professions, the result of this institutionalized subjectivism is the entrenchment of mediocrity. Perhaps this is also its purpose.

OBJECTIVIST CALENDAR

■ On February 16, Ayn Rand began a new series of radio broadcasts for the Columbia University station WKCR (89.9 FM). The series is entitled "Ayn Rand on Campus," and is broadcast every other Sunday, at 7 P.M.

■ On March 16, Nathaniel Branden will address the Graduate Students Association of the University of California, Los Angeles. His subject: "The Political Philosophy of Ayn Rand." Time: 12 noon. Place: Student Union Building, U.C.L.A., Los Angeles. Open to the public, admission free.

■ Beginning on March 30, in New York City, Nathaniel Branden will give public readings of three plays by Ayn Rand. March 30: *The Night of January 16th* (original version). April 6: *Ideal.* April 13: *Think Twice.* Time: 7:30 P.M. Place: Hotel Roosevelt. Advance series tickets may be purchased from NATHANIEL BRANDEN INSTITUTE (120 E. 34 St., N. Y. 16) by mail only; price: $9. Tickets for individual plays will be available at the door; $3.50 per play.

■ On March 9, NBI's Tape Transcription Division began "Basic Principles of Objectivism" in Los Angeles. On March 16, Nathaniel Branden will be in Los Angeles and will deliver lecture #2 of this course in person.

■ In addition, NBI's Tape Transcription Division has scheduled the following starting dates: "Basic Principles of Objectivism" in Columbus, Ohio, February 7; Buena Park, California, March 13; and San Fernando Valley, March 30. "Basic Principles of Objectivist Psychology" in Miami, February 27. "A Critical Analysis of Contemporary Psychology" in San Francisco, April 6. "The Economics of a Free Society" in Chicago, April 3; Washington, D.C., April 13. For details, contact NBI.

■ New American Library published the first printing of the paperback edition of *For the New Intellectual* — 200,000 copies — this past December. In February, it issued the third printing.

—B.B.

Published monthly at 120 East 34th Street, New York 16, N. Y.
Subscription rate: in United States, its possessions, Canada and Mexico, $5 for one year; other countries, $6.
Additional copies of this Newsletter: single copy 50¢ (coins, not stamps); 10 — 99 copies, 25¢ each plus postage (for first-class delivery add 1¢ per copy, for third-class delivery add ½¢ per copy); 100 or more copies, 15¢ each plus postage (same as above).
For change of address send old address and new address with zone number if any. Allow us three weeks to process new subscriptions and change of address.

Ayn Rand and Nathaniel Branden, Editors and Publishers
Barbara Branden, Managing Editor
Elayne Kalberman, Circulation Manager

THE OBJECTIVIST NEWSLETTER

Edited and Published by AYN RAND and NATHANIEL BRANDEN

VOL. 3 NO. 4   APRIL, 1964

CHECK YOUR PREMISES
By AYN RAND

The Property Status of Airwaves

Any material element or resource which, in order to become of use or value to men, requires the application of human knowledge and effort, should be private property — by the right of those who apply the knowledge and effort.

This is particularly true of broadcasting frequencies or waves, because they are produced by human action and do not exist without it. What exists in nature is only the potential and the medium through which those waves must travel. (That medium is not air; in legal discussions it is often referred to by the mythical term of "ether" — to indicate some element in space, at present unidentified.) Without the broadcasting station which generates the waves, that "ether" — on our present level of knowledge — is of no practical use or value to anyone.

Just as two trains cannot travel on the same section of track at the same time, so two broadcasts cannot use the same frequency at the same time in the same area without "jamming" each other. There is no difference in principle between the ownership of land and the ownership of airways. The only issue is the task of defining the application of property rights to this particular sphere. It is on this task that the American government has failed dismally, with incalculably disastrous consequences.

There is no essential difference between a broadcast and a concert: the former merely transmits sounds over a longer distance and requires more complex technical equipment. No one would venture to claim that a pianist may own his fingers and his piano, but the space inside the concert hall — through which the sound waves he produces travel — is "public property" and, therefore, he has no right to give a concert without a license from the government. Yet this is the absurdity foisted on our broadcasting industry.

The chief argument in support of the notion that broadcasting frequencies should be "public property" has been stated succinctly by Justice Frankfurter: "[Radio] facilities are limited; they are not available to all who may wish to use them; the radio spectrum simply is not large enough to accommodate everybody. There is a fixed natural limitation upon the number of stations that can operate without interfering with one another."

The fallacy of this argument is obvious. The number of broadcasting frequencies *is* limited; so is the number of concert halls; so is the amount of oil or wheat or diamonds; so is the acreage of land on the surface of the globe. There is no material element or value that exists in *unlimited* quantity. And if a "wish" to use a certain "facility" is the criterion of the right to use it, then the universe is simply not large enough to accommodate all those who harbor wishes for the unearned.

It is the proper task of the government to protect individual rights and, as part of it, to formulate the laws by which these rights are to be implemented and adjudicated. It is the government's responsibility to define the application of individual rights to a given sphere of activity — to *define* (*i.e.*, to identify), *not* to create, invent, donate or expropriate. The question of defining the application of property rights has arisen frequently, in the wake of major scientific discoveries or inventions, such as the question of oil rights, vertical space rights, etc. In most cases, the American government was guided by the proper principle: it sought to protect all the individual rights involved, *not* to abrogate them.

A notable example of the proper method of establishing private ownership from scratch, in a previously ownerless area, is the Homestead Act of 1862, by which the government opened the Western frontier for settlement and turned "public land" over to private owners. The government offered a 160-acres farm to any adult citizen who would settle on it and cultivate it for five years, after which it would become his property. Although that land was originally regarded, in law, as "public property," the method of its allocation, *in fact*, followed the proper principle (*in fact*, but not in explicit ideological intention). The citizens did not have to *pay* the government as if it were an owner; ownership began with *them*, and they earned it by the method which is the source and root of the concept of "property": by working on unused material resources, by turning a wilderness into a civilized settlement. Thus, the government, in this case, was acting not as the owner but as the *custodian* of ownerless resources who defines objectively impartial rules by which potential owners may acquire them.

This should have been the principle and pattern of the allocation of broadcasting frequencies.

As soon as it became apparent that radio broadcasting had opened a new realm of material resources which, in the absence of legal definitions, would become a wilderness of clashing individual claims, the government should have promulgated the equivalent of a Homestead Act of the airways — an act defining private property rights in the new realm, establishing the rule that the user of a radio frequency would own it after he had operated a station for a certain number of years, and allocating all frequencies by the rule of priority, *i.e.*, "first come, first served."

Bear in mind that the development of commercial radio took many years of struggle and experimentation, and that the goldrush of the "wishers" did not start until the pioneers — who had taken the risks of venturing into the unknown — had built it into a bright promise of great commercial value. By what right, code or standard was anyone entitled to that value except the men who had created it?

If the government had adhered to the principle of private property rights, and the pioneers' ownership had been legally established, then a latecomer who wished to acquire a radio station would have had to *buy* it from one of the original owners (as is the case with every other type of property). The fact that the number of available frequencies was limited would have served, not to entrench the original owners, but to threaten their hold, if they did not make the best economic use of their property (which is what free competition does to every other type of property). With a limited supply and a growing demand, competition would have driven the market value of a radio (and later, TV) station so high that only the most competent men could have afforded to buy it or to keep it; a man unable to make a profit, could not have long afforded to waste so valuable a property. Who, on a free market, determines the economic success or failure of an enterprise? The *public* (the public as a sum of individual producers, viewers and listeners, each making his own decisions – *not* as a single, helpless, disembodied *collective* with a few bureaucrats posturing as the spokesmen of its will on earth).

Contrary to the "argument from scarcity," if you want to make a "limited" resource available to the whole people, make it private property and throw it on a free, open market.

The "argument from scarcity," incidentally, is outdated, even in its literal meaning: with the discovery of ultra-high frequencies, there are more broadcasting channels available today than prospective applicants willing to pioneer in their development. As usual, the "wishers" seek, not to create, but to take over the rewards and advantages created by others.

The history of the collectivization of radio and television demonstrates, in condensed form, in a kind of microcosm, the process and the causes of capitalism's destruction. It is an eloquent illustration of the fact that capitalism is perishing by the philosophical default of its alleged defenders.

Collectivists frequently cite the early years of radio as an example of the failure of free enterprise. In those years, when broadcasters had no property rights in radio, no legal protection or recourse, the airways were a chaotic no-man's land where anyone could use any frequency he pleased and jam anyone else. Some professional broadcasters tried to divide their frequencies by private agreements, which they could not enforce on others; nor could they fight the interference of stray, maliciously mischievous amateurs. This state of affairs was used, then and now, to urge and justify government control of radio.

This is an instance of capitalism taking the blame for the evils of its enemies.

The chaos of the airways was an example, not of free enterprise, but of *anarchy*. It was caused, not by private property rights, but by their absence. It demonstrated why capitalism is incompatible with anarchism, why men do need a government and what is a government's proper function. What was needed was *legality,* not *controls.*

What was imposed was worse than controls: outright nationalization. By a gradual, uncontested process — by ideological default — it was taken for granted that the airways belong to "the people" and are "public property."

If you want to know the intellectual state of the time, I will ask you to guess the political ideology of the author of the following quotation:

"Radio communication is not to be considered as merely a business carried on for private gain, for private advertisement, or for entertainment of the curious. It is a public concern impressed with the public trust and to be considered primarily from the standpoint of public interest in the same extent and upon the basis of the same general principles as our other public utilities."

No, this was not said by a business-hating collectivist eager to establish the supremacy of the "public interest" over "private gain"; it was not said by a socialist planner nor by a communist conspirator; it was said by Herbert Hoover, then Secretary of Commerce, in 1924.

It was Hoover who fought for government control of radio and, as Secretary of Commerce, made repeated attempts to extend government power beyond the limits set by the legislation of the time, attempts to attach detailed conditions to radio licenses, which he had no legal authority to do and which were repeatedly negated by the courts. It was Hoover's influence that was largely responsible for that tombstone of the radio (and the then unborn television) industry known as the Act of 1927, which established the Federal Radio Commission with all of its autocratic, discretionary, undefined and undefinable powers. (That Act — with minor revisions and amendments, including the Act of 1934 that changed the Federal Radio Commission into the Federal Communications Commission — is still, in all essential respects, the basic legal document ruling the broadcasting industry today.)

"What we are doing," said F.C.C. Chairman Newton N. Minow in 1962, "did not begin with the New Frontier." He was right.

The Act of 1927 did not confine the government to the role of a traffic policeman of the air who protects the rights of broadcasters from technical interference (which is all that was needed and all that a government should properly do). It established service to the "public interest, convenience or necessity" as the criterion by which the Federal Radio Commission was to judge applicants for broadcasting licenses and accept or reject them. Since there is no such thing as the "public interest" (other than the sum of the individual interests of individual citizens), since that collectivist catch-phrase has never been and can never be defined, it amounted to a blank check on totalitarian power over the broadcasting industry, granted to whatever bureaucrats happened to be appointed to the Commission.

"The public interest" — that intellectual knife of collectivism's sacrificial guillotine which the operators of broadcasting stations have to test by placing their heads on the block every three years — was not raised over their heads by capitalism's enemies, but by their own leaders.

It was the so-called "conservatives" — including some of the pioneers, some of the broadcasting industry's executives who, today, are complaining and protesting — who ran to the government for regulations and controls, who cheered the notion of "public property" and service to the "public interest," and thus planted the seeds of which Mr. Minow and Mr. Henry are merely the logical, consistent flowers. The broadcasting industry was enslaved with the sanction of the victims — but they were not fully innocent victims.

Many businessmen, of the "mixed economy" persuasion, resent the actual nature of capitalism; they believe that it is safer to hold a position, not by right, but by favor; they dread the competition of a free market and they feel that a bureaucrat's friendship is much easier to win. Pull, not merit, is their form of "social security." They believe that they will always succeed at courting, pressuring or bribing a bureaucrat, who is "a good fellow" they can "get along with" and who will protect them from that merciless stranger: the abler competitor.

Consider the special privileges to be found in the status of a certified servant of the "public interest" and a licensed user of "public property." Not only does it place a man outside the reach of economic competition, but it also spares him the responsibility and *the costs* entailed in private property. It grants him *gratuitously* the use of a broadcasting frequency for which he would have had to pay an enormous price on a free market and would not have been able to keep for long, if he sent forth through the "ether" the kind of unconscionable trash he is sending forth today.

Such are the vested interests made possible by the doctrine of the "public interest" — and such are the beneficiaries of any form, version or degree of the doctrine of "public property."

Now observe the practical demonstration of the fact that without property rights, no other rights are possible. If censorship and the suppression of free speech ever get established in this country, they will have originated in radio and television.

The Act of 1927 granted to a government Commission total power over the professional fate of broadcasters, with the "public interest" as the criterion of judgment — and, simultaneously, forbade the Commission to censor radio programs. From the start, and progressively louder through the years, many voices have been pointing out that this is a contradiction impossible to practice. If a commissioner has to judge which applicant for a broadcasting license will best serve the "public interest," how can he judge it without judging the content, nature and value of the programs the applicants have offered or will offer?

If capitalism had had any proper intellectual defenders, it
(continued on page 16)

INTELLECTUAL AMMUNITION DEPARTMENT

[*Subscribers are invited to send in the questions that they find themselves unable to answer in philosophical or political discussions. As many questions as space permits will be answered. No questions will be answered by mail.*]

■ **With regard to the principle that man is a being of volitional consciousness, does not a man have to be thinking already in order to "choose" to think?**

The primary choice to think — *i.e.*, to focus one's mind, to set it to the purpose of active integration — must be distinguished from any other category of choice. It must be distinguished from the decision to think about a particular subject, which depends on one's values, interests, knowledge and context; and it must be distinguished from the decision to perform a particular physical action, which again depends on one's values, interests, knowledge and context. These decisions involve causal antecedents, of a kind which the choice to focus does not. A man's choice to focus is a primary, a *first cause* in consciousness. (See my articles on volition and determinism in the January 1963 and the May 1962 issues of this NEWSLETTER.)

The principle that man is a being of volitional consciousness has reference, specifically, to the *human* form of consciousness — *i.e.*, to the *conceptual* level of awareness. The perceptual level, which man shares with animals, is automatic. To be aware of the physical concretes of his immediate sensory field, man merely has to be awake (assuming, of course, a normal brain state). But to engage in an active process of cognitive integration—to abstract, conceptualize, relate, infer—to *reason* — man must *focus* his mind, he must *set* it to the task of active integrating. This level of awareness must be achieved and maintained volitionally.

The act of focusing pertains to the *operation* of the faculty of consciousness, to its method of functioning — *not* to its *content*.

To understand the process of focusing, one must understand the concept of "level of awareness." This concept refers to the degree of *active cognitive integration* in which a mind is engaged. This will be reflected in (a) the clarity or vagueness of the mind's contents, (b) the degree to which the mind's activity involves abstractions or is concrete-bound, (c) the degree to which the relevant wider context is present or absent in the process of thinking. Thus, there are *degrees* of awareness, *degrees* of consciousness; the alternative is not simply absolute unconsciousness or optimal consciousness.

The choice to focus (or to think) does not consist of moving from a state of literal unconsciousness to a state of consciousness. This clearly would be impossible. When one is asleep, one cannot suddenly choose to start thinking. To focus is to move from a *lower* level of consciousness to a *higher* level — to move from mental passivity to purposeful mental activity — to initiate a process of directed cognitive integration.

In a state of passive (or relatively passive) awareness, a man can apprehend the need to be in full mental focus. His choice is to evade that knowledge or to exert the effort of raising the level of his awareness.

As focusing involves expanding the range of one's awareness, so evasion consists of the reverse process: of *shrinking* the range of one's awareness. Evasion takes the form of refusing to raise the level of one's awareness, when one knows (clearly or dimly) that one should — or of *lowering* the level of one's awareness, when one knows that one shouldn't.

When a man acts and functions with his mind unfocused, we may, in certain contexts, refer to him as "unconscious." This is a means of indicating that such a man is existing on a level of awareness inadequate to the requirements of human survival — *i.e.*, he is attempting to exist in a state inadequate to the cognition of reality which human survival requires — he is attempting, in effect, to exist on the passive, perceptual level that is appropriate to a lower animal. But this is a specialized use of the term "unconscious."

Speaking literally, of course, when a man is awake and his brain and nervous system are structurally normal, he is conscious — if only passively. This basic level of consciousness is given to him by nature, as it were. Volition pertains to the responsibility of raising this basic level to the active, conceptual level, which is biologically appropriate to *man*.

— NATHANIEL BRANDEN

■ **In the context of the Objectivist ethics, what is the justification for knowingly risking one's life?**

The Objectivist ethics holds "man's life" or "the life appropriate to a rational being" as its standard of value. But this does *not* mean that, in any value-choice, one's only or foremost concern should be immediate, physical self-preservation. Such a policy would be *incompatible* with the standard of man's life.

Life is a process of self-sustaining and self-generated action. The life proper to man is a process of pursuing, achieving and enjoying values — the values which his life as a rational being requires. The pursuit of values entails a *struggle* — and struggle entails *risk*. The pursuit of values necessarily involves the possibility of failure and defeat. A rational man does not rebel against this fact — nor against any *metaphysical* fact of reality. To choose to act for one's values only when no risk is involved, is to forsake values; and to forsake values is to forsake life. A rational man does not venture senselessly, he does not attempt the impossible, he does not indulge in grandiose, empty gestures that can result only in his destruction — but, when crucial values are at stake, he accepts the fact that the risk of his life itself may be necessary.

Thus, the man who consciously and willingly risks his life in the attempt to escape a dictatorship, the man who dies in the effort to achieve freedom — *is* acting on the principle of man's life as the standard of value. He knows what *human* existence is — and he will not accept anything less. He is unwilling to endure and regard as normal a non-human state of being: a state where men act and function with a gun aimed at their heads, with destruction aimed at their values, and with escape from death, not the achievement of life, as the best they can hope for. It is in the name of the life proper to man that a rational person may be willing to die — not as treason to his life, but as the only act of loyalty possible to him.

The man who makes terms with the rulers of a dictatorship, the man who delivers his wife and closest friends to destruction, in exchange for being allowed to survive — does *not* hold man's life as his standard of value. His motive is terror of dying, not passion for living. He is willing to sacrifice every value he had ever found, he is willing to live *without* values — and to surrender that which had been their root: his mind, his independence, his judgment, his love — in order to gain the "security" of a caged animal.

"Man's life" and "value" are very wide abstractions. For each individual man, the value of life is experienced through the *particular* values he has chosen. They constitute the source of his enjoyment of life — and that enjoyment is the emotional fuel that keeps him moving. (See my article on "The Psychology of Pleasure" in the February 1964 issue of this NEWSLETTER.) The greatest of these values are work and love. Such values can be irreplaceable; that is, once holding them, a man may have no desire to live without them. For this reason, a rational man might willingly risk death to save the life of the woman he loves — because the value of life, to him, has become inextricably tied to her existence.

The man who, in any and all circumstances, would place

his physical self-preservation above any other value, is not a lover of life, but an abject traitor to life — to the *human* mode of life — who sees no difference between the life proper to a rational being and the life of a mindless vegetable. His treason is not that he values his life too much, but that he values it *too little*.

Quoting Francisco d'Anconia, "To love a thing is to know and love its nature." To love life is to know and love the nature of life. Since life is a process of self-sustaining action, this means: to love the *process* of self-sustaining action — to love the thought, the effort, the struggle, the challenges that such action entails.

— NATHANIEL BRANDEN

The Property Status of Airwaves (from page 14)

is they who should have been loudest in opposing a contradiction of that kind. But such was not the case: it was the *statists* who seized upon it, not in defense of free speech, but in support of the Commission's *"right"* to censor programs. And, so long as the criterion of the "public interest" stood unchallenged, logic was on the side of the statists.

The result was what it had to be (illustrating once more the power of basic principles): by gradual, unobtrusive, progressively accelerating steps, the Commission enlarged its control over the content of radio and television programs — leading up to the open threats and ultimatums of Mr. Minow, who merely made explicit what had been known implicitly for many years. No, the Commission did not censor specific programs: it merely took cognizance of program content at license-renewal time. What was established was worse than open censorship (which could be knocked out in a court of law): it was the unprovable, intangible, insidious *censorship-by-displeasure* — the usual, and only, result of any non-objective legislation.

(See my articles "Have Gun, Will Nudge" and "Vast Quicksands" in the March 1962 and July 1963 issues of this NEWSLETTER. For a graphic report on the present state of the television industry, see "TV: The Timid Giant" and "Why the Timid Giant Treads Softly," both by Edith Efron, in the May 18 and August 10, 1963 issues of *TV Guide*.)

All media of communication influence one another. It is impossible to compute the extent to which the gray, docile, fear-ridden, appeasement-minded mediocrity of so powerful a medium as television has contributed to the demoralization of our culture.

Nor can the freedom of one medium of communication be destroyed without affecting all the others. When censorship of radio and television becomes fully accepted, as a *fait accompli*, it will not be long before all the other media — books, magazines, newspapers, lectures — follow suit, unobtrusively, unofficially and by the same method: overtly, in the name of the "public interest"; covertly, for fear of government reprisals. (This process is taking place already.)

So much for the relationship of "human" rights to property rights.

Since "public property" is a collectivist fiction, since the public as a whole can neither use nor dispose of its "property," that "property" will always be taken over by some political "elite," by a small clique which will then rule the public — a public of literal, dispossessed proletarians.

If you want to gauge a collectivist theory's distance from reality, ask yourself: by what inconceivable standard can it be claimed that the broadcasting airways are the property of some illiterate share-cropper who will never be able to grasp the concept of electronics, or of some hillbilly whose engineering capacity is not quite sufficient to cope with a corn-liquor still — and that broadcasting, the product of an incalculable amount of scientific genius, is to be ruled by the will of such owners?

Remember that *this literally* is the alleged principle at the base of the entire legal structure of our broadcasting industry.

There is only one solution to this problem, and it has to start at the base; nothing less will do. The airways should be turned over to private ownership. The only way to do it now is to sell radio and television frequencies to the highest bidders (by an objectively defined, open, impartial process) — and thus put an end to the gruesome fiction of "public property."

Such a reform cannot be accomplished overnight; it will take a long struggle; but that is the ultimate goal which the advocates of capitalism should bear in mind. That is the only way to correct the disastrous, atavistic error made by capitalism's alleged defenders.

I say "atavistic," because it took hundreds of centuries before primitive, nomadic tribes of savages reached the concept of private property — specifically, *land* property, which marked the beginning of civilization. It is a tragic irony that in the presence of a new realm opened by a gigantic achievement of science, our political and intellectual leaders reverted to the mentality of primitive nomads and, unable to conceive of property rights, declared the new realm to be a tribal hunting ground.

The breach between man's scientific achievements and his ideological development is growing wider every day. It is time to realize that men cannot keep this up much longer if they continue to retrogress to ideological savagery with every step of scientific progress.

OBJECTIVIST CALENDAR

■ On Sunday, April 19, Ayn Rand will give a talk at the Ford Hall Forum in Boston. Her subject: "Is Atlas Shrugging?" Time: 8 P.M. Place: Jordan Hall, 30 Gainsboro St.

■ On Friday, April 24, Robert A. Hessen will address the Ayn Rand Club of the Drexel Institute of Technology in Philadelphia. His subject: "The Mock War on Poverty." For details, contact NBI, or phone EV 6-6274 (evenings) in Philadelphia. Mr. Hessen will give the same lecture to the Ayn Rand Society of Brooklyn College late in April; for details, phone NBI (LE 2-5787) in New York.

■ On Thursday, April 30, Nathaniel Branden will address The Forum of the Bronx High School of Science. His subject: "Objectivism and Its Applications to Our Society." Time: 3:15 P.M.

■ On Monday, April 20, in New York City, Nathaniel Branden will deliver the opening lecture of a ten-lecture course on "Contemporary Theories of Neurosis and Human Nature." Place: Hotel Roosevelt. Time: 7:30 P.M. Visitors' admission: $3.50.

■ NBI's Tape Transcription Division has scheduled the following starting dates: "Basic Principles of Objectivism" in Montreal, April 14; "The Principles of Efficient Thinking" in Wilmington, April 13, in Philadelphia, April 14, and in Chicago, April 21; "The Esthetics of the Visual Arts" in Los Angeles, May 20. For details, contact NBI.

■ Change of Schedule: "Ayn Rand on Campus" will be broadcast by WKCR on April 5, April 19, May 3 and May 17.

Published monthly at 120 East 34th Street, New York 16, N. Y.
Subscription rate: in United States, its possessions, Canada and Mexico, $5 for one year; other countries, $6.
Additional copies of this Newsletter: single copy 50¢ (coins, not stamps); 10 – 99 copies, 25¢ each plus postage (for first-class delivery add 1¢ per copy, for third-class delivery add ½¢ per copy); 100 or more copies, 15¢ each plus postage (same as above). (Bulk rates apply only to multiple orders of a single issue.)
For change of address send old address and new address with zone number if any. Allow us three weeks to process new subscriptions and change of address.

Ayn Rand and Nathaniel Branden, Editors and Publishers
Barbara Branden, Managing Editor
Elayne Kalberman, Circulation Manager

THE OBJECTIVIST NEWSLETTER

Edited and Published by AYN RAND and NATHANIEL BRANDEN

VOL. 3 NO. 5   MAY, 1964

Pseudo-Self-Esteem

By NATHANIEL BRANDEN

(Part I of a two-part article.)

If one wishes to understand a man's basic motivation — if one wishes to understand the root of the values and goals that direct a man's behavior — the most fundamental question one must answer is: What is the nature and degree of his self-esteem or lack of it?

Self-esteem, the conviction of one's efficacy and worthiness, is man's deepest psychological need. In briefest essence, the basis of this need may be summarized as follows.

Reason is man's basic means of survival — and the exercise of his rational faculty is volitional. Since reality confronts him with constant alternatives, man must *choose* his goals and actions. His life and happiness depend on his making the *right* choices (*i.e.*, choices which are consonant with the facts of reality and with the requirements of his own nature). Man cannot demand omniscience or infallibility of himself. But he does require the conviction that his *method* of choosing and making decisions — *i.e.*, his characteristic manner of using his consciousness — is right, right *in principle*, appropriate to reality. An organism whose consciousness functioned automatically would face no such problem; it could not question the validity of the mental operations which lie behind its actions. But to man, who is a being of *volitional* consciousness, this question is of life-and-death concern.

Man is the one living species who is able to reject, sabotage and betray his means of survival: his mind. Man is free to exercise his rational faculty — or to suspend it; to act in accordance with his best, clearest and most conscientious judgment — or to act against it, moved by blind feelings; to preserve his intellectual independence and integrity — or to surrender in parasitical fear to the authority of others. Thus, man is the one species who must, by volitional effort, make himself into an entity that is *able* to live and *worthy* of living. His need of self-esteem is his need to know that he has succeeded at this task.

To think or not to think, to focus his conceptual faculty or to inactivate it, is man's basic act of choice, the one act solely and directly within man's volitional power. An unbreached determination to use one's mind to the fullest of one's ability, an unbreached refusal ever to place any other consideration above one's perception of reality, is the only rational criterion of virtue, the only justifiable standard of moral perfection, and the only possible basis of authentic self-esteem.

The reasons why man *needs* self-esteem dictate the standard by which self-esteem is to be gauged and the necessary conditions of its attainment.

To the extent that a man fails to attain it, the consequence is a feeling of anxiety, insecurity, self-doubt, the sense of being unfit for reality, inadequate to existence. Anxiety is a psychological alarm-signal, warning of danger to the organism.

In varying degrees of intensity, the experience of such anxiety is the fate of most human beings.

Most men never identify the importance of reason to their existence, they do not judge themselves by the standard of devotion to rationality — and they are not aware of the issue of self-esteem in the terms discussed above. They are aware only of a desperate desire to feel confident and in control, and to feel that they are *good*, good in some basic way which they cannot name. But the cause of that formless fear and guilt which haunts their lives, is a failure which is *psycho-epistemological, i.e.*, a failure in the proper use of their consciousness — a default on the responsibility of reason. The anxiety they experience is part of the price they pay for that default.

These are the persons who, for instance, cannot bear to be alone; who cannot live without sleeping-pills; who jump at every unexpected sound; who drink too much to calm a nervousness that comes too often; who feel a constantly pressing need to be amusing and to entertain; who flee to too many movies they have no desire to see and to too many gatherings they have no desire to attend; who sacrifice any vestige of independent self-confidence to an obsessive concern with what others think of them; who long to be emotional dependents or to be depended upon; who succumb to periodic spells of unaccountable depression; who submerge their existence in the dreary passivity of unchosen routines and unchallenged duties and, as they watch their years slip by, wonder, in occasional spurts of frustrated anguish, what has robbed them of their chance to live; who run from one meaningless sexual affair to another; who seek membership in the kind of collective movements that dissolve personal identity and obviate personal responsibility — a vast, anonymous assemblage of men and women who have accepted fear as a built-in, not-to-be-wondered-about fixture of their soul, dreading even to identify that what they feel is fear or to inquire into the nature of that which they seek to escape.

Since self-esteem is the fundamental need of man's consciousness, since it is a need that cannot be by-passed, men who fail to achieve self-esteem, or who fail to a significant degree, strive to *fake* it — to evade its lack and to seek protection from their state of inner dread behind the barricade of a *pseudo*-self-esteem.

Pseudo-self-esteem, an irrational pretense at self-value, is a neurotic device to diminish anxiety and provide a spurious sense of security — to assuage a man's need of authentic self-esteem while allowing the real causes of its lack to be evaded.

A man's pseudo-self-esteem is maintained by two means: by evading and repressing ideas and feelings that could affect his self-appraisal adversely — and by seeking to derive his sense of efficacy and worth from something *other than* rationality, some *alternative* value or virtue which he experiences as less demanding or more easily attainable, such as "doing one's duty," or being stoical or altruistic or financially successful or sexually attractive.

This complex process of self-deception, on which the neurotic builds his life, holds the key to his motivation, to his values and goals. To understand the nature and form of a particular man's pseudo-self-esteem, is to understand the mainspring of his actions — to know "what makes him tick."

In the psychology of a man of authentic self-value, there is no clash between his perception of reality and the preservation of his self-esteem — since he *bases* his self-esteem on his perception of reality and on the fact that he holds no value or consideration above reality. But to the man of pseudo-self-esteem, reality appears as a threat, as an enemy; he feels, in effect, that it's reality *or* his self-esteem — since his pretense at self-esteem is purchased at the cost of evasion, of entrenched areas of blindness, of cognitive self-censorship. This is why a man may be perfectly rational and lucid, in an

(continued on page 20)

BOOKS

*The Greatest Plot in History**

by Ralph de Toledano

—————————— Reviewed by EDITH EFRON

"Young men in the federal government, researchers and technologists in American industry, and graduate students had made the blinding discovery that Utopia and the Soviet Union were synonymous. In the darkness of their blazing noon, they were eager and ready to make a compound of moral treason and sophistry, excusing the betrayal of principle and common decency with the argument that they were 'helping the working class' or 'fighting fascism'... No longer was a spy a shameful creature, stealthily lurking in the back alleys of society. The Soviet apparat could claim men of stature and intellectual attainment — men who spurned money, and justified their acts as moral."

In *The Greatest Plot in History*, Ralph de Toledano has told the ugliest spy story in the annals of political corruption. It is the story of those "idealistic" American intellectuals who emerged from universities and laboratories, during World War II, to betray this nation — to place its most closely guarded military secret, the atomic bomb, into the hands of espionage agents for a criminal dictatorship.

This is the first complete study of the theft of the atomic bomb to be published; it is invaluable for those who have acquired a splintered and incomplete version of these events from the press. Heavily documented with selections from Army and FBI interviews, transcripts of Congressional hearings, and records of captured spies, it covers every major facet of "the greatest plot in history." It includes: a valuable analysis of the primitive state of atomic science in wartime Russia; a detailed report on the wartime Soviet espionage network in the United States; and a series of remarkable studies of those intellectuals who became spies for Russia.

By far the most significant aspect of Mr. de Toledano's book is its portrayal of the struggle by U.S. security agents to safeguard the atomic bomb; the major enemy in that harrowing and futile struggle was not so much a limited Soviet spy ring, but the entire Roosevelt administration and the "academic community" which viewed the Soviet Union as "idealistic, misunderstood, and more sinned against than sinning."

Nothing more clearly communicates the bias of the governmental and scientific world than the manner in which the U.S. atomic project was staffed. Scientists with open communist sympathies and affiliations were hired for top-level research jobs and directorial posts, with wanton disregard for security rulings; in some cases, thorough investigations were not made; in others, known facts were evaded; and, at times, men were hired in the face of protests from security officers.

A similar laxity characterized the employment procedures on the lower echelons. Much of the scientific and technical personnel was employed through a professional union which was heavily infiltrated with communists. In consequence, as military intelligence was later to discover, there were entrenched communist cells within the major atomic installations and their subsidiary atomic research laboratories.

The presence of this veritable communist garrison was not the only force against which U.S. intelligence officers had to struggle. Many other factors handicapped their attempts to protect the secrets of the bomb. Mr. de Toledano goes into each of these factors in detail, but here only a few can be listed:

— As a group, the scientists, the non-communists as well as the communists, were hostile to security. Most of them considered the requirements of secrecy an infringement of their intellectual freedom by the "fascist military." They broke internal and external security constantly and deliberately, until the atomic projects "leaked like a sieve."

— Security was thwarted by scientists who were often aware that their communist colleagues were spying, but either evaded it or actively protected the spies from the intelligence officers. In several known cases, scientists did not report approaches by Soviet agents, but sheltered their identity. On one occasion, a famous scientist informed military intelligence that four of his colleagues had been approached by a Soviet agent. But he refused, as a matter of "moral principle," to name either the scientists or the agent.

— While intelligence officers were struggling to dam the leaks in the atomic project, they were simultaneously clashing with the Roosevelt administration which was protecting the sanctity of the Lend-Lease airlift at Great Falls, Montana; through this airlift, official shipments of uranium and heavy water, as well as "diplomatic" pouches containing stolen blueprints of atomic installations, were being flown to Russia in U.S. planes.

The culmination of this ignominious internecine war was predictable: Russia received the secrets of the atom bomb. The atomic plants she ultimately constructed were almost complete replicas of our own. At a giant Russian war relief rally, Roosevelt's privy counsellor, Harry Hopkins, had said, in an apostrophe to Stalin, "We are determined that nothing shall stop us from sharing with you all that we have." Nothing did.

The failure of our intelligence officers is understakable. They might have been able to resist the onslaught of foreign agents. But they were helpless under the onslaught of domestic irresponsibility, evasion and treachery, posing as "idealism."

The Greatest Plot in History is a powerful, important and genuinely enlightening book. It should be read by everyone who is attempting to understand the suicidal strains which are increasingly manifest in our culture.

It is, however, incomplete in one critical respect. It describes the Russian motives for the plot against American security, but it does not explain the motives of those American intellectuals who, alone, made the success of the Russian plot possible. It neither tells us why our "intellectual community" dedicated itself to the belief that "the world's most vicious tyranny was an...idealistic experiment in social engineering," nor why the Roosevelt administration blindly evaded the dangers of trusting communist sympathizers with the nation's most critical secrets. Without such explanation, this book, which provides staggering evidence of governmental complicity in the loss of the bomb, will merely feed the shallow conspiracy theory of American politics, which is all too prevalent already in conservative circles.

There is only one reason for which loyalty to the Soviet Union at the expense of our own nation has been so widespread and so successfully rationalized by American intellectuals as "idealistic" and "moral." Communism is the political expression of altruism: the Soviet Union is the moral ideal of altruism incarnate. And so long as the ethics of altruism is enshrined in our culture, it will endlessly serve as a moral cloak for those who are motivated to betray this nation which is still deeply, if inarticulately, committed to a philosophy of individualism and self-interest.

The real horror of "the greatest plot in history" is that it is not yet over. Fully aware of this, Mr. de Toledano ends his book with these words: "Only when communist perfidy has been forever ground into the dust can this chapter be ended." In this, he is mistaken. This chapter will be ended only when Americans understand that their mortal enemy is not mere communist perfidy, but that which gives communist perfidy its moral sanction: the "ideal" of altruism.

---

*Published by Duell, Sloan and Pearce, $4.95. Available from NBI BOOK SERVICE, 120 E. 34th St., New York 16, N.Y., for $4.25. (N.Y.C. residents add 4% sales tax; outside the U.S., add 15¢.)

Edith Efron is a journalist whose articles have appeared in such publications as Life, Look *and* The New York Times Magazine.

INTELLECTUAL AMMUNITION DEPARTMENT

[*Subscribers are invited to send in the questions that they find themselves unable to answer in philosophical or political discussions. As many questions as space permits will be answered. No questions will be answered by mail.*]

■ **What is the Objectivist position in regard to patents and copyrights?**

Patents and copyrights are the legal implementation of the base of all property rights: a man's right to the product of his mind.

Every type of productive work involves a combination of mental and physical effort: of thought and of physical action to translate that thought into a material form. The proportion of these two elements varies in different types of work. At the lowest end of the scale, the mental effort required to perform unskilled manual labor is minimal. At the other end, what the patent and copyright laws acknowledge is the paramount role of mental effort in the production of material values; these laws protect the mind's contribution in its purest form: the origination of an *idea*. The subject of patents and copyrights is *intellectual* property.

An idea as such cannot be protected until it has been given a material form. An invention has to be embodied in a physical model before it can be patented; a story has to be written or printed. But what the patent or copyright protects is not the physical object as such, but the *idea* which it embodies. By forbidding an unauthorized reproduction of the object, the law declares, in effect, that the physical labor of copying is not the source of the object's value, that that value is created by the originator of the idea and may not be used without his consent; thus the law establishes the property right of a mind to that which it has brought into existence.

It is important to note, in this connection, that a *discovery* cannot be patented, only an *invention*. A scientific or philosophical discovery, which identifies a law of nature, a principle or a fact of reality not previously known, cannot be the exclusive property of the discoverer because: (a) he did not *create* it, and (b) if he cares to make his discovery public, claiming it to be true, he cannot demand that men continue to pursue or practice falsehoods except by his permission. He *can* copyright the book in which he presents his discovery and he *can* demand that his authorship of the discovery be acknowledged, that no other man appropriate or plagiarize the credit for it — but he cannot copyright *theoretical* knowledge. Patents and copyrights pertain only to the *practical* application of knowledge, to the creation of a specific object which did not exist in nature — an object which, in the case of patents, *may* never have existed without its particular originator; and in the case of copyrights, *would* never have existed.

The government does not "grant" a patent or copyright, in the sense of a gift, privilege or favor; the government merely *secures* it — i.e., the government certifies the origination of an idea and protects its owner's exclusive right of use and disposal. A man is not forced to apply for a patent or copyright; he may give his idea away, if he so chooses; but if he wishes to exercise his property right, the government will protect it, as it protects all other rights. A patent or copyright represents the formal equivalent of registering a property deed or title. The patent or copyright notice on a physical object represents a public statement of the conditions on which the inventor or author is willing to sell his product: for the purchaser's use, but *not* for commercial reproduction.

The right to intellectual property cannot be exercised in perpetuity. Intellectual property represents a claim, not on material objects, but on the idea they embody, which means: not merely on existing wealth, but on wealth yet to be produced — a claim to payment for the inventor's or author's work. No debt can be extended into infinity.

Material property represents a static amount of wealth already produced. It can be left to heirs, but it cannot remain in their effortless possession in perpetuity: the heirs can consume it or must *earn* its continued possession by their own productive work. The greater the value of the property, the greater the effort demanded of the heir. In a free, competitive society, no one could long retain the ownership of a factory or of a tract of land without exercising a commensurate effort.

But intellectual property cannot be consumed. If it were held in perpetuity, it would lead to the opposite of the very principle on which it is based: it would lead, not to the earned reward of achievement, but to the unearned support of parasitism. It would become a cumulative lien on the production of unborn generations, which would ultimately paralyze them. Consider what would happen if, in producing an automobile, we had to pay royalties to the descendants of all the inventors involved, starting with the inventor of the wheel and on up. Apart from the impossibility of keeping such records, consider the accidental status of such descendants and the unreality of their unearned claims.

The inheritance of material property represents a dynamic claim on a static amount of wealth; the inheritance of intellectual property represents a static claim on a dynamic process of production.

Intellectual achievement, *in fact*, cannot be transferred, just as intelligence, ability or any other personal virtue cannot be transferred. All that can be transferred is the material results of an achievement, in the form of actually produced wealth. By the very nature of the right on which intellectual property is based — a man's right to the product of his mind — that right ends with him. He cannot dispose of that which he cannot know or judge: the yet-unproduced, indirect, potential results of his achievement four generations — or four centuries — later.

It is in this issue that our somewhat collectivistic terminology might be misleading: on the expiration of a patent or copyright, the intellectual property involved does not become "public property" (though it is labeled as "in the public domain"); it ceases to exist *qua* property. And if the invention or the book continues to be manufactured, the benefit of that former property does not go to the "public," it goes to the only rightful heirs: to the producers, to those who exercise the effort of embodying that idea in new material forms and thus keeping it alive.

Since intellectual property rights cannot be exercised in perpetuity, the question of their time limit is an enormously complex issue. If they were restricted to the originator's life-span, it would destroy their value by making long-term contractual agreements impossible: if an inventor died a month after his invention were placed on the market, it could ruin the manufacturer who may have invested a fortune in its production. Under such conditions, investors would be unable to take a long-range risk; the more revolutionary or important an invention, the less would be its chance of finding financial backers. Therefore, the law has to define a period of time which would protect the rights and interests of all those involved.

In the case of copyrights, the most rational solution is Great Britain's Copyright Act of 1911, which established the copyright of books, paintings, movies, etc. for the lifetime of the author and fifty years thereafter.

In the case of patents, the issue is much more complex. A patented invention often tends to hamper or restrict further research and development in a given area of science. Many patents cover overlapping areas. The difficulty lies in defining the inventor's specific rights without including more than he can properly claim, in the form of indirect consequences or yet-undiscovered implications. A lifetime patent could become an unjustifiable barrier to the development of knowledge beyond the inventor's potential power or actual achievement. The legal problem is to set a time limit which would secure for the inventor the fullest possible benefit of his invention without infringing the right of others to pursue independent research. As in many other legal issues, that time limit has to be determined by the principle of defining and protecting all the individual rights involved.

As an objection to the patent laws, some people cite the fact that two inventors may work independently for years on the same invention, but one will beat the other to the patent office by an hour or a day and will acquire an exclusive monopoly, while the loser's work will then be totally wasted. This type of objection is based on the error of equating the potential with the actual. The fact that a man *might* have been first, does not alter the fact that he *wasn't*. Since the issue is one of commercial rights, the loser in a case of that kind has to accept the fact that in seeking to trade with others he must face the possibility of a competitor winning the race, which is true of all types of competition.

Today, patents are the special target of the collectivists' attacks — directly and indirectly, through such issues as the proposed abolition of trademarks, brand names, etc. While the so-called "conservatives" look at those attacks indifferently or, at times, approvingly, the collectivists seem to realize that patents are the heart and core of property rights, and that once they are destroyed, the destruction of all other rights will follow automatically, as a brief postscript.

The present state of our patent system is a nightmare. The inventors' rights are being infringed, eroded, chipped, gnawed and violated in so many ways, under cover of so many non-objective statutes, that industrialists are beginning to rely on secrecy to protect valuable inventions which they are afraid to patent. (Consider the treatment accorded to patents under the antitrust laws, as just one example out of many.)

Those who observe the spectacle of the progressive collapse of patents — the spectacle of mediocrity scrambling to cash-in on the achievements of genius — and who understand its implications, will understand why in the closing paragraphs of Chapter VII, Part II, of *Atlas Shrugged,* one of the guiltiest men is the passenger who said: "Why should Rearden be the only one permitted to manufacture Rearden Metal?"

—AYN RAND

Pseudo-Self-Esteem (from page 17)

area that does not touch on or threaten his pseudo-self-esteem — and be flagrantly irrational, evasive, defensive and *stupid,* in an area which *is* threatening to his self-appraisal. His characteristic response to any potential assault on his pseudo-self-esteem, is unconsciousness. The anxiety triggered off by such an assault acts as a psycho-epistemological disintegrator. Thus, he perpetuates the very process of psycho-epistemological self-sabotaging by which he caused his initial failure of self-esteem.

In this phenomenon, one may see the lead to one index of mental health and illness: A man is psychologically healthy to the extent that there is no clash in him between perceiving reality and preserving his self-esteem; the degree to which such a clash exists, is the degree of his mental illness.

The process of evasion and repression is not sufficient to provide a neurotic with the illusion of self-esteem; that process is only part of the self-fraud he perpetrates. The other part consists of the values he chooses as the means of achieving a sense of personal worth. In the process of choosing values, there is a fundamental difference in principle between the motivation of a man of self-esteem and a man of pseudo-self-esteem.

An individual who develops healthily, derives his cardinal pleasure and pride from the work of his mind — and from the achievements which that work makes possible. Feeling confident of his ability to deal with the facts of reality, he will want a challenging, effortful, *creative* existence. Creativeness will be his highest love, whatever his level of intelligence. Feeling confident of his own value, he will be drawn to self-esteem in others; what he will desire most in human relationships is the opportunity to feel *admiration;* he will want to find men and achievements he can respect, that will give him the pleasure which his own character and achievements can offer others. In the sphere both of work and of human relationships, his base and motor is a firm sense of confidence, of efficacy — and, as a consequence, a love for existence, for the fact of being alive. What he seeks are means to *express* and *objectify* his self-esteem.

The base and motor of the man without self-esteem is not confidence, but fear. Not to live, but to escape his terror of life, is his fundamental goal. Not creativeness, but *safety,* is his ruling desire. And what he seeks from others is not the chance to experience admiration, but an escape from moral values, an escape from moral judgment, a promise to be forgiven, to be accepted, *to be taken care of* — to be taken care of *metaphysically* — to be comforted and protected in a terrifying universe. His values are not the *expression* of his self-esteem, but the confession of its lack.

A man's self-esteem or pseudo-self-esteem determines his *abstract* values, not the *specific* goals he will seek; the latter proceed from a number of factors, such as a man's intelligence, knowledge, premises and personal context. For instance, a man of high self-esteem will desire intellectually challenging work; but whether he chooses to enter business or science or art, depends on narrower, less fundamental considerations. Similarly, a man of pseudo-self-esteem will desire that others protect him from reality; but a variety of factors determine whether he feels more at home among the country club set or the academic set or the underworld set.

The principle that distinguishes the basic motivation of a man of self-esteem from that of a man of pseudo-self-esteem, is the principle of *motivation by love* versus *motivation by fear.* Love of self and of existence — versus the fear that one's self is *unfit* for existence. Motivation by *confidence* — versus motivation by terror.

Here, then, is another index of mental health and illness: A man is psychologically healthy to the extent that he functions on the principle of motivation by confidence; the degree of his motivation by fear, is the degree of his mental illness.
(To be completed in our next issue)

OBJECTIVIST CALENDAR

■ On Wednesday, May 6, Robert A. Hessen will address the Ayn Rand Society of Brooklyn College. His subject: "The Mock War on Poverty." Time: 12 noon. Place: 404 Whitehead Hall.

■ On Wednesday, May 13, Ayn Rand will speak at Brooklyn College. Her subject: "Is Atlas Shrugging?" Time: 12 noon. Place: Walt Whitman Auditorium.

■ Beginning Tuesday, June 16, in New York City, NBI will offer a 13 lecture course on "The History of Modern Philosophy," to be given by Dr. Leonard Peikoff. Further details will be announced in next month's Calendar.

■ NBI's Tape Transcription Division has scheduled "Three Plays by Ayn Rand" in Washington, D.C., on May 17, May 24 and June 7. For details, contact NBI.

Published monthly at 120 East 34th Street, New York 16, N. Y.
Subscription rate: in United States, its possessions, Canada and Mexico, $5 for one year; other countries, $6.
Additional copies of this Newsletter: single copy 50¢ (coins, not stamps); 10 — 99 copies, 25¢ each plus postage (for first-class delivery add 1¢ per copy, for third-class delivery add ½¢ per copy); 100 or more copies, 15¢ each plus postage (same as above). (Bulk rates apply only to multiple orders of a single issue.)
For change of address send old address and new address with zone number if any. Allow us three weeks to process new subscriptions and change of address.

Ayn Rand and Nathaniel Branden, Editors and Publishers
Barbara Branden, Managing Editor
Elayne Kalberman, Circulation Manager

THE OBJECTIVIST NEWSLETTER

Edited and Published by AYN RAND and NATHANIEL BRANDEN

VOL. 3 NO. 6   JUNE, 1964

CHECK YOUR PREMISES
By AYN RAND

The Cult of Moral Grayness

One of the most eloquent symptoms of the moral bankruptcy of today's culture, is a certain fashionable attitude toward moral issues, best summarized as: "There are no blacks and whites, there are only grays."

This is asserted in regard to persons, actions, principles of conduct, and morality in general. "Black and white," in this context, means "good and evil." (The reverse order used in that catch phrase is interesting psychologically.)

In any respect one cares to examine, that notion is full of contradictions (foremost among them is the fallacy of "the stolen concept"). If there is no black and white, there can be no gray—since gray is merely a mixture of the two.

Before one can identify anything as "gray," one has to know what is black and what is white. In the field of morality, this means that one must first identify what is good and what is evil. And when a man has ascertained that one alternative is good and the other is evil, he has no justification for choosing a mixture. There can be no justification for choosing any part of that which one knows to be evil. In morality, "black" is predominantly the result of attempting to pretend to oneself that one is merely "gray."

If a moral code (such as altruism) is, in fact, impossible to practice, it is the code that must be condemned as "black," not its victims evaluated as "gray." If a moral code prescribes irreconcilable contradictions—so that by choosing the good in one respect, a man becomes evil in another—it is the code that must be rejected as "black." If a moral code is inapplicable to reality—if it offers no guidance except a series of arbitrary, groundless, out-of-context injunctions and commandments, to be accepted on faith and practiced automatically, as blind dogma—its practitioners cannot properly be classified as "white" or "black" or "gray": a moral code that forbids and paralyzes moral judgment is a contradiction in terms.

If, in a complex moral issue, a man struggles to determine what is right, and fails or makes an honest error, he cannot be regarded as "gray"; morally, he is "white." Errors of knowledge are not breaches of morality; no proper moral code can demand infallibility or omniscience.

But if, in order to escape the responsibility of moral judgment, a man closes his eyes and mind, if he evades the facts of the issue and struggles *not to know*, he cannot be regarded as "gray"; morally, he is as "black" as they come.

Many forms of confusion, uncertainty and epistemological sloppiness help to obscure the contradictions and to disguise the actual meaning of the doctrine of moral grayness.

Some people believe that it is merely a re-statement of such bromides as "Nobody is perfect in this world"—*i.e.*, everybody is a mixture of good and evil, and, therefore, morally "gray." Since the majority of those one meets are likely to fit that description, people accept it as some sort of natural fact, without further thought. They forget that morality deals only with issues open to man's choice (*i.e.*, to his free will)—and, therefore, that no statistical generalizations are valid in this matter.

If man is "gray" by nature, no moral concepts are applicable to him, including "grayness," and no such thing as morality is possible. But if man has free will, then the fact that ten (or ten million) men made the wrong choice, does not necessitate that the eleventh one will make it; it necessitates nothing—and proves nothing—in regard to any given individual.

There are many reasons why most people *are* morally imperfect, *i.e.*, hold mixed, contradictory premises and values (the altruist morality is one of the reasons), but that is a different issue. Regardless of the reasons of their choices, the fact that most people are morally "gray," does not invalidate man's need of morality and of moral "whiteness"; if anything, it makes the need more urgent. Nor does it warrant the epistemological "package-deal" of dismissing the problem by consigning all men to moral "grayness" and thus refusing to recognize or to practice "whiteness." Nor does it serve as an escape from the responsibility of moral judgment: unless one is prepared to dispense with morality altogether and to regard a petty chiseller and a murderer as morally equal, one still has to judge and evaluate the many shadings of "gray" that one may encounter in the characters of individual men. (And the only way to judge them is by a clearly defined criterion of "black" and "white.")

A similar notion, involving similar errors, is held by some people who believe that the doctrine of moral grayness is merely a re-statement of the proposition: "There are two sides to every issue," which they take to mean that nobody is ever fully right or fully wrong. But that is not what that proposition means or implies. It implies only that in judging an issue, one should take cognizance of or give a hearing to both sides. This does not mean that the claims of both sides will necessarily be equally valid, nor even that there will be some modicum of justice on both sides. More often than not, justice will be on one side, and unwarranted presumption (or worse) on the other.

There are, of course, complex issues in which both sides are right in some respects and wrong in others—and it is here that the "package-deal" of pronouncing both sides "gray" is least permissible. It is in such issues that the most rigorous precision of moral judgment is required to identify and evaluate the various aspects involved—which can be done only by unscrambling the mixed elements of "black" and "white."

The basic error in all these various confusions is the same: it consists of forgetting that morality deals only with issues open to man's choice—which means: forgetting the difference between "unable" and "unwilling." This permits people to translate the catch phrase "There are no blacks and whites" into: "Men are *unable* to be wholly good or wholly evil"—which they accept, in foggy resignation, without questioning the metaphysical contradictions it entails.

But not many people would accept it, if that catch phrase were translated into the actual meaning it is intended to smuggle into their minds: "Men are *unwilling* to be wholly good or wholly evil."

The first thing one would say to any advocate of such a proposition, is: "Speak for yourself, brother!" And *that*, in effect, is what he is actually doing; consciously or subconsciously, intentionally or inadvertently, when a man declares: "There are no blacks and whites," he is making a psychological confession, and what he means is: *"I am unwilling to be wholly good—and please don't regard me as wholly evil!"*

(continued on page 24)

Copyright © 1964 by The Objectivist Newsletter, Inc.

Pseudo-Self-Esteem

By NATHANIEL BRANDEN

(Part II of a two-part article.)

To the extent that a man lacks self-esteem, he lives *negatively* and *defensively*. When he chooses his particular values and goals, his primary motive is, not to afford himself a positive enjoyment of existence, but to defend himself against anxiety, against painful feelings of inadequacy, self-doubt and guilt.

If a man's life is in physical danger, say, if he suffers from some major disease, his primary concern in such an emergency situation is, not with the pursuit of enjoyment, but with the removal of the danger—*i.e.*, with regaining his health, with re-establishing the context in which the pursuit of enjoyment will again be possible and appropriate. But to the man devoid of self-esteem, life is, in effect, a *chronic* emergency; he is *always* in danger—psychologically. He never reaches normality, he never feels free for the enjoyment of life—because his method of combatting the danger consists, not of dealing with it rationally, not of working to remove it, but of *seeking to persuade himself that it does not exist*. Since A is A, since facts are facts and are not to be wiped out by self-made blindness, he can never succeed—but most of his evasions, repressions and self-defeating actions are aimed at this goal.

Fear is the ruling element in such a man's psychology.

Just as fear rules him *psycho-epistemologically*, undercutting the clarity of his perception, distorting his judgments, restricting his cognitive ambition and driving him to ever-wider evasions—so fear rules him *motivationally*, subverting his normal value-development, sabotaging his proper growth, leading him toward goals that promise to support his pretense at efficacy, driving him to passive conformity or hostile aggressiveness or autistic withdrawal, to *any* path that will protect his pseudo-self-esteem against a stern, unknown and unforgiving reality.

Values chosen in this manner may be termed *"defense-values."* A defense-value is one motivated by fear and aimed at supporting a pseudo-self-esteem. It is experienced, in effect, as a means of survival, as a substitute for rationality. It is an *anti-anxiety* device.

Such a value is unhealthy, not necessarily by virtue of its nature, but by virtue of the motivation for choosing it. The value itself may not be irrational; what is irrational is the reason for its selection. Productive work, for instance, is a rational value; but escaping into work as a means of evading one's flaws, shortcomings and conflicts, is *not* rational. Often, however, defense-values are irrational in *both* respects—as in the case of a man who seeks to escape anxiety and fake a sense of efficacy by acquiring power over others.

The extent to which a man lacks self-esteem, is the extent to which defense-values constitute the building-blocks of his soul.

The following example illustrates the process by which defense-values and pseudo-self-esteem develop—and the psychological crisis to which they can lead.

Consider the case of a person who, as a child, is characteristically antipathetic to exerting mental effort: who rebels against the responsibility of thinking, who resents the necessity of judgment, who prefers an undemanding state of mental fog, and drifts at the mercy of unexamined emotions. Whenever feelings of inadequacy or anxiety penetrate his chronic lethargy, warning him of the danger of his course, he seeks to evade them as best he can. He clings to the guidance and authority of those around him, in order to obtain a sense of security and protection.

As a result of his policy of unquestioning obedience, his parents praise him as a "good" boy.

At school, his work is mediocre; and he feels an unadmitted resentment against the brighter boys in his class. He is pleased whenever they show signs of unruliness and are chastised by the teacher; this proves, he feels, that they are *not* "good" boys and that, notwithstanding his intellectual weakness, he is their moral superior.

He enjoys going to church, where he is informed that it is not the head that matters, but the heart—and that "the meek shall inherit the earth."

As he grows to adulthood, he is seldom conscious of the steps by which he selects his values and goals. But, moving like a somnambulist under the direction of subconscious orders, he is guided through all his crucial decisions by his unacknowledged sense of impotence, his fear of independence, his longing for safety and his antipathy to thought. These lead him unerringly to choose friends of undistinguished intelligence, to accept a job in his uncle's hardware store, to join the same political party as his father, and to marry the girl next door whom he has known all his life.

Whenever he feels vaguely guilty over his inertia, or whenever his wife reproaches him for his lack of ambition, and nags him to demand a raise, he responds by summoning the thought that he is a "decent citizen," a "good provider," a "devoted, faithful husband," a "God-fearing man," and that he has done all the things "one is supposed to do." Whenever he feels a surge of envy or hostility toward those men around him who have made more of their lives than he has, he tells himself that *his* cardinal virtue is *humility*—and that people are at fault in not recognizing this and giving him the respect he deserves. It is thus that he makes his existence tolerable psychologically.

At the hardware store, he performs the routine tasks he has been taught, initiating nothing, learning nothing, thinking nothing. But occasionally he dreams of the higher income and enhanced prestige he will enjoy when his uncle dies and leaves him the business; if the moral implications of his wish rise to trouble him, he promptly unfocuses his mind and thus eludes them. However, when the longed-for event finally happens, he does not experience the elation he had imagined. A day after his uncle's funeral, he awakens in the middle of the night, his heart pounding frantically, in a state of acute dread. He does not know how to account for it; he knows only that he feels overwhelmed by a sense of impending disaster.

The evasion and self-deception which have been habitual since childhood, now forbid him to know the meaning of his anxiety. For years, he had been shrinking his perception and the dimensions of the world with which he had to deal—in order to avoid coming face to face with his moral and psychological default, and to escape any potential threat to his precarious inner "security." He has crawled through his life, accepting, nodding, agreeing, obeying, seeking to by-pass the effort and responsibility of thought by making *humility* his *means of survival*, seeking to establish for himself a world in which this would be possible. But now reality has demolished the walls of that world, he has been thrown into a situation where *intellectual responsibility* will be demanded of him, where he will have to exercise *judgment*. Two thoughts have collided within him: "I've *got* to know what to do!" and "I *can't!*" In response to this collision, the chronic fear he had always evaded explodes into terror—the terror of the knowledge that his defense-values are now inadequate to protect him and that there is no longer any place to run.

Just as a rational, psychologically healthy man bases his self-esteem on the use of his mind, and gains an ever-increasing sense of control over his existence by choosing values that demand constant intellectual growth—so this man based his pseudo-self-esteem on his humility, counting on *others* to solve the problem of his survival, and chose values appropriate to this manner of existence, values intended to reassure him of the validity and safety of his course. The terror he feels when he assumes ownership of the hardware store, is the terror of a man suddenly divested of his means of survival, who must act and function in reality without weapons.

A significant characteristic of defense-values is the unreasoning compulsiveness with which they are usually held. Men of pseudo-self-esteem cling to these values with blind tenacity and fanatical devotion—as they would cling to a life-preserver in a stormy sea. Man's greatest fear is not of dying, but of feeling unfit to live. And to escape the agony of that feeling, men will pay any price: they will defy logic, they will sacrifice their practical self-interest, sometimes they will even forfeit their life.

With rare exceptions, they will pay any price except the one that could save them: they will not acknowledge the fraudulence of their defences, and work to achieve an *authentic* self-esteem; they will not accept the responsibility of living as rational beings.

The number of different defense-values which men can adopt, is virtually limitless. Most of these values, however, fall into one broad category: they are values generally held in high regard by the culture or sub-culture in which a person lives. They are "social metaphysical" in nature. (See my article, "Social Metaphysics," in the November 1962 issue of this NEWSLETTER.)

The following examples illustrate common defense-values of this category:

—The man who is obsessed with being popular, who feels driven to win the approval of every person he meets, who clings to the image of himself as "likeable," who, in effect, regards his appealing personality as his means of survival and the proof of his personal worth;

—The woman who has no sense of personal identity and who seeks to lose her inner emptiness in the role of a sacrificial martyr for her children, demanding in exchange only that her children adore her, that their adoration fill the vacuum of the ego she does not possess;

—The man who never forms independent judgments about anything, but who seeks to compensate by making himself authoritatively knowledgeable concerning *other* men's opinions about everything;

—The man who works at being aggressively "masculine," whose other concerns are entirely subordinated to his role as woman-chaser, and who derives less pleasure from the act of sex than from the act of reporting his adventures to the men in the locker room;

—The woman whose chief standard of self-appraisal is the "prestige" of her husband, and whose pseudo-self-esteem rises or falls according to the number of men who court her husband's favor;

—The man who feels guilt over having inherited a fortune, who has no idea of what to do with it and proceeds frantically to give it away, clinging to the "ideal" of altruism and to the vision of himself as a humanitarian, keeping his pseudo-self-esteem afloat by the belief that charity is a moral substitute for competence and courage;

—The man who has always been afraid of life and who tells himself that the reason is his superior "sensitivity," who chooses his clothes, his furniture, his books and his bodily posture by the standard of what will make him appear "idealistic."

Among defense-values, those of a religious nature figure prominently. In such cases, obedience to some religious injunction(s) is made the basis of pseudo-self-esteem. Faith in God, asceticism and systematic self-abnegation, adherence to religious rituals, are devices commonly employed to allay anxiety and purchase a sense of worthiness. (For a discussion of why the precepts of mysticism are especially inimical to authentic self-esteem, see my article, "Mental Health versus Mysticism and Self-Sacrifice," in the March 1963 issue of this NEWSLETTER.)

Still another type of defense-value may be observed in the person who rationalizes behavior of which he feels guilty by telling himself that such behavior "does not represent the *real* me," that "the real me is my *aspirations*." Such a person supports his pseudo-self-esteem by the vision of himself as an *aspirer*—an aspirer who is prevented from acting in accordance with his professed ideals by reasons beyond his control, such as the evil of "the system," the malevolence of the universe, the tragedy of some unspecified "circumstances," "human infirmity," "I never got a break," "I'm too honest and decent for this world," etc. The concept of a "real me" which bears little relation to anything one says or does in reality, is an especially prevalent anti-anxiety device, and often co-exists with other defense-values.

Defense-values and pseudo-self-esteem do not always or necessarily break down in a violent and dramatic form, as in the case of the man discussed above, who collapsed into acute anxiety. Often, the process of psychological erosion and disintegration is quieter, more insidious; the person involved is not brought to a moment of unmistakeable crisis; rather, his energy is slowly drained, he becomes increasingly more subject to fatigue, depression and, perhaps, a variety of minor somatic complaints, his pretense at self-value becomes progressively more frayed and worn—and his life peters out in desolate, meaningless misery, without climaxes, without explosions, with only an occasional, lethargic wonder, wearily evaded, as to what failure could have so impoverished his existence.

No evasion, no defense-values, no strategy of self-deception can ever provide a man with a substitute for authentic self-esteem. The sense of efficacy and virtue men long for, cannot be purchased by any of the self-frauds men perpetrate. Man needs the conviction that he is *right* for reality, right *in principle*—and only an unbreached rationality can achieve it.

Let a man tell himself that self-esteem is to be earned, not by the fullest exercise of his intellect, but by its abandonment in submission to faith—let him hold that efficacy is attained, not by thinking, but by conformity to the beliefs of others—let him hold that efficacy consists of giving love—let him hold that efficacy consists of *gaining* love—let him believe that his basic worth is to be measured by the number of women he sleeps with—or by the number of women he *doesn't* sleep with—or by the people he can manipulate—or by the nobility of his dreams—or by the money he gives away—or by the sacrifices he makes—let him renounce the world—let him lie on a bed of nails—but whatever he may expect to achieve, be it a moment's self-forgetfullness or a temporary illusion of virtue or a temporary amelioration of guilt, he will *not* achieve self-esteem.

The tragedy of most men's lives comes from their attempts to escape this fact.

Self-esteem is the key to man's motivation—by virtue either of its presence or of its absence. And perhaps the most eloquent testimony to the urgency of man's need of self-esteem, is the terror that haunts the lives of those who fail to achieve it, the twisted paths along which that terror drives them—and the inevitable wreckage at the end.

The Cult of Moral Grayness (from page 21)

Just as, in epistemology, the cult of uncertainty is a revolt against reason—so, in ethics, the cult of moral grayness is a revolt against moral values. Both are a revolt against the absolutism of reality.

Just as the cult of uncertainty could not succeed by an open rebellion against reason and, therefore, struggles to elevate the negation of reason into some sort of superior reasoning—so the cult of moral grayness could not succeed by an open rebellion against morality, and struggles to elevate the negation of morality into a superior kind of virtue.

Observe the form in which one encounters that doctrine: it is seldom presented as a positive, as an ethical theory or a subject of discussion; predominantly, one hears it as a negative, as a snap objection or reproach, uttered in a manner implying that one is guilty of breaching an absolute so self-evident as to require no discussion. In tones ranging from astonishment to sarcasm to anger to indignation to hysterical hatred, the doctrine is thrown at you in the form of an accusatory: "Surely you don't think in terms of black-and-white, do you?"

Prompted by confusion, helplessness and fear of the entire subject of morality, most people hasten to answer guiltily: "No, of course, I don't," without any clear idea of the nature of the accusation. They do not pause to grasp that that accusation is saying, in effect: "Surely you are not so unfair as to discriminate between good and evil, are you?"—or: "Surely you are not so evil as to seek the good, are you?"—or: "Surely you are not so immoral as to believe in morality!"

Moral guilt, fear of moral judgment, and a plea for blanket forgiveness, are so obviously the motive of that catch phrase that a glance at reality would be sufficient to tell its proponents what an ugly confession they are uttering. But escape from reality is both the pre-condition and the goal of the cult of moral grayness.

Philosophically, that cult is a negation of morality—but, psychologically, this is not its adherents' goal. What they seek is not amorality, but something more profoundly irrational: a non-absolute, fluid, elastic, middle-of-the-road morality. They do not proclaim themselves "beyond good and evil"—they seek to preserve the "advantages" of both. They are not moral challengers, nor do they represent a medieval version of flamboyant evil-worshipers. What gives them their peculiarly modern flavor is that they do not advocate selling one's soul to the Devil; they advocate selling it piecemeal, bit by bit, to any retail bidder.

They are not a philosophical school of thought; they are the typical product of philosophical default—of the intellectual bankruptcy that has produced irrationalism in epistemology, a moral vacuum in ethics, and a mixed economy in politics. A mixed economy is an amoral war of pressure groups, devoid of principles, values or any reference to justice, a war whose ultimate weapon is the power of brute force, but whose outward form is a game of *compromise*. The cult of moral grayness is the ersatz-morality which made it possible and to which men now cling in a panicky attempt to justify it.

Observe that their dominant overtone is not a quest for the "white," but an obsessive terror of being branded "black" (and with good reason). Observe that they are pleading for a morality which would hold *compromise* as its standard of value and would thus make it possible to gauge virtue by the number of values one is willing to betray.

The consequences and the "vested interests" of their doctrine are visible all around us.

Observe, in politics, that the term *"extremism"* has become a synonym of "evil," regardless of the content of the issue (the evil is not *what* you are "extreme" about, but *that* you are "extreme"—*i.e.*, consistent). Observe the phenomenon of the so-called *"neutralists"* in the United Nations: the "neutralists" are worse than merely neutral in the conflict between the United States and Soviet Russia; they are committed, *on principle*, to see no difference between the two sides, never to consider the merits of an issue, and always to seek a compromise, any compromise in any conflict—as, for instance, between an aggressor and an invaded country.

Observe, in literature, the emergence of a thing called *"anti-hero,"* whose distinction is that he possesses no distinction—no virtues, no values, no goals, no character, no significance—yet who occupies, in plays and novels, the position formerly held by a hero, with the story centered on his actions, even though he does nothing and gets nowhere. Observe that the term "good guys and bad guys" is used as a sneer—and, particularly in television, observe the revolt against happy endings, the demands that the "bad guys" be given an equal chance and an equal number of victories.

Like a mixed economy, men of mixed premises may be called "gray"; but, in both cases, the mixture does not remain "gray" for long. "Gray," in this context, is merely a prelude to "black." There may be "gray" men, but there can be no "gray" moral principles. Morality is a code of black and white. When and if men attempt a compromise, it is obvious which side will necessarily lose and which will necessarily profit.

Such are the reasons why—when one is asked: "Surely you don't think in terms of black-and-white, do you?"—the proper answer (in essence, if not in form) should be: "You're damn right I do!"

OBJECTIVIST CALENDAR

■ Nathaniel Branden's *Who is Ayn Rand?* has been published in a softcover edition by Paperback Library, Inc. First printing: 100,000 copies.

■ On Thursday, June 11, Ayn Rand will deliver lecture #18—"The Esthetics of Literature"—in the current NBI course on "Basic Principles of Objectivism." Time: 7:30 P.M. Place: Hotel Roosevelt, 45th St. & Madison Ave., New York City. Visitor's admission: $3.50.

■ On Tuesday, June 16, Dr. Leonard Peikoff will give the opening lecture of his 13-lecture course on "The History of Modern Philosophy." Time: 7:30 P.M. Place: Hotel Roosevelt, N.Y.C. Admission: $3.50.

■ NBI's Tape Transcription Division has scheduled "Three Plays by Ayn Rand" in Boston, on June 2, 9 and 16. The course on "Principles of Efficient Thinking" will begin in Cincinnati on June 8; "The Esthetics of the Visual Arts" will begin in Washington, D.C., on June 22 and in Indianapolis on June 26. For details, contact NBI.

■ Nathaniel Branden's article, "Mental Health versus Mysticism and Self-Sacrifice" (originally published in this NEWSLETTER, March 1963), has been reprinted in pamphlet form. Price: 25¢. (N.Y.C. residents add 1¢ sales tax.)

Published monthly at 120 East 34th Street, New York 16, N. Y.
Subscription rate: in United States, its possessions, Canada and Mexico, $5 for one year; other countries, $6.
Additional copies of this Newsletter: single copy 50¢ (coins, not stamps); 10 – 99 copies, 25¢ each plus postage (for first-class delivery add 1¢ per copy, for third-class delivery add ½¢ per copy); 100 or more copies, 15¢ each plus postage (same as above). (Bulk rates apply only to multiple orders of a single issue.)
For change of address send old address and new address with zone number if any. Allow us three weeks to process new subscriptions and change of address.

Ayn Rand and Nathaniel Branden, Editors and Publishers
Barbara Branden, Managing Editor
Elayne Kalberman, Circulation Manager

THE OBJECTIVIST NEWSLETTER

Edited and Published by AYN RAND and NATHANIEL BRANDEN

VOL. 3 NO. 7   JULY, 1964

CHECK YOUR PREMISES
By AYN RAND

The Argument from Intimidation

There is a certain type of argument which, in fact, is not an argument, but a means of forestalling debate and extorting an opponent's agreement with one's undiscussed notions. It is a method of by-passing logic by means of psychological pressure. Since it is particularly prevalent in today's culture and is going to grow more so in the next few months, one would do well to learn to identify it and be on guard against it.

This method bears a certain resemblance to the fallacy *ad hominem,* and comes from the same psychological root, but is different in essential meaning. The *ad hominem* fallacy consists of attempting to refute an argument by impeaching the character of its proponent. Example: "Candidate X is immoral, therefore his argument is false."

But the psychological pressure method consists of threatening to impeach an opponent's character by means of his argument, thus impeaching the argument without debate. Example: "Only the immoral can fail to see that Candidate X's argument is false."

In the first case, Candidate X's immorality (real or invented) is offered as proof of the falsehood of his argument. In the second case, the falsehood of his argument is asserted arbitrarily and offered as proof of his immorality.

In today's epistemological jungle, that second method is used more frequently than any other type of irrational argument. It should be classified as a logical fallacy and may be designated as "The Argument from Intimidation."

The essential characteristic of the Argument from Intimidation is its appeal to moral self-doubt and its reliance on the fear, guilt or ignorance of the victim. It is used in the form of an ultimatum demanding that the victim renounce a given idea without discussion, under threat of being considered morally unworthy. The pattern is always: "Only those who are evil (dishonest, heartless, insensitive, ignorant, etc.) can hold such an idea."

The classic example of the Argument from Intimidation is the story *The Emperor's New Clothes.*

In that story, some charlatans sell non-existent garments to the Emperor by asserting that the garments' unusual beauty makes them invisible to those who are morally depraved at heart. Observe the psychological factors required to make this work: the charlatans rely on the Emperor's self-doubt; the Emperor does not question their assertion nor their moral authority; he surrenders at once, claiming that he does see the garments—thus denying the evidence of his own eyes and invalidating his own consciousness—rather than face a threat to his precarious self-esteem. His distance from reality may be gauged by the fact that he prefers to walk naked down the street, displaying his non-existent garments to the people—rather than risk incurring the moral condemnation of two scoundrels. The people, prompted by the same psychological panic, try to surpass one another in loud exclamations on the splendor of his clothes—until a child cries out that the Emperor is naked.

This is the exact pattern of the working of the Argument from Intimidation, as it is being worked all around us today.

We have all heard it and are hearing it constantly:

"Only those who lack finer instincts can fail to accept the morality of altruism."—"Only the ignorant can fail to know that reason has been invalidated."—"Only black-hearted reactionaries can advocate capitalism."—"Only warmongers can oppose the United Nations." — "Only the lunatic fringe can still believe in freedom."—"Only cowards can fail to see that life is a sewer."—"Only the superficial can seek beauty, happiness, achievement, values or heroes."

As an example of an entire field of activity based on nothing but the Argument from Intimidation, I give you modern art—where, in order to prove that they *do* possess the special insight possessed only by the mystic "elite," the populace are trying to surpass one another in loud exclamations on the splendor of some bare (but smudged) piece of canvas.

The Argument from Intimidation dominates today's discussions in two forms. In public speeches and print, it flourishes in the form of long, involved, elaborate structures of unintelligible verbiage, which convey nothing clearly except a moral threat. ("Only the primitive-minded can fail to realize that clarity is over-simplification.") But in private, day-by-day experience, it comes up wordlessly, between the lines, in the form of inarticulate sounds conveying unstated implications. It relies, not on *what* is said, but on *how* it is said—not on content, but on tone of voice.

The tone is usually one of scornful or belligerent incredulity. "Surely you are not an advocate of capitalism, are you?" And if this does not intimidate the prospective victim—who answers, properly: "I am,"—the ensuing dialogue goes something like this: "Oh, you couldn't be! Not *really!*" "Really." "But *everybody* knows that capitalism is outdated!" "I don't." "Oh, come now!" "Since I don't know it, will you please tell me the reasons for thinking that capitalism is outdated?" "Oh, don't be ridiculous!" "Will you tell me the reasons?" "Well, really, if you don't know, I couldn't possibly tell you!"

All this is accompanied by raised eyebrows, wide-eyed stares, shrugs, grunts, snickers and the entire arsenal of non-verbal signals communicating ominous innuendoes and emotional vibrations of a single kind: *disapproval.*

If those vibrations fail, if such debaters are challenged, one finds that they have no arguments, no evidence, no proof, no reasons, no ground to stand on—that their noisy aggressiveness serves to hide a vacuum—that the Argument from Intimidation is a confession of intellectual impotence.

The primordial archetype of that Argument is obvious (and so are the reasons of its appeal to the neo-mysticism of our age): "To those who understand, no explanation is necessary; to those who don't, none is possible."

The psychological source of that Argument is social metaphysics. (See Mr. Branden's article on "Social Metaphysics" in the November 1962 issue of this NEWSLETTER.)

A social metaphysician is one who regards the consciousness of other men as superior to his own and to the facts of reality. It is to a social metaphysician that the moral appraisal of himself by others is a primary concern which supersedes truth, facts, reason, logic. The disapproval of others is so shatteringly terrifying to him that nothing can withstand its impact within his consciousness; thus he would deny the evidence of his own eyes and invalidate his own consciousness for the sake of any stray charlatan's moral sanction. It is only a social metaphysician who could conceive of such absurdity as hoping to win an intellectual argument by hinting: "But people won't *like* you!"

Strictly speaking, a social metaphysician does not conceive of his Argument in conscious terms: he finds it "instinctively" by introspection—since it represents his psycho-epistemological way of life. We have all met the exasperating type of person who does not listen to what one says, but to the emotional vibrations of one's voice, anxiously translating them into approval or disapproval, then answering accordingly. This is a kind of self-imposed Argument from Intimidation, to which a social metaphysician surrenders in most of his human encounters. And thus when he meets an adversary, when his premises are challenged, he resorts automatically to the weapon that terrifies him most: the withdrawal of a moral sanction.

Since that kind of terror is unknown to psychologically healthy men, they may be taken in by the Argument from Intimidation, precisely because of their innocence. Unable to understand that Argument's motive or to believe that it is merely a senseless bluff, they assume that its user has some sort of knowledge or reasons to back up his seemingly self-confident, belligerent assertions; they give him the benefit of the doubt—and are left in helplessly bewildered confusion. It is thus that the social metaphysicians can victimize the young, the innocent, the conscientious.

This is particularly prevalent in college classrooms. Many professors use the Argument from Intimidation to stifle independent thinking among the students, to evade questions they cannot answer, to discourage any critical analysis of their arbitrary assumptions or any departure from the intellectual *status quo*.

"Aristotle? My dear fellow—" (a weary sigh) "if you had read Professor Spiffkin's piece in—" (reverently) "the January 1912 issue of *Intellect* magazine, which—" (contemptuously) "you obviously haven't, you would know—" (airily) "that Aristotle has been refuted."

"Professor X?" (X standing for the name of a distinguished theorist of free-enterprise economics.) "Are you quoting Professor X? Oh *no,* not really!"—followed by a sarcastic chuckle intended to convey that Professor X had been thoroughly discredited. (By whom? Blank out.)

Such teachers are frequently assisted by the liberal goon-squad of the classroom, who burst into laughter at appropriate moments.

In our political life, the Argument from Intimidation is the almost exclusive method of discussion. Predominantly, today's political debates consist of smears and apologies, or intimidation and appeasement. The first is usually (though not exclusively) practiced by the liberals, the second by the conservatives. The champions, in this respect, are the liberal Republicans who practice both: the first, toward their conservative fellow Republicans—the second, toward the Democrats.

All smears are Arguments from Intimidation: they consist of derogatory assertions without any evidence or proof, offered as a substitute for evidence or proof, aimed at the moral cowardice or unthinking credulity of the hearers.

As an example, observe the smear campaign against Barry Goldwater. It consists of blatant misrepresentations, in spite of the fact that his position is on record and that his actual statements have been heard by millions of listeners. What, then, are the smear-squads counting on? They are counting on moral cowardice, self-doubt and social-metaphysical panic among the listeners. They are counting on the kind of mentality that would feel, in effect: "Yeah, I heard him myself and that's not what he said, but maybe I missed something.... If all those important people tell me otherwise, how am I to judge? Who am I to know?"

(It is to be hoped that Sen. Goldwater realizes that such mentalities do not determine the outcome of an election or the course of a country's history. If smears were an effective way of deceiving people, no dictator would ever need to establish censorship.)

I must mention, parenthetically and regretfully, that Sen. Goldwater is helping his enemies whenever he softens his stand. Vagueness lends plausibility to smears. While nothing can justify the misrepresentations on the part of the press, it is unfortunate that Sen. Goldwater has made their job easier by occasional lapses in the precision and consistency of his own statements—as, for instance, in his speech at Madison Square Garden on May 12. Let us hope that the pressure of his enemies will not tempt him to compromise (in regard to the party platform, for instance) and thus to commit political suicide. (If the Republican nomination is stolen from Sen. Goldwater, his supporters cannot, in honor, vote for any Republican substitute, not after the kind of tactics we have witnessed. Such tactics should not be sanctioned by anyone, least of all by the victims.)

The Argument from Intimidation is not new; it has been used in all ages and cultures, but seldom on so wide a scale as today. It is used more crudely in politics than in other fields of activity, but it is not confined to politics. It permeates our entire culture. It is a symptom of cultural bankruptcy.

How does one resist that Argument? There is only one weapon against it: moral certainty.

When one enters any intellectual battle, big or small, public or private, one cannot seek, desire or expect the enemy's sanction. Truth or falsehood must be one's sole concern and sole criterion of judgment — not anyone's approval or disapproval; and, above all, *not* the approval of those whose standards are the opposite of one's own.

Let me emphasize that the Argument from Intimidation does *not* consist of introducing moral judgment into intellectual issues, but of *substituting* moral judgment for intellectual argument. Moral evaluations are implicit in most intellectual issues; it is not merely permissible, but *mandatory* to pass moral judgment when and where appropriate; to suppress such judgment is an act of moral cowardice. But a moral judgment must always *follow,* not *precede* (or supersede), the reasons on which it is based.

When one gives reasons for one's verdict, one assumes responsibility for it and lays oneself open to objective judgment: if one's reasons are wrong or false, one suffers the consequences. But to condemn without giving reasons is an act of irresponsibility, a kind of moral "hit-and-run" driving, which is the essence of the Argument from Intimidation.

Observe that the men who use that Argument are the ones who dread a reasoned moral attack more than any other kind of battle—and when they encounter a morally confident adversary, they are loudest in protesting that "moralizing" should be kept out of intellectual discussions. But to discuss evil in a manner implying neutrality, is to sanction it.

The Argument from Intimidation illustrates why it is important to be certain of one's premises and of one's moral ground. It illustrates the kind of intellectual pitfall that awaits those who venture forth without a full, clear, consistent set of convictions, wholly integrated all the way down to fundamentals — those who recklessly leap into battle, armed with nothing but a few random notions floating in a fog of the unknown, the unidentified, the undefined, the unproved, and supported by nothing but their feelings, hopes and fears. The Argument from Intimidation is their Nemesis. In moral and intellectual issues, it is not enough to be right: one has to *know* that one is right.

The most illustrious example of the proper answer to the Argument from Intimidation was given in American history by the man who, rejecting the enemy's moral standards and with full certainty of his own rectitude, said:

"If this be treason, make the most of it."

Social Metaphysical Fear

By NATHANIEL BRANDEN

Several years ago, I witnessed a quiet little horror story.

A young man came to see me, at the suggestion of a mutual acquaintance who thought that Objectivism might help the young man with his personal and professional problems. After I had answered a number of questions concerning the Objectivist philosophy, the young man looked at me nervously—and then he said: "But if I accept these ideas, my friends will kill me. They won't let me live. No one will let you live."

"Do you mean," I asked, "that you expect your friends to murder you?" "No, of course not!" he answered. "Do you expect them to lock you in a room and starve you to death?" "No!" "Well, then, what *do* you mean?" "I mean, *they won't let me live.*"

I was unable to obtain any other answer from him or any explanation; he kept repeating, "They won't let me live," as if it were a self-evident fact, an axiom understood by everybody and taken for granted. Our mutual acquaintance, who had brought him, was dumbfounded, and kept asking: "What on earth do you mean?" The young man seemed unable to explain. He left, and I never heard from him again. I knew what he meant, but one seldom hears it stated quite so openly.

That boy was projecting the kind of inner hell that most people live with and seldom question. They do not all reach the extreme he had reached, but, in different forms and to varying degrees, most people carry the same fear within them.

To understand the nature of this fear and its role in men's lives, is to understand what makes it possible for men to betray their own rational knowledge, to betray their own self-interest and to surrender the world to evil.

This fear is a symptom of a psychological disorder to which I gave the name of *Social Metaphysics*. In my article on "Social Metaphysics," which appeared in the November 1962 issue of this NEWSLETTER, I discussed the psycho-epistemological default that lies behind this disorder.

In briefest essence, the default consists of rebelling against the responsibility of rational judgment, of resenting the "burden" of cognitive self-reliance—of seeking to exist as a parasite on the consciousnesses of others.

The consequence of this policy is the social metaphysician's profound sense of alienation from reality—the sense of being "a stranger and afraid in a world I never made"—the sense of being a metaphysical outcast, whose survival depends, not on the efficacy of his cognition of reality, but on his skill at grasping and complying with the values, judgments, terms, expectations and frame-of-reference of others—so that the universe in which he lives, the realm of his ultimate concern, is not the world of objective facts, but rather, the world as perceived and interpreted by others.

The incident involving the young man discussed above focuses with unusual clarity the peculiar nature of the social metaphysician's dependence and fear. The dependence is not, fundamentally, material or financial; it is deeper than any practical or tangible consideration; the material forms of parasitism and exploitation that some men practice are merely one of its consequences. The basic dependence is psycho-epistemological, a parasitism of cognition, of judgment, of values—a wish to function within a context established by others, to live by the guidance of rules for which one does not bear ultimate cognitive responsibility—a *parasitism of consciousness*. Since the social metaphysician's pseudo-self-esteem rests on his ability to deal with the-world-as-perceived-by-others, his fear of disapproval or condemnation is the fear of being pronounced inadequate to reality, unfit for existence, devoid of personal worth—a verdict which he hears whenever he is "rejected."

The meaning of the statement, "They won't let me live," was: "They won't keep me alive, they won't take care of me, they'll withdraw their approval, I'll be abandoned in an unknowable reality."

The *non-venal, non-practical* nature of the social metaphysician's dependence is illustrated in the following example:

Consider the case of a social metaphysician who is a multi-millionaire—and who is obsessively concerned with the issue of what everyone thinks of him, even his office boy. He feels driven to win the office boy's approval or liking, he watches eagerly for any signs of a personal response, and any indication of the boy's indifference or dislike makes him feel anxious or depressed. He finds himself being compulsively "charming" in order to win the boy's admiration. Now he certainly has nothing practical to gain from that boy's favor, neither money nor advice nor prestige nor business advantage; in any practical, business sense, the boy is his inferior; yet the multi-millionaire feels that he must win the boy's affection. What significance, then, does the boy have for him? It is not the office boy as an actual person that he seeks to placate or charm, but the office boy as a symbol of other people, of any other people, of mankind at large. The implicit thought behind his compulsion is *not*: "This office boy is a potential provider who will take care of me and guide me"—but: "I am acceptable to other people. People who are non-me, approve of me, they regard me as a good human being."

In order to belong *with* others, the social metaphysician is willing to belong *to* them.

Since, however, he is seeking a manner of survival improper to man by nature, since the intellectual sovereignty he has surrendered is an essential of mental health and self-esteem, he condemns himself to chronic insecurity—and to a fear of other men that is profoundly humiliating. The humiliation he endures—the sense of living under blackmail—is one of the most painful aspects of his plight.

The nature of his humiliation and fear, however, are seldom identified by him—because he would find it too degrading. Most often, he seeks to protect his pseudo-self-esteem by evading the humiliation and *rationalizing* the fear; he commonly attempts to justify his fear by an appeal to allegedly *"practical"* considerations, asserting that his fear is an appropriate response to an actual danger.

This is one of the most prevalently-used devices by which men seek to conceal their dread of independence and their moral cowardice.

The following examples illustrate this practice in various representative areas of life. They illustrate the manner in which men, prompted by a degrading fear they dare not acknowledge and so cannot overcome, invent non-existent dangers or grossly exaggerate minor ones, betray their own minds, sell out whatever authentic rationality they possess, contribute to the spread of values inimical to their own—and acquire a *vested interest* in believing that men are unavoidably evil, that human existence is evil, that the good has no chance on earth.

Consider the case of a professor of philosophy who is an atheist. He knows that the arguments for the existence of a God are thoroughly indefensible, he regards the notion of a supernatural being as irrational and destructive, he despises mysticism and considers himself an advocate of reason. But he evades the issue of atheism versus theism in his books and lectures, refuses to commit himself on the subject publicly, and, every Sunday, attends church with his parents and relatives.

He does not tell himself that his motive is fear, that he is terrified to stand alone against his family, friends and colleagues, that violent arguments of any kind make him panicky—and that he desperately wants to feel "accepted."

Instead, he tells himself that if he were to acknowledge his atheism, his career would be ruined (evading the fact that many professors are known atheists and their careers are unaffected by it). He tells himself that he is reluctant to cause pain to his elderly parents who are devoutly religious and who would be dismayed by his lack of faith (evading the fact that he is not obliged to "convert" his parents, merely to state his own convictions, and that a man who takes ideas seriously does not sacrifice his own judgments, which he knows to be rational, in order to placate people whose beliefs he knows to be irrational).

His rationalizations serve to shield him from a full recognition of his treason. But because it cannot be blanked out entirely, he is condemned to struggle against secret feelings of self-contempt — and he retaliates by cursing the malevolence of "the system" and of reality, since he cannot have his treason and his self-esteem, too.

Consider the case of a successful playwright who selects some important theme as the subject of a play, a theme requiring and deserving a serious dramatic presentation, who then realizes that his viewpoint will antagonize a great many people. He decides, therefore, to write the play as a comedy, making "good-natured fun" of the things he regards as evil, counting on his humor to prevent anyone from taking his views seriously and being offended or antagonized.

He does not tell himself that he dreads to be regarded as "unfashionable." Instead, he tells himself that serious plays dealing with controversial ideas are non-commercial — and dismisses the many exceptions as "freaks" requiring no explanation.

But he cannot entirely elude the knowledge that he has sold out the motive that prompted his desire to write the play in the first place. So he retaliates against his discomfiting sense of moral uncleanliness, by cursing the "stupidity" and "bad taste" of the masses.

Consider the case of a scientist who despises the obscurantist jargon that is rampant in his profession, and the "postulates" underlying that jargon, who is rationally convinced that the theories of many of his most highly regarded colleagues are wrong. But he twists his brain to adopt that jargon in his own writings, dilutes his criticisms in every possible way, and strives to smuggle his own ideas into the minds of his readers in such a manner that no one will notice the extent of his departure from established belief.

He does not tell himself that he is afraid of being ridiculed as an "outsider," or that he abjectly hungers for the esteem of men he regards as pretentious incompetents. Instead, he tells himself that he is "playing it smart," that when he becomes famous *he* will be the term-setter, and that the "practical" way to become famous, to become a *successful* innovator, is to make himself indistinguishable from everyone else.

But he cannot entirely drown the knowledge that this was not the view of science with which he started, and that the youth who had been himself would find it strange to be told that devotion to truth is expressed by catering to falsehood. So he retaliates by cursing the malevolence of a universe in which the concept of a "fashionable innovator" is a contradiction in terms.

Consider, finally, the case of a businessman who recognizes that capitalism is the only rational and just social system. He knows the intelligence, independence and dedication which industrial production requires, he knows that he *earns* his profits, he loves his work and is secretly proud of it. But he apologizes for his success publicly, contributes financially to intellectual organizations explicitly devoted to his destruction, accepts the government's expropriation of his wealth and infringement of his rights without moral protest, and begs mankind at large to forgive him for the sin of possessing ability.

He does not tell himself that he is afraid to challenge the prevailing value-system which damns his way of life as ignoble, selfish and materialistic, even though that value-system has never made sense to him; he does not tell himself that he cannot bear to feel alienated from all those who support that value-system; he does not tell himself that the responsibility of passing independent judgments in the realm of *morality* fills him with dread. Instead, he tells himself that his policy is motivated solely by the desire to protect his business interests, that it is "good sense" not to antagonize government officials, that it is "shrewd public relations" to finance intellectuals of the statist persuasion, so they will see he is a "nice guy," that it is "bad business" to court unpopularity. His secret fear takes the form of imagining that the masses are unthinking brutes, that they are the ultimate masters of reality—they can kill him and take over his property whenever they wish—so they must be placated, they must be told that he works only to serve them, he must restrain them by assuring them that theirs is the right superseding all other rights. This, he tells himself, is "hard-headed realism."

But he cannot entirely escape the disquieting awareness somewhere within him that his appeasement is not prompted by the motives he names, that his "practicality" and "cynicism" are protective affectations masking something worse. So he retaliates by cursing human irrationality and the malevolence of a world which demands that he be concerned with moral issues, one way or the other.

Such is the manner in which men deliver the world to evil.

To the extent that men irrationally surrender to fear, they increase the power of fear over their lives. More and more things acquire the power to *invoke* fear in them. Their self-confidence diminishes and their sense of danger grows. Social metaphysical fear is a cancer that either spreads or (if rationally resisted) contracts; but it does not stand still.

With every surrender to the consciousness of others, with every successive betrayal, the social metaphysician's sense of alienation from reality worsens and his sense of impotence finds confirmation. The shrinking remnants of his self-esteem are drained to appease an endless stream of blackmailers whose demands are inexhaustible — blackmailers who are any human consciousness but his own — blackmailers who, more often than not, are afraid of *his* judgment as he is afraid of *theirs,* who are desperately seeking *his* approval, who are committing the same form of treason and enduring the same humiliation. The grim irony is that all sides involved assure themselves that the grotesque farce of their selfless existence is motivated by considerations of "practicality."

OBJECTIVIST CALENDAR

■ NBI's Tape Transcription Division has scheduled the following starting dates: "Principles of Efficient Thinking" in Denver, July 1, and in Los Angeles, July 29; "The Esthetics of the Visual Arts" in San Francisco, August 4. "Three Plays by Ayn Rand" will be given in Los Angeles on August 3, 10 and 17.

Published monthly at 120 East 34th Street, New York 16, N. Y.

Subscription rate In United States, its possessions, Canada and Mexico: one year, $5; 2 years, $9. Other countries: one year, $6; 2 years, $11.

Additional copies of this Newsletter: single copy 50¢ (coins, not stamps); 10 – 99 copies, 25¢ each plus postage (for first-class delivery add 1¢ per copy, for third-class delivery add ½¢ per copy); 100 or more copies, 15¢ each plus postage (same as above). (Bulk rates apply only to multiple orders of a single issue.)

For change of address send old address and new address with zone number if any. Allow us three weeks to process new subscriptions and change of address.

Ayn Rand and Nathaniel Branden, Editors and Publishers
Barbara Branden, Managing Editor
Elayne Kalberman, Circulation Manager

THE OBJECTIVIST NEWSLETTER

Edited and Published by AYN RAND and NATHANIEL BRANDEN

VOL. 3 NO. 8   AUGUST, 1964

CHECK YOUR PREMISES
By AYN RAND

Is Atlas Shrugging?

(Lecture delivered by Ayn Rand at the Ford Hall Forum, Boston, on April 19, 1964.)

As the title of this discussion indicates, its theme is: the relationship of the events presented in my novel *Atlas Shrugged* to the actual events of today's world.

Or, to put the question in a form which has often been addressed to me: "Is *Atlas Shrugged* a prophetic novel — or a historical one?"

The second part of the question seems to answer the first: if some people believe that *Atlas Shrugged* is a *historical* novel, this means that it was a successful prophecy.

The truth of the matter can best be expressed as follows: although the political aspects of *Atlas Shrugged* are not its central theme nor its main purpose, my attitude towards these aspects — during the years of writing the novel — was contained in a brief rule I had set for myself: *"The purpose of this book is to prevent itself from becoming prophetic."*

The book was published in 1957. Since then, I have received many letters and heard many comments which amounted, in essence, to the following: "When I first read *Atlas Shrugged*, I thought that you were exaggerating, but then I realized suddenly — while reading the newspapers — that the things going on in the world today are exactly like the things in your book."

And so they are. Only more so.

The present state of the world, the political events, proposals and ideas of today are so grotesquely irrational that neither I nor any other novelist could ever put them into fiction: no one would believe them. A novelist could not get away with it; only a politician might imagine that he can.

The political aspects of *Atlas Shrugged* are not its theme, but one of the consequences of its theme. The theme is: *the role of the mind in man's existence* and, as a corollary, the presentation of a new code of ethics — the morality of rational self-interest.

The story of *Atlas Shrugged* shows what happens to the world when the men of the mind — the originators and innovators in every line of rational endeavor — go on strike and vanish, in protest against an altruist-collectivist society.

There are two key passages in *Atlas Shrugged* that give a brief summary of its meaning. The first is a statement of John Galt: "There is only one kind of men who have never been on strike in human history. Every other kind and class have stopped, when they so wished, and have presented demands to the world, claiming to be indispensable — except the men who have carried the world on their shoulders, have kept it alive, have endured torture as sole payment, but have never walked out on the human race. Well, their turn has come. Let the world discover who they are, what they do and what happens when they refuse to function. This is the strike of the men of the mind, Miss Taggart. This is the mind on strike."

The second passage — which explains the title of the novel — is: "'Mr. Rearden,' said Francisco, his voice solemnly calm, 'if you saw Atlas, the giant who holds the world on his shoulders, if you saw that he stood, blood running down his chest, his knees buckling, his arms trembling but still trying to hold the world aloft with the last of his strength, and the greater his effort the heavier the world bore down upon his shoulders — what would you tell him to do?'

"'I...don't know. What...could he do? What would *you* tell him?'

"'To shrug.'"

The story of *Atlas Shrugged* presents the conflict of two fundamental antagonists, two opposite schools of philosophy or two opposite attitudes toward life. As a brief means of identification, I shall call them the "reason-individualism-capitalism axis" versus the "mysticism-altruism-collectivism axis." The story demonstrates that the basic conflict of our age is *not* merely political or economic, but moral and philosophical — that the dominant philosophy of our age is a virulent revolt against reason — that the so-called "redistribution of wealth" is only a superficial manifestation of the mysticism-altruism-collectivism axis — that the real nature and deepest, ultimate meaning of that axis is *anti-man, anti-mind, anti-life*.

Do you think that I was exaggerating?

During — and after — the writing of *Atlas Shrugged*, I kept a file which, formally, should be called a "Research or Documentation File." For myself, I called it "The Horror File." Let me give you a few samples from it.

I shall read to you an example of modern ideology — from an Alumni-Faculty Seminar, entitled "The Distrust of Reason," at Wesleyan University, in June, 1959.

"Perhaps in the future reason will cease to be important. Perhaps for guidance in time of trouble, people will turn not to human thought, but to the human capacity for suffering. Not the universities with their thinkers, but the places and people in distress, the inmates of asylums and concentration camps, the helpless decision makers in bureaucracy and the helpless soldiers in foxholes — these will be the ones to lighten man's way, to refashion his knowledge of disaster into something creative. We may be entering a new age. Our heroes may not be intellectual giants like Isaac Newton or Albert Einstein, but victims like Anne Frank, who will show us a greater miracle than thought. They will teach us how to endure — how to create good in the midst of evil and how to nurture love in the presence of death. Should this happen, however, the university will still have its place. Even the intellectual man can be an example of creative suffering."

Do you think that this is a rare exception, a weird extreme? On January 4, 1963, *Time* magazine published the following news story:

" 'Ultimate performance in society' — not just brains and grades — should be the admissions criterion of top colleges, says Headmaster Leslie R. Severinghaus of the Haverford School near Philadelphia. In the *Journal of the Association of College Admissions Counselors,* he warns against the 'highly intelligent, aggressive, personally ambitious, and socially indifferent and unconcerned egotist.' Because these self-centered bright students have 'little to offer, either now or later,' colleges should be ready to welcome other good qualities. 'Who says that brains and motivated performance represent the dimensions of excellence? Is not social concern a facet of excellence? Is it not exciting to find a candidate who believes that "no man liveth unto himself?" What about leadership? Integrity? The ability to communicate both ideas and friendship? May we discount spiritual eagerness? And why should we pass over cooperation with others in good causes, even at some sacrifice of one's own scholastic achievement? What about graciousness and decency?' None of this shows up on college board scores, chides Severinghaus. 'Colleges must themselves believe in the potential of young people of this sort.' "

Consider the meaning of this. If your husband, wife or child were stricken with a deadly disease, of what use would the doctor's "social concern" or "graciousness" be to you, if that doctor had sacrificed his "own scholastic achievement"? If our country is threatened with nuclear destruction, will our lives depend on the *intelligence* and *ambition* of our scientists, or on their "spiritual eagerness" and "capacity to communicate friendship"?

I would not put a passage of that kind into the mouth of a character in the most exaggerated farce-satire — I would consider it too absurdly grotesque — and yet, this is said, heard and discussed *seriously* in an allegedly civilized society.

Are you inclined to believe that theories of this kind will have no results in practice? I quote from the *Rochester Times Union,* of February 18, 1960, from an article entitled "Is Our Talent Running Out?"

"Is this mighty nation running short of talent?

"At this point in history, with Russia and the United States 'in deadly competition,' could this nation fall behind because of a lack of brainpower?

"Dr. Harry Lionel Shapiro, chairman of the department of anthropology at the American Museum of Natural History in New York City, says, 'There is a growing uneasiness, not yet fully expressed . . . that the supply of competence is running short.'

"The medical profession, he says, is 'profoundly worried' about the matter. Studies have shown that today's medical students, on the basis of grades, are inferior to those of a decade ago.

"Some spokesmen for the profession have been inclined to blame this on the dramatic and financial appeal of other professions in this space age — engineering and other technological fields.

"But, Dr. Shapiro says, 'This seems to be a universal complaint.'

"The anthropologist spoke before a group of science writers at Ardsley-on-Hudson. This same group listened to some 25 scientists over a 2-week period — and heard the same lament from engineers, physicists, a meteorologist and many others.

"These scientists, outstanding spokesmen for their fields, found this subject of far greater importance than the need for more money.

"Dr. William O. Baker, vice president in charge of research at Bell Telephone Laboratories in Murry Hill, N.J., one of the top scientists in the country, said more research is needed — but that it will come not as a result of more money.

" 'It all depends on ideas,' he said, 'not very many, but they have to be new ideas.'

"Dr. Baker argued that the National Institute of Health has continually increased its grants but the results of the work have remained on a level, 'if they are not on the downgrade.'

"Eugene Kone, public relations director of the American Physical Society, said that in physics, 'We are not getting anywhere near enough first-class people.'

"Dr. Sidney Ingram, vice president of the Engineering Manpower Commission, said the situation 'is absolutely unique in the history of Western Civilization.' "

This news story was not given any prominence in our press. It reflects the first symptoms of anxiety over a situation which may still be hidden from the general public. But the same situation in Great Britain has become so obvious that it cannot be hidden any longer, and it is being discussed in terms of headlines. The British have coined a name for it: they call it *"The Brain Drain."*

Let me remind you, parenthetically, that in *Atlas Shrugged,* John Galt states, referring to the strike: "I have done by plan and intention what had been done throughout history by silent default." And he lists the various ways in which exceptional men had perished, in which intelligence had gone on strike against tyranny *psychologically,* deserting any mystic-altruist-collectivist society. You may also remember Dagny's description of Galt before she meets him, which he later repeats to her: "The man who's draining the brains of the world."

No, I do not mean to imply that the British have plagiarized my words. What is much more significant is that they *haven't;* most of them, undoubtedly, have never read *Atlas Shrugged.* What is significant is that they are facing — and groping to identify — the same phenomenon.

I quote from a news story in *The New York Times* of February 11, 1964: "The Labor party is calling for a Government study of the emigration of British scientists to the United States, a problem known here as the 'brain drain.' Labor's action . . . followed the disclosure that Prof. Ian Bush and his research team are leaving Birmingham University for the Worcester Foundation for Experimental Biology in Shrewsbury, Mass.

"Professor Bush, who is 35 years old, heads the department of physiology at Birmingham. His team of nine scientists has been investigating the treatment of mental diseases with drugs.

"Tonight it was learned that a leading physicist, Prof. Maurice Pryce, and a top cancer research pathologist, Dr. Leonard Weiss, would take posts in the United States . . .

"Tom Dalyell, a Labor spokesman on science, will ask

if the Prime Minister, Sir Alec Douglas-Home, will appoint a royal commission 'to consider the whole problem of the training, recruitment and retention of scientific manpower for service in Britain'. . .

"Professor Bush's decision was termed 'tragic' by Sir George Pickering, president of the British Medical Association. He described the professor as the 'most brilliant pupil I ever had and one of the most brilliant people I have ever met.' "

From *The New York Times* of February 12: "The furor over Britain's loss of scientific talent was intensified today when a foremost theoretical physicist said he was leaving for the United States.

"Dr. John Anthony Pople, superintendent of the Basic Physics Division at the National Physical Laboratory, said he was going to the Carnegie Institute of Technology in Pittsburgh in about a month.

"Afternoon newspapers used large headlines to report the move, the 13th since the weekend. One paper's front-page headline read: 'Another One Down the Brain Drain.' "

From *The New York Times* of February 13: "With the announcement today of the impending departure of at least five more scientists from Britain, the nation began searching with new anxiety for root causes of the exodus." The story names two of the departing scientists: Dr. Ray Guillery, 34-year-old associate professor of anatomy at University College, London, and, also from University College, Dr. Eric Shooter, 39, an assistant professor of biochemistry.

From *The New York Times* of February 16: "With Britain in a furor over the steady departure of her scientists, the nation is again searching for the causes of the exodus and demanding remedies. . . .

"The 'brain drain' as the departure of scientists is called here, is not new to Britain. For decades, foreign universities and other institutions of learning and research, especially in the United States, have been drawing scientific talent from Britain.

"In the last academic year Britain lost 160 senior university teachers, about 60 of them to the United States, according to a survey published by the Association of University Teachers. . . .

"British scientists with newly acquired Ph.D.'s have been leaving the country permanently at a rate of at least 140 a year, according to a report last year by the Royal Society. This would be about 12 per cent of the nation's output. . . .

"Most commonly, the scientists who depart permanently explain that funds available for research equipment and staff in the United States cannot be matched at home.

"Some say frankly that they are attracted by salaries two or three times higher than they get in Britain and also by what they consider a greater general regard in the United States for scientific effort and achievement.

"Others complain about the shortage of senior posts in universities, about the administrative jungle through which research grants must pass in Britain and about what they term the mean, controlling hand of the Treasury in all university grants."

What intellectual arguments are being offered to the scientists as an inducement to prevent them from leaving, and what practical remedies are being proposed? Quintin Hogg, Secretary of State for Education and Science, "appealed to the patriotism of scientists to stay at home. 'It is better to be British than anything else,' he said." An earlier story (October 31, 1963) stated that a "report, submitted by a committee headed by Sir Burke Trend, Secretary of the Cabinet, calls for reshaping Britain's civil science set up and for giving *increased powers* to the Minister of Science." (Italics mine.)

There is, of course, a great deal of implicit and explicit indignation against American wealth and big business, which the British seem to regard as chiefly to blame for the flight of their scientific talent.

Now I want to call your attention to two significant facts: the age and the professions of the scientists who were mentioned by name in these stories. Most of them are in their thirties; most of them are connected with theoretical medicine.

Socialized medicine is an established institution of Britain's political system. What future would brilliant young men see under it? Draw your own conclusions about the causes of the "brain drain" — about the future welfare of those left behind in the welfare state — and about the role of the mind in man's existence.

The next time you hear or read reports about the success of socialized medicine in Great Britain and in the other welfare states of Europe — the reports brought by the superficial, concrete-bound mentalities who cannot see beyond the range of the moment and who declare that they observe no change in the conscientious efficiency of the family doctors — remember that the source of the family doctors' efficiency, knowledge and power lies in the laboratories of theoretical medicine, and that that source is drying up. *This* is the real price which a country pays for socialized medicine — a price which does not appear on the cost sheets of the state planners, but which will not take long to appear in reality.

At present, we lag behind Great Britain on the road to the collectivist abyss — but not very far behind. In recent years, our newspapers have been mentioning alarming reports on the state of the enrollment in our medical schools. There was a time when these schools had a much greater number of applicants then could be accepted — and only the ablest students, those with the highest academic grades and records, had a chance to be admitted. Today, the number of applicants is falling — and, according to some reports, will soon be *less* than the number of openings available in our medical schools.

Consider the growth of socialized medicine throughout the world — consider the "Medicare" plan in this country — consider the strike of the Canadian doctors in Saskatchewan, and the recent strike of the doctors in Belgium. Consider the fact that in every instance the overwhelming majority of the doctors fought against socialization and that the moral cannibalism of the welfare-statists did not hesitate to force them into slavery at the point of a gun. The picture was particularly eloquent in Belgium, with thousands of doctors fleeing blindly, escaping from the country — with the allegedly "humanitarian" government resorting to the crude, Nazi-like, militaristic measure of *drafting the doctors into the army* in order to force them back into practice.

Consider it — and then read the statement of Dr. Hendricks in *Atlas Shrugged,* the surgeon who went on strike in protest against socialized medicine: "I have often wondered at the smugness with which people assert their right to enslave me, to control my work, to force my will, to violate my conscience, to stifle my mind — yet what is it that they expect to depend on, when they lie on an operating table under my hands?"

That is the question that should be asked of the altruistic slave-drivers of Belgium.

The next time you hear a discussion of "Medicare," give some thought to the future — particularly to the future of your children, who will live at a time when the best brains available will no longer choose to go into medicine.

Ragnar Danneskjöld, the pirate in *Atlas Shrugged,* said that he was fighting against "the idea that need is a sacred idol requiring human sacrifices — that the need of some men is the knife of a guillotine hanging over others and that the extent of our ability is the extent of our danger, so that success will bring our heads down on the block, while failure will give us the right to pull the cord." *This* is the essence of the morality of altruism: the greater a man's achievement and the greater society's need of him — the more vicious the treatment he receives and the closer he comes to the status of a sacrificial animal.

Businessmen — who provide us with the means of livelihood, with jobs, with labor-saving devices, with modern comforts, with an ever-rising standard of living — are the men most immediately and urgently needed by society. They have been the first victims, the hated, smeared, denounced, exploited scapegoats of the mystic-altruist-collectivist axis. Doctors come next; it is precisely because their services are so crucially important and so desperately needed that the doctors are now the targets of the altruists' attack, on a world-wide scale.

As to the present condition of businessmen, let me mention the following. After completing *Atlas Shrugged,* I submitted it, in galley-proofs, to a railroad expert, for a technical check-up. The first question he asked me, after he had read it, was: "Do you realize that all the laws and directives you invented are on our statute books already?" "Yes," I answered, "I realize it."

And *that* is what I want my readers to realize.

In my novel, I presented these issues in terms of abstractions which expressed the *essence* of government controls and of statist legislation at any time and in any country. But the principles of every edict and every directive presented in *Atlas Shrugged* — such as "The Equalization of Opportunity Bill" or "Directive 10-289"— can be found, and in cruder forms, in our *antitrust laws.*

In that accumulation of non-objective, undefinable, unjudicable statutes, you will find every variant of penalizing ability for being ability, of penalizing success for being success, of sacrificing productive genius to the demands of envious mediocrity. You will find such rulings as: the forced break-up of large companies or the "divorcement" of companies from their subsidiaries (which is my "Equalization of Opportunity Bill") — the forcing of established concerns to share with any newcomer the facilities it had taken them years to create — the compulsory licensing or the outright confiscation of patents — and, on top of this last, the order that the victims *teach* their own competitors how to use these patents.

The only thing that stands between us and the level of social disintegration presented in *Atlas Shrugged* is the fact that the statists do not dare as yet to enforce the antitrust laws to the full extent of their power. But the power is there — and you can observe the accelerating process of its widening application year by year.

Now you might think, however, that the "Railroad Unification Plan" and the "Steel Unification Plan," which I introduced toward the end of *Atlas Shrugged,* have no counterpart in real life. I thought so, too. I invented them — as a development dictated by the logic of events — to illustrate the last stages of a society's collapse. These two plans were typical collectivist devices for helping the weakest members of an industry at the expense of the strongest, by means of forcing them to "pool" their resources. I thought these plans were a bit ahead of our time.

I was wrong.

I quote from a news story of March 17, 1964:

"The three television networks have been asked by the Federal Government to consider a tentative plan under which each would turn over a share of its programs to existing or new TV stations that might operate from a competitive disadvantage. . . .

"A companion suggestion, also put forth for discussion by the [Federal Communications] Commission, would compel some stations now affiliated with one network to accept affiliation with an alternative chain.

"The proposals, which in effect call upon the 'haves' of the television industry to help the 'have nots,' drew strenuous objections over the weekend from the Columbia Broadcasting System. . . .

"The thinking behind the F.C.C. proposals is to help sustain existing ultra-high frequency stations and encourage the start of additional such outlets by guaranteeing them program resources that would win audiences. Most advertisers normally prefer the more powerful very-high frequency stations . . .

"Under the controversial proposals, the total pool of network programming would be carved up among two V.H.F. stations and one U.H.F. station."

The alleged justification for these proposals is the desire to correct "competitive imbalance."

Now observe today's situation in the sphere of labor.

In *Atlas Shrugged,* I showed that at a time of desperate shortages of transportation, due to shortages of motive power, track and fuel, the railroads of the country were ordered to run shorter trains at lower speeds. Today, at a time when the railroads are perishing, with most of them on the brink of bankruptcy, the railroad unions are demanding the preservation of "featherbedding" practices (that is, of useless, un-needed jobs) and of antiquated work and payment rules.

The press comments on this issue were mixed. But one editorial deserves a moment's special attention: it is from the *Star Herald* of Camden, N.J., of August 16, 1963, and it was sent to me by a fan.

"The money-makers, the powerful business leaders of America, have failed to realize that prosperity can be inhuman. They have failed to understand that people take precedence over profits. . . .

"Ambition and the drive for profit is a good thing. It spurs man to higher achievements. But it must be tempered by concern for society and its members. It must be slowed down in the light of human needs. . . .

"These are the thoughts that trouble us when we ponder the railroad stalemate. Crying 'featherbed!' like a war whoop, the managers of the railroads have insisted on eliminating tens of thousands of jobs . . . jobs that are the mainstays of homes . . . jobs that mean the difference between a man's feeling dignified or futile. . . . Before you vote yes for such painful progress, imagine your husband or brother or father as one of those destined to be sacrificed on the altar of progress. Far better, in our view, to have the government nationalize the railroads and prevent another human disaster on their one-way track of making profit at human expense."

This editorial had no by-line, but my anonymous admirer had written on it in penciled block letters: "By Eugene Lawson???"

That kind of "humanitarian" attitude is not directed against profits, but against achievement; it is not directed against the rich, but against the *competent*. Do you think that the only victims of the mystic-altruist-collectivist axis are a few exceptional men on the top of the social pyramid, a few men of financial and intellectual genius?

Here is an old clipping from my "Horror File," a news story dating years back: "Britain is currently stirred by the story of a young coal miner who has quit his job to prevent 2,000 miners from striking at Doncaster.

"Alan Bulmer, 31, got in trouble with his fellow workers when he finished a week's assignment three hours ahead of time. Instead of sitting down for three hours, he started on a new stint of work.

"More than 2,000 miners held a meeting last Sunday to object to his working too hard. They demanded that he be demoted for three months and his pay cut from $36 a week to $25.

"Bulmer quit his job to end the crisis, with the statement that it always has been his belief that 'a man should do a full day's work for a full day's pay.'

"Officials of the government-operated mines say the affair is up to the unions."

Ask yourself, what will become of that young man in the future? How long will he preserve his integrity and his ambition if he knows that they will bring him *punishments,* not rewards? Will he continue to exercise his ability if he is to be *demoted* for it?

This is how a nation loses the best of its men.

Do you remember the scene in *Atlas Shrugged* when Hank Rearden finally decided to go on strike? The last straw, which made the situation clear to him, was James Taggart's statement that he, Rearden, would always find a way to "do something"—even in the face of the most irrational and impossible demands. Compare that with the following quotation in a news story of December 28, 1959—which is a statement by Michael J. Quill, head of the Transport Workers' Union, commenting on a threatened city transit strike: "A lot of people are thinking we are taking this to the brink. But it so happens that every time we went to the well before, there was something there."

In the closing chapters of *Atlas Shrugged,* I described the labor situation of the country as follows: " 'Give us men!' The plea began to hammer progressively louder upon the desk of the Unification Board, from all parts of a country ravaged by unemployment, and neither the pleaders nor the Board dared to add the dangerous words which the cry was implying: 'Give us men of ability!' There were waiting lines years' long for the jobs of janitors, greasers, porters and bus boys; there was no one to apply for the jobs of executives, managers, superintendents, engineers."

An editorial in the July 29, 1963 issue of *Barron's* magazine mentions "the mounting scarcity of skilled labor including, as Dr. Arthur F. Burns noted in a recent critique of official unemployment statistics, 'extensive shortages of scientists, teachers, engineers, doctors, nurses, typists, stenographers, automobile and TV mechanics, tailors and domestic servants.' "

Do you remember the story of the Minnesota harvest disaster in *Atlas Shrugged?* A bumper crop of wheat perished along the roadsides, around the overfilled silos and grain elevators — for lack of railroad freight cars which, by government order, had been sent to carry a harvest of soybeans.

The following news story is from the *Chicago Sun Times* of November 2, 1962: "Illinois farm officials and grain dealers met Thursday in an effort to relieve an acute freight car shortage which is threatening Midwest's bumper grain harvest. . . .

"Farmers and grain dealers agreed that the shortage of railroad boxcars has become 'critical,' and saw little hope of relief for at least two weeks.

"Some grain elevator operators showed the group photographs of corn piled on the ground near elevators plugged up with corn which can't be shipped. . . .

"The boxcar shortage was blamed on the harvesting of three major crops — corn, soybeans and milo — at the same time this year. In addition, there have been heavy movements of government-owned grain."

In *Atlas Shrugged*, Ragnar Danneskjöld denounced Robin Hood as the particular image of evil that he wanted to destroy in men's minds. "He is the man who became the symbol of the idea that need, not achievement, is the source of rights, that we don't have to produce, only to want, that the earned does not belong to us, but the unearned does."

I shall never know whether Ragnar was or was not the inspiration of an article denouncing Robin Hood, which appeared last year in a British journal called *Justice of the Peace and Local Government Review*, a magazine of law and police affairs. The occasion for the article was the revival of the Robin Hood festival. "Having regard to the fact," said the article, "that the exploits of this legendary hero were chiefly concerned with robbing the rich under the specious motive of giving to the poor, a function which, in modern times, has been taken over by the welfare state, it is a question of some doubt whether a Robin Hood festival is not contrary to public policy."

But now we come to a composition that beats anything presented in *Atlas Shrugged*. I concede that I would have been unable to invent it and that no matter how low my estimate of the altruist-collectivist mentalities — and it is *very* low — I would not have believed this possible. It is not fiction — no fiction writer could get away with it. It is a *news story,* which appeared, on March 23, 1964, on the front page of *The New York Times*.

I quote: "Every American should be guaranteed an adequate income as a matter of right whether he works or not, a 32-member group calling itself the Ad Hoc Committee on the Triple Revolution urged today....

"The three revolutions listed in their statement, which they sent to President Johnson, were 'the cybernation revolution,' 'the weaponry revolution' and 'the human rights revolution.'

"'The Fundamental problem posed by the cybernation revolution in the United States is that it invalidates the general mechanism so far employed to undergird *people's rights as consumers*,' the committee said.

"'Up to this time,' it continued, 'economic resources have been distributed on the basis of contributions to production, with *machines and men competing for employment on somewhat equal terms*. In the developing cybernated system, potentially unlimited output can be achieved by systems of machines which will require little cooperation from human beings.'

"'The continuance of the income-through-jobs link as the only major mechanism for distributing effective demand — *for granting the right to consume* — now acts as the main brake on the almost unlimited capacity of a cybernated productive system.'

"The Committee urged that the link be broken by 'an unqualified commitment' by society to provide, through its appropriate legal and governmental institutions, 'every individual and every family *with an adequate income as a matter of right*.'" (All italics mine.)

To be provided — by whom? Blank out.

One would expect a proclamation of this kind to be issued by a group of small-town crackpots dissociated from reality and from any knowledge of economics. Or one would expect it to be issued by a group of rabble-rousers, for the purpose of inciting the lowest elements of the population to violence against any business office that owns an electronic computer and thus deprives them of their "right to consume."

But such was not the case.

This proclamation was issued by a group of professors, economists, educators, writers and other "intellectuals." What is frightening — as a symptom of the present state of our culture — is that it received front page attention, and that apparently-civilized people are willing to regard it as within the bounds of civilized discussion.

What is the cultural atmosphere of our day? See whether the following description fits it. I quote from *Atlas Shrugged* — from a passage referring to a series of accelerating disasters and catastrophies:

"The newspapers did not mention it. The editorials went on speaking of self-denial as the road to future progress, of self-sacrifice as the moral imperative, of greed as the enemy, of love as the solution — their threadbare phrases as sickeningly sweet as the odor of ether in a hospital.

"Rumors went spreading through the country in whispers of cynical terror — yet people read the newspapers and acted as if they believed what they read, each competing with the others on who would keep most blindly silent, each pretending that he did not know what he knew, each striving to believe that the unnamed was the unreal. It was as if a volcano were cracking open, yet the people at the foot of the mountain ignored the sudden fissures, the black fumes, the boiling trickles, and went on believing that their only danger was to acknowledge the reality of these signs."

The purpose of my discussing this today was, not to boast nor to leave you with the impression that I possess some mystical gift of prophecy, but to demonstrate the exact opposite: that that gift is *not* mystical. Contrary to the prevalent views of today's alleged scholars, history is *not* an unintelligible chaos ruled by chance and whim — historical trends *can* be predicted, and changed — men are *not* helpless, blind, doomed creatures carried to destruction by incomprehensible forces beyond their control.

There is only one power that determines the course of history, just as it determines the course of every individual life: the power of man's rational faculty — *the power of ideas*. If you know a man's convictions, you can predict his actions. If you understand the dominant philosophy of a society, you can predict its course. But convictions and philosophy are matters open to man's choice.

There is no fatalistic, predetermined historical necessity. *Atlas Shrugged* is not a prophecy of our unavoidable destruction, but a manifesto of our power to avoid it, if we choose to change our course.

It is the philosophy of the mysticism-altruism-collectivism axis that has brought us to our present state and is carrying us toward a finale such as that of the society presented in *Atlas Shrugged*. It is only the philosophy of the reason-individualism-capitalism axis that can save us and carry us, instead, toward the Atlantis projected in the last two pages of my novel.

Since men have free will, no one can predict with certainty the outcome of an *ideological* conflict nor how long such a conflict will last. It is too early to tell which choice this country will make. I can say only that if part of the purpose of *Atlas Shrugged* was to prevent itself from becoming prophetic, there are many, many signs to indicate that it is succeeding.

OBJECTIVIST CALENDAR

■ NBI's Tape Transcription Division has scheduled "Three Plays by Ayn Rand" in San Fernando Valley, Calif., on August 17, 24 and 31. The course on "Principles of Efficient Thinking" will begin in Washington, D.C. on Sept. 15. For details, contact NBI.

■ Reduced long-term subscription rates are now available for this NEWSLETTER: two years, $9; three years, $13. Overseas rates are: two years, $11; three years, $16.

■ Six articles on economics by Nathaniel Branden, originally published in this NEWSLETTER, have been reprinted as a single pamphlet under the title "Common Fallacies about Capitalism," dealing with such issues as monopolies, depressions, etc. Price: 75¢.

Published monthly at 120 East 34th Street, New York 16, N. Y.
Subscription rate In United States, its possessions, Canada and Mexico: one year, $5; 2 years, $9; 3 years, $13. Other countries: one year, $6; 2 years, $11; 3 years, $16.
Additional copies of this Newsletter: single copy 50¢ (coins, not stamps); 10 – 99 copies, 25¢ each plus postage (for first-class delivery add 1¢ per copy, for third-class delivery add ½¢ per copy); 100 or more copies, 15¢ each plus postage (same as above). (Bulk rates apply only to multiple orders of a single issue.)
For change of address send old address and new address with zone number if any. Allow us three weeks to process new subscriptions and change of address.

Ayn Rand and Nathaniel Branden, Editors and Publishers
Barbara Branden, Managing Editor
Elayne Kalberman, Circulation Manager

THE OBJECTIVIST NEWSLETTER

Edited and Published by AYN RAND and NATHANIEL BRANDEN

VOL. 3 NO. 9　　　　　　　　SEPTEMBER, 1964

CHECK YOUR PREMISES
By AYN RAND

"Extremism"
or
The Art of Smearing

In my article on "The Argument from Intimidation," in the July issue of this NEWSLETTER, I said that that Argument would grow more prevalent in the next few months. I did not, however, expect the extremes it would reach on the issue of "extremism."

Among the many symptoms of today's moral bankruptcy, the performance of the so-called "moderates" at the Republican National Convention was the climax, at least to date. It would be hard to imagine a lower level of brazenly vicious absurdity that men could permit themselves to attempt. It was an attempt to institutionalize smears as an instrument of national policy—to raise those smears from the private gutters of yellow journalism to the public summit of a proposed inclusion in a political party platform. *The "moderates" were demanding a repudiation of "extremism" without any definition of that term.*

Ignoring repeated challenges to define what they meant by "extremism," substituting vituperation for identification, they kept the debate on the level of concretes and would not name the wider abstractions or principles involved. They poured abuse on a few specific groups and would not disclose the criteria by which these groups had been chosen. The only thing clearly perceivable to the public was a succession of snarling faces and hysterical voices screaming with a violent intensity of hatred — while denouncing "purveyors of hate" and demanding "tolerance."

When men feel that strongly about an issue, yet refuse to name it, when they fight savagely for some seemingly incoherent, unintelligible goal—one may be sure that their actual goal would not stand public identification. Let us, therefore, proceed to identify it.

First, observe the peculiar incongruity of the concretes chosen as the objects of the "moderates'" hatred: "the Communist Party, the Ku Klux Klan and the John Birch Society." If one attempts to abstract the common attribute, the *principle,* by which these three groups could be linked together, one finds none—or none more specific than "political group." Obviously, this is not what the "moderates" had in mind.

The common attribute—the "moderates" would snarl at this point—is "evil." Okay, what evil? The Communist Party is guilty of the wholesale slaughter of countless millions spread through every continent of the globe. The Ku Klux Klan is guilty of murdering innocent victims through the mob violence of lynchings. What is the John Birch Society guilty of? The only answer elicited from the "moderates" was: "They accused Gen. Eisenhower of being a communist."

The worst category of crime in which this accusation could be placed is *libel.* Let us leave aside the fact that that libel was allegedly committed by the head of the Birch Society as a private individual and that it has been repeatedly repudiated by the Society. Let us also leave aside the fact that libel is what every anti-welfare-statist is chronically subjected to in public discussions. Let us agree that libel *is* a serious offense and ask only one question: does libel belong to the same category of evil as the actions of the Communist Party and the Ku Klux Klan?

Are we to regard wholesale slaughter, lynch-murders and libel as equal evils?

If one heard a man declaring: "I am equally opposed to bubonic plague, to throwing acid in people's faces and to my mother-in-law's nagging"—one would conclude that the mother-in-law was the only object of his hatred and that her elimination was his only goal. The same principle applies to both examples of the same technique.

No one truly opposed to the Communist Party and the Ku Klux Klan would take their evil so lightly as to equate it with the activities of a futile, befuddled organization whose alleged sin, at worst, might be irresponsible recklessness in making unproved or libelous assertions.

And more: the Communist Party as such is not a campaign issue, neither for the Republicans nor the Democrats nor the electorate at large; virtually everybody is denouncing the Communist Party these days and nobody needs the reassurance of a formal repudiation. The Ku Klux Klan is not a *Republican* issue or problem; its members, traditionally, are Democrats; for the Republicans to repudiate their vote would be like repudiating the vote of Tammany Hall—which is not theirs to repudiate.

This leaves only the John Birch Society as a real issue for a Republican convention. And it *was* the real issue—but in a deeper and more devious sense than might appear on the surface.

The real issue was not the John Birch Society as such: that Society was merely an artificial and somewhat unworthy strawman, picked by the "moderates" as a focal point for the intended destruction of much greater and much more important victims.

Observe that everyone at the Republican Convention seemed to understand the implicit purpose behind the issue of "extremism," but nobody would name it explicitly. The debate was conducted in terms of enormous, undefined "package-deals," as if words were merely approximations intended to *connote* an issue no one dared to *denote.* The result gave the impression of a life-and-death struggle conducted out of focus.

The same atmosphere dominates the public controversy now raging over this issue. People are arguing about "extremism" as if they knew what that word meant, yet no two statements use it in the same sense and no two speakers seem to be talking about the same subject. If there ever was a tower-of-Babel situation, this is surely it. Please note that *that* is an important part of the issue.

In fact, most people do not *know* the meaning of the word "extremism"; they merely sense it. They sense that something is being put over on them by some means which they cannot grasp.

In order to understand *what* is done and *how* it is being done, let us observe some earlier instances of the same technique.

A large-scale instance, in the 1930's, was the introduction of the word *"Isolationism"* into our political vocabulary. It was a derogatory term, suggesting something evil, and it had no clear, explicit definition. It was used to convey two meanings: one alleged, the other real—and to damn both.

The alleged meaning was defined approximately like this: "Isolationism is the attitude of a person who is interested only in his own country and is not concerned with the rest of the world." The real meaning was: "Patriotism and national self-interest."

What, exactly, is *"concern* with the rest of the world"? Since nobody did or could maintain the position that the
(continued on page 37)

Copyright © 1964 by The Objectivist Newsletter, Inc.

BOOKS

A History of Western Philosophy by W. T. Jones*
Philosophic Classics ed. Walter Kaufmann**
A History of Philosophy by Wilhelm Windelband***

Reviewed by **LEONARD PEIKOFF**

The philosophic thinking of the twentieth century is the cause of the present state of the world. But what is the cause of the cause? A major part of the answer lies in the history of philosophic thought from Greece to the present; only a knowledge of this history can give one the background, context and perspective required if one is clearly to understand the theories—and therefore the practices—which dominate today's world. Intellectually, the twentieth century is like the final conclusion of a long chain of syllogisms; the premises are to be found in the history of philosophy.

For those who wish to study the subject, there is no better book with which to begin than *A History of Western Philosophy* by W. T. Jones. This work, a standard college text on the subject for beginning students, presents, in a lucid, accurate and comprehensive manner, the main ideas—in metaphysics, epistemology, psychology, ethics, politics and esthetics—which have shaped Western civilization from the pre-Socratics through Bergson, Dewey, Russell and Whitehead.

Prof. Jones' *History* is not one of those encyclopedic and telegrammatic condensations which the introductory student finds more or less unintelligible; nor does it achieve its intelligibility by omitting crucial but difficult ideas. Rather, it attempts to present only the *central* ideas and concepts, and then to discuss these in sufficient detail to make their meaning fully clear to the uninitiated reader. The book achieves this goal with a high degree of success; among the features which enable it to do so are its constant use of original and intelligent analogies and illustrations designed to concretize the more abstract doctrines; its inclusion of lengthy (and relevant) passages from the philosophers' own writings, followed by an analysis of the meaning of the passages cited; its emphasis upon the arguments offered for and against the views expounded, combined with an attempt to evaluate their validity; and its consideration (more detailed than is usual for an introductory text) of the ways in which the various views of a philosopher are related to each other and to those of his culture, predecessors and followers.

A history of philosophy that is selective and evaluative rather than all-inclusive and non-committal, will necessarily be influenced by the author's own views: his views concerning what problems are of greatest philosophic importance—and concerning what answers are true. In this connection, it must be pointed out that, although Prof. Jones does discuss all the main philosophic issues in his book, he often fails to emphasize topics and problems to which an Objectivist would have given considerably more space and prominence; for instance, Aristotle's epistemology, or the theory of universals, or the relation of consciousness to existence.

On the evaluative level in particular, Objectivists will find much with which to disagree. Prof. Jones specifies at the outset the criteria he employs in appraising a philosophy. These criteria—and consequently the estimates based upon them—are of very unequal worth: some (e.g., self-consistency, systematic integration, comprehensiveness) are objective indices of a philosophy's merit; others (e.g., "consistency with the accumulated experience of the human race" and the ability to "satisfy a large number of people for a relatively long time") are ambiguous and/or irrelevant as evaluative standards. What

---

*Published by Harcourt, Brace & World, $12.50. Available from NBI BOOK SERVICE, 120 East 34th St., New York 16, N. Y., for $10.75.
**Published by Prentice-Hall in two volumes, $10.60 per volume. NBI BOOK SERVICE price, $9.25 per volume.
***Published by Harper Torchbooks in two volumes, paperbound: publisher's and NBI BOOK SERVICE price, $1.75 per volume.
(N.Y.C. residents add 4% sales tax; outside the U.S., add 15¢.)

Leonard Peikoff received his Ph.D. in philosophy from New York University. He is now Assistant Professor of Philosophy at the University of Denver.

---

one sorely misses is the recognition of the one criterion which really counts: i.e., that a good philosophy is a *true* philosophy, one which correctly describes the facts of reality. Prof. Jones, however, rules out this criterion; he believes that "even if there is an ultimate truth, nobody is likely to find it..."

Nevertheless, Prof. Jones does make every effort to be fair in his appraisals (his estimate of Nietzsche, however, is based on doctrines which are not representative of the full content and caliber of Nietzsche's thought); and he very often makes extremely valuable points (his eloquent contrast between the pro-man, pro-this-earth philosophy of Aristotle and its Christian antithesis in Augustine is particularly noteworthy in this connection). Moreover, the evaluation is clearly separated from the exposition, so that one is free to judge the philosophies presented by one's own standards.

No matter how well a historian summarizes a thinker's views, however, a full and detailed understanding of them requires one to read the philosopher's own writings and judge them for oneself. A valuable anthology of selections, covering philosophers from Thales to Kant, has recently been edited by Prof. Walter Kaufmann. Entitled *Philosophic Classics*, it contains the complete text of: four Platonic dialogues, a number of books and chapters from the Aristotelian corpus, Descartes' *Meditations* and Hume's *Enquiry Concerning Human Understanding*—as well as generous excerpts from many other famous works, such as Hobbes' *Leviathan*, Locke's *Essay*, Berkeley's *Principles* and Kant's *Critique of Pure Reason*. The Kaufmann anthology is an ideal companion piece to the Jones book. Since philosophic classics are often notoriously difficult to follow, the best procedure is to alternate between the two volumes, reading Jones' discussion of a given philosopher first as introduction and orientation, and then the appropriate source material in Kaufmann. By this method, each book can be used to illuminate and supplement the other.

A quite different type of history, which cannot be too highly recommended, is *A History of Philosophy* by Wilhelm Windelband, the distinguished nineteenth-century German philosopher and historian of ideas. Windelband's work is—deservedly—one of the great classics on the subject; it is worth reading, not only as a superlative history, but also as a philosophic work of stature in its own right. It will be of greatest value to advanced students, who already have some familiarity with the history of philosophy.

The stars of Windelband's *History* are not men, schools, countries or centuries, but *ideas*. Except in the case of a few philosophers of major importance, no attempt is made to summarize individual philosophic systems. What Windelband does instead is to define—in a way which is often original and always illuminating—the fundamental philosophic *questions* which concerned and united all of the thinkers of a period, no matter to what particular school they adhered; and then to organize his exposition around these questions, presenting and brilliantly interrelating the variety of answers given to them in that period. A few of the subsection titles will illustrate the comprehensiveness and fundamentality of the questions with which the book deals: Conceptions of Being; The Problem of Science; The Criteria of Truth; Spirit and Matter; The Controversy over Universals; The Problem of Values; Natural Right; The Problem of Civilization.

Windelband was a master of philosophic integration, in two key respects: in his ability, in treating a given period, to reveal important logical relationships between the most diverse and apparently unconnected topics; and in his ability to relate different periods, to detect central philosophic similarities uniting thinkers separated by centuries or millenia and often superficially described as fundamental antagonists. The cosmology of the pre-Socratics and Socrates' distinctive quest for ethical definitions; the nature of universals and the function of government; the metaphysics of Augustine and, 1200 years later, the post-Renaissance "problem of the external world"; the epistemological theory that sounds and colors are subjective and the ethics of asceticism; Kant's arguments against the possibility of the human mind knowing "things-in-themselves" and Hegel's development of the dialectic process—these are five instances, drawn at random from a book brimming with others of equal caliber, of the sort of issues which Windelband can join and unite by means of his truly remarkable

(continued on page 40)

Extremism (from page 35)

state of the world is of no *concern* to this country, the term "Isolationism" was a strawman used to misrepresent the position of those who were concerned with this country's interests. The concept of patriotism was replaced by the term "Isolationism" and vanished from public discussion.

The number of distinguished patriotic leaders smeared, silenced and eliminated by that tag would be hard to compute. Then, by a gradual, imperceptible process, the real meaning of the tag took over: the concept of "concern" was switched into *"selfless* concern." The ultimate result was a view of foreign policy which is wrecking the United States to this day: the suicidal view that our foreign policy must be guided, not by considerations of national self-interest, but by concern for the interests and welfare of the world, that is, of all countries except our own.

In the late 1940's, another newly coined term was shot into our cultural arteries: *"McCarthyism."* Again, it was a derogatory term, suggesting some insidious evil, and without any clear definition. Its alleged meaning was: "Unjust accusations, persecutions and character assassinations of innocent victims." Its real meaning was: "Anti-communism."

Senator McCarthy was never proved guilty of those allegations, but the effect of that term was to intimidate and silence public discussions. Any uncompromising denunciation of communism or communists was—and still is—smeared as "McCarthyism." As a consequence, opposition to and exposes of communist penetration have all but vanished from our intellectual scene. (I must mention that I am not an admirer of Sen. McCarthy, but *not* for the reasons implied in that smear.)

Now consider the term *"Extremism."* Its alleged meaning is: "Intolerance, hatred, racism, bigotry, crackpot theories, incitement to violence." Its real meaning is: "The advocacy of capitalism."

Observe the technique involved in these three examples. It consists of creating an artificial, unnecessary and (rationally) unusable term, designed to replace and obliterate some legitimate concepts—a term which sounds like a concept, but stands for a "package-deal" of disparate, incongruous, contradictory elements taken out of any logical conceptual order or context, a "package-deal" whose (approximately) defining characteristic is always a non-essential. This last is the essence of the trick.

Let me remind you that the purpose of a definition is to distinguish the things subsumed under a single concept from all other things in existence; and, therefore, their defining characteristic must always be that essential characteristic which distinguishes them from everything else.

So long as men use language, *that* is the way they will use it. There *is no* other way to communicate. And if a man accepts a term with a definition by non-essentials, his mind will substitute for it the *essential* characteristic of the objects he is trying to designate.

For instance, "concern (or non-concern) with the rest of the world" is *not* an essential characteristic of any theory of foreign relations. If a man hears the term "isolationists" applied to a number of individuals, he will observe that the essential characteristic distinguishing them from other individuals is *patriotism*—and he will conclude that "Isolationism" means "patriotism" and that patriotism is evil. Thus the real meaning of the term will automatically replace the alleged meaning.

If a man hears the term "McCarthyism," he will observe that the best-known characteristic distinguishing Sen. McCarthy from other public figures is an *anti-communist* stand, and he will conclude that anti-communism is evil.

If a man hears the term "extremism" and is offered the innocuous figure of the John Birch Society as an example, he will observe that its best-known characteristic is *"conservatism,"* and he will conclude that "conservatism" is evil—as evil as the Communist Party and the Ku Klux Klan. ("Conservatism" is itself a loose, undefined, badly misleading term—but in today's popular usage it is taken to mean "pro-capitalism.")

Such is the function of modern smear-tags, and such is the process by which they destroy our public communications, making rational discussion of political issues impossible.

The same mentalities that create an "anti-hero" in order to destroy heroes, and an "anti-novel" in order to destroy novels, are creating *"anti-concepts"* in order to destroy concepts.

The purpose of "anti-concepts" is to obliterate certain concepts without public discussion; and, as a means to that end, to make public discussion unintelligible, and to induce the same disintegration in the mind of any man who accepts them, rendering him incapable of clear thinking or rational judgment. No mind is better than the precision of its concepts.

(I call this to the special attention of two particular classes of men who aid and abet the dissemination of "anti-concepts": the academic ivory-tower philosophers who claim that definitions are a matter of arbitrary social whim or convention, and that there can be no such thing as right or wrong definitions—and the "practical" men who believe that so abstract a science as epistemology can have no effect on the political events of the world.)

Of all the "anti-concepts" polluting our cultural atmosphere, "extremism" is the most ambitious in scale and implications; it goes much beyond politics. Let us now examine it in detail.

To begin with, "extremism" is a term which, standing by itself, has no meaning. The concept of "extreme" denotes a relation, a measurement, a degree. The dictionary gives the following definitions: "Extreme, *adj.*—1. of a character or kind farthest removed from the ordinary or average. 2. utmost or exceedingly great in degree."

It is obvious that the first question one has to ask, before using that term, is: a degree—of what?

To answer: "Of anything!" and to proclaim that any extreme is evil because it is an extreme—to hold the *degree* of a characteristic, regardless of its *nature*, as evil—is an absurdity (any garbled aristotelianism to the contrary notwithstanding). Measurements, as such, have no value-significance—and acquire it only from the nature of that which is being measured.

Are an extreme of health and an extreme of disease equally undesirable? Are extreme intelligence and extreme stupidity—both equally far removed "from the ordinary or average"—equally unworthy? Are extreme honesty and extreme dishonesty equally immoral? Are a man of extreme virtue and a man of extreme depravity equally evil?

The examples of such absurdities can be multiplied indefinitely—particularly in the field of morality where only an *extreme* (i.e. unbreached, uncompromised) degree of virtue can be properly called a virtue. (What is the moral status of a man of *"moderate"* integrity?)

But "don't bother to examine a folly—ask yourself only what it accomplishes." What is the "anti-concept" of "extremism" intended to accomplish in politics?

The basic and crucial political issue of our age is: *capitalism versus socialism,* or freedom versus statism. For decades, this issue has been silenced, suppressed, evaded and hidden under the foggy, undefined rubber-terms of "conservatism" and "liberalism" which had lost their original meaning and could be stretched to mean all things to all men.

The goal of the "liberals"—as it emerges from the record of the past decades—was to smuggle this country into welfare statism by means of single, concrete, specific measures, enlarging the power of the government a step at a time, never permitting these steps to be summed up into principles, never permitting their direction to be identified or the basic issue to be named. Thus statism was to come, not by vote or by violence, but by slow rot—by a long process of evasion and epistemological corruption, leading to a *fait accompli.* (The goal of the "conservatives" was only to retard that process.)

The "liberals'" program required that the concept of *capitalism* be obliterated—not merely as if it could not exist any longer, but as if it had never existed. The actual nature, principles and history of capitalism had to be smeared, distorted, misrepresented and thus kept out of public discussion—because socialism has not won and cannot win in open debate, in an uncorrupted market place of ideas, neither on the ground of logic nor economics nor morality nor historical performance. Socialism can win only by default—by the moral default of its alleged opponents.

That blackout seemed to work for a while. But "you can't fool all of the people all of the time." Today, the frayed, worn tags of "conservatism" and "liberalism" are cracking up—and what is showing underneath is: capitalism versus socialism.

The welfare-statists need a new cover. What we are witnessing now is a desperate, last-ditch attempt to put over two "anti-concepts": the *"extremists"* and the *"moderates."*

To put over an "anti-concept," one needs a strawman (or scarecrow or scapegoat) to serve as an example of its *alleged* meaning. That is the role for which the "liberals" have chosen the John Birch Society.

That Society was thrust into public prominence by the "liberal" press, a few years ago, and overpublicized out of all proportion to its actual importance. It has no clear, specific political philosophy (it is not *for* capitalism, but merely *against* communism), no real political program, no intellectual influence; it represents a confused, non-intellectual, "cracker-barrel" type of protest; it is certainly *not* the spokesman nor the rallying point of pro-capitalism or even of "conservatism." *These* precisely are the reasons why it was chosen by the "liberals."

The intended technique was: first, to ignore the existence of any serious, reputable, intellectual advocacy of capitalism and the growing body of literature on that subject, past and present—by literally pretending that it did not and does not exist; then, to publicize the John Birch Society as the only representative of the "right"; then to smear all "rightists" by equating them with the John Birch Society.

An explicit proof of this intention was given in a TV interview last year (September 15, 1963) by Gov. Rockefeller, who later led the attack on "extremism" at the Republican Convention. Asked to define what he meant by "the radical right," he said: "The best illustration was what happened at the Young Republican Convention in San Francisco a number of months ago, where a man was elected, a Young Republican was elected on a platform to abolish the income tax, to withdraw from the United Nations, *I don't know whether he included* impeachment of Earl Warren, *but that is part of this whole concept,* and the idea that General Eisenhower was a crypto-communist." (Italics mine.)

Part of *what* concept?

The first two tenets listed are legitimate "rightist" positions, backed by many valid reasons; the third is a sample of purely Birchite foolishness; the fourth is a sample of the irresponsibility of just one Birchite. The total is a sample of the art of smearing.

Now consider the meaning ascribed to the term *"rightist"* within the "package-deal" of "extremism." In general usage, the terms "rightists" and "leftists" designate advocates of capitalism and socialism. But observe the abnormal, artificial stress of the attempt to associate *racism* and *violence* with "the extreme right"—two evils of which even the strawman, the Birch Society, is not guilty, and which can be much more plausibly associated with the Democratic Party (via the Ku Klux Klan). The purpose is to revive that old saw of pre-World War II vintage, the notion that the two political opposites confronting us, the two *"extremes,"* are: Fascism versus Communism.

The political origin of that notion is more shameful than the "moderates" would care publicly to admit. Mussolini came to power by claiming that that was the only choice confronting Italy. Hitler came to power by claiming that that was the only choice confronting Germany. It is a matter of record that in the German election of 1933, the Communist Party was ordered by its leaders to vote for the Nazis — with the explanation that they could later fight the Nazis for power, but first they had to help destroy their common enemy: capitalism and its parliamentary form of government.

It is obvious what the fraudulent issue of fascism versus communism accomplishes: it sets up, as opposites, two variants of the same political system; it eliminates the possibility of considering capitalism; it switches the choice of "Freedom or dictatorship?" into "Which kind of dictatorship?" — thus establishing dictatorship as an inevitable fact and offering only a choice of rulers. The choice — according to the proponents of that fraud — is: a dictatorship of the rich (fascism) or a dictatorship of the poor (communism).

That fraud collapsed in the 1940's, in the aftermath of World War II. It is too obvious, too easily demonstrable that fascism and communism are not two opposites, but two rival gangs fighting over the same territory — that both are variants of statism, based on the collectivist principle that man is the rightless slave of the state—that both are socialistic, in theory, in practice and in the explicit statements of their leaders— that under both systems, the poor are enslaved and the rich are expropriated in favor of a ruling clique—that fascism is not the product of the political "right," but of the "left"—that the basic issue is not "rich versus poor," but man versus the state, or: individual rights versus totalitarian government— which means: capitalism versus socialism. (See my lecture on "The Fascist New Frontier.")

The smear of capitalism's advocates as "fascists" has failed in this country and, for over a decade, has been moldering in dark corners, seldom venturing to be heard openly, in public—coming only as an occasional miasma from under the ground, from the sewers of actual leftism. And *this* is the kind of notion that the "liberals" are unfastidious enough to attempt to revive. But it is obvious what vested interest that notion can serve.

If it were true that dictatorship is inevitable and that fascism and communism are the two "extremes" at the opposite ends of our course, then what is the safest place to choose? Why, the middle of the road. The safely undefined, indeterminate, mixed-economy, "moderate" middle—with a "moderate" amount of government favors and special privileges to the rich and a "moderate" amount of government handouts to the poor—with a "moderate" respect for rights and a "moderate" degree of brute force—with a "moderate" amount of freedom and a "moderate" amount of slavery—with a "moderate" degree of justice and a "moderate" degree of injustice—with a "moderate" amount of security and a "moderate" amount of terror—and with a moderate degree of tolerance for all, except those "extremists" who uphold principles, consistency, objectivity, morality and who refuse to compromise.

The notion of compromise as the supreme virtue superseding all else, is the moral imperative, the moral pre-condition of a mixed economy. (See my article on "The Cult of Moral Grayness" in the June issue of this NEWSLETTER.) A mixed economy is an explosive, untenable mixture of two opposite elements, which cannot remain stable, but must ultimately go one way or the other; it is a mixture of freedom and controls, which means: not of fascism and communism, but of capitalism and statism (including all its variants). Those who wish to support the un-supportable, distintegrating *status quo,* are screaming in panic that it can be prolonged by eliminating the two *"extremes"* of its basic components; but the two extremes are: capitalism or total dictatorship.

Dictatorship feeds on the ideological chaos of bewildered, demoralized, cynically flexible, unresisting men. But capitalism requires an uncompromising stand. (Destruction can be done blindly, at random; but construction requires strict adherence to specific principles.) The welfare-statists hope to eliminate capitalism by smear and silence—and to "avoid" dictatorship by "voluntary" compliance, by a policy of bargaining and compromise with the government's growing power.

This brings us to the deeper implications of the term "extremism." It is obvious that an uncompromising stand (on anything) is the actual characteristic which that "anti-concept" is designed to damn. It is also obvious that compromise is incompatible with morality. In the field of morality, compromise is surrender to evil.

There can be no compromise on basic principles. There can be no compromise on moral issues. There can be no compromise on matters of knowledge, of truth, of rational conviction.

If an uncompromising stand is to be smeared as "extremism," then that smear is directed at any devotion to values, any loyalty to principles, any profound conviction, any consistency, any steadfastness, any passion, any dedication to an unbreached, inviolate truth—*any man of integrity.*

And it is against all these that that "anti-concept" has been and is being used.

Here we can see the deeper roots, the source that has made the spread of "anti-concepts" possible. The mentally-paralyzed, anxiety-ridden neurotics produced by the disintegration of modern philosophy—with its cult of uncertainty, its epistemological irrationalism and ethical subjectivism—come out of our colleges, broken by chronic dread, seeking escape from the absolutism of reality with which they feel themselves impotent to deal. Fear drives them to unite with slick political manipulators and Pragmatist ward-heelers to make the world safe for mediocrity by raising to the status of a moral ideal that archetypical citizen of a mixed economy: the docile, pliable, moderate Milquetoast who never gets excited, never makes trouble, never cares too much, adjusts to anything and upholds nothing.

It is such anti-intellect intellectuals who serve as the natural transmission-belts of "anti-concepts": ready-made slogans and prefabricated, indigestible "package-deals" are all that their uncritical mentalities can swallow and regurgitate. Who originates "anti-concepts"? Any pressure group that cares to bother —any pressure group of the *left*, since that is the only "mainstream" in which those intellectuals are conditioned to swim. "McCarthyism" was undoubtedly of communist origin. "Extremism," most likely, is the product of the welfare-statists —of the "liberal Establishment," if there is such a thing.

So long as these smear-games are played by private individuals and private organizations, they can be combatted; they are disastrous culturally, but only by default, by the sanction and cowardice of their opponents. It is a different matter when a concerted effort is made to smuggle "anti-conceptual" smears into public institutions, into the province of the government, and to give them official status as part of a major political party's platform.

The same political group who objected to the Attorney General's listing of subversive organizations (a listing supported by careful study and objective evidence), were attempting to establish a proscription or index of forbidden political views—in the calm, deliberative, judicious atmosphere of that contemplative retreat: a political convention.

The brazen effrontery of the attack on "extremism" at that Convention lay in the fact that one thing was clear to everybody, amidst the carefully manipulated fogginess of the rest: the attack was directed at Barry Goldwater and at the great majority of those present who were about to nominate him for the Presidency of the United States. They, the delegates, were asked to endorse the very smear against which they had fought—and won—an inordinately hard battle. It was as if the bad losers were trying their last trick by spitting in the faces of the winners, hoping that the too-lengthily-patient, too generous endurance of the victims would make them forgive it and prevent them from knowing that the spittle was poisonous.

The booing of Gov. Rockefeller was a remarkably restrained, *moderate* response, when one considers the content of what he was saying—and when one remembers that that crusader against unproved, libelous accusations was accusing his opponents, the Goldwater faction, of anonymous threats to bomb his campaign offices.

Yet, typically, the "liberal" press denounced the delegates' response as "extremist"—and praised Gov. Rockefeller's performance as "courageous." The same press raised the howl of "extremist, uncompromising, high-handed" against Sen. Goldwater's remarks on this issue, which expressed his own views in his own acceptance speech. Yet no one mentioned the high-handed, presumptuous impropriety of Gov. Hatfield who—in his keynote address, purportedly speaking for the whole Convention—permitted himself an "anti-extremist" smear, knowing that it had been rejected by the Platform Committee, by the majority of the delegates and by the leading candidate.

If there are any doubts in anyone's mind as to the innocence of the "moderates'" alleged "confusion"—such as their "inability to understand" Sen. Goldwater's position and their demands for "clarification"—observe that the best and most clarifying statement on this issue was made, surprisingly, by Gen. Eisenhower. In a televised interview, on July 13, he said that "extremism" is undesirable except in morals and in matters of exact science. The "moderates," who regard Gen. Eisenhower as their revered standard-bearer, ignored his statement entirely; *The N. Y. Times* omitted it from its report on his interview.

Intentionally or not, Gen. Eisenhower's statement destroys the effectiveness of "extremism" as an "anti-concept." The exemption of morals and exact science from the province of that smear, exempts the entire field of a rational man's values, convictions and concerns; it exempts the field of reason; what is left is only the field of blind emotions, irrational urges and subjective whims—and anyone who acts on such motives (whether to an "extreme" or to a "moderate" degree) certainly deserves to be condemned. (I suspect that Gen. Eisenhower may not classify politics as an exact science; but that is a matter open to debate. It can be demonstrated that all the so-called "humanities" can and should belong to the realm of exact science.)

It is obviously the inclusion of moral issues in the "package-deal" of "extremism" that Sen. Goldwater was fighting when he said: "I would remind you that extremism in the defense of liberty is no vice. And let me remind you also that moderation in the pursuit of justice is no virtue." (This, incidentally, was the best passage in his remarkable acceptance speech.)

In the preceding paragraph, Sen. Goldwater urged Republicans not to be "made fuzzy and futile by unthinking and stupid labels"—which indicated clearly that he was rejecting the undefined, undeclared meaning of a smear tag and was reminding the country of the *actual* meaning of the word "extreme."

A story in *The N. Y. Times* of July 23, admits the following: "Sen. Goldwater believed, sources close to him say, that some critics had defined 'extremism' to mean those Republicans who were strongly conservative.... He wanted, his associates note, to defend the convention delegates and other Republicans who had loyally supported him, and had been given the epithet 'kooks' by some journalistic and political critics.... He was annoyed that the words 'extremist' and 'moderate' had been used tellingly in the debate over his views without ever having been defined."

This was the attitude of a man of integrity. Here—for the first time in thirty years—was a Republican candidate who was not intimidated by the Argument from Intimidation.

Now observe the grotesque indecency of the "moderates'" response: ignoring the clear, specific meaning of his words, they howled that he had endorsed communists, Ku-Kluxers, Birchites, etc.—thus permitting themselves the impertinence of demanding that their hidden, unadmitted context be accepted as an objective one, and that their cowardly corruption of language be used by all, yet never be translated explicitly.

Some "moderates" walked out of the Republican Party in protest against that particular passage of Sen. Goldwater's speech—an action which was not evaluated by the "liberal" press as "intolerant, immoderate, uncompromising or extremist," but as "loyalty to one's conscience and convictions." (!) Ask yourself what was actually at stake—and whether modern politicians would risk their careers over an issue of mere semantic confusion or over a difference of opinion about the Birch Society?

But what *is* serious—deadly serious—as an indication of today's cynical contempt for the veracity and precision of public statements, is the fact that the "moderates" could permit themselves a protest of that kind, which, logically, should be taken to mean that they *do* regard extremism in the defense of liberty as a vice, and moderation in the pursuit of justice as a virtue. What is the state of our public communications, if the literal meaning of words and ideas has been discarded, and a kind of private code of signals, symbols, hints, innuendoes, subjective interpretations, secret signs and hidden meanings has taken over?

And, as if we had not had enough, *The N. Y. Times* is now trying to launch a new "anti-concept"—"*Goldwaterism.*" Draw your own conclusions about its implications.

Some of the newspapermen and TV commentators at the Republican Convention seemed to be genuinely puzzled by the intensity of the delegates' resentment against the press. The tactics described above are the explanation and the cause. How long can the press expect half the country (or more) to put up with that degree of injustice and with being consigned to the status of invisible men?

The "anti-concept" cliques do not represent the majority of the press—they are, probably, a very small minority—but the uncritical acceptance of their lead and their lingo has destroyed the country's respect for the press which is now losing its public influence and power.

In a sense, the press, too, is a victim: by giving currency, innocently or otherwise, to the "anti-concepts" designed to con the public, the press has conned itself. By evading the fact that welfare statism was far from a universally accepted doctrine, by ignoring the opposition and actually believing that only some negligible crackpots represented the political "right"—the press found itself in a state of shock, when confronted by the victory of a movement it had not known existed, yet which had been growing openly in front of its unseeing eyes.

That the press could miss the existence of a nationwide movement significant enough to nominate the presidential candidate of a major party, raises enormous questions about the criteria directing its news coverage. It is as if newsmen, with "their ears to the ground," had heard everything except an earthquake in full progress. There is something very wrong with the press of a free country, if such a situation could occur.

It is only under a dictatorship that the function of the press is to conceal, distort, deceive and mislead; in a free country, the function is to inform, to enlighten—which cannot be done by means of "anti-concepts." It is the moral obligation of all those who write or speak to define their terms with rigorous precision. Both Lenin and Hitler said that the destruction of a free society has to begin with the destruction of language. Without clear, intelligible, objective means of communication, no representative government is possible.

The first step toward a remedy, both for the press and the public, is to check one's premises and vocabulary—to discard all undefined words and "anti-concepts," then to stand on guard against the introduction of any new, derogatory and undefined terms.

As of this writing, it appears likely that the smear-potential of the term "extremism" will be defeated. In his speech of August 12, Sen. Goldwater said: "We repudiate character assassins, vigilantes, Communists and any group such as the Ku Klux Klan that seeks to impose its views through terror or threat of violence." (These are things which he had been repudiating all along.) The John Birch Society—the crux of the "anti-concept's" purpose—was omitted. This leaves the smear with its teeth pulled out. It is regrettable, however, that he used the term "extremism" at all, in that speech. It should not be used by anyone—it should be left to dissolve in the murk from which it came.

In conclusion, let me say that the best proof of an intellectual movement's collapse is the day when it has nothing to offer as an ultimate ideal but a plea for "moderation." Such is the final proof of collectivism's bankruptcy. The vision, the courage, the dedication, the moral fire are now on the barely awakening side of the crusaders for capitalism.

It will take more than an "anti-concept" to stop them.

BOOKS *(from page 36)*

capacity to detect and exhibit similarities, influences and relationships.

When lesser men write histories of philosophy, the reader too often gets the impression of a chaotic succession of unrelated viewpoints. Windelband's presentation reveals, in the history of philosophic developments, a structure, coherence and logic often approaching that of a geometric system. If such feats of integration deserve—as they do—to be called "thinking," then Windelband's English translator, James Tufts, is not exaggerating when he states in his Preface that the main justification for reading the book is "not so much to learn what other men have thought, as to learn to think."

Reading Windelband is not easy. Although the writing is clear and precise, it is also abstract and compressed, with almost no illustrations or examples. Nor is there any particular attempt to evaluate the doctrines which are presented, or to weigh arguments and counter-arguments. (Windelband himself was a Hegelian, and while this to some extent affects his selection of issues and awarding of emphases, his own views rarely appear explicitly in the book.) But for those who study the work with the diligent attentiveness it requires and deserves, the rewards are invaluable. If it is possible to acquire a truly profound understanding of the inner logic of the history of philosophy by reading just one book, then, to my knowledge, that one book would be Windelband's *History*.

Near the end of his work, commenting on the irrationalism and subjectivism which had come to dominate late nineteenth-century philosophy, Windelband warned: "Just this determines the problem of the future. Relativism is the dismissal and death of philosophy. Philosophy can live only as the science of values which are universally valid." In 1900, this was only a "problem of the future"; Windelband could not know what would happen in the next century. We do; the "dismissal and death of philosophy" is now the most firmly entrenched philosophy of all in both Europe and America. In the former, it commonly calls itself Existentialism; in the latter, Linguistic Analysis.

In the face of today's disintegration, historians of philosophy characteristically end their books now on a note somewhere between an amused weariness and an outright desperation. (Prof. Gordon H. Clark, in his *Thales to Dewey*, suggests that the reader turn back to the first page and start again. "This," he says in his final sentence, "will at least stave off suicide for a few days more.")

Writes Prof. Jones, in a section entitled "One More Word": "Now, the history of philosophy is certainly not 'good theater' —in fact, it is not even good melodrama. No handsome hero has emerged in the final chapter, when all is desperate and in doubt, to rescue the heroine, punish the villain, and settle all disputes." For a book which ends with Bertrand Russell, this is an understatement. But the history of philosophy is an ongoing process, and there are one or two chapters yet to be written; so far, we have seen only the second act curtain. Those who read this NEWSLETTER know that a dramatic third act has now been prepared, which awaits inclusion in the histories of philosophy in the next few decades.

OBJECTIVIST CALENDAR

■ On Monday, October 12, Nathaniel Branden's course on "Basic Principles of Objectivism" will begin in New York City. Place: Hotel Biltmore. Time: 7:30 P.M. Ayn Rand will participate in the question period which follows the lecture. For further details and descriptive brochure, contact NBI.

■ NBI's Tape Transcription Division has scheduled "Three Plays by Ayn Rand" in Montreal, on September 23 and 30 and October 7. The course on "Principles of Efficient Thinking" will begin in Youngstown on September 11, and in Washington, D.C., on September 14. For details, contact NBI.

■ An article by Ayn Rand, entitled "Let Us Alone!" appears in the Summer 1964 issue of the Yale Political Magazine. The issue is devoted to the topic: "Government and Business in America." Copies may be obtained (price, 50¢) by writing to: The Circulation Manager, Yale Political Magazine, 2138 Yale Station, New Haven, Connecticut.

Published monthly at 120 East 34th Street, New York 16, N. Y.

Subscription rate in United States, its possessions, Canada and Mexico: one year, $5; 2 years, $9; 3 years, $13. Other countries: one year, $6; 2 years, $11; 3 years, $16.

Additional copies of this Newsletter: single copy 50¢ (coins, not stamps); 10 – 99 copies, 25¢ each plus postage (for first-class delivery add 1¢ per copy, for third-class delivery add ½¢ per copy); 100 or more copies, 15¢ each plus postage (same as above). (Bulk rates apply only to multiple orders of a single issue.)

For change of address send old address and new address with zone number if any. Allow us three weeks to process new subscriptions and change of address.

Ayn Rand and Nathaniel Branden, Editors and Publishers
Barbara Branden, Managing Editor
Elayne Kalberman, Circulation Manager

THE OBJECTIVIST NEWSLETTER

Edited and Published by AYN RAND and NATHANIEL BRANDEN

VOL. 3 NO. 10   OCTOBER, 1964

Psycho-Epistemology

By NATHANIEL BRANDEN

(Part I of a two-part article)

The term "psycho-epistemology" was first introduced by Ayn Rand in *For the New Intellectual*. Since then, we have had many occasions to use it in our writing. The concept has figured prominently in NEWSLETTER articles. It is appropriate, therefore, to discuss in some detail the meaning, need for and importance of this concept.

As a field of scientific study, psycho-epistemology should be classified as a branch of psychology. It may be characterized as *the psychology of thinking*.

Epistemology, of course, is a branch of philosophy; it is the science that studies the nature and means of human knowledge. Its primary purpose is to establish the *criteria* of knowledge, to establish principles of evidence and proof, to enable man to distinguish between that which he may and may not regard as knowledge. Epistemology assumes, or takes as its "given," a normal (meaning: healthy) consciousness; it assumes an intact mind intent on knowing reality. Insofar as it is concerned with the internal operations of mind, with the volitional and automatic functions of consciousness, it is concerned from one standpoint exclusively: the standpoint of relevance to establishing the *criteria of knowledge*. Its basic concern is with the relationship of ideas to reality—not with mental processes *as such*.

The study of mental processes as such is the province of psychology—most particularly, of psycho-epistemology. *Psycho-epistemology is the study of the mental operations that are possible to and that characterize man's cognitive behavior.*

This branch of psychology is concerned with all the possible types of mental operations of which man's mind is capable; and with individual differences among men in their manner of cognitive functioning. This includes the sphere of perception, learning, concept-formation, memory, creativity, and, also, the various *mal*functions of consciousness. The basic interest of psycho-epistemology is with establishing the conditions of mental health, *i.e.*, of biologically appropriate mental functioning.

There is clearly a degree of interpenetration between epistemology and psycho-epistemology. But the following example serves to illustrate the essential difference in the spheres of their concern.

Suppose that a man declares: "The ideas of Mr. X cannot be true, because no one has advocated those ideas before, and because all the acknowledged authorities say Mr. X is wrong." In such a case, epistemology is concerned with the question: Is the process of inference exhibited in this statement logically valid? It answers: No; truth is not a matter of majority vote or authority vote; this argument is invalid and untenable. Psycho-epistemology asks a different question: What are the internal mental processes, what is the nature of the cognitive self-sabotage, that permits a man to make so gross an error? It answers (in essence): When weighing the ideas of Mr. X, the speaker is not focused on the facts of reality; he does not actually *form* a cognitive judgment about the truth of the ideas. His mind registers only that the ideas are unfamiliar, that they go against prevailing opinion, that the "significant others" disagree with them. What passes through the speaker's consciousness is images of those "significant others"—with looks of disapproval or sarcasm or anger on their faces. What dominates the speaker's emotions is a feeling of dread at opposing the authority of those faces. The speaker suspends any effort at independent judgment, the dread is permitted ascendancy—and, in effect, the order sent to the subconscious is to produce an argument that will allow the speaker to reject Mr. X's ideas. (Motivational psychology would ask still another question: What prompts a man to such abject dependence on the minds of others?)

In studying the operations of man's consciousness, psycho-epistemology seeks to identify those mental operations which are characteristic of all men, by virtue of their being human. It aims at discovering general *laws* of mental functioning. This would include, for instance, laws pertaining to the relationship between the volitional and automatic functions involved in thinking, the manner in which memories are retained and reactivated, the way in which ideational material is integrated subconsciously, the effects of conscious, volitional mental acts on subconscious, automatic processes, etc.

Psycho-epistemology seeks, also, to identify the respects in which individual men's mental processes can *differ*. Since man is a being of volitional consciousness, the responsibility is his to determine how he will use it—how he will deal, cognitively, with the material that reality presents to him. For example, one man's thinking can involve abstractions and principles to a high degree, while another man's thinking is narrow and concrete-bound; one man's approach to solving problems can be purposeful, systematic and explicit, while another man's approach is chaotic, random, emotional and unfocused.

Entailed by man's basic choice, to think or not to think, are three broad and fundamental psycho-epistemological alternatives—alternatives in his method of cognitive functioning.

(1) A man characteristically can activate and sustain a sharp intellectual focus, seeking to bring his understanding to an optimal level of precision and clarity—or he characteristically can relax his focus to the level of blurred approximation, in a state of passive, undiscriminating, goal-less mental drifting.

(2) A man characteristically can differentiate between *knowledge* and *feelings*, letting his judgment always be directed by his intellect, not his emotions—or he characteristically can *suspend* his intellect in the face of strong feelings, and deliver himself to the direction of impulses whose validity he does not judge and/or does not care about.

(3) A man characteristically can perform an independent act of analysis, in weighing the truth or falsehood of any claim, or the right or wrong of any issue—or he characteristically can accept, in uncritical passivity, the opinions and assertions of others, substituting their judgment for his own.

These alternatives are what the choice to think or not to think, actually means. *(continued on page 43)*

BOOKS

The God of the Machine by Isabel Paterson*

Reviewed by **AYN RAND**

An eloquently significant characteristic of the twentieth century is the odd combination of two facts: that politics is the paramount concern of our age—and that political philosophy has all but vanished from public consideration, discussion or knowledge.

The subject of politics is virtually absent from philosophical journals; political science textbooks are written predominantly on the intellectual level of a third-rate tabloid editorial; political campaigns are conducted—well, as you can see them being conducted. It is as if our age were bent on committing suicide in loyalty to the premise that the more pressing a problem, the less thought one must give it.

This cultural context adds an extra element of urgency to the importance of *The God of the Machine* by Isabel Paterson—a book which would be of great significance in any period, but which, today, has the effect of a unique phenomenon: it is a work of specifically *political* philosophy.

Originally published in 1943, this book may serve as an example of the fact that ideas are never fully lost in a free or even semi-free society: though out of print for many years, *The God of the Machine* has never been forgotten, its fame has been growing quietly and has led to its re-publication in a welcome and timely new edition.

One of the things that readers will learn from this book, apart from its specific contents, is what constitutes political *thinking*—on what level political issues have to be approached and discussed, what questions have to be answered, what are political *principles*. This may be an astonishing discovery to those reared in the modern belief that science is applicable only to inanimate objects, but when it comes to human life—to millions of human lives—knowledge is unnecessary, principles are irrelevant, causality is inoperative, consequences are unknowable, and the only thing required to create a free, prosperous society is the good intentions of its leaders armed with sufficient power.

The theme of *The God of the Machine* is the fact that a free, prosperous society requires a specific political structure, without which it can neither be created nor maintained.

Let me say at the outset that this is a brilliant and extraordinary book which narrowly misses greatness. It is brilliant in the perceptiveness, the incisiveness, the power, the scope of its analysis that presents—in carefully chosen, dramatically illuminating essentials—the history of man's long quest for freedom, from ancient Greece to World War II. It offers an unforgettable experience: a panorama of the centuries, as seen from the elevation of a truly grand intellectual scale.

But the book misses in one puzzling respect: the author's failure to present her own original theory clearly and unambiguously. Her theory—that political systems must be understood in terms of engineering—is presented in so sketchy, fragmented and confusing a manner that it clouds, rather than illuminates, her text.

According to this theory, men's productive energy, although different in kind from the energy moving the material universe, is subject to the same laws of nature and can be directed toward beneficent ends only through an appropriate type of mechanism. This mechanism is embodied in a country's political system, which, like any other kind of machine using energy, should be constructed according to the principles of mechanics. If a political system is properly constructed, it protects freedom and creates "a long circuit of energy"—of production, communication and trade—required to develop and maintain civilization. If it is improperly constructed, it can "short-circuit," blow up and destroy a human society.

To be fully demonstrated, such a theory would have to define the exact social-political equivalents of the engineering concepts it uses. This, unfortunately, Mrs. Paterson has not done: she uses the literal terms of mechanical engineering in regard to political systems, thus creating the impression of a merely metaphorical discussion.

But it is obviously not intended as a metaphor; it is, perhaps, an attempt to integrate a wide-scale abstraction. As it stands, however, it has to be regarded as a hypothesis, which is suggested and left undeveloped.

The book's paradox lies in the fact that the author's failure to demonstrate her theory does not diminish the actual value of her book. Its theme—that a free society requires a specific political structure—can be demonstrated without reference to engineering, in purely political and historical terms, which Mrs. Paterson does with brilliant eloquence. She discusses, logically and lucidly, what that structure has to be and why, what are the consequences of structural breaches, and why a monolithic, structureless totalitarian state is doomed to productive impotence, bloodshed, chaos and starvation.

The most important achievement of the book is Mrs. Paterson's definition of the nature of government—her demonstration of the fact that the crucial difference between the actions of a government and of private individuals lies in the government's function as an instrument of force.

She explains that a civilized economy, "which consists of production and exchange in a sequence extending through time and space," needs an agency to protect long-term contracts, and that a government is properly empowered by delegated authority to punish or restrain an individual "if he infringes the liberty or takes the property of another . . . That is what government does, and all it can do. It is a prohibitory and expropriative agency."

The great problem, therefore, in devising a proper political system, is to confine the government's function to a *retaliatory* use of force, leaving it no opportunity to expand its power and to grow into tyranny.

If you want to understand the achievement of the Founding Fathers and the importance of constitutional "checks and balances," read Chapter XII, "The Structure of the United States." If you want to know the steps by which that structure was breached, read Chapter XV, "The Fatal Amendments." And if you want to see the relevance of this book to the trends of our day—particularly to the Supreme Court's legislative reapportionment decision—pause on the following example of Mrs. Paterson's prophetic vision: "The final and formal stroke in disestablishing the states was the Seventeenth Amendment, which took the election of Senators out of the State Legislature and gave it to the popular vote. Since then the states have had no connection with the Federal government; representation in both Houses of Congress rests only on dislocated mass. . . . The immediate appearance of an enormous bureaucracy was the natural phenomenon of the structureless nation."

Space does not permit me to discuss all the valuable elements of this book, but I will call your special attention to the following subjects: the discussion of a fundamental difference

---

*Published by Caxton, $4.95. Available from NBI BOOK SERVICE, 120 East 34th St., New York 16, N. Y., for $4.25. (N.Y.C. residents add 4% sales tax; outside the U.S., add 15¢.)

between two antithetic political systems, in Chapter V, "The Society of Status and the Society of Contract"—the brilliant defense of American businessmen, in Chapter XVI, "The Corporations and Status Law"—the devastating critique of collectivism, in Chapter XVII, "The Fiction of Public Ownership" — the unusually simple and lucid presentation of the usually incomprehensible subject of monetary policy, in Chapter XVIII, "Why Real Money Is Indispensable"—and, for its victims (as who isn't?), Chapter XXI, "Our Japanized Educational System."

The God of the Machine is an invaluable arsenal of intellectual ammunition for any advocate of capitalism. It is a sparkling book, with little gems of polemical fire scattered through almost every page, ranging from bright wit to the hard glitter of logic to the quiet radiance of a profound understanding.

Regretfully, I must warn you also about the book's flaws; they are far less than its virtues, but they are there. The book suffers from a faulty organization. It is not written as a consecutive, systematic presentation of a case, but more as a series of essays dealing with various aspects of the theme. This creates a certain confusion, particularly at the start, in the first three chapters.

The chief flaw of the book's content is a touch of mysticism, which comes up once in a rare while, in occasional statements attempting to connect freedom with religion. Such statements are tacked on to the text, in the form of irrelevant and arbitrary assertions, which can be safely ignored, since the author builds her case on the solid ground of earthly logic.

That flaw extends, however, to other, non-mystical subjects, undercutting the intellectual discipline, level and manner of presentation: some issues are treated too briefly and arbitrarily; closely reasoned passages are marred, at times, by unproved assertions thrown in as if they were self-evident. Most of these do not pertain to politics, but to the author's philosophical frame-of-reference, which is far from perfect.

All books have to be read critically, but this is particularly true of *The God of the Machine*. It must be read cautiously, weighing every statement, using one's own judgment, accepting nothing on faith. Its virtues are so great that it is well worth the effort.

The book's last paragraphs state: "The most profound scholar of the past century, Lord Acton, who devoted his life to study of the history of human liberty, said it 'was that which *was not*, until the last quarter of the eighteenth century in Pennsylvania.' The event he denoted was unique in that it was the first time a nation was ever founded on reasoned political principles, proceeding from the axiom that man's birthright is freedom." And: "Whoever is fortunate enough to be an American citizen came into the greatest inheritance man has ever enjoyed. He has had the benefit of every heroic and intellectual effort men have made for many thousands of years, realized at last. . . ."

But the battle is not over—and in that great line of heroic and intellectual effort, *The God of the Machine* itself is another illustrious link.

BOOK REPORT

Since I have expressed admiration for the work of Mickey Spillane in the past, I must inform our readers regretfully that that estimate does not extend to his forthcoming novel, *Day of the Guns*. I feel obliged to state for the record that I object emphatically to the political views expressed in this novel, which are shocking and rationally indefensible.

Spillane's new hero, named "Tiger Mann," is a cross between a secret agent and a plain criminal: he belongs to a *private* organization that works with the unofficial help and sanction of some mysterious, unidentified and, apparently, omnipotent government officials—an organization formed to bypass legality and to fight communist spies by "direct action," which consists predominantly of murder.

All this is allegedly justified by some crude and appallingly ignorant political remarks, tossed in casually once in a while, to the effect that communists can be fought only by "people more ruthless than they are and like poverty protects Communism, money can protect Capitalism." Or: "The bad guys seem to have the edge these days and if you're going to be a bad one, be good and bad." Or: "You can't win with scared diplomacy, but a bullet on the way to somebody's gut doesn't know any fear at all and moves too fast to be stopped. It has a power all its own of changing the shape of things instantly . . ."

If some "liberal" wanted to embody in a single book the worst smears directed at anti-communists, this is the kind of book he would write.

So long as Spillane's former hero, Mike Hammer, was fighting criminals as a private individual, his battle could be taken as an abstract symbol of man's battle against evil. (This includes *One Lonely Night* in which the villains were communist criminals.) But when a cynical version of that battle is transposed into the realm of politics, and the hero is given a semi-official status in a semi-governmental gang, with none of the legal restraints that limit the power of a civilized government—it is no longer symbolic; it is a cheap, unthinking advocacy of force — of the statist philosophy — cheap because so dreadfully casual. One does not treat issues like that, *like that*.

Spillane is obviously not interested in politics. He uses the most awesome questions of our age as a mere backdrop for a rather sordid love story. He never even bothers to tell us what specific goal his hero is pursuing: it has to do with forestalling some communist efforts to damage the "prestige" of this country in the U.N., in connection with some American-British "proposal" which is never revealed to the reader.

The moral fire, the passionate dedication to justice, which was Mike Hammer's most attractive characteristic, is gone. Tiger Mann is a drab, nasty, embittered cynic. The sharp blacks-and-whites of a moral crusader are gone: Mann is as sordidly gray as the villains he fights. And, to refute Spillane's ideology on the basis of his own material: his hero — who believes in the power of guns—comes within two minutes of "righteously" murdering an innocent woman.

A fiction writer does not have to be a philosophical thinker. But there is a limit to the degree of non-thinking he can permit himself. *Day of the Guns* is a sadly eloquent indication of that limit. —AYN RAND

Psycho-Epistemology (*from page 41*)

The choices a man makes with regard to these alternatives are the crucial determinants of his individual psycho-epistemology. For example, the degree to which a man sustains a high level of intellectual focus, seeking precision and clarity in his own mental contents, is the degree to which he will function on the *conceptual* level of awareness, rather than the passive, *sensory* level of awareness. The degree to which a man substitutes the judgment of others for his own, failing to look at reality directly, is the degree to which his mental processes will be alienated from reality and he will function, not by means of concepts, but by means of memorized cue-words, *i.e.*, learned

(*continued on page 44*)

Psycho-Epistemology (*from page 43*)

sounds associated with certain contexts and situations, but lacking authentic cognitive content for their user.

The proper exercise of his rational faculty is not automatic; it is a process that man must direct and control. This fact gives psycho-epistemology its great practical importance. Psycho-epistemological knowledge offers man the means of raising the *efficacy* of his consciousness.

The efficacy of a man's thinking is determined, not merely by the rationality of his volitional mental functions in any given moment, but by his *past* psycho-epistemological policies. The clarity or vagueness of his past identifications, the honesty or evasiveness that he has previously practiced, the order or chaos of his past knowledge—all are part of the implicit context of any new act of thinking, all affect the automatic mental functions which are involved in any thinking process.

Consciousness is volitional, but it is not infinitely elastic; it possesses a nature, it has an identity—it is not a fluid, non-absolute plaything that man can safely maltreat as he wishes. Just as man cannot abuse his body and have it continue to function efficiently, so he cannot with impunity abuse his consciousness. If he characteristically evades, if he maintains a policy of sluggish mental passivity, if he runs from reality into autistic fantasy—if he fills his subconscious with an undigested mess of cue-words, non-understood abstractions, meaningless generalities and brain-disintegrating contradictions—if his deepest operating premise is that wishes matter more than facts and that emotions matter more than knowledge—if he devotes his energy, not to connecting and unifying the contents of his mind, but to never allowing his left hand to know what his right hand is doing—he will find, when he needs his intellect most, that it no longer serves him properly, it is not an efficient or reliable instrument; he will find that the process of thinking has become agonizing, and then he will cry that he lacks intelligence or that reason is "not enough"; and he will not know in what manner he has been his own destroyer.

One of the jobs of psycho-epistemology is to teach him to know.

Another, is to teach him how psycho-epistemological damage of this kind can be corrected.

(To be completed in our next issue)

SPECIAL NOTE

As of this writing, Senator Goldwater's campaign has been conducted so badly that unless he changes his methods, he is moving toward defeat. Those who are active in the campaign should urge him to raise some essential issues, instead of the secondary matters and vague generalities he has been discussing. He has not presented a case for capitalism; he has not demonstrated the statist-socialist trend of his opponents. The basic issue—the choice he had promised to give us—is being left to unspoken implications and will, once more, go by default, without being discussed or considered.

Sen. Goldwater's attitude has fluctuated so often between true courage and the usual Republican method that nothing can be predicted or counted upon with certainty. But I suggest —to those young people who have done their best for Sen. Goldwater—that they call on their philosophical resources *now*, to understand the causes of the bitter disappointment awaiting them and be prepared for it, if it comes.

—AYN RAND

OBJECTIVIST CALENDAR

■ On Sunday, October 4, Ayn Rand will resume her radio program for the Columbia University station WKCR (89.9 FM). The program is entitled "Ayn Rand on Campus" and will be broadcast every other Sunday, at 7 P.M. Some of the scheduled topics are: "Extremism," Oct. 4; "The Objectivist View of Politics," Oct. 18; "The Objectivist View of the Coming Election," Nov. 1.

If an Educational or University radio station in your community is interested in these programs, its representative may write to: Jack M. Kress, Program Director, WKCR-FM, 208 Ferris Booth Hall, Columbia University, New York, N. Y. 10027.

■ On Monday, October 12, Nathaniel Branden's course on "Basic Principles of Objectivism" will begin in New York City. Place: Hotel Biltmore, 43rd St. & Madison Ave. Time: 7:30 P.M. Admission: $3.50, payable at the door. (College and High School students, $2.75.) Ayn Rand will participate in the question period which follows the lecture.

■ On Thursday, October 29, Nathaniel Branden's course on "Basic Principles of Objectivist Psychology" will begin in New York City. Place: Hotel Roosevelt, 46th St. & Madison Ave. Time: 7:30 P.M. Admission: $3.50.

■ On October 20 and 30 respectively, NBI will begin its fall series on "Basic Principles of Objectivism" in Washington, D.C. and Boston. Mr. Branden will deliver both opening lectures in person. Miss Rand will join Mr. Branden in extended question periods following both lectures.

In addition, NBI's Tape Transcription Division has scheduled starting dates for "Basic Principles of Objectivism" in the following cities: Dallas, September 30; Fort Worth, Oct. 2; Denver, Oct. 2; Harrisburg, Oct. 5; San Francisco, Oct. 6; San Diego, Oct. 8; Los Angeles, Oct. 9; Phoenix, Oct. 9; San Jose, Oct. 11; San Gabriel Valley, Oct. 14; Cincinnati, Oct. 14; Detroit, Oct. 15; Chicago, Oct. 16; Anaheim, Oct. 16; San Fernando Valley, Oct. 17; Montreal, Oct. 23; Toronto, Oct. 26; Rockford, Oct. 27; Milwaukee, Nov. 13. Mr. Branden will deliver the opening night's lecture in person in Chicago, Cincinnati, Dallas, Denver, Detroit, Los Angeles, Montreal, San Diego, San Francisco, and Toronto.

Starting dates in additional cities will be listed here as they are scheduled. For further information, contact NBI.

Published monthly at 120 East 34th Street, New York 16, N. Y.

Subscription rate in United States, its possessions, Canada and Mexico: one year, $5; 2 years, $9; 3 years, $13. Other countries: one year, $6; 2 years, $11; 3 years, $16.

Additional copies of this Newsletter: single copy 50¢ (coins, not stamps); 10 – 99 copies, 25¢ each plus postage (for first-class delivery add 1¢ per copy, for third-class delivery add ½¢ per copy); 100 or more copies, 15¢ each plus postage (same as above). (Bulk rates apply only to multiple orders of a single issue.)

For change of address send old address and new address with zone number if any. Allow us three weeks to process new subscriptions and change of address.

Ayn Rand and Nathaniel Branden, Editors and Publishers
Barbara Branden, Managing Editor
Elayne Kalberman, Circulation Manager

THE OBJECTIVIST NEWSLETTER

Edited and Published by AYN RAND and NATHANIEL BRANDEN

VOL. 3 NO. 11   NOVEMBER, 1964

CHECK YOUR PREMISES
By AYN RAND

Introduction to "The Virtue of Selfishness"
(From Miss Rand's forthcoming book, to be
published by New American Library in December.
For details, see Objectivist Calendar.)

The title of this book may evoke the kind of question that I hear once in a while: "Why do you use the word 'selfishness' to denote virtuous qualities of character, when that word antagonizes so many people to whom it does not mean the things you mean?"

To those who ask it, my answer is: "For the reason that makes you afraid of it."

But there are others, who would not ask that question, sensing the moral cowardice it implies, yet who are unable to formulate my actual reason or to identify the profound moral issue involved. It is to them that I will give a more explicit answer.

It is not a mere semantic issue nor a matter of arbitrary choice. The meaning ascribed in popular usage to the word "selfishness" is not merely wrong: it represents a devastating intellectual "package-deal," which is responsible, more than any other single factor, for the arrested moral development of mankind.

In popular usage, the word "selfishness" is a synonym of evil; the image it conjures is of a murderous brute who tramples over piles of corpses to achieve his own ends, who cares for no living being and pursues nothing but the gratification of the mindless whims of any immediate moment.

Yet the exact meaning and dictionary definition of the word "selfishness" is: *concern with one's own interests.*

This concept does *not* include a moral evaluation; it does not tell us whether concern with one's own interests is good or evil; nor does it tell us what constitutes man's actual interests. It is the task of ethics to answer such questions.

The ethics of altruism has created the image of the brute, as its answer, in order to make men accept two inhuman tenets: (a) that any concern with one's own interests is evil, regardless of what these interests might be—and (b) that the brute's activities are *in fact* to one's own interest (which altruism enjoins man to renounce for the sake of his neighbors).

For a view of the nature of altruism, its consequences and the enormity of the moral corruption it perpetrates, I shall refer you to *Atlas Shrugged*—or to any of today's newspaper headlines. What concerns us here is altruism's *default* in the field of ethical theory.

There are two moral questions which altruism lumps together into one "package-deal": (1) What are values? (2) Who should be the beneficiary of values? Altruism substitutes the second for the first; it evades the task of defining a code of moral values, thus leaving man in fact without moral guidance.

Altruism declares that any action taken for the benefit of others is good, and any action taken for one's own benefit is evil. Thus the *beneficiary* of an action is the only criterion of moral value—and so long as that beneficiary is anybody other than oneself, anything goes.

Hence the appalling immorality, the chronic injustice, the grotesque double-standards, the insoluble conflicts and contradictions that have characterized human relationships and human societies throughout history, under all the variants of the altruist ethics.

Observe the absurd indecency of what passes for moral judgments today. An industrialist who produces a fortune, and a gangster who robs a bank are regarded as equally immoral, since they both sought wealth for their own "selfish" benefit. A young man who gives up his career in order to support his parents and never rises beyond the rank of grocery clerk, is regarded as morally superior to the young man who endures an excruciating struggle and achieves his personal ambition. A dictator is regarded as moral, since the unspeakable atrocities he committed were intended to benefit "the people," not himself.

Observe what this beneficiary-criterion of morality does to a man's life. The first thing he learns is that morality is his enemy: he has nothing to gain from it, he can only lose; self-inflicted loss, self-inflicted pain and the gray, debilitating pall of an incomprehensible duty is all that he can expect. He may hope that others might occasionally sacrifice themselves for his benefit, as he grudgingly sacrifices himself for theirs, but he knows that the relationship will bring mutual resentment, not pleasure—and that, morally, their pursuit of values will be like an exchange of unwanted, unchosen Christmas presents, which neither is morally permitted to buy for himself. Apart from such times as he manages to perform some act of self-sacrifice, he possesses no moral significance: morality takes no cognizance of him and has nothing to say to him for guidance in the crucial issues of his life; it is only his own, personal, private, "selfish" life and, as such, it is regarded either as evil or, at best, *amoral.*

If you wonder about the reasons behind the ugly mixture of cynicism and guilt in which most men spend their lives, these are the reasons; cynicism, because they neither practice nor accept the altruist morality — guilt, because they dare not reject it.

To rebel against so devastating an evil, one has to rebel against its basic premise. To redeem both man and morality, it is the concept of *"selfishness"* that one has to redeem.

The first step is to assert *man's right to a moral existence*—that is: to recognize his need of a moral code to guide the course and the fulfillment of his own life.

For a brief outline of the nature and the validation of a
(Continued on page 48)

Psycho-Epistemology

By NATHANIEL BRANDEN

(Part II of a two-part article)

In Part I of this article, I said that the primary concern of psycho-epistemology is with establishing the conditions of mental health. This statement carries an implication which needs to be elaborated—namely, that the issue of mental health is essentially psycho-epistemological.

Contrary to the claims of many psychologists that there is no objectively valid standard of mental health, the standard of mental health—*i.e.*, of biologically appropriate mental functioning—is the same as that of physical health: man's survival and well-being. A mind is healthy to the extent that its method of functioning is such as to provide man with the control over his existence that the support and furtherance of his life require.

"A healthy body is one whose organs function efficiently in maintaining the life of the organism; a diseased body is one whose organs do not. The standard by which health and disease are to be measured is *life*, for it is only the alternative of life or death that makes the concept of health or disease meaningful or possible. Just as medical science evaluates man's body by the standard of whether or not his body is functioning as man's life requires, so psychological science must uphold the standard of life in appraising the health or disease of man's consciousness. The health of man's consciousness must be judged, like the health of any other organ, by how well it performs its proper function; and the function of consciousness is perception, cognition, and the initiation and direction of action. An unobstructed consciousness, an integrated consciousness, a thinking consciousness, is a *healthy* consciousness. A blocked consciousness, an evading consciousness, a self-blinding consciousness, a consciousness disintegrated by fear or immobilized by depression, a consciousness dissociated from reality, is an *unhealthy* consciousness." *(Who is Ayn Rand?)*

That the problem of mental illness is essentially psycho-epistemological, is illustrated in the following examples:

Consider the case of a man who habitually avoids thinking about the causes of any desire or emotion that he suspects to be irrational; he seeks to deny the existence of such feelings by resorting to the devices of evasion and repression; when the feelings persist, he sabotages his consciousness further by surrendering to them blindly, ignoring his reason and intelligence, and resorting to additional devices of self-deception, such as self-justifying rationalizations. The emotional result is a state of neurotic anxiety. But the anxiety is a *consequence*, it is a *symptom* or *warning-signal* of the basic threat to his well-being, which lies in his method of using his consciousness.

Or consider the man who abdicates the responsibility of intellectual independence, and accepts a set of moral rules imposed by others, which he does not genuinely understand; failing to live up to these rules, he finds it easier to damn himself than to re-think his policy, to re-think the issue of morality, and, perhaps, to challenge the precepts his authorities have taught him. The end of his course is neurotic depression. But the core of his mental illness is not the depression as such, but the psycho-epistemological policies that brought him to it and that sustain it.

Or consider the case of a man who characteristically refuses to think about the validity or invalidity of his desires, and about the actions necessary to achieve them; he expects reality and other people "somehow" to provide him with happiness; he reacts to frustration with mindless anger and petulant defiance. His basic sense of life is, inevitably, one of anxiety, helplessness and malevolence. And *this* is inevitably reflected in the values and goals to which he feels himself drawn: values and goals that offer an outlet for his spite, hatred and parasitism. His consequent motivation is clearly "unhealthy"—but that motivation expresses a deeper corruption in his manner of using his consciousness. Again, the basic problem is psycho-epistemological.

A relationship of reciprocal causation exists between unhealthy psycho-epistemological practices, on the one hand, and emotional and motivational disturbances, on the other. That is, emotional and motivational disorders act to *worsen* existing psycho-epistemological errors and, often, to create *new* psycho-epistemological malfunctions.

For example, the anxiety produced by unhealthy cognitive policies, leads to additional and often worse evasions, repressions, rationalizations, flights from reality into fantasy, etc.—which aim at diminishing the anxiety. When a sufferer from neurotic depression, passively under the sway of his emotions, distorts reality in such a way as to find evidence of his worthlessness and depravity everywhere, his psycho-epistemology is *deteriorating* under the impact of his depression. Or again, unhealthy psycho-epistemology leads to unhealthy motivation, *i.e.*, to the formation of irrational values—but the pursuit of irrational values, because they *are* irrational, necessitates further psycho-epistemological self-sabotaging, further cognitive disintegration; which leads to the further pursuit of irrational values, etc.

Therefore, an effective psychotherapy must entail, to a crucial degree, teaching the patient *a new way of thinking*, a new method of cognitive functioning, a new psycho-epistemology—building on the foundation of whatever elements of a rational psycho-epistemology the patient still possesses. If one neglects this task, the best one might accomplish is to remove certain emotional symptoms or change certain specific values, but the underlying illness will remain untouched and will lead to the development of new symptoms.

The value and application of psycho-epistemological knowledge extends far beyond the treatment of mental illness. Since the broadest purpose of psycho-epistemology is to raise the efficacy of man's thinking, the knowledge discovered in this field is needed by *healthy* minds in order to achieve their full intellectual potential.

A healthy mind is one committed to the policy of seeking constantly to expand the range of its awareness, of functioning by the guidance of reason, and of preserving its intellectual sovereignty. But the manner of fully implementing this policy is not self-evident. It is here that psycho-epistemological knowledge is crucially relevant.

For example, in the process of artistic creation or scientific discovery, many complex integrations are made on the subconscious level. How to use one's subconscious, how to make its material readily available to the conscious mind, must be learned. Individual artists or scientists differ enormously in the ease and magnitude of their productiveness, according to their skill at this task. There is a great deal yet to be discovered about the psycho-epistemology of the creative process; as knowledge advances in this field, the productiveness of men's artistic and intellectual efforts will be raised as a consequence.

Why does one man get new ideas readily, while another man of equal intelligence does not? Why is one man intellectually imaginative, while another is not? Why does one man's mind leap to unconventional solutions to problems, while another man's mind is locked within a much narrower range of possibilities? Psycho-epistemological factors clearly are involved here. But what sort of factors? It is with such questions as these that the field of psycho-epistemology is concerned.

Psycho-epistemology is crucially relevant to the field of *ethics*. The Objectivist ethics is a *psycho-epistemological morality;* that is one of its most distinctive features.

I touched upon this issue in *Who is Ayn Rand?*, when I wrote: "The Objectivist ethics is especially significant for the psychotherapist because it is the first *psychological* morality. It is the first morality to define the issue of good and evil in terms of the *actions of one's consciousness*—that is, in terms of the manner in which one *uses* one's consciousness. It ties virtue and vice to the action directly subject to man's volition: the choice to think or not to think. The evils that a man may commit existentially, in action, are made possible only by the primary evil committed inside his consciousness: evasion, the refusal to think, the rejection of reason—just as the good that a man may achieve is made possible by his choice to think, to identify, to integrate, to accept reason as an absolute."

That the Objectivist ethics is a psycho-epistemological morality, may be observed in the fact that *rationality* is the foremost virtue it advocates—the virtue that is the base of all of a man's other virtues.

The central theme of *The Fountainhead* may be defined as a psycho-epistemological issue: the conflict between the first-hander and the second-hander—the man who judges reality independently versus the man who seeks to exist as a parasite on the consciousnesses of others. The basic difference between Roark and Keating is psycho-epistemological.

In *Atlas Shrugged*, the psycho-epistemological orientation is more explicit. The issue of rationality versus irrationality is the central conflict, projected through the psychology and actions of the various characters.

Consider, for example, the scene in James Taggart's office, after the Winston Tunnel catastrophe—specifically, the description of Taggart's internal processes: "He sat looking down at his desk, keeping his eyes and his mind out of focus ... He did not examine the events in Colorado, he did not attempt to grasp their cause, he did not consider the consequences. He did not think. The clogged ball of emotion was like a physical weight in his chest, filling his consciousness, releasing him from the responsibility of thought. The ball was hatred—hatred as his only answer, hatred as the sole reality, hatred without object, cause, beginning or end, hatred as his claim against the universe, as a justification, as a right, as an absolute."

Or again, in another scene involving James Taggart, when the consequences of his irrational actions are closing in on him: "... danger, to him, was a signal to shut off his sight, suspend his judgment and pursue an unaltered course, on the unstated premise that the danger would remain unreal by the sovereign power of his wish not to see it—like a foghorn within him, blowing, not to sound a warning, but to summon the fog."

Consider, by contrast, the many scenes in the novel in which the essence of the heroes' virtue is shown to be their intransigent rationality, realism, cognitive sovereignty, and *respect for facts*—maintained under acute emotional pressure and stress.

Consider, for example, the un-selfpitying conscientiousness of Hank Rearden's unceasing efforts to understand the bewildering irrationality of his family.

Or consider the scene in which Dagny Taggart learns of a new government directive which will have disastrous consequences for her railroad, for Hank Rearden and for Ellis Wyatt. Her mind numb with shock, she nonetheless retains the knowledge that the immediately urgent action she must take concerns Ellis Wyatt. "And because, were she lying crushed under the ruins of a building, were she torn by the bomb of an air raid, so long as she was still in existence she would know that action is man's foremost obligation, regardless of anything he feels—she was able to run down the platform and to see the face of the stationmaster when she found him—she was able to order: 'Hold Number 57 for me!'—then to run to the privacy of a telephone booth in the darkness beyond the end of the platform, and to give the long-distance operator the number of Ellis Wyatt's house."

Or the scene when Dagny sees John Galt for the first time: "... he looked as if his faculty of sight were his best-loved tool and its exercise were a limitless, joyous adventure ..."

Or the scene in the Valley, between Galt and Dagny. She asks: "'You want to hold me here, don't you?' 'More than anything else in the world.' 'You could hold me.' 'I know it.' His voice had said it with the same sound as hers. He waited, to regain his breath ...'It's your acceptance of this place that I want. What good would it do me, to have your physical presence without any meaning? That's the kind of faked reality by which most people cheat themselves of their lives. I'm not capable of it.... And neither are you.'"

One of the most powerful dramatizations of the Objectivist view of morality as psycho-epistemological, is the last sequence of Chapter VII, Part I, in which Hank Rearden learns that the legislature has passed the "Equalization of Opportunity Bill." If anyone wishes to understand, through a single scene, the difference between the Objectivist view of what constitutes moral greatness, and the view upheld by the conventional, mystical ethics, this is the sequence to read.

The sequence does not show a man mortifying his flesh, or giving all his wealth to the poor, or wandering into the jungle to minister to lepers.

It shows a man who has just learned that a major part of his life's work is to be torn away from him by a grossly unjust law, who is in excruciating agony, and who preserves his intellectual clarity—who preserves his capacity and will to think, to create, to move forward—whose answer to suffering and disaster is new heights of intellectual inventiveness and achievement.

Re-read that scene in the context of the present article. It can teach you a great deal about the psycho-epistemology of moral greatness.

It will also help you to understand why the fundamental issue of psychology—as well as of ethics—is a man's method of using his consciousness.

"The Virtue of Selfishness" (from page 45)

rational morality, see my lecture on "The Objectivist Ethics." The reasons why man needs a moral code will tell you that the purpose of morality is to define man's proper values and interests, that *concern with his own interests* is the essence of a moral existence, and that *man must be the beneficiary of his own moral actions*.

Since all values have to be gained and/or kept by men's actions, any breach between actor and beneficiary necessitates an injustice: the sacrifice of some men to others, of the actors to the non-actors, of the moral to the immoral. Nothing could ever justify such a breach, and no one ever has.

The choice of the beneficiary of moral values is merely a preliminary or introductory issue in the field of morality. It is *not* a substitute for morality nor a criterion of moral value, as altruism has made it. Neither is it a moral *primary*: it has to be derived from and validated by the fundamental premises of a moral system.

The Objectivist ethics holds that the actor must always be the beneficiary of his action and that man must act for his own *rational* self-interest. But his right to do so is derived from his nature as man and from the function of moral values in human life — and, therefore, is applicable *only* in the context of a rational, objectively demonstrated and validated code of moral principles which define and determine his actual self-interest. It is not a license "to do as he pleases" and it is not applicable to the altruists' image of a "selfish" brute nor to any man motivated by irrational emotions, feelings, urges, wishes or whims.

This is said as a warning against the kind of "Nietzschean egoists" who, in fact, are a product of the altruist morality and represent the other side of the altruist coin: the men who believe that any action, regardless of its nature, is good if it is intended for one's own benefit. Just as the satisfaction of the irrational desires of others is *not* a criterion of moral value, neither is the satisfaction of one's own irrational desires. Morality is not a contest of whims. (See Nathaniel Branden's articles "Counterfeit Individualism" and "Isn't Everyone Selfish?" in the April 1962 and September 1962 issues of this NEWSLETTER.)

A similar type of error is committed by the man who declares that since man must be guided by his own independent judgment, any action he chooses to take is moral if *he* chooses it. One's own independent judgment is the *means* by which one must choose one's actions, but it is not a moral criterion nor a moral validation: only reference to a demonstrable principle can validate one's choices.

Just as man cannot survive by any random means, but must discover and practice the principles which his survival requires, so man's self-interest cannot be determined by blind desires or random whims, but must be discovered and achieved by the guidance of rational principles. This is why the Objectivist ethics is a morality of *rational* self-interest — or of *rational selfishness*.

Since selfishness is "concern with one's own interests," the Objectivist ethics uses that concept in its exact and purest sense. It is not a concept that one can surrender to man's enemies, nor to the unthinking misconceptions, distortions, prejudices and fears of the ignorant and the irrational. The attack on "selfishness" is an attack on man's self-esteem; to surrender one, is to surrender the other.

A "Thank You" Note

In my lecture "Is Atlas Shrugging?" published in the August 1964 issue of this NEWSLETTER, I mentioned my "Horror File" of clippings on the present state of our culture. In response, I have received and am still receiving a large amount of mail from our readers sending me clippings for that file.

Since there are more letters than I can answer individually, I want to thank you here for your interest and for your judicious selection of material. It represents a valuable—and often "hair-raising"—contribution, and I appreciate it very much.

When and as our schedule permits it, I shall try to write another survey, using many of these clippings.

—AYN RAND

OBJECTIVIST CALENDAR

■ In December, New American Library will publish *The Virtue of Selfishness* by Ayn Rand, with several essays contributed by Nathaniel Branden. This book consists of a new introduction by Miss Rand, her lecture "The Objectivist Ethics" and eighteen essays originally published in THE OBJECTIVIST NEWSLETTER. The essays deal with the Objectivist theory of rational self-interest and clarify many aspects of today's moral and psychological confusion about the issue of egoism versus altruism. In paperback only. Available from NBI BOOK SERVICE, 120 E. 34th St., New York, N. Y. 10016; price 60¢, plus 15¢ postage.

■ The radio program "Ayn Rand on Campus" (on the Columbia University station WKCR-FM) will discuss the following topics: "An Analysis of the Election," Nov. 15; "Popular Fallacies Regarding Capitalism," Nov. 29; "Objectivism Versus Nietzscheanism," Dec. 13.

■ NBI's Tape Transcription Division has scheduled the following starting dates: "Basic Principles of Objectivism" in New Orleans, December 8, and in Seattle, Dec. 11; "Basic Principles of Objectivist Psychology" in St. Louis, November 10, and in Boston, December 1; "The Economics of a Free Society" in Toronto, Nov. 2; "The History of Modern Philosophy" in San Francisco, December 4. For details, contact NBI.

Published monthly at 120 East 34th Street, New York 16, N. Y.

Subscription rate in United States, its possessions, Canada and Mexico: one year, $5; 2 years, $9; 3 years, $13. Other countries: one year, $6; 2 years, $11; 3 years, $16.

Additional copies of this Newsletter: single copy 50¢ (coins, not stamps); 10 – 99 copies, 25¢ each plus postage (for first-class delivery add 1¢ per copy, for third-class delivery add ½¢ per copy); 100 or more copies, 15¢ each plus postage (same as above). (Bulk rates apply only to multiple orders of a single issue.)

For change of address send old address and new address with zone number if any. Allow us three weeks to process new subscriptions and change of address.

Ayn Rand and Nathaniel Branden, Editors and Publishers
Barbara Branden, Managing Editor
Elayne Kalberman, Circulation Manager

THE OBJECTIVIST NEWSLETTER

Edited and Published by AYN RAND and NATHANIEL BRANDEN

VOL. 3 NO. 12   DECEMBER, 1964

CHECK YOUR PREMISES
By AYN RAND

It Is Earlier Than You Think

The OBJECTIVIST NEWSLETTER began publication in January 1962. The first paragraphs of my first article in the first issue read as follows:

"Objectivism is a philosophical movement; since politics is a branch of philosophy, Objectivism advocates certain political principles—specifically, those of laissez-faire capitalism—as the consequence and the ultimate practical application of its fundamental philosophical principles. It does not regard politics as a separate or primary goal, that is: as a goal that can be achieved without a wider ideological context.

"Politics is based on three other philosophical disciplines: metaphysics, epistemology and ethics—on a theory of man's nature and of man's relationship to existence. It is only on such a base that one can formulate a consistent political theory and achieve it in practice. When, however, men attempt to rush into politics without such a base, the result is that embarrassing conglomeration of impotence, futility, inconsistency and superficiality which is loosely designated today as 'conservatism.'"

In my lecture "Conservatism: An Obituary," on December 7, 1960, I said:

"Nothing is as futile as a movement without goals, or a crusade without ideals, or a battle without ammunition. A bad argument is worse than ineffectual: it lends credence to the arguments of your opponents. A half-battle is worse than none: it does not end in mere defeat—it helps and hastens the victory of your enemies."

This is the lesson to be learned from the last presidential election. History has seldom offered so clear, awesome and awful a demonstration of that lesson on so large a scale.

It is not necessary to expect full philosophical consistency from a political candidate. But the extent of the philosophical vacuum exhibited in Barry Goldwater's campaign was unprecedented. In this respect, his campaign was unique.

It was as if history had adopted the method of a scientific laboratory or of fiction writing: the method of eliminating all the variables and presenting a single attribute in naked, dramatized isolation. In former campaigns, Republican candidates had been guilty of compromise, evasion, cowardice, "me-too'ism." Barry Goldwater was not; he had courage, frankness, integrity—and *nothing to say*.

This is what gave the campaign that aura of unreality which now, in retrospect, still makes it hard to believe. None of the usual causes of political disasters were applicable: there were no "vested interests" that could have profited by a campaign of that kind; there were no "practical" reasons for that pointless, aimless performance. There was only one reason: a candidate who had promised to fight on the battlefield of philosophy, but did not know the meaning of that word.

Barry Goldwater did not lack moral courage: what he lacked was *intellectual* courage—a quality one cannot acquire except from a set of firm philosophical convictions. His past record, in that respect, had been mixed, but immeasurably superior to what emerged in the campaign. He was not a leader but a product of today's culture. In a fiction-like manner, he was the personified embodiment of a desperate, incoherent, inarticulate public need. When that need threw him to the crest—not of a "mainstream," but of a churning, direction-less underground current—one of two things had to happen: either the best premises of his mixed ideological equipment had to rise to the occasion and give voice to that current—or, being precariously inadequate, they had to collapse. They collapsed.

There was a brief moment—following his nomination and his acceptance speech—when the country seemed to hold its breath respectfully, sensing, rather than knowing, that it needed the kind of crusade he had promised to lead. The attitude, not of his supporters, but of his enemies was particularly significant and gave an indication of what might have been possible.

The entire campaign can be summed up in two quotations from James Reston, the columnist of *The N.Y. Times*, who is one of the best exponents of the "liberal" consensus.

On July 22, James Reston, who opposed Sen. Goldwater, wrote a column that had an oddly solemn, respectful, almost wistfully hopeful tone. He said, among other things: "Underneath all the popular personal and partisan issues, the Republican Presidential nominee, whether you like him or not, has raised some basic questions that have troubled men since the days of Aristotle.

"What sort of world is this where men aspire to good and yet so often achieve evil? Where lies the source of authority: In the laws of man or nature? What of the relationships of the individual to the community, to the state, and to the eternal? What is man's place in it all, and how are his ideals, and his values, related not only to an increasingly complicated and crowded world but to the universe? . . .

"It has been a long time since we have had a really good debate in the United States on the fundamentals of our society. . . . A savage conflict between the parties on ideological grounds cannot be avoided now, but it can have some real advantages. Ideally, the purpose of an election is to clarify and not to confuse the issues, to destroy and not perpetuate illusion, to make a little clearer what we are and where we are.

"Senator Goldwater has set the stage for this. He has offered his choice. He has arrested the attention of the nation. He may not have the answers, but at least he has raised some good questions, and the Democrats, if they are wise, will stop moaning about Barry and his allies, and start dealing with his arguments."

On October 11, James Reston wrote that Sen. Goldwater's "campaign has descended from philosophy to wisecracks . . .

"He began with the philosophy of 'the whole man' in San Francisco, with Edmund Burke, and the Natural Law, with Hobbes, and the law of the jungle, with Natural Rights, and Adam Smith, and Locke and the Sanctity of Property, and the inequality of man.

"But he is ending up with Bob Hope and the McCarthy charges of 'soft on Communism,' and even with that old gag, originally applied to Nixon: 'Would you buy a used car from Lyndon Johnson?'"

What took place between these two dates was a fantastic waste of an unrepeatable historical opportunity.

The keynote and danger signal was sounded by the campaign's slogan: "In your heart, you know he's right." One could hope that this was merely an ill-advised, embarrassing catch phrase. But it wasn't. Whoever had chosen it, meant it.

The whole of what was to be a philosophical campaign, was devoted to an attempt to by-pass the mind.

From the height of the loftiest forum on earth, the doorstep to the White House—with the whole country and the whole world stopped to hear him—with the country perishing by default, in blind confusion, and the world snarling its ignorant hatred at the social system it had never discovered, the American system, the system of freedom: capitalism—after decades of the totalitarian statists' ferocious struggle to prevent mankind from discovering it—decades of suppressions, misrepresentations, falsehoods, smears—with two months of the world's attention at his command, two months in which to blast through the muck and proclaim capitalism's credo to a desperate world —the champion of capitalism was talking about home, family, prayer and the corruption of government underlings!

The "savage conflict between the parties on ideological

grounds" never materialized. There was *less* ideological content in this campaign than in any of the previous ones. A crusade may be savage, it may be violent, it may be ruthless. But a *boring crusade* is an incredible contradiction in terms. Yet that is what we witnessed.

The only "ideology" that the Republican candidate offered us was like a newspaper consisting of headlines over blank spaces where the facts, the proofs, the explanations should have appeared. The headlines were vague generalities—the worn-out bromides of the past thirty years.

"Big Government Is Bad." Why is it bad? Blank out. "Freedom Is Good." How does it work? Blank out. "Foreign Policy Must Be Firm." What does firmness consist of? Blank out. "The Record Of The Present Administration Is Disastrous." *What is that record?* Blank out.

Observe also the chaotic make-up of the candidate's ideological newspaper—the lack of any *hierarchical* order of importance. On page 1, and without any explanatory or ideological headline—a story proposing to sell the TVA (which is not the worst nor the most urgent example of governmental encroachment). Somewhere on page 27—a headline about "Free Enterprise," without any story. On page 1, a story proposing to give the NATO commander permission to use "conventional" nuclear weapons (a technical military matter, which civilian voters are not qualified to judge). On page 28, a headline about "Winning The Cold War," over a blank space. On page 38, a sub-head announcing that the NATO commander possesses a similar permission already and has possessed it for some time past. Et cetera.

All of this added up to a terrifying jumble of floating abstractions and out-of-context, concrete-bound inessentials—an appalling inability to relate abstractions to concretes, or principles to facts—an inability to grasp what constitutes evidence, demonstration, argument, proof—and, consequently, a senseless shuttling between arbitrary assertions and irrelevant trivia, and a loud, daily confession of philosophical impotence.

There was no discussion of capitalism. There was no discussion of statism. There was no discussion of the blatantly vulnerable record of the government's policies in the last thirty years. There was no discussion. There were no issues.

In psychological, if not existential, fact, the campaign ended in mid-October, when Senator Goldwater chose to concede his defeat in one of the least attractive forms possible. It was the form of a truly shameful switch: the attempt to substitute the question of personal "morals" for all the crucial questions of our age, and offer it as the cardinal issue of the campaign.

The man who had promised us "a choice, not an echo"—a choice between freedom or slavery, between capitalism or socialism, between victory or surrender to Soviet Russia—was offering us, instead, a choice between *his* sidekicks or Mr. Johnson's, was proclaiming so novel an issue as an "honest" administration versus a "dishonest" one, and was warning us that the major threat to our lives and future lay in the personal characters of the Messrs. Baker, Estes and Jenkins.

That was that.

The press had not been fair to Sen. Goldwater and the smear campaign against him had been uncommonly vicious. But a smear does not work and does not stick, unless the victim gives ground for it by his own actions. Nothing that the smear-specialists said about him could ever be as damaging to Sen. Goldwater as that switch to the so-called "morals" issue.

Sen. Goldwater complained that the "trigger-happy" label had hurt his campaign. So it did; and it *was* a smear. But if one wants to reassure the country and prove that one is not an advocate of war, one does not do it by such statements as: "Only men without conscience—only men who deny their creator—would initiate any kind of war" (forgetting that the bloodiest wars of history were religious ones)—or: "I want to remind you that I'm a father. I have two sons of military age. I have two sons-in-law of military age. I have grandchildren. I've been through a war. I never want to see another one. I understand war. And I never want to see your children or mine ever have to go to war again." (As if wars were started by the personal whim of rulers and only of childless rulers.)

This leads us to the climax of the campaign (from which the above is a quotation)—to Sen. Goldwater's last television appearance, on the night before the election. After all of his warnings about the life-or-death importance of this election, with such issues as freedom, slavery, communist conquest, nuclear annihilation hanging in the balance—what we saw was a group of "folks next door," placidly exchanging vapid small talk, of a kind which might have been appropriate at the conclusion of a family picnic, but which could hardly be said to suggest an atmosphere of national danger, dedication or solemnity. I hasten to say that I do not mean to imply anything derogatory to the members of Sen. Goldwater's family: they looked like charming, intelligent people who were as acutely embarrassed by their ordeal as were the members of the TV audience. I mean to place the blame on whoever conceived of that show.

Yet, in a fiction-like way, that show was an appropriate finale: it expressed the spirit and style of the campaign, it summarized the candidate's view of the voters he was addressing.

If you were a dramatist, could you invent a better way to dramatize anti-intellectuality?

Unbelievable as it is, Sen. Goldwater seems actually to have believed that philosophy is a matter of the heart, not of the mind, that ideas are of no importance, and that the most profound ideological conflict in history could be won without recourse to the intellect. He believed, apparently, that the principles of "the American way of life" were a kind of self-evident primary, clearly understood and firmly entrenched in the souls of the people, and that a few old-fashioned slogans were sufficient to bring them forth. He believed, apparently, that statism and collectivism were merely the corrupt aberrations of a small, inconsequential minority: of the intellectuals—but that the broad masses had remained pure in heart, loyal to their American "tradition," and that they needed nothing, in order to save the country, but a chance to rally behind a leader who announced himself as a "conservative."

"Conservatism" is a loose term, embracing many different groups; it cannot be said that Sen. Goldwater represented any one of them. But what he did represent was their common denominator: a folksy, "cracker-barrel," mass-oriented kind of anti-intellectual reliance on faith ("the heart") and on "tradition." The question, of course, is: *what* tradition? And since a "conservative," in the original meaning of the word, is one who seeks to preserve the *status quo,* the question is: *what status quo?*

The *status quo* of today is welfare statism, of a semi-socialist, semi-fascist variety. So is the explicit tradition of the past thirty years (and the implicit one of over a century).

"President Johnson," said an article in *The N. Y. Times* of October 11, "is the true conservative in this campaign—not perhaps in the political sense in which the term has come to be used in this country but in the older and deeper sense that he is the safe candidate, the proponent of the established approach to political problems, the guardian and the champion of the vital center."

The principles of a free society are so thoroughly forgotten today that an advocate of capitalism cannot be a "conservative." He has to challenge the fundamental premises of our age; he has to be a rebel, a radical innovator. Paradoxically enough, *that* is what Sen. Goldwater was taken for; he was regarded—and feared—as the new, the unfamiliar, the unknown. This appraisal was demanded by the inner logic of events, of his position in today's context. But an innovator has to make his principles and policies rigorously clear; he cannot speak in and count on bromides.

Granting the philosophical chaos of our age, was it possible to conduct a better campaign in purely political terms, and did we have a right to expect it? It was and we did. A brief glimpse of it, the best of the campaign, was a speech by Ronald Reagan, televized much too late—in the last week before the election.

All of the candidate's speeches should have been on a level equal to Mr. Reagan's. But none of them approached it.

It is impossible to tell whether a campaign conducted on that level would have won. I think it might have. But what one can say with certainty is that it would not have ended in so devastating a defeat.

As it stands, the most grotesque, irrational and disgraceful consequence of the campaign is the fact that the only section of the country left in the position of an alleged champion of freedom, capitalism and individual rights is the agrarian, feudal, racist South. The Southerners, undoubtedly, were voting on

(Continued on page 52)

A Report to Our Readers – 1964

By NATHANIEL BRANDEN

Last December, in response to inquiries from our readers, I wrote the first "progress report" on the spread of Objectivism. In my report I stated that there were "signs which suggest, rather powerfully, that intense interest in the Objectivist philosophy is growing at a rapidly accelerating pace, that Objectivism has captured the mind and enthusiasm of the younger generation as no other contemporary intellectual trend has succeeded in doing."

The evidence since then, has served only to strengthen this impression.

This article is a sequel to last year's report, and should be read in that context.

Seven years after the publication of *Atlas Shrugged*, and twenty-one years after the publication of *The Fountainhead*, each novel continues to sell between 100,000 and 200,000 copies a year. (During 1964, New American Library, Miss Rand's paperback publisher, printed 200,000 copies of *The Fountainhead* and 225,000 copies of *Atlas Shrugged*.) The 100,000 copy initial printing of *Who is Ayn Rand?*, published last May by Paperback Library, is almost exhausted, and a new printing is imminent.

At present, NATHANIEL BRANDEN INSTITUTE is offering its lecture courses on Objectivism in 54 cities throughout the United States and Canada. (Since last year's report, we have grown by approximately 20 cities.) Between September 1964 and September 1965, about 3,500 students will attend NBI courses—plus several thousand visitors auditing individual lectures.

Plans are now underway to offer NBI courses outside of North America—beginning with Munich in West Germany and, possibly, the Marshall Islands in the South Pacific.

The most startling of NBI's new locations, however, is not on any continent or island on earth—it is somewhere under the Atlantic Ocean. Early in November, a young submariner visited NBI's office in New York; he explained that a group of approximately 25 submariners, all admirers of *Atlas Shrugged*, were shortly to leave for a two-month patrol on a Polaris submarine; he wanted to know if NBI would make "Basic Principles of Objectivism" available to his group, via tape transcription, so that he and his friends could listen to and study the lectures during their free hours aboard the Polaris. It was a proposal to which we were delighted to agree; the young man is now in the process of making the necessary arrangements. There is a large wall-map in Barbara Branden's office, with little colored flags marking the cities where NBI courses are given; set apart from all the others, a lone blue flag stands planted in the middle of the Atlantic Ocean. (If you visit Barbara Branden's office, you had better notice that flag.)

THE OBJECTIVIST NEWSLETTER is following a similar pattern of rapid growth. The NEWSLETTER began publication in January, 1962. Two years later, when I wrote my report last December, our paid circulation stood at 5,000. Now, a year later, it stands at close to 15,000. Except that it is not "standing"; our circulation has been moving steadily upward for the past twelve months and there is every indication that the trend will continue.

As I mentioned in my previous report, it is not an easy task to trace the course of new ideas, or to gauge the extent of their influence, in the early stages of their motion through a culture. The process is often too complex and indirect. The facts presented above are merely the most tangible and easily measurable signs of Objectivism's progress.

On campuses throughout the country, college students—acting on their own initiative, with no connection to or help from NBI—continue to organize Ayn Rand study groups. Steadily increasing numbers of term papers or theses on Objectivism are being written for university courses in philosophy, psychology, literature and political science. *The Fountainhead, Atlas Shrugged* and *For the New Intellectual* are appearing on more and more college lists of required or recommended reading.

An interesting new development of the past year is the growing amount of mail NBI has been receiving from high school students; there has also been a significant increase in the number of high school teachers enrolled in NBI courses.

Another interesting development is the marked increase in the inquiries concerning Objectivism we have been receiving from foreign countries. A letter Miss Rand received recently from a university student in Oslo, Norway, is typical: "A steadily increasing number of people in this country take a greater interest in your thoughts. We know that your novels are read by a great number of students at our universities, and the implications of your philosophical system are a constant object of discussion among us." A student at the University of Virginia wrote to us, mentioning a visiting professor of economics who discussed "her [Ayn Rand's] influence in Great Britain." Requests that NBI courses be offered in Europe come into our office at an ever accelerating rate.

Many of these letters inquire about the availability of Miss Rand's books in foreign translation. Therefore, for the benefit of our foreign subscribers, I offer the following information. *We the Living* has been published in England and in the following languages: Danish, German, Hebrew, Italian and Spanish. *Anthem* has been published in England and in the following languages: Italian and Spanish. *The Fountainhead* has been published in England and in the following languages: Danish, Dutch, French, German, Hebrew, Italian, Norwegian, Portuguese, Spanish and Yugoslavian (a contract was signed for this last country, but we have no way of knowing whether the book was ever published). *Atlas Shrugged* has been published in the following languages: Danish, French, German, Hebrew, Italian and Spanish. Some of these translations have been published in both hard cover and paperback editions. I might mention that the New American Library English-language paperback editions of Miss Rand's books are sold throughout most of the world.

It is of immense importance to the future of Objectivism that a major part of the Objectivist following is among the younger generation. It is from that generation that tomorrow's culture-makers will come.

Ideas move the world and determine the course of history—and if one wishes to challenge the prevailing philosophical-political trend, and to move in a new direction, it is the intellectuals that one has to reach and persuade. Not the intellectuals of the older generation who are committed to the *status quo*, not those whose lives are so heavily invested in the institutions and bromides of our age that they cannot afford (psychologically) to understand what Objectivism is saying—but the *new* intellectuals of the younger generation, those who have not relinquished the conviction that the job of an intellectual is to discover and fight for truth. It is from this group that the strongest response to Objectivism has come.

There are, of course, supporters of Objectivism among the older generation of intellectuals. But they are exceptions. More than one older intellectual has approached us, describing himself as an enthusiast and ally—and then, subsequently, backed away with evasive apologies or evasive defiance, when he fully realized the extent to which he would be alienated from, and in irreconcilable conflict with, his particular intellectual "Establishment."

Even among the younger generation of intellectuals, the advocates and supporters of Objectivism are, at present, a minority. But intellectual history is made by minorities—by those who assume the responsibility of passing judgment on ideological issues.

The power of Objectivism, as a future cultural movement, lies in the fact that its adherents are the one group today whose intellectual fire has not been extinguished by the mind-destroying dogmas of the *status quo*—who have a rational, consistent and comprehensive frame-of-reference in which to judge ideas and events—and who are moved by an authentic *moral* enthusiasm.

It is a long road, whose length no one can calculate in advance, from the formulation of a new philosophy to its translation into practical reality, in art, in science, in politics, in social institutions, in the culture at large. At present, one can hope to see only the first steps down that road. But the signs of motion are there to be seen—and the steps are growing louder.

It is Earlier Than You Think (from page 50)

the basis of "tradition"; but it was hardly a tradition of pro-capitalism. This, perhaps, is the clearest indication of the extent to which Sen. Goldwater had failed to present his case.

It is difficult to draw any conclusions about the ideological state of the country at large. Since no fundamental issues were discussed, since so many contradictions were offered by both sides, it is impossible to tell what the voters thought they were choosing. There were, apparently, as many different motives as there are pressure-groups. It is foolish to imagine—as some Republicans are doing—that all those who voted for Sen. Goldwater were staunch supporters of freedom and capitalism. They obviously were not. It is just as foolish to believe that all those who voted for President Johnson were confirmed statists. But whether wittingly or unwittingly, whether through ignorance, cowardice, confusion or evasion, whether by default or by fully conscious intention, it was capitalism that the voters rejected.

In previous elections, the issue was evaded and left unnamed. This time, it was named. Just that. It was named and left hanging in a foggy vacuum (with both sides paying lip-service to free enterprise, and President Johnson mentioning it more often than did Sen. Goldwater). Whether one interprets the results as a measure of the country's ideological corruption or as a measure of the country's political ignorance, the fact remains that it is welfare statism (and cynical, mixed-economy Pragmatism) that the country has endorsed. And if the statists now wish to claim that they have received a popular mandate, one cannot disprove it.

This is an example of why a half-battle is worse than none.

Those who forget this lesson and start plunging into the "mainstream" or "*dead* center," seeking a compromise with the worst and morally guiltiest group in the country: the "moderate" Republicans—deserve what they will get.

In the March issue of this NEWSLETTER, I said: "An election campaign is not the cause, but the effect and the product of a culture's intellectual trends. It is, perhaps, too early to fight for capitalism on the level of practical politics, in a culture devoid of any intellectual base for capitalism."

What the election has taught me is to remove the "perhaps" from the above sentence.

One may vote, in future elections, for the lesser of two evils, when and if such a choice is offered. But—barring some national catastrophe, such as an economic collapse—one cannot count on an election to reverse the trend toward statism, not for a long time to come.

Yet, bitter as things might seem at the moment, there are certain advantages for the advocates of freedom in the years ahead.

The chief advantage is a *cleaner* road.

One of the pre-election surveys claimed that the largest percentage of support for President Johnson was to be found in the age group of 35 to 49. Although statistical claims cannot be taken as conclusive proof, this one suggests some significant implications.

The majority of those over 49 are the real *"conservatives,"* in the true sense of that word; they are the men who, reared before World War I, took capitalism smugly for granted and, refusing to take notice of its cracking ideological foundations, maintaining an attitude of stubbornly stagnant anti-intellectuality, tried to stem a philosophical flood by means of a few stale slogans—and let freedom slip through their limp fingers. Those between 35 and 49 are the product of the New Deal era, riding a dead intellectual horse. Those under 35 are coming to the cause of freedom, not by "tradition," but by philosophical conviction.

What this election has wiped out are the old-guard, rear-guard "conservatives" of the Coolidge-Hoover-Taft axis, who wanted to go back, not to capitalism, but to the mixed economy of the 19th century, never asking themselves why it vanished in the first place, never admitting that *they*, not the "liberals," started the trend toward government controls, which the "liberals" quite logically took over. The election has wiped out the pretensions of the countless so-called "patriotic" groups, organizations and publications that had never upheld capitalism, but thought it sufficient to be anti-socialist and rely on "tradition." The election has wiped out the illusions of those who believed that capitalism is compatible with altruism, and, dreading the necessity to challenge altruism, thought that capitalism could be purchased at a bargain price.

The political philosophy of America's Founding Fathers is so thoroughly buried under decades of statist misrepresentations on one side and empty lip-service on the other, that it has to be *re-discovered*, not ritualistically repeated. It has to be rescued from the shameful barnacles of platitudes now hiding it. It has to be *expanded*—because it was only a magnificent beginning, not a completed job, it was only a *political* philosophy without a full philosophical and *moral* foundation, which the "conservatives" cannot provide.

The road is now left cleared for those who know that the battle has to be fought on *moral-intellectual* grounds, those who are willing to start from scratch and to build the philosophical foundation which freedom and capitalism had never possessed —those who are not afraid to be a minority.

This is no time for social metaphysicians, band-wagon-climbers, camp-followers, mystics, "traditionalists" or any of the shaky amateurs who believed that "conservatism" is safe, easy or fashionable, and were willing to collaborate with any dubious group so long as it was "anti-socialist." This is no time for the "antis"—it is a time only for the "pros," in both meanings of the term.

The job to be done belongs to professional intellectuals. The battle has to be fought—and won—in colleges and universities, before it can be carried to the voting booths. Not until a *cultural* movement is ready to answer such questions as those listed by James Reston, can the advocates of freedom hope to be heard or understood at the polls.

It is too late for the "conservatives." There is nothing left to "conserve." It was too late for them in the election of 1932. It was much later than they thought. But for us—for the *radical* advocates of capitalism—it is merely the beginning.

In that same column of July 22, James Reston, the voice of "liberalism," wrote: "In almost every great transformation in the lives of nations, it has usually been a small, ardent minority that has prevailed over the indifferent majority." I would add a postscript to his statement: So long as men are free to speak, a small, rational minority will always prevail over an irrational majority.

Do not expect it to be easy. It will be a long battle. It is earlier than you think.

OBJECTIVIST CALENDAR

■ Ayn Rand's lecture, "Is Atlas Shrugging?" published in the August 1964 issue of this NEWSLETTER, has been reprinted by NBI and is now available as a pamphlet. Price: 50¢.

■ The hardcover edition of *Atlas Shrugged*, published by Random House, is now in its seventh printing.

■ NBI's Tape Transcription Division has scheduled the following starting dates: "Basic Principles of Objectivism" in Chapel Hill, N.C., December 13, in Portland, Ore., January 4, and in Rochester, N.Y., January 10; "The History of Modern Philosophy" in Los Angeles on December 16. For details, contact NBI.

Published monthly at 120 East 34th Street, New York 16, N. Y.

Subscription rate in United States, its possessions, Canada and Mexico: one year, $5; 2 years, $9; 3 years, $13. Other countries: one year, $6; 2 years, $11; 3 years, $16.

Additional copies of this Newsletter: single copy 50¢ (coins, not stamps); 10 – 99 copies, 25¢ each plus postage (for first-class delivery add 1¢ per copy, for third-class delivery add ½¢ per copy); 100 or more copies, 15¢ each plus postage (same as above). (Bulk rates apply only to multiple orders of a single issue.)

For change of address send old address and new address with zone number if any. Allow us three weeks to process new subscriptions and change of address.

Ayn Rand and Nathaniel Branden, Editors and Publishers
Barbara Branden, Managing Editor
Elayne Kalberman, Circulation Manager

THE OBJECTIVIST NEWSLETTER

Edited and Published by AYN RAND and NATHANIEL BRANDEN

VOL. 4 NO. 1   JANUARY, 1965

CHECK YOUR PREMISES
By AYN RAND

Bootleg Romanticism

Art (including literature) is the barometer of a culture. It reflects the sum of a society's deepest philosophical values: not its professed notions and slogans, but its actual view of man and of existence. The image of an entire society stretched out on a psychologist's couch, revealing its naked subconscious, is an impossible concept; yet *that* is what art accomplishes: it presents the equivalent of such a session, a transcript which is more eloquent and easier to diagnose than any other set of symptoms.

This does not mean that an entire society is bound by the mediocrities who may choose to posture in the field of art at any given time; but it does mean that if no better men chose to enter the field, this tells us something about the state of that society. There are always exceptions who rebel against the dominant trend in the art of their age; but the fact that they are exceptions tells us something about the state of that age. The dominant trend may not, in fact, express the soul of an entire people; it may be rejected, resented or ignored by an overwhelming majority; but if it is the dominant voice of a given period, this tells us something about the state of the people's souls.

In politics, the panic-blinded advocates of today's *status quo*, clinging to the shambles of their mixed economy in a rising flood of statism, are now adopting the line that there's nothing wrong with the world, that this is a century of progress, that we are morally and mentally healthy, that we never had it so good. If you find political issues too complex to diagnose, take a look at today's art: it will leave you no doubt in regard to the health or disease of our culture.

The composite picture of man that emerges from the art of our time is the gigantic figure of an aborted embryo whose limbs suggest a vaguely anthropoid shape, who twists his upper extremity in a frantic quest for a light that cannot penetrate its empty sockets, who emits inarticulate sounds resembling snarls and moans, who crawls through a bloody muck, red froth dripping from his jaws, and struggles to throw the froth at his own non-existent face, who pauses periodically and, lifting the stumps of his arms, screams in abysmal terror at the universe at large.

Engendered by generations of anti-rational philosophy, three emotions dominate the sense of life of modern man: fear, guilt and pity (more precisely, self-pity). Fear, as the appropriate emotion of a creature deprived of his means of survival, his mind; guilt, as the appropriate emotion of a creature devoid of moral values; pity, as the means of escape from these two, as the only response such a creature could beg for. A sensitive, discriminating man, who has absorbed that sense of life, but retained some vestige of self-esteem, will avoid so revealing a profession as art. But this does not stop the others.

Fear, guilt and the quest for pity combine to set the trend of art in the same direction, in order to express, justify and rationalize the artists' own feelings. To justify a chronic fear, one has to portray existence as evil; to escape from guilt and arouse pity, one has to portray man as impotent and innately loathsome. Hence the competition among modern artists to find ever lower levels of depravity and ever higher degrees of mawkishness — a competition to shock the public out of its wits and jerk its tears. Hence the frantic search for misery, the descent from compassionate studies of alcoholism and sexual perversion to dope, incest, psychosis, murder, cannibalism.

To illustrate the moral implications of this trend — the fact that pity for the guilty is treason to the innocent — I submit an enthusiastic review that commends a current movie for arousing compassion for kidnappers. "One's attention and, indeed, one's anxiety is centered more upon them than upon the kidnapped youngster," states the review. And: "As a matter of fact, the motivation is not so clearly defined that it bears analysis or criticism on psychological grounds. But it is sufficiently established to compel our anguished sympathy for the two incredible kidnappers." (*The N.Y. Times*, Nov. 6, 1964.)

Sewers are not very rich nor very deep, and today's dramatists seem to be scratching bottom. As to literature, it has shot its bolt. There is no way to beat the following, which I reproduce in full from the August 30, 1963, issue of *Time*. The heading is "Books," the sub-head "Best Reading," then: *"Cat and Mouse*, by Günter Grass. Best-selling Novelist Grass (*The Tin Drum*) relates the torment of a young man whose prominent Adam's apple makes him an outcast to his classmates. He strives for achievement and wins it, but to the 'cat'— human conformity — he is still a curiosity."

No, all this is not presented to us "tongue-in-cheek." There is an old French theater that specializes in presenting that sort of stuff "tongue-in-cheek." It is called *"Grand Guignol."* But today the spirit of *"Grand Guignol"* has been elevated into a metaphysical system and demands to be taken seriously. What, then, is *not* to be taken seriously? Any representation of human virtue.

One would think that that maudlin preoccupation with chambers of horror, that Wax-Works-Museum view of life, was bad enough. But there is something still worse and, morally, more evil: the recent attempts to concoct so-called "tongue-in-cheek" thrillers.

The trouble with the sewer school of art is that fear, guilt and pity are self-defeating dead-ends: after the first few "daring revelations of human depravity," people cease to be shocked by anything; after experiencing pity for a few dozen of the depraved, the deformed, the demented, people cease to feel anything. And just as the "non-commercial" economics of modern "idealists" prompts them to take over commercial establishments, so the "non-commercial" esthetics of modern "artists" prompts them to attempt the take-over of commercial (*i.e.*, popular) art forms.

"Thrillers" are detective, spy or adventure stories. Their basic characteristic is *conflict*, which means: a clash of goals, which means: purposeful action in pursuit of *values*. Thrillers are the product, the popular offshoot, of the *Romantic* school of art that sees man, not as a helpless pawn of fate, but as a being of free will whose life is directed by his own value-choices. Romanticism is a value-oriented, morality-centered movement: its material is not journalistic minutiae, but the abstract, the essential, the universal principles of man's nature — and its basic literary commandment is to portray man "as he might be and ought to be."

Thrillers are a simplified, elementary version of Romantic literature. They are not concerned with a delineation of values, but, taking certain fundamental values for granted, they are concerned with only one aspect of a moral being's existence: the battle of good against evil in terms of purposeful action — a dramatized abstraction of the basic pattern of: choice, goal, conflict, danger, struggle, victory.

Thrillers are the kindergarten arithmetic, of which the higher mathematics is the greatest novels of world literature. Thrillers deal only with the skeleton — the plot structure — to which "serious" Romantic literature adds the flesh, the blood, the mind. The plots in the novels of Victor Hugo or Dostoievsky are pure thriller-plots, unequalled and unsurpassed by the best writers of thrillers.

In today's culture, Romantic art is virtually non-existent (but for some very rare exceptions): it requires a view of man incompatible with modern philosophy. The last remnants of Romanticism are flickering only in the field of popular art, like bright sparks in a stagnant gray fog. Thrillers are the last refuge of the qualities that have vanished from modern literature: life, color, imagination — like a mirror still holding an image of man.

Bear that in mind when you consider the meaning of the attempt to present them "tongue-in-cheek."

Humor is not an unconditional virtue; its moral character depends on its object. To laugh at the contemptible, is a virtue; to laugh at the good, is a hideous vice. Too often, humor is used as the camouflage of moral cowardice.

There are two types of cowards in this connection. One type is the man who dares not reveal his profound hatred of existence and seeks to undercut all values under cover of a chuckle, who gets away with offensive, malicious utterances and, if caught, runs for cover by declaring: "I was only kidding."

The other type is the man who dares not reveal or uphold his values and seeks to smuggle them into existence under cover of a chuckle, who tries to get away with some concept of virtue or beauty and, at the first sign of opposition, drops it and runs, declaring: "I was only kidding."

In the first case, humor serves as an apology for evil; in the second — as an apology for the good. Which, morally, is the more contemptible policy?

The motives of both types can be united and served by a phenomenon such as "tongue-in-cheek" thrillers.

What are such thrillers laughing at? At values, at man's struggle for values, at man's capacity to achieve his values, at man. At man the hero.

Regardless of their creators' conscious or subconscious motives, such thrillers, in fact, carry a message or intention of their own, implicit in their nature: to arouse people's interest in some daring venture, to hold them in suspense by the intricacy of a battle for great stakes, to inspire them by the spectacle of human efficacy, to evoke their admiration for the hero's courage, ingenuity, endurance and unswerving integrity of purpose, to make them cheer his triumph — and then to spit in their faces, declaring: "Don't take me seriously — I was only kidding — who are we, you and I, to aspire to be anything but absurd and swinish?"

To whom are such thrillers apologizing? To the sewer school of art. In today's culture, the gutter-worshiper needs and makes no apology. But the hero-worshiper chooses to crawl on his belly, crying: "I didn't mean it, boys! It's all in fun! I'm not so corrupt as to believe in virtue, I'm not so cowardly as to fight for values, I'm not so evil as to long for an ideal — I'm one of you!"

The social status of thrillers reveals the profound gulf splitting today's culture — the gulf between the people and its alleged intellectual leaders. The people's need for a ray of Romanticism's light is enormous and tragically eager. Observe the extraordinary popularity of Mickey Spillane and Ian Fleming. There are hundreds of thriller writers who, sharing the modern sense of life, write sordid concoctions that amount to a battle of evil against evil or, at best, gray against black. None of them have the ardent, devoted, almost addicted following earned by Spillane and Fleming. This is not to say that the novels of Spillane and Fleming project a faultlessly rational sense of life; both are touched by the cynicism and despair of today's "malevolent universe"; but, in strikingly different ways, both offer the cardinal element of Romantic fiction: Mike Hammer and James Bond are *heroes*.

This universal need is precisely what today's intellectuals cannot grasp or fill. A seedy, emasculated, unventilated "elite" — a basement "elite" transported, by default, into vacant drawing-rooms and barricaded behind dusty curtains against light, air, grammar and reality — today's intellectuals cling to the stagnant illusion of their altruist-collectivist upbringing: the vision of a cloddish, humble, inarticulate people whose "voice" (and masters) they were to be.

Observe their anxious, part-patronizing, part-obsequious pursuit of "folk" art, of the primitive, the anonymous, the undeveloped, the unintellectual — or their "lusty," "earthy" movies that portray man as an obscene sub-animal. Politically, the reality of a non-cloddish people would destroy them: the collectivist jig would be up. Morally, the existence, possibility or image of a hero would be intolerable to their overwhelming sense of guilt; it would wipe out the slogan that permits them to go on wallowing in sewers: "I couldn't help it!" A heroes-seeking people is what they cannot admit into their view of the universe.

A sample of that cultural gulf — a small sample of a vast modern tragedy — may be seen in an interesting little article in *TV Guide* (May 9, 1964), under the title "Violence Can Be Fun" and with the eloquent subtitle: "In Britain, everybody laughs at 'The Avengers' — except the audience."

The Avengers is a sensationally successful British television series featuring the adventures of secret agent John Steed and his attractive assistant Catherine Gale — "surrounded by some delightfully ingenious plots..." states the article. "*The Avengers* is compulsive viewing for a huge audience. Steed and Mrs. Gale are household words."

But recently "the secret sorrow of producer John Bryce was revealed: *The Avengers* was conceived as a satire of counter-espionage thrillers, but the British public still insists on taking it seriously."

The manner in which that "revelation" came about is interesting. "The fact that *The Avengers* is satire was probably the best-kept secret in British television for almost a year. It might have remained that way, but the series came up for discussion during another show called *The Critics*..." One of these critics — to the astonishment of the others — declared that "surely everybody realized it was being played for laughs." Nobody had, but the producer of *The Avengers* confirmed that view and "moodily" blamed the public for its failure to understand his intentions: its failure to laugh at his product.

Bear in mind that Romantic thrillers are an exceedingly difficult job: they require such a degree of skill, ingenuity, inventiveness, imagination and logic — such a great amount of talent on the part of the producer or the director or the writer or the cast, or all of them — that it is virtually impossible to fool an entire nation for a whole year. Somebody's values were being shamefully exploited and betrayed, besides the public's.

An American television attempt at something like a counterpart of *The Avengers* is not burdened with talent or success and, therefore, offers a clearer, cruder view of the moral meaning of such alleged satires. It is a peculiarly inept, incoherent, unfocused show entitled "*The Man from U.N.C.L.E.*"

The initials U.N.C.L.E. stand for a fictitious organization named "United Network Command for Law and Enforcement." What kind of organization is it? What sort of "law" is being "enforced" — and by whom? The hero — who bears the subtle name of "Napoleon Solo" — is an agent of "U.N.C.L.E." and seems to be an American. His assistant, another agent, is a Russian named Illya Kuryakin. No other nationalities are indicated. Is this a world government police? Or is it a private group, a kind of international vigilantes? In such episodes of the series as I have seen, no answer or explanation was given.

But offscreen, in an article entitled "With Gun in Hand and Tongue in Cheek" (*TV Guide*, October 24, 1964), one of the show's producers is quoted explaining the matter as follows: "I've been wanting to try something along those lines for quite a while. You know, international intrigue, but with comic overtones. We didn't want to do anything actually connected with the Government because then we'd be doing anti-Communist stuff every week. Instead, we've gone completely fictional, and I came up with the word 'UNCLE.' I thought it was a funny designation, kind of provocative. People might think it stood for Uncle Sam, which it doesn't. Or the U.N., which it doesn't. Finally, so many people wanted to know what the initials stood for, we had to make up something that fit."

This is a very enlightening statement psychologically, but not very helpful politically, and disastrous literarily — since it raises more questions than it answers. (A) How is one to find any "comic overtones" in today's international situation? (B) What would be wrong with "doing anti-Communist stuff every week"? (C) If the nature and goals of the side representing *the good* are unclear, can people be expected to root for it or care? (D) If the good is unspecified, what sort of *evil* can one find for it to fight against?

It is on this last question that *The Man from U.N.C.L.E.* has taken a bad beating and will probably yell "Uncle!" pretty soon. Consider the kind of villains that "U.N.C.L.E.'s" brave agents had to fight:

1. A group of Iowan (or Kansan?) farmers who help a group

of plotters from an unnamed South American country who plot the overthrow of their own unidentified government, which plot requires, for an unspecified reason, that they dig a tunnel to blow up a U.S. nuclear installation or laboratory.

2. The Prime Minister of a mythical, *small Balkan country*, who seeks to provoke a war between East and West, intending — in some inexplicable manner — to profit by such a war.

3. A group of individuals of unspecified origin and purpose, but with American accents and operating on American soil, who are launching missiles loaded with germs to land in Soviet Russia, the germs being intended to destroy the entire Soviet wheat crop by causing it to rot.

As a result of such material, the stories fail to coagulate. It is impossible to tell who is doing what or why. There is no plot structure, no motivation, no goals, no values, no conflict, no suspense—nothing but brute physical danger in the midst of radar screens, nuclear rockets and science-fiction paraphernalia.

Apparently, the creators of this mess thought that in order to laugh, it is not necessary to know what one is laughing at — and in order to satirize, it is not necessary to study the object of one's satire. Had they studied it, they would have discovered that the motivating values of a thriller's antagonists must never be left in doubt and that this is the reason why the expert writers of thrillers rely on simple, established, generalized values, which the audience need not question, which are taken for granted and do not interfere with one's understanding of the action (such as justice vs. crime, in Spillane; or patriotism vs. foreign agents, in Fleming). But "generalized" does not mean "woozy" — and the motivating values in *The Man from U.N.C.L.E.* are so woozily dubious that they overshadow the action, if any, muddling it altogether.

They raise such questions as: If "U.N.C.L.E." is dedicated to international law enforcement, does this mean that it protects indiscriminately any sort of government? The first of the stories summarized above, seems to indicate it — since no ideological identity was given to the South American plotters, no badge of evil other than that they were plotting to overthrow the government of their country. If so, then are we to regard the United States, not as the champion of freedom, not as the land of political asylum, but as the protector of the established order — any kind of established order — against "the plotting" of its victims?

If so, then would "U.N.C.L.E." have protected the Nazi government of Germany against the Jewish refugees? Would it protect Castro's government against the Cuban refugees? Would it protect the Soviet government against the refugees from one-third of the globe? The presence of Illya Kuryakin among the knights of "U.N.C.L.E." would seem to indicate the affirmative, which is pretty sickening.

Aw, it's not supposed to be taken seriously — the producers would probably answer — we're only kidding, it's all "tongue-in-cheek." But the question is: which cheek? Left or right?

The answer is probably: the middle — that is, tongue stuck out at the audience in the name of nothing in particular.

But the show's view of the audience raises further questions. It seems to imply that people do not need to know the motives of villains or heroes, that everybody is terrorized by a mysterious, incomprehensible evil — and, therefore, "conspirators" is the only identification needed for evil, and "anti-conspirators" for the good. This seems to suggest paranoia, or a conspiracy-theory of history, or a kind of John Birch Society influence. Perhaps *The Man from U.N.C.L.E.* is a satire on the U.N.

The performance of Robert Vaughn in the role of "Napoleon Solo" suggests another possibility: that the show is a satire on any viewer who might take him for a hero. In that same article in *TV Guide*, Mr. Vaughn is quoted as declaring that his role "has some parallel with the James Bond role. We have similar impedimenta. But I'm playing Solo lighter than Sean Connery plays Bond." This deserves some sort of prize for the most presumptuous understatement of the year. "Lighter" is not the word for it. Mr. Vaughn giggles, chortles, snickers, leers and sneers without any discernible reason, but with an air of bored, supercilious amusement, throughout an entire show, no matter what action is involved. Occasionally, he does remember that he is supposed to be in danger — and then we see a closeup of a face expressing helpless, neurotic terror, the kind that would be ideal in one of those "serious" modern dramas.

His performance is, however, persuasive in one respect: it conveys so eloquently "If you're interested in any of this, you're a fool," that the most uncritical thriller-fan will believe him and will switch to some cleaner kind of comedy.

It is obvious that the modern intellectuals' rush to the thriller bandwagon was precipitated by the spectacular figure and success of James Bond. But, in keeping with modern philosophy, they want to ride the wagon and spit at it, too.

If you think that the producers of mass-media entertainment are motivated primarily by commercial greed, check your premises and observe that the producers of the James Bond movies seem to be intent on undercutting their own success.

Contrary to somebody's strenuously spread assertions, there was nothing "tongue-in-cheek" about the first of these movies, *Dr. No*. It was a brilliant example of Romantic screen art — in production, direction, writing, photography and, most particularly, in the performance of Sean Connery. His first introduction on the screen was a gem of dramatic technique, elegance, wit and understatement: when, in response to a question about his name, we saw his first closeup and he answered quietly: "Bond. James Bond." — the audience, on the night I saw it, burst into applause.

There wasn't much applause on the night when I saw his second movie, *From Russia with Love*. Here, Bond was introduced pecking with schoolboy kisses at the face of a vapid-looking girl in a bathing suit. The story was muddled and, at times, unintelligible. The skillfully constructed, dramatic suspense of Fleming's climax was replaced by conventional stuff, such as old-fashioned chases, involving nothing but crude physical danger.

I shall still go to see the third movie, the current *Goldfinger*, but with heavy misgivings. The misgivings are based on an article by Richard Maibaum who adapted all three novels to the screen (*The N.Y. Times*, December 13, 1964).

"Fleming's tongue-in-cheek attitude toward his material (intrigue, expertise, violence, love, death) finds a ready mass response in a world where audiences enjoy sick jokes," writes Mr. Maibaum. "Incidentally, it is the aspect of Fleming which the films have most developed." So much for his understanding of the appeal of Romantic thrillers — or of Fleming.

Discussing his own work, Mr. Maibaum remarks: "Do I hear anyone asking sotto voce about the screenwriter's blushes? If he was the blushing type he wouldn't be doing Bond screenplays in the first place. Besides, it's good clean fun, or so he tells himself."

Draw your own conclusions about the nature of the ethical standards involved. Note also that the writer of the movie about "the two incredible [but sympathetic] kidnappers" did not feel called upon to blush.

"The actual characterization of James Bond..." Mr. Maibaum continues, "was also a departure from the novels.... That concept retained a basic super-sleuth, super-fighter, super-hedonist, super-lover of Fleming's, but added another large dimension: humor. Humor vocalized in wry comments at critical moments. In the books, Bond was singularly lacking in this." Which is *not* true, as any reader of the books can ascertain.

And finally: "A bright young producer accosted me one day with glittering eyes. 'I'm making a parody of the James Bond films.' How, I asked myself, does one make a parody of a parody? For that is precisely, in the final analysis, what we have done with Fleming's books. Parodied them. I'm not sure that Ian himself ever completely realized this."

This is said about the work of a man whose talent, achievement and fame gave a group of previously undistinguished persons their chance at distinction and at piles of money.

I do not see why Mr. Maibaum has to strain so hard to prove to the boys that he's one of them. He has proved it.

Observe that in the issue of humor versus thrillers, modern intellectuals are using the term "humor" as an *anti-concept*, that is, as a "package-deal" of two meanings, with the proper meaning serving to cover and to smuggle the improper one into people's minds. The purpose is to obliterate the distinction between "humor" and "mockery," particularly *self-mockery* — and thus bring men to defile their own values and self-esteem, for fear of being accused of lacking "a sense of humor."

Remember that humor is *not* an unconditional virtue and depends on its object. One may laugh *with* a hero, but never *at* him — just as a satire may laugh *at* some object, but *never at itself*. A composition that laughs at itself is a fraud on the audience.

In Fleming's novels, James Bond is constantly making witty,

humorous remarks, which are part of his charm. But, apparently, this is not what Mr. Maibaum meant by the word "humor." What he meant, apparently, was *humor at Bond's expense* — the sort of humor intended to undercut Bond's stature, to make him ridiculous and unheroic, to reduce him to the level of Napoleon Solo, which means: to destroy him.

Such is the basic contradiction — and the terrible, parasitic immorality — of any attempt to create "tongue-in-cheek" thrillers. It requires that one employ all the values of a thriller in order to hold the audience's interest, yet turn these values against themselves, that one damage the very elements one is using and counting on. It means an attempt to cash in on the thing one is mocking, to profit by the audience's hunger for Romanticism while seeking to destroy it. This is not the method of a legitimate satire: a satire does not share the values of that which it denounces; it denounces by means and in the context of an *opposite* set of values.

The failure to understand the nature and appeal of Romanticism is an eloquent measure of the modern intellectuals' epistemological disintegration. Only an appallingly concrete-bound, anti-conceptual mentality would lose its faculty of abstraction to such an extent as to be incapable of grasping an abstract meaning which an unskilled laborer can grasp and a United States President can enjoy. Only an arrested modern mentality would go on protesting that the events portrayed in a thriller are incredible or improbable, that there are no heroes, that "life is not like that"—all of which is thoroughly irrelevant.

Nobody takes thrillers literally, nor cares about their specific events, nor harbors any frustrated desire to become a secret agent or a private eye. Thrillers are taken symbolically; they dramatize one of man's widest and most crucial abstractions: the abstraction of *moral conflict*.

What people seek in thrillers is the spectacle of *man's efficacy:* of his ability to fight for his values and to achieve them. What they see is a condensed, simplified pattern, reduced to its essentials: a man fighting for a vital goal — overcoming one obstacle after another — facing terrible dangers and risks — persisting through an excruciating struggle — and winning. Far from suggesting an easy or "unrealistic" view of life, a thriller suggests the necessity of a difficult struggle; if the hero is "larger-than-life," so are the villains and the dangers.

An abstraction has to be "larger-than-life" — to encompass any concretes that individual men may be concerned with, each according to the scale of his own values, goals and ambition. The scale varies; the psychological relationships involved remain the same. The obstacles confronting an average man are, to him, as formidable as Bond's adversaries; but what the image of Bond tells him is: "It can be done."

What men find in the spectacle of the ultimate triumph of the good is the inspiration to fight for one's own values in the moral conflicts of one's own life.

If the proclaimers of human impotence, the seekers of automatic security, protest that "life is not like that, happy endings are not guaranteed to man" — the answer is: a thriller is more realistic than such views of existence, it shows men the *only* road that can make any sort of happy ending *possible*.

Here, we come to an interesting paradox. It is only the superficiality of the naturalists that classifies Romanticism as "an escape"; this is true only in the very superficial sense of contemplating a glamorous vision as a relief from the gray burden of "real-life" problems. But in the deeper, metaphysical-moral-psychological sense, it is *Naturalism* that represents an escape — an escape from choice, from values, from moral responsibility — and it is *Romanticism* that trains and equips man for the battles he has to face in reality.

In the privacy of his own soul, nobody identifies himself with the folks next door, unless he has given up. But the generalized abstraction of a hero permits every man to identify himself with James Bond, each supplying his own concretes which are illuminated and supported by that abstraction. It is not a conscious process, but an emotional integration, and most people may not know that *that* is the reason of the enjoyment they find in thrillers. It is *not* a leader or a protector that they seek in a hero, since his exploits are always highly individualistic and un-social. What they seek is profoundly personal: self-confidence and self-assertion. Inspired by James Bond, a man may find the courage to rebel against the impositions of his in-laws — or to ask for a deserved raise — or to change his job — or to propose to the girl he loves — or to embark on the career he wants — or to defy the whole world for the sake of his new invention.

This is what naturalistic art can never give him.

For example, consider one of the best works of modern naturalism — Paddy Chayefsky's *Marty*. It is an extremely sensitive, perceptive, touching portrayal of an humble man's struggle for self-assertion. One can feel sympathy for Marty, and a sad kind of pleasure at his final success. But it is highly doubtful whether anyone — including the thousands of real-life Martys — would be inspired by his example. Nobody could feel: "I want to be like Marty." Everybody (except the most corrupt) can feel: "I want to be like James Bond."

Such is the meaning of that popular art form which today's "friends of the people" are attacking with such hysterically virulent hatred.

The guiltiest men involved — both among the professionals and the public — are the moral cowards who do not share that hatred, but seek to appease it, who are willing to regard their own Romantic values as a secret vice, to keep them underground, to slip them furtively to blackmarket customers, and to pay off the established intellectual authorities, in the currency demanded: self-mockery.

The game will continue, and the bandwagon-riders will destroy James Bond, as they have destroyed Mike Hammer, as they have destroyed Eliot Ness, then will look for another victim to "parody" — until some future sacrificial worm turns and declares that he'll be damned if he'll allow Romanticism to be treated as bootleg merchandise.

The public, too, will have to do its share: it will have to cease being satisfied with esthetic speakeasies, and demand the repeal of the Joyce-Kafka Amendment, which prohibits the sale and drinking of clean water, unless denatured by humor, while unconscionable rot-gut is being sold and drunk at every bookstore counter.

OBJECTIVIST CALENDAR

■ Beginning Tuesday, January 26, in New York City, NBI will offer a ten-lecture course on "The Economics of a Free Society," to be given by Alan Greenspan. Time: 7:30 P.M. Place: Sheraton-Atlantic Hotel, Broadway at 34th Street. Admission: $3.50, payable at the door.

■ On January 11, NBI will begin its series on "Basic Principles of Objectivist Psychology" in Los Angeles. Nathaniel Branden will deliver the opening lecture in person. The rest of the course will be given via tape transcription. (The January 11 lecture of the N.Y. course will be given by Ayn Rand.)

In addition, NBI's Tape Transcription Division has scheduled the following starting dates: "Basic Principles of Objectivist Psychology" in Pittsburgh, January 17, and in San Jose, February 11 — "Basic Principles of Objectivism" in Houston, January 11; Princeton, January 13; Providence, January 15; Pittsburgh, January 15; Las Vegas, February 1; Philadelphia, February 1—"The Principles of Efficient Thinking" in Chicago, January 10, and in Toronto, January 25 — "Contemporary Theories of Neurosis" in Denver, February 3. For details, contact NBI.

■ An interview with Ayn Rand, originally published in the March, 1964, issue of *Playboy*, has been reprinted by NBI and is now available as a pamphlet. Price: 50¢. (N.Y.C. residents add 2¢ sales tax.)

Published monthly at 120 East 34th Street, New York 16, N. Y.

Subscription rate in United States, its possessions, Canada and Mexico: one year, $5; 2 years, $9; 3 years, $13. Other countries: one year, $6; 2 years, $11; 3 years, $16.

Additional copies of this Newsletter: single copy 50¢ (coins, not stamps); 10 - 99 copies, 25¢ each plus postage (for first-class delivery add 1¢ per copy, for third-class delivery add ½¢ per copy); 100 or more copies, 15¢ each plus postage (same as above). (Bulk rates apply only to multiple orders of a single issue.)

For change of address send old address and new address with zone number if any. Allow us three weeks to process new subscriptions and change of address.

Ayn Rand and Nathaniel Branden, Editors and Publishers
Barbara Branden, Managing Editor
Elayne Kalberman, Circulation Manager

THE OBJECTIVIST NEWSLETTER

Edited and Published by AYN RAND and NATHANIEL BRANDEN

VOL. 4 NO. 2   FEBRUARY, 1965

Rogues' Gallery

By NATHANIEL BRANDEN

(Part I of a two-part article)

"Social metaphysics" is a psychological disorder from which the majority of men suffer in varying degrees of intensity and destructiveness. I first wrote of this phenomenon in the November 1962 issue of this NEWSLETTER. Since then, I have received many requests for a further discussion of the problem. There are many types of social metaphysicians. In this article, I shall delineate some of the most prevalent of these types.

Social metaphysics is the psychological syndrome that characterizes an individual who holds the consciousnesses of other men, not objective reality, as his ultimate psycho-epistemological frame-of-reference.

The traits or symptoms common to *all* social metaphysicians are the following: (1) the absence of a firm, unyielding concept of existence, facts, reality, *as apart from* the judgments, beliefs, opinions, feelings of others; (2) a sense of fundamental helplessness or impotence, a feeling of *metaphysical* inefficacy; (3) a profound fear of other people, and an implicit belief that other people control that unknowable realm: reality; (4) a self-esteem—or, more precisely, a *pseudo*-self-esteem—that is tied to and dependent on the responses of the "significant others"; (5) a tragic or malevolent sense of life, a belief that the universe is essentially inimical to one's interests. (This last symptom is not restricted exclusively to social metaphysicians.)

The most fundamental of these traits, the one that makes all the others inevitable, is: the absence of a firm, independent sense of *objective reality*.

This is the vacuum that is filled by the consciousnesses of others—and this is the void that is responsible for that desolate feeling of *alienation* which is every social metaphysician's chronic torture.

Since social metaphysics represents a flight from the responsibility of independent judgment (particularly in the realm of *values*), and represents an attempt to live through and by others—the most common and easily identifiable type of social metaphysician is the person whose values and view of life are a direct reflection and product of his particular culture (or sub-culture). This is the person who, today, is sometimes described as a "conformist." I shall designate this type as the *Conventional* social metaphysician.

This is the person who accepts the world and its prevailing values ready-made; his is not to reason why. What is true? What others say is true. What is right? What others believe is right. How should one live? As others live. Why does one work for a living? Because one is *supposed* to. Why does one get married? Because one is *supposed* to. Why does one have children? Because one is *supposed* to. Why does one go to church? Oh, please don't start discussing religion, you might offend someone.

This is George F. Babbitt, this is Peter Keating, this is the Organization Man. This is the person for whom reality *"is"* the world as interpreted by the "significant others" of his social environment—the person whose sense of identity and personal worth is *explicitly* a function of his ability to satisfy the values, terms and expectations of those omniscient and omnipresent "others." I am "as you desire me"—such is the formula of his existence, such is the "genetic code" controlling his soul's development.

"Always be what people want you to be," Peter Keating tells Howard Roark. "Then you've got them where you want them." On a superficial level, Keating might appear to be more conscious of his motives than are many social metaphysicians. But he deludes himself in the belief that he fakes his person for others in order to gain practical advantages. This is a rationalization, masking a truth that is more humiliating. In fact, there *is* no real person beneath the fake: there is only a shapeless fear and an abject selflessness—and, at times, a convulsive cry of agonized despair from the embryo of an unactualized human potential.

The Conventional social metaphysician is the type of man who lends surface credibility to the doctrine of environmental determinism. Such a man *is* the product of his background—but through his own default.

In a culture where science is held as a value, such a man may become a scientist; if scientists are expected (occasionally and within limits) to think independently and sometimes challenge the views of their colleagues, he may do it; he may take pains to be an "individualist" and may actually discover new knowledge. If he is taught that the day of the lone innovator is past and that all future scientific progress depends on "teamwork," then he will seek to establish his qualifications as a scientist, not through the productive quality of his thinking, but through his expertise at "human relations."

In a culture where initiative, ambition and business ability are held as values, he may enter business and perhaps function productively; he may even succeed in making a fortune. In a culture where these things are *dis*valued, he may go to Washington instead.

In a culture such as the present one, with its disintegrating values, its intellectual chaos, its moral bankruptcy—where the familiar guideposts and rules are vanishing, where the authoritative mirrors reflecting "reality" are splintering into a thousand unintelligible subcults, where "adjustment" is becoming harder and harder—the Conventional social metaphysician is the first to run to a psychiatrist, crying that he has lost his identity, because he no longer knows unequivocally what he is supposed to do and be.

This is the type of man without whom no dictatorship could establish itself or remain in existence. He is the man who, in a society moving toward statism, "swims with the current" —and is carried into the abyss. He is the man who, in response to advance signs of danger, closes his eyes—lest he be compelled to pass independent *value-judgments* and to recognize that his world is not safe, that action and protest are demanded of him, that the policies and goals of his leaders are evil, that *the "significant others" are wrong*. In the midst of atrocities, he tells himself that the authorities "must have their reasons" —in order to escape the terror of knowing to whom and to what he has surrendered his existence. It is this same man who—

Copyright © 1965 by The Objectivist Newsletter, Inc.

usually when it is too late—will sometimes rebel in hysterical indignation, when the atrocities have come too close and cannot be evaded any longer, and he may die senselessly, in ineffectual protest, screaming at the malevolent omnipotence of the enemy, and wondering who or what had made the enemy's power possible.

There are, of course, immense differences among Conventional social metaphysicians—differences in their intelligence, honesty, ambition, ability and independence (within the limits of "the system"). And, in a culture that contains a diversity of values and models, there are significant differences in the discrimination and judgment exercised by Conventional social metaphysicians with regard to their choice of authorities.

The Conventional type is the most blatant and uncomplicated species of social metaphysician; he represents the "paradigm case," so to speak—the basic pattern, example or prototype that serves as a reference-point with regard to which other species of social metaphysicians may be understood.

A psychologically healthy man of sovereign consciousness bases his self-esteem on his rationality: on his dedication to knowing what is true and what is right *in fact and in reality*, and on acting consistently with his knowledge. A social metaphysician, in contradistinction, substitutes the consciousnesses of others for reality, as the realm and object of his ultimate concern; his pseudo-self-esteem depends on grasping and acting in accordance with what others *believe* to be true and right; thus, the approval he elicits from others becomes the gauge and proof of his efficacy and worth. But success is not guaranteed to him; here, too, as in dealing with objective reality, effort, struggle, risk and the possibility of failure are unavoidably involved. The Conventional type is not undisturbed by this, but he accepts it. What, however, if a social metaphysician feels inadequate to this task, just as he feels inadequate to dealing with reality? What if he finds the challenge and the demands too overwhelming? Then a *new* line of neurotic defenses and self-deceptive practices may be developed, to protect his pseudo-self-esteem against collapse. This is the phenomenon that one may observe in another type of social metaphysician: the *Power-seeker*.

In this type, fear of others is especially pronounced; he finds his fear intolerable—and his reaction is an over-riding emotion of *hatred*. The hatred is aimed at those who invoke his fear. Resentment and hostility are his dominant emotional traits. (These emotions, of course, sometimes are operative in the Conventional social metaphysician also, but they do not play the same central role in his motivation, they are not the motor of his development and goals.)

To this type, the Conventional social metaphysician's path to pseudo-self-esteem is too frighteningly precarious; the spectre of possible failure and defeat looms too large to be endurable. The Power-seeking social metaphysician feels too unsure of his ability to gain the love and approval he desires; his sense of inferiority is overwhelming. And the humiliation of his dependence—of his *unrequited* dependence, so to speak—infuriates him. He longs for an escape from the uncertainty of "free market" social metaphysical competition, where he must win men's *voluntary* esteem. He wants to deceive, to manipulate, to coerce the minds of others; to leave them no choice in the matter. He wants to reach a position where he can *command* respect, obedience, love.

As an example, King Frederick William of Prussia—who would beat his subjects while shouting at them: "You must not fear me, you must love me!"

This is Ellsworth Toohey, this is James Taggart, this is any dictator from Hitler to Stalin to Khrushchev to Castro. This is the man whose formula is: "If you can't join them, lick them."

The hatred that such men feel toward other human beings extends ultimately to reality as such, to a universe which does not allow them to have their irrationality and their self-esteem too, a universe which inexorably links irrationality to pain and guilt. To defeat the reality they have never chosen to grasp, to defy reason and logic, to *succeed* at the irrational, *to get away with it*—which means: to make their will omnipotent—becomes a burning lust, a lust to experience the only sort of "efficacy" they can project. And since, for social metaphysicians, reality means other people, the goal of their existence becomes to impose their will on others, to compel others to provide them with a universe in which the irrational will *not* be unattainable.

The extent of such men's alienation from reality, the extent to which objective facts have no status in their consciousness, may be observed in the following spectacle: a brute standing on the balcony of his palace, the blood of millions dripping from his fingers, beaming down at a ragged mob gathered there to honor him—the brute knowing that the scene is a fraud of his own staging, that the mob is there solely by virtue of his soldiers' bayonets—but his chest swelling in satisfaction nonetheless, while, self-hypnotized, he basks in the warmth of his victims' "adoration." (This is the creature whom other social metaphysicians, in their own alienation from reality, call *practical*.)

Fear is the emotion which Power-seeking social metaphysicians understand best, the emotion on which they are authorities—by introspection. Fear is the social atmosphere in which they feel most at home, and the absence of fear in any man they deal with robs them of their delusion of efficacy; their sense of personal identity tends to evaporate in such a man's presence. One can manipulate uncertainty and self-doubt; one cannot manipulate self-esteem. One can manipulate a Peter Keating or a Mr. Mowen; one cannot manipulate a Howard Roark or a John Galt. This is why self-confidence and independence are the human qualities that most strongly incite the hostility of Power-seeking social metaphysicians; their most frenetic hatred is directed at the man who possesses these qualities. *He* is the man beyond their reach, he is the man who will call them to the bar of judgment, he is the enemy and the danger—whom the Power-seeking social metaphysician recognizes as such, not by means of conceptual knowledge or conscious identification, but by means of his own reaction of impotence and dread. It is in this manner that an Ellsworth Toohey recognizes a Howard Roark, or a James Taggart recognizes a John Galt; the "instinctiveness" of their animosity reflects, not the sensitivity of their perceptiveness, but the intensity of their terror.

While social metaphysicians of the Power-seeking variety will often be attracted to the political or military sphere, the type may be found in every profession and on every level of society—from the corporation president who promotes his executives, not according to their ability, but according to their capacity for obsequiousness—to the professor who enjoys undercutting the intellectual self-confidence of his students, by tossing off incomprehensible contradictions as knowledge—to the vicious little sadist browbeating her troup of Girl Scouts. Differences in ambition, skill and interests obviously are relevant here.

Also, there is the matter of *opportunity*. In a politically free society, the Power-seeking type is severely limited in opportunities for "self-expression." But in a statist society, or in a society moving toward statism, formerly repressed and inhibited little Power-seekers start crawling from under rocks in startling quantities.   *(To be completed in our next issue)*

INTELLECTUAL AMMUNITION DEPARTMENT

[*Subscribers are invited to send in the questions that they find themselves unable to answer in philosophical or political discussions. As many questions as space permits will be answered. No questions will be answered by mail.*]

■ **Who is the final authority in ethics?**

There are certain questions that must be questioned—that is, challenged at their root—because they consist of smuggling a false premise into the mind of a careless listener. "Who created the universe?" is one such question. "Do you still beat your wife?" is another. And so is the question above.

It comes up in many different ways, directly and indirectly. It is usually asked in some formulation such as: "Who *decides* what is right or wrong?"

Students of Objectivism are not likely to ask this question, but they may hear it from others and fail to understand its nature. I was astonished, however, to find it addressed to this department, in the following form: "Is it intellectual plagiarism to accept and even to use philosophical principles and values discovered by someone else?"

It may not appear to be the same question, but it is—in the sense that it comes from the same fundamental error.

The nature of the error will become apparent if one applies that question to the physical sciences: "Who *decides* what is right or wrong in electronics?" Or: "Is it scientific plagiarism to accept and even to use medical principles and therapeutic techniques discovered by someone else?"

It is obvious that the root of such questions is a certain kind of conceptual vacuum: the absence of the concept of *objectivity* in the questioner's mind.

Objectivity is both a metaphysical and an epistemological concept. It pertains to the relationship of consciousness to existence. Metaphysically, it is the recognition of the fact that reality exists independent of any perceiver's consciousness. Epistemologically, it is the recognition of the fact that a perceiver's (man's) consciousness must acquire knowledge of reality by certain means (reason) in accordance with certain rules (logic). This means that although reality is immutable and, in any given context, only one answer is true, the truth is not automatically available to a human consciousness and can be obtained only by a certain mental process which is required of every man who seeks knowledge—that there is no substitute for this process, no escape from the responsibility for it, no shortcuts, no special revelations to privileged observers—and that there can be no such thing as a final "authority" in matters pertaining to human knowledge. Metaphysically, the only authority is reality; epistemologically—one's own mind. The first is the ultimate arbiter of the second.

The concept of objectivity contains the reason why the question "Who decides what is right or wrong?" is wrong. Nobody "*decides*." Nature does not *decide*—it merely *is*; man does not *decide*, in issues of knowledge, he merely *observes* that which is. When it comes to applying his knowledge, man decides what he chooses to do, according to what he has learned, remembering that the basic principle of rational action in *all* aspects of human existence, is: "Nature, to be commanded, must be obeyed." This means that man does not *create* reality and can achieve his values only by making his decisions consonant with the facts of reality.

Who "decides" what is the right way to make an automobile, to cure an illness or to live one's life? Any man who cares to acquire the appropriate knowledge and to judge, at and for his own risk and sake. What is his criterion of judgment? Reason. What is his ultimate frame-of-reference? Reality. If he errs or evades, who penalizes him? Reality.

It took centuries (and the influence of Aristotle) for men to acquire a precarious hold on the concept of objectivity in regard to the physical sciences. How precarious that hold actually is, can be observed in the fact that most men are incapable of extending that concept to *all* human knowledge including the so-called humanities, the sciences dealing with man. In regard to the humanities, consciously or subconsciously, explicitly or implicitly, most people revert to the epistemology of prehistorical savages, *i.e.*, to *subjectivism*.

Subjectivism is the belief that reality is not a firm absolute, but a fluid, plastic, indeterminate realm which can be altered, in whole or in part, by the consciousness of the perceiver—*i.e.*, by his feelings, wishes or whims. It is the doctrine which holds that man—an entity of a specific nature, dealing with a universe of a specific nature—can, somehow, live, act and achieve his goals apart from and/or in contradiction to the facts of reality, *i.e.*, apart from and/or in contradiction to his own nature and the nature of the universe. (This is the "mixed," moderate or middle-of-the-road version of subjectivism. Pure or "extreme" subjectivism does not recognize the concept of identity, *i.e.*, the fact that man or the universe or anything possesses a specific nature.)

Morality has been the monopoly of mystics, *i.e.*, of subjectivists, for centuries—a monopoly reinforced and reaffirmed by the neo-mystics of modern philosophy. The clash between the two dominant schools of ethics, the mystical and the social, is only a clash between personal subjectivism and social subjectivism: one substitutes the supernatural for the objective, the other substitutes the collective for the objective. Both are savagely united against the introduction of objectivity into the realm of ethics.

Most men, therefore, find it particularly difficult to regard ethics as a science and to grasp the concept of a rational, *objective* ethics that leaves no room for anyone's arbitrary "decision."

Subjectivism is the smuggled premise at the root of both variants of the question under discussion. Superficially, the two variants may appear to come from opposite motives. Actually, they are two sides of the same subjectivist coin.

The man who asks: "Who decides what is right or wrong?" is obviously a subjectivist who believes that reality is ruled by human whims and who seeks to escape from the responsibility of independent judgment by one of two means: either by cynicism or by blind faith, either by negating the validity of all moral standards or by looking for an "authority" to obey.

But the man who asks: "Is it intellectual plagiarism to accept and even to use philosophical principles and values discovered by someone else?" is not a sovereign consciousness seeking independence from others, as he wants to make himself appear. He has no better grasp of objectivity than the first man; he is a subjectivist who sees reality as a contest of whims and wants it to be ruled by *his* whims—which he proposes to accomplish by discarding as false everything discovered by others. His primary concern, in regard to philosophical principles, is not: "Is it true or false?" but: "Who discovered it?"

On such a premise, he would have to make fire by rubbing sticks together (if he discovers that much), since he is not Edison and cannot accept electric light. He would have to maintain that the earth is flat, since Columbus beat him to the demonstration of its shape. He would have to advocate statism, since he is not Adam Smith. And he would have to discard the laws of logic, since he is obviously not Aristotle.

The division of labor in the pursuit of knowledge—the fact that men can transmit knowledge and learn from one another's discoveries—is one of man's great advantages over all other living species. Only a subjectivist, who equates *facts* with *arbitrary assertions*, could imagine that to *"learn"* means to *"accept on faith"*—as this questioner seems to imply.

It is also possible that the motive of such a mentality is the wish, not to discard the ideas of others, but to *appropriate* them. "Plagiarism" is a concept that pertains, not to the acceptance, but to the *authorship* of an idea. Needless to say, to accept someone's idea and then to pose as its originator, *is* plagiarism of the lowest order. But this has nothing to do with a legitimate, rational process of learning. The truth of an idea and its authorship are two separate issues, which are not difficult to keep apart.

This particular variant of the question was worth noting only as an extreme example of subjectivism—of the degree to which ideas have no reality and no connection to reality in a subjectivist's mind. It is an illustration of the extent to which the concept of objectivity is still alien to a great many men, and of the extent to which mankind needs it.

Observe that most modern collectivists—the alleged advocates of human brotherhood, benevolence and cooperation—are committed to subjectivism in the humanities. Yet reason—and, therefore, *objectivity*—is the only common bond among men, the only means of communication, the only universal frame-of-reference and criterion of justice. No understanding, communication or cooperation is possible to men on the basis of unintelligible feelings and subjective "urges"; nothing is possible but a contest of whims resolved by the rule of brute force.

In politics, the subjectivist question of "Who 'decides'?" comes up in many forms. It leads many alleged champions of freedom to the notion that "the will of the people" or of the majority is the ultimate sanction of a free society, which is a contradiction in terms, since such a sanction represents the doctrine of unlimited majority rule.

The answer, here as in all other moral-intellectual problems, is that nobody *"decides."* Reason and reality are the only valid criteria of political theories. Who determines which theory is true? *Any man who can prove it.*

Theories, ideas, discoveries are not created collectively; they are the products of individual men. In politics, as in every other field of human endeavor, a group can only accept or reject a product (or a theory); it cannot, *qua* group, participate in its creation. The participants are those who choose that particular field of activity, each to the extent of his ability and ambition. And, when men are free, irrational theories can win only temporarily and only through the errors or the default of the thinkers, *i.e.*, of those who do seek the truth.

In politics, as in every other field, the men who do not care to think are merely ballast: they accept, by default, whatever the intellectual leaders of the moment have to offer. To the extent to which men do think, they follow the man who offers the best (*i.e.*, the most rational) idea. This does not happen instantaneously nor automatically nor in every specific case and detail, but this is the way knowledge spreads among men, and this has been the pattern of mankind's progress. The best proof of the power of ideas—the power of reason for men of all levels of intelligence—is the fact that no dictatorship was ever able to last without establishing censorship.

The number of its adherents is irrelevant to the truth or falsehood of an idea. A majority is as fallible as a minority or as an individual man. A majority vote is not an epistemological validation of an idea. Voting is merely a proper political device—within a strictly, constitutionally delimited sphere of action—for choosing the practical *means* of implementing a society's basic principles. But those principles are not determined by vote. By whom, then, are they determined? By the facts of reality—as identified by those thinkers who chose the field of political philosophy. This was the pattern of the greatest political achievement in history: the American Revolution.

In this connection, it is important to note the *epistemological* significance of a free society. In a free society, the pursuit of truth is protected by the free access of any individual to any field of endeavor he may choose to enter. (A free access does not mean a guarantee of success, nor of financial support, nor of anyone's acceptance and agreement—it means the absence of any forced restrictions or legal barriers.) This prevents the formation of any coercive "elite" in any profession—it prevents the legalized enforcement of a "monopoly on truth" by any gang of power-seekers—it protects the free market place of ideas—it keeps all doors open to man's inquiring mind.

Who "decides"? In politics, in ethics, in art, in science, in philosophy—in the entire realm of human knowledge—it is *reality* that sets the terms, through the work of those men who are able to identify its terms and to translate them into *objective* principles.

—AYN RAND

OBJECTIVIST CALENDAR

■ On Monday, February 15, Ayn Rand will begin the first of six 15-minute radio programs for the *Commentary* series on Station WBAI (99.5 FM) in New York, at 7:45 P.M. The program will be rebroadcast on the following morning, at 10 A.M. The rest of her programs will be broadcast and rebroadcast on consecutive Mondays and Tuesdays, at 7:45 P.M. and 10 A.M. respectively.

These programs may also be broadcast by the Los Angeles and San Francisco stations of the Pacifica Foundation; check locally for information.

■ On Tuesday, February 16, Nathaniel Branden's course on "Basic Principles of Objectivism" will begin in New York City. Place: Hotel Biltmore, 43rd St. & Madison Ave. Time: 7:30 P.M. Admission: $3.50, payable at the door. (College and High School students, $2.75.) Ayn Rand will participate in the question period which follows the lecture.

■ NBI's Tape Transcription Division has scheduled the following starting dates: "Basic Principles of Objectivist Psychology" in San Jose, February 11; "The Economics of a Free Society" in San Diego, February 14, and in Los Angeles, March 19; "The Principles of Efficient Thinking" in Dallas, March 5; "The History of Modern Philosophy" in Washington, March 22; "Three Plays by Ayn Rand" in Phoenix, March 1. For details, contact NBI.

■ NBI is planning a Ball, tentatively scheduled for April 16, in N.Y.C., for students and their guests. All present and former NBI students will receive more information shortly.

Published monthly at 120 East 34th Street, New York 16, N. Y.
Subscription rate in United States, its possessions, Canada and Mexico: one year, $5; 2 years, $9; 3 years, $13. Other countries: one year, $6; 2 years, $11; 3 years, $16.
Additional copies of this Newsletter: single copy 50¢ (coins, not stamps); 10 – 99 copies, 25¢ each plus postage (for first-class delivery add 1¢ per copy, for third-class delivery add ½¢ per copy); 100 or more copies, 15¢ each plus postage (same as above). (Bulk rates apply only to multiple orders of a single issue.)
For change of address send old address and new address with zone number if any. Allow us three weeks to process new subscriptions and change of address.

Ayn Rand and Nathaniel Branden, Editors and Publishers
Barbara Branden, Managing Editor
Elayne Kalberman, Circulation Manager

THE OBJECTIVIST NEWSLETTER

Edited and Published by AYN RAND and NATHANIEL BRANDEN

VOL. 4 NO. 3   MARCH, 1965

CHECK YOUR PREMISES
By AYN RAND
Art and Moral Treason

When I saw Mr. X for the first time, I thought that he had the most tragic face I had ever seen: it was not the mark left by some specific tragedy, not the look of a great sorrow, but a look of desolate hopelessness, weariness and resignation that seemed left by the chronic pain of many lifetimes. He was 26 years old.

He had a brilliant mind, an outstanding scholastic record in the field of engineering, a promising start in his career — and no energy to move farther. He was paralyzed by so extreme a state of indecision that any sort of choice filled him with anxiety—even the question of moving out of an inconvenient apartment. He was stagnating in a job which he had outgrown and which had become a dull, uninspiring routine. He was so lonely that he had lost the capacity to know it, he had no concept of friendship, and his few attempts at a romantic relationship had ended disastrously—he could not tell why.

At the time I met him, he was undergoing psychotherapy, struggling desperately to discover the causes of his state. There seemed to be no existential cause for it. His childhood had not been happy, but no worse and, in some respects, better than the average childhood. There were no traumatic events in his past, no major shocks, disappointments or frustrations. Yet his frozen impersonality suggested a man who neither felt nor wanted anything any longer. He was like a gray spread of ashes that had never been on fire.

Discussing his childhood, I asked him once what he had been in love with (*what*, not *whom*). "Nothing," he answered —then mentioned uncertainly a toy that had been his favorite. On another occasion, I mentioned a current political event of shocking irrationality and injustice, which he conceded indifferently to be evil. I asked whether it made him indignant. "You don't understand," he answered gently. "I never feel indignation about anything."

He had held some erroneous philosophical views (under the influence of a college course in contemporary philosophy), but his intellectual goals and motives seemed to be a confused struggle in the right direction, and I could not discover any major ideological sin, any crime commensurate with the punishment he was suffering.

Then, one day, as an almost casual remark in a conversation about the role of human ideals in art, he told me the following story. Some years earlier, he had seen a certain semi-Romantic movie and had felt an emotion he was unable to describe, particularly in response to the character of an industrialist who was moved by a passionate, intransigent, dedicated vision of his work. Mr. X was speaking incoherently, but conveying clearly that what he had experienced was more than admiration for a single character: it was the sense of seeing a different kind of universe—and his emotion had been exaltation. "It was what I wanted life to be," he said. His eyes were sparkling, his voice was eager, his face was alive and young—he *was* a man in love, for the span of that moment. Then, the gray lifelessness came back and he concluded in a dull tone of voice, with a trace of tortured wistfulness: "When I came out of the theater, I felt guilty about having felt this." "*Guilty? Why?*" I asked. He answered: "Because I thought that what made me react this way to the industrialist, is the part of me that's wrong... It's the impractical element in me... Life is not like that..."

What *I* felt was a cold shudder. Whatever the root of his problems, *this* was the key; it was the symptom, not of amorality, but of a profound moral treason. To what and to whom can a man be willing to apologize for the best within him? And what can he expect of life after that?

(Ultimately, what saved Mr. X was his commitment to reason; he held reason as an absolute, even if he did not know its full meaning and application; an absolute that survived through the most excruciating periods he had to endure in his struggle to regain his psychological health—to remake and release the soul he had spent his life negating. Due to his determined perseverance and to the unusual competence of his psychologist, he won his battle. Today—after quitting his job and taking many calculated risks—he is a brilliant success, in a career he loves, and on his way up to an ever-increasing range of achievement. He is still struggling with some remnants of his past errors. But, as a measure of his recovery and of the distance he has travelled, I would suggest that you re-read my opening paragraph before I tell you that I saw a recent snapshot of him which caught him smiling, and of all the characters in *Atlas Shrugged* the one whom the quality of that smile would suit best is Francisco d'Anconia.)

The case of Mr. Y was strikingly similar, though the two men were quite different in most respects. Mr. Y was a nuclear physicist who had a distinguished name in his profession and many notable achievements to his credit while still in his early thirties. On the surface, he appeared to be a "well-adjusted" man who, outside his laboratory, led a "normal," thoroughly conventional life. His manner seemed poised, quietly self-confident, at times charmingly witty, and merely a bit too stiff. He had an extraordinary intelligence, and his passionate love for his work was one of his most attractive qualities.

Yet he was quietly going to pieces, and the form he gave to his problem (though this was not its real nature) was: doubt of his own intelligence and doubt of the efficacy of science.

He, too, was struggling to discover the roots of his inner conflicts. I did not know him too well, so it was inadvertently that I contributed an important clue to his problem. One evening, I interrupted a conversation with him to tune in for a moment on a certain TV movie: I explained to him that I wanted to hear a piece of music used in that movie, which I loved and could not obtain in record form. It was a popular number of the pre-World War I era and it was *my* kind of music: gay, melodic, rhythmically ingenious and projecting a totally unclouded sense of life.

I was startled by the look of his face when the first bars of that music came on: it was shock, recognition, amusement—an almost paternal amusement directed at me—bitterness, wistfulness and a terrible kind of pain. I asked him what was the matter. He was shaken by such an inner explosion that he could not speak for a while. Then, gradually, he told me.

He knew the place that my kind of music occupied in my life. In *his* life, that place was held by the art and music of ballet. This had been his great love. At one time, he had attended every performance of a good ballet company he could find. The emotion he had then experienced was a state of intense exaltation. He had regarded *this* as his guilty secret. He had tried to stifle it. He had not permitted himself to grasp the meaning of his love. He had sought to give it no place in his life and no importance in his own eyes—in the unstated hope that he could destroy it, not by eliminating it, but worse: by refusing to take it seriously. Acting, in effect, as the executioner of his own soul, he had branded it as "ludicrous."

He still loved music and he owned a large collection of records, which he played frequently—for an esthetic pleasure that conveyed no personal meaning to him and evoked no personal emotion; all the records were classics such as Bach, Haydn, Mozart; *he did not own a single record of ballet music.*

"Why?" I asked. He answered: "Because I am afraid of myself in that mood."

Afraid of what? Of his inability to negate his own values and to comply with the conventional standards he had been forcing on himself all his life. And the thing that had hit him, at the sound of my music, was a sudden insight telling him the meaning of what he was repressing and the full extent of his moral treason.

(Needless to say, I played ballet music for him for the rest of that evening. He has since bought the records he wanted. His problems are not yet solved, but he is improving and coming back to life month by month; and the personality that is now emerging has an authentic self-assurance that inspires enormous confidence, and a kind of subtle intellectual charm that is inimitably his own.)

There are countless cases similar to these; these two are merely the most dramatically obvious in my experience and involve two men of unusual stature. But the same tragedy is repeated all around us, in many hidden, twisted forms—like a secret torture chamber in men's souls, from which an unrecognizable cry reaches us occasionally and then is silenced again. The person, in such cases, is both "man the victim" and "man the killer." And certain principles apply to them all.

Man is a being of self-made soul—which means that his character is formed by his basic premises, particularly by his basic value-premises. In the crucial, formative years of his life—in childhood and adolescence—Romantic art is his major (and, today, his only) source of a *moral* sense of life. (In later years, Romantic art is often his only experience of it.)

Please note that art is not his only source of *morality*, but of a *moral sense of life*. This requires careful differentiation.

A *"sense of life"* is a pre-conceptual equivalent of metaphysics—an emotional, subconsciously integrated appraisal of man's nature and the nature of reality, summing up one's view of man's relationship to existence. *Morality* is an abstract, conceptual code of values and principles.

The process of a child's development consists of acquiring knowledge, which requires the development of his capacity to grasp and deal with an ever-widening range of abstractions. This involves the growth of two interrelated, but different chains of abstractions, two hierarchical structures of concepts, which should be integrated, but seldom are: the *cognitive* and the *normative*. The first deals with knowledge of the facts of reality—the second, with the evaluation of these facts. The first forms the epistemological foundation of science—the second, of morality and of art.

In today's culture, the development of a child's *cognitive* abstractions is assisted to some minimal extent, even if ineptly, half-heartedly, with many hampering, crippling obstacles (such as anti-rational doctrines and influences which, today, are growing worse). But the development of a child's *normative* abstractions is not merely left unaided, it is all but stifled and destroyed. The child whose valuing capacity survives the moral barbarism of his upbringing, has to find his own way to preserve and develop his sense of values.

Apart from its many other evils, conventional morality is not concerned with the formation of a child's character. It does not teach or show him *what kind of man he ought to be*, and why; it is concerned only with imposing a set of rules upon him—concrete, arbitrary, contradictory and, more often than not, incomprehensible rules, which are mainly prohibitions and duties. A child whose only notion of morality (*i.e.*, of *values*) consists of such matters as: "Wash your ears!"—"Don't be rude to Aunt Rosalie!"—"Do your homework!"—"Help papa to mow the lawn (or mama to wash the dishes)!"—faces the alternative of: either a passively *amoral* resignation, leading to a future of hopeless cynicism, or a blind rebellion. Observe that the more intelligent and independent a child, the more unruly he is in regard to such commandments. But, in either case, the child grows up with nothing but resentment and fear or contempt for the concept of morality which, to him, is only "a phantom scarecrow made of duty, of boredom, of punishment, of pain . . . a scarecrow standing in a barren field, waving a stick to chase away [his] pleasures . . ." (*Atlas Shrugged*)

This type of upbringing is the best, not the worst, that an average child may be subjected to, in today's culture. If parents attempt to inculcate a moral ideal of the kind contained in such admonitions as: "Don't be selfish—give your best toys away to the neighbors' children!" or if parents go "progressive" and teach a child to be guided by his whims—the damage to the child's moral character may be irreparable.

Where, then, can a child learn the concept of moral values and of a moral character in whose image he will shape his own soul? Where can he find the evidence, the material from which to develop a chain of *normative* abstractions? He is not likely to find a clue in the chaotic, bewildering, contradictory evidence offered by the adults in his day-by-day experience. He may like some adults and dislike others (and, often, dislike them all), but to abstract, identify and judge their *moral* characteristics is a task beyond his capacity. And such moral principles as he might be taught to recite are, to him, floating abstractions with no connection to reality.

The major source and demonstration of moral values available to a child is Romantic art (particularly Romantic literature). What Romantic art offers him is *not* moral rules, not an explicit didactic message, but the image of a moral *person*—*i.e.*, the *concretized abstraction* of a moral ideal. It offers a concrete, directly perceivable answer to the very abstract question which a child senses, but cannot yet conceptualize: What kind of person is moral and what kind of life does he lead?

It is not abstract principles that a child learns from Romantic art, but the pre-condition and the incentive for the later understanding of such principles: the emotional experience of

(*Continued on page 12*)

Rogues' Gallery

By NATHANIEL BRANDEN

(Part II of a two-part article)

Faced with the question, "What am I to do with my life?" or "What will make me happy?"—the Conventional social metaphysician seeks the answer among the standard values of his culture: respectability, financial success, marriage, family, professional competence, prestige, etc.

Faced with the question, "How am I to make my existence endurable?"—the Power-seeking social metaphysician seeks the answer in aggressive and destructive action aimed at the external object of his fear: other people.

While his desire is to control the consciousnesses of others, he does not necessarily resort to physical force, even when opportunities exist. Manipulation, trickery and deceit are often chosen by him, not as *adjuncts* to coercion, but as preferred *alternatives*. There are several reasons for this. First, not all men of this type have the "stomach" for physical violence: they cannot bear the vision of themselves resorting to such means. Second, devices such as manipulation and deceit do not ordinarily entail the physical risks and dangers inherent in the use of violence. Third, to some Power-seekers, these non-violent devices represent a *superior* form of efficacy, a more "intellectual" form, so to speak. But what must be recognized is that these devices spring from the same root as the impulse to violence: the desire to by-pass and overcome the *voluntary* judgment of others, to affect others through the imposition of one's own will, *against* their desires, knowledge and interests—to gain a sense of triumph by cheating reason and reality. The desire to manipulate other men is the desire to manipulate reality and to make one's wishes omnipotent.

Consider, now, the psychology of the *Spiritual* social metaphysician. This type does not seek to please and placate people, in the manner of a Peter Keating, or to gain power over them, like an Ellsworth Toohey. This type often does virtually nothing at all. His chief virtue, he proclaims or implies, is that he is too good for this world. He must not be expected to conform to conventional standards. He must not be expected to achieve anything *tangible*. His friends and acquaintances must love and respect him, not for anything he does—*doing* is so vulgar—but for what he is. What *is* he? Not everything can be communicated, after all. Some things—the important things—can only be *felt*.

To put it another way: the Spiritual social metaphysician's claim to esteem rests on his alleged possession of a superior kind of *soul*—a soul that is not his mind, not his thoughts, not his values, not anything specifiable, but an ineffable composite of undefinable longings, incommunicable insights and impenetrable mystery.

So long as the influence of mysticism falls as a shadow across our culture, this sort of "solution" to the problem of self-esteem will attract a certain number of social metaphysicians. It spares them the necessity of effort or struggle (except, of course, the dreadful struggle to preserve this fraud *in their own eyes*). They know that the inferiority feelings of their fellow social metaphysicians offer them a "market" for their Spiritual role.

The "market" is a limited one, however; and it is distressingly unpredictable. The Spiritual type has an answer to this, *i.e.*, he has his rationalization ready. If and when he fails to receive the acceptance and esteem he craves, he explains to himself that people are not fine enough to appreciate the "real" him. He may even prefer to be alone, to avoid people—the better to dream, undisturbed and unchallenged, about how he would be admired and loved if only people knew what he was "really" like, deep inside. (It should be added that there are moments when the thought of people knowing what he is *really* like fills him with terror.) An over-active fantasy-life is often characteristic of this type: he sees himself as a religious saint, or an inspired statesman, or a renowned poet, or (forgetting that he is supposed to be spiritual) a sexually irresistible Don Juan.

The extreme case of this mentality, carried to the edge of psychosis (and sometimes beyond), is a *sub*-type which may be designated as the *Religious lunatic* social metaphysician. This type of person can disassociate himself from the human race altogether, he may become a hermit or anchorite —with *God* as his "significant other," as the object of his social metaphysical attachment. Having despaired of impressing his fellow men, it is God whom he seeks to impress. Since God cannot frown at him, or snub him socially, or inquire as to why he doesn't get a job, the Religious lunatic type is free to imagine that God is smiling down at him, blessing and protecting him, responding to the true nobility of his soul, which everyone on earth is too superficial or corrupt to do.

Then there is the *Independent* social metaphysician. This is the counterfeit individualist, the man who rebels against the status quo for the sake of being rebellious, the man whose pseudo-self-esteem is tied to the picture of himself as a defiant non-conformist.

This is the "rebel" who fulfills his concept of profundity and self-expression by proclaiming regularly that "Everything stinks." This is the nihilist, this is the Beatnik, this is the non-objective "artist," this is the "individualist" who proves it by scorning money, marriage, jobs, baths and haircuts. This is the son who leaves home to join the anarchist movement, because his father suggested to him that perhaps it is time to start earning a living, now that he, the son, is approaching forty.

Overwhelmed by feelings of inadequacy in relation to the conventional standards of his culture, this type of person retaliates with the formula "Whatever is, *is wrong*." Overwhelmed by the belief that no one can possibly like or accept him, he goes out of his way to insult people—lest they imagine that he desires their approval. Overwhelmed with humiliation at feeling himself an outcast, he struggles to conquer his sense of non-identity by maintaining that to be an outcast is proof of one's superiority.

The fact he evades is that there are two opposite reasons why a man may be "outside" of society: because his standards are *higher* than those of society—or because they are *lower;* because he is above society—or below it; because he is too good—or not good enough.

To the Independent social metaphysician, existence is a clash between his whims and the whims of others. Reason, objectivity, reality as such have no meaning to him, no importance inside his skull. The only question that concerns him is: "Whose whims do I follow—mine or theirs?"

While he may profess devotion to some particular idea or goal, or even posture as a dedicated crusader, his primary motivation is negative rather than positive; he is *against* rather than *for*. He does not originate or struggle for positive values of his own, he merely rebels against the values and standards of others—as if the *absence* of passive conformity, rather than the *presence* of independent, rational judgment, were the hallmark of self-reliance and spiritual sovereignty. It is by means of this delusion that he seeks to escape the fact of his inner emptiness.

The Independent social metaphysician is the brother-in-spirit of the Power-seeker. Often, it is merely the accident of historical circumstances that determines whether a social metaphysician becomes one type or the other. Nazism and communism, for instance, attracted many Independent social metaphysicians who made an instantaneous and effortless transition to the psychology of the Power-seeking type; they found a form of "togetherness" for which they were eagerly willing to relinquish their "independence."

In a culture where rationality, productiveness and simple sanity are dominant values, if only on a common sense level, social metaphysicians of the Independent type tend to remain on the fringes of society. But in a culture such as ours, the pressure resulting from the intellectual vacuum can fling them up from their cellars to the pinnacles of prestige, in an extended "Fools' Day" orgy. Then one sees the triumphant spread of pretentiously eccentric mediocrity, one sees the drunken glorification of unconsciousness—one sees unintelligible splashes of paint, representing nothing, displayed on the walls of famous museums—one sees unkempt young men, in sweaters and loafers, lecturing on Zen Buddhism in distinguished universities—one sees whims for the sake of whims, absurdity for the sake of absurdity, destruction for the sake of destruction, becoming *fashionable*.

When and to the extent that this occurs, the Independent social metaphysicians involved may react in one of several ways. They may switch to the role of Conventional social metaphysicians, eager to be respectable conformists within the context of their newly established sub-culture, and may then proceed to sneer at all those who do not "belong." Or: They may switch to the psychology of open Power-seekers, struggling to be accepted as leaders of the new elite, scheming and manipulating in order to protect their positions, trembling lest their status be usurped by more effective or aggressive rivals. Or: Feeling too insecure to strive for *any* fixed position within *any* sub-culture, they may abandon the system or movement that they themselves helped to launch, and adopt some *new* posture that will *guarantee* their role as outcasts, so that they will never have to endure the anticipatory panic of possible rejection.

There is, finally, a type of social metaphysician that differs in important respects from all the foregoing varieties I have described. I call this type: the *Ambivalent* social metaphysician.

This is the person who, notwithstanding a major psycho-epistemological surrender to the authority of others, has still preserved a significant degree of intellectual sovereignty. While no one, not even the most abject conformist, can renounce his mind completely, the Ambivalent type retains a far greater measure of authentic independence than any other species of social metaphysician.

His intellectual self-abdication is far more limited; it tends to center on that most sensitive area in which all social metaphysicians are especially vulnerable: the realm of values.

The Ambivalent type seldom dares to question the fundamental values of his social environment, but he is often indifferent to these values, paying them only perfunctory respect. In the areas of life to which these values pertain, he does not assert counter-values of his own, he merely withdraws, surrendering those aspects of reality to others. He tends to restrict his activity and concern to the sphere of his work, where his self-reliance and sovereignty are greatest.

His bondage to social metaphysics is revealed in his quietly persistent sense of alienation from reality, in his lack of confidence and freedom with regard to passing value judgments, in his implicit belief that the world is controlled by others, that others possess a knowledge forever unknowable to him, and in his humiliating desire for "approval" and "acceptance." His superiority to other social metaphysicians is evidenced, not only by his greater independence, but also by his desire to *earn*, through objective achievements, the esteem he longs for, by his relative inability to find real pleasure in an admiration not based on standards he can respect—and by his tortured disgust at his own fear of the disapproval of others. Often, he tries to fight his fear, refusing to act on or surrender to it, exercising immense will-power and discipline—but never winning his battle fully, never setting himself free, because he does not go to the roots of his problem, does not identify the psycho-epistemological base of his betrayal, does not accept full and ultimate intellectual responsibility for his own life and goals.

Among this type, one will find men of distinguished achievements and outstanding creative originality—whose treason and tragedy lie in the contrast between their private lives and their lives as creators. These are the men who have the courage to challenge the *cognitive* judgments of world figures, but lack the courage to challenge the *value* judgments of the folks next door.

It must be understood that none of the social metaphysical types I have described are intended to represent mutually exclusive categories; any particular social metaphysician may possess characteristics of several types. The purpose of such a typological description is to isolate, by a process of abstraction, *certain dominant trends* among social metaphysicians, and make those trends intelligible motivationally.

The forms which social metaphysics can take are virtually unlimited. But if one grasps the basic *principles* involved, one will find oneself far less bewildered when contemplating the spectacle of human irrationality throughout history—or in our modern world—or in one's personal encounters.

Art and Moral Treason (from page 10)

admiration for man's highest potential, the experience of *looking up* to a hero—a view of life motivated and dominated by values, a life in which man's choices are practicable, effective and crucially important—that is, a *moral* sense of life.

While his home environment taught him to associate morality with *pain*, Romantic art teaches him to associate it with *pleasure*—an inspiring pleasure which is his own, profoundly personal discovery.

The translation of this sense of life into adult, conceptual terms would, if unimpeded, follow the growth of the child's knowledge—and the two basic elements of his soul, the cognitive and normative, would develop together in serenely harmonious integration. The ideal which, at the age of seven, was personified by a cowboy, may become a detective at twelve, and a philosopher at twenty—as the child's interests progress from comic strips to mystery stories to the great sunlit universe of Romantic literature, art and music.

But whatever his age, morality is a *normative* science—*i.e.*, a science that projects a value-goal to be achieved by a series of steps, of choices—and it cannot be practiced without a clear vision of the goal, without a concretized image of the ideal to be reached. If man is to gain and keep a moral stature, he needs an image of the ideal, from the first thinking day of his life to the last.

In the translation of that ideal into conscious, philosophical terms and into his actual practice, a child needs intellectual assistance or, at least, a chance to find his own way. In today's culture, he is given neither. The battering which his precarious, unformed, barely glimpsed *moral sense of life* receives from parents, teachers, adult "authorities" and little social metaphysical goons of his own generation is so intense and so evil that only the toughest hero can withstand it—so evil that of the many sins of adults toward children, *this* is the one for which they deserve to burn in hell, if such a place existed.

Every form of punishment—from outright prohibition to threats to anger to condemnation to crass indifference to mockery—is unleashed against a child at the first signs of his Romanticism (which means: at the first signs of his emerging sense of moral values). "Life is not like that!" and "Come down to earth!" are the catchphrases which best summarize the motives of the attackers, as well as the view of life and of this earth which they seek to inculcate.

The child who withstands it and damns the attackers, not himself and his values, is a rare exception. The child who merely *supresses* his values, avoids communication and withdraws into a lonely private universe, is almost as rare. In most cases, the child *represses* his values and gives up. He gives up the entire realm of valuing, of value choices and judgments—without knowing that what he is surrendering is *morality*.

The surrender is extorted by a long, almost imperceptible process, a constant, ubiquitous pressure which the child absorbs and accepts by degrees. His spirit is not broken at one sudden blow: it is bled to death in thousands of small scratches.

The most devastating part of this process is the fact that a child's moral sense is destroyed, not only by means of such weaknesses or flaws as he might have developed, but by means of his barely emerging virtues. An intelligent child is aware that he does not know what adult life is like, that he has an enormous amount to learn and is anxiously eager to learn it. An ambitious child is incoherently determined to make something *important* of himself and his life. So when he hears such threats as "Wait till you grow up!" and "You'll never get anywhere with those childish notions!" it is his virtues that are turned against him: his intelligence, his ambition and whatever respect he might feel for the knowledge and judgment of his elders.

Thus the foundation of a lethal dichotomy is laid in his consciousness: the *practical* versus the *moral*, with the unstated, pre-conceptual implication that practicality requires the betrayal of one's values, the renunciation of ideals.

His rationality is turned against him by means of a similar dichotomy: *reason* versus *emotion*. His Romantic sense of life is only a *sense*, an incoherent emotion which he can neither communicate nor explain nor defend. It is an intense, yet fragile emotion, painfully vulnerable to any sarcastic allegation, since he is unable to identify its real meaning.

It is easy to convince a child, and particularly an adolescent, that his desire to emulate Buck Rogers is ridiculous: he knows that it isn't exactly Buck Rogers he has in mind and yet, simultaneously, it *is*—he feels caught in an inner contradiction—and this confirms his desolately embarrassing feeling that *he is* being ridiculous.

Thus the adults—whose foremost moral obligation toward a child, at this stage of his development, is to help him understand that what he loves is an abstraction, to help him break through into the *conceptual* realm—accomplish the exact opposite. They stunt his conceptual capacity, they cripple his normative abstractions, they stifle his *moral ambition, i.e.,* his desire for virtue, *i.e.,* his self-esteem. They arrest his value-development on a primitively literal, concrete-bound level: they convince him that to be like Buck Rogers means to wear a space helmet and blast armies of Martians with a disintegrator-gun, and that he'd better give up such notions if he ever expects to make a respectable living. And they finish him off with such gems of argumentation as: "Buck Rogers—ha-ha! never gets any colds in the head. Do you know any real people who never get them? Why, *you* had one last week. So don't you go on imagining that you're better than the rest of us!"

Their motive is obvious. If they actually regarded Romanticism as an "impractical fantasy," they would feel nothing but a friendly or indifferent amusement—*not* the passionate resentment and uncontrollable rage which they do feel and exhibit.

While the child is thus driven to fear, mistrust and repress his own emotions, he cannot avoid observing the hysterical violence of the adults' emotions unleashed against him in this and other issues. He concludes, subconsciously, that *all* emotions as such are dangerous, that they are the irrational, unpredictably destructive element in people, which can descend upon him at any moment in some terrifying way for some incomprehensible purpose. This is the brick before last in the wall of repression which he erects to bury his own emotions. The last is his desperate pride misdirected into a decision such as: "I'll never let them hurt me again!" The way never to be hurt, he decides, is never to feel anything.

But an emotional repression cannot be complete; when all other emotions are stifled, a single one takes over: fear. (There are men who, when they grow up, are thrown into panic by a display of *any* strong emotion in others, negative or positive.)

The element of fear was involved in the process of the child's moral destruction from the start. His victimized virtues were not the only cause; his faults were active as well: fear of others, particularly of adults, fear of independence, of responsibility, of loneliness—as well as self-doubt and the desire to be accepted, to "belong." But it is the involvement of his virtues that makes his position so tragic and, later, so hard to correct.

As he grows up, his amorality is reinforced and reaffirmed. His intelligence prevents him from accepting any of the current schools of morality: the mystical, the social or the subjective. An eager young mind, seeking the guidance of reason, cannot take the supernatural seriously and is impervious to mysticism. It does not take him long to perceive the contradictions and the sickeningly self-abasing hypocrisy of the social school of morality. But the worst influence of all, for him, is the subjective school.

He is too intelligent and too honorable (in his own twisted, tortured way) not to know that the *subjective* means the arbitrary, the irrational, the blindly emotional. *These* are the elements which he has come to associate with people's attitudes in moral issues, and to dread. When formal philosophy tells him that morality, by its very nature, is closed to reason and can be nothing but a matter of subjective choice, this is the kiss or seal of death on his moral development. His conscious conviction now unites with his subconscious feeling that value choices come from the mindless element in people and are a dangerous, unknowable, unpredictable enemy. His conscious decision is: not to get involved in moral issues; its subconscious meaning is: *not to value anything* (or worse: not to value anything *too much*, not to hold any irreplaceable, non-expendable values).

From this to the policy of a moral coward existentially and to an overwhelming sense of guilt psychologically, is not a very long step for an intelligent man. The result is such men as the two I described.

Let it be said to their credit that they were unable to "adjust" to their inner contradictions—and that it was precisely their early professional success that broke them psychologically: it exposed their value-vacuum, their lack of personal purpose and thus the self-abnegating futility of their work.

They knew—even though not in fully conscious terms—that they were achieving the opposite of their original, preconceptual goals and motives. Instead of leading a *rational* (*i.e.*, reason-guided and reason-motivated) life, they were gradually becoming moody, subjectivist whim-worshipers, acting on the range of the moment, particularly in their personal relationships—by default of any firmly defined values. Instead of reaching independence from the irrationality of others, they were being forced—by the same default—either into actual social metaphysics or into an equivalent code of behavior, into blind dependence on and compliance with the value-systems of others, into a state of abject conformity. Instead of pleasure, the glimpse of any higher value or nobler experience brought them pain, guilt, terror—and prompted them, not to seize it and fight for it, but to escape, to evade, to betray it (or to *apologize* for it) in order to placate the standards of the conventional men whom they despised. Instead of "man the victim," as they had largely been, they were becoming "man the killer."

The clearest evidence of it was provided, in both cases, by their attitude toward Romantic art. A man's treason to his art values is not the primary cause of his neurosis (it is a contributory cause), but it becomes one of its most revealing symptoms.

This last is of particular importance to the man who seeks to solve his psychological problems. The chaos of his personal relationships and values may, at first, be too complex for him to untangle. But Romantic art offers him a clear, luminous, impersonal abstraction—and thus a clear, objective test of his inner state, a clue available to his conscious mind.

If he finds himself fearing, evading and negating the highest experience possible to man, a state of unclouded exaltation, he can know that he is in profound trouble and that his only alternatives are: either to check his value-premises from scratch, from the start, from the repressed, forgotten, betrayed figure of his particular Buck Rogers, and painfully to reconstruct his broken chain of normative abstractions—or to become completely the kind of monster he is in those moments when, with an obsequious giggle, he tells some fat Babbitt that exaltation is impractical.

Just as Romantic art is a man's first glimpse of a moral sense of life, so it is his last hold on it, his last lifeline.

Romantic art is the fuel and the spark plug of a man's soul; its task is to set a soul on fire and never let it go out. The task of providing that fire with a motor and a direction, belongs to philosophy.

In conclusion, let me give you a different kind of case history. It is the story of a man who withstood the tortures of childhood and made his own way to the discovery of moral abstractions. At the age of seven, his ideal was The Lone Ranger. At the age of nine, it was Superman. At the age of twelve, it was The Scarlet Pimpernel. Then he asked himself a crucial question; he realized that he had no desire to save French aristocrats from the guillotine and that there were no guillotines around, and he asked himself: how does one apply the things he admired in The Scarlet Pimpernel to one's own life and how does one practice them in the modern world? He found the answer two years later. At the age of fourteen, he read *The Fountainhead*.

His name is Nathaniel Branden.

OBJECTIVIST CALENDAR

■ On Wednesday, March 10, Nathaniel Branden will deliver two lectures at Albion College in Albion, Michigan. In the afternoon, his subject will be: "The Role of Consciousness in Psychology—A Critique of Behaviorism." In the evening, as part of a symposium on "Psychology and Religion," his topic will be: "Mental Health Versus the Religious View of Life." For further details, contact Albion College.

■ Beginning Monday, March 22, in New York City, NBI will offer a ten-lecture course on "The Principles of Efficient Thinking," to be given by Barbara Branden. Time: 7:30 P.M. Place: Sheraton-Atlantic Hotel, Broadway at 34th Street. Admission: $3.50, payable at the door.

■ NBI's Tape Transcription Division has scheduled the following starting dates: "Basic Principles of Objectivism" in Indianapolis, March 5; Tucson, March 12; Baltimore, March 16; St. Anthony, Idaho, March 23—"The Principles of Efficient Thinking" in Dallas, March 5; Phoenix, March 19; Detroit, March 26; San Francisco, April 2; Los Angeles, April 21—"The Economics of a Free Society" in Los Angeles, March 19—"The Esthetics of the Visual Arts" in Chicago, April 4—"The History of Modern Philosophy" in San Diego, March 10; Chicago, March 21; Washington, D.C., March 22.

■ The following radio stations have obtained for broadcast the current series of "Ayn Rand on Campus" programs, which are broadcast in New York and syndicated by the Columbia University Station WKCR: Radio Station WRSB, Shimer College, Box 312, Mt. Carroll, Illinois; Radio Station WBKY, University of Kentucky, Lexington, Kentucky; Radio Station WTBS, Mass. Institute of Technology, Cambridge, Mass.; Radio Station KCAP, 9 North Last Chance Gulch, Helena, Montana; Radio Station of the College of William and Mary, Williamsburg, Va.; Radio Station KRAB, Seattle, Washington. For the day and hour of these broadcasts, check with your local station.

■ NBI's 1965 Ball has now been definitely scheduled for April 16. The Ball is for NBI students and their guests; students will receive detailed information by mail and are requested to make their reservations no later than April 1. After that date, if there is still space available, reservations will also be accepted from NEWSLETTER subscribers who are not NBI students. — B.B.

THE OBJECTIVIST NEWSLETTER is interested in learning more about the Ayn Rand clubs and discussion groups on Objectivism which, we hear, have been formed on college campuses throughout the country. We would appreciate it if chairmen or members of such groups would write to us about their activities.

Published monthly at 120 East 34th Street, New York, N.Y. 10016.
Subscription rate in United States, its possessions, Canada and Mexico: one year, $5; 2 years, $9; 3 years, $13. Other countries: one year, $6; 2 years, $11; 3 years, $16.
Additional copies of this Newsletter: single copy 50¢ (coins, not stamps); 10 — 99 copies, 25¢ each plus postage (for first-class delivery add 1¢ per copy, for third-class delivery add ½¢ per copy); 100 or more copies, 15¢ each plus postage (same as above). (Bulk rates apply only to multiple orders of a single issue.)
Please include zip code number with your address.
For change of address, send old and new address. Allow us three weeks to process new subscriptions and change of address.

Ayn Rand and Nathaniel Branden, Editors and Publishers
Barbara Branden, Managing Editor
Elayne Kalberman, Circulation Manager

THE OBJECTIVIST NEWSLETTER

Edited and Published by AYN RAND and NATHANIEL BRANDEN

VOL. 4 NO. 4   APRIL, 1965

CHECK YOUR PREMISES
By AYN RAND

The Psycho-Epistemology of Art

The position of art in the scale of human knowledge is, perhaps, the most eloquent symptom of the gulf between man's progress in the physical sciences and his stagnation (or, today, his *retrogression*) in the humanities.

The physical sciences are still ruled by some remnants of a rational epistemology (which is rapidly being destroyed), but the humanities have been virtually abandoned to the primitive epistemology of mysticism. While physics has reached the level where men are able to study subatomic particles and interplanetary space, a phenomenon such as art has remained a dark mystery, with little or nothing known about its nature, its function in human life or the cause of its tremendous psychological power. Yet art is of passionately intense importance and profoundly *personal* concern to most men — and it has existed in every known civilization, accompanying man's steps from the early hours of his prehistorical dawn, earlier than the birth of written language.

While, in other fields of knowledge, men have outgrown the practice of seeking the guidance of mystic oracles whose qualification for the job was unintelligibility, in the field of esthetics this practice has remained in full force and is becoming more crudely, crassly obvious today. Just as savages took the phenomena of nature for granted, as an irreducible primary not to be questioned or analyzed, as the exclusive domain of unknowable demons—so today's epistemological savages take art for granted, as an irreducible primary not to be questioned or analyzed, as the exclusive domain of a special kind of unknowable demons: their emotions. The only difference is that the prehistorical savage's error was innocent.

One of the grimmest monuments to altruism is man's culturally-induced *selflessness:* his willingness to live with himself as with the unknown, to ignore, evade, repress the personal (the *non-social*) needs of his soul, to know least about the things that matter most, and thus to consign his deepest values to the impotent underground of *subjectivity* and his life to the dreary wasteland of chronic guilt. (See my article on "Art and Moral Treason" in the March 1965 issue of this NEWSLETTER.)

The cognitive neglect of art has persisted precisely because the function of art is non-social. (This is one more instance of altruism's inhumanity, of its brutal indifference to the deepest needs of man—of an actual, individual man. It is an instance of the inhumanity of *any* moral theory that regards moral values as a purely social matter.) Art belongs to a non-socializable aspect of reality, which is universal (*i.e.*, applicable to all men) but non-collective: to the basic nature of man's consciousness.

One of the distinguishing characteristics of a work of art (including literature, *i.e.*, fiction), is that it serves no practical, material end, but is an end in itself; it serves no purpose other than contemplation—and the pleasure of that contemplation is so intense, so deeply personal that a man experiences it as a self-sufficient, self-justifying primary and, often, resists or resents any suggestion to analyze it: the suggestion, to him, has the quality of an attack on his identity, on his deepest, essential self.

No human emotion can be causeless, nor can so intense an emotion be causeless, irreducible and unrelated to the source of emotions (and of values): to the needs of a living entity's survival. Art *does* have a purpose and *does* serve a human need; only it is not a material need, but a need of man's consciousness. Art *is* inextricably tied to man's survival—not to his physical survival, but to that on which his physical survival depends: to the preservation and survival of his consciousness.

The source of art lies in the fact that man's cognitive faculty is *conceptual*—*i.e.*, that man acquires knowledge and guides his actions, not by means of single, isolated percepts, but by means of *abstractions*.

To understand the nature and function of art, one must understand the nature and function of concepts.

A *concept* is a mental integration of two or more perceptual concretes which are isolated by a process of abstraction and united by means of a specific definition. By organizing his perceptual material into concepts, and his concepts into wider and still wider concepts, man is able to grasp and retain, to identify and integrate, an unlimited amount of knowledge, a knowledge extending beyond the immediate concretes of any given, immediate moment.

In any given moment, concepts enable man to hold in the focus of his conscious awareness much more than his purely perceptual capacity would permit. The range of man's perceptual awareness—the number of percepts he can deal with at any one time—is limited. He may be able to visualize four or five units—as, for instance, five trees. He cannot visualize a hundred trees or a distance of ten light years. It is only his conceptual faculty that makes it possible for him to deal with knowledge of that kind.

Man retains his concepts by means of language. With the exception of proper names, every word we use is a concept that stands for an unlimited number of concretes of a certain kind. A concept is like a mathematical series of *specifically defined units*, going off in both directions, open at both ends and including *all* units of that particular kind. For instance, the concept "man" includes all men who live at present, who have ever lived or will ever live—a number of men so great that one would not be able to perceive them all visually, let alone to study them or discover anything about them.

Language is a code of visual-auditory symbols that serves the psycho-epistemological function of converting abstractions into concretes or, more precisely, into the psycho-epistemological equivalent of concretes, into a manageable number of specific units.

Consider the enormous conceptual integration involved in any statement, from the conversation of a child to the discourse of a scientist. Consider the long conceptual chain that starts from simple, ostensive definitions and rises to higher and still higher concepts, forming a hierarchical structure of knowledge so complex that no electronic computer could approach it. It is by means of such chains that man has to acquire and retain his knowledge of reality.

Yet this is the simpler part of his psycho-epistemological task. There is another part which is still more complex.

The other part consists of *applying* his knowledge — *i.e.*, evaluating the facts of reality, choosing his goals and guiding his actions accordingly. To do that, man needs another chain of concepts, derived from and dependent on the first, yet separate and, in a sense, more complex: a chain of *normative* abstractions.

While cognitive abstractions identify the facts of reality, normative abstractions evaluate the facts, thus prescribing a choice of values and a course of action. Cognitive abstractions deal with that which *is;* normative abstractions deal with that which *ought to be* (in the realms open to man's choice).

Ethics, the normative science, is based on two cognitive branches of philosophy: metaphysics and epistemology. To prescribe what man ought to do, one must first know *what* he is and *where* he is—*i.e.*, what is his nature (including his means of cognition) and the nature of the universe in which he acts. (It is irrelevant, in this context, whether the metaphysical base of a given system of ethics is true or false; if it is false, the error will make the ethics impracticable. What concerns us here is only the dependence of ethics on metaphysics.)

Is the universe intelligible to man, or unintelligible and unknowable? Can man find happiness on earth, or is he doomed to frustration and despair? Does man have the power of *choice*, the power to choose his goals and to achieve them, the power to direct the course of his life—or is he the helpless plaything of forces beyond his control, which determine his fate? Is man, by nature, to be valued as good, or to be despised as evil? These are *metaphysical* questions, but the answers to them determine the kind of *ethics* men will accept and practice. These questions represent the link between metaphysics and ethics; the answers define *man's relationship to existence*. And although metaphysics as such is not a normative science, the answers to this category of questions assume, in man's mind, the function of metaphysical value-judgments, since they form the foundation of all of his moral values.

Consciously or subconsciously, explicitly or implicitly, man knows that he needs a comprehensive view of existence to integrate his values, to choose his goals, to plan his future, to maintain the unity and coherence of his life—and that his metaphysical value-judgments are involved in every moment of his life, in his every choice, decision and action.

Metaphysics—the science that deals with the fundamental nature of reality—involves man's widest abstractions. It includes every concrete he has ever perceived, it involves such a vast sum of knowledge and such a long chain of concepts that no man could hold it all in the focus of his immediate conscious awareness. Yet he needs that sum and that awareness to guide him—he needs the constant power to summon them into full, conscious focus.

That power is given to him by art.

Art is a selective re-creation of reality according to an artist's metaphysical value-judgments.

By a selective re-creation, art isolates and integrates those aspects of reality which represent man's fundamental view of himself and of his relationship to existence. Out of the countless number of concretes—of single, disorganized and (seemingly) contradictory attributes, actions and entities—an artist isolates the things which he regards as metaphysically essential and integrates them into a single new concrete that represents an embodied abstraction.

For instance, consider two statues of man: one as a Greek god, the other as a deformed Oriental monstrosity. Both are metaphysical estimates of man; both are projections of the artist's view of man's nature; both are concretized representations of the philosophy of their respective cultures.

Art is a concretization of metaphysics. *Art brings man's concepts to the perceptual level of his consciousness and allows him to grasp them directly, as if they were percepts.*

This is the psycho-epistemological function of art and the reason of its importance in man's life (and the crux of the Objectivist esthetics).

Just as language converts abstractions into the psycho-epistemological equivalent of concretes, into a manageable number of specific units—so art converts man's metaphysical abstractions into the equivalent of concretes, into specific entities open to man's direct perception. The claim that "art is a universal language" is not an empty metaphor, it is literally true—in the sense of the psycho-epistemological function performed by art.

Observe that in mankind's history, art began as an adjunct (and, often, a monopoly) of religion. Religion was the primitive form of philosophy: it provided man with a comprehensive view of existence. Observe that the art of those primitive cultures was a concretization of their religion's metaphysical and ethical abstractions.

The best illustration of the psycho-epistemological process involved in art can be given by one aspect of one particular art: by characterization in literature. Human character—with all of its innumerable potentialities, virtues, vices, inconsistencies, contradictions—is so complex that man is his own most bewildering enigma. It is very difficult to isolate and integrate human traits even into purely *cognitive* abstractions and to bear them all in mind when seeking to understand the men one meets.

Now consider the figure of Sinclair Lewis' Babbitt. He is the concretization of an abstraction that covers an incalculable sum of observations and evaluations of an incalculable number of characteristics possessed by an incalculable number of men of a certain type. Lewis has isolated their essential traits and has integrated them into the concrete form of a single character—and when you say of someone: "He's a Babbitt," your appraisal includes, in a single judgment, the enormous total conveyed by that figure.

When we come to *normative* abstractions—to the task of defining moral principles and projecting what man *ought to be*—the psycho-epistemological process required is still harder. The task demands years of study—and the results are almost impossible to communicate without the assistance of art. An exhaustive philosophical treatise defining moral values, with a long list of virtues to be practiced, will not do it; it will not convey what an ideal man would be like and how he would act: no mind can deal with so immense a sum of abstractions. When I say "deal with" I mean retranslate all the abstractions into the perceptual concretes for which they stand—*i.e.*, reconnect them to reality—and hold it all in the focus of one's conscious awareness. There is no way to integrate such a sum without projecting an actual human figure—an integrated concretization that illuminates the theory and makes it intelligible.

Hence the sterile, uninspiring futility of a great many theoretical discussions of ethics, and the resentment which many people feel toward such discussions: moral principles remain in their minds as floating abstractions, offering them a goal they cannot grasp and demanding that they reshape their souls in its image, thus leaving them with a burden of undefinable moral guilt. *Art is the indispensable medium for the communication of a moral ideal.*

Observe that every religion has a mythology—a dramatized concretization of its moral code embodied in the figures of men who are its ultimate product. (The fact that some of these figures are more convincing than others depends on the comparative rationality or irrationality of the moral theory they exemplify.)

This does not mean that art is a substitute for philosophical thought: without a conceptual theory of ethics, an artist would not be able successfully to concretize an image of the ideal. But without the assistance of art, ethics remains in the position of theoretical engineering: art is the model-builder.

Many readers of *The Fountainhead* have told me that the character of Howard Roark helped them to make a decision when they faced a moral dilemma. They asked themselves: "What would Roark do in this situation?"—and, faster than their mind could identify the proper application of all the complex principles involved, the image of Roark gave them the answer. They sensed, almost instantly, what he would or would not do—and this helped them to isolate and to identify the reasons, the moral principles that would have guided him. Such is the psycho-epistemological function of a personified (concretized) human ideal.

It is important to stress, however, that even though moral values are inextricably involved in art, they are involved only as a consequence, *not* as a causal determinant: the primary focus of art is metaphysical, not ethical. Art is not the "handmaiden" of morality, its *basic* purpose is not to educate, to reform or to advocate anything. The concretization of a moral ideal is not a textbook on how to become one. The basic purpose of art is *not* to teach, but to *show*—to hold up to man a concretized image of his nature and his place in the universe.

Any metaphysical issue will necessarily have an enormous influence on man's conduct and, therefore, on his ethics; and, since every art work has a theme, it will necessarily convey some conclusion, some "message," to its audience. But that influence and that "message" are only secondary consequences. *Art is not the means to any didactic end.* This is the difference between a work of art and a morality play or a propaganda poster. The greater a work of art, the more profoundly universal its theme. *Art is not the means of literal transcription.* This is the difference between a work of art and a news story or a photograph.

The place of ethics in any given work of art depends on the metaphysical views of the artist. If, consciously or subconsciously, an artist holds the premise that man possesses the

(Continued on page 18)

A Message To Our Readers
By NATHANIEL BRANDEN

We have received many inquiries concerning the various groups and publications which have sprung up during the past several years and which claim or imply some connection with the philosophy of Objectivism. Some of these inquiries come from NEWSLETTER subscribers and/or NBI students who wish to know our views about these organizations. Other inquiries come from the heads of the organizations, who seek our advice or sanction.

The purpose of this article is to answer the kind of questions we receive most often—and to put our position on record.

In her *Los Angeles Times* column (8/26/62), Ayn Rand stated: "Please take the following as an official 'Public Notice.' The only authentic sources of information about Objectivism are: My own works. *Who Is Ayn Rand?* by Nathaniel Branden . . . The Objectivist Newsletter . . . The lecture courses on Objectivism given by Nathaniel Branden Institute . . . and the publications of that Institute." Miss Rand's purpose was to disassociate Objectivism from any misrepresentations on the part of its enemies. But her "Notice" has a wider application: it is equally relevant to any possible misrepresentations on the part of Objectivism's professed friends.

On behalf of Miss Rand and myself, therefore, I wish to emphasize the following: *No group, organization, newsletter, magazine, book or other publication — with the exception of those named above — is endorsed or recognized by us as a qualified spokesman for Objectivism.*

The fact that a person describes himself as an admirer of *Atlas Shrugged*, or subscribes to this NEWSLETTER, or has attended NBI courses, guarantees *nothing* about his intellectual qualifications. These depend on individual factors about which, in most cases, we can have no personal knowledge.

Should we ever wish to endorse (fully or in part) any group, publication or activity, you will read the endorsement in this NEWSLETTER. If you do *not* read it here, we have given no endorsement.

In view of the spread of Objectivism through the culture, it was inevitable that, sooner or later, groups and publications in sympathy with Objectivism would begin to appear. While this phenomenon has, to a certain extent, an obvious positive cultural significance, it is *not* an unmixed blessing. The intellectual competence, philosophical consistency and moral stature of the persons involved in these activities vary from individual to individual. A new philosophy, that challenges the cultural status quo, will necessarily attract many different types of people, who are prompted by a broad variety of motives.

We suggest, therefore, that one never give one's intellectual or material support to any organization or activity *merely* on the grounds of its leaders' professed agreement with Objectivism. Tags or labels are not adequate criteria. Each case should be judged on its own merits—on the basis of the objective evidence.

During the past several years, as I have reported previously, Ayn Rand study clubs have been springing up on campuses around the country. They are not organized by Miss Rand or me, nor do we have any connection with them; they are formed by college students acting independently, on their own initiative, for the purpose of studying and discussing Ayn Rand's philosophy.

So long as this is their purpose, these clubs are a worthy undertaking. One of their valuable functions, no doubt, is to provide a means by which individual college students of the same philosophical views can discover one another.

Most of these groups call themselves by such names as "The Ayn Rand Society," "The Ayn Rand Study Club," "Students of Objectivism," etc. This is the right policy—and the one that I suggest when and if I am approached for advice in the matter. Such names make it clear that the members of the club are students and admirers of Ayn Rand's work, but not her representatives.

A name to be *avoided*—Miss Rand has asked me to stress this — is any designation such as "The John Galt Society." As a fiction character, John Galt is Miss Rand's property; he is *not* in the public domain.

Another name to be avoided is any designation such as "The Objectivist Society." An "Objectivist Society" with which Miss Rand has no connection, and of which she has no knowledge, is misrepresentation and entails a misappropriation of her intellectual property. No admirer of her work can wish to be guilty of this.

In this same connection, there is another, more general point that should be made. In the future, when Objectivism has become an intellectual and cultural movement on a wider scale, when a variety of authors have written books dealing with some aspect of the Objectivist philosophy—it could be appropriate for those in agreement to describe themselves as "Objectivists." But at present, when the name is so intimately and exclusively associated with Miss Rand and me, it is not. At present, a person who is in agreement with our philosophy should describe himself, not as an Objectivist, but as a student or a supporter of Objectivism. In any context where he is presenting his philosophical ideas, he should make it clear that he is discussing Objectivism *as he understands it*, and that he speaks for no one but himself.

So long as individuals or organizations do not make claims, explicitly or implicitly, to be spokesmen for or representatives of Objectivism, we are not obliged to repudiate them publicly. But should such claims be made, and should we learn of them, we will be obliged to issue a public repudiation—in order to protect the integrity of our own intellectual position.

A growing number of on-campus and off-campus pro-Objectivist groups are starting to issue newsletters and other publications. We are often asked by these groups how they should deal with their relationship to Objectivism: on the one hand, they do not wish to represent their publications as official Objectivist organs; on the other hand, they do not wish to deny or conceal the nature and source of their philosophical frame of reference. We suggest that these publications carry, as a permanent notice in each issue, some statement such as the following: "The editors of this publication are in agreement with the philosophy of Objectivism; however, we are not an official organ of Objectivism, we speak for no one but ourselves, and we alone are responsible for the views expressed here."

All of the foregoing pertains to those who *are* in agreement with Objectivism, and who wish to act for their convictions in a rational, conscientious and honorable manner.

But it is necessary to discuss an entirely different category of persons and organizations. I refer to some rather unappetizing band-wagon climbers who seek to use Objectivism for non-Objectivist ends.

Some allegedly pro-capitalism groups, it appears, have been impressed with the size and quality of the Objectivist following, and—succumbing to what can be described only as delusions of grandeur—have decided to launch a special effort to "convert" Objectivist students. Having no understanding of what has made the growth of Objectivism possible, dismissing philosophy as irrelevant, they seek to cash in on the effects while remaining unconcerned with the cause.

There are not many of them. But these are the types whom no honest student of Objectivism should approach or deal with or sanction in any manner.

I refer to any person or group who chooses to borrow some ideas from Objectivism and attempts to combine them with some hairbrained theories or "practical" schemes which are entirely incompatible with Objectivism. They seek to con students of Objectivism into supporting such ventures—and, when cornered and confronted with the contradictions involved, make sulking sounds to the effect that "nobody has a monopoly on truth" and that "originality" and "independence" are being persecuted.

I refer to any organization or school which professes to be fighting for laissez-faire capitalism, but which *in fact* (though seldom by admission) advocates political *anarchism*—and which seeks to enlist students of Objectivism under the guise of a common cause. (A brief expose of these anarchists may be found in Miss Rand's article, "The Nature of Government," which appeared in the December 1963 issue of this NEWSLETTER and is reprinted in *The Virtue of Selfishness*.)

I refer to any person or group who claims to agree with Objectivism but who declares that the names "Objectivism" and "Ayn Rand" are "too controversial" and "provoke too much unreasoning antagonism," and, therefore, that one can advocate the ideas more successfully by never identifying their source. The position of these craven parasites amounts to the following: the desire to have Rearden Metal without Rearden, to advance the cause of reason by pandering to men's irrationality, and to advance a morality of rational self-interest by treating its originator as an object of sacrifice.

Reports have reached me about one group that has descended to what is, perhaps, an unprecedented low in offensive absurdity. This group has decided that a large section of the public cannot be reached by abstract ideas or rational arguments, and, besides, political education takes too long, so the group will strike a major blow for freedom by taking a "practical" short-cut: it will buy or lease an island, establish a free enterprise system on it, and become so prosperous that the other nations of the world will be converted to capitalism *by example*. (The history of the United States, or the contrast between West and East Germany, does not provide a sufficiently persuasive example, it seems.) A few emissaries from this group have shown up at NBI Tape Transcription lectures, soliciting the interest of students; local NBI Business Representatives have instructions to sweep them out when and if they appear—along with emissaries from any other such organizations.

Such groups have nothing to offer anyone, and without the sanction of those who do take ideas seriously, will fall of their own weight — or, more precisely, of their own weightlessness.

In conclusion, let me remind you that your moral-intellectual sanction is one of your most precious possessions and, according to how and when you grant or withhold it, one of your most powerful weapons. Do not treat it lightly.

The Psycho-Epistemology of Art (from page 16)

power of volition, it will lead his work to a value orientation (to Romanticism). If he holds the premise that man's fate is determined by forces beyond his control, it will lead his work to an anti-value orientation (to Naturalism). The philosophical and esthetic contradictions of determinism are irrelevant in this context, just as the truth or falsehood of an artist's metaphysical views is irrelevant to the nature of art as such. An art work may project the values man is to seek and hold up to him the concretized vision of the life he is to achieve. Or it may assert that man's efforts are futile and hold up to him the concretized vision of defeat and despair as his ultimate fate. In either case, the esthetic means — the psycho-epistemological processes involved—remain the same.

The existential consequences, of course, will differ. Amidst the incalculable number and complexity of choices that confront a man in his day-by-day existence, with the frequently bewildering torrent of events, with the alternation of successes and failures, of joys that seem too rare and suffering that lasts too long—he is often in danger of losing his perspective and the reality of his own convictions. Remember that abstractions as such do not exist: they are merely man's epistemological method of perceiving that which exists—and that which exists is concrete. To acquire the full, persuasive, irresistible power of reality, man's metaphysical abstractions have to confront him in the form of concretes—*i.e.*, in the form of art.

Consider the difference it would make if—in his need of philosophical guidance or confirmation or inspiration — man turns to the art of ancient Greece or to the art of the Middle Ages. Reaching his mind and emotions simultaneously, with the combined impact of abstract thought and of immediate reality, one type of art tells him that disasters are transient, that grandeur, beauty, strength, self-confidence are his proper, natural state. The other tells him that happiness is transient and evil, that he is a distorted, impotent, miserable little sinner, pursued by leering gargoyles, crawling in terror on the brink of an eternal hell.

The consequences of both experiences are obvious—and history is their practical demonstration. It is not art alone that was responsible for the greatness or the horror of those two eras, but art as the voice of philosophy—of the particular philosophy that dominated those cultures.

As to the role of emotions in art and the subconscious mechanism that serves as the integrating factor both in artistic creation and in man's response to art, they involve a psychological phenomenon which we call a *sense of life*. A sense of life is a pre-conceptual equivalent of metaphysics, an emotional, subconsciously integrated appraisal of man's relationship to existence. But this is a different, though corollary, subject which I will discuss at some later date. The present subject is only the psycho-epistemological role of art. (See Nathaniel Branden's article on "Psycho-Epistemology" in the October and November 1964 issues of this NEWSLETTER, where he defines psycho-epistemology as "the study of the mental operations that are possible to and that characterize man's cognitive behavior.")

A question raised at the start of this discussion should now be clear. The reason why art has such a profoundly *personal* significance for men is that art confirms or denies the efficacy of a man's consciousness, according to whether an art work supports or negates his own fundamental view of reality.

Such is the meaning and the power of a medium which, today, is predominantly in the hands of practitioners who boastfully offer, as their credentials, the fact that they do not know what they are doing.

Let us take them at their word: they don't. We do.

OBJECTIVIST CALENDAR

■ *The Virtue of Selfishness* was published by New American Library in December, 1964. It has recently gone into its fifth printing, bringing the total number of copies in print to 416,000 —in less than four months.

■ On Sunday, April 18, Ayn Rand will give a talk at the Ford Hall Forum in Boston. Her subject: "The New Fascism: Rule by Consensus." Time: 8 P.M. Place: Jordan Hall, 30 Gainsboro Street.

■ On Tuesday, April 20, Nathaniel Branden will address the student body of West Chester State College in West Chester, Pa., on the subject of Objectivism. Time: 10 A.M. For further information, contact Miss Bernice Bernatz, Chairman, Lecture Committee, Dept. of Public Instruction, West Chester State College, West Chester, Pa.

■ On Tuesday, April 27, Ayn Rand will begin a new series of *Commentary* programs for Radio Station WBAI (99.5 FM) in New York. These 30-minute programs will be broadcast at 7:30 P.M. every other Tuesday and will be re-broadcast at 10 A.M. the following Wednesday.

■ On Thursday, April 29, Nathaniel Branden will give a talk at the Baruch School of Business, City College of New York. His subject: "Alienation and the Critics of Capitalism." Time: 12 noon. For further information, contact Mr. Mel Siegel, Free Enterprise Society, Baruch School of Business, C.C.N.Y., 17 Lexington Avenue, New York City.

■ On Thursday, May 6, in New York City, Nathaniel Branden will deliver the opening lecture of a ten-lecture course on "Contemporary Theories of Neurosis." Time: 7:30 P.M. Place: Sheraton-Atlantic Hotel, Broadway at 34th Street. Admission: $3.50, payable at the door.

■ NBI's Tape Transcription Division has scheduled the following starting dates: "Basic Principles of Objectivist Psychology" in Orange County (Calif.), April 9; Rockford (Ill.), April 13; Youngstown, May 7—"The Principles of Efficient Thinking" in Columbus, April 11; Los Angeles, April 21—"The Esthetics of the Visual Arts" in Chicago, April 4; Boston, May 10— "Three Plays by Ayn Rand" in San Francisco, May 8; Toronto, May 10. For details, contact NBI.

■ NBI is now accepting reservations for its April 16 Ball, from NEWSLETTER subscribers who are not NBI students. For information, contact NBI.

Published monthly at 120 East 34th Street, New York, N.Y. 10016.
Subscription rate in United States, its possessions, Canada and Mexico: one year, $5; 2 years, $9; 3 years, $13. Other countries: one year, $6; 2 years, $11; 3 years, $16.
Additional copies of this Newsletter: single copy 50¢ (coins, not stamps); 10 – 99 copies, 25¢ each plus postage (for first-class delivery add 1¢ per copy, for third-class delivery add ½¢ per copy); 100 or more copies, 15¢ each plus postage (same as above). (Bulk rates apply only to multiple orders of a single issue.)
Please include zip code number with your address.
For change of address, send old and new address. Allow us three weeks to process new subscriptions and change of address.

Ayn Rand and Nathaniel Branden, Editors and Publishers
Barbara Branden, Managing Editor
Elayne Kalberman, Circulation Manager

THE OBJECTIVIST NEWSLETTER

Edited and Published by AYN RAND and NATHANIEL BRANDEN

VOL. 4 NO. 5   MAY, 1965

CHECK YOUR PREMISES
By AYN RAND

The New Fascism: Rule by Consensus

(This is the first part of an article based on a lecture given at The Ford Hall Forum, Boston, on April 18, 1965.)

I shall begin by doing a very unpopular thing that does not fit today's intellectual fashions and is, therefore, "anti-consensus": I shall begin by defining my terms, so that you will know what I am talking about.

Let me give you the dictionary definitions of three political terms: socialism, fascism and statism:

"*Socialism*—a theory or system of social organization which advocates the vesting of the ownership and control of the means of production, capital, land, etc. in the community as a whole."

"*Fascism*—a governmental system with strong centralized power, permitting no opposition or criticism, controlling all affairs of the nation (industrial, commercial, etc.) . . ."

"*Statism*—the principle or policy of concentrating extensive economic, political, and related controls in the state at the cost of individual liberty."

(These definitions are from *The American College Dictionary*, 1957.)

It is obvious that "statism" is the wider, generic term, of which the other two are specific variants. It is also obvious that statism is the dominant political trend of our day. But which of those two variants represents the specific direction of that trend?

Observe that both "socialism" and "fascism" involve the issue of property rights. The right to property is the right of use and disposal. Observe the difference in those two theories: socialism negates private property rights altogether, and advocates "the vesting of *ownership and control*" in the community as a whole, *i.e.*, in the state; fascism leaves *ownership* in the hands of private individuals, but transfers *control* of the property to the government.

Ownership without control is a contradiction in terms: it means "property" without the right to use it or to dispose of it. It means that the citizens retain the responsibility of holding property, without any of its advantages, while the government acquires all the advantages without any of the responsibility.

In this respect, socialism is the more honest of the two theories. I say "more honest," *not* "better"—because, *in practice*, there is no difference between them: both come from the same collectivist-statist principle, both negate individual rights and subordinate the individual to the collective, both deliver the livelihood and the lives of the citizens into the power of an omnipotent government—and the differences between them are only a matter of time, degree and superficial detail, such as the choice of slogans by which the rulers delude their enslaved subjects.

Which of these two variants of statism are we moving toward: socialism or fascism?

To answer this question, one must first ask: Which is the dominant ideological trend of today's culture?

The disgraceful and terrifying answer is: *there is no ideological trend today*. There is no ideology. There are no political principles, theories, ideals or philosophy. There is no direction, no goal, no compass, no vision of the future, no intellectual element of leadership. Are there any *emotional* elements dominating today's culture? Yes. One. *Fear*.

A country without a political philosophy is like a ship drifting at random in mid-ocean, at the mercy of any chance wind, wave or current, a ship whose passengers huddle in their cabins and cry: "Don't rock the boat!"—for fear of discovering that the captain's bridge is empty.

It is obvious that a boat which cannot stand rocking is doomed already and that it had better be rocked hard, if it is to regain its course—but this realization presupposes a grasp of facts, of reality, of principles and a long-range view, all of which are precisely the things that the "non-rockers" are frantically struggling to evade.

Just as a neurotic believes that the facts of reality will vanish if he refuses to recognize them—so, today, the neurosis of an entire culture leads men to believe that their desperate need of political principles and concepts will vanish if they succeed in obliterating all principles and concepts. But since, *in fact*, neither an individual nor a nation can exist without some form of ideology, this sort of *anti-ideology* is now the formal, explicit, dominant ideology of our bankrupt culture.

This anti-ideology has a new and very ugly name: it is called "*Government by Consensus*."

If some demagogue were to offer us, as a guiding creed, the following tenets: that statistics should be substituted for truth, vote-counting for principles, numbers for rights, and public polls for morality—that pragmatic, range-of-the-moment expediency should be the criterion of a country's interests, and that the number of its adherents should be the criterion of an idea's truth or falsehood—that any desire of any nature whatsoever should be accepted as a valid claim, provided it is held by a sufficient number of people—that a majority may do anything it pleases to a minority—in short, gang rule and mob rule —if a demagogue were to offer it, he would not get very far. Yet all of it is contained in—and camouflaged by—the notion of "Government by Consensus."

This notion is now being plugged, not as an ideology, but as an *anti-ideology;* not as a principle, but as a means of obliterating principles; not as reason, but as rationalization, as a verbal ritual or a magic formula to assuage the national anxiety neurosis—a kind of pep pill or goof ball for the "non-boat-rockers," and a chance to play it deuces wild, for the others.

It is only today's lethargic contempt for the pronouncements of our political and intellectual leaders that blinds people to the meaning, implications and consequences of the notion of "Government by Consensus." You have all heard it and, I suspect, dismissed it as politicians' oratory, giving no thought to its actual meaning. But *that* is what I urge you to consider.

A significant clue to that meaning was given in an article by Tom Wicker in *The New York Times* (October 11, 1964). Referring to "what Nelson Rockefeller used to call 'the mainstream of American thought,'" Mr. Wicker writes: "That mainstream is what political theorists have been projecting for years as 'the national consensus'—what Walter Lippman has aptly called 'the vital center.' . . . Political moderation, almost by definition, is at the heart of the consensus. That is, the consensus generally sprawls over all acceptable political views—all ideas that are not totally repugnant to and do not directly threaten some major segment of the population. Therefore, acceptable ideas must take the views of others into account and that is what is meant by moderation."

Now let us identify what this means. "The consensus generally sprawls over all *acceptable* political views . . ." Acceptable—to whom? To the consensus. And since the government is to be ruled by the consensus, this means that political views are to be divided into those which are "acceptable" and those which are "unacceptable" to the government. What would be the criterion of "acceptability"? Mr. Wicker supplies it. Observe that the criterion is *not* intellectual, not a question of whether certain views are true or false; the criterion is *not* moral, not a question of whether the views are right or wrong; the criterion is *emotional*: whether the views are or are not "repugnant." To whom? "To some *major* segment of the population." There is also the additional proviso that those views must not "*directly* threaten" that major segment.

What about the *minor* segments of the population? Are the views that threaten *them* "acceptable"? What about the smallest segment: the individual? Obviously, the individual and the minority groups are not to be considered; no matter how repugnant an idea may be to a man and no matter how gravely it may threaten his life, his work, his future, he is to be ignored or sacrificed by the omnipotent consensus and its government—unless he has a gang, a *sizeable* gang, to support him.

What exactly is a "direct threat" to any part of the population? In a mixed economy, every government action is a direct threat to some men and an indirect threat to all. Every government interference in the economy consists of giving an unearned benefit, extorted by force, to some men at the expense of others. By what criterion of justice is a consensus-government to be guided? By the size of the victim's gang.

Now note Mr. Wicker's last sentence: "Therefore, acceptable ideas must take the views of others into account and that is what is meant by moderation." And just *what* is meant here by "the views of others?" Of which others? Since it is not the views of individuals nor of minorities, the only discernible meaning is that every "major segment" must take into account the views of all the other "major segments." But suppose that a group of socialists wants to nationalize all factories, and a group of industrialists wants to keep its properties? What would it mean, for either group, to "take into account" the views of the other? And what would "moderation" consist of, in such a case? What would constitute "moderation" in a conflict between a group of men who want to be supported at public expense—and a group of taxpayers who have other uses for their money? What would constitute "moderation" in a conflict between the member of a smaller group, such as a Negro in the South, who believes that he has an inalienable right to a fair trial—and the larger group of Southern racists who believe that the "public good" of their community permits them to lynch him? What would constitute "moderation" in a conflict between *me* and a communist (or between our respective followers), when *my* views are that I have an inalienable right to my life, liberty and happiness—and *his* views are that the "public good" of the state permits him to rob, enslave or murder me?

There can be no meeting ground, no middle, no compromise between *opposite principles*. There can be no such thing as "moderation" in the realm of reason and of morality. But reason and morality are precisely the two concepts abrogated by the notion of "Government by Consensus."

The advocates of that notion would declare at this point that any idea which permits no compromise constitutes "extremism"—that any form of "extremism," any uncompromising stand, is evil—that the consensus "sprawls" only over those ideas which *are* amenable to "moderation"—and that "moderation" is the supreme virtue, superceding reason and morality.

This is the clue to the core, essence, motive and real meaning of the doctrine of "Government by Consensus": the cult of *compromise*. Compromise is the pre-condition, the necessity, the imperative of a mixed economy. The "consensus" doctrine is an attempt to translate the brute facts of a mixed economy into an ideological—or anti-ideological—system and to provide them with a semblance of justification.

A mixed economy is a mixture of freedom and controls—with no principles, rules or theories to define either. Since the introduction of controls necessitates and leads to further controls, it is an unstable, explosive mixture which, ultimately, has to repeal the controls or collapse into dictatorship. A mixed economy has no principles to define its policies, its goals, its laws—no principles to limit the power of its government. The *only* principle of a mixed economy—which, necessarily, has to remain unnamed and unacknowledged—is that no one's interests are safe, everyone's interests are on a public auction block, and anything goes for anyone who can get away with it. Such a system—or, more precisely, anti-system—breaks up a country into an ever-growing number of enemy camps, into economic groups fighting one another for self-preservation in an indeterminate mixture of *defense* and *offense*, as the nature of such a jungle demands. While, *politically*, a mixed economy preserves the semblance of an organized society with a semblance of law and order, *economically* it is the equivalent of the chaos that had ruled China for centuries: a chaos of robber gangs looting—and draining—the productive elements of the country.

A mixed economy is rule by pressure groups. It is an amoral, institutionalized civil war of special interests and lobbies, all fighting to seize a momentary control of the legislative machinery, to extort some special privilege at one another's expense by an act of government—*i.e.*, by force. In the absence of individual rights, in the absence of any moral or legal principles, a mixed economy's only hope to preserve its precarious semblance of order, to restrain the savage, desperately rapacious groups it itself has created, and to prevent the legalized plunder from running over into plain, unlegalized looting of all by all—is *compromise;* compromise on everything and in every realm—material, spiritual, intellectual—so that no group would step over the line by demanding too much and topple the whole rotted structure. If the game is to continue, nothing can be permitted to remain firm, solid, absolute, untouchable; everything (and everyone) has to be fluid, flexible, indeterminate, approximate. By what standard are anyone's actions to be guided? By the expediency of any immediate moment.

The only danger, to a mixed economy, is any not-to-be-compromised value, virtue or idea. The only threat is any uncompromising person, group or movement. The only enemy is integrity.

It is unnecessary to point out who will be the steady winners and who the constant losers in a game of that kind.

It is also clear what sort of unity (of *consensus*) that game requires: the unity of a tacit agreement that anything goes, anything is for sale (or for "negotiation")—and the rest is up to the free-for-all of pressuring, lobbying, manipulating, favor-swapping, public-relation'ing, give-and-taking, double-crossing, begging, bribing, betraying, and chance, the blind chance of a war in which the prize is the privilege of using legal armed force against legally disarmed victims.

Observe that this type of prize establishes one basic interest held in common by all the players: the desire to have a strong government—a government of unlimited power, strong enough to let the winners and would-be winners get away with whatever they're seeking; a government uncommitted to any policy, unrestrained by any ideology, a government that hoards power, an ever-growing power, power for power's sake—which means: for the sake and use of any "major" gang who might seize it momentarily to ram their particular piece of legislation down the country's throat. Observe, therefore, that the doctrine of "compromise" and "moderation" applies to everything except one issue: any suggestion to limit the power of the government.

Observe the torrents of vilification, abuse and hysterical hatred unleashed by the "moderates" against any advocate of freedom, *i.e.*, of capitalism. Observe that such designations as "extreme middle" or "militant middle" are being used by people seriously and self-righteously. Observe the inordinately vicious intensity of the smear-campaign against Senator Goldwater, which had the overtones of panic: the panic of the "moderates," the "vital-centrists," the "middle-of-the-roaders" in the face of the possibility that a real, pro-capitalism movement might put an end to their game. A movement, incidentally, which does not exist, as yet, since Senator Goldwater was not an advocate of capitalism—and since his meaningless, unphilosophical, unintellectual campaign has contributed to the entrenchment of the consensus-advocates. But what is significant here is the nature of their panic: it gave us a glimpse of their vaunted "moderation," their "democratic" respect for the people's choices and their tolerance of disagreements or opposition.

In a letter to *The New York Times* (June 23, 1964), an assistant professor of political science, fearing Goldwater's nomination, wrote as follows: "The real danger lies in the divisive campaign which his nomination would provoke. . . . The result of a Goldwater candidacy would be a divided and embittered electorate. . . . To be effective, American government requires a high degree of consensus and bipartisanship on basic issues. . . ."

When and *by whom* has statism been accepted as the basic principle of America—and as a principle which should now be placed beyond debate or dissension, so that no basic issues are to be raised any longer? Isn't that the formula of a one-party government? The professor did not specify.

Another letter-writer in *The New York Times* (June 24, 1964), identified in print as a "Liberal Democrat," went a little farther. "Let the American people choose in November.

(Continued on page 22)

BOOKS

Economics and The Public Welfare: Financial and Economic History of the United States, 1914-1946 by Benjamin M. Anderson*

Reviewed by **MARTIN ANDERSON**

Benjamin Anderson possessed a rare combination of personal characteristics; he was highly intelligent, he had a high degree of moral integrity, he understood economic theory thoroughly, and he was intimately acquainted with many of the men who made and influenced economic policy in the United States from 1914 to 1946. Perhaps no one was better qualified than Anderson to chronicle economic events during this period.

Economics and The Public Welfare is an economic history of the United States from 1914 to 1946. In a clear, readable style, the author combines theory and fact, emphasizing names, dates, places, amounts, decisions made and the consequences of those decisions. In his own words: "This book, therefore, represents not the researches of a scholar remote from the field of activity, working primarily with the documents and the writings of other men, but rather, in very considerable measure, the records and recollections of a participant in the history."

Anderson died about two months after he finished this work and never saw it in print. But he left a great legacy for anyone who wishes to understand the economic events of this crucially important period.

Anderson covers this 34-year period in five broad segments: the war economic policy of World War I; the postwar boom, crisis, and revival from 1919 to 1923; the first phase of the New Deal from 1924 to 1932; the New Deal in maturity from 1933 to 1939; and finally the war economic policy of World War II.

The main theme of the book is that governmental interference in the private market economy has far-reaching, disastrous consequences. Armed with an expert's grasp of economic theory, he develops a devastating case against government interference. He shows how government monetary policy and tariff policy during the 1920's were responsible for the great depression of 1929, and how the economic policies of the New Deal held the economy down during the 1930's.

Following World War I, the United States changed from a debtor to a creditor nation, exporting more goods than it imported. Under these circumstances, we needed a low tariff policy to make it possible for other nations to send us goods in exchange. Instead, the government adopted a high tariff policy designed to protect special interests, and thereby created a condition of disequilibrium between our export industries, especially agriculture, and our other industries. Partly in an effort to offset this, the government introduced policies to generate artificially cheap money. For a time, this gave us a great export trade and a hyper-active economy.

Anderson traces in detail what happened when the Federal Reserve Board stepped in and tried to keep credit plentiful and cheap by the creation of excess reserves in the banking system by buying government securities on the open market. The first of three great purchasing moves came in 1922, primarily to maintain the revenue of the banks, the second came in 1924 for the purpose of expanding bank credit, the third followed in 1927 for the same purpose of expanding bank credit. And, as Anderson demonstrates, the moves worked; bank credit did expand enormously, with a great deal of it going into security loans and bank investments in securities. The Federal Reserve attempted to reverse its policy in the winter of 1927-1928, but the rise in stock market prices and the lure of stock market profits had caught the imagination of too many people. The demand for money remained high and, despite sharply rising rates of interest, the volume of loans increased sharply.

---

*Published by D. Van Nostrand Co., $8.00. Available from NBI BOOK SERVICE, INC., 120 East 34th St., New York, N. Y. 10016, for $6.75. (N.Y.C. residents add 4% sales tax; outside the U.S. add 15¢.)

Martin Anderson is Assistant Professor of Finance at the Graduate School of Business, Columbia University. He received a Ph.D. in Industrial Management from M.I.T. He is the author of The Federal Bulldozer, *a critical analysis of the urban renewal program, which has aroused nationwide attention and debate.*

The great stock market crash was inevitable. The prices of stocks had been bid up to such an extraordinarily high level that as soon as a considerable number of investors shook themselves free from the hysteria of the market and appraised the situation calmly and reasonably, a decline was in order. It came in late October, 1929 and the trading swamped the ticker.

After the major break in 1929, the government, instead of letting the market correct itself, stepped in and attempted to hold up wages and prices generally. Tariffs were raised further and many New Deal "remedies" were applied, all of which tended to impair the freedom and efficiency of the capital markets, to frighten off venture capital, and to create frictions and uncertainties which acted as impediments to individual and corporate action.

What was needed in 1929 was a period of drastic readjustment as individuals and corporations took the painful corrective action that would have been necessary for a normal revival. In Anderson's words: "The country and the world were probably strong enough, despite the folly of the years preceding, to have gone through an orderly liquidation and readjustment, with a normal revival, if we had recognized our mistakes in policy in late 1929 and proceeded forthwith to change them. But the Administration at Washington was dead set against any such readjustment. It turned instead to frantic governmental economic planning. Governmental economic planning is back seat driving by a man who doesn't know how to drive and who, except in wartime, doesn't know where he wants to go."

His coverage of the events of the New Deal is very thorough. He carefully selects the determining events, both national and international, and weaves them together, explaining their interrelationships. Among the many issues and events covered are: the banking holiday, intergovernmental debts, the reopening of the banks, Roosevelt's abandonment of the gold standard, the Banking Act of 1933, the National Industrial Recovery Act, the Gold Reserve Act of 1934, the repeal of the NRA, taxation policies, the S.E.C., the crisis of 1937 and the severe depression of 1937-38.

One fascinating set of figures presented by Anderson shows the effect that the passage of the National Industrial Recovery Act in June of 1933 had on the economy. The codes put into effect were concerned with shorter hours, with minimum wages, with increased employment, and with price fixing. Initially some misguided businessmen had seen in the price fixing aspect of the Act a way to restrict competition by means of government power and had favored it; but the final form of the bill also included many of the demands by labor leaders for increased wages, which eventually led to a drastic increase in production costs for the businessmen. Anderson writes: "From March, 1933, to July, 1933, there was an increase in factory employment of 23%, and an increase of factory payrolls of 35%. NRA came. Hours were shortened. Wages were raised arbitrarily. With what result? There was, between July and December of 1933, a further increase in factory employment of 3%, and a further increase in factory payrolls of 6%. NRA made this addition to the buying power of factory labor. Did this increase production and business activity? The answer is startlingly clear. From July, 1933, to December, 1933, industrial production dropped 25%." The NRA was in force for almost two years, and, during this time, industrial production never rose as high as it had been in July of 1933. The NRA was declared unconstitutional by the Supreme Court in May of 1935, and it was not until that autumn that the first real recovery came.

Throughout the book Anderson demonstrates the importance of the roles played by influential men, showing how strong and weak individuals influenced the course of history by their decisions. He writes: "The young student of economics, sociology, and history is easily impressed with the doctrine that history is made by impersonal social forces, irresistible in character. When one sees history being made from the inside, it is impossible to avoid the conclusion that a vast deal depends upon the strengths and weaknesses of the leading participants."

There are a few points on which Anderson fails to maintain the high degree of consistency which is characteristic of the book. For example, while denouncing the high marginal rates of individual taxation initiated during the New Deal, he maintains that vast fortunes may involve undesirable political and social potentialities, and, to a certain extent, should be held down.

But except for some minor reservations, this book should be noted as a classic of economic history. It should be read for its clear, logical presentation of facts, for its strong emphasis on the important, determining events during this period, and for its demonstration of how heroic men can influence the course of history by their actions. But it is most valuable for its clear demonstration of how governmental interference caused a strong, viable economy to spiral downward into the depths of the great depression of 1929 and kept it there until World War II.

The New Fascism: Rule by Consensus (from page 20)

If they choose overwhelmingly for Lyndon Johnson and the Democrats, then once and for all the Federal Government can get on, with no excuses, with the job millions of Negroes, unemployed, aged, sick and otherwise handicapped persons expect it to do—to say nothing of our overseas commitments.

"If the people choose Goldwater, then it would seem the nation was hardly worth saving after all.

"Woodrow Wilson once said that there is such a thing as being too proud to fight; then he had to go to war. Once and for all let us have it out, while the battle yet can be fought with ballots instead of bullets."

Does this gentleman mean that if we don't vote his way, he will resort to bullets? Your guess is as good as mine.

The New York Times, which had been a conspicuous advocate of "Government by Consensus," said some curious things in its comment on President Johnson's victory. Its editorial of November 8, 1964, stated: "No matter how massive the electoral victory—and it was massive—the Administration cannot merely ride the crest of the popular wave rolling along on a sea of platitudinous generalizations and euphoric promises . . . now that it has a broad popular mandate, it has the moral as well as the political obligation not to try to be all things to all men but to settle down to a hard, concrete, purposeful course of action."

What kind of purposeful action? If the voters were offered nothing but "platitudinous generalizations and euphoric promises," how can their vote be taken as a "broad popular mandate"? A mandate for an *unnamed* purpose? A political blank check? And if Mr. Johnson did win a massive victory by trying "to be all things to all men," then which things is he now expected to be, which voters is he to disappoint or betray—and what becomes of the broad popular consensus?

Morally and philosophically, that editorial is highly dubious and contradictory. But it becomes clear and consistent in the context of a mixed economy's anti-ideology. The president of a mixed economy is not expected to have a specific program or policy. *A blank check on power* is all that he asks the voters to give him. Thereafter, it's up to the pressure-group game, which everybody is supposed to understand and endorse, but never mention. Which things he will be to which men depends on the chances of the game—and on the "major segments of the population." His job is only to hold the power—and to dispense the favors.

In the 1930's, the "liberals" had a program of broad social reforms and a crusading spirit, they advocated a planned society, they talked in terms of abstract principles, they propounded theories of a predominantly socialistic nature—and most of them were touchy about the accusation that they were enlarging the government's power; most of them were assuring their opponents that government power was only a temporary means to an end—a "noble end," the liberation of the individual from his bondage to material needs.

Today, nobody talks of a planned society in the "liberal" camp; long-range programs, theories, principles, abstractions and "noble ends" are not fashionable any longer. Modern "liberals" deride any political concern with such large-scale matters as an entire society or an economy as a whole; they concern themselves with single, concrete-bound, range-of-the-moment projects and demands, without regard to cost, context or consequences. "Pragmatic"—*not* "idealistic"—is their favorite adjective when they are called upon to justify their "stance," as they call it, not "stand." They are militantly opposed to political philosophy; they denounce political concepts as "tags," "labels," "myths," "illusions"—and resist any attempt to "label"

—*i.e.,* to *identify*—their own views. They are belligerently anti-theoretical and—with a faded mantle of intellectuality still clinging to their shoulders—they are anti-intellectual. The only remnant of their former "idealism" is a tired, cynical, ritualistic quoting of shopworn "humanitarian" slogans, when the occasion demands it.

Cynicism, uncertainty and fear are the insignia of the culture which they are still dominating by default. And the only thing that has not rusted in their ideological equipment, but has grown savagely brighter and clearer through the years, is their lust for power—for an autocratic, statist, totalitarian government power. It is not a crusading brightness, it is not the lust of a fanatic with a mission—it is more like the glassy-eyed brightness of a somnambulist whose stuporous despair has long since swallowed the memory of his purpose, but who still clings to his mystic weapon in the stubborn belief that "there ought to be a law," that everything will be all right if only somebody will pass a law, that every problem can be solved by the magic power of brute force. . . .

Such is the present intellectual state and ideological trend of our culture.
(To be completed in our next issue.)

OBJECTIVIST CALENDAR

■ On Sunday, May 16, Dr. Leonard Peikoff will give a talk at Stanford University. His subject: "Ayn Rand's Concept of Egoism." Time: 4:15 P.M. For further information, contact Mr. Peter M. Brown, Box 7086, Stanford, California. At 12 noon that day, Dr. Peikoff will be interviewed on "The Weekend Show," Radio Station KZSU (Stanford University student station).

■ Beginning on Friday, May 21, in New York City, Nathaniel Branden will give public readings of three plays by Ayn Rand. May 21: *The Night of January 16th* (original version). May 28: *Ideal.* June 4: *Think Twice.* Time: 7:30 P.M. Place: Sheraton-Atlantic Hotel, Broadway at 34th Street. Advance series tickets may be purchased from NATHANIEL BRANDEN INSTITUTE (120 E. 34 St., N.Y. 10016) by mail only; price: $9. Tickets for individual plays will be available at the door; $3.50 per play.

■ On Friday, May 28, NBI's Montreal Business Representative will present a showing of the film *The Fountainhead.* Place: Laurentien Hotel, Montreal. Time: 8:00 P.M. (Latecomers will not be admitted until the intermission.) Admission: $1.00. For advance tickets, Montreal residents may telephone Anne Rivard at 935-8666.

■ On Tuesday, June 8, Ayn Rand will deliver lecture #17—"The Esthetics of Literature"—in the current NBI course on "Basic Principles of Objectivism," in New York City. Time: 7:30 P.M. Place: Hotel Biltmore, 43rd Street & Madison Avenue, New York City. Visitor's admission: $3.50.

■ NBI's Tape Transcription Division has scheduled the following starting dates: "Basic Principles of Objectivism" in Albuquerque, May 28—"The Principles of Efficient Thinking" in Atlanta, May 16—"Contemporary Theories of Neurosis" in Los Angeles, May 28—"The Esthetics of the Visual Arts" in Boston, May 10; Phoenix, June 11 — "Three Plays by Ayn Rand" in Toronto, May 10; St. Louis, May 16. For details, contact NBI.

■ Nathaniel Branden's article, "Psycho-Epistemology" (originally published in two parts in the October and November 1964 issues of this NEWSLETTER), has been reprinted in pamphlet form. Price: 50¢. (N.Y.C. residents add 2¢ sales tax.)
—B.B.

Published monthly at 120 East 34th Street, New York, N.Y. 10016.

Subscription rate in United States, its possessions, Canada and Mexico: one year, $5; 2 years, $9; 3 years, $13. Other countries: one year, $6; 2 years, $11; 3 years, $16.

Additional copies of this Newsletter: single copy 50¢ (coins, not stamps); 10 — 99 copies, 25¢ each plus postage (for first-class delivery add 1¢ per copy, for third-class delivery add ½¢ per copy); 100 or more copies, 15¢ each plus postage (same as above). (Bulk rates apply only to multiple orders of a single issue.)

Please include zip code number with your address.

For change of address, send old and new address. Allow us three weeks to process new subscriptions and change of address.

Ayn Rand and Nathaniel Branden, Editors and Publishers
Barbara Branden, Managing Editor
Elayne Kalberman, Circulation Manager

THE OBJECTIVIST NEWSLETTER

Edited and Published by AYN RAND and NATHANIEL BRANDEN

VOL. 4 NO. 6   JUNE, 1965

CHECK YOUR PREMISES
By AYN RAND

The New Fascism: Rule by Consensus

(*This is the second and final part of an article based on a lecture given at The Ford Hall Forum, Boston, on April 18, 1965.*)

Now I shall ask you to consider the question I raised at the beginning of this discussion: Which of these two variants of statism are we moving toward: socialism or fascism?

Let me submit in evidence, as part of the answer, a quotation from an editorial that appeared in the *Washington Star* (October, 1964). It is an eloquent mixture of truth and misinformation, and a typical example of the state of today's political knowledge:

"Socialism is quite simply the state ownership of the means of production. This has never been proposed by a major party candidate for the Presidency and is not now proposed by Lyndon Johnson. [*True*]

"There is, however, a whole series of American legislative acts that increase either government regulation of private business or government responsibility for individual welfare. [*True*] It is to such legislation that warning cries of 'socialism!' refer.

"Besides the Constitutional provision for Federal regulation of interstate commerce, such 'intrusion' of government into the market-place begins with the anti-trust laws. [*Very true*] To them we owe the continued existence of competitive capitalism and the non-arrival of cartel capitalism. [*Untrue*] Inasmuch as socialism is the product, one way or another, of cartel capitalism, [*Untrue*] it may reasonably be said that such government interference with business has in fact prevented socialism. [*Worse than untrue*]

"As to welfare legislation, it is still light years away from the 'cradle to grave' security sponsored by contemporary socialism. [*Not quite true*] It seems much more like ordinary human concern for human distress than like an ideological program of any kind." [*The last part of this sentence is true: it is not an ideological program. As to the first part, ordinary human concern for human distress does not manifest itself ordinarily in the form of a gun aimed at the wallets and earnings of one's neighbors.*]

This editorial did not mention, of course, that a system in which the government does *not* nationalize the means of production, but assumes total control over the economy is *fascism*.

It is true that the welfare-statists are not socialists, that they never advocated or intended the socialization of private property, that they want to "preserve" private property—with government control of its use and disposal. But *that* is the fundamental characteristic of fascism.

Here is another piece of evidence. This one is less crudely naive than the first and much more insidiously wrong. This is from a letter to *The New York Times* (November 1, 1964), written by an assistant professor of economics:

"Viewed by almost every yardstick, the United States today is more committed to private enterprise than probably any other industrial country and is not even remotely approaching a socialist system. As the term is understood by students of comparative economic systems and others who do not use it loosely, socialism is identified with extensive nationalization, a dominant public sector, a strong cooperative movement, egalitarian income distribution, a total welfare state and central planning.

"In the United States not only has there been no nationalization, but Government concerns have been turned over to private enterprise. . . .

"Income distribution in this country is one of the most unequal among the developed nations, and tax cuts and tax loopholes have blunted the moderate progressivity of our tax structure. Thirty years after the New Deal, the United States has a very limited welfare state, compared with the comprehensive social security and public housing schemes in many European countries.

"By no stretch of the imagination is the real issue in this campaign a choice between capitalism and socialism or between a free and a planned economy. The issue is about two differing concepts of the role of government within the framework of an essentially private enterprise system."

The role of government in a private enterprise system is that of a policeman who protects man's individual rights (including property rights) by protecting men from physical force; in a free economy, the government does not control, regulate, coerce or interfere with men's economic activities.

I do not know the political views of the writer of that letter; he may be a "liberal" or he may be an alleged defender of capitalism. But if he is this last, then I must point out that such views as his—which are shared by many "conservatives"—are more damaging and derogatory to capitalism than the ideas of its avowed enemies.

Such "conservatives" regard capitalism as a system compatible with government controls, and thus help to spread the most dangerous misconceptions. While full, laissez-faire capitalism has not yet existed anywhere, while some (unnecessary) government controls were allowed to dilute and undercut the original American system (more through error than through theoretical intention)—such controls were minor impediments, the mixed economies of the 19th century were predominantly free, and it is this unprecedented freedom that brought about mankind's unprecedented progress. The principles, the theory and the actual practice of capitalism rest on a free, unregulated market, as the history of the last two centuries has amply demonstrated. No defender of capitalism can permit himself to ignore the exact meaning of the term "laissez-faire"—and of the term "mixed economy," which clearly indicates the two opposite elements involved in the mixture: the element of economic freedom, which is capitalism, and the element of government controls, which is statism.

An insistent campaign has been going on for years to make us accept the Marxist view that all governments are tools of economic class interests and that capitalism is not a free economy, but a system of government controls serving some privileged class. The purpose of that campaign is to distort economics, rewrite history and obliterate the existence and the possibility of a free country and an uncontrolled economy. Since a system of nominal private property ruled by government controls is *not* capitalism, but *fascism*, the only choice this obliteration would leave us is the choice between fascism and socialism (or communism)—which all the statists in the world, of all varieties, degrees and denominations, are struggling frantically to make us believe. (The destruction of freedom is their common goal, after which they hope to fight one another for power.)

It is thus that the views of that professor and of many "conservatives" lend credence and support to the vicious leftist propaganda which equates capitalism with fascism.

But there is a bitter kind of justice in the logic of events. That propaganda is having an effect which may be advantageous to the communists, but which is the opposite of the effect intended by the "liberals," the welfare-statists, the socialists, who share the guilt of spreading it: instead of smearing capitalism, that propaganda has succeeded in white-washing and disguising fascism.

In this country, few people care to advocate, to defend or even to understand capitalism; yet fewer still wish to give up its advantages. So if they are told that capitalism is compatible with controls, with the particular controls which further their

Copyright © 1965 by The Objectivist Newsletter, Inc.

particular interests—be it government handouts, or minimum wages, or price-supports, or subsidies, or antitrust laws, or censorship of dirty movies—they will go along with such programs, in the comforting belief that the results will be nothing worse than a "modified" capitalism. And thus a country which does abhor fascism is moving by imperceptible degrees—through ignorance, confusion, evasion, moral cowardice and intellectual default—not toward socialism or any mawkish altruistic ideal, but toward a plain, brutal, predatory, power-grubbing, *de facto* fascism.

No, we have not reached that stage. But we are certainly *not* "an essentially private enterprise system" any longer. At present, we are a disintegrating, unsound, precariously unstable mixed economy—a random, mongrel mixture of socialistic schemes, communistic influences, fascist controls, and shrinking remnants of capitalism still paying the costs of it all—the total of it rolling in the direction of a fascist state.

Consider our present Administration. I don't think I'll be accused of unfairness if I say that President Johnson is *not* a philosophical thinker. No, he is not a fascist, he is not a socialist, he is not a pro-capitalist. Ideologically, he is not anything in particular. Judging by his past record and by the consensus of his own supporters, the concept of an *ideology* is not applicable in his case. He is a *politician*—a very dangerous, yet very appropriate phenomenon in our present state. He is an almost fiction-like, archetypical embodiment of the perfect leader of a mixed economy: a man who enjoys power for power's sake, who is expert at the game of manipulating pressure groups, of playing them all against one another, who loves the process of dispensing smiles, frowns and favors, particularly *sudden* favors, and whose vision does not extend beyond the range of the next election.

Neither President Johnson nor any of today's prominent groups would advocate the socialization of industry. Like all his predecessors in office, Mr. Johnson knows that businessmen are the milch-cows of a mixed economy and he does not want to destroy them, he wants them to prosper and to feed his welfare projects (which the next election requires) while they, the businessmen, are eating out of his hand, as they seem to be anxiously eager to do. The business lobby is certain to get its fair share of influence and of recognition—just like the labor lobby or the farm lobby or the lobby of any "major segment"—on his own terms. He will be particularly adept at the task of creating and encouraging the type of businessmen whom I call "the aristocracy of pull." This is not a socialistic pattern; it is the typical pattern of fascism.

The political, intellectual and *moral* meaning of Mr. Johnson's policy toward businessmen was summed up eloquently in an article in *The New York Times* of January 4, 1965:

"Mr. Johnson is an out-and-out Keynesian in his assiduous wooing of the business community. Unlike President Roosevelt, who delighted in attacking businessmen until World War II forced him into a reluctant truce, and President Kennedy, who also incurred business hostility, President Johnson has worked long and hard to get businessmen to join ranks in a national consensus for his programs.

"This campaign may perturb many Keynesians, but it is pure Keynes. Indeed, Lord Keynes, who once was regarded as a dangerous and Machiavellian figure by American businessmen, made specific suggestions for improving relations between the President and the business community.

"He set down his views in 1938 in a letter to President Roosevelt, who was running into renewed criticism from businessmen following the recession that took place the previous year. Lord Keynes, who always sought to transform capitalism in order to save it, recognized the importance of business confidence and tried to convince Mr. Roosevelt to repair the damage that had been done.

"He advised the President that businessmen were not politicians and did not respond to the same treatment. They are, he wrote, 'much milder than politicians, at the same time allured and terrified by the glare of publicity, easily persuaded to be "patriots," perplexed, bemused, indeed terrified, yet only too anxious to take a cheerful view, vain perhaps but very unsure of themselves, pathetically responsive to a kind word.'...

"He was confident that Mr. Roosevelt could tame them and make them do his bidding, provided he followed some simple Keynesian rules.

" 'You could do anything you liked with them,' the letter continued, 'if you would treat them (even the big ones), not as wolves and tigers, but as domestic animals by nature, even though they have been badly brought up and not trained as you would wish.'

"President Roosevelt ignored his advice. So, apparently, did President Kennedy. But President Johnson seems to have got the message.... By kind words and frequent pats on the head, he had had the business community eating out of his hand.

"Mr. Johnson appears to agree with Lord Keynes's view that there is little to be gained by carrying on a feud with businessmen. As he put it, 'If you work them into the surly, obstinate, terrified mood of which domestic animals, wrongly handled, are capable, the nation's burden will not get carried to market; and in the end, public opinion will veer their way.' "

The view of businessmen as *"domestic animals"* who carry "the nation's burden" and who must be "trained" by the President "to do his bidding" is certainly not a view compatible with capitalism. It is not a view applicable to socialism, since there are no businessmen in a socialist state. It is a view that expresses the economic essence of fascism, of the relationship between business and government in a fascist state.

No matter what the verbal camouflage, such is the actual meaning of any variant of *"transformed"* (or "modified" or "modernized" or "humanized") capitalism. In all such doctrines, the "humanization" consists of turning some members of society (the most productive ones) into beasts of burden.

The formula by which the sacrificial animals are to be fooled and tamed is being repeated today with growing insistence and frequency: businessmen, it is said, must regard the government, not as an enemy, but as a "partner." The notion of a "partnership" between a private group and public officials, between business and government, between production and force, is a linguistic corruption (an "anti-concept") typical of a fascist ideology—an ideology that regards force as the basic element and ultimate arbiter in all human relationships.

" 'Partnership' is an indecent euphemism for 'government control.' There can be no partnership between armed bureaucrats and defenseless private citizens who have no choice but to obey. What chance would you have against a 'partner' whose *arbitrary* word is law, who may give you a hearing (if your pressure group is big enough), but who will play favorites and bargain your interests away, who will always have the last word and the legal 'right' to enforce it on you at the point of a gun, holding your property, your work, your future, your life in his power? Is *that* the meaning of 'partnership'?" (*The Fascist New Frontier*)

But there are men who may find such a prospect attractive; they exist among businessmen as among every other group or profession: the men who dread the competition of a free market and would welcome an armed "partner" to extort special advantages over their abler competitors; men who seek to rise, not by merit but by pull, men who are willing and eager to live not by right, but by favor. Among businessmen, this type of mentality was responsible for the passage of the antitrust laws and is still supporting them today.

A substantial number of Republican businessmen switched to the side of Mr. Johnson in the last election. Here are some interesting observations on this subject, from a survey by *The New York Times* (September 16, 1964): "Interviews in five cities in the industrial Northeast and Midwest disclose striking differences in political outlook between officials of large corporations and men who operate smaller businesses.... The business executives who expect to cast the first Democratic Presidential vote of their lives are nearly all affiliated with large companies.... There is more support for President Johnson among business executives who are in their 40's and 50's than there is among either older or younger businessmen.... Many businessmen in their 40's and 50's say they find relatively little shifting toward support of Mr. Johnson on the part of younger business executives. Interviews with those in their 30's confirm this.... The younger executives themselves speak with pride of their generation as the one that interrupted and reversed the trend toward more liberalism in younger persons.... It is on the issue of Government deficits that the division of opinion between small and large businessmen emerges most dramatically. Officials of giant corporations have a far greater

(Continued on page 25)

From the "Horror File"

(For those who may have wondered whether the intellectual level of today's culture is as low as we charge, the following documentation should prove illuminating. From time to time, we will offer additional documents of this kind.)

"We are accustomed to the naive notion that 'objects' 'exist,' but in the modern world there is an epistemological consensus that objects are created by the symbols of the language in which the objects are discussed." Harley C. Shands, *Thinking and Psychotherapy*, Cambridge: Harvard University Press, 1961, p. 65.

* * *

"*The great error of individualistic psychology is the supposition that man thinks*. . . . A chain of errors; for it is not man himself who thinks but his social community; the source of his thoughts is in the social medium in which he lives, the social atmosphere which he breathes, and he cannot think ought else than what the influences of his social environment concentrating upon his brain necessitate . . .

"The individual simply plays the part of the prism which receives the rays, dissolves them according to fixed laws and lets them pass out again in a predetermined direction and with a predetermined color . . .

"The premises of 'inalienable human rights,' rest upon the most unreasonable self-deification of man and overestimation of the value of human life . . ." Ludwig Gumplowicz, *The Outlines of Sociology*, Philadelphia: American Academy of Political and Social Science, 1899. (Quoted in *The Broken Image* by Floyd W. Matson, New York: George Braziller, 1964, pp. 41-42).

* * *

"Sacrifice, like gravity, is built into the structure of the universe.

"All life exists at the expense of other life. You will be able to eat your next meal because some creature has died. All dishes of meat, fowl or fish represent the sacrifice of one life that your life might be sustained. . . . From microscopic amoeba to man, this rule runs like a scarlet thread through the tapestry of nature: all life is sustained through the sacrifice of other life. . . .

"But 'sacrifice' has higher, holier meanings. . . . In religious terms a sacrifice is anything that is dedicated to a divine being, thus taking on a sacred significance. . . .

"Whether it is a lamb slain on an altar or money placed in an offering plate, a sacrifice is man's acknowledgement that his life is not his own. . . . All religious sacrifices of a high order are but outward symbols of this essential truth that the universe and all things in it are God's to be used for God's purposes. . . .

"In the spiritually mature person this is God's world; people are God's children; every event is God's affair. Attention is shifted from self to God and to other people. This change makes joyous, sacrificial living possible.

"When this conversion occurs a person is ready to accept risks of pain and death for the sake of others and for God's sake. He can do this because, unlike the self-centered person, he feels the world is more important than his own little concerns and that the world will not fall apart if pain, tragedy or death should visit him. He is God's as everything else is God's. He is not here to be spared but to be spent. If he must give his energy, time, money or life for the sake of the common good and for God's sake, he has the conviction he is doing right because he belongs to God and God's children anyway, and not to himself." The Rev. Harold E. Kohn, "The Meaning of Sacrifice," a newspaper column. (This clipping was sent to us by a reader who did not supply the name and date of the newspaper.)

* * *

"We believe Comrade Augusto Martinez Sanchez could not have consciously committed this act, since every revolutionary knows that he does not have the right to deprive his cause of a life that does not belong to him, and that he can only sacrifice against an enemy." Cuban Government communique on attempted suicide of the Labor Minister. *The New York Times*, December 9, 1964.

* * *

"The despot must wield his power for the good of others. If he takes any step which reduces the sum total of human happiness, his power is reduced by a like amount. What better check against a malevolent despotism could you ask for?" B. F. Skinner, *Walden Two*, New York: Macmillan, 1948, p. 220.

* * *

"Schools should de-emphasize the 'Three R's' and concentrate primarily on teaching students how to be 'warm, loving human beings,' one of the world's most famous social scientists declared. . . .

"Dr. [Ashley] Montagu said scientists have determined that the strongest need—and the need most often unfilled—is love.

"'Love has been the most important factor in the evolution of man,' he said, 'and I am not talking about sex. There is no connection whatever. The love to which I refer is behavior calculated to confer survival benefits on other people in a creatively enlarging manner; in other words, an involvement, a continuing interest and concern in their welfare.'

"He noted: 'We were born to live as if to live and love were one. If we fail in loving, then, we fail in living.'

"For that reason, he contended, schools should really be institutes for teaching the art of human relations, the 'theory, art and sciences of practicing ability to love.'

"Such presently emphasized subjects as reading, writing and arithmetic, he said, should be regarded only as 'ancillary, secondary skills.'" *The Sun* (Lowell, Mass.), February 4, 1965.

* * *

"Not the human mind, not the individual understanding are the true subjects of the notions and verities of human existence. Society, however, gifted with a kind of collective mind, different from the individual's, is imbued with such knowledge. The individual, the human being is nothing; society alone exists. It is the soul of the moral world. It alone has reality, while individuals are only phenomena . . ." Maine de Biran, quoted in *The Broken Image*, p. 51.

* * *

"I once asked [Bertrand] Russell if he was willing to die for his beliefs. 'Of course not,' he replied. 'After all, I may be wrong.'" Leonard Lyons, *The New York Post*, June 23, 1964.

This true story was sent to us by Al Ramrus of Los Angeles.

A man who attends a Los Angeles university overheard the following conversation in a hallway:

Student: In other words, what you're saying is that the only kind of productive economy is one controlled by the law of supply and demand, and with profit as its goal?

Instructor: That's right. Laissez-faire capitalism.

Student: And that's the only way for a country to be prosperous?

Instructor: Correct.

Student: But isn't there some solution to this?

The New Fascism: Rule by Consensus (from page 24)

tendency to accept the idea that budget deficits are sometimes necessary and even desirable. The typical small businessman, however, reserves a very special scorn for deficit spending . . ."

This gives us an indication of who are the vested interests in a mixed economy—and what such an economy does to the beginners or the young.

An essential aspect of the socialistically inclined mentality is the desire to obliterate the difference between the earned and the unearned, and, therefore, to permit no differentiation between such businessmen as Hank Rearden and Orren Boyle. To a concrete-bound, range-of-the-moment, primitive socialist mentality—a mentality that clamors for a "redistribution of wealth" without any concern for the origin of wealth—the enemy is all those who are rich, regardless of the source of their riches. Such mentalities, those aging, graying "liberals" who had been the "idealists" of the 30's, are clinging desperately to the illusion that we are moving toward some sort of socialist state inimical to the rich and beneficial to the poor—while frantically evading the spectacle of *what kind of rich* are being destroyed and what kind are flourishing under the system they, the "liberals," have established. The grim joke is on them: their alleged "ideals" have paved the way, not toward socialism, but toward fascism. The collector of their efforts is not the helplessly, brainlessly virtuous "little man" of their flat-footed imagination and shopworn fiction, but the worst type of predatory rich, the rich-by-force, the rich-by-political-privilege, the type who has no chance under capitalism, but who is always there to cash in on every collectivist "noble experiment."

It is the creators of wealth, the Hank Reardens, who are destroyed under any form of statism, socialist, communist or fascist; it is the parasites, the Orren Boyles, who are the privileged "elite" and the profiteers of statism, particularly of fascism. (The special profiteers of socialism are the James Taggarts; of communism—the Floyd Ferrises.) The same is true of their psychological counterparts among the poor and among the men of all the economic levels in-between.

The particular form of economic organization, which is becoming more and more apparent in this country, as an outgrowth of the power of pressure groups, is one of the worst variants of statism: *guild socialism.* Guild socialism robs the talented young of their future—by freezing men into professional castes under rigid rules. It represents an open embodiment of the basic motive of most statists, though they usually prefer not to confess it: the entrenchment and protection of mediocrity from abler competitors, the shackling of the men of superior ability down to the mean average of their professions. That theory is not too popular among socialists (though it has its advocates)—but the most famous instance of its large-scale practice was Fascist Italy.

In the 1930's, a few perceptive men said that Roosevelt's New Deal was a form of guild socialism and that it was closer to Mussolini's system than to any other. They were ignored. Today, the evidence is unmistakable.

It was also said that if fascism ever came to the United States, it would come disguised as socialism. In this connection, I recommend that you read or re-read Sinclair Lewis' *It Can't Happen Here*—with special reference to the character, style and ideology of Berzelius Windrip, the fascist leader.

Now let me mention, and answer, some of the standard objections by which today's "liberals" attempt to camouflage (to differentiate from fascism) the nature of the system they are supporting.

"*Fascism requires one-party rule.*" What will the notion of "Government by Consensus" amount to in practice?

"*Fascism's goal is the conquest of the world.*" What is the goal of those global-minded, bipartisan champions of the United Nations? And, if they reach it, what positions do they expect to acquire in the power-structure of "One World"?

"*Fascism preaches racism.*" Not necessarily. Hitler's Germany did; Mussolini's Italy did not.

"*Fascism is opposed to the welfare state.*" Check your premises and your history books. The father and originator of the welfare state, the man who put into practice the notion of buying the loyalty of some groups with money extorted from others, was Bismarck—the political ancestor of Hitler. Let me remind you that the full title of the Nazi party was: the National Socialist Workers party of Germany.

Let me remind you also of some excerpts from the political program of that party, adopted in Munich, on February 24, 1920:

"We ask that the government undertake the obligation above all of providing citizens with adequate opportunity for employment and earning a living."

"The activities of the individual must not be allowed to clash with the interests of the community, but must take place within its confines and be for the good of all. Therefore, we demand: . . . *an end to the power of the financial interests.*"

"We demand profit sharing in big business."

"We demand a broad extension of care for the aged."

"We demand . . . the greatest possible consideration of small business in the purchases of the national, state, and municipal governments."

"In order to make possible to every capable and industrious [citizen] the attainment of higher education and thus the achievement of a post of leadership, the government must provide an all-around enlargement of our entire system of public education. . . . We demand the education at government expense of gifted children of poor parents . . ."

"The government must undertake the improvement of public health—by protecting mother and child, by prohibiting child labor . . . by the greatest possible support for all clubs concerned with the physical education of youth."

"[We] combat the . . . materialistic spirit within and without us, and are convinced that a permanent recovery of our people can only proceed from within on the foundation of
"The Common Good Before the Individual Good."

For many more quotations of this kind, revealing the altruist-collectivist base of the Nazi and fascist ideology, I refer you to my lecture *The Fascist New Frontier.*

There is, however, one difference between the type of fascism toward which we are drifting, and the type that ravaged European countries: ours is not a militant kind of fascism, not an organized movement of shrill demagogues, bloody thugs, hysterical third-rate intellectuals and juvenile delinquents—ours is a tired, worn, cynical fascism, fascism by default, not like a flaming disaster, but more like the quiet collapse of a lethargic body slowly eaten by internal corruption.

Did it have to happen? No. Can it still be averted? Yes.

If you doubt the power of philosophy to set the course and shape the destiny of human societies, observe that our mixed economy is the literal, faithfully carried out product of *Pragmatism*—and of the generation brought up under its influence. Pragmatism is the philosophy which holds that there is no objective reality or permanent truth, that there are no absolute principles, no valid abstractions, no firm concepts, that anything may be tried by rule-of-thumb, that objectivity consists of collective subjectivism, that whatever people wish to be true, *is* true, whatever people wish to exist, *does* exist—provided a *consensus* says so.

If you want to avert the final disaster, it is this type of thinking—every one of those propositions and all of them—that you must face, grasp and reject. Then you will have grasped the connection of philosophy to politics and to the daily events of your life. Then you will have learned that no society is better than its philosophical foundation. And then—to paraphrase John Galt—you will be ready, not to *return* to capitalism, but to *discover* it.

OBJECTIVIST CALENDAR

■ Beginning Monday, June 21, in New York City, NBI will offer a ten-lecture course on "The History of Ancient Philosophy," to be given by Dr. Leonard Peikoff. Time: 7:30 P.M. Place: Sheraton-Atlantic Hotel, Broadway at 34th St. Admission: $3.50, payable at the door.

■ NBI's Tape Transcription Division has scheduled the following starting dates: "The Esthetics of the Visual Arts" in Phoenix, June 11; Los Angeles, July 7—"The Principles of Efficient Thinking" in Seattle, June 21—"The Economics of a Free Society" in Philadelphia, June 29. For details, contact NBI.

■ On the evening of April 24, Dr. and Mrs. Allan Blumenthal gave a joint concert-art show at the Barbizon Plaza Hotel in New York City. Allan Blumenthal is a pianist by avocation, while Joan Mitchell Blumenthal is a rising young artist. The occasion was planned as a private event, by invitation only, but it attracted an enthusiastic audience of 500 NBI students, whose response gave it a special significance. It was like a small preview of the future, a demonstration of what an evening of esthetically integrated, Romantic art can accomplish—and of the great emotional need it can satisfy. We offer our congratulations to Dr. and Mrs. Blumenthal.

—B.B.

Published monthly at 120 East 34th Street, New York, N.Y. 10016.
Subscription rate in United States, its possessions, Canada and Mexico: one year, $5; 2 years, $9; 3 years, $13. Other countries: one year, $6; 2 years, $11; 3 years, $16.
Additional copies of this Newsletter: single copy 50¢ (coins, not stamps); 10 — 99 copies, 25¢ each plus postage (for first-class delivery add 1¢ per copy, for third-class delivery add ½¢ per copy); 100 or more copies, 15¢ each plus postage (same as above). (Bulk rates apply only to multiple orders of a single issue.)
Please include zip code number with your address.
For change of address, send old and new address. Allow us three weeks to process new subscriptions and change of address.

Ayn Rand and Nathaniel Branden, Editors and Publishers
Barbara Branden, Managing Editor
Elayne Kalberman, Circulation Manager

THE OBJECTIVIST NEWSLETTER

Edited and Published by AYN RAND and NATHANIEL BRANDEN

VOL. 4 NO. 7   JULY, 1965

CHECK YOUR PREMISES
By AYN RAND

The Cashing-in: The Student "Rebellion"

(Part I of a two-part article)

The so-called student "rebellion," which was started and keynoted at the University of California at Berkeley, has profound significance, but not of the kind that most commentators have ascribed to it. And the nature of the misrepresentations is part of its significance.

The events at Berkeley began, in the fall of 1964, ostensibly as a student protest against the University administration's order forbidding political activity—specifically, the recruiting, fund-raising and organizing of students for political action off-campus—on a certain strip of ground adjoining the campus, which was owned by the University. Claiming that their rights had been violated, a small group of "rebels" rallied thousands of students of all political views, including many "conservatives," and assumed the title of the "Free Speech Movement." The Movement staged "sit-in" protests in the administration building, and committed other acts of physical force, such as assaults on the police and the seizure of a police car for use as a rostrum.

The spirit, style and tactics of the rebellion are best illustrated by one particular incident. The University administration called a mass meeting, which was attended by 18 thousand students and faculty members, to hear an address on the situation by the University President, Clark Kerr; it had been expressly announced that no student speakers would be allowed to address the meeting. Kerr attempted to end the rebellion by capitulating: he promised to grant most of the rebels' demands; it looked as if he had won the audience to his side. Whereupon, Mario Savio, the rebel leader, seized the microphone, in an attempt to take over the meeting, ignoring the rules and the fact that the meeting had been adjourned. When he was—properly—dragged off the platform, the leaders of the F.S.M. admitted, openly and jubilantly, that they had almost lost their battle, but had saved it by provoking the administration to an act of "violence" (thus admitting that the victory of their publicly proclaimed goals was not the goal of their battle).

What followed was nation-wide publicity, of a peculiar kind. It was a sudden and, seemingly, spontaneous out-pouring of articles, studies, surveys, revealing a strange unanimity of approach in several basic aspects: in ascribing to the F.S.M. the importance of a national movement, unwarranted by the facts —in blurring the facts by means of unintelligible generalities— in granting to the rebels the status of spokesmen for American youth, acclaiming their "idealism" and "commitment" to political action, hailing them as a symptom of the "awakening" of college students from "political apathy." If ever a "puff-job" was done by a major part of the press, this was it.

In the meantime, what followed at Berkeley was a fierce, three-cornered struggle among the University administration, its Board of Regents and its faculty, a struggle so sketchily reported in the press that its exact nature remains fogbound. One can gather only that the Regents were, apparently, demanding a "tough" policy toward the rebels, that the majority of the faculty were on the rebels' side and that the administration was caught in the "moderate" middle of the road.

The struggle led to the permanent resignation of the University's Chancellor (as the rebels had demanded)—the temporary resignation, and later reinstatement, of President Kerr—and, ultimately, an almost complete capitulation to the F.S.M., with the administration granting most of the rebels' demands. (These included the right to advocate illegal acts and the right to an unrestricted freedom of speech *on campus*.)

To the astonishment of the naive, this did not end the rebellion: the more demands were granted, the more were made. As the administration intensified its efforts to appease the F.S.M., the F.S.M. intensified its provocations. The unrestricted freedom of speech took the form of a "Filthy Language Movement," which consisted of students carrying placards with four-letter words, and broadcasting obscenities over the University loudspeakers (which Movement was dismissed with mild reproof by most of the press, as a mere "adolescent prank").

This, apparently, was too much even for those who sympathized with the rebellion. The F.S.M. began to lose its following—and was, eventually, dissolved. Mario Savio quit the University, declaring that he "could not keep up with the *undemocratic* procedures that the administration is following" (italics mine)—and departed, reportedly to organize a nation-wide revolutionary student movement.

This is a bare summary of the events as they were reported by the press. But some revealing information was provided by volunteers, outside the regular news channels, such as in the letters-to-the-editor columns.

An eloquent account was given in a letter to *The N.Y. Times* (March 31, 1965) by Alexander Grendon, a biophysicist in the Donner Laboratory, University of California:

"The F.S.M. has always applied coercion to insure victory. One-party 'democracy,' as in the Communist countries or the lily-white portions of the South, corrects opponents of the party line by punishment. The punishment of the recalcitrant university administration (and more than 20,000 students who avoided participation in the conflict) was to 'bring the university to a grinding halt' by physical force.

"To capitulate to such corruption of democracy is to teach students that these methods are right. President Kerr capitulated repeatedly. . . .

"Kerr agreed the university would not control 'advocacy of illegal acts,' an abstraction until illustrated by examples: In a university lecture hall, a self-proclaimed anarchist advises students how to cheat to escape military service; a nationally known Communist uses the university facilities to condemn our Government in vicious terms for its action in Vietnam, while funds to support the Vietcong are illegally solicited; propaganda for the use of marijuana, with instructions where to buy it, is openly distributed on campus.

"Even the abstraction 'obscenity' is better understood when one hears a speaker, using the university's amplifying equipment, describe in vulgar words his experiences in group sexual intercourse and homosexuality and recommend these prac-

Copyright © 1965 by The Objectivist Newsletter, Inc.

tices, while another suggests students should have the same sexual freedom on campus as dogs....

"Clark Kerr's 'negotiation'—a euphemism for surrender—on each deliberate defiance of orderly university processes contributes not to a liberal university but to a lawless one."

David S. Landes, Professor of History, Harvard University, made an interesting observation in a letter to *The N.Y. Times* (December 29, 1964). Stating that the Berkeley revolt represents potentially one of the most serious assaults on academic freedom in America, he wrote:

"In conclusion, I should like to point out the deleterious implications of this dispute for the University of California. I know personally of five or six faculty members who are leaving, not because of lack of sympathy with 'free speech' or 'political action,' but because, as one put it, who wants to teach at the University of Saigon?"

The clearest account and most perceptive evaluation were offered in an article in the *Columbia University Forum* (Spring 1965), entitled "What's Left at Berkeley," by William Petersen, professor of sociology at the University of California at Berkeley.

He writes: "The first fact one must know about the Free Speech Movement is that it has little or nothing to do with free speech.... If not free speech, what then is the issue? In fact, preposterous as this may seem, the real issue is the seizure of power....

"That a tiny number, a few hundred out of a student body of more than 27,000, was able to disrupt the campus is the consequence of more than vigor and skill in agitation. This miniscule group could not have succeeded in getting so many students into motion without three other, at times unwitting, sources of support: off-campus assistance of various kinds, the University administration and the faculty.

"Everyone who has seen the efficient, almost military organization of the agitators' program has a reasonable basis for believing that skilled personnel and money are being dispatched into the Berkeley battle.... Around the Berkeley community a dozen *ad hoc* committees to support' this or that element of the student revolt sprang up spontaneously, as though out of nowhere.

"The course followed by the University administration... could hardly have better fostered a rebellious student body if it had been devised to do so. To establish dubious regulations and when they are attacked to defend them by unreasonable argument is bad enough; worse still, the University did not impose on the students any sanctions that did not finally evaporate.... Obedience to norms is developed when it is suitably rewarded, and when noncompliance is suitably punished. That professional educators should need to be reminded of this axiom indicates how deep the roots of the Berkeley crisis lie.

"But the most important reason that the extremists won so many supporters among the students was the attitude of the faculty. Perhaps their most notorious capitulation to the FSM was a resolution passed by the Academic Senate on December 8, by which the faculty notified the campus not only that they supported all of the radicals' demands but also that, in effect, they were willing to fight for them against the Board of Regents, should that become necessary. When that resolution passed by an overwhelming majority—824 to 115 votes—it effectively silenced the anti-FSM student organizations....

"The Free Speech Movement is reminiscent of the Communist fronts of the 1930's, but there are several important differences. The key feature, that a radical core uses legitimate issues ambiguously in order to manipulate a large mass, is identical. The core in this case, however, is not the disciplined Communist party, but a heterogeneous group of radical sects."

Professor Petersen lists the various socialist, Trotskyist, communist and other groups involved. His conclusion is: "The radical leaders on the Berkeley campus, like those in Latin American or Asian universities, are not the less radical for being, in many cases, outside the discipline of a formal political party. They are defined not by whether they pay dues to a party, but by their actions, their vocabulary, their way of thinking. The best term to describe them, in my opinion, is Castroite." This term, he explains, applies primarily to their choice of tactics, to the fact that "in critical respects all of them imitate the Castro movement....

"At Berkeley, provocative tactics applied not against a dictatorship but against the liberal, divided, and vacillating University administration proved to be enormously effective. Each provocation and subsequent victory led to the next."

Professor Petersen ends his article on a note of warning: "By my diagnosis... not only has the patient [the University] not recovered but he is sicker than ever. The fever has gone down temporarily, but the infection is spreading and becoming more virulent."

Now let us consider the ideology of the rebels, from such indications as were given in the press reports. The general tone of the reports was best expressed by a headline in *The N.Y. Times* (March 15, 1965): "The New Student Left: Movement Represents Serious Activists in Drive for Changes."

What kind of changes? No specific answer was given in the almost full-page story. Just "changes."

Some of these activists "who liken their movement to a 'revolution,' want to be called radicals. Most of them, however, prefer to be called 'organizers.'"

Organizers—of what? Of "deprived people." For what? No answer. Just "organizers."

"Most express contempt for any specific labels, and they don't mind being called cynics.... The great majority of those questioned said they were as skeptical of Communism as they were of any other form of political control.... 'You might say we're a-Communist,' said one of them, 'just as you might say we're amoral and a-almost everything else.'"

There are exceptions, however. A girl from the University of California, one of the leaders of the Berkeley revolt, is quoted as saying: "At present the socialist world, even with all its problems, is moving closer than any other countries toward the sort of society I think should exist. In the Soviet Union, it has almost been achieved."

Another student, from the City College of New York, is quoted as concurring: "'The Soviet Union and the whole Socialist bloc are on the right track,' he said."

In view of the fact that most of the young activists were active in the civil rights movement, and that the Berkeley rebels had started by hiding behind the issue of civil rights (attempting, unsuccessfully, to smear all opposition as of "racist" origin), it is interesting to read that: "There is little talk among the activists about racial integration. Some of them consider the subject passé. They declare that integration will be almost as evil as segregation if it results in a complacent, middle-class interracial society."

The central theme and basic ideology of all the activists is: *anti-ideology*. They are militantly opposed to all "labels," definitions and theories; they proclaim the supremacy of the immediate moment and commitment to action—to subjectively, emotionally motivated action. Their anti-intellectual attitude runs like a stressed leitmotif through all the press reports.

"The Berkeley mutineers did not seem political in the sense of those student rebels in the Turbulent Thirties," declares an article in *The N.Y. Times Magazine* (Feb. 14, 1965), "they
(Continued on page 31)

Alienation

By NATHANIEL BRANDEN

(*Part I of a three-part article*)

"And how am I to face the odds
of man's bedevilment and God's?
I, a stranger and afraid
in a world I never made."

In the writings of contemporary psychologists and sociologists, one encounters these lines from A. E. Housman's poem more and more often today—quoted as an eloquent summation of the sense of life and psychological plight of twentieth century man.

In book after book of social commentary, one finds the same message: modern man is overwhelmed by anxiety, modern man suffers from an "identity crisis," modern man is *alienated*. " 'Who am I?' 'Where am I going?' 'Do I belong?': these are the crucial questions man asks himself in modern mass society," declares the sociologist and psychoanalyst Hendrik M. Ruitenbeek, in *The Individual and the Crowd—A Study of Identity in America*. (New York: Mentor Books, New American Library, 1965, p. 15.)

The concept of *alienation*, in its original psychiatric usage, denoted the mentally ill, the severely mentally ill—often, particularly in legal contexts, the insane. It conveyed the notion of the breakdown of rationality and self-determination, the notion of a person driven by forces which he cannot grasp or control, which are experienced by him as compelling and alien, so that he feels estranged from himself.

Centuries earlier, medieval theologians had spoken with distress of man's alienation from God—of an over-concern with the world of the senses that caused man to become lost to himself, estranged from his proper spiritual estate.

It was the philosopher Hegel who introduced the concept of alienation (outside of its psychiatric context) to the modern world. The history of man, maintained Hegel, is the history of man's self-alienation: man is blind to his true essence, he is lost in the "dead world" of social institutions and of property, which he himself has created, he is estranged from the Universal Being of which he is a part—and human progress consists of man's motion toward that Whole, as he transcends the limitations of his individual perceptions.

"Alienation" was taken over by Karl Marx and given a narrower, less cosmic meaning. He applied the concept primarily to the worker. The worker's alienation was inevitable, he asserted, with the development of the division of labor, specialization, exchange, and private property. The worker must sell his services; thus he comes to view himself as a "commodity," he becomes alienated from the product of his own labor, and his work is no longer the expression of his powers, of his inner self. The worker, who is alive, is ruled by that which is "dead" (*i.e.*, capital, machinery). The consequence, says Marx, is spiritual impoverishment and mutilation: the worker is alienated from himself, from nature and from his fellow-men; he exists only as an animated *object*, not as a human being.

Since the time of Marx, the idea of alienation has been used more and more extensively by psychologists, sociologists and philosophers—gathering to itself a wide variety of usages and meanings. But from Hegel and Marx onward, there appears to be an almost universal reluctance, on the part of those who employ the term, to define it precisely; it is as if one were expected to *feel* its meaning, rather than to grasp it conceptually. In a two-volume collection of essays entitled *Alienation*, the editor, Gerald Sykes, specifically scorns those who are too eager for a definition of the term; haste for a definition, he declares, reveals that one suffers from "an advanced case of—alienation." (New York: George Braziller, Inc., 1964, Introduction, xiii.)

Certain writers—notably those of a Freudian or Jungian orientation—declare that the complexity of modern industrial society has caused man to become "over-civilized," to have lost touch with the deeper roots of his being, to have become alienated from his "instinctual nature." Others—notably those of an Existentialist or Zen Buddhist orientation—complain that our advanced technological society compels man to live too intellectually, to be ruled by abstractions, thus alienating him from the real world which can be experienced in its "wholeness" only via his emotions. Others—notably those of a petulant mediocrity orientation—decry specifically the alienation of the artist; they assert that, with the vanishing of the age of patrons, with the artist thrown on his own resources to struggle in the marketplace—which is ruled by "philistines"—the artist is condemned to fight a losing battle for the preservation of his spiritual integrity: he is too besieged by material temptations.

Most of these writers declare that the problem of alienation —and of man's search for identity—is not new, but has been a source of anguish to man in every age and culture. But they insist that today, in Western civilization—above all, in America —the problem has reached an unprecedented severity. It has become a crisis.

What is responsible for this crisis? What has alienated man and deprived him of identity? The answer given by most writers on alienation is not always stated explicitly, but—in their countless disparaging references to "the dehumanizing effects of industrialism," "soul-destroying commercialism," "the arid rationalism of a technological culture," "the vulgar materialism of the West," etc.—the villain in their view of things, the destroyer whom they hold chiefly responsible, is not hard to identify. It is *capitalism*.

This should not be startling. Since its birth, capitalism has been made the scapegoat responsible for almost every real or imagined evil denounced by anyone. As the distinguished economist, Ludwig von Mises, observes: "Nothing is more unpopular today than the free market economy, *i.e.*, capitalism. Everything that is considered unsatisfactory in present-day conditions is charged to capitalism. The atheists make capitalism responsible for the survival of Christianity. But the papal encyclicals blame capitalism for the spread of irreligion and the sins of our contemporaries, and the Protestant churches and sects are no less vigorous in their indictment of capitalist greed. Friends of peace consider our wars as an offshoot of capitalist imperialism. But the adamant nationalist warmongers of Germany and Italy indicted capitalism for its 'bourgeois' pacifism, contrary to human nature and to the inescapable laws of history. Sermonizers accuse capitalism of disrupting the family and fostering licentiousness. But the 'progressives' blame capitalism for the preservation of allegedly out-dated rules of sexual restraint. Almost all men agree that poverty is an outcome of capitalism. On the other hand many deplore the fact that capitalism, in catering lavishly to the wishes of people intent upon getting more amenities and a better living, promotes a crass materialism. These contradictory accusations of capitalism cancel one another. But the fact remains that there are few people left who would not condemn capitalism altogether." (*Socialism*, New Haven: Yale University Press, 1951, p. 527.)

It is true that a great many men suffer from a chronic feeling of inner emptiness, of spiritual impoverishment, the sense of lacking personal identity. It is true that a great many men feel alienated—*from something*—even if they cannot say from what—from themselves or other men or the universe. And it is profoundly significant that capitalism should be blamed for this. Not because there is any justification for the charge, but because, by analyzing the reasons given for the accusation, one can learn a good deal about the nature and meaning of men's sense of alienation and non-identity—and, simultaneously, about the psychological motives that give rise to hostility toward capitalism.

The writers on alienation, as I have indicated, are not an intellectually homogeneous group. They differ in many areas: in their view of what the problem of alienation exactly consists of, in the aspects of modern industrial society and a free market economy which they find most objectionable, in the explicitness with which they identify capitalism as the villain, and in the details of their own political inclinations. Some of these writers are socialists, some are fascists, some are medievalists, some are supporters of the welfare state, some scorn politics altogether. Some believe that the problem of alienation is largely or entirely solvable by a new system of social organization; others believe that the problem, at bottom, is metaphysical and that no entirely satisfactory solution can be found.

Fortunately for the purposes of this analysis, however, there is one contemporary writer who manages to combine in his books virtually all of the major errors perpetrated by commentators in this field: psychologist and sociologist Erich Fromm. Let us, therefore, consider Fromm's view of man and his theory of alienation in some detail.

Man, declares Erich Fromm, is "the freak of the universe."

This theme is crucial and central throughout his writings: man is radically different from all other living species, he is "estranged" and "alienated" from nature, he is overwhelmed by a feeling of "isolation" and "separateness"—he has lost, in the process of evolution, the undisturbed tranquillity of other organisms, he has lost the "pre-human harmony" with nature which is enjoyed by an animal, a bird or a worm. The *source* of his curse is the fact that he possesses a mind.

"Self-awareness, reason and imagination," Fromm writes in *Man for Himself*, "have disrupted the 'harmony' which characterizes animal existence. Their emergence has made man into an anomaly, into the freak of the universe." Man cannot live as an animal: he is not equipped to adapt himself automatically and unthinkingly to his environment. An animal blindly "repeats the pattern of the species," its behavior is biologically prescribed and stereotyped, it "either fits in or it dies out"—but it does not have to *solve* the problem of survival, *it is not conscious of life and death as an issue*. Man does and is; this is his tragedy. "Reason, man's blessing, is also his curse...." (New York: Rinehart, 1947, pp. 39, 40.)

In *The Art of Loving*, he writes: "What is essential in the existence of man is the fact that he has emerged from the animal kingdom, from instinctive adaptation, that he has transcended nature—although he never leaves it; he is part of it—and yet once torn away from it, he cannot return to it; once thrown out of paradise—a state of original oneness with nature—cherubim with flaming swords block his way, if he should try to return." (New York: Harper & Brothers, 1956, p. 7.)

That man's rational faculty deprives man of "paradise," alienating and estranging him from nature, is clearly revealed, says Fromm, in the "existential dichotomies" which his mind dooms man to confront—"contradictions" inherent in life itself. What are these tragic "dichotomies?" He names three as central and basic. Man's mind permits him to "visualize his own end: death"—yet "his body makes him want to be alive." (*Man for Himself*, p. 40.) Man's nature contains innumerable potentialities—yet "the short span of his life does not permit their full realization even under the most favorable circumstances." (p. 42.) Man "must be alone when he has to judge and to make decisions solely by the power of his reason"—yet "he cannot bear to be alone, to be unrelated to his fellow men." (p. 43).

These "contradictions," says Fromm, constitute the dilemma of the "human situation"—contradictions with which man is compelled to struggle, but which he can never resolve or annul, *and which alienate man from himself, from his fellow men and from nature.*

If the logic of the foregoing is not readily perceivable, the reason does not lie in the brevity of the synopsis. It lies in the unmitigated arbitrariness of Fromm's manner of presenting his ideas; he writes, not like a scientist, but like an oracle who is not obliged to give reasons or proof.

It is true that man differs fundamentally from all other living species, by virtue of possessing a rational, conceptual faculty. It is true that, for man, survival is a problem to be solved—by the exercise of his intelligence. It is true that no man lives long enough to exhaust his every potentiality. It is true that every man is alone, separate and unique. It is true that thinking requires independence. These are the facts that grant glory to man's existence. Why would one choose to regard these facts as a terrifying cosmic paradox and to see in them the evidence of monumentally tragic human problems?

There *are* men who resent the fact that their life is their responsibility and that the task of their reason is to discover how to maintain it. Large numbers of such men—men who prefer the state of animals—may be found (or used to be found) sleeping on the benches of any public park; they are called tramps. There *are* men who find thought abnormal and unnatural. Large numbers of such men may be found in mental institutions; they are called morons. There *are* men who suffer a chronic preoccupation with death; who bitterly resent the fact that they cannot simultaneously be a concert pianist, a business tycoon, a railroad engineer, a baseball player and a deep-sea diver; who find their existence as separate, independent entities an unendurable burden. Large numbers of such men may be found in the offices of psychotherapists; they are called neurotics. But why does Fromm choose tramps, morons and neurotics as his symbols of humanity, as his image of man —and why does he choose to claim that *theirs* is the state in which all men are destined to start, and out of which they must struggle to rise?

Fromm does not tell us. Nowhere does he establish any logical connection between the facts he observes and the conclusions he announces.

If we are *not* to regard his conclusions as arbitrary, as mystical revelations, in effect—then we must assume that he does not bother to give reasons for his position because he regards his conclusions as virtually self-evident, as irresistibly conveyed by the facts he cites, easily available to everyone's experience and introspection. But if he feels it is readily apparent, by introspection, that the facts he cites constitute an agonizing problem for man—the most appropriate answer one can give is: "Speak for yourself, brother!"

Reason, Fromm insists, and the self-awareness which reason makes possible, turns man's "separate, disunited existence" into an "unbearable prison"—and man "would become insane could he not liberate himself from this prison and reach out, unite himself in some form or other with men, with the world outside." (*The Art of Loving*, p. 8.)

The following paragraph is typical of what Fromm considers an explanation:

"The experience of separateness arouses anxiety; it is, indeed, the source of all anxiety. Being separate means being cut off, without any capacity to use my human powers. Hence to be separate means to be helpless, unable to grasp the world—things and people—actively; it means that the world can invade me without my ability to react. Thus, separateness is the source of intense anxiety. Beyond that, it arouses shame and the feeling of guilt. This experience of guilt and shame in separateness is expressed in the Biblical story of Adam and Eve. After Adam and Eve have eaten of the 'tree of knowledge of good and evil,' after they have disobeyed ... after they have become human by having emancipated themselves from the original harmony with nature, *i.e.*, after their birth as human beings—they saw 'that they were naked—and they were ashamed.' Should we assume that a myth as old and elementary as this has the prudish morals of the nineteenth-century outlook, and that the important point the story wants to convey to us is the embarassment that their genitals were visible? This can hardly be so, and by understanding the story in a Victorian spirit, we miss the main point, which seems to be the following: after man and woman have become aware of themselves and of each other, they are aware of their separateness, and of their difference, inasmuch as they belong to different sexes. But while recognizing their separateness they remain strangers, because they have not yet learned to love each other (as is also made very clear by the fact that Adam defends himself by blaming Eve, rather than trying to defend her). *The awareness of human separation, without reunion by love—is the source of shame. It is at the same time the source of guilt and anxiety."* (*The Art of Loving*, p. 9.)

All social institutions, all cultures, all religions and philosophies, all progress, asserts Fromm, are motivated by man's need to escape the terrifying sense of helplessness and aloneness to which his reason condemns him. *"The necessity to find ever-new solutions for the contradictions of his existence, to find ever-higher forms of unity with nature, his fellowmen and himself, is the source of all psychic forces which motivate man . . ."* (*The Sane Society*, New York: Rinehart, 1955, p. 25.)

In *Man for Himself*, Fromm states that only through "reason, productiveness and love" can man solve the problem of his "separateness" and achieve a "new union" with the world around him. Fromm's claim to be an advocate of *reason* is disingenuous, to say the least. He speaks of reason and love as being "only two different forms of comprehending the world." (p. 97.) As if this were not an unequivocal proof of his mysticism, he goes on to speak, in *The Art of Loving*, of the "paradoxical logic" of Eastern religions, which, he tells us approvingly, is not encumbered by the Aristotelian law of contradiction and which teaches that "man can perceive reality only in contradictions." (p 77.) (Hegel and Marx, he asserts—correctly—belong to this "paradoxical" epistemological line.) His discussion of what he means by "productiveness" is scarcely more gratifying.

In *The Art of Loving*, written some years after *Man for Himself*, he declares that reason and productive work, though certainly important, provide only partial and, by themselves, very unsatisfactory solutions: the "unity" they achieve is "not interpersonal," and the "desire for interpersonal fusion is the most powerful striving in man." (p. 18.) Fromm pulls an unexplained switch at this point. What began as a problem between man and nature is now to be solved (in some unspecified manner) by human "togetherness." One is not surprised; in reading Fromm, this is the sort of pronouncement for which one is waiting—there is a sense of inevitability about it. Love and love alone, he tells us with wonderful originality, can allay man's terror—"Love is the only sane and satisfactory answer to the problem of human existence." (p. 133.)

Only through "relating" oneself positively to others, only through feeling "care and responsibility" for them—while preserving one's personal integrity, he adds somewhat mysteriously—can man establish new ties, a new union, that will release him from alienated aloneness.

The cat is now ready to be let fully out of the bag. The preceding is Fromm's view of alienation as a *metaphysical* problem; its full meaning and implication become clear when one turns to his *social-political* analysis of alienation. In the context of the latter, one can see clearly what sort of "ties," what sort of "union" and what sort of "love" Fromm has in mind. (*To be continued in our next issue*)

The Cashing-in: The Student "Rebellion" (from page 28)

are too suspicious of all adult institutions to embrace wholeheartedly even those ideologies with a stake in smashing the system. An anarchist or I.W.W. strain seems as pronounced as any Marxist doctrine. 'Theirs is a sort of political existentialism,' says Paul Jacobs, a research associate at the university's Center for the Study of Law and Society, who is one of the F.S.M.'s applauders. 'All the old labels are out. . . .' "

And: "The proudly immoderate zealots of the F.S.M. pursue an activist creed—that only commitment can strip life of its emptiness, its absence of meaning in a great 'knowledge factory' like Berkeley."

An article in *The Saturday Evening Post* (May 8, 1965), discussing the various youth groups of the left, quotes a leader of Students for a Democratic Society:

"We began by rejecting the old sectarian left and its ancient quarrels, and with a contempt for American society, which we saw as depraved. We are interested in direct action and specific issues. We do not spend endless hours debating the nature of Soviet Russia or whether Yugoslavia is a degenerate workers' state." And: "With sit-ins we saw for the first time the chance for direct participation in meaningful social revolution."

"In their off-picket-line hours," states the same article, "the P.L. [Progressive Labor] youngsters hang out at the experimental theaters and coffee shops of Manhattan's East Village. Their taste in reading runs more to Sartre than to Marx."

With an interesting touch of unanimity, a survey in *Newsweek* (March 22, 1965) quotes a young man on the other side of the continent: " 'These students don't read Marx,' said one Berkeley Free Student Movement leader. 'They read Camus.' "

"If they are rebels," the survey continues, "they are rebels without an ideology, and without long-range revolutionary programs. They rally over issues, not philosophies, and seem unable to formulate or sustain a systematized political theory of society, either from the left or right."

"Today's student seeks to find himself through what he does, not what he thinks," the survey declares explicitly—and quotes some adult authorities in sympathetic confirmation. " 'What you have now, as in the 30's,' says New York Post editor James A. Wechsler, 'are groups of activists who really want to function in life.' But not ideologically. 'We used to sit around and debate Marxism, but students now are working for civil-rights and peace.' " Richard Unsworth, chaplain at Dartmouth, is quoted as saying: "In the world of today's campus 'the avenue now is doing and then reflecting on your doing, instead of reflecting, then deciding, and then doing, the way it was a few years ago.' " Paul Goodman, described as writer, educator and "one of the students' current heroes," is quoted as hailing the Berkeley movement because: "The leaders of the insurrection, he says, 'didn't play it cool, they took risks, *they were willing to be confused,* they didn't know whether it all would be a success or a failure. Now they don't want to be cool any more, they want to take over.' " (Italics mine. The same tribute could be paid to any drunken driver.)

The theme of "taking over" is repeated again and again. The immediate target, apparently, is the take-over of the universities. *The N.Y. Times Magazine* article quotes one of the F.S.M. leaders: "Our idea is that the university is composed of faculty, students, books and ideas. In a literal sense, the administration is merely there to make sure the sidewalks are kept clean. It should be the servant of the faculty and the students."

The climax of this particular line was a news-story in *The N.Y. Times* (March 29, 1965) under the heading: "Collegians adopt a 'Bill of Rights.'"

"A group of Eastern college students declared here [in Philadelphia] this weekend that college administrators should be no more than housekeepers in the educational community.

"The modern college or university, they said, should be run by the students and the professors; administrators would be 'maintenance, clerical and safety personnel whose purpose is to enforce the will of faculty and students.'"

A manifesto to this effect was adopted at a meeting held at the University of Pennsylvania and attended by 200 youths "from 39 colleges in the Philadelphia and New York areas, Harvard, Yale, the University of California at Berkeley, and from schools in the Midwest."

"A recurring theme in the meeting was that colleges and universities had become servants of the 'financial, industrial, and military establishment,' and that students and faculty were being 'sold down the river' by administrators.

"Among the provisions of the manifesto were declarations of freedom to join, organize or hold meetings of any organization . . . abolition of tuition fees; control of law enforcement by the students and faculty; an end to the Reserve Officer Training Corps; abolition of loyalty oaths; student-faculty control over curriculum. . . ."

The method used to adopt that manifesto is illuminating: "About 200 students attended the meeting, 45 remaining until the end when the 'Student Bill of Rights' was adopted." So much for "democratic procedures" and for the activists' right to the title of spokesmen for American youth.

What significance is ascribed to the student rebellion by all these reports and by the authorities they choose to quote? Moral courage is not a characteristic of today's culture, but in no other contemporary issue has moral cowardice been revealed to such a naked, ugly extent. Not only do most of the commentators lack an independent evaluation of the events, not only do they take their cue from the rebels, but of all the rebels' complaints, it is the most superficial, irrelevant and, therefore, the *safest*, that they choose to support and to accept as the cause of the rebellion: the complaint that the universities have grown "too big."

As if they had mushroomed overnight, the "bigness" of the universities is suddenly decried by the consensus as a national problem and blamed for the "unrest" of the students, whose motives are hailed as youthful "idealism." In today's culture, it has always been safe to attack "bigness." And since the meaningless issue of mere *size* has long served as a means of evading real issues, on all sides of all political fences, a new catch phrase has been added to the list of "Big Business," "Big Labor," "Big Government," etc.: "Big University."

For a more sophisticated audience, the socialist magazine *The New Leader* (Dec. 21, 1964) offers a Marxist-Freudian appraisal, ascribing the rebellion primarily to "alienation" (quoting Savio: "Somehow people are being separated off from something") and to "generational revolt" ("Spontaneously the natural idiom of the student political protest was that of sexual protest against the forbidding university administrator who ruled *in loco parentis*").

But the prize for expressing the moral-intellectual essence of today's culture should go to Governor Brown of California. Remember that the University of California is a state institution, that its Regents are appointed by the Governor and that he, therefore, was the ultimate target of the revolt, including all its manifestations, from physical violence to filthy language.

"Have we made our society safe for students with ideas?" said Gov. Brown at a campus dinner. (*The N.Y. Times,* May 22, 1965.) "We have not. Students have changed but the structure of the university and its attitudes towards its students have not kept pace with that change.

"Therefore, some students felt they had the right to go outside the law to force the change. But in so doing, they displayed the height of *idealistic hypocrisy*. [Italics mine.] On the one hand, they held up the Federal Constitution, demanding their rights of political advocacy. But at the same time, they threw away the principle of due process in favor of direct action.

"In doing so, they were as wrong as the university. This, then, is the great challenge that faces us, the challenge of change."

Consider the fact that Gov. Brown is generally regarded as a powerful chief executive and, by California Republicans, as a formidable opponent. Consider the fact that "according to the California Public Opinion Poll, 74 per cent of the people disapprove of the student protest movement in Berkeley." (*The New Leader*, April 12, 1965.) Then observe that Gov. Brown did not dare denounce a movement led or manipulated by a group of 45 students—and that he felt obliged to qualify the term "hypocrisy" by the adjective "idealistic," thus creating one of the weirdest combinations in today's vocabulary of evasion.

Now observe that in all that mass of comments, appraisals and interpretations (including the ponderous survey in *Newsweek* which offered statistics on every imaginable aspect of college life) not one word was said about the *content* of modern education, about *the nature of the ideas* that are being inculcated by today's universities. Every possible question was raised and considered, except: *What are the students taught to think?* This, apparently, was what no one dared discuss.

This is what we shall discuss next month.

(To be completed in our next issue)

OBJECTIVIST CALENDAR

■ NBI's Tape Transcription Division has scheduled the following starting dates: "The Esthetics of the Visual Arts" in Los Angeles, July 7—"The Principles of Efficient Thinking" in Portland, July 8; Indianapolis, July 29—"Three Plays by Ayn Rand" in Pittsburgh, July 14; Dallas, July 17; Los Angeles, August 13. For details, contact NBI. —B.B.

Published monthly at 120 East 34th Street, New York, N.Y. 10016.
Subscription rate in United States, its possessions, Canada and Mexico: one year, $5; 2 years, $9; 3 years, $13. Other countries: one year, $6; 2 years, $11; 3 years, $16.
Additional copies of this Newsletter: single copy 50¢ (coins, not stamps); 10 — 99 copies, 25¢ each plus postage (for first-class delivery add 1¢ per copy, for third-class delivery add ½¢ per copy); 100 or more copies, 15¢ each plus postage (same as above). (Bulk rates apply only to multiple orders of a single issue.)
Please include zip code number with your address.
For change of address, send old and new address. Allow us three weeks to process new subscriptions and change of address.

Ayn Rand and Nathaniel Branden, Editors and Publishers
Barbara Branden, Managing Editor
Elayne Kalberman, Circulation Manager

THE OBJECTIVIST NEWSLETTER

Edited and Published by AYN RAND and NATHANIEL BRANDEN

VOL. 4 NO. 8   AUGUST, 1965

CHECK YOUR PREMISES

By AYN RAND

The Cashing-in: The Student "Rebellion"

(Part II of a three-part article)*

If a dramatist had the power to convert philosophical ideas into real, flesh-and-blood people and attempted to create the walking embodiments of modern philosophy—the result would be the Berkeley rebels.

These "activists" are so fully, literally, loyally, devastatingly the products of modern philosophy that someone should cry to all the university administrations and faculties: "Brothers, you asked for it!"

Mankind could not expect to remain unscathed after decades of exposure to the radiation of intellectual fission-debris, such as: "Reason is impotent to know things as they are—reality is unknowable—certainty is impossible—knowledge is mere probability—truth is that which works—mind is a superstition—logic is a social convention—ethics is a matter of subjective commitment to an arbitrary postulate"—and the consequent mutations are those contorted young creatures who scream, in chronic terror, that they know nothing and want to rule everything.

If that dramatist were writing a movie, he could justifiably entitle it "Mario Savio, Son of Immanuel Kant."

With rare and academically neglected exceptions, the philosophical "mainstream" that seeps into every classroom, subject and brain in today's universities, is: epistemological agnosticism, avowed irrationalism, ethical subjectivism. Our age is witnessing the ultimate climax, the cashing-in on a long process of destruction, at the end of the road laid out by Kant.

Ever since Kant divorced reason from reality, his intellectual descendants have been diligently widening the breach. In the name of reason, Pragmatism established a range-of-the-moment view as an enlightened perspective on life, context-dropping as a rule of epistemology, expediency as a principle of morality, and collective subjectivism as a substitute for metaphysics. Logical Positivism carried it farther and, in the name of reason, elevated the immemorial psycho-epistemology of shyster-lawyers to the status of a scientific epistemological system—by proclaiming that knowledge consists of linguistic manipulations. Taking this seriously, Linguistic Analysis declared that the task of philosophy is, not to identify universal principles, but to tell people what they mean when they speak, which they are otherwise unable to know (which last, by that time, was true—in philosophical circles). This was the final stroke of philosophy breaking its moorings and floating off, like a lighter-than-air balloon, losing any semblance of connection to reality, any relevance to the problems of man's existence.

(Correction: last month, we announced erroneously that this article consisted of two parts.)

No matter how cautiously the proponents of such theories skirted any reference to the relationship between theory and practice, no matter how coyly they struggled to treat philosophy as a parlor or classroom game—the fact remained that young people went to college for the purpose of acquiring *theoretical* knowledge to guide them in *practical* action. Philosophy teachers evaded questions about the application of their ideas to reality, by such means as declaring that "reality is a meaningless term," or by asserting that philosophy has no purpose other than the amusement of manufacturing arbitrary "constructs," or by urging students to temper every theory with "common sense"—the common sense they had spent countless hours trying to invalidate.

As a result, a student came out of a modern university with the following sediment left in his brain by his four to eight years of study: existence is an uncharted, unknowable jungle, fear and uncertainty are man's permanent state, skepticism is the mark of maturity, cynicism is the mark of realism and, above all, the hallmark of an intellectual is the denial of the intellect.

When and if academic commentators gave any thought to the practical results of their theories, they were predominantly united in claiming that uncertainty and skepticism are socially valuable traits which would lead to tolerance of differences, flexibility, social "adjustment" and willingness to compromise. Some went so far as to maintain explicitly that intellectual certainty is the mark of a dictatorial mentality, and that chronic *doubt*—the absence of firm convictions, the lack of absolutes—is the guarantee of a peaceful, "democratic" society.

They miscalculated.

It has been said that Kant's dichotomy led to two lines of Kantian philosophers, both accepting his basic premises, but choosing opposite sides: those who chose reason, abandoning reality—and those who chose reality, abandoning reason. The first delivered the world to the second.

The collector of the Kantian rationalizers' efforts—the receiver of the bankrupt shambles of sophistry, casuistry, sterility and abysmal triviality to which they had reduced philosophy—was *Existentialism*.

Existentialism, in essence, consists of pointing to modern philosophy and declaring: "Since *this* is reason, to hell with it!"

In spite of the fact that the pragmatists-positivists-analysts had obliterated reason, the existentialists accepted them as reason's advocates, held them up to the world as examples of rationality and proceeded to reject reason altogether, proclaiming its impotence, rebelling against its "failure," calling for a return to reality, to the problems of human existence, to values, to action—to subjective values and mindless action. In the name of reality, they proclaimed the moral supremacy of "instincts," urges, feelings—and the cognitive powers of stomachs, muscles, kidneys, hearts, blood. It was a rebellion of headless bodies.

The battle is not over. The philosophy departments of today's universities are the battleground of a struggle which, in fact, is only a family quarrel between the analysts and the existentialists. Their progeny are the activists of the student rebellion.

If these activists choose the policy of "doing and then reflecting on your doing"—hasn't Pragmatism taught them that truth is to be judged by consequences? If they "seem unable to formulate or sustain a systematized political theory of society," yet shriek with moral righteousness that they propose to achieve their social goals by physical force—hasn't Logical Positivism taught them that ethical propositions have no cognitive meaning and are merely a report on one's feelings or the equivalent of emotional ejaculations? If they are savagely blind to everything but the immediate moment—hasn't Logical Positivism taught them that nothing else can be claimed with certainty to exist? And while the Linguistic Analysts are busy demonstrating that "The cat is on the mat" does *not* mean that "the mat" is an attribute of "the cat," nor that "on-the-mat" is the genus to which "the cat" belongs, nor yet that "the-cat" equals "on-the-mat"—is it any wonder that students storm the Berkeley campus with placards inscribed "Strike now, analyze later"? (This slogan is quoted by Professor Petersen in the *Columbia University Forum*.)

On June 14, CBS televised a jumbled, incoherent, unintelligible—and for these very reasons, authentic and significant—documentary entitled "The Berkeley Story." There is method in every kind of madness—and for those acquainted with modern philosophy, that documentary was like a display of sideshow mirrors throwing off twisted reflections and random echoes of the carnage perpetrated in the academic torture-chambers of the mind.

"Our generation has no ideology," declared the first boy interviewed, in the tone of defiance and hatred once reserved for saying: "Down with Wall Street!"—clearly projecting that the enemy now is not the "Robber Barons," but *the mind*. The older generation, he explained scornfully, had "a neat little pill" to solve everything, but the pill didn't work and they merely "got their hearts busted." "We don't believe in pills," he said.

"We've learned that there are no absolute rules," said a young girl, hastily and defensively, as if uttering an axiom—and proceeded to explain inarticulately, with the help of gestures pointing inward, that "we make rules for ourselves" and that what is right for *her* may not be right for others.

A girl described her classes as "words, words, words, paper, paper, paper"—and quietly, in a tone of authentic despair, said that she stopped at times to wonder: "What am I doing here? I'm not learning anything."

An intense young girl who talked volubly, never quite finishing a sentence nor making a point, was denouncing society in general, trying to say that since people are social products, society has done a bad job. In the middle of a sentence, she stopped and threw in, as a casual aside: "Whatever way I turn out, I still am a product," then went on. She said it with the simple earnestness of a conscientious child acknowledging a self-evident fact of nature. It was not an act: the poor little creature meant it.

The helpless bewilderment on the face of Harry Reasoner, the commentator, when he tried to sum up what he had presented, was an eloquent indication of why the press is unable properly to handle the student rebellion. "Now—immediacy—any situation must be solved *now*," he said incredulously, describing the rebels' attitude, neither praising nor blaming, in the faintly astonished, faintly helpless tone of a man unable to believe that he is seeing savages running loose on the campus of one of America's great universities.

Such are the products of modern philosophy. They are the type of students who are too intelligent not to see the logical consequences of the theories they have been taught—but not intelligent nor independent enough to see through the theories and reject them.

So they scream their defiance against "The System," not realizing that they are its most consistently docile pupils, that theirs is a rebellion against the *status-quo* by its archetypes, against the intellectual "Establishment" by its robots who have swallowed every shopworn premise of the "liberals" of the 1930's, including the catchphrases of altruism, the dedication to "deprived people," to such a safely *conventional* cause as "the war on poverty." A rebellion that brandishes banners inscribed with bromides is not a very convincing nor very inspiring sight.

As in any movement, there is obviously a mixture of motives involved: there are the little shysters of the intellect who have found a gold mine in modern philosophy, who delight in arguing for argument's sake and stumping opponents by means of ready-to-wear paradoxes—there are the little role-players who fancy themselves as heroes and enjoy defiance for the sake of defiance—there are the nihilists who, moved by a profound hatred, seek nothing but destruction for the sake of destruction—there are the hopeless dependents who seek to "belong" to any crowd that would have them—and there are the plain hooligans who are always there, on the fringes of any mob action that smells of trouble. Whatever the combination of motives, *neurosis* is stamped in capital letters across the whole movement, since there is no such thing as rejecting reason through an innocent error of knowledge. But whether the theories of modern philosophy serve merely as a screen, a defense-mechanism, a rationalization of neurosis or are, in part, its cause—the fact remains that modern philosophy has destroyed the best in these students and fostered the worst.

Young people do seek a comprehensive view of life, *i.e.*, a philosophy, they do seek meaning, purpose, ideals—and most of them take what they get. It is in their teens and early twenties that most people seek philosophical answers and set their premises, for good or evil, for the rest of their lives. Some never reach that stage; some never give up the quest; but the majority are open to the voice of philosophy for a few brief years. These last are the permanent, if not innocent, victims of modern philosophy.

They are not independent thinkers nor intellectual originators; they are unable to answer or withstand the flood of modern sophistries. So some of them give up, after one or two unintelligible courses, convinced that thinking is a waste of time—and turn into lethargic cynics or stultified Babbitts by the time they reach twenty-five. Others accept what they hear; they accept it blindly and *literally;* these are today's activists. And no matter what tangle of motives now moves them, every teacher of modern philosophy should cringe in their presence, if he is still open to the realization that it is by means of the best within them, by means of their twisted, precarious groping for ideas, that he has turned them into grotesque little monstrosities.

Now what happens to the better minds in modern universities, to the students of above average intelligence who are actually eager to learn? What they find and have to endure is a long, slow process of psycho-epistemological torture.

Directly or indirectly, the influence of philosophy sets the epistemological standards and methods of teaching for all departments, in the physical sciences as well as in the humanities. The consequence, today, is a chaos of subjective whims setting the criteria of logic, of communication, demonstration, evidence, proof, which differ from class to class, from teacher to teacher. I am not speaking of a difference in viewpoint or content, but of the absence of *basic epistemological principles* and the consequent difference in the method of functioning required of a student's mind. It is as if each course were given in a different language, each requiring that one *think* exclusively in that language, none providing a dictionary. The result—to the extent that one would attempt to comply—is intellectual disintegration.

Add to this: the opposition to "system-building," *i.e.*, to the integration of knowledge, with the result that the material taught in one class contradicts the material taught in the others, each subject hanging in a vacuum and to be accepted out of context, while any questions on how to integrate it are rejected, discredited and discouraged.

Add to this: the arbitrary, senseless, haphazard conglomeration of most curricula, the absence of any hierarchical structure of knowledge, any order, continuity or rationale—the jumble of courses on out-of-context minutiae and out-of-focus surveys—the all-pervading unintelligibility—the arrogantly self-confessed irrationality—and, consequently, the necessity to memorize, rather than learn, to recite, rather than understand, to hold in one's mind a cacophony of undefined jargon long enough to pass the next exam.

Add to this: the professors who refuse to answer questions—the professors who answer by evasion and ridicule—the professors who turn their classes into bull-sessions on the premise that "we're here to mull things over together"—the professors who *do* lecture, but, in the name of "anti-dogmatism," take no stand, express no viewpoint and leave the students in a maze of contradictions with no lead to a solution—the professors who *do* take a stand and invite the students' comments, then penalize dissenters by means of lower grades (particularly in political courses).

Add to this: the moral cowardice of most university administrations, the policy of permanent moral neutrality, of compromising on anything, of evading any conflict at any price—and the students' knowledge that the worst classroom injustice will remain uncorrected, that no appeal is practicable and no justice is to be found anywhere.

Yes, of course, there are exceptions—there *are* competent educators, brilliant minds and rational men on the university staffs—but they are swallowed in the rampaging "mainstream" of irrationality and, too often, defeated by the hopeless pessimism of bitter, long-repressed frustration.

(Continued on page 38)

Alienation

By NATHANIEL BRANDEN

(Part II of a three-part article)

Every society, as a system of human relationships, may be evaluated by how well it satisfies man's basic psychological needs, says Fromm—*i.e.*, he explains, by the possibilities for love, relatedness and the experience of personal identity which it offers man.

Capitalism, Fromm declares, has been disastrous in this regard: far from solving the problem of man's alienation, it worsens it immeasurably in many respects. In liberating man from medieval regulation and authority, in breaking the chains of ecclesiastical, economic and social tyranny, in destroying the "stability" of the feudal order, capitalism and individualism thrust upon man an unprecedented freedom that was "bound to create a deep feeling of insecurity, powerlessness, doubt, aloneness and anxiety." (*Escape from Freedom*, New York: Rinehart, 1941, p. 63.)

Scratch a collectivist and you will usually find a medievalist. Fromm is not an exception. Like so many socialists, he is a glamorizer of the Middle Ages. He perfunctorily acknowledges the faults of that historical period—but in contrasting it with the capitalism that succeeded it, he is enchanted by what he regards as its virtues.

"What characterizes medieval in contrast to modern society is its lack of individual freedom.... But although a person was not free in the modern sense, neither was he alone and isolated. In having a distinct, unchangeable, and unquestionable place in the social world from the moment of birth, man was rooted in a structuralized whole, and thus life had a meaning which left no place, and no need, for doubt. A person was identical with his role in society; he *was* a peasant, an artisan, a knight, and not *an individual* who *happened* to have this or that occupation. The social order was conceived as a natural order, and being a definite part of it gave man a feeling of security and of belonging. There was comparatively little competition. One was born into a certain economic position which guaranteed a livelihood determined by tradition, just as it carried economic obligations to those higher in the social hierarchy. But within the limits of his social sphere the individual actually had much freedom to express his self in his work and in his emotional life. Although there was no individualism in the modern sense of the unrestricted choice between many possible ways of life (a freedom of choice which is largely abstract), there was a great deal of *concrete individualism in real life*." (*Escape from Freedom*, pp. 41, 42.)

It is not uncommon to encounter this sort of perspective on the Middle Ages, among writers on alienation. But what makes the above passage especially shocking and offensive, in the case of Fromm, is that he repeatedly professes to be a lover of freedom and a valuer of human life.

The complete lack of control over any aspect of one's existence, the ruthless suppression of intellectual freedom, the paralyzing restrictions on any form of individual initiative and independence—these are cardinal characteristics of the Middle Ages. But all of this is swept aside by Fromm—along with the famines, the plagues, the exhausting labor from sunrise to sunset, the suffocating routine, the superstitious terror, the attacks of mass-hysteria afflicting entire towns, the nightmare brutality of men's dealings with one another, the use of legalized torture as a normal way of life—all of this is swept aside, so entranced is Fromm by the vision of a world in which men did not have to invent and compete, they had only to submit and obey.

Nowhere does he tell us what specifically the medieval man's *"concrete individualism"* consisted of. One is morbidly curious to know what he would say.

With the collapse of medievalism and the emergence of a free market society, Fromm declares, man was compelled to assume total responsibility for his own survival: he had to produce and to trade—he had to think and to judge—he had no authority to guide him, and nothing but his own ability to keep him in existence. No longer could he, by virtue of the class into which he was born, *inherit* his sense of personal identity: henceforward, he had to *achieve* it. This posed a devastating psychological problem for man, intensifying his basic feeling of isolation and separateness.

"It is true," Fromm remarks, "that the capitalistic mode of production is conducive to political freedom, while any centrally planned social order is in danger of leading to political regimentation and eventually to dictatorship." (*The Sane Society*, p. 138.) Capitalism, he further concedes, has proven itself superlatively capable of producing goods and of raising men's material standard of living to undreamed-of heights. But a "sane society" must have more to offer man than political freedom and material well-being. Capitalism, Fromm insists, is destructive of man's *spirit*. He offers several reasons for this charge, which are very revealing.

(1) Like Marx, Fromm decries the humiliating predicament of the worker who has to *sell* his *services*. Capitalism condemns the worker to experience himself, not as a man, but as a commodity, as a thing to be traded. Furthermore, since he is only a tiny part of a vast production process, since, for example, he does not build an entire automobile himself (and then drive home in it), but builds only a small part of it (the total being subsequently sold to some unknown, distant party), the worker feels alienated from the product of his own labor and, therefore, feels alienated from his own labor as such—unlike the artisan of the Middle Ages, whose labor could express the "full richness" of his personality.

It is an elementary fact of economics that specialization and exchange, under a division of labor, make a level of productivity possible which otherwise would not be remotely attainable. In pre-capitalist centuries, when a man's economic well-being was limited by the goods he himself could produce with his own primitive tools, an unconscionable amount of labor was required to make or acquire the simplest necessities—and the general standard of living was appallingly low: human existence was a continual, exhausting struggle against imminent starvation. About half of the children born, perished before the age of ten. But with the development of the wages system under capitalism, the introduction of machinery and the opportunity for a man to sell his labor, life (to say nothing of an ever-increasing standard of material well-being) was made possible for millions who could have had no chance at survival in pre-capitalist economies. However, for Fromm and those who share his viewpoint, these considerations are, doubtless, too "materialistic." To offer men a chance to enjoy an unprecedented material well-being, is, evidently, to sentence them to alienation; whereas to hold them down to the stagnant level of a medieval serf or guildsman, is to offer them spiritual fulfillment.

(2) Fromm decries the "anonymity of the social forces ... inherent in the structure of the capitalistic mode of production." (p. 138.) The laws of the market, of supply and demand, of economic cause and effect, are ominously impersonal: no single individual's *wishes* control them. Is it the worker who determines how much he is to be paid? No. It is not even the employer. It is that faceless monster, the market. *It* determines the wage level in some manner beyond the worker's power to grasp. As for the capitalist, his position is scarcely better: he, too, is helpless. "The individual capitalist expands his enterprise not primarily because he *wants* to, but because he *has* to, because ... postponement of further expansion would mean regression." (p. 86.) If he attempts to stagnate, he will go out of business. Under such a system, asks Fromm, how can man *not* feel alienated?

Consider what Fromm is denouncing. Under capitalism, the wages paid to a man for his work are determined *objectively*—by the law of supply and demand. The market—reflecting the voluntary judgments of all those who participate in it, all those who buy and sell, produce and consume, offer or seek employment—establishes the general price level of goods and services. This is the context which men are obliged to consider in setting the prices they will ask for their work or offer for the work of others; if a man demands more than the market value of his work, he will remain unemployed; if a particular employer offers him less than the market value of his work, the man will seek—and find—employment elsewhere. The same principle applies to the capitalist who offers his goods for sale. If the prices and quality of his goods are comparable or superior to those of other men in the same field of production, he will be able to compete; if others can do better than he can, if they can offer superior goods and/or lower prices, he will be obliged to improve, to grow, to equal their achievement, or else he will lose his customers. The standard determining a producer's success or failure is the *objective* value of his product—as judged, within the context of the market (and of their knowledge), by those to whom he offers his product. This is the only rational and just principle of exchange. But *this* is what Fromm considers evil.

What he rebels against is *objectivity*. How—he demands—can a man not feel alienated in a system where his wishes are not omnipotent, where the unearned is not to be had, where growth is rewarded and stagnation is penalized?

It is clear from the foregoing that Fromm's basic quarrel is with *reality*—since nature confronts man with the identical conditions, which a free economy merely reflects: nature, too, holds man to the law of cause and effect; nature, too, makes constant growth a condition of successful life.

There are writers on alienation who recognize this and do not bother to center their attacks on capitalism: they damn nature outright. They declare that man's life is intrinsically and inescapably *tragic*—since reality is "tyrannical," since contradictory desires cannot be satisfied, since objectivity is a "prison," since time is a "net" that no one can elude, etc. Existentialists, in particular, specialize in this sort of pronouncement.

(3) As *consumer* in a capitalist economy, Fromm contends, man is subject to further alienating pressures. He is overwhelmed with innumerable products among which he must choose. He is bewildered and brainwashed by the blandishments of advertisers, forever urging him to buy their wares. This staggering multiplicity of possible choices is threatening to his sanity. Moreover, he is "conditioned" to consume for the sake of consuming—to long for an ever-higher standard of living—merely in order to keep the "system" going. With automatic washing-machines, automatic cameras and automatic can-openers, modern man's relationship to nature becomes more and more remote. He is increasingly condemned to the nightmare of an *artificial* world.

No such problem confronted the feudal serf.

This much is true: sleeping on an earthern floor, the medieval serf—to say nothing of the caveman—was much *closer* to nature, in one uncomfortable and unhygienic sense of the word.

The above criticism of capitalism has become very fashionable among social commentators. What is remarkable is that almost invariably, as in the case of Fromm, the criticism is made by the same writers who are loudest in crying that man needs more *leisure*. Yet the purpose of the "gadgets" they condemn is, specifically, to liberate man's time. Thus they wish to provide man with more leisure, while damning the material means that make leisure possible.

As for the charge—equally popular—that the multiplicity of choices offered to man in capitalistic society is threatening to his mental equilibrium, it should be remembered that *fear* of choices and decisions is a basic symptom of mental illness. To whose mentality, then, do these critics of capitalism demand that society be adjusted?

(4) The development of a complex, highly industrialized society requires an extreme degree of quantification and abstraction in men's method of thinking, observes Fromm—and this, in still another way, estranges man from the world around him: he loses the ability to relate to things "in their concreteness and uniqueness." (p. 114.)

One can agree with Fromm in part: an industrial technological society demands the fullest development and exercise of man's *conceptual* faculty, *i.e.*, of his distinctively *human* form of cognition. The *sensory-perceptual* level of consciousness—the level of an animal's cognition—will not do.

Those who assert that the conceptual level of consciousness alienates man from the real world, merely confess that their concepts bear no relation to reality—or that they do not understand the relation of concepts to reality. But it should be remembered that the capacity to abstract and conceptualize offers man—to the extent that he is rational—a means of "relating" to the world around him immeasurably superior to that enjoyed by any other species. It does not "alienate" man from nature, it makes him nature's master: an animal obeys nature *blindly;* man obeys her *intelligently*—and thereby acquires the power to command her.

(5) Finally, and most alienating of all, perhaps, are the sort of relationships that exist among men under capitalism, says Fromm. "What is the modern man's *relationship to his fellow man?* It is one between two abstractions, two living machines who use one another. The employer uses the ones whom he employs; the salesman uses his customers.... There is not much love or hate to be found in human relations of our day. There is, rather, a superficial friendliness, and a more than superficial fairness, but behind that surface is distance and indifference.... The alienation between man and man results in the loss of those general and social bonds which characterize medieval as well as most other precapitalist societies." (p. 139.)

Fromm is claiming that there existed, in pre-capitalist societies, a mutual good will among men, an attitude of respect and benevolent solidarity, a regard for the value of the human person, that vanished with the rise of a free market society. This is worse than false. The claim is absurd historically and disgraceful morally.

It is notorious that, in the Middle Ages, human relationships were characterized by mutual suspiciousness, hostility and cruelty: everyone regarded his neighbor as a potential threat; and nothing was held more cheaply than human life. Such invariably is the case in *any* society where men are ruled by brute force. In putting an end to slavery and serfdom, capitalism introduced a social benevolence that would have been impossible under earlier systems. Capitalism valued a man's life as it had never been valued before. Capitalism is the politico-economic expression of the principle that a man's life, freedom and happiness are his by moral right.

There is a passage in *The Fountainhead* that bears on this issue. "Civilization is the progress toward a society of privacy. The savage's whole existence is public, ruled by the laws of his tribe. Civilization is the process of setting man free from men."

Under capitalism, men are free to *choose* their "social bonds" —meaning: to choose whom they will associate with. Men are not trapped within the prison of their family, tribe, caste, class or neighborhood. They choose whom they will value, whom they will befriend, whom they will deal with, what kind of relationships they will enter. This implies and entails man's responsibility to form independent value-judgments. It implies and entails, also, that a man must *earn* the social relationships he desires. But this, clearly, is anathema to Fromm.

"Love," he has told us, "is the only sane and satisfactory answer to the problem of human existence"—but, he asserts, love and capitalism are *inimical*. "The *principle* underlying capitalistic society and the *principle* of love are incompatible." (*The Art of Loving,* p. 131.) The principle of capitalism, says Fromm, is that of "fairness ethics," of *trade*, of the exchange of values, without recourse to force or fraud; individuals deal with one another only on the premise of mutual self-interest; they engage only in those transactions from which they expect a profit, reward or gain. "It may even be said that the development of fairness ethics is the particular ethical contribution of capitalist society." (p. 129.)

But to approach love with any concern for one's self-interest is—he asserts—to negate the very essence of love. To love an individual is to feel care and responsibility for him; it is not to appraise his character or personality as a "commodity" from which one expects pleasure. To love "ideally" is to love "unconditionally"—it is to love a human being, not for the fact of *what* he is, but for the fact *that* he is—it is to love without reference to values or standards or judgment. "In essence, all human beings are identical. We are all part of One, we are One. This being so, it should not make any difference whom we love." (p. 55.)

It should not, in other words, make any difference whether the person we love is a being of stature or a total nonentity, a genius or a fool, a hero or a scoundrel. "We are all part of One." Is it necessary to point out who stands to gain and who to lose by this view of love?

The desire to be loved "unconditionally," the desire to be loved with no concern for his objective personal worth, is one of man's "deepest longings," Fromm insists; whereas to be loved on the basis of *merit*, "because one deserves it," invokes doubt and uncertainty, since merit has to be struggled for and since such love can be withdrawn should the merit cease to exist. "Furthermore, 'deserved' love easily leaves a bitter feeling that one is not loved for oneself, that one is loved *only* because one pleases..." (p. 42.)

It is typical of Fromm that he should deliver what is in fact (though not in Fromm's estimate) a deadly insult to human nature, without offering any justification for his charge. He assumes that all men, by nature, are so profoundly lacking in self-esteem that they crave a love which bears no relation to their actions, achievements or character, a love not to be earned but to be received only as a free gift.

What does it mean to be loved "for oneself?" In reason, it can mean only: to be loved for the values one has achieved in one's character and person. The highest compliment one can be paid by another human being is to be told: "Because of what you are, you are essential to my happiness." But this is the love that, according to Fromm, leaves one with "a bitter feeling."

It is the capitalistic culture, he declares, that inculcates such concepts as the "deserved" and the "undeserved"—the earned and the unearned—and thus poisons the growth of proper love. Proper love, Fromm tells us, should be given solely out of the richness of the spirit of the giver, in demonstration of the giver's "potency." Fromm nowhere reveals the exact nature of this "potency," of course. "Love is an act of faith..." (p. 128.) Proper love should raise no questions about the virtue or character of its object; it should desire no joy from such virtue as the object might possess—for, if it does, it is not proper love, it is only capitalistic selfishness.

But, Fromm asks, "how can one act within the framework of existing society and at the same time practice love?" (pp. 130, 131.) He does not declare that love is *impossible* under capitalism—merely that it is exceptionally difficult.

Commenting, in *Who is Ayn Rand?*, on Fromm's theory of love, I wrote: "To love... is to *value;* love, properly, is the consequence and expression of admiration—'the emotional price paid by one man for the joy he receives from the virtues of another.' [*Atlas Shrugged*] Love is not alms, but a moral tribute.

"If love did *not* imply admiration, if it did not imply an acknowledgement of moral qualities that the recipient of love possessed—what meaning or significance would love have, and why would Fromm or anyone consider it desirable? Only one answer is possible, and it is not an attractive one: when love is divorced from values, then 'love' becomes, not a tribute, but a moral blank check: a promise that one will be forgiven anything, that one will not be abandoned, that one will be taken care of."

This view of love is not, of course, peculiar to Fromm; it is a central component of the mystic-altruist tradition—and is as prevalent among psychologists, sociologists and philosophers as it is among religionists. Perhaps the simplest and most eloquent answer to this view of love is one sentence of John Galt in *Atlas Shrugged:* "A morality that professes the belief that the values of the spirit are more precious than matter, a morality that teaches you to scorn a whore who gives her body indiscriminately to all men—this same morality demands that you surrender your soul to promiscuous love for all comers."

To divorce love from values (and value-judgments), is to confess one's longing for the unearned. The idealization of this longing as a proper moral goal is a constant theme running through Fromm's writing.

That the underlying motive is the desire to be taken care of, the desire to be spared the responsibility of independence, is revealed explicitly in Fromm's socio-political "solution" to the problem of alienation.

In order that man may be enabled to conquer his feeling of aloneness and alienation, to practice love and to achieve a full sense of personal identity, a new social system must be established, Fromm declares.

Private ownership of the means of production must be abolished. The profit motive must be forbidden. Industry must be de-centralized. Society should be divided into self-governing industrial guilds; factories should be owned and run by all those who work in them.

Why—according to Fromm's social philosophy—should a janitor in an industrial plant not have the same right to determine its management as the man who happened to create the plant? Does not the personality of the janitor require as much self-expression as anyone else's?

Under capitalism, says Fromm, men are overwhelmed by and are the pawns of a complex industrial machine whose omnipotent forces and laws are beyond their comprehension or control. Under the de-centralized, "democratic" system he proposes—which is some sort of blend of Guild Socialism and Syndicalism—industrial establishments will be broken down into units whose function is within everyone's easy comprehension, with no "alienating" demands made on anyone's abstract capacity.

Under this system, he explains, every person will be provided with his minimum subsistence, whether the person wishes to work or not. This is necessary if man is to develop healthily and happily. However, to discourage parasitism, Fromm suggests that this support should not extend beyond two years. Who is to provide this support, whether they will be willing to do so, and what will happen if they are not willing, are questions Fromm does not discuss.

So long as men are occupied with the problem of survival, Fromm feels, their spiritual concerns—the concerns that really *matter*—are almost inevitably neglected. How can the worker's personality not be impoverished, if he must face daily the necessity of earning a livelihood? How can the businessman develop his creative potentialities, if he is in bondage to his obsession with production? How can the artist preserve his soul's integrity, if he is plagued with temptations by Hollywood and Madison Avenue? How can the consumer cultivate individual tastes and preferences, if he is surrounded by the standardized commodities begotten by mass production?

If one wishes to understand the relevance of epistemology to politics, one should observe what is gained for Fromm by that "paradoxical logic" of which he writes so approvingly. If, as it teaches, "man can perceive reality only in contradictions," then Fromm does not have to be troubled by the conflict between his claim to be an advocate of reason and his enthusiasm for Eastern mysticism—nor does he have to be troubled by the conflict between his claim to be a defender of individualism and his advocacy of political collectivism. His disdain for the law of contradiction permits him to announce that true individualism is possible only in the collectivized community—that true freedom is possible only when production is taken out of the hands of private individuals and placed under the absolute control of the group—that men will cease to be objects of "use" by others, only when they are willing to renounce personal profit and make *social usefulness* the goal of their lives. (For the most detailed presentation of these doctrines, see *The Sane Society*.)

Fromm calls his proposed system "Humanistic Communitarian Socialism." Under it, he maintains, man will achieve "a new harmony with nature" to replace the one he has lost—man will enjoy the tranquillity and self-fulfillment of the animals whose state Fromm finds so enviable.

If, often, Fromm is more than a little disingenuous in the presentation of his views, he is, nonetheless, extremely *explicit*. This is what is unusual about him. Most writers of his persuasion twist themselves for pages and pages in order to obscure their advocacy of the ideas—and contradictions—which he announces openly. With rare exceptions, one will find comparable candor only among the Existentialists and Zen Buddhists, many of whose premises Fromm shares.

His explicitness notwithstanding, he is very representative culturally and should be recognized as such. The recurrent themes running through the literature on alienation — and through today's social commentary generally—are the themes which Fromm brings into naked focus: that reason is "unnatural," that a noncontradictory, objective reality "restricts" one's individuality, that the necessity of *choice* is an awesome burden, that it is "tragic" not to be able to eat one's cake and have it, too, that self-responsibility is frightening, that the achievement of personal identity is a *social* problem — that "love" is the omnipotent solution—and that the political implementation of this solution is socialism.

The transparent absurdity or the unintelligibility of most discussions of alienation might tempt one to believe that the issue is entirely illusory. But this would be an error. Although the explanations offered for it are spurious, the problem of alienation is real. A great many men do recognize the painful emotional state which writers on alienation describe. A great many men do lack a sense of personal identity. A great many men do feel themselves to be strangers and afraid in a world they never made.

But *why*? What *is* the problem of alienation? What *is* personal identity? Why should so many men experience the task of achieving it as a dreaded burden? And what is the significance of the attacks on capitalism in connection with this issue? These are the questions we must proceed to answer.

(To be completed in our next issue)

The Cashing-in: The Student "Rebellion" *(from page 34)*

And further: most professors and administrators are much more competent and rational as individuals than they are in their collective performance. Most of them realize and, privately, complain about the evils of today's educational world. But each of them feels individually impotent before the enormity of the problem. So they blame it on some nameless, disembodied, almost mystical power, which they designate as "The System"—and too many of them take it to be a *political* system, specifically *capitalism*. They do not realize that there is only one human discipline which enables men to deal with large-scale problems, which has the power to integrate and unify human activities—and that that discipline is *philosophy*, which they have set, instead, to the task of disintegrating and destroying their work.

What does all this do to the best minds among the students? Most of them endure their college years with the teeth-clenched determination of serving out a jail sentence. The psychological scars they acquire in the process are incalculable. But they struggle as best they can to preserve their capacity to think, sensing dimly that the essence of the torture is an assault on their mind. And what they feel toward their schools ranges from mistrust to resentment to contempt to hatred—intertwined with a sense of exhaustion and excruciating boredom.

To various extents and various degrees of conscious awareness, these feelings are shared by the entire pyramid of the student body, from intellectual top to bottom. *This* is the reason why the handful of Berkeley rebels was able to attract thousands of students who did not realize, at first, the nature of what they were joining and who withdrew when it became apparent. Those students were moved by a desperate, incoherent frustration, by a need to protest, not knowing fully against what, by a blind desire to strike out at the university somehow.

I asked a small group of intelligent students at one of New York's best universities—who were ideologically opposed to the rebels—whether they would fight for the university administration, if the rebellion came to their campus. All of them shook their heads, with faint, wise, bitter smiles.

The philosophical impotence of the older generation is the reason why the adult authorities—from the Berkeley administration to the social commentators to the press to Gov. Brown—were unable to take a firm stand and had no rational answer to the Berkeley rebellion. Granting the premises of modern philosophy, logic was on the side of the rebels. To answer them would require a *total* philosophical re-evaluation, down to basic premises—which none of those adults would dare attempt.

Hence the incredible spectacle of brute force, hoodlum tactics and militantly explicit irrationality being brought to a university campus—and being met by the vague, uncertain, apologetic concessions, the stale generalities, the evasive platitudes of the alleged defenders of academic law and order.

In a civilized society, a student's declaration that he rejects reason and proposes to act outside the bounds of rationality, would be taken as sufficient grounds for immediate expulsion—let alone if he proceeded to engage in mob action and physical violence on a university campus. But modern universities have long since lost the moral right to oppose the first—and are, therefore, impotent against the second.

The student rebellion is an eloquent demonstration of the fact that when men abandon reason, they open the door to physical force as the only alternative and the inevitable consequence.

The rebellion is also one of the clearest refutations of the argument of those intellectuals who claimed that skepticism and chronic doubt would lead to social harmony. "When men reduce their virtues to the approximate, then evil acquires the force of an absolute, when loyalty to an unyielding purpose is dropped by the virtuous, it's picked up by scoundrels—and you get the indecent spectacle of a cringing, bargaining, traitorous good and a self-righteously uncompromising evil." *(Atlas Shrugged)*

Who stands to profit by that rebellion? The answer lies in the nature and goals of its leadership, which we shall examine next month.

(To be completed in our next issue)

From the "Horror File"

"When you listen to the conversation of nervous, depressed, unhappy people, it cannot help striking you how often you hear the pronoun 'I' and 'me'. . .

"But when you listen to the conversation of happy, hearty, self-confident people, you rarely hear the pronoun 'I' and 'me.' They're too busy about their work, too much interested in other people to be fussing about themselves.

"It's a basic principle of mental health that the unwholesome personality integrates around the self; the wholesome personality around his life task, serving other people.

"As we truly mature we accept the message of the great religious sages that the self is a burden and the less attention paid to it the better. . . .

"As we absorb ourselves in our life task, especially if it is in the service of other people, we escape much of the evil of life simply by having no mind for it. . . .

"Children are naturally selfish and can only gradually be weaned from self-centeredness. A child has to be selfish before he can learn to be unselfish. But in time he can grow up to this if tactfully, lovingly directed.

"Meantime don't indulge your children—as so many present-day parents do—with an excess of luxuries and comforts. Let 'em live lean and they'll grow up strong." Dr. David Goodman, "Don't Pamper Your Children," a newspaper column. (This clipping was sent to us by a reader who did not supply the name and date of the newspaper.)

"The New Fascism: Rule by Consensus," a lecture delivered by Ayn Rand and recorded at the Ford Hall Forum, Boston, on April 18, 1965, is now available on a single LP record. This record will be of special interest to college discussion groups and political clubs. May be purchased from NBI BOOK SERVICE, 120 East 34th Street, New York, New York 10016; price: $3.75.

OBJECTIVIST CALENDAR

■ NBI's Tape Transcription Division has scheduled the following starting dates: "Three Plays by Ayn Rand" in Los Angeles, August 13; "Basic Principles of Objectivist Psychology" in Detroit, August 20; "Basic Principles of Objectivism" in Kwajalein (Marshall Islands), August 31. For details, contact NBI.

Published monthly at 120 East 34th Street, New York, N.Y. 10016.

Subscription rate in United States, its possessions, Canada and Mexico: one year, $5; 2 years, $9; 3 years, $13. Other countries: one year, $6; 2 years, $11; 3 years, $16.

Additional copies of this Newsletter: single copy 50¢ (coins, not stamps); 10 – 99 copies, 25¢ each plus postage (for first-class delivery add 1¢ per copy for third-class delivery add ½¢ per copy); 100 or more copies, 15¢ each plus postage (same as above). (Bulk rates apply only to multiple orders of a single issue.)

Please include zip code number with your address.

For change of address, send old and new address. Allow us three weeks to process new subscriptions and change of address.

Ayn Rand and Nathaniel Branden, Editors and Publishers
Barbara Branden, Managing Editor
Elayne Kalberman, Circulation Manager

THE OBJECTIVIST NEWSLETTER

Edited and Published by AYN RAND and NATHANIEL BRANDEN

VOL. 4 NO. 9   SEPTEMBER, 1965

CHECK YOUR PREMISES
By AYN RAND

The Cashing-in: The Student "Rebellion"

(Part III of a three-part article)

If the rank-and-file of the college rebels are victims, at least in part, this cannot be said of their leaders. Who are their leaders? Any and all of the statist-collectivist groups that hover, like vultures, over the remnants of capitalism, hoping to pounce on the carcass—and to accelerate the end, whenever possible. Their minimal goal is just "to make trouble"—to undercut, to confuse, to demoralize, to destroy. Their ultimate goal is to take over.

To such leadership, the college rebels are merely cannon-fodder, intended to stick their headless necks out, to fight on campuses, to go to jail, to lose their careers and their future—and eventually, if the leadership succeeds, to fight in the streets and lose their "non-absolute" lives, paving the way for the absolute dictatorship of whoever is the bloodiest among the thugs scrambling for power. Young fools who refuse to look beyond the immediate *"now,"* have no way of knowing whose long-range goals they are serving.

The communists are involved, among others; but, like the others, they are merely the manipulators, not the cause, of the student rebellion. This is an example of the fact that whenever they win, they win by default—like germs feeding on the sores of a disintegrating body. They did not create the conditions that are destroying American universities—they did not create the hordes of embittered, aimless, neurotic teen-agers—but they *do* know how to attack through the sores which their opponents insist on evading. They are professional ideologists and it is not difficult for them to move into an intellectual vacuum and to hang the cringing advocates of "anti-ideology" by their own contradictions.

For its motley leftist leadership, the student rebellion is a trial balloon, a kind of cultural-temperature-taking. It is a test of how much they can get away with and what sort of opposition they will encounter.

For the rest of us, it is a miniature preview—in the microcosm of the academic world—of what is to happen to the country at large, if the present cultural trend remains unchallenged.

The country at large is a mirror of its universities. The practical result of modern philosophy is today's mixed economy with its moral nihilism, its range-of-the-moment pragmatism, its anti-ideological ideology and its truly shameful recourse to the notion of "Government by Consensus." (See my article in the May and June issues of this NEWSLETTER.)

Rule by pressure groups is merely the prelude, the social conditioning for mob rule. Once a country has accepted the obliteration of moral principles, of individual rights, of objectivity, of justice, of reason, and has submitted to the rule of legalized brute force—the elimination of the concept "legalized" does not take long to follow. Who is to resist it—and in the name of what?

When numbers are substituted for morality, and no individual can claim a right, but any gang can assert any desire whatever, when *compromise* is the only policy expected of those in power, and the preservation of the moment's "stability," of peace at any price, is their only goal—the winner, necessarily, is whoever presents the most unjust and irrational demands; the system serves as an open invitation to do so. If there were no communists or other thugs in the world, such a system would create them.

The more an official is committed to the policy of compromise, the less able he is to resist anything: to give in, is his "instinctive" response in any emergency, his basic principle of conduct, which makes him an easy mark.

In this connection, the extreme of naive superficiality was reached by those commentators who expressed astonishment that the student rebellion had chosen Berkeley as its first battleground and President Kerr as its first target *in spite of* his record as a "liberal" and as a renowned mediator and arbitrator. "Ironically, some of the least mature student spokesmen...tried to depict Mr. Kerr as the illiberal administrator," said an editorial in *The N. Y. Times* (March 11, 1965). "This was, of course, absurd in view of Mr. Kerr's long and courageous battle to uphold academic freedom and students' rights in the face of those right-wing pressures that abound in California." Other commentators pictured Mr. Kerr as an innocent victim caught between the conflicting pressures of the "conservatives" on the Board of Regents and the "liberals" on the faculty. But, in fact and in logic, the middle of the road can lead to no other final destination—and it is clear that the rebels chose Clark Kerr as their first target, not *in spite of,* but *because of* his record.

Now project what would happen if the technique of the Berkeley rebellion were repeated on a national scale. Contrary to the fanatical belief of its advocates, compromise does not satisfy, but *dissatisfies* everybody; it does not lead to general fulfillment, but to general frustration; those who try to be all things to all men, end up by not being anything to anyone. And more: the partial victory of an unjust claim, encourages the claimant to try further; the partial defeat of a just claim, discourages and paralyzes the victim. If a determined, disciplined gang of statists were to make an assault on the crumbling remnants of a mixed economy, boldly and explicitly proclaiming the collectivist tenets which the country had accepted by tacit default—what resistance would they encounter? The disspirited, demoralized, embittered majority would remain lethargically indifferent to any public event. And many would support the gang, at first, moved by a desperate, incoherent frustration, by a need to protest, not knowing fully against what, by a blind desire to strike out somehow at the suffocating hopelessness of the *status-quo.*

Who would feel morally inspired to fight for Johnson's "consensus"? Who fought for the aimless platitudes of the Kerensky government in Russia—of the Weimar Republic in Germany—of the Nationalist government in China?

But no matter how badly demoralized and philosophically disarmed a country might be, it has to reach a certain psychological turning point before it can be pushed from a state of semi-freedom into surrender to full-fledged dictatorship. And *this* was the main ideological purpose of the student rebellion's leaders, whoever they were: *to condition the country to accept force as the means of settling political controversies.*

Observe the ideological precedents which the Berkeley rebels were striving to establish: all of them involved the abrogation of rights and the advocacy of force. These notions have been publicized, yet their meaning has been largely ignored and left unanswered.

1. The main issue was the attempt to make the country accept *mass civil disobedience* as a proper and valid tool of political action. This attempt has been made repeatedly in connection with the civil rights movement. But there the issue was confused by the fact that the Negroes *were* the victims of legalized injustice and, therefore, the matter of breaching legality did not become unequivocally clear. The country took it as a fight for justice, not as an assault on the law.

Civil disobedience may be justifiable, in some cases, when and if an individual disobeys a law in order to bring an issue to court, as a test case. Such an action involves respect for legality and a protest directed only at a particular law which the individual seeks an opportunity to prove to be unjust. The same is true of a group of individuals when and if the risks involved are their own.

But there is no justification, in a civilized society, for the kind of mass civil disobedience that involves the violation of the rights of others—regardless of whether the demonstrators' goal is good or evil. The end does *not* justify the means. No one's rights can be secured by the violation of the rights of others. Mass disobedience is an assault on the concept of rights: it is a mob's defiance of legality as such.

The forcible occupation of another man's property or the obstruction of a public thoroughfare is so blatant a violation of rights that an attempt to justify it becomes an abrogation of morality. An individual has no right to do a "sit-in" in the home or office of a person he disagrees with—and he does not acquire such a right by joining a gang. Rights are not a matter of numbers—and there can be no such thing, in law or in morality, as actions forbidden to an individual, but permitted to a mob.

The only power of a mob, as against an individual, is greater muscular strength—*i.e.,* plain, brute physical force. The attempt to solve social problems by means of physical force is what a civilized society is established to prevent. The advocates of mass civil disobedience admit that their purpose is intimidation. A society that tolerates intimidation as a means of settling disputes—the *physical* intimidation of some men or groups by others—loses its moral right to exist as a social system, and its collapse does not take long to follow.

Politically, mass civil disobedience is appropriate only as a prelude to civil war—as the declaration of a total break with a country's political institutions. And the degree of today's intellectual chaos and context-dropping was best illustrated by some "conservative" California official who rushed to declare that he objects to the Berkeley rebellion, but respects civil disobedience as a valid American tradition. "Don't forget the Boston Tea Party," he said, forgetting it.

If the meaning of civil disobedience is somewhat obscured in the civil rights movement—and, therefore, the attitude of the country is inconclusive—that meaning becomes blatantly obvious when a sit-in is staged on a university campus. If the universities—the supposed citadels of reason, knowledge, scholarship, civilization—can be made to surrender to the rule of brute force, the rest of the country is cooked.

2. To facilitate the acceptance of force, the Berkeley rebels attempted to establish a special distinction between *force* and *violence:* force, they claimed explicitly, is a proper form of social action, but violence is not. Their definition of the terms was as follows: coercion by means of a *literal* physical contact is "violence" and is reprehensible; any other way of violating rights is merely "force" and is a legitimate, peaceful method of dealing with opponents.

For instance, if the rebels occupy the administration building, that is "force"; if policemen drag them out, that is "violence." If Savio seizes a microphone he has no right to use, that is "force"; if a policeman drags him away from it, that is "violence."

Consider the implications of that distinction as a rule of social conduct: if you come home one evening, find a stranger occupying your house and throw him out bodily, he has merely committed a peaceful act of "force," but *you* are guilty of "violence" and *you* are to be punished.

The theoretical purpose of that grotesque absurdity is to establish a moral inversion: to make the *initiation* of force moral, and *resistance* to force immoral—and thus to obliterate *the right of self-defense.* The immediate practical purpose is to foster the activities of the lowest political breed: the provocateurs, who commit acts of force and place the blame on their victims.

3. To justify that fraudulent distinction, the Berkeley rebels attempted to obliterate a legitimate one: the distinction between *ideas* and *actions.* They claimed that freedom of speech means freedom of action and that no clear line of demarcation can be drawn between them.

For instance, if they have the right to advocate any political viewpoint—they claimed—they have the right to organize, on campus, any off-campus activities, even those forbidden by law. As Professor Petersen put it, they were claiming the right "to use the University as a sanctuary from which to make illegal raids on the general community."

The difference between an exchange of ideas and an exchange of blows is self-evident. The line of demarcation between freedom of speech and freedom of action is established by the ban on the initiation of physical force. It is only when that ban is abrogated that such a problem can arise—but when that ban is abrogated, no political freedom of any kind can remain in existence.

At a superficial glance, the rebels' "package-deal" may seem to imply a sort of anarchistic extension of freedom; but, in fact and in logic, it implies the exact opposite—which is a grim joke on those unthinking youths who joined the rebellion in the name of "free speech." If the freedom to express ideas were equated with the freedom to commit crimes, it would not take long to demonstrate that no organized society can exist on such terms and, therefore, that the expression of ideas has to be curtailed and some ideas have to be forbidden, just as criminal acts are forbidden. Thus the gullible would be brought to concede that the right of free speech is undefinable and "impracticable."

4. An indication of such a motive was given by the rebels' demand for unrestricted freedom of speech on campus—with the consequent "Filthy Language Movement."

There can be no such thing as the right to an unrestricted freedom of speech (or of action) *on someone else's property.* The fact that the university at Berkeley is owned by the state, merely complicates the issue, but does not alter it. The owners of a state university are the voters and taxpayers of that state. The university administration, appointed (directly or indirectly) by an elected official, is, theoretically, the agent of the owners —and has to act as such, so long as state universities exist. (Whether they *should* exist, is a different question.)

In any undertaking or establishment involving more than one man, it is the owner or owners who set the rules and terms of appropriate conduct; the rest of the participants are free to go elsewhere and seek different terms, if they do not agree. There can be no such thing as the right to act on whim, to be exercised by some participants at the expense of others.

Students who attend a university have the right to expect that they will not be subjected to hearing the kind of obscenities for which the owner of a semi-decent barroom would bounce hoodlums out on the street. The right to determine what sort of language is permissible, belongs to the administration of a university—fully as much as to the owner of a barroom.

The technique of the rebels, as of all statists, was to take advantage of the principles of a free society in order to undercut them by an alleged demonstration of their "impracticability"— in this case, the "impracticability" of the right of free speech. But, in fact, what they have demonstrated is a point farthest removed from their goals: that *no rights of any kind can be exercised without property rights.* *(Continued on page 43)*

Alienation

By NATHANIEL BRANDEN

(Part III of a three-part article)

The problem of alienation and the problem of personal identity are inseparable. The man who lacks a firm sense of personal identity feels alienated; the man who feels alienated lacks a firm sense of personal identity.

Pain is an organism's alarm-signal, warning of danger; the particular species of pain which is the feeling of alienation announces to a man that he is existing in a psychological state improper to him—*that his relationship to reality is wrong.*

No animal faces such questions as: What should I make of myself? What manner of life is proper to my nature? Such questions are possible only to a rational being, *i.e.*, a being whose characteristic method of cognitive functioning (of apprehending reality) is conceptual, who is not only conscious but also self-conscious, and whose power of abstraction enables him to project many alternative courses of action. Further, such questions are possible only to a being whose cognitive faculty is exercised *volitionally* (thinking is not automatic)—a being who is self-directing and self-regulating in thought and in action, and whose existence, therefore, entails a constant process of *choice*.

As a living entity, man is born with specific needs and capacities; these constitute his *species* identity, so to speak—*i.e.*, they constitute his human nature. How he exercises his capacities to satisfy his needs—*i.e.*, how he deals with the facts of reality, how he chooses to function, in thought and in action—constitutes his *personal* or *individual* identity. His sense of himself—his implicit concept or image of the kind of person he is (including his self-esteem or lack of it)—is the cumulative product of the choices he makes. This is the meaning of Ayn Rand's statement that "man is a being of self-made soul."

A man's "I," his ego, his deepest self, is his faculty of awareness, his capacity to think. To choose to think, to identify the facts of reality—to assume the responsibility of judging what is true or false, right or wrong—is man's basic form of *self-assertiveness*. It is his acceptance of his own nature as a rational being, his acceptance of the responsibility of intellectual independence, his commitment to the efficacy of his own mind.

The essence of *selflessness* is the suspension of one's consciousness. When and to the extent that a man chooses to evade the effort and responsibility of thinking, of seeking knowledge, of passing judgment, his action is one of *self-abdication*. To relinquish thought, is to relinquish one's ego—and to pronounce oneself unfit for existence, incompetent to deal with the facts of reality.

To the extent that a man chooses to think, his premises and values are acquired first-hand and they are not a mystery to him; he experiences himself as the *active cause* of his character, behavior and goals. To the extent that a man attempts to live without thinking, he experiences himself as *passive*, his person and actions are the accidental products of forces he does not understand, of his range-of-the-moment feelings and random environmental influences. When a man defaults on the responsibility of thought, he is left at the mercy of his involuntary, subconscious reactions—and *these* will be at the mercy of the outside forces impinging upon him, at the mercy of whoever and whatever is around him. By his default, such a person turns himself into the social determinists' view of man: into an empty mold waiting to be filled, into a will-less robot waiting to be taken over by any environment and any conditioners.

A strong sense of personal identity is the product of two things: a policy of independent thinking and, as a consequence, the possession of an integrated set of values. Since it is his values that determine a man's emotions and goals, and give direction and meaning to his life, a man experiences his values as an extension of himself, as an integral part of his identity, as crucial to that which makes him himself.

"Values," in this context, refers to fundamental and abstract values, not to concrete value-judgments. For example, a man holding rationality as his abstract value may choose a friend who appears to embody this value; if, subsequently, he decides that he was mistaken in his judgment, that his friend is not rational and that their relationship should be ended, this does not alter his personal identity; but if, instead, he decides that he no longer values rationality, his personal identity *is* altered.

If a man holds contradictory values, these necessarily do violence to his sense of personal identity. They result in a splintered sense of self, a self broken into unintegratable fragments. To avoid this painful experience of a splintered identity, a man whose values are contradictory will commonly seek to escape knowledge of his contradictions by means of evasion, repression, rationalization, etc. Thus, to escape a problem created by a failure of thought, he suspends thinking. To escape a threat to his sense of personal identity, *he suspends his ego*—he suspends his self *qua* thinking, judging entity.

Thus, he displaces his sense of self *downward*, so to speak, from his reason, which is the active, initiating element in man, to his emotions, which are the passive, reactive element. Moved by feelings whose source he does not understand, and by contradictions whose existence he does not acknowledge, he suffers a progressive sense of self-estrangement, of self-alienation. A man's emotions are the product of his premises and values, of the thinking he has done or has failed to do. But the man who is run by his emotions, attempting to make them a substitute for rational judgment, experiences them as alien forces. The paradox of his position is this: his emotions become his only source of personal identity, but his experience of identity becomes: *a being ruled by demons.*

It is important to observe that the experience of self-alienation and the feeling of being alienated from reality, from the world around one, proceed from the same cause: one's default on the responsibility of thinking. The suspension of proper cognitive contact with reality and the suspension of one's ego, are a single act. A flight from reality is a flight from self.

One of the consequences is a feeling of alienation from other men, the sense that one is not part of the human race—that one is, in effect, a freak. In betraying one's status as a human being, one makes oneself a metaphysical outcast. This is not altered by the knowledge that many other human beings have committed the same betrayal. One feels alone and cut off—cut off by the unreality of one's own existence, by one's desolate inner sense of spiritual impoverishment.

The same failure of rationality and independence by which men rob themselves of personal identity leads them, most commonly, to the self-destructive policy of seeking a *substitute* for identity—or, more precisely, seeking a *second-hand* identity—through mindless conformity to the values of others. This is the psychological phenomenon which I have designated as social metaphysics. In an article dealing with different types of social metaphysicians ("Rogues Gallery," February 1965, this NEWSLETTER), I commented on the type most relevant to the present context, the Conventional social metaphysician:

"This is the person who accepts the world and its prevailing values ready-made; his is not to reason why. What is true? What others say is true. What is right? What others believe is right. How should one live? As others live... [This is] the person whose sense of identity and personal worth is *explicitly* a function of his ability to satisfy the values, terms and expectations of those omniscient and omnipresent 'others'... In a culture such as the present one, with its disintegrating values, its intellectual chaos, its moral bankruptcy—where the familiar guideposts and rules are vanishing, where the authoritative mirrors reflecting 'reality' are splintering into a thousand unintelligible subcults, where 'adjustment' is becoming harder and harder—the Conventional social metaphysician is the first to run to a psychiatrist, crying that he has lost his identity, because he no longer knows unequivocally what he is supposed to do and be."

It would never occur to a person of self-esteem and independent judgment that one's "identity" is a thing to be gained from or determined by others. To a person untouched by profound self-doubt, the wails heard today about the anguish of modern man as he confronts the question, "Who am I?", are incomprehensible. But in the light of the above, the wailing becomes more intelligible. It is the cry of social metaphysicians who no longer know which authorities to obey—and who are moaning that it is *someone's* duty to herd them to a sense of self, that "the system" must provide them with self-esteem.

This is the psychological root of the modern intellectuals' mystique of the Middle Ages, of the dazed longing for that style of life—and of the massive evasion concerning the actual conditions of existence during that period. The Middle Ages represents the social metaphysician's unconfessed dream: a system in which his dread of independence and self-responsibility is proclaimed to be a virtue and made a social imperative.

When—in any age—a man attempts to evade the responsibility of intellectual independence, and to derive his sense of identity from "belonging," he pays a deadly price in terms of the sabotaging of his mental processes thereafter. The degree to which a man substitutes the judgment of others for his own, failing to look at reality directly, is the degree to which his mental processes are alienated from reality. He functions, not by means of concepts, but by means of memorized cue-words, *i.e.*, learned *sounds* associated with certain contexts and situations, but lacking authentic cognitive content for their user. This is the unidentified, unrecognized phenomenon that prompts unthinking people today to grant validity to the charge that modern man lives "too abstractly," "too intellectually," and that he needs to "get back to nature." They sense dimly that they are out of contact with reality, that something is wrong with their grasp of the world around them. But they accept an entirely fallacious interpretation of their problem. The truth is not that they are lost among "abstractions," but that they have failed to discover the nature and proper use of abstractions; they are not lost among concepts, they are lost among *cue-words*. They are cut off from reality not because they attempt to grasp it too intellectually, but because they attempt to grasp it *only as seen by others;* they attempt to grasp it *second-hand*. And they move through an unreal world of verbal rituals, mouthing the slogans and phrases they hear repeated by others, falsely imagining that those empty words are concepts, and never apprehending the proper use of their conceptual faculty, never learning what firsthand, conceptual knowledge consists of. Then they are ready for the Zen-Buddhist who tells them that the solution to their alienation from reality is to empty their mind of all thought and sit for an hour, cross-legged, contemplating the pattern of veins on a leaf.

It is a well-known psychological fact that when men are neurotically anxious, when they suffer from feelings of dread for which they cannot account, they often attempt to make their plight more tolerable by directing their fear at some external object: they seek to persuade themselves that their fear is a rational response to the threat of germs, or the possible appearance of burglars, or the danger of lightning, or the brain-controlling radiations of Martians. The process by which men decide that the cause of their alienation is capitalism, is not dissimilar.

There are reasons, however, why capitalism is the target for their projection and rationalization.

The alienated man is fleeing from the responsibility of a volitional (*i.e.*, self-directing) consciousness: the freedom to think or not to think, to initiate a process of reason or to evade it, is a burden he longs to escape. But since this freedom is inherent in his nature as man, there is no escape from it; hence his guilt and anxiety when he abandons reason and sight in favor of feelings and blindness. But there is another level on which man confronts the issue of freedom: the existential or social level—and here escape *is* possible. *Political* freedom is not a metaphysical given: it has to be *achieved*—hence it can be rejected. The psychological root of the revolt against freedom in one's existence, is the revolt against freedom in one's consciousness. *The root of the revolt against self-responsibility in action is the revolt against self-direction in thought*. The man who does not want to think, does not want to bear responsibility for the consequences of his actions nor for his own life.

It is appropriate, in this connection, to quote a passage from *Who is Ayn Rand?* in which I discuss the similarity of the attacks against capitalism launched by nineteenth-century medievalists and socialists:

"In the writings of both medievalists and socialists, one can observe the unmistakable longing for a society in which man's existence will be automatically guaranteed to him—that is, in which man will not have to bear responsibility for his own survival. Both camps project their ideal society as one characterized by that which they call 'harmony,' by freedom from rapid change or challenge or the exacting demands of competition; a society in which each must do his prescribed part to contribute to the well-being of the whole, but in which no one will face the necessity of making choices and decisions that will crucially affect his life and future; in which the question of what one has or has not earned, and does or does not deserve, will not come up; in which rewards will not be tied to achievement and in which someone's benevolence will guarantee that one need never bear the consequences of one's errors. The failure of capitalism to conform to what may be termed this *pastoral* view of existence, is essential to the medievalists' and socialists' indictment of a free society. It is not a Garden of Eden that capitalism offers men."

Today, of course, capitalism has largely been abandoned in favor of a "mixed economy," *i.e.*, a mixture of freedom and statism—moving steadily in the direction of increasing statism. Today, we are far closer to the "ideal society" of the socialists than when Marx first wrote of the worker's "alienation." Yet with every advance of collectivism, the cries concerning man's alienation grow louder. The problem, we are told, is getting worse. In communist countries, when such criticisms are allowed to be voiced, some commentators are beginning to complain that the Marxist solution to the worker's alienation has failed, that man under communism is still alienated, that the "new harmony" with nature and one's fellow-men has not come.

It didn't come to the medieval serf or guildsman, either—the propaganda of commentators such as Erich Fromm notwithstanding.

Man cannot escape from his nature, and if he establishes a social system which is inimical to the requirements of his nature—a system which forbids him to function as a rational, independent being—psychological and physical disaster is the result.

A free society, of course, cannot automatically guarantee the mental well-being of all its members. Freedom is not a *sufficient* condition to assure man's proper fulfillment, but it is a *necessary* condition. And capitalism—laissez-faire capitalism—is the only system which provides that condition.

The problem of alienation is not metaphysical; it is not man's natural fate, never to be escaped, like some sort of Original Sin; it is a *disease*. It is not the consequence of capitalism or industrialism or "bigness"—and it cannot be legislated out of existence by the abolition of property rights. The problem of alienation is *psycho-epistemological:* it pertains to how man chooses to use his own consciousness. It is the product of man's revolt against thinking—which means: against reality.

If a man defaults on the responsibility of seeking knowledge, choosing values and setting goals—if this is the sphere he surrenders to the authority of others—*how is he to escape the feeling that the universe is closed to him?* It is. By his own choice.

The proper answer to the question—
"And how am I to face the odds
of man's bedevilment and God's?
I, a stranger and afraid
in a world I never made"
—is: *Why didn't you?*

The Cashing-in: The Student "Rebellion" (from page 40)

It is only on the basis of property rights that the sphere and application of individual rights can be defined in any given social situation. Without property rights, there is no way to solve or to avoid a hopeless chaos of clashing views, interests, demands, desires and whims.

There was no way for the Berkeley administration to answer the rebels except by invoking property rights. It is obvious why neither modern "liberals" nor "conservatives" would care to do so. It is not the contradictions of a free society that the rebels were exposing and cashing-in on, but the contradictions of a mixed economy.

As to the question of what ideological policy should properly be adopted by the administration of a state university, it is a question that has no answer. There are no solutions for the many contradictions inherent in the concept of "public property," particularly when the property is directly concerned with the dissemination of ideas. This is one of the reasons why the rebels would choose a state university as their first battleground.

A good case could be made for the claim that a state university has no right to forbid the teaching or advocacy of any political viewpoint whatever, as, for instance, of communism, since some of the taxpaying owners may be communists. An equally good case could be made for the claim that a state university has no right to permit the teaching and advocacy of any political viewpoint which (as, for instance, communism) is a direct threat to the property, freedom and lives of the majority of the taxpaying owners. Majority rule is not applicable in the realm of ideas; an individual's convictions are not subject to a majority vote; but neither an individual nor a minority nor a majority should be forced to support their own destroyers.

On the one hand, a government institution has no right to forbid the expression of any ideas. On the other hand, a government institution has no right to harbor, assist and finance the country's enemies (as, for instance, the collectors of funds for the Vietcong).

The source of these contradictions does not lie in the principle of individual rights, but in their violation by the collectivist institution of "public property."

This issue, however, has to be fought in the field of constitutional law, not on campus. As students, the rebels have no greater rights in a state university than in a private one. As taxpayers, they have no greater rights than the millions of other California taxpayers involved. If they object to the policies of the Board of Regents, they have no recourse except at the polls at the next election—if they can persuade a sufficient number of voters. This is a pretty slim chance—and this is a good argument *against* any type of "public property." But it is not an issue to be solved by physical force.

What is significant here is the fact that the rebels—who, to put it mildly, are *not* champions of private property—refused to abide by the kind of majority rule which is inherent in public ownership. *That* is what they were opposing when they complained that universities have become servants of the "financial, industrial and military establishment." It is the rights of these particular groups of taxpayers (the right to a voice in the management of state universities) that they were seeking to abrogate.

If anyone needs proof of the fact that the advocates of public ownership are not seeking "democratic" control of property by majority rule, but control by dictatorship—this is one eloquent piece of evidence.

5. As part of the ideological conditioning for that ultimate goal, the rebels attempted to introduce a new variant on an old theme that has been the object of an intense drive by all statist-collectivists for many years past: the obliteration of the difference between private action and government action.

This has always been attempted by means of a "package-deal" ascribing to private citizens the specific violations constitutionally forbidden to the government, and thus destroying individual rights while freeing the government from any restrictions. The most frequent example of this technique consists of accusing private citizens of practicing "censorship" (a concept applicable only to the government) and thus negating their right to disagree. (See my article on "Man's Rights" in the April 1963 issue of this NEWSLETTER.)

The new variant provided by the rebels was their protest against alleged "double jeopardy." It went as follows: if the students commit illegal acts, they will be punished by the courts and must not, therefore, be penalized by the university for the same offense.

"Double jeopardy" is a concept applicable only to *one* branch of the government, the judiciary, and only to a specific judiciary action: it means that a man must not be put on trial twice for the same offense.

To equate private judgment and action (or, in this context, a government official's judgment and action) with a court trial, is worse than absurd. It is an outrageous attempt to obliterate the right to moral judgment and moral action. It is a demand that a lawbreaker suffer no *civil* consequences of his crime.

If such a notion were accepted, individuals would have no right to evaluate the conduct of others nor to act according to their evaluation. They would have to wait until a court had decreed whether a given man was guilty or innocent—and even after he was pronounced guilty, they would have no right to change their behavior toward him and would have to leave the task of penalizing him exclusively to the government.

For instance, if a bank employee were found guilty of embezzlement and had served his sentence, the bank would have no right to refuse to give him back his former job—since a refusal would constitute "double jeopardy."

Or: a government official would have no right to watch the legality of the actions of his department's employees, nor to lay down rules for their strict observance of the law, but would have to wait until a court had found them guilty of law-breaking—and would have to reinstate them in their jobs, after they had served their sentences for influence-peddling or bribe-taking or treason.

The notion of *morality as a monopoly of the government* (and of a single branch or group within the government) is so blatantly a part of the ideology of a dictatorship that the rebels' attempt to get away with it is truly shocking.

6. The rebels' notion that universities should be run by students and faculties was an open, explicit assault on the right attacked implicitly by all their other notions: the right of private property. And of all the various statist-collectivist systems, the one they chose as their goal is, politico-economically, the least practical; intellectually, the least defensible; morally, the most shameful: *Guild Socialism*.

Guild socialism is a system that abolishes the exercise of individual ability by chaining men into groups according to their line of work, and delivering the work into the group's power, as its exclusive domain, with the group dictating the rules, standards and practices of how the work is to be done and who shall or shall not do it.

Guild socialism is the concrete-bound, routine-bound mentality of a savage, elevated into a social theory. Just as a tribe of savages seizes a piece of jungle territory and claims it as a monopoly by reason of the fact of being there—so guild socialism grants a monopoly, not on a jungle forest or water-hole, but on a factory or a university—not by reason of a man's ability, achievement or even "public service," but by reason of the fact that he is there.

Just as savages have no concept of causes or consequences, of past or future, and no concept of efficacy beyond the muscular power of their tribe—so guild socialists, finding themselves in the midst of an industrial civilization, regard its institutions as phenomena of nature and see no reason why the gang should not seize them.

If there is any one proof of a man's incompetence, it is the stagnant mentality of a worker (or of a professor) who, doing some small, routine job in a vast undertaking, does not care to look beyond the lever of a machine (or the lectern of a classroom), does not choose to know how the machine (or the classroom) got there or what makes his job possible, and proclaims that the management of the undertaking is parasitical and unnecessary. Managerial work—the organization and integration of human effort into purposeful, large-scale, long-range activities—is, in the realm of action, what man's conceptual faculty is in the realm of cognition. It is beyond the grasp and, therefore, is the first target of the self-arrested, sensory-perceptual mentality.

If there is any one way to confess one's own mediocrity, it is the willingness to place one's work in the absolute power of a group, particularly a group of one's *professional colleagues.* Of any forms of tyranny, this is the worst; it is directed against a single human attribute: the mind—and against a single enemy: the innovator. The innovator, by definition, is the man who challenges the established practices of his profession. To grant a professional monopoly to any group, is to sacrifice human ability and abolish progress; to advocate such a monopoly, is to confess that one has nothing to sacrifice.

Guild socialism is the rule of, by and for mediocrity. Its cause is a society's intellectual collapse; its consequence is a quagmire of stagnation; its historical example is the guild system of the Middle Ages (or, in modern times, the fascist system of Italy under Mussolini).

The rebels' notion that students (along with faculties) should run universities and determine their curricula is a crude absurdity. If an ignorant youth comes to an institution of learning in order to acquire knowledge of a certain science, by what means is he to determine what is relevant and how he should be taught? (In the process of learning, he can judge only whether his teacher's presentation is clear or unclear, logical or contradictory; he cannot determine the proper course and method of teaching, ahead of any knowledge of the subject.) It is obvious that a student who demands the right to run a university (or to decide who should run it) has no knowledge of the concept of knowledge, that his demand is self-contradictory and disqualifies him automatically. The same is true—with a much heavier burden of moral guilt—of the professor who taught him to make such demands and who supports them.

Would you care to be treated in a hospital where the methods of therapy were determined by a vote of doctors and patients?

Yet the absurdity of these examples is merely more obvious—not more irrational nor more vicious—than the standard collectivist claim that workers should take over the factories created by men whose achievement they can neither grasp nor equal. The basic epistemological-moral premise and pattern are the same: the obliteration of reason obliterates the concept of reality, which obliterates the concept of achievement, which obliterates the concept of the distinction between *the earned* and *the unearned.* Then the incompetent can seize factories, the ignorant can seize universities, the brutes can seize scientific research laboratories—and nothing is left in a human society but the power of whim and fist.

What makes guild socialism cruder than (but not different from) most statist-collectivist theories is the fact that it represents the other, the usually unmentioned, side of altruism: it is the voice, not of the givers, but of the receivers. While most altruistic theorists proclaim "the common good" as their justification, advocate self-sacrificial service to the "community," and keep silent about the exact nature or identity of the recipients of sacrifices—guild socialists brazenly declare themselves to be the recipients and present their claims to the community, demanding its services. If they want a monopoly on a given profession, they claim, the rest of the community must give up the right to practice it. If they want a university, they claim, the community must provide it.

And if "selfishness" is taken, by the altruists, to mean the sacrifice of others to self, I challenge them to name an uglier example of it than the pronouncement of the little Berkeley collectivist who declared: "Our idea is that the university is composed of faculty, students, books and ideas. In a literal sense, the administration is merely there to make sure the sidewalks are kept clean. It should be the servant of the faculty and the students."

What did that little disembodied mystic omit from his idea of a university? Who pays the salaries of the faculty? Who provides the livelihood of the students? Who publishes the books? Who builds the classrooms, the libraries, the dormitories—and the sidewalks? Leave it to a modern "mystic of *muscle*" to display the kind of contempt for "vulgar material concerns" that an old-fashioned mystic would not quite dare permit himself.

Who—besides the university administration—is to be the voiceless, rightless "servant" and sidewalk-sweeper of the faculty and students? No, not only the men of productive genius who create the material wealth that makes universities possible, not only the "tycoons of big business," not only the "financial, industrial, and military establishment"—but every taxpayer of the state of California, every man who works for a living, high or low, every human being who earns his sustenance, struggles with his budget, pays for what he gets, and does not permit himself to evade the reality of "vulgar material concerns."

Such is the soul revealed by the ideology of the Berkeley rebellion. Such is the meaning of the rebels' demands and of the ideological precedents they were trying to establish.

Observe the complexity, the equivocations, the tricks, the twists, the intellectual acrobatics performed by these avowed advocates of unbridled feelings—and the ideological consistency of these activists who claim to possess no ideology.

The first round of the student rebellion has not gone over too well. In spite of the gratuitous "puff-job" done by the press, the attitude of the public is a mixture of bewilderment, indifference and antagonism. Indifference—because the evasive vagueness of the press reports was self-defeating: people do not understand what it is all about and see no reason to care. Antagonism—because the American public still holds a profound respect for universities (as they might be and ought to be, but are not any longer), and the commentators' half-laudatory, half-humorous platitudes about the "idealism of youth" have not succeeded in whitewashing the fact that brute physical force was brought to a university campus. That fact has aroused a vague sense of uneasiness in people, a sense of undefined, apprehensive condemnation.

The rebellion's attempt to invade other campuses did not get very far. There were some disgraceful proclamations of appeasement by some university administrators and commencement orators this spring, but no discernible public sympathy.

There were a few instances of a proper attitude on the part of university administrations—an attitude of firmness, dignity and uncompromising severity—notably at Columbia University. A commencement address by Dr. Meng, president of Hunter College, is also worth noting. Declaring that the violation of the rights of others "is intolerable" in an academic community and that any student or teacher guilty of it deserves "instant expulsion," he said: "Yesterday's ivory tower has become today's foxhole. The leisure of the theory class is increasingly occupied in the organization of picket lines, teach-ins, think-ins, and stake-outs of one sort or another." *(The N. Y. Times,* June 18, 1965.)

But even though the student rebellion has not aroused much public sympathy, the most ominous aspect of the situation is the fact that it has not met any *ideological opposition,* that the implications of the rebels' stand have neither been answered nor rejected, that such criticism as it did evoke was, with rare exceptions, evasively superficial.

As a trial balloon, the rebellion has accomplished its leaders' purpose: it has demonstrated that they may have gone a bit too far, bared their teeth and claws a bit too soon, and antagonized many potential sympathizers, even among the "liberals"—but that the road ahead is empty, with no intellectual barricades in sight.

The battle is to continue. The long-range intentions of the student rebellion have been proclaimed repeatedly by the same activists who proclaim their exclusive dedication to the immediate moment. The remnants of the "Free Speech Movement" at Berkeley have been reorganized into a "Free Student Union," which is making militant noises in preparation for another assault. No matter how absurd their notions, the rebels' assaults are directed at the most important philosophical-political issues of our age. These issues cannot be ignored, evaded or bribed away by compromise. When brute force is on the march, compromise is the red carpet. When reason is attacked, common sense is not enough.

Neither a man nor a nation can exist without some form of philosophy. A man has the free will to think or not; if he does not, he takes what he gets. The free will of a nation is its intellectuals; the rest of the country takes what they offer; they set the terms, the values, the course, the goal.

In the absence of intellectual opposition, the rebels' notions will gradually come to be absorbed into the culture. The uncontested absurdities of today are the accepted slogans of tomorrow. They come to be accepted by degrees, by precedent, by implication, by erosion, by default, by dint of constant pressure on one side and constant retreat on the other—until the day when they are suddenly declared to be the country's official ideology. That is the way welfare statism came to be accepted in this country.

What we are witnessing today is an acceleration of the attempts to cash-in on the ideological implications of welfare statism and to push beyond it. The college rebels are merely the commandos, charged with the task of establishing ideological beachheads for a full-scale advance of all the statist-collectivist forces against the remnants of capitalism in America; and part of their task is the take-over of the ideological control of America's universities.

If the collectivists succeed, the terrible historical irony will lie in the fact that what looks like a noisy, reckless, belligerent confidence is, in fact, a hysterical bluff. The acceleration of collectivism's advance is not the march of winners, but the blind stampede of losers. Collectivism has lost the battle for men's minds; its advocates know it; their last chance consists of the fact that no one else knows it. If they are to cash-in on decades of philosophical corruption, on all the gnawing, scrapping, scratching, burrowing to dig a maze of philosophical rat-holes which is about to cave in, it's now or never.

As a cultural-intellectual power and a moral ideal, collectivism died in World War II. If we are still rolling in its direction, it is only by the inertia of a void and the momentum of disintegration. A social movement that began with the ponderous, brain-cracking, dialectical constructs of Hegel and Marx, and ends up with a horde of morally unwashed children stamping their foot and shrieking: "I want it *now!*"—is through.

All over the world, while mowing down one helpless nation after another, collectivism has been steadily losing the two elements that hold the key to the future: the brains of mankind and its youth. In regard to the first, observe Britain's "brain drain." In regard to the second, consider the fact (which was not mentioned in the press comments on the student rebellion) that in a predominant number of American universities, the political views of the faculty are perceptibly more "liberal" than those of the student body. (The same is true of the youth of the country at large—as against the older generation, the 35 to 50 age bracket, who were reared under the New Deal and who hold the country's leadership, at present.) That is one of the facts which the student rebellion was intended to disguise.

This is not to say that the anti-collectivists represent a *numerical* majority among college students. The passive supporters of the *status-quo* are always the majority in any group, culture, society or age. But it is not by passive majorities that the trends of a nation are set. Who sets them? Anyone who cares to do so, if he has the intellectual ammunition to win on the battlefield of ideas, which belongs to those who *do* care. Those who don't, are merely social ballast by their own choice and predilection.

The fact that the "non-liberals" among college students (and among the youth of the world) can be identified at present only as "anti-collectivists" is the dangerous element and the question mark in today's situation. They are the young people who are not ready to give up, who want to fight against a swamp of evil, but do not know what is the good. They have rejected the sick, worn platitudes of collectivism—(along with all of its cultural manifestations, including the cult of despair and depravity—the studied mindlessness of jerk-and-moan dancing, singing or acting—the worship of anti-heroes—the experience of looking up to the dissection of a psychotic's brain, for inspiration, and to the bare feet of an inarticulate brute, for guidance—the stupor of reduction to sensory stimuli—the sense of life of a movie such as *Tom Jones*)—but they have found, as yet, no direction, no consistent philosophy, no rational values, no long-range goals. Until and unless they do, their incoherent striving for a better future will collapse before the final thrust of the collectivists.

Historically, we are now in a kind of intellectual no man's land—and the future will be determined by those who venture out of the trenches of the *status-quo*. Our direction will depend on whether the venturers are crusaders fighting for a new Renaissance or scavengers pouncing upon the wreckage left of yesterday's battles. The crusaders are not yet ready; the scavengers are.

That is why—in a deeper sense than the little zombies of college campuses will ever grasp—"Now, now, now!" is the last slogan and cry of the ragged, bearded stragglers who had once been an army rallied by the promise of a *scientifically* (!) planned society.

The two most accurate characterizations of the student rebellion, given in the press, were: "Political Existentialism" and "Castroite." Both are concepts pertaining to intellectual bankruptcy: the first stands for the abdication of reason—the second, for that state of hysterical panic which brandishes a fist as its sole recourse.

In preparation for its published survey (March 22, 1965), *Newsweek* conducted a number of polls among college students at large, on various subjects, one of which was the question of who are the students' heroes. The editors of *Newsweek* informed me that my name appeared on the resultant list, and sent an interviewer to question me about my views on the state of modern universities. For reasons best known to themselves, they chose not to publish any part of that interview. What I said (in briefer form) was what I am now saying in this article—with the exception of the concluding remarks which follow and which I want to address most particularly to those college students who chose me as one of their heroes.

Young people are constantly asking what they can do to fight today's disastrous trends; they are seeking some form of action, and wrecking their hopes in blind alleys, particularly every four years, at election time. Those who do not realize that the battle is ideological, had better give up, because they have no chance. Those who do realize it, should grasp that the student rebellion offers them a chance to train themselves for the kind of battle they will have to fight in the world, when they leave the university; a chance, not only to train themselves, but to win the first rounds of that wider battle.

If they seek an important cause, they have the opportunity to fight the rebels, to fight *ideologically*, on *moral-intellectual* grounds—by identifying and exposing the meaning of the rebels' demands, by naming and answering the basic principles which the rebels dare not admit. The battle consists, above all, of providing the country (or all those within hearing) with *ideological answers*—a field of action from which the older generation has deserted under fire.

Ideas cannot be fought except by means of better ideas. The battle consists, not of opposing, but of exposing; not of denouncing, but of disproving; not of evading, but of boldly proclaiming a full, consistent and radical alternative.

This does not mean that rational students should enter debates with the rebels or attempt to convert them: one cannot argue with self-confessed irrationalists. The goal of an ideological battle is to enlighten the vast, helpless, bewildered majority in the universities—and in the country at large—or, rather, the minds of those among the majority who are struggling to find answers or those who, having heard nothing but collectivist sophistries for years, have withdrawn in revulsion and given up.

The first goal of such a battle is to wrest from a handful of beatniks the title of "spokesmen for American youth," which the press is so anxious to grant them. The first step is to make oneself heard, on the campus and outside. There are many civilized ways to do it: protest meetings, public petitions, speeches, pamphlets, letters-to-editors. It is a much more important issue than picketing the United Nations or parading in support of the House Un-American Activities Committee. And while such futile groups as Young Americans for Freedom are engaged in such undertakings, they are letting the collectivist vanguard speak in their name—in the name of American college students—without any audible sound of protest.

But in order to be heard, one must have something to say. To have that, one must know one's case. One must know it fully, logically, consistently, all the way down to philosophical fundamentals. One cannot hope to fight nuclear experts with Republican pea-shooters. And the leaders behind the student rebellion *are* experts at their particular game.

But they are dangerous only to those who stare at the issues out of focus and hope to fight ideas by means of faith, feelings and fund-raising. You would be surprised how quickly the ideologists of collectivism retreat when they encounter a confident, *intellectual* adversary. Their case rests on appealing to human confusion, ignorance, dishonesty, cowardice, despair. Take the side they dare not touch: appeal to human intelligence.

Collectivism has lost the two crucial weapons that raised it to world power and made all of its victories possible: intellectuality and idealism, or reason and morality. It had to lose precisely at the height of its success, since its claim to both was a fraud: the full, actual reality of socialist-communist-fascist states has demonstrated the brute irrationality of collectivist systems and the inhumanity of altruism as a moral code.

Yet reason and morality are the only weapons that determine the course of history. The collectivists dropped them, because they had no right to carry them. Pick them up; you have.

From the "Horror File"

"In 'New American Story'... ten authors give fiction another chance to go on. The stories... are to be read for their linguistic rather than their semantic potential. For too long, readers of the novel have been like viewers who refused to look at a painting unless they could find a picture in it; writing has been for them merely a means to a plot. At the back of the book is a section with notes by the contributors. William Burroughs explains his fold-in method. He takes a page of text—his own or someone else's—folds it down the middle and places it on another page of text, then reads the composite text across. He says: 'I have made and used fold-ins from Shakespeare, Rimbaud, from newspapers, magazines, conversations and letters, so that the novels I have written using this method are in fact composites of many writers.'" (*The New York Times*, August 28, 1965.)

OBJECTIVIST CALENDAR

■ Due to the unusual success of *The Virtue of Selfishness* in its paperback edition, New American Library is publishing a hardcover edition which will be available in late October.

■ On Monday, October 11, Nathaniel Branden's course on "Basic Principles of Objectivism" will begin in New York City. Time: 7:30 P.M. Place: Sheraton-Atlantic Hotel. Ayn Rand will participate in the question period which follows the lecture. For further details, contact NBI.

■ On Friday, October 15, NBI will begin its Fall series on "Basic Principles of Objectivism" in Boston. Mr. Branden will deliver the opening lecture in person. Miss Rand will join Mr. Branden in an extended question period following the lecture. (The rest of the course will be given via tape transcription.)

In addition, NBI's Tape Transcription Division has scheduled starting dates for "Basic Principles of Objectivism" in the following cities: Dallas, Sept. 27; Kansas City, Kansas, Oct. 1; Richmond, Oct. 1; Seattle, Oct. 4; San Francisco, Oct. 5; San Diego, Oct. 6; Los Angeles, Oct. 8; Phoenix, Oct. 9; Houston, Oct. 10; Long Beach, Oct. 12; Orange, Oct. 15; Hartford, Oct. 15; Chicago, Oct. 19; Detroit, Oct. 21. Mr. Branden will deliver the opening night's lecture in person in Chicago, Detroit, Houston, Los Angeles, Phoenix, San Diego, San Francisco and Seattle. "The Economics of a Free Society" will begin in Baltimore on Sept. 7. "Basic Principles of Objectivist Psychology" will begin in Dallas, Oct. 1; Philadelphia, Oct. 5. "The Principles of Efficient Thinking" will begin in Pittsburgh on Oct. 1. "The Esthetics of the Visual Arts" will begin in Youngstown on Oct. 1.

Starting dates in additional cities will be listed here as they are scheduled. For further information, contact NBI.

Dr. Leonard Peikoff, Assistant Professor of Philosophy at the University of Denver, is giving a course on Objectivism in the Graduate College of the University of Denver this fall. The course is a Graduate Seminar, entitled: *Objectivism's Theory of Knowledge*. It deals with the fundamentals of Objectivist epistemology. The course carries five hours of academic credit and is open only to regularly-enrolled students at the University of Denver who fulfill the University's requirements for admission to graduate level study.

Published monthly at 120 East 34th Street, New York, N.Y. 10016.
Subscription rate In United States, its possessions, Canada and Mexico: one year, $5; 2 years, $9; 3 years, $13. Other countries: one year, $6; 2 years, $11; 3 years, $16.
Additional copies of this Newsletter: single copy 50¢ (coins, not stamps); 10 – 99 copies, 25¢ each plus postage (for first-class delivery add 1¢ per copy, for third-class delivery add ½¢ per copy); 100 or more copies, 15¢ each plus postage (same as above). (Bulk rates apply only to multiple orders of a single issue.)
Please include zip code number with your address.
For change of address, send old and new address. Allow us three weeks to process new subscriptions and change of address.

Ayn Rand and Nathaniel Branden, Editors and Publishers
Barbara Branden, Managing Editor
Elayne Kalberman, Circulation Manager

THE OBJECTIVIST NEWSLETTER

Edited and Published by AYN RAND and NATHANIEL BRANDEN

VOL. 4 NO. 10   OCTOBER, 1965

CHECK YOUR PREMISES
By AYN RAND

The Obliteration of Capitalism

In my article on " 'Extremism' or The Art of Smearing," in the September 1964 issue of this NEWSLETTER, I discussed the subject of "anti-concepts"—*i.e.*, artificial, unnecessary, undefined and (rationally) unusable terms intended to replace and obliterate certain legitimate concepts in people's minds.

I said that the "liberals" are coining and spreading "anti-concepts" in order to smuggle this country into statism by an imperceptible process—and that the primary target marked for obliteration is the concept of "capitalism" which, if lost, would carry away with it the knowledge that a free society can and did exist.

But there is something much less attractive (and, politically, much more disastrous) than capitalism's enemies: its alleged defenders—some of whom are muscling in on the game of manufacturing "anti-concepts" of their own.

Have you ever felt a peculiar kind of embarrassment when witnessing a grossly inappropriate human performance, such as the antics of an unfunny comedian? It is a depersonalized, almost metaphysical embarrassment at having to witness so undignified a behavior on the part of a member of the human species.

That is what I feel at having to hear the following statement of Governor Romney, which was his alleged answer to the communists' boast that they would bury capitalism:

"But what they do not understand—and what we have failed to tell the world—is that Americans buried capitalism long ago, and moved on to consumerism."

The implications of such a statement are too sickeningly obvious. The best comment on it came from The Richardson Digest (Richardson, Texas, April 28, 1965), from the column "Lively Comments" by Earl Lively, who wrote: "Afraid to stand alone, even on his knees, Romney then tells the rest of us that we do not know the definition of capitalism, we do not understand our economic principles, and we'd be better off if we quit going around defending such an unpopular concept as capitalism."

Mr. Lively is admirably precise in his description of the posture involved. But Mr. Romney is not alone in it. A number of intellectually more reputable men (including some distinguished free-enterprise economists) have adopted the same stance and the same line for the same psychological reasons.

There are the economists who proclaim that the essence (and the moral justification) of capitalism is *"service* to others—to the consumers," that the consumers' wishes are the absolute edicts ruling the free market, etc. (This is an example of what a definition by non-essentials accomplishes, and of why a half-truth is worse than a lie: what all such theorists fail to mention is the fact that capitalism grants economic recognition to only one kind of consumer: the producer—that only traders, *i.e.*, producers who have something to offer, are recognized on a free market, not "consumers" as such—that, in a capitalist economy, as in reason, in justice and in reality, production is the pre-condition of consumption.)

There are the businessmen who spend fortunes on ideological ads, allegedly in defense of capitalism, which assure the public that all but a tiny fraction of an industry's income goes to labor (wages), to government (taxes) etc., with these shares represented as big chunks in full-color process, and, lost among them, an apologetic little sliver is marked "2½ percent" and labelled "profits."

Since none of these attempts can succeed in disguising the nature of capitalism nor in degrading it to the level of an altruistic stockyards, their sole result is to convince the public that capitalism hides some evil secret which imbues its alleged defenders with such an aura of abject guilt and hypocrisy. But, in fact, the secret they are struggling to hide is capitalism's essence and greatest virtue: that it is a system based on the recognition of individual rights—on man's right to exist (and to work) for his own sake—*not* on the altruistic view of man as a sacrificial animal. Thus it is capitalism's *virtue* that the public is urged—by such defenders—to regard as evil, and it is *altruism* that all their efforts help to reinforce and reaffirm as the standard of the good.

What they dare not allow into their minds is the fact that capitalism and altruism are incompatible; so they wonder why the more they propagandize, the more unpopular capitalism becomes. They blame it on people's stupidity (because people refuse to believe that a successful industrialist is an exponent of altruistic self-sacrifice)—and on people's greed for the unearned (because, after being battered with assurances that the industrialist's wealth is "morally" theirs, people do come to believe it).

No "anti-concept" launched by the "liberals" goes so far so crudely as the tag "consumerism." It implies loudly and clearly that the status of "consumer" is separate from and superior to the status of "producer"; it suggests a social system dedicated to the service of a new aristocracy which is distinguished by the ability to "consume" and vested with a special claim on the caste of serfs marked by the ability to produce. If taken seriously, such a tag would lead to the ultimate absurdity of the communists proclaiming: "Who does not toil, shall not eat"—and the alleged representatives of capitalism replying: "Oh yes, he shall!" And if the Ad Hoc Committee on the Triple Revolution propounds such a moral obscenity as *"the right to consume"*—who inspired it, Karl Marx or Governor Romney?

It is true that we are not a capitalist system any longer: we are a mixed economy, *i.e.*, a mixture of capitalism and statism, of freedom and controls. A mixed economy is a country in the process of disintegration, a civil war of pressure-groups looting and devouring one another. In this sense, "consumerism" might be the appropriate name for it.

Now to whom is it that the friends, the semi-friends and even the acquaintances of capitalism are so anxiously apologizing?

As the clearest illustration of the psychological motives, the

---

Announcing
THE OBJECTIVIST
The Journal of the philosophy of Objectivism

We are pleased to announce that the growing circulation of THE OBJECTIVIST NEWSLETTER has permitted us to enlarge it and to adopt a magazine format. THE OBJECTIVIST will begin publication in January, 1966.

As of that date, subscribers to THE OBJECTIVIST NEWSLETTER will receive the new monthy magazine. There will be no increase in the subscription price.

THE OBJECTIVIST will continue to feature articles by Ayn Rand, Nathaniel Branden and other contributors, on ethics, political economy, psychology, literature—as well as reviews of recommended books, and reports on Objectivist activities.

moral meaning and the intellectual technique involved in the manufacture of "anti-concepts," I offer you a column by C. L. Sulzberger, entitled "Should the Old Labels Be Changed," in the July, 1964, issue of *The New York Times.*

"A research report of the United States Information Agency," writes Mr. Sulzberger, "has ruefully discovered that the more our propaganda advertises the virtues of 'capitalism' and attacks 'Socialism,' the less the world likes us.... Confused semantics make bad public relations.... Having analyzed conclusions of its poll-takers in both hemispheres, the U.S.I.A. study observes: ' "Capitalism is evil. The United States is the leading capitalist country. Therefore, the United States is evil." It would be difficult to exaggerate the harm that this line of thinking has done. In the Soviet Union and Communist China it sustains attitudes and actions that greatly increase the danger of thermonuclear war.' "

What is meant here by such a foggy expression as "sustains attitudes and actions"? The smear of capitalism as evil was originated and is constantly reiterated by the communists. Does the above mean that their own smear sustains their attitudes? And does it mean that the way to avoid thermonuclear war is for us to agree that the smear is true?

The report does not say. It merely goes on: " 'In the non-Communist world it tends to poison the atmosphere in which we are trying to carry on our aid programs and other international cooperation.' "

This means that the harm, to us, lies in the danger that the recipients of our charity might refuse to take our money—and that in order to gain their "cooperation," we must spit in our own face and join in smearing the system which produced the wealth which is saving their lives.

" 'Capitalism' is a dirty word to millions of non-Marxists who see 'Socialism' as vaguely benevolent. When the U.S.I.A. sampled foreign opinion it found that to the majority 'Socialism' did not mean government ownership and was not necessarily related to communism. Rather it seemed to imply a system favoring welfare of common people."

If you have doubted that the philosophy of Pragmatism actually teaches that truth is to be established by public polls —here is a sample of it, in pure and naked form. Volumes of theory, a century of history and the bloody practice of five continents to the contrary notwithstanding, "socialism" does not mean government ownership and is not related to communism—because a sampling of majority opinion said so. And what is meant by "a system favoring welfare of common people?" How does one "favor" the "common people"? At the expense of the uncommon? A "favor" means the unearned— since the earned is a right, not a favor. Whose rights and earnings are to be abrogated and expropriated—for whose benefit? The only variant of socialism that can distribute "favors" without government ownership, is fascism. Draw your own conclusions about the political inclinations of the moral cannibals involved in that poll.

"Most foreigners apparently don't regard 'capitalism' as descriptive of an efficient economy or a safeguard of individual rights. To them it means little concern for the poor, unfair distribution of wealth and undue influence of the rich."

How does one combine the safeguard of individual rights with a government-enforced "concern for the poor" and a government-distributed wealth and "influence"? No answer.

"U.S.I.A. found an impressive percentage of British, West Germans, Italians, Japanese, Mexicans and Brazilians have a favorable opinion of 'Socialism' and a strongly unfavorable opinion of 'capitalism.' "

Consider the philosophical trends, the intellectual commitments, the moral records of these countries—and *their political results.* Germany, Italy and Japan were fascist dictatorships; their claims to political wisdom consist of giving the world a demonstration of horror equalled only by their ideological brothers in Soviet Russia and Red China. Britain, Mexico and Brazil are mixed economies which have long since gone over the borderline state of mixture into the category—and the economic bankruptcy—of socialistic countries. And *these* are the nations whose opinions we are asked to value, whose favor we are asked to court—these are the moral authorities to whom we must apologize for the noblest political system in history: ours —these are the judges whom we must placate by denying our system, dishonoring its record and obliterating its name.

Is there any conceivable motive that could prompt a nation to so base a betrayal? Conceivable—no, if one refers to the realm of rational concepts. But—

" 'Capitalism' abroad is frequently a pejorative word. Efforts to purge it of negative connotations by phrases like 'people's capitalism' have failed.... But 'Socialism' is chic. [Yes, *chic.*] Even in Britain and West Germany, where private ownership is the mode, the majority expressed itself sympathetic to 'Socialism,' while abhoring Communism."

If the term "social metaphysics" occurs to you at this point, you would be right—except that even that term seems too clean, almost too innocent, to explain the following:

"Leaders of underdeveloped nations, spurning 'capitalism,' boast of special brands of 'Socialism.' Leopold Senghor of Senegal says 'Socialism is a sense of community which is a return to Africanism.' Julius Nyerere of Tanganyika insists 'no underdeveloped country can afford to be anything but "Socialist." ' Tunisia's Habib Bourguiba claims Mohammed's companions 'were Socialists before the invention of the word.' And Cambodia's Prince Norodom Sihanouk contends 'our Socialism is first and foremost an application of Buddhism.' "

The above is true, totally true, true all the way down to the deepest philosophical, psychological, political and moral fundamentals. And *this* is the most damning indictment of socialism that a rational person could need to see. Socialism *is* a regression to primitive barbarism. But that is not the appraisal or the conclusion of the U.S.I.A. report. It is to the Mohammedans, the Buddhists and the cannibals (the literal *cannibals,* this time) —to the underdeveloped, the undeveloped, and the not-to-be-developed cultures—that the Capitalist United States of America is asked to apologize for her skyscrapers, her automobiles, her plumbing and her smiling, confident, un-tortured, un-skinned-alive, un-eaten young men!

The column ends as follows: "The study concludes that foreigners attribute to the U.S.A. 'a high degree of capitalist exploitation and of capitalist power over the society as a whole, as well as (U.S.I.A.'s own italics) *a great absence of those social welfare measures which, to them, are the decisive criterion of Socialism.'*

"There is surely no sense in proclaiming our philosophy in terms that are unsalable and peculiarly vulnerable to our opponents' attacks....

"Our system of capitalism has evolved immensely from the outmoded economic doctrine to which the label was originally applied by Marx and other 19th-century thinkers. Might not the U.S.I.A. attempt another survey seeking ways of announcing our social and political system in a manner more acceptable to those abroad whose opinions we would influence?"

Influence—how? In what direction? To what purpose? If, for the sake of appeasement, we renounce our philosophy and adopt theirs, if we discard the last remnants of capitalism and proclaim ourselves to be a "National Socialist Welfare State," who would have "influenced"—and buried—whom?

A great many things may be observed about this unusually revealing column. It is true, of course, that if American propagandists are defending capitalism abroad as they do at home, the results would be precisely as described in that U.S.I.A. study, or worse. At home, it is the "conservatives" who are appeasing the "liberals" and losing the battle, because they dare not uphold the true nature of capitalism. Abroad, it is the "liberals" who are appeasing the communists and losing the battle, for the same reason: there is no way to defend capitalism without upholding man's right to exist, which means, without rejecting altruism.

Observe the appalling indifference to the issue of truth or falsehood, on the part of capitalism's alleged defenders. They attach no significance to such contradictions as sympathizing with socialism while abhoring communism—or to the fact that capitalism is the only opposite of and the only defense against communism. They attach no significance to the ignorance, the dishonesty, the injustice, the irrationality of capitalism's critics. In the face of a moral-philosophical issue, their response is an immediate, uncritical acceptance of the critics' terms, a surrender to ignorance, dishonesty, injustice, irrationality. In the face of the knowledge that capitalism is being smeared by the communists, by the very enemy they intend to fight, their policy is not to blast the smear, not to enlighten the world, not to defend the victim, not to speak out for justice—but to sanction the smear, to hide the truth, to sacrifice the victim, to join

(Continued on page 50)

BOOKS

The Democrat's Dilemma by Philip M. Crane*

Reviewed by **JOAN MELTZER**

In 1905 a dedicated group of one hundred intellectuals banded together and issued an ideological death warrant. Their prey was capitalism.

In 1962 a member of the group proudly proclaimed that they, and hundreds of thousands like them, had largely achieved their goal. The free enterprise system had been "condemned, sentenced and executed."

How?

The Democrat's Dilemma provides a major clue: American socialists discovered the value of education as the means to successful political action.

In this informative book, Philip M. Crane examines the numerous groups working to educate Americans to accept socialism, discusses their means of cultural indoctrination and political permeation, and proves that such educational groups are largely responsible for America's frenzied orgy of legislation during the last forty-five years.

In tracing the genesis of both their ideology and methodology, the author points out that American socialists enthusiastically emulated the English Fabian Society. This scholarly group, organized in 1882, took its name and purpose from the following motto:

"For the right moment you must wait, as Fabius did most patiently when warring against Hannibal; but when the time comes you must strike hard, as Fabius did, or your waiting will be in vain and fruitless."

Translated into a principle for political action, this motto meant: Slowly educate, then brutally legislate.

British Fabian and economist John Maynard Keynes concisely stated the theme of the Fabian movement when he wrote in his book *The General Theory of Employment, Interest, and Money*: "The ideas of economists and political philosophers, both when they are right and when they are wrong, are more powerful than is commonly understood. Indeed, the world is ruled by little else. Practical men, who believe themselves to be quite exempt from any intellectual influences, are usually the slaves of some defunct economist."

The one hundred men who organized the Intercollegiate Socialist Society (I.S.S.) in 1905, were the first Americans to adopt and relentlessly pursue this Fabian doctrine. Under the leadership of novelist Upton Sinclair, they maintained that if socialist legislation were to be successfully enacted, socialism first had to become the new orthodoxy within the academic world. Zealously dedicating itself to this task, the Society zeroed in on the marketplace of ideas, the university.

The I.S.S. found a fertile desert—scholars and students alike offered only a feeble defense for capitalism. Thus, the Society easily and systematically injected socialist ideology into the soil and watched it flower. By 1910, writes Dr. Crane, fifteen I.S.S. study groups thrived on college campuses—the two most flourishing led by Walter Lippman, a student at Harvard, and Charles A. Beard, an historian at Columbia. Only five years later, sixty I.S.S. study groups were collecting and collectivizing 35,000 young minds a year. The I.S.S. was but one of hundreds of such educational organizations.

Dr. Crane goes on to say that the Socialist party bolstered the work of the I.S.S. by establishing the Rand School for Social Science in New York City. He calls it a "West Point for turning out well-indoctrinated socialist leaders." Its purpose was to make young men and women intellectually fit for effective socialist leadership on the pulpit, in classrooms, in congressional halls and in labor unions.

Labor was a particularly important area for socialist educators, because they saw the working class as the springboard to control of the Government. As a member of the League for Industrial Democracy (an off-shoot of the I.S.S.) wrote: "The Government is the head of a human society and directs and coerces the members of society the same as the brain is the head of the human body and directs and disciplines its members. Whatever dominates the head, dominates the body. The only way then to destroy economic privilege and establish Industrial Democracy is to secure political control of the public head—the Government."

To this end, educators indoctrinated workers with a strong sense of class warfare by means of the following ideas:

—Businessmen acquire great wealth only by imposing hardships, suffering and misery on others.

—To avoid exploitation, workers must advocate political rather than private decisions in economic issues.

—A judicious social order acknowledges the supremacy of human need rather than private profit as its organizing principle.

Unlimited variations of these ideas were ground out in vast quantities of leaflets, pamphlets, books, newsletters, magazines, films, not only during an election year, but every day and month of every year. Dr. Crane conservatively estimates that these ideas reached sixty million workers directly and influenced more than twice that many votes. No opportunity for the dissemination of socialist ideology was overlooked. As one L.I.D. member boasted: "We socialists don't run for office primarily to get elected, we go into politics for the educational advantages of a campaign."

Their main goal, however, was to draw into government circles the best socialist brains of the country and let them educate the practical politicians. Their first significant success, notes the author, was the formation of Franklin Roosevelt's "brain trust." Indeed, they were so successful under Roosevelt's administration that Upton Sinclair predicted: "It will be the Democratic Party which will bring the great change to America."

Subsequent legislation has demonstrated that he was right. And, according to Dr. Crane, these educational groups significantly shaped and successfully sold to the public the policies not only of Roosevelt's "New Deal," but Truman's "Fair Deal" and Kennedy's "New Frontier."

The predictable climax of the story is the virtual take-over of all political thought in America. When Fabian-oriented socialists began their educational campaign, they found that this country's free enterprise system was operating in an intellectual vacuum. So well did they fill that vacuum that today our most prominent political leaders righteously champion collectivism.

"My only regret in this heart-warming anniversary celebration is that Rand Schools do not dot the land from New England to California," said Vice President Hubert H. Humphrey, at a Rand School anniversary dinner in New York, 1961.

"Surely we have reached the point where we can say, for our time at least, that Jefferson was wrong: That government is *not* best which governs least," wrote Senator Joseph S. Clark in a pamphlet entitled *The Elite and the Electorate*.

"Government by the people is possible but highly improbable. The experience of modern times shows us that when the passengers take over the navigation of the ship it is likely to go on the rocks," wrote Senator J. William Fulbright in the same pamphlet, *The Elite and the Electorate*.

Although Dr. Crane has assembled valuable and richly-documented material, he has failed to identify and to discuss explicitly its true significance: its implicit testimony to the power of ideas. Too much of his book is devoted to a mass of details on the internal structure and underground financing of political action groups, and not enough attention is given to the real cause of their success: their relentless educational work. Only at the conclusion of the book does he attempt to offer an explanation: "American Fabians expended the effort the average American did not—to educate themselves to a philosophical conviction and do a remarkable job of selling it." The average American, however, cannot be expected to educate himself philosophically. That, precisely, is the job of professional intellectuals, and *their* default is responsible for our present political state.

Dr. Crane shares their default to some extent: his attempted defense of capitalism is superficial and unconvincing, offering nothing but the claim that capitalism is "practical."

Nevertheless, *The Democrat's Dilemma* is a valuable reference book. It is particularly recommended to the so-called "political activists" who are eager to fight for capitalism by rushing into "practical" action without any knowledge of what caused the collectivist trend and what is required to reverse it.

---

*Published by Henry Regnery Co., $4.95. Available from NBI BOOK SERVICE, 120 East 34th St., New York, N.Y. 10016, for $4.25. N.Y. State residents add sales tax; outside the U.S., add 15¢.

The Obliteration of Capitalism (from page 48)

the lynching. What they feel is: Of what account is truth in the face of such a consideration as "people don't like us?" What they cry is: "But this is the way we'll make people like the victim!"—after we've helped them grind her to bits in the mud. Then they wonder why contempt is all they earn, from betrayed allies and sworn enemies alike. Moral cowardice is not an attractive nor an inspiring nor a very practical trait.

Observe the obscenity of those Europeans who—in this day and age, in the rising tide of global bloodshed, in the face of the unspeakable atrocities of the "newly emerging" nations—dare prattle about "little concern for the poor" and criticize the United States for *that*. Whatever their motives, concern for human suffering is not one of them.

We may observe all that, but it seems almost irrelevant beside the one central, overwhelming fact: the intellectual leaders of today's world are willing to condone and accept anything, they are willing to recognize the right of Buddhism and Africanism to their boastfully asserted traditions (remember the nature and record of those traditions)—but they make one exception. There is one country—the United States of America—who is not acceptable to them, who must renounce *her* tradition and, in atonement, must crawl on her knees, begging the savages of five continents to choose a new name for her system, which would obliterate the guilt of her past. What is her guilt? That for one brief moment in human history, she offered the world the vision of unsacrificed man in a non-sacrificial way of life.

When one grasps *this*, one knows that it is no use arguing over political trivia, or wondering about the nature of altruism, and why the reign of the altruists is leading the world to an ever widening spread of horror. *This* is the nature of altruism, *this*—not any sort of benevolence, good will or concern for human misfortune. Hatred of man, not the desire to help him—hatred of life, not the desire to further it—hatred of *the successful state of life*—and that ultimate, apocalyptic evil: *hatred of the good for being the good*.

What every succesful man (successful at any human value, spiritual or material) has encountered, has sensed, has been bewildered by, but has seldom identified, can now be seen in the open, with nations, instead of individual men, re-enacting the same unspeakable evil on a world scale where it cannot be hidden any longer. It is not for her flaws that the United States of America is hated, but *for her virtues*—not for her weaknesses, but *for her achievements*—not for her failures, but *for her success*—her magnificent, shining, life-giving success.

"It is not your wealth that they're after. Theirs is a conspiracy against the mind, which means: against life and man. It is a conspiracy without leader or direction, and the random little thugs of the moment who cash in on the agony of one land or another are chance scum riding the torrent from the broken dam of the sewer of centuries, from the reservoir of hatred for reason, for logic, for ability, for achievement, for joy, stored by every whining anti-human who ever preached the superiority of the 'heart' over the mind." (*Atlas Shrugged*)

With most of the world in ruins, with the voice of philosophy silent and the last remnants of civilization vanishing undefended, in an unholy alliance of savagery and decadence, bloody thugs are fighting over the spoils, while the cynical pragmatists left in charge and way out of their depth, are trying to drown their panic at Europe's cocktail-parties, where emasculated men and hysterical, white-lipped women determine the fate of the world by declaring that socialism is chic.

This is the face of our age. To attempt to fight it by means of compromise, conciliation, equivocation and circumlocution is worse than grotesque. This is not a battle to be fought by joining the enemy in any manner—nor by borrowing any of his slogans or his bloody ideological equipment—nor by deluding the world about the nature of the battle—nor by pretending that one is "in" with that sort of crowd.

It is a battle only for those who know why it is necessary to be "out"—as far out of that stream as words will carry—why, when moral issues are at stake, one must begin by blasting the enemy's base and cutting off any link to it, any bridge, any toehold—and if one is to be misunderstood, let it be on the side of intransigence, not on the side of any resemblance to any part of so monstrous an evil.

It is a battle only for those who—paraphrasing a character in *Atlas Shrugged*—are prepared to say:

"Capitalism was the only system in history where wealth was not acquired by looting, but by production, not by force, but by trade, the only system that stood for man's right to his own mind, to his work, to his life, to his happiness, to himself. If this is evil, by the present standards of the world, if this is the reason for damning us, then we—we, the champions of man —accept it and choose to be damned by that world. We choose to wear the name 'Capitalism' printed on our foreheads, proudly, as our badge of nobility."

This is what the battle demands. Nothing less will do.

OBJECTIVIST CALENDAR

■ The hardcover edition of *The Virtue of Selfishness* is now scheduled for publication by The New American Library on November 29. Advance copies will be available from NBI BOOK SERVICE (120 E. 34th St., New York, N.Y. 10016) for delivery in late October. Publishers price: $4.50; NBI price: $3.85. (N.Y. State residents add sales tax.)

■ Ayn Rand's article "The Cashing-In: The Student 'Rebellion' " (originally published in three parts in the July, August and September 1965 issues of this NEWSLETTER) has been reprinted in pamphlet form. Price: 75¢. (N.Y. State residents add sales tax.)

■ On Thursday, October 14, at 7 P.M., Radio Station KUOW (94.9 FM) of the University of Washington in Seattle will broadcast the first of twelve "Ayn Rand on Campus" programs. This series was originally broadcast in New York City by Columbia University Station WKCR. The programs will continue over Station KUOW on alternate Thursdays.

■ On Tuesday, October 19, Ayn Rand will be interviewed on "Dayline," Radio Station WTOP in Washington, D.C. Time: 3:10-3:55 P.M.

■ On Friday, October 22, Ayn Rand will be interviewed on "On Call," Radio Station WCFL in Chicago. Time: 10:15 P.M.-midnight.

■ On Tuesday, October 26, NBI will begin its fall series on "Basic Principles of Objectivism" in Washington, D.C. Mr. Branden will deliver the opening lecture in person. Miss Rand will join Mr. Branden in an extended question period.

In addition, NBI's Tape Transcription Division has scheduled starting dates for "Basic Principles of Objectivism" in: Tulsa, Oct. 17; Chicago, Oct. 19; Detroit, Oct. 21; Toronto, Oct. 22; Montreal, Oct. 23; Denver, Nov. 1; Huntsville, Ala, Nov. 1; Austin, Nov. 8; Ann Arbor, Nov. 8; New Haven, Nov. 16. Mr. Branden will deliver the opening lecture in person in Chicago, Detroit, Montreal and Toronto.

The following starting dates have also been scheduled: "Contemporary Theories of Neurosis" in Toronto, Oct. 19—"The Principles of Efficient Thinking" in Orange, Oct. 21; Rockford, Nov. 2—"Basic Principles of Objectivist Psychology" in Portland, Oct. 26—"The History of Ancient Philosophy" in Los Angeles, Nov. 10. For further information, contact NBI.

■ On Thursday, Nov. 11, Nathaniel Branden's course on "Basic Principles of Objectivist Psychology" will begin in New York City. Time: 7:30 P.M. Place: Sheraton-Atlantic Hotel, 34th St. and Broadway. Admission: $3.50. (College and High School students, $2.75.)

■ Ayn Rand's *Commentary* programs on Radio Station WBAI in New York will now be broadcast every other Thursday at 7:30 P.M. and re-broadcast the following Friday at 10 A.M. The next broadcast will be on October 28.

Published monthly at 120 East 34th Street, New York, N.Y. 10016.
Subscription rate in United States, its possessions, Canada and Mexico: one year, $5; 2 years, $9; 3 years, $13. Other countries: one year, $6; 2 years, $11; 3 years, $16.
Additional copies of this Newsletter: single copy 50¢ (coins, not stamps); 10 – 99 copies, 25¢ each plus postage (for first-class delivery add 1¢ per copy, for third-class delivery add ½¢ per copy); 100 or more copies, 15¢ each plus postage (same as above). (Bulk rates apply only to multiple orders of a single issue.)
Please include zip code number with your address.
For change of address, send old and new address. Allow us three weeks to process new subscriptions and change of address.

Ayn Rand and Nathaniel Branden, Editors and Publishers
Barbara Branden, Managing Editor
Elayne Kalberman, Circulation Manager

THE OBJECTIVIST NEWSLETTER

Edited and Published by AYN RAND and NATHANIEL BRANDEN

VOL. 4 NO. 11   NOVEMBER, 1965

CHECK YOUR PREMISES
By AYN RAND
What Is Capitalism?

(Part I of a two-part article)

The disintegration of philosophy in the 19th century and its collapse in the 20th have led to a similar, though much slower and less obvious, process in the course of modern science.

Today's frantic development in the field of technology has a quality reminiscent of the days preceding the economic crash of 1929: riding on the momentum of the past, on the unacknowledged remnants of an Aristotelian epistemology, it is a hectic, feverish expansion, heedless of the fact that its theoretical account is long since overdrawn—that in the field of scientific theory, unable to integrate or interpret their own data, scientists are abetting the resurgence of a primitive type of mysticism. In the humanities, however, the crash is past, the depression has set in, and the collapse of science is all but complete.

The clearest evidence of it may be seen in such comparatively young sciences as psychology and political economy. In psychology, one may observe the attempt to study human behavior without reference to the fact that man is conscious. In political economy, one may observe the attempt to study and to devise social systems without reference to *man*.

It is philosophy that defines and establishes the epistemological criteria to guide human knowledge in general and specific sciences in particular. Political economy came into prominence in the 19th century, in the era of philosophy's post-Kantian disintegration, and no one rose to check its premises or to challenge its base. Implicitly, uncritically and by default, political economy accepted as its axioms the fundamental tenets of collectivism.

Political economists—including the advocates of capitalism—defined their science as the study of the management or direction or organization or manipulation of a "community's" or a nation's "resources." The nature of these "resources" was not defined; their communal ownership was taken for granted—and the goal of political economy was assumed to be the study of how to utilize these "resources" for "the common good."

The fact that the principal "resource" involved was man himself, that he was an entity of a specific nature with specific capacities and requirements, was given the most superficial attention, if any. Man was regarded simply as one of the factors of production, along with land, forests or mines—as one of the less significant factors, since more study was devoted to the influence and quality of these others than to *his* role or quality.

Political economy was, in effect, a science starting in midstream: it observed that men were producing and trading, it took for granted that they had always done so and always would—it accepted this fact as the given, requiring no further consideration—and it addressed itself to the problem of how to devise the best way for the "community" to dispose of human effort.

There were many reasons for this tribal view of man. The morality of altruism was one; the growing dominance of political statism among the intellectuals of the 19th century was another. Psychologically, the main reason was the soul-body dichotomy permeating European culture: material production was regarded as a demeaning task of a lower order, unrelated to the concerns of man's intellect, a task assigned to slaves or serfs since the beginning of recorded history. The institution of serfdom had lasted, in one form or another, till well into the 19th century; it was abolished, politically, only by the advent of capitalism; politically, but not intellectually.

The concept of man as a free, independent individual was profoundly alien to the culture of Europe. It was a tribal culture down to its roots; in European thinking, the tribe was the entity, the unit, and man was only one of its expendable cells. This applied to rulers and serfs alike: the rulers were believed to hold their privileges only by virtue of the services they rendered to the tribe, services regarded as of a noble order, namely armed force or military defense. But a nobleman was as much chattel of the tribe as a serf: his life and property belonged to the King. It must be remembered that the institution of private property, in the full, legal meaning of the term, was brought into existence only by capitalism. In the pre-capitalist eras, private property existed *de facto*, but not *de jure, i.e.*, by custom and sufferance, not by right or by law: in law and in principle, all property belonged to the head of the tribe, the King, and was held only by his permission, which could be revoked at any time, at his pleasure. (The King could and did expropriate the estates of recalcitrant noblemen throughout the course of Europe's history.)

The American philosophy of the Rights of Man was never grasped fully by European intellectuals. Europe's predominant idea of emancipation consisted of changing the concept of man as a slave of the absolute state embodied by a King, to the concept of man as a slave of the absolute state embodied by "the people" — *i.e.*, switching from slavery to a tribal chief into slavery to the tribe. A non-tribal view of existence could not penetrate the mentalities that regarded the privilege of ruling material producers by physical force as a badge of nobility.

Thus Europe's thinkers did not notice the fact that during the 19th century, the galley slaves had been replaced by the inventors of steamboats, and the village blacksmiths by the owners of blast furnaces, and they went on thinking in such terms (such contradictions in terms) as "wage slavery" or "the antisocial selfishness of industrialists who take so much from society without giving anything in return"—on the unchallenged axiom that wealth is an anonymous, social, tribal product.

That notion has not been challenged to this day; it represents the implicit assumption and the base of contemporary political economy.

As an example of this view and its consequences, I shall cite the article on "Capitalism" in the *Encyclopaedia Britannica*, 1964, Volume 4, pp. 839-845.

The article gives no definition of its subject; it opens as follows: "CAPITALISM, a term used to denote the economic system that has been dominant in the western world since the breakup of feudalism. Fundamental to any system called capitalist are the relations between private owners of nonpersonal means of production (land, mines, *industrial plants*, etc., collectively known as capital) [italics mine] and free but capitalless workers, who sell their labour services to employers. . . . The resulting wage bargains determine the proportion in which the total product of society will be shared between the class of labourers and the class of capitalist entrepreneurs."

(I quote from Galt's speech in *Atlas Shrugged*, from a passage describing the tenets of collectivism: "An industrialist—blank-out—there is no such person. A factory is a 'natural resource,' like a tree, a rock or a mud-puddle.")

The success of capitalism is explained by the *Britannica* as follows: "Productive use of the 'social surplus' was the special virtue that enabled capitalism to outstrip all prior economic systems. Instead of building pyramids and cathedrals, those in command of the social surplus chose to invest in ships, warehouses, raw materials, finished goods and other material forms of wealth. The social surplus was thus converted into enlarged productive capacity."

This is said about a time when Europe's population subsisted in such poverty that child mortality approached 50 per cent, and periodic famines wiped out the "surplus" *population* which the pre-capitalist economies were unable to feed. Yet, making no distinction between tax-expropriated and industrially produced wealth, the *Britannica* asserts that it was the *surplus wealth* of that time that the early capitalists "commanded" and "chose to invest"—and that this investment was the cause of the stupendous prosperity of the age that followed.

What is a "social surplus"? The article gives no definition or explanation. A "surplus" presupposes a norm; if subsistence on a chronic starvation level is above the implied norm, what is that norm? The article does not answer.

There is, of course, no such thing as a "social surplus." All wealth is produced by somebody and belongs to somebody. And "the special virtue that enabled capitalism to outstrip all prior economic systems" was *freedom* (a concept eloquently absent from the *Britannica's* account), which led, not to the expropriation, but to the *creation* of wealth.

I shall have more to say later about that disgraceful article (disgraceful on many counts, not the least of which is scholarship). At this point, I quoted it only as a succinct example of the tribal premise that underlies today's political economy. That premise is shared by the enemies and the champions of capitalism alike; it provides the former with a certain inner consistency, and disarms the latter by a subtle, yet devastating aura of moral hypocrisy—as witness, their attempts to justify capitalism on the ground of "the common good" or "service to the consumer" or "the best allocation of resources." (*Whose* resources?)

If capitalism is to be understood, it is this *tribal premise* that has to be checked—and challenged.

Mankind is not an entity, an organism or a coral bush. The entity involved in production and trade is *man*. It is with the study of man—not of the loose aggregate known as a "community"—that any science of the humanities has to begin.

This issue represents one of the epistemological differences between the humanities and the physical sciences, one of the causes of the former's well-earned inferiority complex in regard to the latter. A physical science would not permit itself (not yet, at least) to ignore or by-pass the nature of its subject. Such an attempt would mean: a science of astronomy that gazed at the sky, but refused to study individual stars, planets and satellites—or a science of medicine that studied disease, without any knowledge or criterion of health, and took, as its basic subject of study, a hospital as a whole, never focusing on individual patients.

A great deal may be learned about society by studying man; but this process cannot be reversed: nothing can be learned about man by studying society—by studying the inter-relationships of entities one has never identified or defined. Yet that is the methodology adopted by most political economists. Their attitude, in effect, amounts to the unstated, implicit postulate: "Man is that which fits economic equations." Since he obviously does not, this leads to the curious fact that in spite of the practical nature of their science, political economists are oddly unable to connect their abstractions to the concretes of actual existence.

It leads also to a baffling sort of double standard or double perspective in their way of viewing men and events: if they observe a shoemaker, they find no difficulty in concluding that he is working in order to make a living; but as political economists, on the tribal premise, they declare that his purpose (and duty) is to provide society with shoes. If they observe a panhandler on a street corner, they identify him as a bum; in political economy, he becomes "a sovereign consumer." If they hear the communist doctrine that all property should belong to the state, they reject it emphatically and feel, *sincerely,* that they would fight communism to the death; but in political economy, they speak of the government's duty to effect "a fair redistribution of wealth," and they speak of businessmen as the best, most efficient trustees of the nation's "natural resources."

This is what a basic premise (and philosophical negligence) will do; this is what the tribal premise has done.

To reject that premise and begin at the beginning—in one's approach to political economy and to the evaluation of various social systems—one must begin by identifying man's nature, *i.e.,* those essential characteristics which distinguish him from all other living species.

Man's essential characteristic is his rational faculty. Man's mind is his basic means of survival—his only means of gaining knowledge. "Man cannot survive, as animals do, by the guidance of mere percepts. . . . He cannot provide for his simplest physical needs without a process of thought. He needs a process of thought to discover how to plant and grow his food or how to make weapons for hunting. His percepts might lead him to a cave, if one is available—but to build the simplest shelter, he needs a process of thought. No percepts and no 'instincts' will tell him how to light a fire, how to weave cloth, how to forge tools, how to make a wheel, how to make an airplane, how to perform an appendectomy, how to produce an electric light bulb or an electronic tube or a cyclotron or a box of matches. Yet his life depends on such knowledge—and only a volitional act of his consciousness, a process of thought, can provide it." (*The Objectivist Ethics.*)

A process of thought is an enormously complex process of identification and integration, which only an individual mind can perform. There is no such thing as a collective brain. Men can learn from one another, but learning requires a process of thought on the part of every individual student. Men can cooperate in the discovery of new knowledge, but such cooperation requires the independent exercise of his rational faculty by every individual scientist. Man is the only living species that can transmit and expand his store of knowledge from generation to generation; but such transmission requires a process of thought on the part of the individual recipients. As witness, the breakdowns of civilization, the dark ages in the history of mankind's progress, when the accumulated knowledge of centuries vanished from the lives of men who were unable, unwilling or forbidden to think.

In order to sustain its life, every living species has to follow a certain course of action required by its nature. The action required to sustain human life is primarily intellectual: everything man needs has to be discovered by his mind and produced by his effort. Production is the application of reason to the problem of survival.

If some men do not choose to think, they can survive only by imitating and repeating a routine of work discovered by others—but those others had to discover it, or none would have survived. If some men do not choose to think or to work, they can survive (temporarily) only by looting the goods produced by others—but those others had to produce them, or none would have survived. Regardless of what choice is made, in this issue, by any man or by any number of men, regardless of what blind, irrational or evil course they may choose to pursue—the fact remains that reason is man's means of survival and that men prosper or fail, survive or perish in proportion to the degree of their rationality.

Since knowledge, thinking and rational action are properties of the individual, since the choice to exercise his rational faculty or not depends on the individual, man's survival requires that those who think be free of the interference of those who don't. Since men are neither omniscient nor infallible, they must be free to agree or disagree, to cooperate or to pursue their own independent course, each according to his own rational judgment. Freedom is the fundamental requirement of man's mind.

A rational mind does not work under compulsion; it does not subordinate its grasp of reality to anyone's orders, directives or controls; it does not sacrifice its knowledge, its view of the truth, to anyone's opinions, threats, wishes, plans or "welfare." Such a mind may be hampered by others, it may be silenced, proscribed, imprisoned or destroyed; it cannot be forced; a gun is not an argument. (An example and symbol of this attitude is Galileo.)

It is from the work and the inviolate integrity of such minds —from the intransigent innovators—that all of mankind's knowledge and achievements have come. (See *The Fountainhead.*) It is to such minds that mankind owes its survival. (See *Atlas Shrugged.*)

The same principle applies to all men, on every level of ability and ambition. To the extent that a man is guided by his rational judgment, he acts in accordance with the requirements of his nature and, to that extent, succeeds in achieving a human form of survival and well-being; to the extent that he acts irrationally, he acts as his own destroyer.

The social recognition of man's rational nature—of the connection between his survival and his use of reason — is the concept of *individual rights*.

I shall remind you that "rights" are a moral principle defining
(Continued on page 54)

INTELLECTUAL AMMUNITION DEPARTMENT

[*Subscribers are invited to send in the questions that they find themselves unable to answer in philosophical or political discussions. As many questions as space permits will be answered. No questions will be answered by mail.*]

■ **What is psychological maturity?**

"Maturity," in the broadest sense, is the state of being fully grown or developed. A living organism is mature when its normal process of development is completed, and it functions on the "adult" level appropriate to its species.

"*Psychological* maturity," then, is a concept pertaining to the successful development of man's consciousness, to the attainment of a level of functioning appropriate to man *qua* man.

Man is a rational being; to be guided in action by a *conceptual* form of consciousness, is his distinctive characteristic among living species. His psychological maturity is an issue of the proper growth and development of his conceptual faculty; it is a *psycho-epistemological* matter.

At first, a child knows only perceptual concretes; he does not know abstractions or principles. His world is only the immediate *now;* he cannot think, plan or act long-range; the future is largely unreal to him. At this stage, he is a total dependent, necessarily: his method of functioning (although biologically inevitable at this period of his life) is inadequate to the requirements of survival as an independent entity.

As the child grows, his intellectual field widens: he learns language, he begins to grasp abstractions, he generalizes, he makes increasingly subtle discriminations, he looks for principles, he acquires the ability to project a distant and more distant future—he rises from the sensory-perceptual level of consciousness to the conceptual level. His power to deal independently with the world around him, with the facts of reality, rises accordingly—in step with his increasing knowledge and increasing proficiency at conceptual mental functioning.

The first and basic index of psychological maturity is *the ability to think in principles*.

More broadly, the basic index of successfully achieved adulthood is the policy of conceptualizing. This means: "an actively sustained process of identifying one's impressions in conceptual terms, of integrating every event and every observation into a conceptual context, of grasping relationships, differences, similarities in one's perceptual material and of abstracting them into new concepts, of drawing inferences, of making deductions, of reaching conclusions, of asking new questions and discovering new answers and expanding one's knowledge into an ever-growing sum." (Ayn Rand, *The Objectivist Ethics.*)

It must be stressed that this practice constitutes evidence of maturity only when it operates in all the areas of one's life and not exclusively in the area of one's professional work: there are men who are brilliant at conceptualizing and thinking in principles when their focus is on higher mathematics or some distant galaxy or some business activity—but who become helpless, concrete-bound children, blind to any abstractions or principles, seeing nothing but the immediate moment, when their focus is on, say, current politics or, worse still, a problem in their personal life. Maturity is evidenced by the ability to think in principles *about oneself*.

All other aspects of psychological maturity are derivatives and consequences of the foregoing.

(1) A man who deals with the facts of reality on the conceptual level of consciousness has accepted the responsibility of a *human* manner of existence—which entails his acceptance of responsibility for his own life and actions.

A child cannot accept such responsibility — certainly not fully; he is still in the process of acquiring the knowledge and skills necessary for independence. But an adult who expects others to take care of him—and/or who habitually cries, when the consequences of his actions catch up with him, "I couldn't help it!"—is a case of self-arrested development, a person who has defaulted on the process of human maturation.

(2) The acceptance of responsibility for one's own life requires a policy of planning and acting long-range, so that one's actions are integrated to one another and to one's future. It is a child who, in large measure, "lives for the moment." A healthy adult plans and acts in terms of a lifespan.

This policy entails a corollary: the willingness to defer immediate pleasure or rewards and to tolerate frustration, when and if necessary. One will find many examples of this in the heroes of Ayn Rand's novels; a long-range perspective and a capacity to handle frustration with unself-pitying realism are among the heroes' most conspicuous and psychologically important traits.

An infant's typical reaction to frustration is crying. If a child learns that he cannot go to the circus on the day he had expected to, he may, understandably, feel crushed; next week, to him, seems like an infinite time away. But a healthy adult does not view his life and goals in this manner. He does not repress his frustrations; if he can find a way to overcome them, he does; if he cannot, he moves on, he is not paralyzed by them.

(3) A cardinal characteristic of maturity is emotional stability. This trait is the consequence of one particular aspect of the policy of conceptual functioning: the ability to preserve the full context of one's knowledge under conditions of stress —frustration, disappointment, fear, anguish, shock. It is the ability, under the pressure of such emotions, to preserve one's capacity to think. The opposite of this state is described as "going to pieces."

One of the unmistakable signs of *im*maturity is the characteristic of being habitually swamped, mentally, by the concrete problem of the moment, so that one loses one's abstract or long-range perspective, one loses the wider context of one's knowledge, and one is taken over by feelings of anger or panic or despair that paralyze thought.

A young person's hold on an abstract perspective, under conditions of stress, is, at best, tenuous; that perspective is still in the process of being formed and of growing firm. But a properly developed adult's perspective has hardened and does not normally crack under pressure.

An impressive example, in *Atlas Shrugged*, of this kind of maturity and strength, is John Galt's attitude when Dagny comes to his room, when Galt knows that she has been followed and that he will be arrested in a few minutes.

(This kind of emotional stability must be distinguished sharply from that counterfeit form of stability which is achieved by emotional repression. The repressor, who is so fearful of losing control that he dares not let himself know what he feels, is not an exponent of maturity.)

(4) Finally, there is an aspect of psychological maturity that is profoundly important and that few adults fully achieve. It pertains to one's attitude toward the unknown—not to knowledge which has not yet been discovered by anyone, but to knowledge which is available but which one does not possess.

To a child, the world around him is—necessarily—an immense unknown. He is aware that adults possess knowledge far in excess of his own and that there are many things he is not yet able to understand. He knows that he does not yet know the wider context of his life and actions. He tells himself, in effect: "I will have to wait until I grow up. There are many things I cannot understand now. They are known to other people, but they are beyond me at present."

It is this attitude that a genuinely mature adult does not permit himself. He does not tolerate such a category as that which is known to others but *unknowable* to him; he does not accept the validity of such a concept. This does not mean that his goal is to possess encyclopedic knowledge. It means that, within the sphere of his first-hand concerns, of his own actions and goals, he regards himself as competent to know that which he needs to know and he acquires whatever knowledge his interests and purposes demand. It means that he does not resign himself to the permanently unknown, when and if the knowledge is available and is relevant to his activities. It means that he does not regard himself as a second-class citizen, epistemologically. It is this attitude, consistently maintained, that marks a man's entry into full adulthood, which means: into full self-responsibility.

Such are the basic characteristics of psychological maturity.

They may serve as one more illustration of why Objectivism holds that the act of thinking is the root of all virtue—and of mental health.

—**NATHANIEL BRANDEN**

What is Capitalism? (from page 52)

and sanctioning a man's freedom of action in a social context, that they are derived from man's nature as a rational being and represent a necessary condition of his particular mode of survival. I shall remind you also that the right to life is the source of all rights, including the right to property. (For a fuller discussion of rights, I refer you to my articles "Man's Rights" and "Collectivized 'Rights' " in the April and June, 1963, issues of this NEWSLETTER.)

In regard to political economy, this last requires special emphasis: man has to work and produce in order to support his life. He has to support his life by his own effort and by the guidance of his own mind. If he cannot dispose of the product of his effort, he cannot dispose of his effort; if he cannot dispose of his effort, he cannot dispose of his life. Without property rights, no other rights can be practiced.

Now, bearing these facts in mind, consider the question of what social system is appropriate to man.

A social system is a set of moral-political-economic principles embodied in a society's laws, institutions and government, which determine the relationships, the terms of association, among the men living in a given geographical area. It is obvious that these terms and relationships depend on an identification of man's nature, that they would be different if they pertain to a society of rational beings or to a colony of ants. It is obvious that they will be radically different if men deal with one another as free, independent individuals, on the premise that every man is an end in himself—or as members of a pack, each regarding the others as the means to *his* ends and to the ends of "the pack as a whole."

There are only two fundamental questions (or two aspects of the same question) that determine the nature of any social system: Does a social system recognize individual rights?—and: Does a social system ban physical force from human relationships? The answer to the second question is the practical implementation of the answer to the first.

Is man a sovereign individual who owns his person, his mind, his life, his work and its products—or is he the property of the tribe (the state, the society, the collective) that may dispose of him in any way it pleases, that may dictate his convictions, prescribe the course of his life, control his work and expropriate his products? Does man have the *right* to exist for his own sake—or is he born in bondage, as an indentured servant who must keep buying his life by serving the tribe but can never acquire it free and clear?

This is the first question to answer. The rest is consequences and practical implementations. The basic issue is only: Is man free?

In mankind's history, capitalism is the only system that answers: Yes.

Capitalism is a social system based on the recognition of individual rights, including property rights, in which all property is privately owned.

The recognition of individual rights entails the banishment of physical force from human relationships: basically, rights can be violated only by means of force. In a capitalist society, no man or group may *initiate* the use of physical force against others. The only function of the government, in such a society, is the task of protecting man's rights, *i.e.*, the task of protecting him from physical force; the government acts as the agent of man's right of self-defense, and may use force only in retaliation and only against those who initiate its use; thus the government is the means of placing the retaliatory use of force under *objective control*. (For a fuller discussion of this subject, see my article "The Nature of Government" in the December 1963 issue of this NEWSLETTER.)

It is the basic, metaphysical fact of man's nature—the connection between his survival and his use of reason—that capitalism recognizes and protects.

In a capitalist society, all human relationships are *voluntary*. Men are free to cooperate or not, to deal with one another or not, as their own individual judgments, convictions and interests dictate. They can deal with one another only in terms of and by means of reason, *i.e.*, by means of discussion, persuasion and *contractual* agreement, by voluntary choice to mutual benefit. The right to agree with others is not a problem in any society; it is *the right to disagree* that is crucial. It is the institution of private property that protects and implements the right to disagree—and thus keeps the road open to man's most valuable attribute (valuable personally, socially and *objectively*): the creative mind.

This is the cardinal difference between capitalism and collectivism.

The power that determines the establishment, the changes, the evolution and the destruction of social systems is philosophy. The role of chance, accident or tradition, in this context, is the same as their role in the life of an individual: their power stands in inverse ratio to the power of a culture's (or an individual's) philosophical equipment, and grows as philosophy collapses. It is, therefore, by reference to philosophy that the character of a social system has to be defined and evaluated. Corresponding to the four branches of philosophy, the four keystones of capitalism are: metaphysically, the requirements of man's nature and survival — epistemologically, reason — ethically, individual rights—politically, freedom.

This, in substance, is the base of the proper approach to political economy and to an understanding of capitalism—not the tribal premise inherited from prehistorical traditions.

The "practical" justification of capitalism does not lie in the collectivist claim that it effects "the best allocation of national resources." Man is *not* a "national resource" and neither is his mind—and without the creative power of man's intelligence, raw materials remain just so many useless raw materials.

The *moral* justification of capitalism does not lie in the altruist claim that it represents the best way to achieve "the common good." It is true that capitalism does—if that catch phrase has any meaning—but this is merely a secondary consequence. The moral justification of capitalism lies in the fact that it is the only system consonant with man's rational nature, that it protects man's survival *qua* man, and that its ruling principle is: *justice*.

(To be completed in our next issue)

OBJECTIVIST CALENDAR

■ On Sunday, October 31, Ayn Rand resumed her radio program for the Columbia University radio station WKCR (89.9 FM). The program is entitled "Ayn Rand on Campus" and is broadcast on alternate Sundays at 10 P.M.

If an educational or university radio station in your community is interested in these programs, its representatives may write to: Arthur Gandolfi, WKCR, 208 Ferris Booth Hall, Columbia University, New York, N. Y. 10027.

■ On Wednesday, November 24, Nathaniel Branden will address the Michigan Society of Consulting Psychologists, in Detroit. His subject: "Psychotherapy and the Objectivist Ethics." Time: 8 P.M. Place: Sheraton-Cadillac Hotel. Open to the public; admission free.

■ On Friday, December 3, NBI will begin a ten-lecture course on "The Esthetics of the Visual Arts," to be given by Mary Ann Rukavina in New York City. Time: 7:30 P.M. Place: Sheraton-Atlantic Hotel, 34th St. and Broadway. Admission: $3.50.

■ NBI's Tape Transcription Division has scheduled the following starting dates: "Basic Principles of Objectivism" in Indianapolis, Nov. 19; St. Louis, Nov. 22; Anchorage, Dec. 1; Bloomington, Dec. 7—"Basic Principles of Objectivist Psychology" in Indianapolis, Nov. 23; Phoenix, Dec. 3; Las Vegas, Dec. 5—"The History of Modern Philosophy" in Boston, Nov. 29—"The Principles of Efficient Thinking" in New Orleans, Dec. 7. For further information, contact NBI.

Published monthly at 120 East 34th Street, New York, N.Y. 10016.
Subscription rate in United States, its possessions, Canada and Mexico: one year, $5; 2 years, $9; 3 years, $13. Other countries: one year, $6; 2 years, $11; 3 years, $16.
Additional copies of this Newsletter: single copy 50¢ (coins, not stamps); 10 – 99 copies, 25¢ each plus postage (for first-class delivery add 1¢ per copy, for third-class delivery add ½¢ per copy); 100 or more copies, 15¢ each plus postage (same as above). (Bulk rates apply only to multiple orders of a single issue.)
Please include zip code number with your address.
For change of address, send old and new address. Allow us three weeks to process new subscriptions and change of address.

Ayn Rand and Nathaniel Branden, Editors and Publishers
Barbara Branden, Managing Editor
Elayne Kalberman, Circulation Manager

THE OBJECTIVIST NEWSLETTER

Edited and Published by AYN RAND and NATHANIEL BRANDEN

VOL. 4 NO. 12   DECEMBER, 1965

CHECK YOUR PREMISES
By AYN RAND

What Is Capitalism?
(Part II of a two-part article)

Every social system is based, explicitly or implicitly, on some theory of ethics. The tribal notion of "the common good" has served as the moral justification of most social systems—and of all tyrannies—in history. The degree of a society's enslavement or freedom corresponded to the degree to which that tribal slogan was invoked or ignored.

"The common good" (or "the public interest") is an undefined and undefinable concept: there is no such entity as "the tribe" or "the public"; the tribe (or the public or society) is only a number of individual men. Nothing can be good for the tribe as such; "good" and "value" pertain *only* to a living organism—to an individual living organism—not to a disembodied aggregate of relationships.

"The common good" is a meaningless concept, unless taken literally, in which case its only possible meaning is: the sum of the good of *all* the individual men involved. But in that case, the concept is meaningless as a moral criterion: it leaves open the question of what *is* the good of individual men and how does one determine it?

It is not, however, in its literal meaning that that concept is generally used. It is accepted precisely for its elastic, undefinable, mystical character which serves, not as a moral guide, but as an escape from morality. Since the good is not applicable to the disembodied, it becomes a moral blank check for those who attempt to embody it.

When "the common good" of a society is regarded as something apart from and superior to the individual good of its members, it means that the good of *some* men takes precedence over the good of others, with those others consigned to the status of sacrificial animals. It is tacitly assumed, in such cases, that "the common good" means "the good of the *majority*" as against the minority or the individual. Observe the significant fact that that assumption is *tacit*: even the most collectivized mentalities seem to sense the impossibility of justifying it morally. But "the good of the majority," too, is only a pretense and a delusion: since, in fact, the violation of an individual's rights means the abrogation of all rights, it delivers the helpless majority into the power of any gang that proclaims itself to be "the voice of society" and proceeds to rule by means of physical force, until deposed by another gang employing the same means.

If one begins by defining the good of individual men, one will accept as proper only a society in which that good is achieved and *achievable*. But if one begins by accepting "the common good" as an axiom and regarding individual good as its possible but not necessary consequence (not necessary in any particular case), one ends up with such a gruesome absurdity as Soviet Russia, a country professedly dedicated to "the common good," where, with the exception of a miniscule clique of rulers, the entire population has existed in subhuman misery for over two generations.

What makes the victims and, worse, the observers accept this and other similar historical atrocities, and still cling to the myth of "the common good"? The answer lies in philosophy—in philosophical theories on the nature of moral values.

There are, in essence, three schools of thought on the nature of the good: the intrinsic, the subjective and the objective. The *intrinsic* theory holds that the good is inherent in certain things or actions as such, regardless of their context and consequences, regardless of any benefit or injury they may cause to the actors and subjects involved. It is a theory that divorces the concept of "good" from beneficiaries, and the concept of "value" from valuer and purpose—claiming that the good is good in, by and of itself.

The *subjectivist* theory holds that the good bears no relation to the facts of reality, that it is the product of a man's consciousness, created by his feelings, desires, "intuitions" or whims, and that it is merely an "arbitrary postulate" or an "emotional commitment."

The intrinsic theory holds that the good resides in some sort of reality, independent of man's consciousness; the subjectivist theory holds that the good resides in man's consciousness, independent of reality.

The *objective* theory holds that the good is neither an attribute of "things in themselves" nor of man's emotional states, but *an evaluation* of the facts of reality by man's consciousness according to a rational standard of value. (Rational, in this context, means: derived from the facts of reality and validated by a process of reason.) The objective theory holds that *the good is an aspect of reality in relation to man*—and that it must be discovered, not invented, by man. Fundamental to an objective theory of values is the question: Of value, to whom and for what? An objective theory does not permit context-dropping or "concept-stealing"; it does not permit the separation of "value" from "purpose," of the good from beneficiaries, and of man's actions from reason.

Of all the social systems in mankind's history, *capitalism is the only system based on an objective theory of values.*

The intrinsic theory and the subjectivist theory (or a mixture of both) are the necessary base of every dictatorship, tyranny or variant of the absolute state. Whether they are held consciously or subconsciously—in the explicit form of a philosopher's treatise or in the implicit chaos of its echoes in an average man's feelings—these theories make it possible for a man to believe that the good is independent of man's mind and can be achieved by physical force.

If a man believes that the good is intrinsic in certain actions, he will not hesitate to force others to perform them. If he believes that the human benefit or injury caused by such actions is of no significance, he will regard a sea of blood as of no significance. If he believes that the beneficiaries of such actions are irrelevant (or interchangeable), he will regard wholesale slaughter as his moral duty in the service of a "higher" good. It is the intrinsic theory of values that produces a Robespierre,

Copyright © 1965 by The Objectivist Newsletter, Inc.

a Lenin, a Stalin or a Hitler. It is not an accident that Eichmann was a Kantian.

If a man believes that the good is a matter of arbitrary, subjective choice, the issue of good or evil becomes, for him, an issue of: *my* feelings or *theirs*? No bridge, understanding or communication is possible to him. Reason is the only means of communication among men, and an objectively perceivable reality is their only common frame of reference; when these are invalidated (*i.e.*, held to be irrelevant) in the field of morality, force becomes men's only way of dealing with one another. If the subjectivist wants to pursue some social ideal of his own, he feels morally entitled to force men "for their own good," since he *feels* that he is right and that there is nothing to oppose him but their misguided feelings.

Thus, in practice, the proponents of the intrinsic and the subjectivist schools meet and blend. (They blend in terms of their psycho-epistemology as well: by what means do the moralists of the intrinsic school discover their transcendental "good," if not by means of special, non-rational intuitions and revelations, *i.e.*, by means of their feelings?) It is doubtful whether anyone can hold either of these theories as an actual, if mistaken, conviction. But both serve as a rationalization of power-lust and of rule by brute force, unleashing the potential dictator and disarming his victims.

The objective theory of values is the only moral theory incompatible with rule by force. Capitalism is the only system based implicitly on an objective theory of values—and the historic tragedy is that this has never been made explicit.

If one knows that the good is *objective*—*i.e.*, determined by the nature of reality, but to be discovered by man's mind—one knows that an attempt to achieve the good by physical force is a monstrous contradiction which negates morality at its root by destroying man's capacity to recognize the good, *i.e.*, his capacity to value. Force invalidates and paralyzes a man's judgment, demanding that he act against it, thus rendering him morally impotent. A value which one is forced to accept at the price of surrendering one's mind, is not a value to anyone; the forcibly mindless can neither judge nor choose nor value. An attempt to achieve the good by force is like an attempt to provide a man with a picture gallery at the price of cutting out his eyes. Values cannot exist (cannot be valued) outside the full context of a man's life, needs, goals and *knowledge*.

The objective view of values permeates the entire structure of a capitalist society.

The recognition of individual rights implies the recognition of the fact that the good is not an ineffable abstraction in some supernatural dimension, but a value pertaining to reality, to this earth, to the lives of individual human beings (note the right to the pursuit of happiness). It implies that the good cannot be divorced from beneficiaries, that men are not to be regarded as interchangeable, and that no man or tribe may attempt to achieve the good of some at the price of the immolation of others.

The free market represents the *social* application of an objective theory of values. Since values are to be discovered by man's mind, men must be free to discover them—to think, to study, to translate their knowledge into physical form, to offer their products for trade, to judge them and to choose, be it material goods or ideas, a loaf of bread or a philosophical treatise. Since values are established contextually, every man must judge for himself, in the context of his own knowledge, goals and interests. Since values are determined by the nature of reality, it is reality that serves as men's ultimate arbiter: if a man's judgment is right, the rewards are his; if it is wrong, he is his only victim.

It is in regard to a free market that the distinction between an intrinsic, subjective and objective view of values is particularly important to understand. The market value of a product is *not* an intrinsic value, not a "value in itself" hanging in a vacuum. A free market never loses sight of the question: Of value, *to whom*? And, within the broad field of objectivity, the market value of a product does not reflect its *philosophically objective* value, but only its *socially objective* value.

By "philosophically objective," I mean a value estimated from the standpoint of the best possible to man, *i.e.*, by the criterion of the most rational mind possessing the greatest knowledge, in a given category, in a given period and in a defined context (nothing can be estimated in an undefined context). For instance, it can be rationally proved that the airplane is *objectively* of immeasurably greater value to man (to *man at his best*) than the bicycle—and that the works of Victor Hugo are *objectively* of immeasurably greater value than true-confession magazines. But if a given man's intellectual potential can barely manage to enjoy true confessions, there is no reason why his meager earnings, the product of *his* effort, should be spent on books he cannot read—or on subsidizing the airplane industry, if his own transportation needs do not extend beyond the range of a bicycle. (Nor is there any reason why the rest of mankind should be held down to the level of his literary taste, his engineering capacity and his income. Values are not determined by fiat nor by majority vote.)

Just as the number of its adherents is not a proof of an idea's truth or falsehood, of an art work's merit or demerit, of a product's efficacy or inefficacy—so the free market value of goods or services does not necessarily represent their philosophically objective value, but only their *socially objective* value, *i.e.*, the sum of the individual judgments of all the men involved in trade at a given time, the sum of what *they* valued, each in the context of his own life.

Thus, a manufacturer of lipstick may well make a greater fortune than a manufacturer of microscopes—even though it can be rationally demonstrated that microscopes are scientifically more valuable than lipstick. But—valuable, *to whom*?

A microscope is of no value to a little stenographer struggling to make a living; a lipstick is; a lipstick, to her, may mean the difference between self-confidence and self-doubt, between glamor and drudgery.

This does not mean, however, that the values ruling a free market are *subjective*. If the stenographer spends all her money on cosmetics and has none left to pay for the use of a microscope (for a visit to the doctor) *when she needs it*, she learns a better method of budgeting her income; the free market serves as her teacher: she has no way to penalize others for her mistakes. If she budgets rationally, the microscope is always available to serve her own specific needs *and no more*, as far as she is concerned: she is not taxed to support an entire hospital, a research laboratory or a space ship's journey to the moon. Within her own productive power, she does pay a part of the cost of scientific achievements, *when and as she needs them*. She has no "social duty," her own life is her only responsibility—and the only thing that a capitalist system requires of her is the thing that *nature* requires: rationality, *i.e.*, that she live and act to the best of her own judgment.

Within every category of goods and services offered on a free market, it is the purveyor of the best product at the cheapest price who wins the greatest financial rewards *in that field*

(Continued on page 59)

A Report to Our Readers — 1965
By NATHANIEL BRANDEN

In October, 1964, Ayn Rand received a letter from L. Quincy Mumford, Librarian of Congress, which reads, in part, as follows:

"Among the most widely discussed philosophies of our time is that associated with your writings. In your fiction and essays you have made the Objectivist philosophy an issue affecting many levels of public discourse. When the history of our times is written, your work will have a prominent place.

"In order to insure that your work will be the subject of informed study, I invite you to place your manuscripts and personal papers in the Library of Congress. Here they will join a distinguished manuscript collection which includes the papers of most of the Presidents, statesmen, jurists, artists, writers, scientists, and philanthropists. In fact, all phases of our national past are documented through materials in the Library's Manuscript Division."

Miss Rand replied that she would be honored to accept the invitation.

This past year has been a very interesting and active one, from the point of view of the spread of Objectivism through the culture.

Eight years after the publication of *Atlas Shrugged*, and twenty-two years after the publication of *The Fountainhead*, each novel continues to sell between 100,000 and 200,000 copies a year. *The Virtue of Selfishness*, published a year ago, has gone through several printings, amounting in total to approximately 500,000 copies. Originally published in softcover, the book has been so successful that New American Library issued a hardcover edition this fall. A sequel to *The Virtue of Selfishness*, dealing with the subject of political economy, is being prepared for publication in the fall of 1966.

At present, NATHANIEL BRANDEN INSTITUTE is offering its lecture courses on Objectivism in close to eighty cities throughout the United States and Canada. Between September 1965 and September 1966, approximately 5,000 students will attend NBI courses; in addition, several thousand visitors will audit individual lectures. NBI has grown, not only in the number of cities in which its courses are offered, but also in the average size of enrollment in any given city. In New York City, the introductory course, "Basic Principles of Objectivism," currently has an enrollment of close to 200 students.

Last year, I reported that NBI's "Basic Principles" course was being offered aboard a Polaris submarine. This year, I have another new location to report that is no less startling: we are, at present, making arrangements to offer the "Basic Principles" course to interested American soldiers who have requested it —in Vietnam. (Less startling, perhaps, but worth mentioning, is the fact that we have just appointed an NBI Business Representative to organize our courses in Greenland, and expect shortly to appoint one in Pakistan.)

As we announced in the October issue, the successful growth of THE OBJECTIVIST NEWSLETTER has permitted us to enlarge it and to adopt a magazine format. THE OBJECTIVIST will begin publication in January, 1966. It will continue to feature articles by Miss Rand, other contributors and myself, on ethics, political economy, psychology, literature—as well as reviews of recommended books, and reports on Objectivist activities.

With regard to the spread of Objectivism on the college campuses, the trend I reported last year continues in full force: "On campuses throughout the country, college students—acting on their own initiative, with no connection to, or help from, NBI—continue to organize Ayn Rand Study Groups. Steadily increasing numbers of term papers or theses on Objectivism are being written for university courses in philosophy, psychology, literature and political science. *The Fountainhead, Atlas Shrugged* and *For The New Intellectual* [and now *The Virtue of Selfishness*] are appearing on more and more college lists of required or recommended reading." We receive increasing numbers of requests for additional material from teachers and professors who wish to include a discussion of Objectivism in their courses.

An event of particular importance took place in the academic world this fall: the first presentation of a course on the philosophy of Objectivism at an American university. Dr. Leonard Peikoff, Assistant Professor of Philosophy at the University of Denver, gave a course on "Objectivism's Theory of Knowledge" in the Graduate College of the University of Denver. As its title indicates, the course dealt with the fundamentals of Objectivist epistemology.

We have received many inquiries about this course from our readers. We hope to arrange to have Dr. Peikoff give the course for NBI in New York City. It would then be tape-recorded and made available to NBI Tape Transcription groups throughout the country.

As to student activities, I should like to quote from a very interesting letter we received from a student at Rice University in Houston:

"At Rice University, there has been an institution called the Book of the Semester. In previous years there have been dull books, dull official discussions, and dull reactions by the students. This last fall, I decided to recommend *Ninety-Three*. [He refers to the Bantam edition of Victor Hugo's novel, with an introduction by Ayn Rand.] . . . . [A] professor agreed to make the official wheels turn if I went ahead and ordered a number [of books] in my name. I ordered one hundred copies of *Ninety-Three*. . . . [With the help of a friend], I began advertising . . . by posting signs which gave the good points of the book: a complex, logically surprising plot; a heroic sense of life; a theme consisting of man's loyalty to values. The initial reaction was disbelief. Students at Rice, brought up on the sewer school of literature, flocked up to ask: 'The signs look serious but can such a book possibly exist? Was such literature ever written? Did anyone ever really *care* about such things?' The older liberals began to go around saying: 'It's not true. Life's not like that. Such books were never written.' The sale of copies expanded with its reputation by word-of-mouth. A political science professor 'assigned it optionally' to one class to read—and liberals confessed being afraid to read it on the grounds that [it is] hopelessly right wing! . . . The book sold, at bookstores all over town, and then it developed that this was *not* the Book of the Semester! . . . The Rice Campus Store made such a profit that they said any book [that] could sell like *that* didn't *have* to be official.

"The big payoff [is that] the Book of *this* Semester is *The Virtue of Selfishness!*"

Another example of unusual initiative and tenacity displayed by students of Objectivism in fighting for their ideas, took place this fall at the University of Virginia. I was invited by the John Randolph Society to deliver a lecture on Objectivism. I accepted—and then the trouble began. Part of the story is told by the Richmond *News Leader* (November 16) as follows: "All was well until the Randolph Society approached the proper University authorities seeking financial aid for their program.

Their requests for funds from the Student Activities Fund was approved by both the Student Council Organizations and Publications Committee and the Council itself. Next, it went to the Faculty Student Activities Committee, which has final say in such matters. The faculty committee gave the Society a flat 'No!' ... The faculty committee, according to Dean Runk, felt the expense simply was not justified: There might be other programs of greater value to be considered at later dates.

"Obviously, the faculty committee is out of touch with the outside world: There are 40,000 persons currently receiving material from the Branden Institute. Ayn Rand's novels sell in the millions.... By anyone's measure, Miss Rand's Objectivism has a following.... Naturally, this makes her not so popular with the arbiters of the academic community who prefer to see their students led down a single intellectual path. Such is the 'academic freedom' of the liberal-dominated campus of today. ... Certainly, it is not to be supposed that the faculty committee ever would be truly receptive to Miss Rand's Objectivism. It does seem, however, that they occasionally could muster some objectivity as they decide whom the University committee can and cannot hear."

But the students of the John Randolph Society who had invited me were not stopped. Led by a graduate economics student, Earl Good, they launched an independent publicity campaign for my appearance and announced that—contrary to their usual policy of free admission—they would charge an admission of 25¢ to cover expenses. The press picked up the story and gave it considerable publicity. I am gratified to say that the lecture was an unqualified success. I am told that the audience that attended was conspicuously larger than most of those drawn by the speakers acceptable to the faculty committee. As of this writing, I understand that the controversy over my appearance still continues; it seems that there are a significant number of people who do not share the view that "academic freedom" is a concept applying exclusively to speakers of a leftist persuasion.

Our readers often send me newspaper clippings and other items of interest relevant to the impact of Objectivism on the culture. I appreciate this very much. Recently, I received an interesting clipping from the Toronto Globe and Mail (November 22). It is a column by Richard J. Need, who had previously invited his readers to write to him on the subject of who were their personal heroes. Mr. Need begins his column by quoting one of his readers as follows: "I think it is much harder to be a hero in this continent, where so many of our natural instincts and drives are being killed off or crippled by this society of conformity and complacency. Here, to be yourself, to be true to yourself, means to be an outcast!" Then Mr. Need declares that perhaps this reader "would be consoled by the number of young Canadians who bestow their heroic award on Ayn Rand."

Of the seven young people whose choice of hero Mr. Need discusses, four chose Ayn Rand. One of them gave the reasons of her choice as follows: "[Ayn Rand] has given me the glimpse and incentive of all the high and noble experiences of life, and shown me the method of seizing and fighting for them. That method is reason." Another writes: "In Ayn Rand's works, her persuasively genuine characters are motivated by values which project man as he might be and ought to be, not as he is. Focusing on intelligence, ability, integrity and achievement, she has raised a gleaming goal for man to climb toward." Another writes: "She views existence as rational, and man as a being capable of reason, heroism and almost infinite joy. Thanks to her, so do I." The fourth writes: "Ayn Rand doesn't just protest, as do most of today's young people and their heroes. She's not anti-something: she's pro-freedom, pro-reason, etc. She offers a positive solution for the world's predicament.... Ayn Rand gives us hope—hope based on reason, not on mystical beliefs."

On the other side of the ledger, our readers have sent me clippings from various religious publications which denounce Objectivism for its "dangerous" influence on the young. One such publication, These Times, after quoting Miss Rand to the effect that man can perceive and understand reality only by means of reason (as against any form of mystical faith or revelation), declares: "That premise turns an ever-increasing number of young people away from Christianity and our churches—young people who have neither the experience nor the background to recognize and ward off such manifest nonsense." If religionists describe the advocacy of reason as "manifest nonsense," one does not have to wonder that young people are turning away from religion. Another publication, Catholic World, complains: "Objectivists ... are far more zealous and numerous than it is comfortable for us to admit."

In view of the fact that most of these attacks declare or imply that atheism is the most important and central feature of the Objectivist philosophy, a brief comment is perhaps appropriate. As uncompromising advocates of reason, Objectivists are, of course, atheists. We are intransigent atheists, *not* militant ones. We are *for* reason; therefore, as a consequence, we are opposed to any form of mysticism; therefore, we do not grant any validity to the notion of a supernatural being. But atheism is scarcely the center of our philosophical position. To be known as crusaders for atheism would be acutely embarrassing to us; the adversary is too unworthy.

On the lighter side, I received, earlier this fall, a clipping from the New York Herald Tribune which tells of a former FBI agent, engaged in undercover work, who identifies himself as an admirer of Ayn Rand's philosophy and who, in his contacts with the FBI, used "Wesley Mouch" as his alias. He explained that several of his friends in the FBI, also engaged in undercover work, "have been using the names of 'heavies' in Miss Rand's books, as FBI aliases."

There is one final item, relevant to the progress of Objectivism, which I should like to report.

This fall, lecturing in various cities, I encountered a good deal of interest, among psychologists and psychiatrists, in the application of Objectivism to their work. I also met a considerable number of graduate students in psychology who are Objectivist in their psychological and philosophical orientation. From both these groups, I received requests to provide workshops in our theories and methods of psychotherapy.

In November, I addressed the Michigan Society of Consulting Psychologists on the subject of "Psychotherapy and the Objectivist Ethics," and was immensely gratified by the number of people who expressed interest in learning more about our psychological theories. Dr. Roger Callahan, a practicing psychologist in Detroit, is arranging for my colleague, psychiatrist Dr. Allan Blumenthal, to give a workshop in our therapeutic methods, in Detroit early in 1966.

New projects are now being planned by us that will be of special interest to those working in the mental health field, who desire information about and training in Objectivist psychology. One of our long-range goals is the establishment of a national psychotherapy referral system. I am taking this opportunity to extend an invitation to professionals and students in the mental health field—psychology, psychiatry, psychiatric social work, etc.—to write to me, if they would like to receive information on these projects.

What is Capitalism? *(from page 56)*

—not automatically nor immediately nor by fiat, but by virtue of the free market, which teaches every participant to look for the *objective* best within the category of his own competence, and penalizes those who act on irrational considerations.

Now observe that a free market does not level men down to some common denominator—that the intellectual criteria of the majority do not rule a free market or a free society—and that the exceptional men, the innovators, the intellectual giants, are not held down by the majority. In fact, it is the members of this exceptional minority who lift the whole of a free society to the level of their own achievements, while rising further and ever further.

A free market is a *continuous process* that cannot be held still, an upward process that demands the best (the most rational) of every man and rewards him accordingly. While the majority have barely assimilated the value of the automobile, the creative minority introduces the airplane. The majority learn by demonstration, the minority is free to demonstrate. The "philosophically objective" value of a new product serves as the teacher for those who are willing to exercise their rational faculty, each to the extent of his ability. Those who are unwilling, remain unrewarded—as well as those who aspire to more than their ability produces. The stagnant, the irrational, the subjectivist have no power to stop their betters.

(The small minority of adults who are *unable*, rather than unwilling to work, have to rely on voluntary charity; misfortune is not a claim to slave labor; there is no such thing as the *right* to consume, control and destroy those without whom one would be unable to survive. As to depressions and mass unemployment, they are not caused by the free market, but by government interference into the economy.)

The mental parasites—the imitators who attempt to cater to what they think is the public's known taste—are constantly being beaten by the innovators whose products raise the public's knowledge and taste to ever higher levels. It is in this sense that the free market is ruled, not by the consumers, but by the producers. The most successful ones are those who discover new fields of production, fields which had not been known to exist.

A given product may not be appreciated at once, particularly if it is too radical an innovation; but, barring irrelevant accidents, it wins in the long run. It is in this sense that the free market is not ruled by the intellectual criteria of the majority, which prevail only at and for any given moment; the free market is ruled by those who are able to see and plan long-range—and the better the mind, the longer the range.

The economic value of a man's work is determined, on a free market, by a single principle: by the voluntary consent of those who are willing to trade him their work or products in return. This is the moral meaning of the law of supply and demand; it represents the total rejection of two vicious doctrines: the tribal premise and altruism. It represents the recognition of the fact that man is not the property nor the servant of the tribe, that *a man works in order to support his own life* —as, by his nature, he must—that he has to be guided by his own rational self-interest, and if he wants to trade with others, he cannot expect sacrificial victims, *i.e.*, he cannot expect to receive values without trading commensurate values in return. The sole criterion of what is commensurate, in this context, is the free, voluntary, uncoerced judgment of the traders.

The tribal mentalities attack this principle from two seemingly opposite sides: they claim that the free market is "unfair" both to the genius and to the average man. The first objection is usually expressed by a question such as: "Why should Elvis Presley make more money than Einstein?" The answer is: Because men work in order to support and enjoy their own lives—and if many men find value in Elvis Presley, they are entitled to spend their money on their own pleasure. Presley's fortune is not taken from those who do not care for his work (I am one of them) nor from Einstein—nor does he stand in Einstein's way—nor does Einstein lack proper recognition and support in a free society, on an appropriate intellectual level.

As to the second objection, the claim that a man of average ability suffers an "unfair" disadvantage on a free market— "Look past the range of the moment, you who cry that you fear to compete with men of superior intelligence, that their mind is a threat to your livelihood, that the strong leave no chance to the weak in a market of voluntary trade....When you live in a rational society, where men are free to trade, you receive an incalculable bonus: the material value of your work is determined not only by your effort, but by the effort of the best productive minds who exist in the world around you....

"The machine, the frozen form of a living intelligence, is the power that expands the potential of your life by raising the productivity of your time.... Every man is free to rise as far as he's able or willing, but it's only the degree to which he thinks that determines the degree to which he'll rise. Physical labor as such can extend no further than the range of the moment. The man who does no more than physical labor, consumes the material value-equivalent of his own contribution to the process of production, and leaves no further value, neither for himself nor others. But the man who produces an idea in any field of rational endeavor—the man who discovers new knowledge—is the permanent benefactor of humanity.... It is only the value of an idea that can be shared with unlimited numbers of men, making all sharers richer at no one's sacrifice or loss, raising the productive capacity of whatever labor they perform....

"In proportion to the mental energy he spent, the man who creates a new invention receives but a small percentage of his value in terms of material payment, no matter what fortune he makes, no matter what millions he earns. But the man who works as a janitor in the factory producing that invention, receives an enormous payment in proportion to the mental effort that his job requires of *him*. And the same is true of all men between, on all levels of ambition and ability. The man at the top of the intellectual pyramid contributes the most to all those below him, but gets nothing except his material payment, receiving no intellectual bonus from others to add to the value of his time. The man at the bottom who, left to himself, would starve in his hopeless ineptitude, contributes nothing to those above him, but receives the bonus of all of their brains. Such is the nature of the 'competition' between the strong and the weak of the intellect. Such is the pattern of 'exploitation' for which you have damned the strong." (*Atlas Shrugged*)

And such is the relationship of capitalism to man's mind and to man's survival.

The magnificent progress achieved by capitalism in a brief span of time—the spectacular improvement in the conditions of man's existence on earth—is a matter of historical record. It is not to be hidden, evaded or explained away by all the propaganda of capitalism's enemies. But what needs special emphasis is the fact that this progress was achieved by *non-sacrificial* means.

Progress cannot be achieved by forced privations, by squeezing a "social surplus" out of starving victims. Progress can come only out of *individual surplus, i.e.,* from the work, the energy, the creative over-abundance of those men whose ability produces more than their personal consumption requires, those who are intellectually and financially able to seek the new, to improve on the known, to move forward. In a capitalist society, where such men are free to function and take their own risks, progress is not a matter of sacrificing to some distant future, it is part of the living present, it is the normal and natural, it is achieved as and while men live—and *enjoy*—their lives.

Now consider the alternative—the tribal society, where all men throw their efforts, values, ambitions and goals into a tribal pool or common pot, then wait hungrily at its rim, while the leader of a clique of cooks stirs it with a bayonet in one hand and a blank check on all their lives in the other. The most consistent example of such a system is the Union of Socialist Soviet Republics.

Half a century ago, the Soviet rulers commanded their subjects to be patient, bear privations and make sacrifices for the sake of "industrializing" the country, promising that this was only temporary, that industrialization would bring them abundance, and Soviet progress would surpass the capitalistic West.

Today, Soviet Russia is still unable to feed her people—while the rulers scramble to copy, borrow or steal the technological achievements of the West. Industrialization is not a static goal; it is a dynamic process with a rapid rate of obsolescence. So the wretched serfs of a planned tribal economy, who starved while waiting for electric generators and tractors, are now starving while waiting for atomic power and interplanetary travel. Thus, in a "people's state," the progress of science is a threat to the people, and every advance is taken out of the people's shrinking hides.

This was not the history of capitalism.

America's abundance was not created by public sacrifices to "the common good," but by the productive genius of free men who pursued their own personal interests and the making of their own private fortunes. They did not starve the people to pay for America's industrialization. They gave the people better jobs, higher wages and cheaper goods with every new machine they invented, with every scientific discovery or technological advance—and thus the whole country was moving forward and profiting, not suffering, every step of the way.

Do not, however, make the error of reversing cause and effect: the good of the country was made possible precisely by the fact that it was not forced on anyone as a moral goal or duty; it was merely an effect; the cause was a man's right to pursue his own good. It is this right—not its consequences—that represents the moral justification of capitalism.

But this right is incompatible with the intrinsic or the subjectivist theory of values, with the altruist morality and the tribal premise. It is obvious which human attribute one rejects when one rejects objectivity; and, in view of capitalism's record, it is obvious against which human attribute the altruist morality and the tribal premise stand united: against man's mind, against intelligence — particularly against intelligence applied to the problems of human survival, *i.e.,* productive ability.

While altruism seeks to rob intelligence of its rewards, by asserting that the moral duty of the competent is to serve the incompetent and sacrifice themselves to anyone's need—the tribal premise goes a step further: it denies the existence of intelligence and of its role in the production of wealth.

It is morally obscene to regard wealth as an anonymous, tribal product and to talk about "redistributing" it. The view that wealth is the result of some undifferentiated, collective process, that we all did something and it's impossible to tell who did what, therefore some sort of equalitarian "distribution" is necessary—might have been appropriate in a primordial jungle with a savage horde moving boulders by crude physical labor (though even there someone had to initiate and organize the moving). To hold that view in an industrial society—where individual achievements are a matter of public record—is so crass an evasion that even to give it the benefit of the doubt is an obscenity.

Anyone who has ever been an employer or an employee, or has observed men working, or has done an honest day's work himself, knows the crucial role of ability, of intelligence, of a focused, competent mind—in any and all lines of work, from the lowest to the highest. He knows that ability or the lack of it (whether the lack is actual or volitional) makes a difference of life-or-death in any productive process. The evidence is so overwhelming—theoretically and practically, logically and "empirically," in the events of history and in anyone's own daily grind—that no one can claim ignorance of it. Mistakes of this size are not made innocently.

When great industrialists made fortunes on a *free* market (*i.e.,* without the use of force, without government assistance or interference), they *created* new wealth—they did not take it from those who had *not* created it. If you doubt it, take a look at the "total social product"—and the standard of living—of those countries where such men are not permitted to exist.

Observe how seldom and how inadequately the issue of human intelligence is discussed in the writings of the tribal-statist-altruist theoreticians. Observe how carefully today's advocates of a mixed economy avoid and evade any mention of intelligence or ability in their approach to politico-economic issues, in their claims, demands and pressure-group warfare over the looting of "the total social product."

It is often asked: Why was capitalism destroyed in spite of its incomparably beneficent record? The answer lies in the fact that the lifeline feeding any social system is a culture's dominant philosophy and that capitalism never had a philosophical base. It was the last and (theoretically) incomplete product of an Aristotelian influence. As a resurgent tide of mysticism engulfed philosophy in the 19th century, capitalism was left in an intellectual vacuum, its lifeline cut. Neither its moral nature nor even its political principles had ever been fully understood or defined. Its alleged defenders regarded it as compatible with government controls (*i.e.,* government interference into the economy), ignoring the meaning and implications of the concept of "laissez-faire." Thus, what existed in practice, in the 19th century, was not pure capitalism, but variously mixed economies. Since controls necessitate and breed further controls, it was the statist element of the mixtures that wrecked them; it was the free, capitalist element that took the blame.

Capitalism could not survive in a culture dominated by mysticism and altruism, by the soul-body dichotomy and the tribal premise. No social system (and no human institution or activity of any kind) can survive without a moral base. On the basis of the altruist morality, capitalism had to be—and was—damned from the start. (For a discussion of the philosophers' default in regard to capitalism, see the title essay in *For the New Intellectual.*)

For those who do not fully understand the role of philosophy in politico-economic issues, I offer—as the clearest example of today's intellectual state—some further quotations from the *Encyclopaedia Britannica's* article on capitalism.

"Few observers are inclined to find fault with capitalism as an engine of production. Criticism usually proceeds either from *moral* or *cultural* disapproval of certain features of the capitalist system, or from the short-run vicissitudes (crises and depressions) with which long-run improvement is interspersed." (*Italics mine.*)

The "crises and depressions" were caused by government interference, not by the capitalist system. But what was the nature of the "moral or cultural disapproval"? The article does not tell us explicitly, but gives one eloquent indication:

"Such as they were, however, both tendencies and realizations [of capitalism] bear the unmistakable stamp of the businessman's interests and still more the businessman's type of mind. Moreover it was not only policy but the philosophy of national and individual life, the scheme of cultural values, that bore that stamp. Its materialistic utilitarianism, its naive confidence in progress of a certain type, its actual achievements in the field of pure and applied science, the temper of its artistic creations, may all be traced to *the spirit of rationalism* that emanates from the businessman's office." (*Italics mine.*)

The author of the article, who is not "naive" enough to believe in a capitalistic (or *rational*) type of progress, holds, apparently, a different belief:

"At the end of the middle ages western Europe stood about where many underdeveloped countries stand in the 20th century. [This means that the culture of the Renaissance was about the equivalent of today's Congo; or else, it means that people's intellectual development has nothing to do with economics.] In underdeveloped economies the difficult task of statesmanship is to get under way a cumulative process of economic development, for once a certain momentum is attained, further advances appear to follow more or less automatically."

Some such notion underlies every theory of a planned economy. It is on some such "sophisticated" belief that two generations of Russians have perished, waiting for *automatic* progress.

The classical economists attempted a tribal justification of capitalism on the ground that it provides the best "allocation" of a community's "resources." Here are their chickens coming home to roost:

"The market theory of resource allocation within the private sector is the central theme of classical economics. The criterion for allocation between the public and private sectors is formally the same as in any other resource allocation, namely that the community should receive equal satisfaction from a marginal increment of resources used in the public and private spheres. ... Many economists have asserted that there is substantial, perhaps overwhelming, evidence that total welfare in capitalist United States, for example, would be increased by a reallocation of resources to the public sector—more schoolrooms and fewer shopping centers, more public libraries and fewer automobiles, more hospitals and fewer bowling alleys."

This means that some men must toil all their lives without adequate transportation (automobiles), without an adequate number of places to buy the goods they need (shopping centers), without the pleasures of relaxation (bowling alleys)—in order that other men may be provided with schools, libraries and hospitals.

If you want to see the ultimate results and full meaning of the tribal view of wealth—the total obliteration of the distinction between private action and government action, between production and force, the total obliteration of the concept of "rights," of an individual human being's reality, and its replacement by a view of men as interchangeable beasts of burden or "factors of production"—study the following:

"Capitalism has a bias against the public sector for two reasons. First, all products and income accrue [?] initially to the private sector while resources reach the public sector through the painful process of taxation. Public needs are met only by sufferance of consumers in their role as taxpayers [what about *producers?*], whose political representatives are acutely conscious of their constituents' tender feelings [!] about taxation. That people know better than governments what to do with their income is a notion more appealing that the contrary one, that people get more for their tax money than for other types of spending. [By what theory of values? By whose judgment?] ...

"Second, the pressure of private business to sell leads to the formidable array of devices of modern salesmanship which influence consumer choice and bias consumer values toward private consumption ... [This means that your desire to spend the money you earn rather than have it taken away from you, is a mere *bias*.] Hence, much private expenditure goes for wants that are not very urgent in any fundamental sense. [Urgent—to whom? Which wants are "fundamental," beyond a cave, a bearskin and a chunk of raw meat?] The corollary is that many public needs are neglected because these superficial private wants, artificially generated, compete successfully for the same resources. [*Whose* resources?] ...

"A comparison of resource allocation to the public and private sectors under capitalism and under socialist collectivism is illuminating. [It is.] In a collective economy all resources operate in the public sector and are available for education, defense, health, welfare and other public needs without any transfer through taxation. Private consumption is restricted to the claims that are *permitted* [by whom?] against the *social product*, much as public services in a capitalist economy are limited to the claims permitted against the private sector. [*Italics mine.*] In a collective economy public needs enjoy the same sort of built-in priority that private consumption enjoys in a capitalist economy. In the Soviet Union teachers are plentiful, but automobiles are scarce, whereas the opposite condition prevails in the United States."

Here is the conclusion of that article: "Predictions concerning the survival of capitalism are, in part, a matter of definition. One sees everywhere in capitalist countries a shifting of economic activity from the private to the public sphere ... At the same time [after World War II] private consumption appeared destined to increase in communist countries. [Such as the consumption of wheat?] The two economic systems seemed to be drawing closer together by changes converging from both directions. Yet significant differences in the economic structures still existed. It seemed reasonable to assume that the society which invested more in people would advance more rapidly and inherit the future. In this important respect capitalism, in the eyes of some economists, labours under a fundamental but not inescapable disadvantage in competition with collectivism."

The collectivization of Soviet agriculture was achieved by means of a government-planned famine; Soviet Russia's enemies claim that 15 million peasants died in that famine; the Soviet government admits the death of 7 million.

At the end of World War II, Soviet Russia's enemies claimed that 30 million people were doing forced labor in Soviet concentration camps (and were dying of planned malnutrition, human lives being cheaper than food); Soviet Russia's apologists admit to the figure of 12 million people.

This is what the *Encyclopaedia Britannica* refers to as "investment in people."

In a culture where such a statement is made with intellectual impunity and with an aura of moral righteousness, the guiltiest men are not the collectivists; the guiltiest men are those who, lacking the courage to challenge mysticism or altruism, attempt to by-pass the issues of reason and morality and to defend the only rational and moral system in mankind's history—capitalism—on any grounds other than rational and moral.

A RECOMMENDATION. One cannot recommend a magazine or a periodical over whose future content one has no control —except conditionally or provisionally, in the form of a mere hypothesis based on past performance. Since there is no automatic guarantee of philosophical consistency, one can recommend a periodical only with the following warning to the readers: this publication deserves your attention, but we cannot guarantee or underwrite its future ideological position; judge for yourself.

With this reservation, I want to recommend to your attention a modest little periodical which I have watched for almost a year and found to be excellent in its particular field. It is called *Persuasion*. It is published monthly, in mimeographed form, by a private group, edited by Joan Kennedy Taylor, and distributed by the Metropolitan Young Republican Club.

Although Miss Taylor and some of the contributors are former NBI students, *Persuasion* is their own independent venture, speaks only for itself and has no connection with Objectivism other than the fact that its contributors may have accepted some Objectivist principles.

It is not a philosophical or theoretical, but specifically a *political* publication. Its value lies in an intellectual approach to concrete political problems. It does a remarkable educational job in tying current political issues to wider principles, evaluating specific events in a rational frame-of-reference, and maintaining a high degree of consistency. It is of particular interest and value to all those who are eager to fight on the level of practical politics, but flounder hopelessly for lack of proper material.

I recommend it especially to the attention of Young Republican Clubs and other political youth groups—or to those among them who are seriously concerned with the art of political argumentation.

For further details, contact Joan Kennedy Taylor, *Persuasion*, Inc., 260 West 86th Street, New York, N.Y. 10024.

—AYN RAND

OBJECTIVIST CALENDAR

■ "Psychotherapy and the Objectivist Ethics," a lecture delivered by Nathaniel Branden before the Michigan Society of Consulting Psychologists and recorded in Detroit on November 24, 1965, is now available on tape (3¾ IPS, seven-inch reel; the lecture is one hour and fifteen minutes in length). Available from NBI BOOK SERVICE, 120 East 34th St., New York, New York 10016; price: $6.00. (N.Y. State residents add sales tax.)

■ Nathaniel Branden's article "Alienation" (originally published in three parts in the July, August and September 1965 issues of this NEWSLETTER) has been reprinted in pamphlet form. Price: 75¢. (N.Y. State residents add sales tax.)

■ On Wednesday, January 12, NBI will begin a ten-lecture course on "The Economics of a Free Society," to be given by Alan Greenspan in New York City. Time: 7:30 P.M. Place: Sheraton-Atlantic Hotel, 34th St. and Broadway. Admission: $3.50.

■ On Friday, January 21, Nathaniel Branden will address the Ayn Rand Society at Stanford University in Stanford, Calif. His subject: "Alienation and the Critics of Capitalism." Time: 4:15 P.M. Place: Cubberly Auditorium. Open to the public; admission free.

■ On January 22 and 26 respectively, NBI will begin its series on "Basic Principles of Objectivist Psychology" in San Francisco and Los Angeles. Nathaniel Branden will deliver both opening lectures in person. The rest of the course will be given via tape transcription.

In addition, NBI's Tape Transcription Division has scheduled the following starting dates: "Basic Principles of Objectivism" in Minneapolis, Jan. 7; Columbus, Jan. 8; Vancouver, Jan. 9; Akron, Jan. 10; Ithaca, Jan. 11; Pittsburgh, Jan. 28; Des Moines, Jan. 30; Tampa, Feb. 1; Riverside, Calif., Feb. 2—"The History of Modern Philsophy" in Toronto, Jan. 4—"The Principles of Efficient Thinking" in San Diego, Jan. 7—"The Economics of a Free Society" in Pittsburgh, Jan. 30. For further information, contact NBI.

Published monthly at 120 East 34th Street, New York, N.Y. 10016.
Subscription rate in United States, its possessions, Canada and Mexico: one year, $5; 2 years, $9; 3 years, $13. Other countries: one year, $6; 2 years, $11; 3 years, $16.
Additional copies of this Newsletter: single copy 50¢ (coins, not stamps); 10 — 99 copies, 25¢ each plus postage (for first-class delivery add 1¢ per copy, for third-class delivery add ½¢ per copy); 100 or more copies, 15¢ each plus postage (same as above). (Bulk rates apply only to multiple orders of a single issue.)
Please include zip code number with your address.
For change of address, send old and new address. Allow us three weeks to process new subscriptions and change of address.

Ayn Rand and Nathaniel Branden, Editors and Publishers
Barbara Branden, Managing Editor
Elayne Kalberman, Circulation Manager

www.ingramcontent.com/pod-product-compliance
Lightning Source LLC
Chambersburg PA
CBHW080514090426
42734CB00015B/3053